AWAKENING
Youth Discipleship

AWAKENING
Youth Discipleship

Christian Resistance in a Consumer Culture

Brian J. Mahan
Michael Warren
David F. White

with a foreword by Don C. Richter

 CASCADE *Books* · Eugene, Oregon

AWAKENING YOUTH DISCIPLESHIP
Christian Resistance in a Consumer Culture

Cascade Books
A Division of Wipf and Stock Publishers
199 W. 8th Ave., Suite 3
Eugene, OR 97401

ISBN13: 978-1-55635-136-5

Cataloging-in-Publication data:

Mahan, Brian J.
Awakening youth discipleship : Christian resistance in a consumer culture / Brian J.
Mahan, Michael Warren, and David F. White. With a foreword by Don C. Richter.

      xii + 126 p.; 23 cm.
      ISBN13: 978-1-55635-136-5

1. Youth—Religious life. 2. Youth (Christian theology). 3. Church work with youth. I.
Warren, Michael. II. White, David F. III. Richter, Don C. IV. Title.

BV4447 .M33 2008

Manufactured in the U.S.A.

Contents

Foreword by Don C. Richter / *vii*
Introduction: Practicing Resistance / *xi*

PART ONE by David F. White
CONSUMERISM IN THE CULTURAL CONTEXT 1
1 The Social Construction of Adolescence 3
2 Pedagogy for the Unimpressed 21

PART TWO by Michael Warren
IMAGINING AN INCONVENIENT CHURCH 39
3 The Imaginations of Youth 41
4 Youth Ministry in an Inconvenient Church 61

PART THREE by Brian J. Mahan
THE DEVIL IS IN THE DETAILS 75
5 Advanced Placement and the Kingdom of God 77
6 Youth Ministry and the Practice of Sacred Commiseration 93

PART FOUR
CONCLUSION 107
7 Talking It Out: Further Musings on Youth Ministry 109

Foreword

BRIAN MAHAN, Mike Warren, and David White are troublemakers.

I mean that as a compliment.

Maria Harris, of blessed memory, writes about "the ministry of trouble-making" in her 1981 classic, *A Portrait of Youth Ministry*.[1] Troublemaking is how Maria describes *diakonia*, the Greek word for "service" that gave rise to the office of "deacon" in the early church. Serving in the name of Christ, deacons shared food and money with suffering, poor, and neglected people. Throughout history, deacons have been "troublemakers" when their ministry calls attention to systemic injustice, oppression, and inequality. Standing in solidarity with those on the margins, deacons stir up trouble for those who sit comfortably in the centers of power and privilege—including those of us who serve the institutional church.

Brian, Mike, and David stir up trouble by standing in solidarity with young people who are idolized yet sidelined by a consumer society, lauded yet too often domesticated by the church. These three coconspirators don't serve up standard, predictable youth ministry fare in the following pages. They don't dish out a smorgasbord of glitzy games with a side of seven habits of highly effective youth ministers. Instead, these authors invite us to join them at table for a nourishing feast of insights and life-centering conversation about what it means—for adults as well as for teenagers—to be faithful followers of Jesus in our day and time. They've spent years thoughtfully preparing this meal for us.

Mike Warren has been in the kitchen a long time. I met Mike through his writings before I met him in person. Three decades ago, when the entire

1. Maria Harris, *Portrait of Youth Ministry* (Eugene: Wipf & Stock, 2004).

field of youth ministry was taking a "developmental journey" with teens, the voice of one crying in the wilderness proclaimed, "Pay attention to the social contexts of youth, to the cultural scripts we give them, to the ways they are manipulated by the media, the marketeers, the military!" Mike is indeed a modern-day John the Baptist, urging us to repent from viewing adolescence as an exotic life stage, regarding young people as *consumers* rather than as *persons*. Mike calls us to name and resist all life-draining cultural captivities in light of gospel grace and freedom.

I met Brian and David in person before getting to know them as scholars. Courageously, perhaps foolishly, they both signed on as faculty for the fledgling Youth Theological Initiative, which I directed at Emory University (see chapters 5 and 6). Over the course of several seasons, I witnessed their passion for exploring theology with seventeen-year-olds. They probed Walter Wink's analysis of powers and principalities; they reflected on the ethics of ambition; they made pilgrimages to serve and worship with communities throughout Atlanta; they even slogged to a Braves game through a hurricane. Through it all, Brian and David became conversation partners, close colleagues, confidants.

Brian is a modern-day Evagrius, that fourth-century monastic who portrayed "the eight deadly thoughts"—later called "the seven deadly sins"—that impede all disciples in their faith pilgrimage. When Brian describes our penchant for "invidious comparison," for instance, he recalls that ancient tug of envy (*invidia*), the insatiable craving for what others have that we ourselves lack. As you'll see in these essays, Brian's charism is to eschew abstraction and call attention to the particular details of one's own spiritual struggles. He reminds us that saints cultivate virtue by acknowledging the persistent allure of vices that weigh down their souls. He invites us to join with youth in honest, humble confession that leaves us crying and laughing at our silly strivings.

David taught me to view the passions of youth in relation to prophetic *pathos,* God's own passion to repair the world. David's careful historical research describes how over the past century, the energy and talents of young people have been "anesthetized" by the broader culture, especially media culture. Like Toto in the *Wizard of Oz,* David pulls back the curtain to demystify "the great and powerful wizard" of contemporary social forces that hold youth in thrall. He does so by asking big questions, such as "Who benefits from the ways teens are socially constructed as adolescents? How have teens been disconnected from life-giving work that makes a difference and brings joy? What practices can faith communities nurture to remedy the loss of apprenticeship between teenagers and adults?" Artfully and playfully, David engages these big questions with youth by drawing on pedagogues such as Paulo Freire and Augusto Boal.

In a lineup of "the usual suspects" in youth ministry, you would likely skip over Brian, Mike, and David. These guys are white males, they're over fifty, and they make no evident effort to be "hip" or "with it." They are who they are, transparent and without pretension. And they look rather harmless. But when you listen awhile to what they say, you'll realize they are troublemakers. They stir things up, pointing out who gets access to life-giving resources, power, and privilege . . . and who does not. They don't play the trendy youth ministry game, dropping the latest buzzwords. Yet young people always seem to be at the center of their attention. You might describe them as life-long advocates for youth, exercising what Maria Harris calls "the ministry of advocacy" (*kerygma*) as well as *diakonia*. And you would be right.

So pull up a chair to the table. Join the conversation. The first course is ready to be served.

DON C. RICHTER
MARCH 14, 2007

Introduction:
Practicing Resistance

How should the Church engage young people in vital partnership with Christ, as Christ's disciples in the contemporary world?

This is not a new question. It is nonetheless a question that must be posed anew for each generation. In our own time, there is little doubt that the ubiquity and power of the culture of consumerism—so evident in mass media, in the marketplace, in our own habits of being and doing—threatens to obscure the scandalous beauty and sublimity of the gospel, as well as its power to challenge business as usual—the status quo.

In moments of private rumination or while commiserating with others ministering to youth, we sometimes find ourselves asking if resistance is really possible, if in fact we might only be going through the motions.

Shortly before his death, the eminent youth minister Mike Yaconelli expressed his own doubts on the matter: "Young people flock to Christian concerts, cheer Jesus at large events, and work on service projects. Unfortunately, it's not because of Jesus; it's because they're young!" Yaconelli says, "The most important function of youth ministry is longevity. Long-term discipleship."[2]

But what is to be done? How, in the face of the quantitative superiority of the deformative power of the culture of consumerism (and militarism), can we truly encourage young men and women to embrace Christian discipleship fully, passionately and, as Mike Yaconelli challenges us, *for the long term?*

Awakening Youth Discipleship addresses itself to these questions. The six essays and "talking chapter" that follow are the product of ongoing conversations

2. Mike Yaconelli, "The Failure of Youth Ministry," *YouthWorker Journal* (May/June 2003).

among the three authors, conversations that started nearly a decade ago during annual meetings of the Association of Professors and Researchers in Religious Education (APRRE) and continued with meetings over the last few years at St. Ignatius Jesuit Retreat House in Manhasset, New York; at Glastonbury Abbey, a Benedictine monastery in Hingham, Massachusetts; and at Simpsonwood, a Methodist retreat center in Norcross, Georgia.

The consensus animating our conversations is a shared sense of the need to both complement and move beyond current "communitarian-narrativist" approaches to youth ministry. Theorists, including Alasdair MacIntyre, Stanley Hauerwas and John Westerhoff, have given renewed attention to formative Christian practices such as Sabbath-keeping, hospitality to strangers, forgiveness, testimony and most importantly critical reflection on Scripture and tradition. These practices have served to place Christian community back at the center of Christian formation and have provided a bulwark against the hegemony of consumerist society.

It is our contention, however, that the individual and communal practices of sacred remembering central to communitarian-narrativist pedagogies need to be complemented and extended by practices of discernment and disciplined conversation—practices that actively deconstruct cultural distortions.

To the communitarian-narrativist practices of *anamnesis*, centered as they are in the retrieval of traditional practices of sacred remembering, should be added the *ascesis* of individual and communal practices of resistance, practices that encourage Christian youth to actively dehabituate themselves from the toxic images and beliefs of consumer culture. Taken together, such remembering and resisting constitute what Daniel Berrigan has called "the upside-down hermeneutics of Jesus Christ."[3]

---

3. A paraphrase from a statement of Daniel Berrigan's, from his *Steadfastness of the Saints: A Journal of Peace and War in Central and North America* (Maryknoll, NY: Orbis, 1985) 22.

PART ONE
Consumerism in the Cultural Context

David White's two essays, "The Social Construction of Adolescence" and "Pedagogy for the Unimpressed," provide a theoretical backdrop for the volume as a whole.

In the first essay, David illustrates how various social structures throughout history—especially economic and political ones—have influenced social constructions of adolescence, which have in turn spawned misleading and harmful assumptions about youth and youth ministry, many of which remain in force today. David's detailed and closely worked historical overview also provides the scholarly groundwork for challenging the widely held assumption that current pedagogies aimed at domesticating youth, and youth ministry as well, are inevitable and irreversible.

In his second essay, David builds upon and extends his theoretical analysis by introducing several practices of resistance that engage youth in studying the complex social, cultural, and economic systems that impinge so powerfully and incessantly on their lives. These practices of resistance, though essential, are not conceived as ends in themselves, but as serving to free youth to respond more fully and compassionately to the deep call of God upon their lives.

1

The Social Construction
of Adolescence

DAVID F. WHITE

Contemporary Context of Youth and Ministry

A LOOK at the public face of contemporary youth ministry reveals that there are available more resources, books, curricula, videos, and conferences than ever before in the history of the world. Youth ministry, like contemporary Christian music, has become a significant industry in the U.S. In this youth ministry market we see high energy, high visibility, and high budget programs, promising high yield youth ministry. And for some, and in a certain way, this seems to work—we have even learned how, for example, with enough resources to attract great numbers of young people, to get them to make professions of faith. And yet, a recent report of the National Study of Youth and Religion (NSYR) indicates that sixty percent, or the majority of American teenagers—who are overwhelmingly mainline Protestant and Roman Catholic—hold attitudes toward religion described as "benign positive regard." In other words, they believe religion is *good,* but *inconsequential.*[1] As the project's principle investigator, Christian Smith, a sociologist at the University of North Carolina-Chapel Hill, put it, "Most religious communities' central problem is not teen rebellion but teenagers' benign 'whateverism.'"[2] Most of these youth call themselves

1. Oral summary of NSYR findings, by Melinda Denton, presentation to United Methodist youth workers, Myrtle Beach, SC, February 2004.

2. Christian Smith and Melinda Lundquist Denton, *Soul Searching: The Religious and*

3

Christians, regularly attend worship, and are involved in Christian education and youth ministry programs. But they have virtually no religious language to prove it, nor do they understand central doctrines of historically orthodox Christianity. The version of Christian faith they have internalized does not, for the most part, influence the shape of their lives, their relationships, or perspectives on vocation. This NSYR report represents something of a wake-up call to those doing youth ministry as usual, and a challenge to reconsider what counts for most congregations as youth ministry.

While a better plan for more effective youth ministry is far from clear, one clue to our way forward involves understanding the relationship of Christian faith to culture, including how culture clarifies or distorts the gospel, and whether we should celebrate or resist the cultural milieu in which we minister with youth. And importantly, historical perspective is necessary if we are not to simply reify our current cultural forms, imagine them as normal and appropriate, as the way the world has always been. If we ignore the historical development of cultural institutions, the stories of their rise to prominence and the particular influences that shaped them, we may assume as normal such social institutions as slavery, racism, misogyny, classism—or adolescence.

Since the invention of the social institution of adolescence over a hundred years ago, adolescence has rarely been questioned, apart from the rise of developmental theories that have largely served to establish it as normal in the popular mind. And, until recent years, the bargain of adolescence—*dependence and education now, responsibility and independence later*—has worked reasonably well for many, due primarily to its brief span and the certain reward of middle-class employment. However, recent cultural developments have made problematic this unwritten treaty with youth. These developments relegate most youth to institutions in which they have less than full power for longer than any age cohort in the history of the world, leaving them considerably less free to make their distinctive mark on history, and are quickly shaping them as passive consumers rather than active agents and shapers of history. Further, cultural observers recognize a subtle hostility toward youth, in which youth are unfairly blamed for everything from rising rates of violent crime to high rates of teen pregnancy.[3] In recent legislation, more than fifteen states have criminalized youth behavior once considered experimental, such as public mischief,

Spiritual Lives of American Teenagers (Oxford: Oxford University Press, 2005) 266.

3. Mike Males, *The Scapegoat Generation* (Monroe, ME: Common Courage, 1996), and *Framing Youth: 10 Myths about the Next Generation* (Monroe, ME: Common Courage, 1999).

minor vandalism, and gang affiliation, placing increasing numbers of youth alongside adults in courtrooms and prisons.[4]

Unfortunately, these and other troubling social conditions do not remain outside the church door, regardless of our resolve to ignore them, but they impact our church youth and our youth ministry. Discussions of church youth ministry are often framed too narrowly and assume as normal the social location of adolescence. As a result, the church has often adopted approaches to ministry that further domesticate and marginalize youth. As a society and as the church we have too long neglected questions like these: How and for what purposes was the institution of adolescence shaped? Who has benefited from it? What should be the church's response?

This chapter will illuminate a series of watershed moments in the history of adolescence, in which the social location of youth significantly shifted.

Organic Preindustrial Society

PREINDUSTRIAL YOUTH and their families experienced life as interrelated—connected with each other and the greater public good. In preindustrial America, youth and adults worked side by side for the benefit of families and their communities. The rhythms of life for the young were largely defined by work and their capacity for it. As far back as the seventeenth century, children as young as six or seven were often sent out to work in the homes of nearby relatives or neighbors. Some young children were bound out as servants, but were, by age fifteen or sixteen, often apprenticed to learn the intricacies of a craft. The work of children and youth was important, at least in part as a form of social security and unemployment insurance for aging parents. But youth work also had larger social purposes. According to Thomas Hines, the traditional story of the birth of America has emphasized how generations of adults have sacrificed themselves for their children but has neglected the labor of teenagers and the very large role it played in the development of North America.[5] Hines states, "Work was not punishment, but part of a larger purpose: It helped sustain the

---

4. See, for example, California's Proposition 21, passed in the spring of 2000. Among other provisions, Prop 21 takes the discretion for trying juveniles as adults away from judges and places the decision in the hands of prosecutors who are often elected on their record for being tough on crime. Further, Prop 21 includes a range of typical adolescent behaviors as aggravating factors for prosecution—including gang affiliation, loosely defined as two or more people with similar clothing or gestures.

5. Thomas Hines, *The Rise and Fall of the American Teenager* (New York: Avon, 1999) 57.

family, the larger community, and many believed, God's plan."[6] Hines offers a corrective to the story of preindustrial labor.

> For most of our history, child labor was not a social horror but simply a fact of life. . . . The exploitation and abuse we now attach to the term did not exist until work moved from the home and into the factories that began to appear at the turn of the nineteenth century. . . . Americans were very, very slow to condemn it. Most developed serious moral scruples about child labor only after industrialists concluded it was inefficient, and labor unions sought to keep wages up by preventing its reappearance.[7]

In addition to the importance of the work of youth for family and society, there were also considerable compensations for youth themselves. Hines argues, "They had the satisfaction of doing real work and making a difference—experiences that modern teenagers often miss."[8] The entire idea and experience of work has become so distorted by industrial work that we fail to grasp that work was often a source of great joy, power, connection, and creativity. A worker who tilled the soil with his family developed deep understandings of and connections to the earth, the seasons, the sun and moon, the growing cycles, and appreciation of human strengths and his or her signature gifts.

The family was the primary economic unit, the location of production, and the chief policing authority—the only safety net. If individuals became estranged from their family, prison was the only other social institution they were likely to encounter.[9] In fact, each of the New England colonies had laws that forbade living outside family government.[10] If you did not have a family, the law required that you establish living arrangements with a family. Without the contemporary structures of social welfare and security, youth often passed from the care of their family into that of their master craftsman, a second family. Apprenticeship was also a source of education, as many masters were required to teach their apprentices to read and write, and often their catechism.[11]

In addition to work, young people once held important political and civic roles. In preindustrial communities, convention dictated that young people be quickly exposed to the religious, political, and emotional concerns of adults. According to Joseph Kett, "Public political gatherings were likely to attract chil-

---

6. Ibid., 63.

7. Ibid., 58.

8. Ibid., 59.

9. Ibid., 62.

10. In Southern colonies, which were settled by individuals rather than families, indentured servitude provided a structure of authority that replaced the family.

11. Hines, *Rise and Fall*, 67.

dren and youth as well as adults."[12] Indeed, youth were often politically aware and took up causes alongside adults, especially when work was undervalued or exploited by landowners or later by industrialists. Youth were politically aware enough to understand civic injustices—and often turned holidays and festivals, such as May Day, Midsummer's festival, Guy Fawkes Night, and Feast of Fools into occasions for social protest and political street drama. In such festivals, it was common for feasting, singing, and dancing to evolve into social activism—for example, marching en masse to the home of a man who had been beating his wife, hanging him in effigy, singing bawdy songs, and stigmatizing him by placing a big X on his front door to further dissuade him.[13]

These strong public roles for youth were made possible in part by young people's natural desire to understand and act in their world. In his book *The Underground History of American Education,* John Taylor Gatto provides numerous examples of young people in early American history who lacked formal education but, led by their hunger to learn about their world, became empowered to act on behalf of their own benefit and the common good.[14] For example, Benjamin Franklin left school at age ten and yet, as a writer, politician, scientist, and businessman, had few equals among the educated of his day. At an age equivalent to American junior high youth, Franklin read *Pilgrim's Progress*, R. Burton's historical collections (all fifty of them), Plutarch's *Lives,* Defoe's *Essay on Projects*, and Dr. Mather's *Essays to Do Good*.[15] Thomas Edison went to work on a train at age twelve, and by the age of thirteen he had set up his own newspaper, which became a main conduit of news during the Civil War. Gatto reminds us that the men who won the American Revolution were barely beyond high school age: Alexander Hamilton was twenty, Aaron Burr twenty-one, Light Horse Harry Lee twenty-one, Jean Lafayette nineteen. Hines notes, "What amounted to a college class rose up and struck down the British Empire, afterwards helping to write the most sophisticated documents in modern history."[16] These examples are not exceptions, but illustrate a norm of educated and empowered young people in early American history. Their intelligence was born of a natural hunger for knowledge and the desire to

12. Joseph Kett, *Rites of Passage: Adolescence in America 1790 to the Present* (New York: Basic, 1977) 43.

13. The example is from Kett's book—see footnote 11. However, this is a theme that runs through many historical accounts of adolescence, including John Taylor Gatto's book (see footnote 14), especially in chapter 1—page 4 and following.

14. John Taylor Gatto, *The Underground History of American Education: A Schoolteacher's Intimate Investigation Into the Problems of Modern Schooling* (New York: Oxford Village, 2000).

15. Ibid., 28.

16. Ibid., 25.

build a radically new kind of nation—rather than the artificial requirements of obtaining a passing grade.

These examples should not be understood as arguing for a return to a pre-industrial "golden age," since, along with a stronger role for youth, the world was often harsh for young and old, women and slaves. Yet it is important to know that whatever might have been gained in the shift to industrialization, there were also significant losses.

Industrial Capitalism and Fragmentation of Organic Life

BY THE end of the eighteenth century, an industrial capitalist economy was fast replacing agricultural and domestic industries. Many youth migrated to cities seeking factory jobs, prompting the death of many of the older customs that had sustained rural communities for centuries—as, for example, primogeniture and apprenticeships. In rural American communities, it was the Great Depression of the 1930s that proved destructive for a preindustrial way of life, as family farms in great numbers failed due to labor shortages, weather cycles, shifting market forces, demand crises, and the increasing centralization of land ownership by corporations.

What was lost in the shift from rural agrarian life to urban industrial life? As opposed to the earlier craft/agricultural vocations, industrial workers had no choice concerning what they made or how it was made. Thus, work is no longer a creative activity in which individual personality can be expressed. Not only is the worker's product an alien thing to him or her, but in this new context the worker loses comprehension of his or her real and material relationships with other workers, including how dependent they are on each other for the materials that sustain life. Instead, now competition has fundamentally shaped the character of relationships.[17] These losses are not incidental to human life but strike at the heart of what it means to be human and faithful as a Christian disciple.

But for youth, there were additional losses. As work shifted from farms to urban factories, families naturally assumed that children and youth would take their place alongside adults, as they had in villages for centuries. Ultimately, however, compassion for youth working in harsh conditions, combined with the greed of adult labor unions seeking higher wages, displaced youth from industry jobs. Thus, the market subverted longstanding traditions of apprenticeship and mentorship as the competition for wages came to outweigh the value of their traditional roles. By the early decades of the 1900s, youth were

17. Bertell Ollman, *Alienation: Marx's Conception of Man in Capitalist Society*, 2nd ed. (Cambridge: Cambridge University Press, 1976) 136.

largely unwelcome in factories, and by the end of the 1930s, also displaced from traditional work on family farms. This displacement of youth created a new level of alienation and anomie—now abstracted from families, traditional communities, fulfilling work, and from any significant social role. This displacement would also be a key motivation for new common school and high school movements in the U.S., movements that came to prescribe the contours of modern adolescence. Significantly, it was in this context that the Christian Endeavor Movement, the first ministry dedicated especially for youth, was created at the Williston Congregational Church of Portland, Maine, in 1881 under the leadership of Frances Clark. While this was initially a para-church movement, mainline Protestant denominations quickly followed suit and organized denominational and congregational youth ministry programs. It is important to note that this youth ministry movement could not have emerged a century earlier and only gained momentum from the displacement of youth from other social roles.

Adolescence and Market-shaped Identity

INDUSTRIAL PRODUCTION forces its own mode of alienating work and social relationships. But the impact of the commercial market does not end there. Market culture includes pressure to shape everything with aesthetic or sensual value into a commodity.[18] Thus, items or experiences having intrinsic aesthetic value—nature, music, art, literature—things that organic communities had for centuries generously shared, might in a commodity culture be shaped all the more convincingly as a commodity for sale. For example, the natural wilderness, once valued for its inspirational beauty and endless resources for life, became a commodity to be used and exploited for profit rather than appreciated and protected as a partner in human flourishing. Literature that once addressed a full range of issues, including science and politics, became formulaic thrillers

---

18. In its original usage, "aesthetic" referred to that which touched the senses as distinguished from more purely cognitive intellectual activity. In the original discourse of aesthetics by German philosopher Alexander Baumgarten, "the term did not in the first place refer to art, but as the Greek *aisthesis* would infer, to the whole region of human perception and sensation." See Alexander Baumgarten, *Reflections on Poetry*, trans. K. Aschenbrenner and W. B. Holther (Berkeley: University of California Press, 1954) 43. This mid-eighteenth-century distinction was concerned to distinguish the material from the immaterial, things from thoughts, sensations from ideas. It is precisely this understanding of the aesthetic that has shifted substantially over the last two centuries to connote instead the "constructed" aesthetic form—as in decorative art products and artifacts. This shift is not accidental but parallels a social shift in which human life and work became increasingly alienated in its sensual forms—reflecting the capitalist, industrialist shift in material conditions of human work, removing playful, sensual and intrinsically fulfilling human activity from the center of human life to its margins.

for profit, to make our blood pump faster when the rest of life is so thoroughly managed. Paintings are transformed from expressions of deepest human vision into expensive decorations for bank lobbies. A similar commodifying logic colonized adolescents whose lives became increasingly reduced as producers, consumers, and targets of advertising.

In part, G. Stanley Hall, the first theorist of adolescence, contributed to the recognition of the intrinsic beauty of youth and also to their exploitation as commodities. For instance, in his 1904 treatise *On Adolescence*, the first scientific theory of adolescence, he lavishly romanticized youth as a "golden age of life":

> This golden stage (*adolescence*) when life glistens and crepitates . . . has wrought a great work in the world and infected it with love of beauty everywhere. It is the vernal season of the heart and the greatest stimuli for the imagination. It opens the world of fancy which is superimposed upon that of reality, and which is the totalizing faculty that supplements the limitations of individuality and makes the age of love the natal hour of esthetic appreciation.[19]

Hall asserted that adolescence is a critical juncture in the human life cycle as it recapitulates a critical period of human history in which the race turned from ego-centeredness to altruism. The intensity of the aesthetic, the power of love, beauty and truth in adolescence, sensitizes the soul to the influences of nature, making it a factor in the evolution of art, literature, natural religion, and science. According to Hall,

> everything men strive for—fame, wealth, knowledge, power, love—are only specialized forms of the will to attain and to feel the maximum of vitality. The intensity of adolescent feelings serves to draw them out of their ego-centrism to a higher commitment to the good, the beautiful and the true. In adolescence, intense feelings for nature ultimately lead toward a higher and more precise systematic explanation of the world. It is the intensity of adolescence that provides impetus for the arts and sciences: In youth, "Everything is pregnant, and things about us seem to fairly cry out for some higher explanation. . . . Love and enthusiasm for nature if it is ever to arise, is now in order."[20]

Yet, while praising youth as a "golden era" of life, he also sought ways of capturing that energy for the good of the new industrial world. He depicted youth in the following way:

19. G. Stanley Hall, *Adolescence: Its Psychology and its Relation to Physiology, Anthropology, Sociology, Sex, Crime, Religion and Education*, vol. 1 (New York: Appleton, 1922) 131.

20. Ibid., 145.

> Life is . . . a stream flowing from high mountain ranges which wring
> it from the clouds, coursing down through all the manifold ways
> in which the water comes down at Lodore to the sea of eternity.
> Adolescence is the chief rapids in this river of life which may cut
> a deep canyon and leave its shores a desert. Educational methods,
> from those of the statesman and the religious founder to those of the
> artist and man of science, and even the pedagogue, are hydrographic
> engineering which builds a series of well-located and well-devised
> dams to irrigate wide and arid areas or turn the mills of life, or that
> its floods be stored up against drought and need, so that nothing is
> lost. Seepage is the waste of licensed vice in otherwise happy fami-
> lies or prosperous civilizations. Youthful dissipation is the wreckage
> of a spring freshet which wears away the dams, makes deep gullies,
> and may restore the primitive desert.[21]

While adolescence, like a mountain river, represents a deep reservoir of genera-
tive energy, in Hall's view, expert pedagogues must channel it for the good of
humanity and prevent its waste. His theory was instrumental in channeling
youth for, among other things, the good of commercial forces. The two main
bulkheads against what Hall understood as adolescent precocity and waste
were the high school and the needs of the market.

As youth settled comfortably into high schools, corporations saw opportunities for exploiting these energies of youth for their own purposes. According
to Grace Palladino, "during the Great Depression there were 4 million young
Americans aged sixteen to twenty-four who were looking for work, and about
40 percent of them—1 million boys and 750,000 girls—were high school age."[22]
Many of these young people took to the road seeking work in the 1930s, in
part to keep from being a drain on their families struggling to make ends meet.
Palladino argues that

> youth had the energy and the anger to spark a social revolution—or
> at least a full-fledged explosion in the streets, and some adults were
> beginning to fear that they had the necessary political organiza-
> tion, too . . . concerned Americans began to fear the influence of
> street-corner socialists and communists, who were busy organizing
> anyone willing to listen—workers, college students, farmers, the
> unemployed.[23]

In the Spring of 1935 FDR launched the National Youth Administration (NYA)
to provide training camps for out-of-school youth who needed to develop
marketable skills and a pleasant personality in order to compete for jobs. They

21. Ibid., 143.
22. Palladino, *Teenagers: An American History* (New York: Basic, 1996) 36.
23. Ibid., 37.

had to be willing to learn the middle-class habits of self-discipline, ambition, and work. In fact, the NYA "fully intended to transmit the values and habits of middle-class families to those who had never experienced them."[24] The ultimate goal of the NYA camps was to channel into high schools these hordes of young people displaced by the Great Depression. At the beginning of 1930 only about twenty percent of all young people attended high school, but by the end of 1940 that figure had risen to nearly ninety percent. The NYA and FDR thus avoided a much-feared revolution.[25]

Without a doubt, the economic depression of the 1930s put a practical spin on the process of growing up. A key learning of the depression, according to Grace Palladino, was that "when the margin of error was painfully small, youth's high spirits could prove expensive. The crucial thing for the working class youngster was to find a job, any job . . . for a middle-class child, it was to get that high school diploma that could lead to a white-collar job."[26] The seriousness of the Great Depression has not only deeply impacted middle-class values, but especially the shape of normal adolescence. For boys, high school was promoted by advice and character-building literature as a time to "buckle down" and get serious about building a career, preferably a professional career that could only be attained by education. For boys and girls coming of age in the dominance of middle-class norms the focus was on the future and increasingly away from the intrinsic value of life. Boys and girls were warned away from sexual activity and other frivolities as distractions from a secure future. Ambition for middle-class status took the place of any yearnings to experience the intrinsic goodness of ordinary life, whether delight, adventure, or heroism. And lost was an expectation of youth in roles as agents on behalf of the common good.

For girls, delayed gratification took a different form. It was assumed that girls would not be entering professions, and so most of the advice and character-building literature guided girls in how to attract boys that would be suitable for marriage—especially those boys who could provide economically. Girls were encouraged to present themselves in a way so as not to diminish their value as marriage material by controlling their own and regulating their boyfriends' sexual urges, thus enhancing their reputations. For girls, a good reputation could mean the difference between a life of poverty and affluence.[27] Boys were expected to shape themselves as commodities for the job market, while girls were to shape themselves as commodities for the marriage market, including winsome social skills, makeup and grooming, home decorating, and

24. Ibid., 39.
25. Ibid., 41.
26. Ibid., 17.
27. Ibid., 26–27.

the art of polite casual conversation. Prosperous and comfortable middle-class families could rely on the promise of a good marriage and attractive future to keep them in line, while working poor had no such assurances.

While high school emerged in response to the need to find spaces for youth displaced in the farm and job crises of the 1930s and to quell the rising unrest among young people, the popularity of high school can in part be attributed to two significant movements: (1) the realization that youth confined to high school were ready targets for commercial exploitation and (2) the identification of education as a credential for professional white-collar and middle-class employment. Often these two movements functioned symbiotically. For example, teachers and parents came to view consumerism among youth as an ideal means of creating a youth subculture capable of keeping youth in school long enough to get their credentials for professional middle-class employment. While fashionable commodities—music, clothing, movies, food, etc.—ultimately became hallmarks of this new youth subculture, they were at first resisted by parents who resented the commercial exploitation of their children. However, parents ultimately capitulated to the whims of marketers who hawked their wares in scholastic journals and teen magazines as a means of softening the impact of newly enforced high school attendance standards.

As the lives of youth were increasingly distracted from the authority and guidance of families, communities, and congregations, into this void, a youth subculture was substituted. Whereas culture has, in the best of times, fostered human flourishing within particular contexts and communities, the subculture of youth, including its music, entertainment, and fashion, has cut young people loose from identities related to their local communities and sent them soaring in an autonomous youth culture—one likely as not originating in Hollywood and increasingly incomprehensible and irrelevant to their parents and local communities.

Postmodern Adolescence

THE HALLMARK of postmodern youth culture is its mixed blessing of destabilization—of meaning, social institutions, traditions, and personal identity. This destabilization has various sources and effects. On one hand, postmodern scholars of culture have appropriately celebrated the destabilization of "master narratives" that depict the white, Eurocentric, and male version of reality as normative. In this culture new space has been opened in which women and minorities can legitimately seek and gain equal rights and privileges. But on the other hand, alongside these new zones of freedom has emerged another kind of instability, having more to do with the iconoclasm and promiscuity of the market. In order to create new profits, corporations have established "planned obsolescence" in the hearts and minds of American consumers, in which old fashions become passé overnight and new ones are designated as trendy. When the voracious need for market share depends upon keeping unsettled our self-identity and esteem, in order to sell us "new and better" products, the result is an overheated, protean, and unstable culture in which identity is threatened and community fragmented. Market culture, in addition to replacing oppressive master narratives, also decimates those traditions that promote faith, relationship, trust, and the common good.

American life, until recent decades, has involved pursuit of a great deal more than riches and the lifestyle they afford, such as art, religion, the common good, knowledge, care of the earth and relationships. In fact, those who organized their commitments so exclusively around greed were stigmatized by the church and society.[28] However, much of contemporary human life has now been rationalized by the values of the market—values that include frenetic work for economic reward, exploitation of wage labor and natural resources, sensationalism, marketing on the basis of image (style over substance), individualism and competition, conspicuous consumption, and success at all costs. The unbridled forces of the commercial market have pervaded human life in North America and across the globe. This global movement has impacted young people in particular ways. Listed below are some recent developments that have destabilized the identity and roles of youth.

- One way postmodern commercial culture has impacted youth involves the vastly diminished social roles allowed for youth. Today adolescence begins with an earlier puberty and extends longer than ever before—often beyond the age of thirty if we allow the sociological definition of adulthood as achieving a significant social role, marriage, and steady employment. In part, we can account for this prolongation by the escalating pressure to obtain undergraduate and graduate educational credentials. This prolongation leaves youth in situations in which they have less than full power for longer than any other age cohort in history. Whereas historically youth were at the forefront of those who took responsibility for creating a just social environment in which human life can flourish, today many young people are relegated to marginal social roles that discourage or inhibit such engagement.

- Adolescence is further destabilized by the realization that the promises of education no longer hold the guarantee of middle-class security. This

28. See, for example, Albert O. Hirschman, *The Passions and the Interests* (Princeton: Princeton University Press, 1977).

guarantee is threatened in part by the sheer numbers of young people competing for professional jobs and middle-class employment. While the costs and expectations of education have risen significantly, its real value for vocational training has diminished. Many jobs that parents and grandparents held with only a high school diploma now require college or graduate degrees. Ironically, young people report that many corporate jobs secured after college could be easily managed without a college degree and with less than three weeks of on-the-job training! The expensive college degree, key to middle class employment and life-style, has become a necessary but insufficient credential.

- Uncertainty about the future includes uncertainty about the potential for upward mobility in the workplace. Whereas it was once possible with hard work and perseverance to eventually achieve advancement from low skill jobs to upper management positions, today the concentration of upper-level and lower-level jobs has thinned out middle-level jobs, effectively limiting possibilities of advancing within the corporate world. This "declining middle" has concentrated wealth and opportunity among the middle-aged and seniors. This situation is mirrored in the political habit of communities to limit the means for young people to achieve upward mobility by voting against school bond issues and for a low minimum wage. Sociologists Cote and Allahar reveal that the middle-aged and seniors have for over thirty years consolidated their wealth and power at the expense of the young, enforcing a prolonged and anxious adolescence lacking certainty of a future in the middle class, burdened with huge amounts of student loan debt.[29]

- Along with the anxiety and uncertainty of middle-class youth, under-class youth are stripped of their earning power, as they must compete with labor exported to developing countries.

- Destabilization of adolescence has been further catalyzed by states that misunderstand the nature of this crisis and have reacted to the displace-

29. James E. Côté and Alton L. Allahar, *Generation on Hold: Coming of Age in the Late Twentieth Century* (New York: New York University Press, 1996). These authors suggest that youth have become the new source of cheap labor for businesses that have capitalized on the diminished status of youth and have restructured the wage scale. There is an increased concentration of jobs at the bottom and upper-middle segments of wage distribution. There is a resulting decline in the wage-base of young people due to an increase in middle age workers who consolidated their position in the upper middle class for whom the average wages rose 6%. The result is an increase in unemployment and poverty among youth. Since 1973 there has been a relative decrease in wages (declined 26% since 1973). Youth now on average earn less than 70% of what adult white males make, as opposed to 94% in 1967.

ment of young people from past social roles, and now from institutions of education, care, and meaningful work, with more severe laws criminalizing behaviors of youth once considered experimental. More than fifteen states now prosecute as felonies offenses previously judged as juvenile misdemeanors, filling prisons to overflowing with displaced young people. In California, the growth of prisons—one of the fastest growing industries in the state and populated disproportionately by young people—is quickly outstripping the state's investment in its universities.[30]

- Adolescence is still further destabilized by the decline in the number of adult mentors and sponsors—a void now filled by the entertainment media that ushers young people into a specious adulthood. Relegating youth to media-driven peer culture and isolating them from adult relationships and centers of adult influence leaves youth with a vague yearning for more influence or social agency, but without the opportunities or skills that come through experience in negotiating complex practical and social problems. Without opportunity as agents and without adult mentors, young people often lack a sense of loyalty to social institutions characteristic of their parents and grandparents.

- There has also been a steady decline in the general capacity of young people to think critically and with depth. Some attribute the weakening of curiosity and critical intelligence to the exploitation of youth by the entertainment industry. Robert McChesney in the PBS Frontline documentary *The Merchants of Cool* explains that with dozens of new cable channels competing for viewers and advertising dollars, producers rely on sex and violence as tried and true strategies for getting viewers' attention.[31] With only scant seconds to grab the attention of channel-surfing viewers with remote controls in hand, programmers have no time to develop intricate plots or establish complex characters that would challenge the minds of viewers. In this environment, not only is it more difficult to be informed about complex world or local events, but such inattention to complexity becomes a habit of mind among American youth and adults. As noted by Neal Postman and Marshall McLuhan, our very consciousness is shaped by the expectation of titil-

30. For details about this movement to criminalize adolescence see Males, *Scapegoat Generation*.

31. *The Merchants of Cool* (airdate: 2/27/01), directed by Barak Goodman, written by Rachel Dretzin, produced by Barak Goodman and Rachel Dretzin, correspondent and consulting producer Douglas Rushkoff. A Frontline Co-Production with 10/20 Productions, LLC.

lation.[32] When we and our youth are held captive by entertainment, we suppress our innate curiosity and forget the delights of intellectual endeavor. Combine this habit of mind forged in a culture of entertainment with the prevailing approaches of education in America that often fail to make learning relevant, and we see more clearly why young people eschew learning in our churches. The love of learning experienced by Franklin, Edison, and countless other early Americans has never been awakened in many youth. Sadly, many churches capitulate to youth's alienation from their intellects by portraying a simplistic gospel as an easily consumable product that does not require our best thinking.

- In this postmodern culture, adolescence is also marked by its symbiotic relationship with the entertainment industry. Scholars at Calvin College have documented the historic rise of the entertainment industry and its systematic exploitation of youth and their discretionary dollars.[33] One impact of this relentless exploitation has been to make identity formation among young people problematic. Not only did young people once look to a stable set of commonly held beliefs about God, their world, and their place in it as important resources for establishing identity, but local authorities, such as homes, churches, neighborhoods, and families were once sources for stories, symbols, and ideas that funded identity. Today, an overheated media culture replaces these local authorities as sources of identity. However, the images and ideas communicated in a variety of means—through television, movies, music, internet, magazines—are not only vastly more numerous and diverse than in previous decades, but additionally, young people are confronted by them at an alarming and increasing rate. Today identity is a much more fluid and elusive thing for adolescents, and negotiating this vast set of images and values is more challenging due to the dearth of adults and critical skills.

- Finally, the changing character of adolescent work is another development of the market that militates against stable identity for adolescents. As mentioned earlier, prior to the twentieth century young people were regularly apprenticed to mentoring adults who taught them skills for a trade, and as late as the 1950s in the United States, young people as

32. See, for example, Marshall McLuhan and Quentin Fiore, *The Medium is the Message* (New York: Bantam/Random House, 1967) and Neil Postman, *Technopoly: The Surrender of Culture to Technology* and *Amusing Ourselves to Death: Public Discourse in the Age of Show Business* (San Francisco: Vintage, 1993).

33. See *Dancing in the Dark: Youth, Popular Culture and the Electronic Media* (Grand Rapids: Eerdmans, 1990).

young as fifteen regularly served as apprentices. While these roles were often difficult for young learners, they were also compensated by the recognition of their role as significant and respected by their communities. Today, adolescent work can be characterized as low-skilled, service-sector work with little or no adult interaction or respect by the community. As hordes of teenagers migrate from one service-sector job to another, we fail to provide for them important resources for establishing identity in community.

A half century ago, Erik Erikson maintained that group identity precedes individual identity and specifically that adolescents determine their identities by immersion in community. He held that healthy adolescent identity development requires supportive social groups whose members introduce young people to religio-cultural traditions while also encouraging adolescents to learn, act, and think for themselves in ways continuous with those traditions. Erikson's concept of identity overlaps with the Christian notion of vocation—the unique ways we are called to love God and neighbor. It is in and through the uniqueness of identity that God calls us to vocation. Today, however, Erikson's confidence in Western cultural institutions as promoters of adolescent well-being is increasingly difficult to maintain. Commodification of culture, the entertainment industry's proliferation of diverse norms and values, social fragmentation, mercurial shifts of job markets, and the privatization of common goods all threaten adolescent identity achievement and pose new pedagogical and theological challenges to churches committed to supporting youth.

Conclusions: The Abstractions of Youth

THIS BRIEF survey of the history of adolescence is intended not as an exhaustive account, but to point to some of the watershed moments in the creation of adolescence. In summary, I want to identify a theme—*the abstractions of youth*—that has run through this history as a key dynamic. Through this history we see that young people have been subjected to forces that have removed them as actors/agents in history. For example, the history of adolescence reveals the following:

1. Youth were abstracted from *significant social roles* in communities. (Youth roles are now limited to education, consumption, peer relationships.)

2. Youth were abstracted from *networks of care* in communities. (Youth are largely relegated to peer relationships with little adult involvement.)

3. Youth were abstracted from *attention to the common good*. (Youth today are seduced by marketers to a focus upon commodities and sumptuous lifestyles.)

4. Youth were abstracted from *families and other local authorities*. (Youth are relegated primarily to peer groups.)

5. Youth were abstracted from *innate "passions and sensibilities,"* described by G. Stanley Hall as intellectual curiosity, compassion, passion for life, beauty, and justice. (Many youth experience curiosity and passion as unnecessary and irrelevant for vocational advancement.)

6. Youth were abstracted from *expectation to fully attend to the call of God* upon their lives. (For many youth, the need for security and desire for consumption drives lifestyle and vocational choices.)

7. Youth were abstracted from *faith communities*. (Youth are relegated to special but marginal status as adolescents.)

8. Youth were abstracted from *their own powers as agents of God in history*, shaping a better world. (School and other social roles do not expect or challenge youth to explore their powers and abilities.)

Significantly, the theme of abstraction bears upon the Christian theology of salvation and the Kingdom of God. To whatever extent the gospel of Jesus concerns human flourishing and the flourishing of creation in the Kingdom of God, we cannot afford a narrow view of youth ministry as simply inviting young people into personal salvation. The history of adolescence reveals a fragmentation and alienation that requires congregations to engage in critical and theological discernment, to resist the dominant and domesticating version of adolescence, to invite young people as partners in life and mission, to restore mentoring relationships between adults and youth, to resist vocations that distort the call of God, and to focus Christian practice on embodying the work of Jesus on earth as in heaven. Only this kind of youth ministry can move beyond being simply a means of domestication for youth and towards engaging youth and adults as partners with God.

2

Pedagogy for the Unimpressed

David F. White

"I can't believe this is so much fun! I've never had fun using my mind before!" The unusually excited speaker was Roberto, a sixteen-year-old African-American young man. It was July in Southern California, and we were in the third week of a four-week program of the Youth Discipleship Project at the Claremont School of Theology in which sixty high school youth explored their lives through theological lenses. In the beginning days of the program we encouraged young people, who were working in small groups of twelve, to tell us about their lives. What made them angry, sad, frustrated, joyful, loved, appreciated, or connected? Roberto was among a group of young men that seemed to literally ache to investigate a particular burning question: Why were young men in their urban Los Angeles community continually being harassed by police? Each day, as the group gathered to tell stories about life in their communities, Roberto and his friends told story after story that brought this question into greater focus. According to Roberto and his friends, Samuel and Miguel, the police in their neighborhood rousted them daily, stopped them in their cars for no reason (a phenomenon that has come to be described somewhat tongue in cheek as "driving while black"!), and surveiled them suspiciously as they shopped at local malls. And they told stories about friends who were serving sentences in prison or in the juvenile detention center. From the stories these boys told our group, it was clear that the world they inhabited was much more dangerous than my world in suburban Claremont, where the most dangerous

21

thing I could imagine was misfiling my income taxes or failing to mow my lawn, incurring the ire of neighbors. Even though the neighborhoods in which these young men lived were geographically only about thirty miles away from my own, the differences in how we experienced life were stark. In my arrogance, I had imagined that I had much to teach these young men but did not imagine that they had much to teach me about how societies marginalize some and privilege others.

Our study group at the Youth Discipleship Project summer academy, composed of twelve young men and women and me, was visibly moved—some to tears or anger, but all clearly beyond apathy by the stories of Roberto's neighborhood—and so we decided to join him and his friends in exploring these questions. Over the first three weeks of the summer academy, our group designed and implemented their own research in which they interviewed white and minority youth at a local mall, visited local attorneys who worked with juveniles, participated in discussions at the local American Civil Liberties Union (ACLU) about the increasing criminalization of adolescents, sat in on local town council meetings investigating a recent shooting of a young black boy by local police, read from books and newspapers, and conducted internet searches, all for the purpose of trying to make sense of the questions raised by Roberto and his friends. My role was to facilitate their research by making suggestions about how and where to explore specific questions, such as statistics on black men and the justice system, and setting up appointments with various experts. Their findings were stunning—more about this later.

In his 1904 treatise on adolescence, G. Stanley Hall observed that young people are naturally curious:

> During adolescence . . . a suddenly widened area of life is governed and perhaps reconstructed by intelligence. . . . Their bud is curiosity, often seen in the animal world, and in the infant as its first dim preclusion is the reflex victimization of the eye by any patch of light. Staring, experimenting with sensation, surprise, active observation, the passion to touch, handle, taste everything, often apparent cruelty due to the lust to know . . . anxiety to know the origin of life that is suppressed to stealthiness at about the same age when it really grows more intense, baffling theological queries, interest in death and in theological questions, in the how of mechanical processes that often motivates what seems destructiveness, desire to travel, the conquests of timidity by curiosity, its function in prompting to take the first drink . . . truancy, and runaways . . . ; all these expressions of a pure desire for knowledge are phenomena of the crepuscular dawn that precedes the sunrise of reason in adolescence.[1]

1. G. Stanley Hall, *Adolescence: Its Psychology and its Relations to Physiology, Anthropology,*

Hall's perspective represents a radical contrast to popular media portrayals of youth as apathetic slackers: he likens youth to detectives, always on an adventure, seeking clues to life. Hall's assessment of the intellectual curiosity of youth still rings true, even if that curiosity is buried beneath layers of distractions and expectations that seduce young people from their own curiosity. At the Youth Discipleship Project, we had somehow tapped into Roberto's hidden lust for knowledge. Roberto's joy was visible. This young man who early in the summer hid during meeting times, requiring frustrated seminary students to flush him from various hiding places around campus, now showed up ten minutes early and spoke excitedly about his findings and theories. Indeed, now our whole group wanted to speak at once: the room seemed on fire with intellectual curiosity. For some, using their minds in this way was not new—having been turned on to learning by a teacher, parent, or adult mentor. But for others, their excitement seemed to signal something like a conversion, a qualitative shift in their capacity for learning about themselves and their world, the discovery of a new delight that involved more than the passive consumption promoted in our culture as the sole source of pleasure.

This intellectual conversion was particularly striking since many in our group had earlier confessed to struggling academically—some failed multiple grades in school, and nearly all disliked it. I couldn't help but wonder about the disparity between their academic failures and their now passionate interest in learning. Why were they and Roberto not learning to use their minds in school or church or at home? Through informal conversations, I sensed that they were all very bright and capable of thinking creatively and complexly. One young woman explained to me, "At school, all we do is read about ideas, facts, and formulas that have no apparent connection to our daily lives." Another said, "The only motivation we have for studying is the hope of good grades, good colleges, and good jobs—for some of us, that is not enough." It seems that many schools have failed to make learning more immediately relevant; at least this seems to be the experience of these young people.

Not only have schools failed to spark intellectual curiosity and capacity, but many of our churches have also failed to engage young people in using their minds as an act of faith. I recall being asked to help a particular congregation in California that was seeking a way forward in their ministry with youth. Over the course of two years in conversations, I heard young people and adults repeat in various forms, "We work so hard in school all week that we don't want to work on Sundays. We don't want to have to think!" Some adults and youth viewed the church as a sanctuary, a haven protecting them from the competition and alienation of school life, and anything that felt like school was

Sociology, Sex, Crime, Religion and Education, vol. 2 (New York: Appleton, 1904) 450.

suspect to them. Others were not so generous and accused their church youth ministry of "warehousing" or "ghettoizing" young people—removing them from experiencing or considering the complexities of this broken world and the skills necessary for them to become agents of faith in healing the world. They claimed that popular youth ministry creates warehouses or ghettos by entertaining youth, holding them within the church attic or basement, not inviting them to join working committees of the church, never allowing them to experience or explore the world—its brokenness and beauty—and in so doing, to discover their own powers. It is no wonder that many adults imagine youth as vapid, irresponsible, and apathetic. Youth are caught in institutions that do not believe them capable of intellectual vigor and consider the only worthwhile thoughts as those that pertain to making grades and getting jobs.

It is tragic to think how many youth may never discover, like Roberto, the delights of using their minds in identifying the forces important in shaping their lives. Sadly, there is not much in secular or church culture that encourages the use of our minds. For instance, a recent PBS Frontline special revealed how the increasing competition in cable television has intensified a reliance on sex and violence to catch the attention of channel surfing teens, making complex plots that challenge our minds a relic of the past.[2] Indeed, the very logic of consumer culture obscures analysis. Commodities are sold to us on the basis of sex appeal or some other basic compulsion, but not on the basis of reflection on how we can become better people or more responsible to a broken world. As a matter of fact, entire political campaigns are now run on the basis of emotional sound bites or images, designed not to argue points but to passionately assert ideas as self-evidently true, patriotic, moral, or Christian on their face.

However problematic in this culture, Christian faith at its core is concerned with how we understand the workings of the world. Even though there prevails an anti-intellectual ethos among many American churches—including a retreat to forms of youth ministry and worship that are emotionally and physically lively but at the same time humanly superficial—the life of the mind is an important dimension of Christian faith, and intelligent reflection is at the heart of Christian practice. Roberto's discovery that he could, by using his mind, name and contest the demons plaguing his community was consistent with, and not contrary to, his Christian faith. And a key finding of the Youth Discipleship Project is that there is something energizing about learning that engages the concrete life of young people—just ask Roberto!

2. *The Merchants of Cool* (airdate: 2/27/01), directed by Barak Goodman, written by Rachel Dretzin, produced by Barak Goodman and Rachel Dretzin, correspondent and consulting producer Douglas Rushkoff. A Frontline Co-Production with 10/20 Productions, LLC.

Love God with Your Mind

WHEN THE Pharisees attempted to lure Jesus into a series of legal traps by raising tricky questions about taxes and marriage, they concluded their inquiry by asking him for a summary of the law. Jesus responded by quoting Deuteronomy 6, the Shema, "Love the Lord your God with all your heart, and your soul, and your strength." But according to the Markan account, Jesus included an additional imperative, "Love God with your mind." The Greek word for *mind* used in this New Testament text is not *nous* but *dianoia,* which does not suggest abstract intellectualization but instead includes the meaning, "love God by the way you put things together."[3] It has the meaning of coherence, or how we make sense of our discrete experiences. This injunction makes how we put the world together, how we envision the parts of our world in relationship to the whole, a matter of faith and a means of loving God. This is the dimension of faith that Roberto and his friends were discovering—the creation of a story of their world in which they and God are actors.

The Whole and the Parts

JAMES FOWLER, in his seminal work *Stages of Faith,* echoes this concern for how we "put things together." He argues that faith is a kind of imagination, a way of seeing our everyday life in relation to holistic images of what he calls the ultimate environment. He says, "We shape our action (our responses and initiatives) in accordance with what we see to be going on."[4] The "ultimate environment" involves "our images of that largest theater of action in which we act out our lives. You might say that our images of the ultimate environment determine the ways we arrange the scenery and grasp the plot in our lives' plays. Furthermore, images of our ultimate environments change as we move through life. They expand and grow, and the plots get blown open or have to be linked in with other plots."[5] Fowler asserts that imagination is a powerful force underlying all knowing.

Imagination composes comprehensive images of the ultimate conditions of existence and gives character and shape to our particular reality. In fact, how we imagine the largest frame in which we understand the drama of our lives to be set makes an enormous difference in defining the character of our lives. For example, if we imagine the world constituted by individuals fighting to get as

3. Inaugural address of Thomas Trotter, the interim president of Claremont School of Theology, in 2000.

4. James Fowler, *Stages of Faith: The Psychology of Human Development and the Quest for Meaning* (San Francisco: Harper and Row, 1981) 24.

5. Ibid., 29.

many of the goodies as possible before they die, then individual life is likely to be grasped as a life spent in acquiring and consuming. Or if we view this world as corrupt, evil, and devoid of redeeming possibilities, doomed for destruction, and await a blissful life in a heavenly beyond, then this vision of life's signifi-cance will not likely result in an attempt to heal the broken world. Or, if we, like the Brazilian peasants with whom Paulo Freire worked, view our poor, broken, oppressed lives as fated by the gods, then we are not likely to feel empowered to resist our poverty. But if we, like Mother Teresa, view our lives as an extension of God's work of loving the wretched and broken, and see the beauty of God in these little ones, then we are likely to joyfully give our lives in service to others. These various ultimate environments describe particular ways of putting things together, of making narrative sense of discrete experiences. Individuals' lives, feelings, and behaviors are filtered through the lens of these various visions, limiting or expanding their partnership with God.

Prior to their Youth Discipleship Project summer, Roberto and his friends viewed the world as a mysterious place in which forces and powers move at will, sometimes maliciously, without any clear rationale. And they viewed their lives as inextricably caught in the movement of these malicious forces. Educator Paulo Freire called this type of thinking naïve consciousness, because it lacks an understanding of the various structures and forces that impact life and it leaves them unchallenged. The discussions engaged at the Youth Discipleship Project challenged their naïve consciousness. Although the analysis by Roberto and his friends was by no means exhaustive, it set their lives in a world constituted by complex relationships with schools, banks, police, families, media, neighbor-hoods, and prevailing myths, some of which they have the means to change. It broke open for them a mysterious world, rendering it more understandable and malleable, subject to their investigation and transformation. This type of consciousness Freire would call critical consciousness.

The Parts of the Whole

WHILE VERSIONS of reality for children or youth may descend whole from on high, from parents or communities, if these versions are to become more accurate and faithful, they require a good deal of thought to piece together. Roberto and his friends conveyed initial understandings of their world that featured a jumble of competing myths about how the world works, including American success stories that promised success as a reward of education and hard work, and competing myths that African Americans are helpless victims and should not expect to succeed because there are so many obstacles in their way. Some myths involved roles appropriate for black males that minimized the importance of education and glamorized violence and crime. Other myths involved the expectation that teenagers should desire, and are entitled to, a wealth of consumer commodities, and that these make life worthwhile. But alongside these consumerist myths, the odd story of Jesus' life, death, and resurrection sometimes challenged all other myths, but came to be interpreted in ways that confirm myths of hard work, politeness, and consumption. Few of these myths influenced people's thinking about the forces that determine their lives or encouraged their role as agents and partners with God. These myths allowed them to assume that the world was simply too inflexible and opaque to permit them to change their circumstances to any great degree. Nevertheless, their anger and frustration opened a way to create new, more adequate myths by which to make sense of their lives.

Fowler describes the content of faith as including (1) centers of value—the causes, concerns, or persons that command greatest worth, (2) images of power—how we understand and align ourselves in relationship to various forms of power, and (3) master stories—those characterizations of power in action that disclose the ultimate meaning for our lives. Fowler points to a variety of influences that determine the content of our faith: cognitive and other developmental factors that shape consciousness, the communally held stories and their versions of norms, values and beliefs, sponsors and mentors, and the mystery of God. But in addition to factors in our environment unnoticed and thus beyond our control, Fowler affirms the central place of reflection—paying deliberate attention to our master stories, images of power, and centers of value. He says,

> The operative contents of our faiths—whether explicitly religious or not—shape our perceptions, interpretations, priorities and passions. They constitute our characters as persons and communities of faith. Few things could be more important than serious reflection on how we form and commit ourselves to and through the contents of our faiths. Few things could be more important than serious reflection on what constitutes worthy, life-giving and life-enhancing master stories and centers of value and power.[6]

For Roberto and his friends the world was a dangerous and mysterious place in which people of color are naturally oppressed. This was their master story. Yet, as they explored the various causes for their lot, a new master story emerged in which people of color are oppressed, but in which people in partnership with God can also mobilize to change structures. For example, one finding from Roberto's study revealed that many young black males end up in prison or juvenile detention due to their lack of care and support, and

6. Ibid., 281.

that overworked and impersonal justice systems cannot provide needed care. In exploring this situation, they learned that their experience was only one dimension of a systemic problem of how law enforcement and justice systems relate to men of color. They learned that young black men are overrepresented in the justice and prison system in the United States, due to a number of causes, including structural racism and poverty which prevent young black men from having access to the same legal representation as white youth. But they also discovered that when peers provide positive support, such as through teen courts, many offenders do not repeat their crimes. Teen courts are a recent invention of a California attorney who learned that the recidivism rate of juvenile justice systems in California topped 91 percent. He arranged for juvenile judges to organize high school classes as juvenile courts for first-time offenders. In teen courts, high school students, for academic credit, learn about roles and processes of the court system and serve as attorneys, jurors, and judges for first-time offenders. Teen court participants across the United States report that recidivism rates for juvenile offenders are at least cut in half in comparison to the juvenile justice system.[7] Roberto and his friends enacted their faith by starting teen courts in their high schools to create a fairer environment for young black offenders. By studying the parts of their lives, they came to have a more adequate view of the whole of their lives, a more adequate master story. You might say that the plots of their lives' plays were blown open and linked in with other plots. Their study of the parts, the various concrete causes and situations of their world, shifted the images of the ultimate environment that determined how they arranged the scenery and grasped the plot in their lives' plays. In breaking open the stories of their lives, these young people suddenly found themselves alongside other allies working on their behalf, but also found themselves pitted against forces destructive to their flourishing. These sets of allies and adversaries sometimes included surprises. For example, those counted as allies sometimes included figures perhaps once seen as nerdy or uncool, such as the odd teacher or neighborhood adult who raised important questions about life and the common good, while adversaries sometimes included peers or family members who encouraged apathy or escapism.

---

7. Jeffrey A. Butts, Jeneen Buck, and Mark B. Coggeshall, "The Impact of Teen Court on Young Offenders," research report of the Urban Institute Justice Policy Center, April 2002.

Powers and Principalities: Redeeming Allies and Adversaries

ANOTHER WAY of grasping the theological importance of the work of the mind and the allies and adversaries formed as we break open our stories, is through Walter Wink's exegesis of Ephesians 6:12, which states, "For our struggle is not against enemies of blood and flesh, but against the rulers, against the authorities, against the cosmic powers of this present darkness, against the spiritual forces of evil in the heavenly places." Wink explains,

> The Powers . . . have long since been identified as an order of angelic beings in heaven, or as demons flapping about in the sky. Most people have simply consigned them to the dustbin of superstition. Others sensing the tremendous potential in the concept of the Powers for interpreting social reality have identified them without remainder as institutions, structures, and systems. The Powers are the simultaneity of an outer, visible structure and an inner, spiritual reality. The Powers properly speaking are not just the spirituality of institutions, but their outer manifestations as well. The New Testament uses the language of power to refer now to the outer aspect, now to the inner aspect, now to both together. . . . It is the spiritual aspect, however, that is so hard for people inured to materialism to grasp.[8]

Wink, in asserting that Powers are both spiritual and structural, perceptible and analyzable, suggests two means for knowing them: affective means and cognitive means. He notes that in a prescientific world, the power of the occupying Roman army was sensual and spiritual. In prescientific Palestine, for want of any greater explanatory powers, people projected their felt intuitions of the structures of evil onto the screen of the universe as disembodied spirits. Alternately, with the dawn of the Enlightenment and scientific method, we abandoned as superstition our felt sense of the powers and relied exclusively upon intellectual analysis. Wink insists that discernment involves both intuiting the powers and analyzing their various causal dimensions, how they impact the common good and our love of God and neighbor. Just as first-century Jews felt the spiritual presence of Roman occupation and projected their feelings as "legion" spirits, Roberto and his friends sensed the distorted relationship of the justice system to young black men. In fact, they felt so strongly about their perception of evil that they convinced other youth of the urgency of studying this problem. However, Wink does not merely *demonize* powers but insists, "The powers are good, the powers are fallen, and the powers can be redeemed." Similarly, Roberto and his friends struggled to grasp the working dimensions of this system of powers in order to redeem it. Finally, if the Kingdom of God

8. Walter Wink, *Engaging the Powers: Discernment and Resistance in a World of Domination* (Minneapolis: Fortress, 1992) 7.

involves infusing the fallen power of the world with the Holy Spirit, then we must learn, like Roberto and his friends, to understand and work in the power of this Spirit to change the world.

Risks of Loving God with Our Minds

YET, ENGAGING young people in using their minds involves risks. About nine months after the summer program in which Roberto and his friends so deftly analyzed their context, I got a call from the office of Phil Amerson, the President of Claremont School of Theology, inviting me to come for a chat. I could tell by the tone of the invitation that this was no social event. I approached the president's office with the trepidation of a fourth-grader summoned to the principal's office for a "who knows what" misdemeanor. I sat on Phil's sofa and he handed me a letter from an irate parent whose daughter had attended our summer program. It seems that this young woman, Jennie, had been in a group that had explored how youth are exploited by the entertainment and fashion industries. Jennie had gone home and over the next few months gradually dismantled her former life—she had removed from her bedroom walls posters of popular musicians, given much of her wardrobe to the Salvation Army, and stopped going to hang out at the mall with her friends. She was instead volunteering to work at the nearby homeless shelter. All were done as acts of faith prompted by her study of her life and how she related to entertainment and fashion. Her parents' complaint? Though their love for their daughter was evident, they seemed disturbed by her radical changes subsequent to her summer at the Youth Discipleship Project. They seemed to have preferred a daughter with a lesser dose of religion—enough to make her compliant, respectable, and securely middle class, but not so much as to make her stand out among her friends, or make it difficult to find lucrative employment. Jennie's present behavior was clearly out of step with their expectations for her life.[9]

Jennie's situation points to the importance of involving entire church communities, parents, and youth in habits of learning together. This process of mapping and understanding our world is best done in communities of youth and adults, parents and children, in which we reflect, discuss, and recreate together an increasingly accurate picture of the world and how it works. It is crucial that these conversations include the range of voices and experiences of youth and adults of a particular community, to give a fuller sense of the many sides of the situation. Through such discussions, youth and adults cre-

---

9. Certainly, there is a risk of using knowledge as a sort of moral elitism ("my spirituality is better than yours"). This is why Brian Mahan's work is so important, in order to help keep our knowing in proportion to our loving of God and neighbor, not as a weapon against them.

ate common visions of their world, enhancing their perspective on the world. Youth and adults can become lively coinvestigators of their world, and especially since my summer with Roberto, I am a witness to the power of adults co-learning with youth. And due to our failure to engage Jennie's family as partners in learning, we had inadvertently set her at odds with her family and church. I now grasp the urgency of inviting families and congregations into conversations about powers and principalities.

Key Questions for Pulling Things Apart and Putting Them Together

SOME FIND it helpful to think of the world as a woven cloth held together by many threads. We might understand the process of investigating the world as "unraveling" or illuminating the constituent parts that make up the whole. While the cloth of our lives may appear seamless, when we pull on these threads one by one we can better see how the garment is constructed, how it holds together. The root question that guides the work of exploring a problem is "What forces and relationships impact the situation we are trying to understand?" We can break the root question into several specific questions. A serious attempt to understand a situation might include a range of questions such as:

- Why does the situation exist?
- What forces have aligned in order to allow this situation?
- What individual decisions were made?
- What community decisions were made?
- How do social institutions, expectations and pressures impact this situation?
- What is the role of economic pressures?
- What is the role of political forces?
- What is the role of cultural forces?
- What is the role of religious expectations, norms, values, and beliefs?
- What is the role of racial/ethnic expectations, norms, values and beliefs?
- What is the role of human psychology in creating this situation, including deep fears and hopes?

Rarely do we step out of the flow of our lives in order to see and understand how we are in relationship to each of these forces, how they impact us and we them. Can we, in and through these relationships, find an opportunity to be in partnership with God in the healing of the world, by supporting, resisting, or challenging the relationships that surround us and constitute us?

Below are some creative ways of engaging youth in this critical and constructive work of the mind.

"BUT WHY?" METHOD   A simple way to introduce youth to the idea of mapping or problematizing is articulated in the series *Training for Transformation* by Hope and Timmel.[10] In the "But why?" method people are led through a process of how to question a particular situation. Young people might begin with a situation they already have some clarity about. For example, I have frequently used the situation "Rosa Parks's feet hurt." This theme captures an historical situation that has many root causes that can be explored with youth as an exercise. The facilitator probes the group, "*But why* did Rosa Parks's feet hurt?" The group might respond, "Because she had to give up her seat on the bus in Alabama in 1961." The facilitator might push, "*But why* did she have to give up her seat?" The group might respond, "Because of the racist policies of the city of Montgomery that required her to sit at the back of the bus." The facilitator might counter, "*But why* were there racist policies?" The group might say, "Because the folks in power were white, and they had a history of seeing black people as inferior." The facilitator might push behind this, "*But why* did they have a history of seeing black people as inferior?" Depending on their understanding of history, they might respond, "Because they owned slaves to make cotton crops profitable for the South." The conversation might not be linear or include only direct causation, but causes might branch out in many parallel directions that include psychological, ethnic, cultural, economic, political, or religious causes. As the group fleshes out the causes for a particular theme in this way, the facilitator may depict the causes in some kind of chart form for all to follow along. The chart develops into a full-blown map of a theme as the group contributes their understandings of the problem, perhaps resulting in a flow chart with arrows and devices to indicate relationships be-

---

10. Anne Hope and Sally Timmel, *Training for Transformation: A Handbook for Community Workers*, vols. 1–4 (Warwickshire, UK: ITDG, 2000).

tween the causes. In this way, a facilitator can prepare a group for doing this kind of mapping with any theme.

THEATER GAMES

Augusto Boal, Brazilian activist, educator, and performer, has explored with great success the use of drama and theater games by communities who wish to problematize their life-world.[11] He assumes that our rational minds are limited in their awareness of how we are present to our daily lives. For example, much as we drive a car without having to think about it, we sleepwalk through most of our lives without being conscious about the ways we participate in either life or death. Boal practices a number of ways of enabling people to surface the felt experiences of their lives, to make them conscious in order to become objects of their reflection. His theater games have been useful in surfacing unconscious experiences of racism, oppression, and injustice. For many youth, the activities involved in analysis can be tedious and dry. But Boal's use of drama helps young people reflect upon social structures and relationships in a way that is energizing rather than draining, drawing upon the primary sources of their own experience in the world.[12]

PROFESSIONS

In Boal's game "Professions," each player receives a piece of paper with the name of a profession on it, such as doctor, lawyer, prostitute, bartender, teacher, and so on. When the facilitator gives a signal, all actors start playing their professions at the same time, with actions and sounds but no words. As they perform they should seek to illuminate as many details about the activities of the profession as they can. To help this evolve as a game, the facilitator should ask them to find others who have something in common with them. As the actors form groups of four or five, depending upon how they conceive of commonalities, they will stand together in the room. At some point the facilitator will ask each group to come to the front of the room and perform their actions, still without words. Observers in the room are asked if they can guess what the portrayals of professions have in common. People make connections that those

11. See Augusto Boal, *Theatre of the Oppressed* (New York: Theatre Communications, 1985), and *Games for Actors and Non-Actors* (New York: Routledge, 1992).

12. Boal has written several volumes, any of which might be helpful for youth ministers or educators. The one that includes the most inclusive list of games is *Games for Actors and Non-Actors* (New York: Routledge, 1992).

depicting the professions and forming common groupings never imagined. The conversations that emerge around commonalities are a form of reflection on the ways professions are situated in relation to each other—how the businessman relates to the prostitute, how the teacher relates to the principal, how the doctor relates to the lawyer, etc. Each group performs the actions of their professions as observers guess and discuss the commonalities. You can make this game more relevant when the professions are related to the themes that young people are investigating. For example, if the theme is related to the frustration of youth in high schools, then the professions might include student, teacher, principal, and parents.

IMAGE THEATER

Boal utilizes images to freeze social situations that are pregnant with emotional energy and multiple relationships. For example, young people might be invited to create a machine, either a frozen image or a machine with interrelated moving parts. So the machine for the theme "high school" might contain images of young people struggling, teachers frustrated, and principals wielding power or parents crying. Such a machine might also include an image of a corporation standing outside of the school machine symbolizing some set of expectations or pressures felt in the high school. Youth may be invited to join the machine one by one, to contribute some dimension that represents their experience of the truth of the theme. By allowing the machine to have moving parts, youth are allowed to more fully represent relationships and their interaction. For example, a teacher making a violent pointing action toward youth contains much symbolic meaning. When fifteen or twenty young people have joined the machine, they have created something resembling the true situation of the theme under consideration. Another dynamization of the machine might include allowing each to say one phrase that captures the essence of their relationship to the whole: "I'm so tired of your behavior!" or "I don't understand why we have to do this assignment!" or "Why can't you teach our children?" Such a machine has the potential for making young people more conscious of social relationships.

DRAWINGS

I once participated with a group of Los Angeles day laborers who were trying to raise the awareness of other laborers and employers about their interrelationships within the community. A small, ingenious group of Mexican day laborers drew a beautiful four-by-four-foot picture depicting the different neighborhoods of their city. They indicated police stations, parks, schools, factories, retail stores, bus stops, and suburban neighborhoods. The drawing was not inflammatory, but accurately depicted the way the city was laid out. The men asked a group composed of laborers and employers to simply walk around the drawing and make notes about what they saw. After almost an hour of observing the very rich painting, the participants were asked to contribute their insights. For almost another hour, laborers and employers made connection after connection identifying things they had never seen before—inequities in bus routes, placement of police stations, the dearth of parks in urban neighborhoods where workers lived, the distance between the urban apartments of the workers and the suburban homes of the employers, and so on. The employers gained a different sense of what the workers' lives must be like. They also came to understand the inequity of public policies in their area. They came to understand in a more real way their need for each other and the necessity of forming coalitions, and significantly, of the employers seeking more just wages and conditions for the workers. With such drawings, young people can reflect upon their social location in relation to schools, entertainment markets, service-sector employment, family pressures, etc.

CODES AND DECODING

Brazilian educator Paulo Freire went into poor communities and took photographs of various situations in which people lived.[13] He took photos of people growing crops, taking grain to sell to the co-op, washing clothes in a stream, walking to work or school, etc. He showed these to small groups of citizens and asked, What do you see? What is happening here? What are they feeling? What is your experience of this? Does this happen in your community? Freire observed that some photos would be discussed matter-of-factly, while others would generate much emotion and energy. Freire learned that those pictures that generated energy, "that set the room on fire," or caused everyone to talk at once were the most important to focus upon. In these discussions, Freire learned a great deal

13. Paulo Freire, *Pedagogy of the Oppressed* (New York: Continuum, 2000).

about the people's experiences, their relationships with merchants, landowners, factories, and politicians. In our work at
the Youth Discipleship Project, we employed Freire's approach
with much success among youth. Usually, we were able to discern with some accuracy the situations in the lives of young
people that constituted situations of limit or fullness. Often,
these could be depicted through simple drawings. In the same
way that Freire showed pictures to small groups of citizens, we
showed drawings to groups of youth and adults as a way of
stimulating conversation about the situations. For example,
one drawing depicted a young girl in her room. Her room was
decorated with ballet slippers, trophies and pictures, indicating
her strong interest in ballet. From the doorway her father is
looking through with a frown on his face. In his hand is an
application to the local business school of the university. From
his expression it is clear they were in an argument. She was sad,
with her head in her hands. He was adamant. This picture generated much discussion about the pressure for young people to
be successful in financial terms, the limits our society places on
vocation, and the pressures parents feel to be validated by their
children's success. Such conversations can open discussions
about the fears and hopes of parents and youth and how youth
are formed in our culture.

Conclusions

OVER RECENT decades in the United States, popular youth ministry has adopted as its most urgent tasks attracting numbers of youth to the church and
cultivating among them Christian identity. While youth ministry has been
successful, to some degree, in introducing large numbers of youth in commitment to Jesus, we often contradict our hopes of forming youth in the way of his
gospel by reinforcing their relationship with popular culture and habits that engage young people as passive consumers of sensational products like concerts,
CDs, T-shirts, and an easily consumable gospel. These commodities, like junk
food, address immediate cravings, but do not adequately evoke their deepest
hunger for God and neighbor. In reality, our youth live in a culture increasingly
incongruous with the gospel of Jesus, making difficult the practice of Christian
discipleship, and making obsolete routine youth ministry approaches of simply
attracting and inspiring youth without helping them to adequately discern the

powers and principalities that shape their outer and inner life. In such a hostile cultural climate, youth ministers must think deliberately about how to form youth for a life attuned to the profound call of God upon their lives, which is always a bit at odds with the culture.

Youth ministry, at its best, seeks not to introduce youth to the nice but unrealistic story of the gospel or to cultivate a Christian identity indistinguishable from popular notions of national or commercially manufactured identity, but engages youth as partners in the Kingdom of God, mobilizing the skills, practices, and attitudes to sustain a countercultural Christian faith beyond adolescence into adulthood. Today, joining one's life in partnership with God requires that we consider our commitment to the gospel not as a private possession but as a challenge to the worlds of work, commerce, community, relationships, leisure, and politics. Prior to the Youth Discipleship Project summer, Roberto and his friends practiced Christian faith in a way that was largely limited to very personal and interpersonal dimensions of their lives. Their congregations had encouraged a Christian faith that was lively and passionate but obscured certain power relations and master narratives that held their lives in thrall. In using their minds to explore their world, Roberto and his friends expanded their view of God's work in the world and became partners with God. If Christian faith in youth is to involve more than a marginal practice (reserved for the available edges of life—Sundays, selected holy days or infrequent prayer times) stapled onto a life oriented to popular myths, such as those that encourage pursuit of wealth, status, distraction, and the status quo, then we must explore how to foster in young people a sustainable faith grounded in love for God and neighbor. In a culture such as ours, which is hostile to the gospel and which obscures conditions that inhibit human faith and flourishing, congregational youth ministry must explore the tools necessary for equipping youth to respond to God's call upon their lives. One such tool involves reminding youth to love God with their minds. And, as Roberto reminds us, rigorous thinking about the world is not only faithful, but represents one of the yearnings and delights that makes us fully human, capable of transcending our current humanity in seeking compassion or justice in partnership with God.

PART TWO
IMAGINING AN INCONVENIENT CHURCH

In his first essay, "The Imaginations of Youth," Michael Warren examines and details ways in which the church often imagines youth and youth ministry. After arguing that youth ministry at times appears more beholden to the techniques and assumptions of marketers and entertainers than to the gospel, he proposes alternative ways of imagining youth and youth ministry grounded in an empowering and transformative memory of "a Galilean Jew of the early first century."

Michael's second essay, "Youth Ministry in an Inconvenient Church," expands on his initial analysis of the hidden influence of consumerism on contemporary models of youth ministry and proposes additional practices of resistance centered around the Eucharist and moving outward toward the world, especially through service to the poor and the active confrontation of injustice wherever it is encountered.

Michael's two essays provide a bridge between David White's theoretical backdrop and Brian Mahan's more practical orientation, exemplifying what Columbia sociologist Robert Merton has called "middle theory."

3

The Imaginations of Youth

MICHAEL WARREN

Introduction: The Imagination in Youth Ministry

WHEN WE come to ministry with the young, how do we imagine or approach what we are doing? When youth ministries gather young people, they gather them around various "logics" or rationales.[1] Even initiatives that look very similar can have quite different "logics" driving them—different assumptions about youth, about youth ministry, about the church, about the role of youth leaders, about the place of prayer and worship, and about the social issues that affect youth; different imaginations of what it means to be young and of how the young should act. Often not articulated, these assumptions and imaginations deserve to be named and considered—and if necessary, reconsidered. My own logic about youth ministry is framed by three convictions about the church.

---

1. David White uses different language but gets at the same issue of viewpoints in his essay "The Social Construction of Adolescence." What I call "logics" in youth ministry refers to a network of convictions understood not so much as specific mental images but as a network of ideas, images, and convictions that together ground our reading of concrete situations and how they might be addressed. For example, when second-year and third-year students at Northport High School on Long Island sojourn to Nicaragua for two weeks with the social studies program, there is a different "logic" at work than when the main youth activity in a given parish is a car wash intended to raise money for a January ski trip. This notion of "logics" is similar to Charles Taylor's "inescapable frameworks."

The first is about the character of the church's ministries. When the church gathers people, it does so because of its fidelity to the Jesus of the gospel. What the church does, it does because fidelity compels it. When the church invites young people to consider and practice what it means to be a follower of Jesus, the effort's originating impulses and purposes, like fidelity, should be clear. Living out fidelity can be complicated. The church, for example, for all its concern for social realities, is not an employment agency engaged in help-ing people find work. It is a community committed to the transformation of persons and social systems in the light of the wisdom of Jesus. That wisdom is concerned with both the character of work and how the conditions of work can heal (or harm) the Self who works.

The second conviction is that the prototypical assembly of people wishing to follow Jesus' Way is the Eucharistic assembly. Here, the community seek-ing fidelity to the teachings of Jesus meets to remember their failures, to ask forgiveness, to remember his life, death, and resurrection, and to proclaim him as a sign of God's goodness. Should the other comings-together forget the focal position of the Eucharistic assembly they have lost their center. The centrality of the Eucharist does not necessarily mean that it comes first in time, but means that when the Eucharistic assembly does gather, it is a gathering joined in the Spirit of Jesus Christ—an intergenerational assembly struggling to discern, over bread and wine, its deeper call to fidelity.

A third conviction: Youth ministry initiatives are a way of recognizing the dignity of each young person, while inviting each, with all the delicacy implied by a true invitation, to move deeper into the circle of faith. Youth ministry focuses on the uniqueness of each person, on that person's gifts and difficul-ties. It also seeks to create life-giving gatherings where people are affirmed just as they are, even as they are challenged to deepen their commitments to God and neighbor.

These central convictions—about fidelity, the Eucharist, and the dignity of each person—raise questions about what happens when a group of young people gathers under church auspices for any kind of event. What sort of imag-ination of their world and of the church, or of themselves as persons, do these events suggest? What sort of images of who Jesus was and of what it means to be followers of Jesus do the leaders of these events celebrate? Such questions are necessarily addressed by all who minister to youth.

Jesus' own teaching is filled with questions for his disciples. Who is your neighbor; how should you use money; how do you practice forgiveness; what does God ask of us? Jesus challenged the imagination of his time with such questions, and they continue down to our day.[2] Still, one might ask, how focal are these questions in ministry with the young today?

The issue of imagination is prominent in writings about "the spiritual life," about the practices needed for the following of Jesus. A classic instance is the writing of Ignatius of Loyola, especially his *Spiritual Exercises*—which are an intensive effort to lead people to an imagination steeped in the words and deeds of Jesus. In the Exercises the life of Jesus is pondered within a strongly imagined narrative.[3] Concern for directing the imagination has been part of the ordinary practice of Roman Catholic spirituality, at least until recently. Religious orders, especially, followed centuries-old procedures intended to transform the imagination. To take just one example, the last words heard before going to bed were to be the main points of the following morning's meditation, which started the day. The practice called the "night silence," a committed effort not to speak to anyone before going to bed, prepared one's imagination for prayer, and the meditative prayer fixed the morning meditation in one's "mind and heart" for the entire day. Such procedures show concern for the imagination as a feature of any systematic gospel-centered life.

We are slow to realize that the shriveled imagination often means a diminished spirit as well. Ironically, the persons today most concerned with influencing the imagination of youth are not religious persons but the marketing specialists aware of how a properly stirred imagination can mean big sales.[4] They give special attention to people's imaginations. Carefully crafted metaphors and images can distort reality and sway people's minds and hearts.

2. Besides the gospels themselves, this is seen most clearly in Jesus' constant use of images and counter-images in the gospels. See Alan Kreider, *The Change of Conversion and the Origin of Christendom*, Christian Mission and Modern Culture Series (Harrisburg, PA: Trinity Press International, 1999), especially his section on how the early communities helped the catechumens learn new narratives and new controlling images, 26ff.

3. See Joseph A. Tetlow's introduction to his *Ignatius Loyola: Spiritual Exercises* (New York: Crossroad, 1992), 15–56, esp. 32–34. The entirety of the Exercises is about getting in touch with our inner lives, and work in the imagination is a key part of that effort. To get a sense of this feature, see the very first exercise for its emphasis on what Ignatius calls "the composition of place" effected by visual imagination, in George E. Ganss SJ, et al., *Ignatius of Loyola: The Spiritual Exercises and Selected Works* (New York: Paulist, 1991) 136–38, and the commentary, 396–400, on the first week. From studying the Exercises, one can see why one of the great current-day exercisers of the prophetic imagination, Daniel Berrigan, and one of the great theoreticians of the imagination, William F. Lynch, both Jesuits, have taken up this matter. Loyola's stress on imagination is a standard feature of many recent works on prayer. See also Edward Leen, *Progress Through Mental Prayer* (New York: Sheed and Ward, 1935) 204–5, 250–51.

4. Three titles to underscore this claim: Stuart Ewen, *All Consuming Images: The Politics of Style in Contemporary Culture* (New York: Basic, 1988); Stuart Ewen, *PR! A Social History of Spin* (New York: Basic, 1996); Leslie Savan, *The Sponsored Life: Ads, TV, and American Culture* (Philadelphia: Temple University Press, 1994).

The Social Imagination

A SOCIETY'S values and aims are not just those of a collection of random individuals. Individuals in a given culture have common social codes, so ingrained they often go unnoticed. The "commonness" of these codes is found in the social behavior everyone finds acceptable or unacceptable. I once was driving a young woman to her home in Ireland, when I honked at a poky driver. My companion immediately slouched in her seat, not wishing to be seen with one who broke a social code against honking in impatience. Taken for granted in New York, that behavior was not acceptable in Cork. Even more, it was marked by a "how dare you" and "this is not the way we do things." My friend politely pointed out, "Most people around here wouldn't imagine doing that." The social codes I have in mind are found in the way people speak about their lives, in the kinds of images and folk-sayings they use, and in the kinds of stories they tell—and in what is allowed and not allowed via such images and sayings.

In some societies, hospitality is such a prized feature of life that a family will go without food in order to provide for the visitor. Once in the South Pacific a restaurant owner told me he would be insulted if I left a tip on the table. "You can buy my food and I must be able to make a profit. But my hospitality is between us as human beings. It is not for sale and has no price." This man thought differently about what happens in a restaurant than most people in the U.S. do. He then put his conviction about hospitality into a story framework, an astonishing one. He said, "My great-grandfather was a cannibal and ate human flesh. Today people would consider him a savage, even though he also followed the very code of hospitality among friends I just explained to you. And so you can ask whether he was less a savage or more a savage than some today, who calmly unleash bombs from high in the air and kill people they cannot see but who would be horrified at eating human flesh." How do such differences arise, and what do they mean for us?

What I am calling attention to here is the power of a society's unifying myth or worldview, often named a "paradigm." A paradigm is a socially constructed way of thinking about and of imagining the world. It is a "story," a master-narrative that a society tells itself about its life. But since everyone is immersed in this narrative and lives it, it is rarely laid out in a beginning–middle–end kind of story. For all who accept it, a paradigm unifies the social world in which they live. For example, a widely shared paradigm in the United States is that our society provides a haven of freedom and opportunity for our own citizens. Our nation is a place where you can fulfill your dreams, as long as you are willing to work hard. Such paradigms evolve socially over long periods of time, creating the way we look at the world. Once seen for what it is, a paradigm can provide a platform for self-reflection.

My own hunch about paradigms is that most people make use of layers of master-narratives, now applying one to a situation, and then applying another. Paradigms are not fixed-in-place but mobile and shifting, the way bubbles of oil float around in water. Another hunch is that several "master"-narratives operate at any one time, with a particular one taking the actual master position at a particular moment or in a particular context, sort of like children playing "king of the mountain" and endlessly displacing one another.

We like to think that our religious convictions fully direct our lives. We may consider ourselves practicing Christians, may know the gist of the gospel story, but be unaware how little this story actually guides our lives. Our first allegiance may in fact be to economic security, an issue constantly preoccupying our attention and determining which social issues seem important to us, how we vote, how we read the newspaper—even which newspaper we read. In fact, the very question about the true priorities among our allegiances might unnerve and anger us.

As the above example suggests, the generalities of paradigms are more easily described than their particularities. Whether we are alert to it or not, a paradigm (or master-narrative) is a feature of the imagination of every person the church reaches out to in its ministries, including youth and young adults, but also of those who do the reaching out. If we choose to ignore the imagination, then a powerful directive force in people's lives is left unnamed, unacknowledged, and possibly untouched. The Good News proclaimed by Jesus can be layered on top of an imagination instead of suffusing and transforming it.[5] Lacking that transformation, only superficial change is possible.

Those who work with young people in the churches do well to ask themselves this question: Is their hands-on master-narrative one about a devout Jew killed for his protests against injustice or a story about psychological maturity? Has the gospel-based paradigm been replaced with a psychological one?

Paradigms about Youth

AGAIN, MY concern in this essay is with the way Christian adults imagine the world of youth. We see youth through a lens, fitting them into a story about life in general. Within such a story some elements are more important than others. If we can understand what those elements are and why, we get a better grasp

5. For a powerful account of the process of transformation worked out in the fourth century for those seeking to be Christians, see Thomas M. Finn, "It Happened One Saturday Night: Ritual and Conversion in Augustine's North Africa," in Michael Warren, ed., *Sourcebook for Modern Catechetics*, vol. 2 (Winona, MN: St. Mary's, 1997) 12–38.

of how we organize in our own imaginations what it means to be young today. How do we imagine the young? A different but related matter concerns how the young imagine themselves and the purposes of their own lives. What is their master-narrative? How do we wish to influence that narrative?

In some church literature, the world of youth is the world of interior struggle for identity, the world of psychological integration, an inner world of psychic tasks one must face as a self. These tasks are seen as a series of sequential steps upward to higher levels. It is almost as if the religious task is impossible until the psychological one is completed. The psychological task becomes a religious task in the sense of its being an indispensable, prior condition needing completion before any deep religious transformation is possible. When the psychological struggle/steps are successfully completed, the person has reached human wholeness. One particular step, achieving identity and coming to know who one is, is seen as the narrow gate though which young people pass before proceeding to the further tasks in the life cycle.

The basic metaphors in such thinking are those of height and depth, of going higher and deeper. For those who work with youth, these metaphors often represent the "standard account"—that is, the most common set of assumptions guiding their efforts. For those who accept it, this account imagines the condition of the young today and names the religious tasks to be faced. Those religious tasks are mainly psychological, inner tasks. The psychological foundation of this "standard account" is, I believe, based on a few writings of Erik Erikson and an inadequate grasp of his approach to the human situation.

I question this account's adequacy for guiding church work with youth or even as providing an account of the situation of youth today. I believe church people should at least examine the standard account's assumptions. Here I will use a one-paragraph example to show how the standard account can be found in church statements about youth, even in good ones. The document in which it appears has important things to say about the role of parents, family, local church, and church schools in the Christian formation of youth, and, of course, about the active role of youth themselves in that process. I cite the statement only as an example of the standard account.

The Roman Catholic pastoral statement on ministry with youth begins with these words:

> All human beings experience change during adolescence. This change can be exciting if it awakens a deeper sense of self-identity, leads to the expansion of authentic freedom, enhances our ability to relate to others, and promotes greater maturity. However, the

changes of adolescence can also be depressing, alienating and filled
with self-doubt and anxiety.[6]

Here, deeper self-identity makes change "exciting"; authentic freedom is to be
expanded; our relational abilities are to be enhanced, with maturity promoted.
If this does not happen, the opposite of "exciting" can result: depression, alienation, self-doubt, and anxiety.

Encapsulated in these three sentences is what I have called the generalized
"standard account" of what it means to be young today and what the needs
of the young are. Offering a framework for thinking about youth, it imagines
young persons as abstracted beings undergoing the challenge of change in an
inner world, inhabited only by the self. That story is one of inner, psychic turmoil and a preoccupation with a search for who one really is. The story is both
individual and developmental, each person meant to move toward ever-fuller
functioning: awakened, deepened, expanded, enhanced, promoted, etc. Each
person needs to resolve these struggles before moving on to the next stage in
the progression. Starting a reflection on youth in the church in such a way is like
starting to button your coat with the wrong button: all the buttons go wrong.

Absent from this paragraph are parents, brothers and sisters, aunts and
uncles, and friends: the circle of those who might be expected to love us and
to encourage us to become loving, trustworthy human beings. There are no
conversations about everyday problems and struggles. There are no faces that
see in us a particular person with particular gifts and deficiencies. There is no

6. The statement is "The Challenge of Adolescent Catechesis: Maturing in Faith," published by the National Federation of Catholic Youth Ministry in 1986. I am making a single
point about it: its starting paragraph. Here the condition of young people is defined by the
psychological struggles of adolescents. By helping young people deal with these struggles, the
Christian community helps the young grow as "persons and believers." This document was
never adopted by the U.S. bishops as their own statement. Had it been, I presume it would
have been revised. At it stands, it is an anomaly. Its starting point is the inner psychological
struggle. Almost all "official" Roman Catholic ecclesial statements begin with assessments
of the social conditions of life, not the psychological, inner world. The anomaly deserves
scrutiny. The collection of documents in which my copy of the "Challenge of Adolescent
Catechesis" appears is *The Catechetical Documents: With Commentary and Index* (Chicago:
Liturgy Training Publications, 1996). Here twelve church-related documents are reprinted.
An examination of each document's framework shows that they all start with a social framework: What situation in the church (and/or) in society gives rise to this document? Readers
should check this assertion for themselves, while being aware that some introductions give
the history of the writing of the document, while others put those matters into a preface. The
actual start of the document is the contextualizing of the issue(s) being addressed. I consider
it most important for readers to know that "The Challenge of Adolescent Catechesis," was
replaced in 1997 with a much more nuanced and satisfactory text, "Renewing the Vision:
A Framework for Catholic Youth Ministry," *Origins* 27:9 (July 31, 1997) 133/135–48. I use
the older text here as an example of how much the psychological angle has dominated our
imagination of what the ministry to and with youth entails.

social wisdom, no religious commitments, no intuitions about the presence of God; no loving adults as kinds of midwives helping birth the more alive and enhanced self and its relationships. Yet, these psychological needs of youth are meant to set the stage for church efforts to invite the young—to what?

What we have here is a psychological paradigm. Youth are individuals in psychological pain needing psychological healing and little more. Missing from this opening paragraph is an awareness of the outer world of culture and social systems.

Eventually, the document I've quoted here, "The Challenge of Adolescent Catechesis," was revised and replaced by a much better, broader statement, "Renewing the Vision." A friend who attended the conference that "celebrated" the new document remarked that two conferences were going on in the hotel at once. One was the Catholic conference on youth ministry and youth catechesis; the second was a conference on military weaponry. He ducked into the second conference and heard what he considered some hair-raising statements about the "kill-ratios" of certain weapons. He returned to the youth conference to hear a discussion of "youth assets." His response was intriguing. He claimed there was nothing in the youth assets presentation that could raise any questions about what was going on in the next room, about weapons. The "youth assets" perspective as he heard it offered no angle from which to critique the "new and better weapons" perspective.

Questioning the Critique

Some may find my way of dealing with the above statement, "All human beings experience change during adolescence," etc., arbitrary and subjective, a cheap attack on a few lines about the young. However, I did not pick this particular statement at random. I chose it because I was asked to be a consultant to the writing of the document in which the statement appears. In correspondence with the committee drafting the document, I noted it would be good to start where nearly all church documents start, with the social situation in which the church exists and in which those addressed by the document exist. The social situation of young people is not defined by their "inner turmoil" alone. Taking "inner turmoil" as the starting point gets pastoral action off on the wrong foot. As a consultant, I suspected that the more critical "turmoil" was being created by commercial attempts to corner the "youth market" or by celebratory depictions of violence and sexual exploitation.

Let me move beyond mere criticism here, however, and offer a constructive statement of my own. Everybody's life is marked by the human condition. Even young children come to see that nobody is happy all the time. Moments of happiness are matched by times of disappointment and sadness. In one's teen years the joy in friendship and emotional connections sometimes can be blunted or destroyed by betrayal, indifference, or emotional manipulation. Still, in the lives of most of us, young and old alike, are persons who we know love us and who encourage us to be our best selves. We cherish these people as gifts. They help us imagine ourselves in the future. We also trust that in our future are persons, as yet unknown to us, who will also love us and whom we will love. Best of all we know that there are some whose lives are happier because we exist and are "there" for them. This knowledge gives us courage when things seem hopeless. Some of us have also come to understand the goodness of life as a gift of God, and God as a loving presence. All who love us provide a kind of invisible circle of love around us, encouraging us to be our best selves and protecting us from our worst impulses. They give us hope as we face the future and contemplate how we too might contribute something to the world.

A person's life can be fundamentally shaped by betrayal, unresponsiveness, emotional manipulation, physical abuse, and inhuman deprivation of basic necessities like safety, food, and shelter. These deficits often represent an invisible circle of hostility around the self not easily overcome or healed. Still, even in the face of such harms, human beings have resources that can find hope. Nurturing love, found in human connectedness, is one such resource. Religious conviction is another.

Of course, there are social issues also tied to this human condition. Some, especially young people, are frightened when they consider the condition of the world of their future. Will the world be destroyed by nuclear, biological, or chemical weapons? Why is there so much global injustice? Who is paying attention to these matters? Is the purpose of life achieved by wealth and endless winter and summer holidays? Who are the adults working to solve *these* problems?

Another Example of the Standard Account: Young Adults

IN NOVEMBER 1996, the U.S. Catholic bishops formally adopted for publication a pastoral plan for ministry with young adults, entitled "Sons and Daughters of the Light."[7] This plan was not authored by the bishops themselves but by a committee of persons working with young adults between eighteen and thirty-five years of age. A year and a half later, in 1998, an independent group concerned for ministry to young adults produced an additional document—a guide for

---

7. For the original plan, see U.S. Bishops Meeting, "Sons and Daughters of the Light: A Pastoral Plan for Ministry with Young Adults," *Origins* 26:24 (November 28, 1996) 384–402.

implementing the 1996 Plan. This "Guide" provides a second encapsulated version of the "standard account" about young people.[8]

The Guide introduces the movement from youth to mature adulthood as a "long transition in the United States . . . , [occurring over] a wide age range of 18–35."[9] While young adults of such differing ages are not a homogeneous population, they are seen as having certain specific "developmental tasks" in common. Mature adulthood, in this document, is achieved sometime before or near age thirty-five. The Guide goes on to list specific tasks as activities appropriate for a person's age or vocation. A person becomes "ripe" for the learning experience required for a particular task. On completing it the young person achieves a degree of happiness and experiences readiness to move on to the next level.

The Guide lists four task areas, each with specific subtasks. The four areas are personal identity, relationships, work, and spiritual life. What is the source of this listing of tasks and subtasks? Its source can be found in note 12 of "Sons and Daughters of the Light," the original Bishops' plan of November 1996: "Robert Havinghurst pioneered the notion of 'developmental tasks' at various stages of development. The work of developmentalists such as Erik Erikson, Jean Piaget, Lawrence Kohlberg, Carol Gilligan, William Perry and Kenneth Keniston has been used in identifying 10 developmental tasks."

The document does not explicitly say that young adults are "nowhere" or "not fully adult" or "incomplete," but the clear implication of "developmental tasks at various stages of development" is that something important is missing. Just what is this something? It seems to be that people in this age group are "developmentally" undeveloped. The Guide (and even the Plan on which the

8. Here I am dealing mostly with the guide, not with the more nuanced and more socially attentive plan, "Sons and Daughters," published in November 1996.

9. To me it is ironic that this phrase, "transition to adulthood," echoes the title of a very important book, published in 1974, James S. Coleman, et al., *Youth: Transition to Adulthood (Report of the Panel on Youth of the President's Science Advisory Committee)* (Chicago: University of Chicago Press, 1974). Those interested in this "move" to adulthood do well to attend to "Part 2: Background," 9–125 and its seven subsections: 1. History of Age Grouping in America (9–29); 2. Rights of Children and Youth (29–45); 3. The Demography of Youth (45–64); 4. Economic Problems of Youth (64–75); 5. Current Educational Institutions (76–91); 6. Biological, Psychological and Socio-Cultural Aspects of Adolescence and Youth (91–111); 7. Youth Culture (112–25). The first of these sections, and possibly the second, was almost certainly written by Joseph F. Kett, the eminent University of Virginia historian, who three years after this report published *Rites of Passage: Adolescence in America, 1790 to the Present* (New York: Basic, 1977). The Coleman and Kett books break the dominance of the psychological master-narrative about youth quite decisively. Both books suggest that the "reality" of the young is much more complex than one can grasp from even the best of psychology. Much that is written about youth would have never seen the light of day had the writers been more aware of social realities lived by the young.

Guide is commenting) appears to define young adulthood as a period of four "lacks" or deficiencies, a period of personal incompleteness, a kind of precondition for adulthood.

Language describing a person by a series of "not yets" can be questioned for its helpfulness for understanding the human situation for any age group. Does this language truly help either those ministering with such people or the people themselves understand what it means to be a Self or more importantly what sort of self one hopes to be? Is there not lurking here an illusory imagination of oneself as one-day fully "developed," of having scaled the Everest of humanization, the peak of human development?

Craig Dykstra, in his critique of developmentalism as applied to moral growth, points out that developmental theory seems to set out a universally predetermined path, implying that growth means moving ever forward on that upward path:

> A developmental approach to moral growth tends to hide . . . the lapses, vacillations, and even prolonged regressions that are common to our moral striving. Moral development sees moral growth as a matter of moving progressively and irreversibly through a hierarchy of stages. But we do not experience the moral life this way. We have moments of clear vision and corresponding appropriate action. But following on these, we then also experience times of great moral darkness in which we can neither see what is going on nor have any strength to respond. The quality of our moral lives does not necessarily improve in a linear progressive fashion. . . . [W]e can become more egocentric, despairing, and defensive, more insulated from and distrusting of other people, more shallow and less discerning than we were at earlier times in our lives.[10]

Speaking from personal experience, I have met teens, even children, who, in relationships, identity, work, and spiritual life, seem more proficient than many adults in their fifties and sixties. Such young people seem more large-hearted, more willing to share the pain of others, more committed to issues and people they have never met, than many people three and four times their ages. Are they complete? Of course not. Incompleteness is the character of the human condition. But they are certainly not to be defined by what they lack rather than who they are.

What is most interesting about the Guide's actual "guidance" for ecclesial interventions with young people eighteen to thirty-five is that more than twelve pages of its text are about the four specific "task areas"—identity, relationships,

10. Craig Dykstra, *Vision and Character: A Christian Educator's Alternative to Kohlberg* (New York: Paulist, 1981) 65.

work, and spiritual life—with each task subdivided and explained in detail for its "implications." These pages are followed by details from consumer research about the "social and cultural characteristics" of young adults and what they are looking for. The subtext of this section seems to be this: Young adults need to have their social and cultural characteristics "massaged" so they can see the church as the place where these needs will be met.

This section of the Guide ends with twelve "implications for ministry," each one beginning with "we must" or "we need to," all cast as vague exhortations, a rhetorical flourish masking a lack of insight. The goals and needs implied in these "implications" could be set out for young adult members of the Rotary Club, the Lions Club, or the Knights of Pythias, or even for increasing a more intimate clientele of a singles bar in the Hamptons. For example, Implication 6: "We *need to assist* [emphasis added] young adults in establishing new relationships with their families of origin, in re-negotiating their relationships with their parents in an adult-to-adult way. They also need our support in finding ways of being intimate with others—family, friends, members of the opposite sex—which are healthy, holy, and age-appropriate."

My questions:

1. Who are the "We" who will undertake this task?
2. Specifically, how are such "new relationships" to be established and nourished?
3. What particular forms of "support" for "being intimate with others" do the writers of Implication 6 have in mind, and who will provide them, and how?
4. What are some of the "healthy, holy, and age-appropriate" ways of being intimate?

Riches of the Assembly for Youth

THE CHURCH is not a club. Its fundamental goals are not entertainment-centered. Its purpose is not to invite members to make themselves their own pets.[11] Ecclesial practice is ordered toward human flourishing. Where it exhibits the way of Jesus, the church is often unsettling, especially to those who are new to its practices and convictions. The church gathers to remember the dangerous life and cruel death of a Galilean Jew, and the continuing presence of the Spirit of Jesus Christ. Persons live in the Spirit of God when they feed the hungry,

11. See Donald Evans, *Struggle and Fulfillment: The Inner Dynamics of Religion and Morality* (New York: Collins, 1979). The passage on making oneself one's own pet is on 144, in a section dealing with self-indulgence. This book has important pastoral implications. Readers working with the young may want particularly to read chapters 7 and 8, 111–53.

clothe the naked, visit the imprisoned, shelter the homeless, forgive debts, and offer the poor the Good News: that their misery is not God's intention. The church's word is one of life and hope. The church's appeal is this: Come and walk with us in this journey to humanization by prizing the sacredness of others. Readers do well to ask if this is indeed a valid version of "the agenda" and, if not, what version they themselves would propose. However readers decide, they should consider that this paragraph's gospel-framed rendition of ministry with young adults is lacking in the Guide.

Still, the church does not ask for a full, all-at-once commitment. Like its ritual of penance in the Eucharist (gradual, incremental, and never-ending, echoing in the Our Father, the Lamb of God refrain, and in the pre-communion, "Lord, I am not worthy"), one's place in gospel practice is gradual, invitational, but self-implicating. The church says, "Walk with us as we try to become healers." Such an invitation is clearly welcoming, not manipulative like a marketing strategy, but it is also clear that the invitation is to the practice of the beatitudes and the kinds of "recognitions" of who the proxies of Jesus are, as found in Matthew 25. It would be ironic if Alcoholics Anonymous were able to put right out front its agenda of sobriety, while ecclesial groups were reluctant to do the same with their agenda of discipleship and living the beatitudes.

A basic metaphor for life in the church is apprenticeship.[12] All are apprentices in trying to live the gospel, always learning a more proficient exhibiting of the practices of discipleship. Together, members embody a community of practice of the struggle to be faithful to the teachings and ways of Jesus. Apprenticeship is about learning how to work at normative practice. When you do the things of gospel apprenticeship, the church readily admits you may not always feel good about yourself. Actually you may find some of these tasks inconvenient and distasteful. The purpose is to give comfort to others. Not exhibited in the Guide, whose most inept section, in my judgment, is entitled "Spiritual Life," issues of gospel apprenticeship are far more clearly set out in the "Sons and Daughters" Pastoral Plan done by the bishops.[13]

The church is not saying to young people, "If only you had faith you could see what we are about." Instead, it says to young people (and everybody else) something like this: Even if you have trouble believing in the traditional teachings, you can still see the gospel being lived. It is observable, discernable, and visible. You might not want to be part of it, or you might judge it to be insane or stupid, but the "it" cannot be denied. That was the way Jesus himself spoke

12. See the *General Directory for Catechesis* (1998) for its use of the metaphor of apprenticeship.

13. One of the best sections of the "Sons and Daughters" pastoral plan is Part II: "A Vision of Faith for Young Adults," 390–92 of the *Origins* text.

to the disciples of the Baptist when they asked him if he were the promised one. "The blind recover their sight, cripples walk, lepers are cured, the deaf hear, dead people are raised to life, and the poor have the good news preached to them" (Matt 11:5; Luke 7:22). And so any announcement of the local church as sacrament of the living spirit of Jesus points to something tangible and actual. As the blind man in John's gospel in effect says to the better-educated scoffers, "It's the deeds, stupid!" or as Jesus himself suggested in a timeless analogy, "You will know there is yeast in the dough when you see the loaf is in fact rising," the church endorses a pastoral strategy of effective living signs. In fact, effective living signs are its core catechetical message.

What is the program being suggested here for young adults? Perhaps what I have in mind is best described by Paul as he encourages the faith-filled in Thessalonica to honor and live according to what they already know, but "even more" deeply:

> Brothers and sisters, may the Lord make you increase and abound in love for one another and for all, just as we have for you, so as to strengthen your hearts, to be blameless in holiness before our God and Father at the coming of our Lord Jesus with all his holy ones. Amen. Finally, brothers and sisters, we earnestly ask and exhort you in the Lord Jesus, that as you received from us how you should con- duct yourselves to please God—and as you are conducting your- selves—you do so even more. For you know what instructions we gave you through the Lord Jesus. (1 Thess 3:11–13; 4:1–2)

Misuses of Erikson's Notion of Identity in Youth Ministry

AT THIS point I return to the psychological paradigm, but in doing so, I must make clear my appreciation of the work of Erik Erikson. Though some have tended to take his theoretical essay on the epigenetic stages of life for a factual, step-by-step actuality, he himself always held to it as a theoretical exercise, helpful as a way of conceptualizing human development, but no more than that. The very placement of "The Eight Ages of Man" in his *Childhood and Society* suggests the nuance of his thought. His famous taxonomy of epigen- etic stages in "Eight Ages" is sandwiched between two essays, one, "Toys and Reasons," about the role of play and family life in a child's development, the other, "Reflections on the American Identity," about how a national identity can be self-deceiving and poisonous, unless properly critiqued. Erikson's field has always seemed to me to be social psychology and the social sources of iden- tity. For Erikson identity is an active synthesis of a person's essence as worked out in community. Identity is a process *"located" in the core of the individual* and yet also *in the core of . . . communal culture,* a process which establishes, in fact, the identity of those two identities [individual and communal]. . . . [Identity] becomes ever more inclusive as the individual grows aware of a widening circle of others significant to him [or her], from the maternal person to "[hu]mankind."[14]

However, to read some accounts of his work, his main interest was in "stage theory," with its semi-mechanistic tendencies. Such accounts distort his ideas.[15] Those who base their theoretical propositions about the conditions of youth and identity on this or that essay of Erikson may have missed the nuance of his genius. If they extract from his work the narrative of psychological development I am calling "the standard account," they have missed his point. My fear is that some who in a graduate course about youth have read a few of Erikson's essays, especially "The Eight Ages," attempt to spin out a rendition of the human condition that centers on "moreness" and "fuller functioning" that is at root quite vague.

Though Erikson has been misinterpreted, his ideas have also been given critical study, especially his very concept of "identity." Erikson himself may have unwittingly fostered the misunderstanding so many take from his writings. In *The Radical Spirit: Essays on Psychoanalysis and Society,*[16] Joel Kovel both credits and critiques Erikson. He credits him with taking psychology out of the hothouse aura that had come to surround psychoanalysis and with connecting psychology with what Erikson called "actuality." Single-handedly, Erikson invented the field of psychohistory. He exposed the developmental side of human phenomena in a manner that made it accessible and credible to many. Neither did he flinch in facing the dilemma Freud was unable to solve: how unconscious mental life affects events outside the self and, conversely, how social situations affect the unconscious. Erikson broke free of Freud's deterministic insistence on the primacy of the struggles of early childhood.

These affirmations notwithstanding, Kovel critiques Erikson for failing to address the full complexities of human choice and for downplaying the place

14. Erik Erikson, *Identity, Youth, and Crisis* (New York: Norton, 1968) 22–23 (emphasis his).

15. See for example, *Identity, Youth, and Crisis,* ch. 2: "Foundations in Observation," 44–90, particularly 84–85, for his observations on the destructiveness of treating persons (and life itself) as a machine. The first chapter, "Reflections on the Revolt of Humanist Youth," 193–224, of *Life History and the Historical Moment* (New York: Norton, 1975), has a "classic" quality to its memorable summons to the young to face their own responsibility for those younger than they. These aspects of his thinking do not show up in applications of his thought to youth ministry.

16. Joel Kovel, *The Radical Spirit: Essays on Psychoanalysis and Society* (London: Free Association, 1988), "Erik Erikson's Psychohistory," 68–115.

of evil in human interactions. For Kovel, then, Erikson opts for an unhelpful optimism described in the following two passages:

> [I]f as Erikson holds, we are always renewing ourselves, if we are not trapped in origins but remake the world, and make a community in so doing, then hope is not only a legitimate aspiration, but becomes, along with trust, initiative, fidelity, and the other virtues postulated by Erikson, part of the determining matrix of life.[17]

> [For Erikson] goodness resides in drawing together, in the whole-ness of a situation rather than in any particular part. Badness lies in moralistic exclusion, condemnation of the other as a "dirty speck in our moral vision." Fortunately, development tends towards whole-ness, greater inclusivity. "What is" and "what ought to be" converge, aided by truth-telling, as in psychoanalysis, or the great religious insights that succeed in re-establishing links between the adult reasoning mind and the well-spring of infantile trust as well as the ineffable mysteries of life.[18]

What Kovel is saying here is that Erikson nearly deifies the concept of iden-tity: "He compulsively makes identity both a manifestation of the summum bonum and an active force,"[19] making it impervious to any major critique. Examining Erikson's use of "identity" in various contexts of his writings, Kovel finds that the concept of identity is often "fuzzy" and vague—and overused.[20] The world of social structures is more complex and dangerous for Kovel than for Erikson.[21]

A good complement, or even alternative, to the Eriksonian concept of "identity" is the concept of "the self," as set out in Charles Taylor's *Sources of the Self: The Making of the Modern Identity*.[22] While also connecting identity and

17. Ibid., 70.

18. Ibid., 71.

19. Ibid., 72.

20. As I was working on this essay, I came across a previously unpublished letter written by Erikson to a woman who had inquired about his own religious identity and, specifically, his Christian identity. Readers may want to examine this letter for its vague, unspecific char-acter. See "Letter: Erikson on his own identity," *Doubletake* 6:4 (Fall 2000) 32–34.

21. I encourage readers to examine the cogency of Kovel's position on Erikson, but to also read "Therapy in Late Capitalism," chapter 7 of his *The Radical Spirit*. Kovel's critique of Erikson, at the least, invites thoughtful youth ministers to reconsider what they mean when they speak about the identity of youth.

22. (Cambridge: Harvard University Press, 1989). See also his important, *The Ethics of Au-thenticity* (Cambridge: Harvard University Press, 1992). Readers who teach courses about youth and the church might consider replacing some Erikson readings with material from either of these two books. It is time to shift the canonical or "must" readings. I also recommend Nancy Sherman, *The Fabric of Character: Aristotle's Theory of Virtue* (Oxford: Clarendon Press, 1989).

self, Taylor's approach to identity is more focused and specific than Erikson's and opens up the religious and moral dimensions of identity's most spontaneous expression: Who am I?

The deeply felt question "Who am I?" helps us know where we stand and for what and whom we stand. Our identities are formed by our commitments and our way of naming and judging the world. These commitments and ways of naming reality provide the framework for our world and the horizon from which we see it.

Here we come back to the issue that opened this essay: paradigms and narrative frameworks. Taylor says, "My identity is defined by the commitments and identifications which provide the frame or horizon within which I can try to determine from case to case what is good, or valuable, or what ought to be done, or what I endorse or oppose. In other words, it is the horizon from which I am capable of taking a stand."[23] Taylor later notes that to lose this orientation, or never to have found it, is to not know who one is.[24] From this perspective an "identity crisis" can be understood as a kind of disorientation or radical uncertainty about where one stands and what one stands for.

The "who am I" question never disappears. One has to reengage the question over and over again.[25] Commitments need to be continually renegotiated and reaffirmed as true expressions of the self. Again, to suggest that such renegotiation is done alone in the supposed solitude of the self is to overlook the social, communal character of the "commitments and identifications" that frame our world. In my view, many people between the ages of eighteen and thirty-five are searching for wisdom about those commitments and identifications. They have hunches about the direction in which wisdom is found, and a validating ecclesial chorus of wisdom can help them trust these hunches and follow them. Lacking such a chorus they can be overwhelmed by the incessant counter-wisdom found in commercial media's omnipresent counter-chorus.

Though not writing out of or about a church context, Taylor offers a challenge to any ecclesial assembly espousing the wisdom of Jesus. "Deciding for yourself but not by yourself" seems to be the appropriate motto for those in ministry with young adults. Many ministries with young adults never pose or even advert to the pressing questions about choices and decisions surging in the very young adults these ministries are to serve. The skills of young adult ministry are those of setting up contexts where the vital questions affecting young adults can be asked as part of a prayerful communal search for wisdom.

---

23. Taylor, *Sources*, 27.

24. Ibid., 29.

25. See "Conclusion: The Conflicts of Modernity," 502–13 of Taylor's *Sources*.

Lacking such contexts some young people may later say, "We asked for bread and you gave us a stone."

The Market Economy and Youth Ministry

IF CHARLES Taylor helps provide youth ministry with images of human responsibility and flourishing, there are other forces impinging on the lives of youth that do quite the opposite. Young adults in Western societies are a fiercely contested market, whose inclinations and impulses are given intense scrutiny. After all, their collective income is in the multibillion-dollar range. The marketers, in my view, are offering neither bread nor stones, but Twinkies. Religious people cannot suppose young adults are any the less influenced by the "production of desire" of the marketing industry than they themselves are. If they wish to invite young adults to consider seriously the option of the gospel, they may have to introduce these young people to a set of "commitments and identifications" they may not have yet considered. These proposals are often unsettling, even to those who propose them. One of the most difficult "developmental tasks" will be the often gradual one of proposing a gospel framework embodied in relationships, in work, and in attitudes toward money.

On the question of relationships, those of us ministering to youth may need to raise the touchy issue of to what extent erotic relationships are imagined for many today by market forces. In an earlier time, marriage expressed the values of real estate, and fidelity was connected to the economic importance of not having to divide and/or sell off the land. But in a new kind of market today, land is no longer the dominant issue. Moving one's capital quickly but intelligently so as to make the greatest return on investment is now a prime skill. In a society where capital is free to move wherever it pleases so long as it increases, the sexual desire also trades on itself, intending to get the greatest return on its search for pleasure. "Fidelity" becomes first fidelity to self, to one's own interests, to one's expanded satisfactions. One's investment must show profit if one is not to withdraw it and invest it elsewhere. "This whole approach to sexuality and sexual desire reproduces, while desiring to fight against, a model of liberal capitalism founded on the free circulation of money (i.e., desire) and free trade."[26] More generally, the creation of desire is so much a part of the market economy that many persons are confused about what they really want from relationships, from work, from love.

---

26. See Eric Fuchs, *Sexual Desire and Love* (New York: Seabury, 1983) 17. I have paraphrased a section of this page.

Conclusion: Fidelity, Eucharist, and Human Dignity

WHEN I had the youth catechesis desk at the United States Catholic Conference in the 1970s, ministry to young adults was just getting the attention of various denominations. I was on the mailing list for the newsletters of many diocesan young adult ministry offices and read those newsletters with great interest. The impression I got from most of these communications—but not all—was that young adult ministry was being run as a church-sponsored singles club. Most (but not all) of the events reported were entertainment-related: dances, events related to holidays like Christmas, and various kinds of trips: to shopping malls, ski resorts, music festivals and theater, sports events, and so forth. Whether such events aided the "developmental tasks" I could not be sure, but of their fun and entertainment value there seemed to be no doubt. My questions at that time were: Could one do these activities and still rest happily in the arms of the marketers? Are vital energies being squandered here? When, in these groups, will there be any whispering of the secrets of Jesus-faith? What actual communities of radical gospel practice will help these persons take on an identity shaped by Jesus' beatitudes?

In conclusion, let me return to the three convictions that form the framework of this essay. First, fidelity is at the heart of any gathering in the name of Jesus. Fidelity to what? To the good news Jesus proclaimed to the poor and the captives and to the way of living embodied in Jesus' own life.

Second, as I stressed at the outset, the prototypical assembly of Christians, the Eucharist, also offers guidance for ministry with youth. The Eucharist defines Christian life as double-sided: offering thanks for the Spirit of Jesus present in the assembly and begging forgiveness for not recognizing the face of Jesus in the hungry, the thirsty, the sick, and the imprisoned, in those without shelter or clothing. It is where we name God's goodness, remember what Jesus endured in the name of justice, and ask for help in living the beatitudes. The Eucharist is the gathering suffused with Jesus' imagination. In this way the Eucharist undermines the Entitled Self of consumer capitalism.[27] It establishes a struggle between God's call to be healers in a broken world and our own worst impulses.

The third conviction regarding youth ministry concerns recognizing the dignity of each young person—honoring the often slow movement of ourselves and others toward the full humanization represented by the imagination of Jesus, recognizing the possibilities in each of more fully embodying the gospel. These very possibilities are what encourage us to propose to young people alter-

---

27. For more on the entitled self, see Michael Warren, "The Bottom Line of Youth Ministry: Fostering Self-Esteem," *The Living Light* 36:3 (Spring 2000) 53–65.

native sensibilities or ways of processing everyday experiences and alternative judgments about which things in life are of greater or lesser value.

Sensibility is about "how things hit us." When persons see violence, not only acted out but also cheered by others, and find themselves unable to join in the cheering or even able to watch the violence, then they exhibit a distinctive way of understanding and judging human actions, a distinctive way of being in the world. When they respond that way because of the example of Jesus, then they show a gospel sensibility. If character is defined by the things we will not let ourselves do, then it is also defined by the things we find funny or admirable and the things we find tear-wrenching or horrible. Ministry that cherishes each person's dignity is attentive to sensibility and judgment. In short, a gospel sensibility rejoices in what enhances the "human thing" in each person and, of course, in groups. Youth ministry is a ministry to sensibility and judgment.

4

Youth Ministry in an Inconvenient Church

Michael Warren

THIS ESSAY revisits issues set out in "The Imaginations of Youth" but with a more specific look at the actual practices of youth ministry. What might churches do to reverse or counter the commodification of youth that David White explains so compellingly in his essays? Some readers might puzzle over my title, particularly its phrase "in an inconvenient church." In my view, ministry to and with youth loses its coherence unless it embraces its "inconvenient" character.

A proper grasp of ministry today demands understanding two realities: mission and manners. Ministry in the churches cannot be properly understood outside of *mission*, the mission of Jesus, which he did not originate but which was given to him by God. We find that mission in the gospels and other New Testament writings. Jesus' mission marked him with a particular character, even defined him. Jesus' mission was not only laborious and inconvenient, it was dangerous. As the prophets showed, one could be killed for it, and Jesus was. What exactly was that mission? It can be found in various of Jesus' words in the gospels, but a stunning summary is in Matthew 11, when the jailed John the Baptist sends his followers to Jesus to ask him, "Are you the one who is to come, or should we look for someone else?" Jesus' answer is about his mission, and it is interesting how it moves to a crescendo: "Go back and report to John what you hear and see: the blind recover their sight, cripples walk, lepers are cured, the deaf hear, dead people are raised to life, and"—and what? what is

61

the last sign that Jesus' mission is truly of God?—"the poor have the good news preached to them" (Matt 11:4–6). And what is that good news? That their misery is not God's will but a human abomination.

The earliest churches took on that mission, and the result was various ministries all tied to being a disciple of Jesus and announcing a new flowering of God's mercy in a particular time and place. Those ministries were not programs of managerial efficiency; they were expressions of who they were as an embodiment of Jesus' mission. Their mission and ministries defined them.

Today, fulfilling the ecclesial mission is also impossible without proper attention to *manners,* a word I am using here to refer to culture. Just as Jesus' was, our mission today is defined in part by the challenges of our societal manners or culture. The cultural backdrop of Jesus' own ministry—the worldview, the mythology, and the theology—are not the backdrop of our own ministry. The religious and moral assumptions of former times that helped reinforce religious teaching and practice are simply not present. Today, if we wish to adopt Jesus' own convictions, we can do so only by articulating and living a personal and communal vision that may never again become the sort of public reality that it was in Jesus' own day or in the Middle Ages. If I am correct, the church has a special task in fostering attitudes of heart that will seem odd in our culture.[1] Jesus-inspired attitudes and practices today call for carefully focused intention by the churches.

Today much of what is called youth ministry does not flow from the life of the local church and the sort of intentionality I have in mind. Most youth ministry is reduced to a program of a particular church, rather than an organic statement of its inner life. It is not what a church does when it *is* a mission and when it *is* a unity of ministries. When a local church's ministry is organic, flowing from its very life, and endemic (literally, in the *demos* or crowd or community, flowing from the very nature of the group), then *its ministry to youth* is organic and endemic. When youth ministry becomes a gesture of welcome to youth within the church that says, "This is who we are; this is how we live; we invite you to be part of our living discipleship," then it has an organic and endemic character. "Now that you are moving to a time of fuller agency in your

---

1. Charles Taylor writes: "Virtually nothing in the domain of mythology, metaphysics, or theology stands in this fashion [i.e., of earlier ages] as publicly available background today. But that doesn't mean that there is nothing in any of those domains that poets may not want to reach out to in order to say what they want to say, nor moral sources they descry there that they want to open for us. What it does mean is that their opening these domains, in default of being a move against a firm background, is an articulation of personal vision. It is one that we might come to partake in as well, as a personal vision." It can never become again an invoking of public reference, short of an almost unimaginable return—some might say regression—to a new age of faith. Charles Taylor, *Sources of the Self: The Making of the Modern Identity* (Cambridge: Harvard University Press, 1989) 491–92.

life, we invite you to walk with us in our own efforts to become better disciples of Jesus. You can enrich these efforts." As I hope to make clear, when the local church is a living sign of the good news, then its ministry to youth is likewise a living sign, flowing out of what the church is living.

But back to the New Testament churches: none of that ministry was convenient in those churches. It was about as convenient as trying to sneak food into the Warsaw ghetto, which is to say that early on, ministry was dangerous, and you could be killed for it—many were. That mission questioned policies of the state, often by refusing to go along with them, as when a baptized man had to refuse service in the emperor's army. The mission exposed injustices that were tolerated because civic leaders profited by those injustices. That's why it was dangerous. It pointed to the social castoffs and insisted they were the proxies of God's own self. These New Testament churches denounced greed, giving numerous examples of why it was evil to feast sumptuously while your household dogs ate better than the beggar starving at your gates. In today's terms, maybe we can ask why it is a social abomination when automobiles are housed in spacious heated garages while the homeless freeze on the pavements of our sidewalks,[2] or why corporations are given generous financial gifts like "corporate welfare" tax breaks, while impoverished women with small children are punished for being poor.

Youth Ministry and Discipleship

EXAMINED THROUGH the lens of the New Testament churches, one can see that much (but not all) youth ministry in today's churches lacks this character of inconvenience—let alone danger. It is a ministry of enticement by way of fun. Its goal is to get the young to love the church and to know that the church loves them. The young are to feel good about the church and to feel good about themselves. The ministry is vague about the gospel but clear about its goals: have a good time under the aegis of the church. In some (but not all) youth ministry programs, the most significant event of the year is the annual ski trip to Mt. Bliss. Although there has been an important recent redirection of youth ministry toward meeting and serving the poor, that redirection is more the exception than the rule of youth ministry in most parishes.

---

2. This comment of mine is inspired by St. John Chrysostom, who said to the comfortable Christians of Antioch, "Your dog is fed to fullness while Christ wastes with hunger. Christ has nowhere to lodge, but goes about as a stranger, and naked and hungry, and you set up houses out of town, and baths and terraces and chambers without number, in thoughtless vanity; and to Christ you give not even a share of a little hut." As quoted by Dolores Greeley, "St. John Chrysostom," in *Studia Patristica* (Elmsford, NY: Pergamon, 1982) vol. 17, pt. 3: 1163–68.

What might be the character of a youth ministry in a church of radical discipleship? What *is* a church of radical discipleship? How would the young get from A to Z in the pursuit of discipleship? How would they go from being spectators to full members in the household of the Spirit? How would they get from commitment to products in a consumerist culture to commitment to the outcasts and to gospel simplicity? How would they master the skills of discipleship? (And just what are those skills?) What changes would have to be made to make radical discipleship accessible to the young? These questions are about dilemmas that do not go away and decisions that must be made.

In dealing with these questions and arriving at wise decisions, local congregations might consider the distinction between their primary and secondary doctrines.[3] The primary doctrines of a church are about how to be a person in the world based on a religious imagination of life's purposes. These doctrines are about life's specific circumstances and how to deal with them in religiously wise and coherent ways. These are not so much the doctrines we have memorized or can recite. They are the deeper core message of the church that gets inside us and causes us to react the way we do to events in our life. They are the well from which our religious reactions and attitudes bubble forth. They form our sense of what is truly right and proper in life, how we think about life and death, what we name as good and what we say is evil. The primary doctrines are what cause certain things to hit us in a certain way. For example, the phrase "the good life" for us may not name a life filled with purchased goodies but one that takes seriously the human dignity of all persons. The primary doctrines are an indispensable pair of religious lenses that help us see with greater clarity and thus walk a more careful path. They shape a basic stance toward the world and a basic way of living and behaving.

It is possible for someone to have a solid grasp of the secondary doctrines (the doctrines about doctrines) but little grasp of the habits of the heart and basic gestures and behaviors fostered by the primary doctrines. Primary doctrines only become truly primary not so much when we grasp them as when they grasp us and determine which of the secondary doctrines we see as most important. Secondary doctrines govern the development of the community's larger body of doctrines. Such rules are one step removed from practice. This fact does not make secondary doctrines unimportant, but it does point out that they are not primary. When a community's espousal of its secondary doctrines loses touch with its primary doctrines, the community's inner life and its outer coherence are endangered and compromised. The philosopher William Christian says that if we had to choose between doctrines about doctrines

3. Here I am following some of the ideas of William A. Christian Sr., *Doctrines of Religious Communities* (New Haven: Yale University Press, 1999) ch. 1.

(secondary doctrines) and proposals about courses of action, he would opt for the second. He implies that the real danger lies in the secondary doctrines displacing the primary practical doctrines. Should the catechism displace the Beatitudes, the primary religious path has been lost. My reflections on youth ministry here seek to recover for the youth in the church the primary practical wisdom about the Jesus Way.

Looking to the Behaviors of Gospel Practice

A QUESTION over which many in the churches agonize is, *How* can we transmit to the rising generation the convictions that are meant to direct the church: the teachings and practices of Jesus whom we name Christ, and of the Jesus-tradition? British novelist David Lodge lays out in several of his novels the difficulties young adults brought up in traditional Catholic faith have in translating that faith into action today. In the old teaching, they are unable to find guidance for their current situations. "The values presented to them with much conviction in secondary school and which were taken to be the truth"[4] have little place in their current lives. The teachings, regardless of the emphatic way they have been communicated to a young person, have little later directive power in the face of daily adult choices. The question of course is, *Why?* Why have religious learnings that were so energetically proposed and to some degree embraced, so quickly evaporated? Are there conditions necessary if religious ideas are to migrate from being concepts to being convictions that intelligently guide one's life? Is teaching about religious doctrines necessary but, by itself, insufficient to communicate doctrinal truth as a compelling guide to living one's life? An even deeper question than either the *how* or *why* is *who* will whisper to them the secrets of the Jesus Way and under what credible conditions.

Ellen Charry warns about making a "forced choice" between insight-oriented and practice-oriented ways of fostering Christian virtue. Actually most people learning new skills shift constantly between reflection about action and the practice of the action itself. Charry encourages us to adopt *sapience* as the word that keeps both poles connected. She defines *sapience* as "engaged knowledge that emotionally connects the knower to the known."[5] Sapience, wisdom about living, was the form of engagement in the Christian way proposed by the church's most celebrated early teachers. Research on the outcomes of the religious teachings given in church-related schools shows emotional engage-

4. Herman Lombaerts, "From Generation to Generation" (unpublished paper, 1999) 1. Lombaerts, a multilingual pastoral theologian, teaches at the University of Louvain in Belgium.

5. Ellen T. Charry, *By the Renewing of Your Minds: The Pastoral Function of Christian Doctrine* (New York: Oxford University Press, 1997) 4.

ment backed by religious practice at home and in a local church to be essential for any lasting influence.[6] But for my present purposes, the key idea is that this intoning of proposals about Christian living is a necessary but generally insufficient condition for the actual living out of the proposal. The most basic form of teaching practical skills is by exhibiting the behavior or skills you would like people to adopt, explaining why they are good or helpful, and then coaching those desiring these skills in these same behaviors. I fear that in most churches people never get to these kinds of basics. Once that phrase is said, about getting to the basics, some people begin an inner chant deploring that so many young people don't know the basics of their faith: they can't even recite the Creed, for God's sake. But I am not talking about the basics as verbal formulas or abstract truths. By "basics" I mean the basic habits or skills needed to be a disciple of Jesus. Some of these are gestures. Today the gestures of discipleship contrast with the gestures of consumerism and, in my view, cannot take hold without some degree of confrontation with consumerism. Consider how the gestures of consumerism contrast with the gestures of the gospel.

Consumerist Gestures and Gospel Gestures

WHAT ARE the gestures of consumer capitalism? The key gesture is the closed fist. The fist that grabs, as in "grab all the gusto you can get." Or the closed fist that does not grab but that grasps, as a fundamental gesture about life: "Everything I have is mine; I earned it, and I intend to keep it," or "I'm not giving up my hard-earned money to support the lazy on welfare." Readers might be able to think of countless specific ads on TV or in print that in various ways embody this gesture. Another gesture is sometimes called "the flip," or what I prefer to call an obscene finger gesture, and as most know, it can take other forms as well. It is a dismissive gesture that says, "You got in my way. How dare you, when you are nothing. I am the only important person in this event." Verbally, the gesture is often accompanied by offensive sentences that begin with "Go . . . ," but it is also found in the bumper sticker message, "Get outta my way."

A third gesture might be "the scowl," meaning "Who do you think you are?" or "What are you doing in my neighborhood?" It is the gesture of seeing the other as the enemy. These gestures are habitual and, as habits, not so easy to break. They characterize a way of being in the world, a stance. They also point to an unpleasant imagination of our connections to others.

---

6. See Leslie J. Francis and Josephine Egan, "Catholic Schools and the Communication of Faith," *Catholic School Studies* 60, no. 2 (1987) 27–34; and "'The Catholic School as 'Faith Community'—An Empirical Inquiry," *Religious Education* 84, no. 4 (Fall 1990) 588–603.

What are the gestures of those who accept Jesus' imagination of what it means to be human? Are there gestures that are not distinctively Christian (used only by Christians) but are at least characteristically Christian, that accompany people who try to imitate the gestures of Jesus? I say there are such gestures, and most of us recognize them when we see them.

Instead of the closed fist that grabs, it is the open hand that offers food to the hungry or comfort to those in pain. It says, pass around what you have and let's see how far it goes. Open hands are a fundamental Christian gesture, and a fundamental one for public as well as private prayer. Before we take food into our hands to eat, we open our hands in thanksgiving to God for the gift of food. Instead of the obscenely raised finger, it is the healing gesture of embracing we find in the father of the Prodigal Son, or in the helping gesture of raising up that we find in the Samaritan who recognized the humanity of the injured one. Instead of the scowl, it is the look of attentive acceptance of the other, the kind of look Jesus must have had in his encounter with the woman at the well and the woman taken in adultery, or in seeing the widow giving her mite in the temple. Or it is the smile of joy at seeing the face of someone we love.

There are other gestures, but we all might do well to ponder what they are. Gestures are effective nonverbal ways of speaking. They signal attitudes wordlessly. Many of the gestures prompted by Jesus' imagination of the human have to do with food, with people in pain, with the doubtful, with the sick or dying. All these gestures—both the consumerist ones and those I am saying are gospel-inspired ones—represent learned physical ways of communicating, skillful ways of getting our point across.

Skills in General and the Skills of Discipleship

WHAT ARE the skills of discipleship appropriate to a self who has moved beyond childhood, and how will they be exhibited by a community of discipleship in such a way that the young might wish to imitate them, seeking out those most skilled in these practices as mentors? By what criteria will a person know if she or he has moved to a skill level appropriate to her or his age? These are the questions that show themselves when we ask about the kind of self inspired by Jesus and by the credible community of his followers. Can these questions be asked in a youth ministry context?

I have been struck by how young people themselves judge the importance of skills in their lives. In certain endeavors skills are clearly needed. The first of these is sports. Everyone knows you cannot walk onto an athletic field and demand to be on a sports team. You need to exhibit the skills of that sport at a level equal or nearly equal to that of the team. In most instances the skills are not just individual skills because you don't qualify for team membership unless your individual skills can be blended into team play. It is important to note here that the pursuit of ever-enhanced athletic skills, though exhausting and even tedious, is no dour endeavor. That pursuit takes place in a celebrative atmosphere, where levels of competence are openly appreciated, acknowledged, and celebrated. Whatever exhaustion is caused by the exercise of the skills is compensated for by exhilaration in achievement.

Another recognized skill regards schooling, with grades exhibiting to some degree one's level of academic proficiency. Few will deny that one must know how to write standard English prose in order to qualify for high school or college. A third uncontested zone demanding skills is work. To secure paid employment, you must show you have the skills for the position. There is no argument about these points; society has successfully taught them. I have never heard a young person even question these convictions about the need for skills.

There are, however, areas where young people don't consider the need for skills. Again, young people don't invent this conviction; society itself hands it on to them. The first of these unskilled areas is love relationships. As a nineteen-year-old once told me at the start of a semester (with considerable insight), "I don't need no marriage course to tell me the kind of person I like." Of course I like to think he eventually came to see that recognizing the kind of person one likes does not represent a full range of interpersonal skills. Another unskilled area is parenting, where love for a baby is thought to give a person a full range of parenting competence. As a new young mother said to me (again with some insight) when informed I was sending her two books about parenting, "I don't need no books to teach me how to love my baby." The third unskilled area is my concern here: religion.

Most (but not all) young people I meet see religion, particularly Christianity, as an area devoid of skill, a conviction successfully taught them by religion itself. Religion is an optional interior attitude: having nice thoughts or loving thoughts about God. The idea that a religion is a discrete set of practices that forges a distinct way of being in the world—more like an athlete's skills than a set of thoughts—is one that many young people have never considered. If there is a practice to religion, it is thought to consist of a single activity, and one they reject: attending religious services. In this equation, if you love God who knows all, God knows of your love, and you don't have to be part of a religious assembly to show that love. However, if you do assemble but don't love God, you are a hypocrite. And so, to avoid hypocrisy, don't assemble. To repeat: Where this common conviction exists, it has been successfully communicated by religion itself, by communities who have misunderstood the nature of their own religiousness.

Can ministry to youth reclaim its connection to the tradition of formation in discipleship as a set of practices necessary for "seeing the Lord"?[7] Can youth ministry do so unless the ecclesial assembly itself embraces these practices and celebrates them in ways that are credible with the young? Here I offer two examples: a negative example of the use of practices, and a positive one. In 1998, World Vision, a Christian program designed to alleviate hunger and poverty in economically distressed areas of the world, publicized its attempt to involve thousands of American youth in a fast to raise money for starving children in the world's poorest countries. Clearly aimed at youth themselves, the ad read in part:

> Make your mark through the planet's coolest event! More than 600,000 young people in the U.S. will be part of it. Twenty-one other countries will do it. It's a gathering of global proportions! It's World Vision's 30 Hour Famine—the worldwide event you and your group won't want to miss. It's fun. It's free. And best of all, the 30 Hour Famine lets you make your mark on a world that's seriously hungry. *So hungry that 33,000 kids die every single day from hunger and hunger-related causes.* Kids you and your group can help save. How? When your group goes without food for 30 hours to raise money for hungry kids, you will save kids' lives! That's what makes the 30 Hour Famine a good event. Don't miss out on the fun. You *can* make a difference—you *can* save kids' lives.

Not exactly a youth ministry message, this ad can be examined from many angles. Its language speaks for itself. The event is cool, it's fun, it's free, so don't miss out. It also misnames a fast as a famine, trivializing thereby the horrors of famine. Famine is a very different kind of event from a fast, and for those caught in it, not "a cool event" in any sense. I am not denying that a fast of solidarity might raise consciousness about world poverty and hunger and help the young reconsider what hunger feels like. My questions are these: Can this be done without trivializing youth's energies and capacity for thought the way this ad does? What other ways, less manipulative and truer to their capacities, might help the young come to understand the global collusion in the deaths of children by hunger? My other questions are about how variations of such an ad, with the same message that efforts toward solidarity with victims is fun and entertaining, can be found in youth ministry literature across the country. Like what?, you might ask. I answer that question with a question: What do the young themselves see as the supreme sacramental moment of their youth ministry gatherings over a particular year?

---

7. Exploring the practices for "seeing the Lord" is the underlying concern of Marianne Sawicki, *Seeing the Lord* (Minneapolis, MN: Fortress, 1994).

A Specific Example

A STUDENT in graduate theology, a former restaurateur, merchant seaman, butcher, and barman-cum-bouncer, accepts a part-time position in youth ministry at a suburban New York church. In his first meeting with the small group of young people who gather to meet him, he proposes they go once a week to a soup kitchen and serve meals. He also proposes they meet another day each week and prepare some simple but large nourishing dish for the hungry. None of the young people has ever been to such a place, and they are interested, though unsure their parents will approve. Neither have any of them done much cooking at home and certainly not the preparation of a large quantity of food. He explains to them that Jesus called his followers to feed the hungry, and that's what they will be doing.

When they meet the next week to cook, he doesn't need any icebreakers or group-building activities. They set to work cooking. He explains to them how to go about it. They have only so much time to complete the task: making a huge bowl of potato salad. Everybody gets busy, and they break the ice with each other as they go about their task of peeling, cutting, cooking, and so forth. When they finish about two hours later, they sit for a moment of prayer.

Two days later, at the moment for bringing the food to the soup kitchen, the young people are somewhat anxious about what is going to happen. Their mentor reassures them they will be fine, and during the forty-five minute van trip he details exactly what it will be like and what they will do. Basically, he answers their questions. They arrive, serve meals, including the one they had prepared themselves, and tumble back into the van. On the trip back to suburbia, their mentor responds to their questions about how it happens that in their area such a large group of people come to the soup kitchen to eat. They also sing songs and tell favorite jokes. In subsequent trips, the group doubles and triples as more and more young people want to cook and serve. Parents have to volunteer their vehicles and their own service as drivers. On arriving back at their church, they always spend a few minutes in prayer for those they met that day.

The questions, conversations, songs, and jokes go on for weeks and weeks of food-runs to the hungry, each trip offering an hour and a half of conversation about themselves, their world, the poor who don't eat, the rich who haul their newest purchases in their front doors and, when they no longer satisfy, out the back door to the yard sales. Implicit in the miles of driving and the hours of conversation are questions about who our neighbors are, about what those who gather to worship do in the spaces between times of worship, about the purpose of life, about discipleship, and most important of all, what it means to be a self who takes Jesus' proposals seriously. The rest is for a lengthy report. The group grows in various ways and finally agrees to spend a whole weekend learning about how certain social groups come to be beaten down, about the deeper problems of change, and about what the gospel and the church have to say about such matters. Whether the young ever state that what they did was cool or fun or free, I do not know. What I do know is that their action was not a one-time cool event but a continual, ever more attentive, ever more appreciative set of activities, sort of like a season on a soccer team.

Their action, however, did not flow from the life of their church so much as from the imagination and wisdom of their leader. What actually happened was that the youth group's efforts to feed the hungry influenced their own church, especially through parents who became part of a cadre of drivers transporting the young. The parish became more aware of hunger in their area and of the gospel call to feed the hungry, a gift brought to the Eucharistic assembly by the young.

What follows is a list of some of the practices of a parish committed to the way of living proposed by Jesus. Each ends with a recognition or an awareness needed for the practices to become actual.

Practices of a Community of Disciples

1. LOVE of Neighbor, as seen in individual and communal acts:
   - Feeding the hungry
   - Sheltering the homeless
   - Caring for and healing the wounded
   - Warming the frozen
   - Visiting the imprisoned
   - Comforting those in anguish
   - Confronting the oppressor(s)
   - Siding with the oppressed
   - Attending to the needs of those whose lives are diminished
   - A stance of doing no harm, physical or spiritual, to others
   - Counseling and/or educating the confused and the ignorant
   - *Recognition:* Seeing others as the proxies of Jesus and as the locus of God's presence

2. LOVE of the relationship between self and neighbor:
   - Forgiving wrongs done to self and others

- Seeking forgiveness for wrongs done to others
- Responding to insults and injury with kindness and compassion
- Recovering and prizing our common humanity
- Bonding with all persons of good will and seeking good will in those lacking it
- Replacing violence with peaceful sister- and brotherhood
- Fostering loving, committed relationships between life partners and between parents and children
- Resisting greed and misuse of the world's goods
- Resisting the temptation to judge the motives of others
- *Recognition*: God's presence is found in human loving-kindness

3. WORSHIP:

- A habit of communal worship based on a need to come together with others of like mind to celebrate their common faith
- The desire to so assemble
- Frequent unscripted moments of communion with God, and regular periods of prayer
- Ongoing reflection on the sacred writings
- *Recognition*: God's loving presence presses us toward a basic stance of giving thanks

Basic Principle (from *Sesame Street*): PUT DOWN THE DUCKY IF YOU WANT TO PLAY THE SAXPHONE. (You can't learn the saxophone if you insist on holding onto your rubber ducky.)

OTHERS:

- Maintaining emotional bonds in disputes
- Moderation instead of excess
- Fasting instead of addiction
- Sharing instead of hoarding
- Openhandedness instead of greed
- Generosity instead of tightfistedness

Here at the end, I can hear someone ask the following question: "Okay, Mr. Professor, I am sorry, but you have given lots of bits of ideas but only one detailed example, that of one parish you happen to know. But in my neighborhood or my church or my situation of ministry with young people in a school, cooking up bowls of macaroni for a soup kitchen just won't work. What help do you give me and my kids?"

This is an appropriate question (and not just because I have thought to ask it). I claim that any of the points within the three areas above: love of a neighbor in affliction as seen in particular acts; love of neighbor as a commitment to maintaining the relationship with neighbor; or worship can all be opened out to a skills-based effort.

Take prayer as an example. Consider developing a skills-based approach. Set up a NEXUS group ("new encounter with Christ using scripture"). It cannot be done in a vacuum or out of the blue. But when you find young people ready for prayer, wanting to know what personal prayer is all about and ready to develop some prayer skills, show them how to find space in their own home where they can quiet themselves, slow themselves down each day for ten minutes, and then pick at random a passage from the New Testament, reflect on it for five minutes, and then talk to Jesus about how it hits them, perhaps writing a few words in their journal. Then each week they come together to do the same thing in a group, sharing what they wish of their own journal reflections with the group. So they are learning to get their feet wet in private prayer and also in group prayer.

Or take the matter of maintaining interpersonal relationships. Bring young people together to develop skills of conflict resolution (using a lot of role playing), until they do it so well that they could role play these skills for younger kids. Older teens—those sixteen and older—might want to learn how to do conflict resolution in cross-gender relationships. There is some skill involved in listening to another, not getting defensive, and trying to see the situation from the others' perspective. Harriet Lerner's books *The Dance of Intimacy* and *The Dance of Anger* could be very useful in such a program particularly because they make clear God's call to love one another. I myself think there is much work to be done with young people on the skills of friendship.

Another example might be visiting the imprisoned. Philip Berrigan was seventy-six years old and spent almost two years in jail in Maine for protesting U.S. weapons production. Berrigan and others like him could be comforted with letters from young people. These ideas offered here are not theoretical. They are realizable in the real world. Are they inconvenient? Yes. But then the conviction behind this essay is that the gospel is inconvenient. In a consumerist culture, inconvenience is considered an abomination and seen as worse than the abomination of the hungry standing at our gates. Is Jesus inconvenient? Remember that the disciples on their way to Emmaus were headed away from Jerusalem, but after meeting Jesus, they returned the way they had come. Was that an inconvenient turnaround? Possibly.

PART THREE
THE DEVIL IS IN THE DETAILS

Consumerism does not announce itself by name. How could it? It has no existence of its own, none apart from us—apart, that is, from the idiosyncratic specificity of our inscribed needs and wants, our scripted dreams and disappointments, our assigned achievements and failures. Nor does consumerism care if we speak out against it, preach against it, teach against it. As long as we don't turn our analysis back upon ourselves and the institutions dearest to us, consumerism will continue to distort and diminish our lives and the lives of those to whom we minister. As is often the case, the devil is in the details. In the case of consumerism, the details are in us.

In his first essay, "Advanced Placement and the Kingdom of God," Brian Mahan names several "culture tricks" that confuse and alienate his students, before confessing that these same culture tricks confuse and alienate him too. Brian's second essay, "Youth Ministry and the Practice of Sacred Commiseration," outlines a pedagogical strategy for diagnosing and resisting these vexing and inhibiting social mechanisms.

5

Advanced Placement and the Kingdom of God

Brian J. Mahan

The Youth Theological Initiative: An Introduction

THE SUMMER Academy of the Youth Theological Initiative (YTI) takes place at Emory University in Atlanta during the month of July. There is a subtropical feel about the place, and academic routines give way to the exuberant and colorful rhythms of tennis camps, wrestling camps, and soccer camps. The youthful energies are more endorphin-based than caffeinated, and the voices are younger, louder, more exultant than during the academic year. The "scholars," the young men and women who attend YTI, fit right in. They too have found others passionate about the things they are passionate about. Their conversations are as animated, as enthusiastic and loud, as any. But there is this difference between the YTI scholars and the campers. The young men and women who play tennis, wrestle, and take to the soccer field are not surprised to find one another. Most were members of similar cliques and teams at their schools of origin. The YTI scholars, on the other hand, never quite get over the fact that they have found one another. Sadly, movingly, many are surprised to find a place where intelligent inquiry and the love of God are not set at odds, where they can be both inquisitive and faithful.

At night prayer, there are candles and Taizé chants, prolonged silences, the soaring and wounding beauty of black spirituals, the word of God preached by young hearts on fire, and music, and more music. There is a zeal at the academy that may rival that of missionaries and martyrs—a profound enthusiasm that reminds older, more jaded fellow travelers of the obscured depths of our own deepest longings and commitments.

All this is not to say that you would confuse the YTI Summer Academy with the fullness of the realized Kingdom of God. The academy represents a kind of liminal space, a place where social roles are put on hold for a time, where things that would matter profoundly otherwise are not quite so important as they were a few weeks before arriving at YTI. But this is America, after all, and there is no hiding from certain intrusive realities that pervade any and all environments, however constituted. What realities? Racial tension is one. The ubiquitous spirit of competition is another.

Clearly, racism, and the wounds, tensions and misunderstandings that accrue from it, are present in the Summer Academy. Over time, however, we've learned that racism and the inevitable hurt feelings and sporadic confrontations growing from it are not, as we first thought, interruptions of our curriculum but something essential to it. Christian love and forgiveness, reconciliation and compassion, after all, are not achieved by pronouncements that we are all one in the Lord or by the mere dispensing of information about race and racism. What is called for, rather, is hard work, self-referential work, work that hurts even as it transforms.

As for the spirit of competition—the subtle and not so subtle intrusion of what Old Testament scholar Walter Brueggemann calls "the world of competence and competition,"[1] into the *communitas* of the summer academy—that's another matter. With race, we know we have a problem, and we've made a start at addressing it. As for competition with one another, we're beyond all that, aren't we? We are fittingly reticent to merely repeat Paul's reminder that "in the one Spirit we were all baptized into one body—Jews or Greeks, slaves or free—and we were all made to drink of one Spirit," or that in Christ "there is no longer Jew or Greek, there is no longer slave or free, there is no longer male and female,"[2] as an adequate response to our embeddedness in the calculus of racial privilege and discrimination. We are more sanguine, however, about the culture of competence and competition. We tell each other, "Seek first the Kingdom" or "Do nothing from selfish ambition or conceit, but in humility regard others as better than yourselves,"[3] and tend to leave it at that. In other words, when it comes to competition, to ambition, to getting ahead—especially

1. Walter Brueggemann speaks of "the world of competence and competition" in his *The Prophetic Imagination* (Philadelphia: Fortress, 1978) 91. The term seems to be synonymous, or nearly so, with the phrase "royal consciousness." Also see chapters 2 and 5.

2. 1 Cor 12:13; Gal 3:28.

3. Matt 6:33; Phil 2:3.

in an environment populated by rising high school seniors, many of whom will soon be applying to elite colleges and all of whom have a keen eye for disparities in achievement and talent—there is a tendency, a temptation really, to sweep things under the rug, to say that those kinds of things don't really matter to Christians, that we're beyond all that, that we need not concern ourselves.

The Narrative

I TAUGHT at the YTI Summer Academy for three years, leaving finally because of a failure of athletic capacity: the Summer Academy in some ways resembles a month-long sprint, and I just didn't have the legs for it anymore. During the first year, my energy still high, I taught an "exploratory course" and also led a "covenant group." In covenant group, scholars check in with one another, talk about how things are going for them and how they're making sense of it all. Each scholar keeps a running journal in which they write observations— "pensées," inspired by Pascal's classic of Christian apologetics—linking their experiences with the enveloping truths and traditions of Christian faith. Faculty serve as facilitators and, every once in a while, as referees.

Conversations in covenant group, most days, are animated and free-flowing. There are exceptions of course. The morning in question, the one I need to tell you about, is one of these. To start with, three or four of the twelve scholars didn't show up. That was unusual. The counselors are uncompromising when rousing drowsy teens from sleep and getting them off to class: "Hey, you all: it was *your* decision to stay up until four in the morning talking about whether Gandhi got to heaven or not. It's not my problem. Get up!"

"So where is everybody?" I asked the faithful remnant. There was some hesitation, some throat clearing, a few exchanged glances before it finally came out: "We got our AP scores back yesterday."

I hadn't known that the scholars received these scores during the Summer Academy. But there it was—an unwelcome and unmentioned intrusion of the wider culture into the liminality of the Summer Academy. As it turned out, many of the scholars had been calling home every day, hoping to get their scores. This intense but hidden preoccupation shared by all, or nearly all, of the YTI scholars hung in the air, unnamed, empowered by its anonymity. "Not everybody did so well, so not everyone came to class this morning," someone said.

A few within the group who had showed up that morning hadn't done so well either. Others had performed spectacularly. Two of those who were distressed by their scores finally spoke up. Both of them told us, through tears, how their plans had been ruined and what a disappointment they were to their parents and guidance counselors.

Though the rest of us listened attentively and sat for a moment or two in silence after they'd finished, our attempts at consolation and commiseration fell flat. Our assurances were just a little too quick and formulaic. I don't remember the conversation in detail, but I do remember that we tried to comfort our disappointed classmates by assuring them that AP scores were, after all, of very little importance in the larger scheme of things, especially for Christians: "God closes some doors in order to open others."

What I remember most vividly is that our conversation became more and more awkward and strained as it unfolded. To compensate for the intensifying discomfort, we stated our assurances ever more aggressively and earnestly. Of course, that only made matters worse. Soon, we'd managed to ratchet up our collective discomfort to nearly unbearable levels.

So what went wrong? Why the intense discomfort? I could hardly disagree with what the scholars and I said that day in our floundering attempts at consolation. Surely, AP scores are ultimately insignificant in the larger scheme of things.[4] Not only that, but I (and the scholars) do truly believe that we can trust in God to open new doors when old doors close: "I will instruct you and teach you the way you should go; I will counsel you with my eye upon you."[5]

Again: What went wrong? One thing that occurred to me later was how difficult it must have been for the two young scholars to be consoled by others still flushed with success over their own excellent scores. I also found myself wondering if our words of consolation were not in fact construed as vaguely accusatory. Were we implying that had these young people been stronger in their faith, they would have been less upset about their scores?

But the pedagogical clue that proved most fruitful was one already mentioned—the fact that the more earnestly we repeated our assurances, the greater our collective discomfort. Why was that? Why couldn't we extract ourselves from that infernal loop of accelerating dis-ease.

Interpretation of the Narrative: Overview

My sense is that the escalating level of discomfort that day was due largely to the scholars' and my growing if inarticulate suspicion that the consolations

---

4. Not only that, but AP scores are not SATs and do not carry the weight of grades or recommendations. Their importance to the scholars appears to be more symbolic than functional. That is to say, the AP scores seem to symbolize, to specify, their comparative standing with their peers as the competition for admission to the schools of their choice is about to get under way. The AP scores are perhaps tantamount to the release of preelection polling results.

5. Ps 32:8.

based on our contention that AP scores didn't really matter felt disingenuous. We sensed, or at least began to sense, that we were using Christian faith to argue away—to rationalize—the emotional significance of failing at the competitive culture game of standardized testing. At some point during our conversation the unspoken suspicion reached a critical point. After that, our hearts were no longer in it. Nonetheless, in order to hide this uncomfortable fact from ourselves, we kept repeating the same tired assurances, turning up the volume in hopes of drowning out our growing suspicion.

Was it our fault? Were we reenacting the dialogue of Job and his friends? Hard to say. My own take on the matter would be to admit to a degree of culpability, while suggesting at the same time that we were all playing out parts in a social script, one we did not write, one we found difficult even to acknowledge, let alone resist.

We were, I believe, unwittingly rehearsing and rehashing two distinct social mechanisms, what I'll call "culture tricks." These culture tricks are so widespread and pervasive, so taken-for-granted, so embedded in the cultural air we breathe, that we were more or less oblivious to the power they held over us.

The first of these—and here I am following the lead of historian Richard Huber—is the "true success" mechanism.[6] In the true success mechanism, the language of faith or other forms of idealism is deployed to hide or disguise deep emotional investment in culture's ascendant images of success and failure. I'll have more to say about this shortly, but for now, it will be enough to suggest an image. Picture, if you will, a politician about to be indicted for corruption who suddenly leaves office "to spend more time with his family." The politician's suggestion that spending more time with the family has suddenly revealed itself as urgently important, more important, say, than the everyday success associated with the power of office, is clearly suspect. Though most would agree that commitment to family is in fact more important than holding office, we will, generally speaking, on hearing a politician make this claim, suspect a sleight of hand. We suspect, in other words, that the mechanism of true success is being deployed to put a favorable spin on things, to avoid public shame and humiliation.

But what is of greater interest here than the true success mechanism itself is the emergence of a second, more subtle culture trick related to it. Let's call this second mechanism "the accusation of religious resentment." "The accusation of religious resentment" is a kind of reaction-formation, a second-level

---

6. See Richard M. Huber, *The Idea of American Success* (New York: McGraw-Hill, 1971) especially 105–6. Also, see my *Forgetting Ourselves on Purpose: Vocation and the Ethics of Ambition* (San Francisco: Jossey-Bass, 2002) 46 (hereafter cited as *FOOP*).

suspicion, growing out of our initial suspicion concerning the motives of the soon-to-be-indicted politician.

It works like this. Over time, having seen the mechanism of true success spun out over and again, a suspicion begins to grow that resorting to the language of faith to critique the powerful images of success and failure ascendant in our culture may be disingenuous, one more instance of the true success mechanism. We may begin to wonder if religiously inspired claims to "transcend" our attachments to the calculus of worldly success are often, if not usually, rationalizations of failure or the expectation of failure to achieve what our culture deems essential for happiness.

Once the suspicion of the mechanism of true success is internalized and linked to the language of faith—once, that is, it becomes a habitual pattern of perception and judgment—the accusation of religious resentment takes hold and represents a profound inhibition to living out and living into Christian vocation. At the very moment we begin to discern some alternative vision for life, one that calls the social scripts of success ascendant in consumer culture into question, one that places the love of God and neighbor and the stunning and ineffable beauty of the emergent Kingdom of God at the center of things—at this very moment, the inhibitive voice of this mechanism will kick in. "C'mon, you know better than that. People only talk that way when things aren't going well, when they don't think they can win, when they finally begin to recognize that they're losers, like when their AP scores just don't measure up."

Because of the power of the accusation of religious resentment to forestall the full embrace of Christian discipleship, the point of transition between unselfconscious deployment of the true success mechanism and the growing suspicion of it represents a crucial moment in the process of Christian formation and, therefore, of youth ministry.

Many of us, perhaps most of us, have learned to cover up, to hide, first from ourselves and then from others, our inevitable emotional investment in test scores, admission to prestigious colleges, and other prized elements constitutive of success within the culture of competence and competition. This is hardly surprising, given the church's own inevitable, if inadvertent, commitment to credible deniability regarding how thoroughly the culture of competence and competition, with its stress on numbers and dogmatic optimism, defines its own sense of mission and identity, its own successes and failures.

Nonetheless, as Walter Brueggemann argues, if the church is to exercise its prophetic ministry, "to nurture, nourish and evoke a consciousness and perception alternative to the consciousness and perception of the dominant culture around us," it will need "to recognize that it is also, both individuals and the institutional church itself, claimed by false fields of perception and idolatrous systems of language and rhetoric."[7]

Of course, the trouble is that the church (and we who constitute it) can usually only manage to confess sinfulness in a general sort of way. Speaking out against consumerism and militarism, while laudatory, has in the final analysis all the formative punch of taking a stand against black holes. The "false fields of perception," including the social mechanisms, the culture tricks, that disguise and protect them, will need to be stated precisely and in detail before they can be efficaciously resisted. We cannot be absolved from our particular attachments by way of a general confession. We need to name them and to help the young men and women we teach to do the same.

Scapegoating Christian Faith: Taking a Closer Look at Culture Tricks

WITH THIS duty or call to "in-detail" confession and repentance in mind, let me take a first step in that direction by taking a closer look at the relations, the interactions, between the two mechanisms mentioned earlier: the true success mechanism and "the accusation of religious resentment." I've said that our growing suspicion of the true success mechanism can give rise to the accusation of religious resentment. But how does this happen, and what can we do about it?

First of all, it is important to note that as Huber says, the true success mechanism serves an important social function in American culture. For those who have failed at ordinary success by society's standards, at achieving a degree of fame, fortune, or power—or perfect or near-perfect AP scores—the shame of having fallen short can be reduced by being redefined or denied. What's so ingenious about this culture trick is its near universal appeal. For those who have failed at so-called worldly success, this mechanism presents the opportunity to save face. We need not fail at anything in the mundane order if we simply adhere to Paul's admonition to be ambitious for the spiritual things. But there are benefits here for the powerful and successful as well. Those who have succeeded at worldly success are spared the resentment of their fellows and the potential political implications of the alienation of those the systems of power and prestige have not treated so kindly.[8]

Clearly, during that ill-fated AP conversation, we were rehearsing the true success mechanism, availing ourselves of the consolation and appeasement we

---

7. Brueggemann, *Prophetic Imagination*, 13.
8. Again, see Huber, 105–6.

hoped it might provide, as it encouraged and guided the self-interested collusion of both those who succeeded and those who did not.

The trouble is, we assured those who had "failed" at this particular competition in our culture's games that they need not feel the way they were, in fact, feeling. After all, true success in our Christian context—seeking first the Kingdom of God, "being ambitious for the spiritual things"—is what really counts.

Still, even as we remained partially embedded in the true success mechanism, we were also beginning to suspect that something was wrong. Our suspicion, inasmuch as it can be specified, was that in having claimed to transcend the power of social scripts of success and failure by fiat, we were in fact evading the hard work of Christian repentance and resistance. Clearly, if we are to be more fully liberated from the power that cultural symbols of success and failure inevitably exercise over our imaginations, we need first to admit our attachment to them, our caughtness in them. The derivation of the word *transcend,* after all, does not connote rising above, but traveling across.[9] Transcending attachments, in other words, is a hands-on activity, one in which we are well-advised to move slowly and deliberately, making sure we have a good toehold before we push on. Again, I believe we sensed this fact, though we were not able to articulate it well enough at the time.

What I think Huber's analysis may have missed is that like many things in our culture, the true success mechanism is constructed for planned obsolescence. Its collapse is inevitable. It is only a matter of time until we (and the youth we minister to) will see through it. What occurs at this moment of suspicion and enlightenment is crucial for ongoing Christian formation. The reason for this is that culture, if I may be allowed to speak of culture anthropomorphically, will attempt to shift the blame for the true success mechanism from itself to religion, to faith, to Christianity. If this cultural sleight of hand is not spotted and resisted as it emerges, it poses a toxic threat to Christian formation.

Central to this cultural trick is making sure that youth (and the rest of us as well) congratulate ourselves on discovering the true success mechanism in the first place. The culture will have us believe that we have now been initiated into critical thinking and are no longer bound by childish fantasies and belief systems. Once we reach this realization, once the true success mechanism fails to serve the culture of competence and competition, it will, at that very moment, be disavowed, condemned, cast aside, by the very culture that created it.

---

9. Luke Timothy Johnson reminds us that "transcendence connotes not only a 'going beyond,' but also a 'going across.' It suggests not only distance but also closeness." See Luke Timothy Johnson, *Religious Experience in Earliest Christianity* (Minneapolis, MN: Augsburg Fortress, 1998) 59.

If I were to put a voice to this cultural dynamic, as it counsels and seduces us away from our faith commitment, it might sound something like this:

"Why yes, of course, the true success mechanism is a deception, a rationalization. Didn't you know that? Well, anyway we're glad you finally caught on. This deception, of course, is concocted by Christians and other idealists who think it is their job to protect the weak and the lazy from full recognition of their failures and shortcomings. You and I both know, of course, that what everyone *really* wants, however they might deny or qualify it, is the honor, the prestige, and, yes, the wealth and power, associated with the American Dream.[10]

"By the way, no one will object if you choose to go through the motions. In fact, we encourage it. Stay in church, raise your kids there. But don't be naive. Condemn things only in the abstract—consumerism, racism, and the rest. Forget the details. You may even wish to act sporadically against these evils. You'll feel better if you do. The key here, however, is to stay preoccupied with what really counts: success as defined by us, by the culture of competence and competition. Oh, yes, please continue to give to charity, and remember to vote your conscience. Just don't get carried away. The key word here is preoccupation, not opinion.[11] Believe what you want, do what you must. But make sure you remain preoccupied with, focused upon, attached to what we tell you is important in life. If you do, everything will work out just fine."

By saddling faith, religion, and other embodiments of youthful idealism with responsibility for the creation of the true success mechanism, the culture trick called the accusation of religious resentment clears the way for culture to place faith at the periphery of things and to diminish its significance.[12]

Joseph Epstein is tone-perfect in his sadly sympathetic evocation of the fatalistic mood of the now-internalized accusation of religious resentment:

> Exhortations to slow down, attacks on the shallowness of success
> as an empty idea, were—and continue to be—unavailing. People,
> men and women, see life as a smorgasbord of choices: a Mercedes
> or a Plymouth, a daughter at Harvard or at secretarial school, first
> cabin to le Harvre or Greyhound to Yellowstone, to be the boss or

10. If you think you are hearing echoes of Nietzsche here, you are. But these echoes are muted by the assimilation and distortion of Nietzsche's thought by an admixture of Darwinism, pop psychology, and popular renderings of economic determinism often called Social Darwinism.

11. See *FOOP*, 183–85.

12. It is important to note that when religious educators, youth ministers, and others encourage youth to claim early and easy transcendence over cultural distortions, they are playing directly into the hands of distorted elements of the culture. It is precisely the compensatory character of such early denials of the power of social scripts that sponsors later suspicion of the efficacy of faith to resist cultural distortions of being and doing.

the bossed. Who, given a choice, wouldn't know which to pick? In America, moreover, the Mercedes, Harvard, first cabin, being the boss, along with being preferable are also altogether possible.[13]

Youthful Vocation and the Internalized Accusation of Religious Resentment

IN MY judgment, the sense of the inevitability of surrendering to the smorgasbord world of power and prestige recommends that we achieve a kind of congruence with the contours of a radically reduced universe of meaning and possibility. For many of the undergraduates I taught before arriving at YTI, the smorgasbord world already was, or was quickly becoming, an uncontested reality—just the way things are. At first I didn't make the connection between undergraduates and the young men and women at YTI. Only slowly did I begin to connect the dots.

One reason I may have failed to see the similarities between these sixteen- and seventeen-year-old rising high school seniors and their older peers at college was my tendency to idealize the young men and women who showed up at YTI. As one who shared their faith, I too wished to believe that they were less prone to the formative and deformative power of the social scripts associated with the culture of competence and competition. After all, they were giving up summer employment or soccer camp or computer camp to study, of all things, theology. Not only that, but the YTI scholars truly attempted to put their faith at the center of things. The trouble is, I'd simply underestimated what they were up against. I'd fallen for the same mechanisms, the same culture tricks that had a hold on them.

Years ago, when I was still teaching undergraduates, a young woman approached me after class, saying that she was confused about something and wanted to talk. She had decided she wanted to be an English major but had delayed her decision because she felt reluctant to tell her friends and family about her decision. The problem? She had been planning to attend medical school and feared that "everyone" would think that she really couldn't hack it, that she'd failed to achieve her personal goal, that her putative "decision" to major in English was simply an attempt to put a brave face on things, that she was making the best of a bad situation. So pervasive, so strong, was this young woman's fear that she was unable to take a symbolic first step toward realizing her new dream—dropping calculus, a course she loathed and would no longer need: "I have an A in there, but if I drop it, everyone will think I'm failing."

---

13. Joseph Epstein, *Ambition the Secret Passion* (Chicago: Dee, 1980) 17.

Of course, there may well be good reasons to stay in a calculus class. I'm not arguing against that. All things being equal, why not complete what you've started? But that's not the issue here. The young woman's confusion and her inability to act on what she felt and thought was best for herself is what's at issue. She heard the internalized voices accusing her of rationalization, of copping out, of weakness, of failure: "You're going to be an English major because you couldn't hack it in pre-med."

It's not difficult to see why this young woman arrived at the conclusion that it's easier to just stay the course, proving herself competent and successful before "indulging" her love of literature.[14]

There is a great deal written about discerning vocation these days. Much of it is valuable, inspiring even. But I am becoming more and more aware that discerning vocation is one thing and that living it out, even beginning to live it out, is quite another. In fact, it may be that it is precisely at moments of vocational clarity, moments of epiphanal insight about our lives, that profound inhibitive forces are most likely to gather strength and assault us.[15] I value Frederick Buechner's description of vocation: "the place where God calls you to is the place where your deep gladness and the world's deep hunger meet."[16] I quote it frequently. But I have come to believe that the smorgasbord world and its faithful vassal, the internalized accusation of religious resentment, exert profound pressure that often succeeds in forestalling vocational commitment. As in the case of the young woman who was unable to drop calculus, moments of self-discovery, of calling, though often liberating and joyful, all too soon yield to self-doubt and internal recrimination, the biographical equivalent of revisionist history: "Do I *really* want to live that way? Is it realistic? Maybe I'm just being selfish."[17]

14. In the next essay I will speak about the culture trick (or social mechanism) of "self-serving procrastination." In this young woman's case, self-serving procrastination dictated that she ought to stay in the course in order to avoid the appearance of failure. Again, it may or may not have been a good thing that she completed the course.

15. Gerald May has noticed a phenomenon of "ego-backlash" after retreatants have a profound religious experience during a retreat. Gerald May, *Will and Spirit* (New York: HarperSanFrancisco, 1982) 112–13. I think something similar may be at work when we experience momentary clarity about personal vocation.

16. Frederick Buechner, *Wishful Thinking: A Theological ABC* (New York: Harper & Row, 1973) 95.

17. Notice how the power of the culture tricks of true success and self-serving procrastination end up inverting values. Giving up her own vocational insight ends up being deemed virtuous.

Beyond Discernment: Remembering and Resistance

For Christians, the ultimate Source of resistance to the deep cultural inhibitions to faith is not self-generated. The Holy Spirit, moving amidst the faithful, inspiring and sustaining, discerning and acting, is more than a match for the materialist spirit of our age. Ultimately, the culture of consumerism is not the irresistible force we often believe it to be. The images and commonsense pronouncements of consumerist culture, though glitzy, loud and incessant, are in the final analysis superficial and vacuous. Ultimately, they lead to alienation, to confusion, to despair. The culture of competence and competition, as we know in moments of clarity, is finally a severely truncated vision of the possibilities for human life, a shallow take on what really counts and on Who it is that can be counted upon.

We and the young people to whom we minister are often and inevitably forgetful of the power and beauty of Christian faith as lived, as practiced. Nonetheless, in comparison with the Christian witness of the saints, both those celebrated and those unknown, those living and those dead, lives defined by shallow and evanescent attachments to consumerism are at best second-rate. The lives of the saints wound us and inspire us; they call us back to ourselves and to the incomparable beauty of God, ineffable, blindingly brilliant and alluring. The intermittent and self-conscious highs of making the grade in consumerist culture compare poorly with the eternal and self-forgetful beauty that whispers to each of us of a different kind of life. Pseudo-Dionysius the Areopagite speaks of this divine beauty with power and conviction:

> For beauty is the cause of harmony, of sympathy, of community. Beauty unites all things and is the source of all things. It is the great creating cause which bestirs the world and holds all things in existence by the longing inside them to have beauty. And there it is ahead of all as Goal, as the Beloved, as the Cause toward which all things move, since it is the longing for beauty which actually brings them into being.[18]

Of course, it is possible to question whether Pseudo-Dionysius's eloquence only serves to provide better cover for the true success mechanism. It is precisely what the purveyors of the smorgasbord vision of life and meaning would have us believe. "Yes, all that God-talk can be appealing, even beautiful. But take another look; pay attention to the way people act, not to what they say." But this objection is, in the final analysis, a last-gasp survival mechanism of the consumerist culture. The response to such inhibitive accusations, I would suggest, need not always be direct, need not be apologetic. On occasion, though

18. Pseudo Dionysius, *The Complete Works* (Mahwah, NJ: Paulist, 1987) 77.

not on all occasions, we may refuse to address certain questions, especially those posed in bad faith. There is a time to argue, to take on the accusation of religious resentment on its own terms, to philosophize, to theologize, even to apologize. But we need not allow ourselves or the youth we minister to, to be smart-talked out of what we and they already know to be true. Sometimes it is best to take a break from intellectual analysis and simply recall a prayer or a hymn, perhaps one learned in childhood, that has over time spoken to you in the depth of your heart, one that has stayed with you over these many years.

Listen, for example, to these closing words from John Wesley's covenant service, often celebrated on New Year's. Attend especially to the power of such communal remembering in comparison with the thin intellectualization of the accusation of religious resentment:

> I am no longer my own, but thine. Put me to what thou wilt, rank me with whom thou wilt; put me to doing, put me to suffering; let me be employed for thee or laid aside for thee, exalted for thee or brought low for thee; let me be full, let me be empty; let me have all things, let me have nothing; I freely and heartily yield all things to thy pleasure and disposal.
>
> And now, O glorious and blessed God, Father, Son and Holy Spirit, thou art mine, and I am thine. So be it.
>
> And the covenant which I have made on earth, let it be ratified in heaven. Amen.[19]

When tempted by our own internalized versions of the accusation of religious resentment, it is essential, even as we take these on, name, analyze and resist them, to also remember the transformative power of prayer, both individual and communal. The spiritual resources of the church—the sacraments, the preached word, group prayer and study—all these move us to remember what we already know to be true: that we long to love God with our whole heart and our whole soul and all our strength and to love our neighbors as ourselves.

The great power of these ancient practices is not quantitative, but qualitative. We too often discourage ourselves and the youth entrusted to us by calculating and endlessly repeating the number of hours young people hang out in the mall or watch television, assuming, it seems, that the images and thoughts they encounter there are of equal power and depth to those at the heart of our shared faith. Consumerism has the numbers and the glitz, but God is Beauty beyond beauty, and draws all these to the Godhead.

Still, having said this, it is nonetheless essential that youth be enabled to recognize, diagnose, and resist the cultural mechanisms that undermine faith, social mechanisms that all too often induce a kind of aesthetic amnesia con-

19. "John Wesley's Covenant Service" (Nashville, TN: Discipleship Resources).

cerning the great beauty and power of Christian faith. We are called upon to tutor young people in religious resistance as well as in spiritual remembering. For this reason, I have, through a brief analysis of the inhibitive social mechanisms of true success and the internalized accusation of religious resentment, attempted to accentuate the former in service of the latter.

Of course, mere resistance, without ongoing repentance and renewal, soon degenerates into a kind of moral drudgery, tragically inattentive to the joy of the emergent Kingdom of God and ultimately indistinguishable from the baptized equivalent of liberal guilt, what Jonathan Kozol calls "inert concern."[20] But it is also and simultaneously true that Christian spirituality, if unaligned with studied and systematic resistance to the cultural forces that undermine and inhibit the life of faith, however deeply felt and compellingly imaged, is finally ineffectual—a subtle collaborator with the very structures it claims to have already transcended.

Perhaps I'm a slow learner. But looking back on the day the YTI scholars and I puzzled over the relation of AP scores to the emergent Kingdom of God, I can at least say I've learned this lesson. I had, in the past, tended to view my relationship with my students dialectically. What I had to contribute was based on the fact that I've been around a little longer and perhaps know a little more. I'd driven down a few more dead ends and navigated a few more roundabouts than they. On the other hand, the sense expressed best by the words "we expect a little more from you, Brian," reminds me, often enough, of the prophetic voice of the faithful youth I've encountered over the years.

But I have learned that my students and I are often caught up in the same inhibitions and confusions, the same infernal social mechanisms that frustrate and confuse our individual and collective intention to more fully embrace the life of Christian discipleship. Like those Venn diagrams with their overlapping circles, there are areas of our lives, of our hopes and our dreams, but also of our biases, blind spots and confusions, that share space and emotion. When we are stalled, as we were the day after the AP scores arrived on the scene, in the netherworld of shared confusion, none of us is really teaching. We are, all of us, being taught. It is the situation itself that is doing the teaching. It is life that is teaching. It is, if we invite Her, the Spirit of Wisdom that is teaching. Often on these occasions, as on that summer morning at YTI, we know full well that there is something wrong, something we can't quite put to words but can't quite dismiss either, something we had better talk about nonetheless if we're going to learn anything.

---

20. Jonathan Kozol, *Night Is Dark and I Am Far from Home: Political Indictment of U.S. Public School* (New York: Bantam, 1977).

What I now say at these moments, even though I do not yet, in the midst of them, know what I am talking about, is "There's something a little off here, isn't there? I'm not sure what it is. Any thoughts? Images? Sentence fragments? Feelings? Should we pray?" I have come to regard these questions as an invitation of sorts, an invitation to what I've come to call "sacred commiseration." I recommend this practice to you.

6

Youth Ministry and the Practice of Sacred Commiseration

BRIAN J. MAHAN

Introductory Comment

THERE IS a tendency to speak of youth culture in a manner that implies that youth ministers stand outside the culture, like cheerleaders at the edge of a maze yelling instruction to youth who have lost their way. But if youth ministers are to respond to the prophetic call to form youth for the long run, we'd do well to remember that we and the youth to whom we minister are fellow travelers. We, too, remain embedded in the culture of consumerism, materialism, and militarism, and we cannot address the particular cultural distortions inhibiting the full embrace of faith and vocation among youth without simultaneously addressing them in our own lives.

For this reason, in this essay I will speak in some detail about the continuing force of the "culture tricks" that distressed and confused the young scholars of the Youth Theological Initiative (YTI) as they continue to distress and confuse me. I will, as I did in the previous essay, provide a brief narrative—this time autobiographical. I will then interpret the narrative, attending to the idiosyncratic manner in which the culture tricks play out in my own life. Finally, I will speak briefly about what I call the practice of "sacred commiseration," in the context of youth ministry.

The Narrative

IT HAS been nearly ten years now since my wife, Kim, came home from a two-day silent retreat at Green Bough House of Prayer in middle Georgia. I asked her how it went. "Well," she said, "I really like the place. It reminds me of a Jesuit retreat center decorated by Grandma, if you know what I mean." I did know what she meant, and it was not long before we returned to Green Bough together. Over the last decade, we have become fixtures at the place, family really. We spent weekends at first, and then stayed for seven months during my pre-tenure leave from Candler School of Theology in 2002. At that time, Kim and I were engaged in ongoing conversation with Fay Key and Steve Bullington, Green Bough's founders and permanent residents, exploring the possibility of living at Green Bough for a more extended period. We often met after Morning Prayer as we discerned together, and I kept a journal of these conversations and my reflections.

Toward the end of my leave, I arranged for an appointment to speak with Russ Richey, the dean at Candler, in the hope that I would be able to reduce my full-time appointment to a half-time position, so that Kim and I could spend half our time at Green Bough. A few months after this initial conversation, I was able to share the good news, first with Kim, Fay, and Steve and then with friends and retreatants at Green Bough. I had received a two-year, half-time, renewable appointment with benefits. We could not have been more certain of the rightness of our decision or been better supported by friends.

That said, I need to admit something to you, something that may appear at odds with what I just said. My own certainty, and Kim's, and the support of friends did not prevent me from spending anxious hours reviewing our decision, wondering what people might think, projecting all kinds of unwelcome consequences, especially financial ones, into a menacing future. It was not that I was second-guessing myself. The decision had been made, and I knew it was the right one, insofar as I am capable of knowing anything. Still, the voices of doubt remained, and I experienced, as my students had, the power of the culture tricks that confuse and complicate all vocational decisions, all attempts to live out one's commitments, one's faith.

Paradoxically, the relative peace and quiet of the retreat center at first only made things worse. Weekend guests at Green Bough sometimes assume that living there is like being on an extended retreat—peaceful, recollected, vacation-like. Sometimes it's like that for me too. But at other times, I find myself thrown back against myself, disrupted, knocked off balance altogether. Silence can do that. There were dozens of times, nights especially, when I was assaulted by intense internal conversations—conversations that did not finally abate until

I returned to Candler and started my new half-time position nearly a year after we'd made our decision. Extended litanies of self-doubt, chanted incessantly by a chorus of menacing internal accusers, were not uncommon. Exasperated by my "voices" and the frequency of their attendance at chapel, I once found myself yelling out loud, "Oh shut up, the bunch of you!"

It was to no avail. They just continued: "Moving to Green Bough is just your way of avoiding the tenure process, the pain of it." "You've always feared rejection, and now you're running away with your tail between your legs."

Or alternatively: "You're just afraid you might actually *get* tenure, Mr. Holy Joe. You're trying to act like you're beyond all that, holier than Thou, yeah, a Holy Joe, just like your father called you when you were a kid. He was right, nobody likes a Holy Joe." Intimidating composite figures—colleague-collages, I've come to call them—compared me to themselves, always to my disadvantage. Each composite figure was balanced, well-groomed, brilliant, productive, and an altogether better person than I, both morally and spiritually. They had children, they voted in every election, they got things done on time. Given their own elevated status—tenured and renowned, though invariably low-key about their achievements—they were particularly put off by even a hint that my decision was the product of what they labeled "higher motives."

I tried to point out to the colleague-collage that many of their accusations conflicted, even contradicted one another. Doesn't that count for something? Shouldn't it make them wonder a little if there might be something about my decision that got to them? "Not really. Who cares *why* you're wrong, Brian? That's not the point. The point is that you *are* wrong—wrong as usual. We all agree on that."

Once or twice, I got a little aggressive and tried to turn the tables on my colleague-collage. Since these composite figures were, for the most part, theological educators and scholars, I sought to discredit the lot of them with a prophetic invective borrowed proximately from the first chapter of my dissertation and ultimately from the pages of William James's classic *The Varieties of Religious Experience*:

> When I was a boy, I used to think that a closet-naturalist must be the vilest type of wretch under the sun. But surely the systematic theologians are the closet naturalists of the deity. What is their deduction of metaphysical attributes but a shuffling and matching of pedantic dictionary-adjectives, aloof from morals, aloof from human needs, something that might be worked out from the mere word "God" by one of those logical machines of wood and brass which recent ingenuity has contrived as well as by a man of flesh and blood. They have the trail of the serpent over them. One feels that in the theologians' hands, they are only a set of titles obtained

by a mechanical manipulation of synonyms; verbality has stepped into the place of vision, professionalism into that of life. Instead of bread, we have a stone; instead of a fish, a serpent.[1]

But my colleague-collage knew resentment when they heard it. They'd all read William James, too, but they'd read Nietzsche as well and favored his approach. "If you were a little more successful at your own professional pursuits—with publishing, in particular—you wouldn't have to bother criticizing those of us who have actually contributed something to the world of scholarship. Sour grapes. We've heard it all before. All your thoughts and arguments are just more of the same."[2]

In the final analysis, however, it was not what might be called the "tough-cop" insults of my colleague-collage that proved most effective. The "good-cop" aspect was at once more powerful and insidious. Feigning disdain for the tough-cop dismissals of my vocational commitment, the good cop was empowered to offer me what amounts to an academic plea bargain. Maybe the accusations could be dropped—he'd see what he could do—if only I would co-operate a little. "As far as I'm concerned, all you'll need to do is admit that you didn't look before you leapt, that you made a bad decision leaving tenure-track and going half-time. We all get a little tired of the game. Once you've done that—admitted your mistake—you probably could get off with little more than a three-year rehab program consisting of full-time work and an extra committee assignment or two."

"Look, Brian, your sincere discernment, eventuating in your decision to move to Green Bough, is just fine, perhaps even praiseworthy. Nobody is really questioning that. People *like* you around here, Brian, please try to understand that. We really do, most of us, and you have a good sense of humor, too. There's just a widespread sense that your decision is a little premature. That's all. You're doing so well, and look at this third-year review. It's excellent. So let me ask you, and be careful about how you answer this: Are you really sure your decision is not a little precipitous? Why not just come back next year and think it over?"

Self-Serving Procrastination as Culture Trick

I ONCE heard a story attributed to the great Chicago activist Saul Alinsky. Alinsky, so the story goes, had asked a young Catholic priest, reputedly one of the best interns he'd ever mentored, if he might stay on with him as a commu-

---

1. William James, *The Varieties of Religious Experience* (New York: Penguin, 1982) 446.

2. Here I'm describing my own struggles with "the internalized accusation of religious resentment" which also played a central role in the conversation around AP scores in my previous essay.

nity organizer.[3] But the priest turned down the offer, saying that he would first go off and do whatever he had to do to become a bishop. Having once attained that exalted office, he could bring a bishop's power to bear on the issues of their shared concern. He'd then be Alinsky's most powerful ally in one of America's largest Catholic archdioceses. Alinsky countered that by the time the young priest did whatever he'd need to do to become a bishop, he'd very probably have lost enthusiasm for working with the likes of him.

Maybe the story is apocryphal. Frankly, I don't even remember where I heard it. Accurate or inaccurate, the story has something important to say. The social mechanism of "self-serving procrastination"[4] is as deceptively appealing in the short term as it is disastrous in the long: "Why expend the energy to more fully embrace the life you are invited to embrace at this very moment, when doing something else might well prove invaluable further down the line? If you wish to work in the inner city now, why not wait until you're a bishop? Then you'll really be able to change things."

That's what the good-cop component of my colleague-collage was selling: "So why not wait two or three more years before going to Green Bough? Receiving tenure would still the accusatory voices and provide you with a little more money. Nothing wrong with that, as far as I can tell. It would only delay moving to Green Bough by a few years. You'd still be relatively young."

Of course, there's nothing *wrong* with that, with delaying things a bit. But reflect on the matter for a minute. Morality, right and wrong, isn't at issue here. Maintaining that a certain life trajectory is not immoral hardly recommends it as the best course of action, the more faithful choice. Indeed, I suspect that the conflation of moral rectitude with vocational discernment is itself a culture trick—a way of keeping us where we are well after we should be elsewhere. In fact, though there are exceptions, it is my considered opinion that adopting the strategy of self-serving procrastination, once you have a strong sense about what direction your life might take, is almost invariably a bad call.

This does not mean that once embraced, self-serving procrastination is either fatal to vocation or irreversible—who needs that kind of pressure? Nonetheless, the danger of adopting the strategy of self-serving procrastination in the first place resides in the fact that the strategy is self-perpetuating, habit-

3. See Saul Alinsky, *Rules for Radicals* (New York: Vintage, Random House, 1989) 13. In a footnote early in this text, Alinsky, in speaking to a seminarian who is concerned about keeping faith with his commitment to social justice and community organizing, says the following: "When you go out that door, just make your own personal decision about whether you want to be a bishop or a priest, and everything else will follow." This passage may or may not be the source of this story.

4. Cf. Brian J. Mahan. *Forgetting Ourselves on Purpose: Vocation and the Ethics of Ambition* (San Francisco: Jossey-Bass, 2002) 187–88 (hereafter cited as *FOOP*).

forming, if you will. Unless named and resisted at the outset, the mechanism of self-serving procrastination will inevitably reassert itself again and again until it gets a hearing. Waiting patiently for a moment of weakness and confusion to make its pitch, it intends nothing less than the death of vocational insight sealed by a final and irrevocable commitment to something else, something not quite right, though never obviously wrong either.[5]

Assume I took the good cop's advice and came back for a couple of years in order to get tenure. Would that satisfy my internalized colleague-collage? I doubt it: "There is—is there not, Brian?—a measure of shame attached to not receiving a full professorship after you've received tenure. So why stop there? Why not wait another four or five years and get that under your belt too? In fact, why not wait just a little longer before moving to Green Bough? Who's to say you won't live into your nineties? Scholarly types do that all the time. There's plenty of time."

And if I take that advice: "Beyond that—of course, I'm only mentioning this, no need to feel pressured—there is always the possibility of an endowed chair. I'm just saying that it might be better to wait and see how this all works out. For now, why not use your imagination and try this one on for size, just to see how it feels: 'Brian J. Mahan, the Edward W. and Candace B. Sterling Professor of Vocational Discernment.'"

I admit, I like the sound of that. My mother would have been so proud. And Green Bough? Well, it isn't going anywhere, is it?

Come to think of it, once I've got a title like that, why not position myself with another decade's hard work, a couple more books (well-reviewed), a few more grants, and a lucky break here and there, and maybe—who's to say—I might make it onto the *New York Times* obituary page. As for Green Bough, I don't see why I couldn't add a rider to my living will specifying that my ashes be scattered behind the guest house, just to the left of the church bell as you're facing it. A plaque would be nice but not essential.

The Temptations of Professionalism

I REGARD the foregoing narrative as an act of sacred commiseration. It reflects my own growing recognition that in ministering to youth, I remain deeply attached to the opinions of my colleagues in academia and that, at times, this attachment runs counter to my deeper commitment to live out my faith. I

---

5. I once read, in a place that I cannot remember, that Satan's most powerful and most often used lie is that "it is too late." I believe that it is never too late. So whenever self-serving procrastination is recognized and resisted, including on one's death bed, it leaves plenty of time. Still, I have to say, more often than not, the sooner we can discover and resist, the better it is for us and all others concerned for us.

recognize, also, that others may well be less concerned about such things than I am, less attached, stronger in faith.[6] But there's no use torturing myself about it. It makes no sense to wait around for a stronger, better, holier Brian to emerge. The best thing for me to do, as far as I can see, is simply to acknowledge, with an edge of sadness, but without hint of despair, my inability to free myself through my own power from my attachments, my sinfulness.

Given this, and given especially the need for the company of fellow travelers, I find myself indebted to, inspired by, and informed by a prior act of sacred commiseration I stumbled upon in Walter Brueggemann's *The Prophetic Imagination*:

> As I reflect on ministry, especially my ministry, I know in the hidden places that the real restraints are not in my understanding or in the receptivity: I discover that I am as bourgeois and obdurate as any to whom I might minister. I, like most of the others, am unsure that the royal road is not the best and the royal community the one that governs all the goodies. I, like most others, am unsure that the alternative community inclusive of the poor, the hungry and grieving is really the wave of God's future.[7]

Clearly, what Brueggemann confesses about the restraints on his own ministry is applicable to youth ministers as well. I am sure Brueggemann would not deny the importance of diagnostic perspectives on culture, including youth culture, would not deny, either, that many of our youth and others we minister to may themselves be deeply caught up in the distortions of what he calls "the culture of competition and competency." What Brueggemann sees most clearly, however, is that he, too, is implicated, as are we, in the same cultural distortions he criticizes.

However passionately, however sincerely, however frequently we issue warnings and condemnations about the culture that endangers the lives and souls of youth, we must not avoid confrontation with the idiosyncratic details of our own entanglements in the same. Recrimination is no substitute for repentance, and social analysis is incomplete without a corresponding spiritual

6. I recognize, of course, that there is a social function for such concern. If standards are to be upheld, the methods that "maintain standards" must be internalized and promulgated. Because of this, we all frequently and necessarily report to internalized peer reviews of one sort or another at regular intervals. In the present context, however, I am pointing to the toxic consequences of conflating success or failure in social or professional roles with the full embrace (or failure to embrace) of authentic selfhood. The cannibalization of authentic selfhood by this or that social role is the distilled essence of alienation and all too often of despair itself.

7. Walter Brueggemann, *The Prophetic Imagination* (Minneapolis, MN: Fortress, 1978) 111–12.

analysis—without, that is to say, a thorough examination of both conscience and consciousness.

Given this, I would like to suggest that you consider occasionally setting aside a little time for the practice of sacred commiseration in your own work with youth. This may challenge the widespread tendency of youth ministers to cultivate the caffeinated high of mere optimism at the expense of obscuring the more sustained and deep-seated, if also more solemn, joy intrinsic to Christian hope. The practice of sacred commiseration leaves room for "downs" as well as "ups," for confusion as well as for certainty, for failure as well as for success, for confession as well as for encouragement. This is the lesson I learned the day the AP scores arrived on the scene.

My friend and co-author Michael Warren has noted that "without speaking to one another of our struggles toward gospel fidelity, there will be lagging fidelity. Lacking such speech about struggles, the field of the local church tends to be an arid one. The religious speech I am describing is rooted in uncertainty, in struggles, and a desire for better fidelity. The letters of holy people like Simone Weil and Flannery O'Connor are filled with this discourse of struggling uncertainty."[8]

For Warren, shared conversation about our struggles toward gospel fidelity always entails an ongoing analysis of the social forces that inhibit faithfulness. We would do well to analyze in detail, for the sake of future resistance, the often evasive particulars of how the images, voices and attitudes of the culture of competence and competition distort our individual and collective commitments to authentic Christian witness.[9]

Walter Brueggemann agrees:

> The contemporary American church is so largely enculturated to the American ethos of consumerism that it has little power to believe or to act. This enculturation is in some way true across the spectrum of church life, both liberal and conservative. . . . That enculturation is true not only of the institution of the church but also of us as persons. Our consciousness has been claimed by false fields of perception and idolatrous systems of language and rhetoric.[10]

8. Michael Warren, *At This Time, In This Place* (Harrisburg, PA: Trinity, 1999) 94–95.

9. I need to stress here that such conversations are not to be understood in isolation from worship, prayer, or the singing of hymns. The practice of sacred commiseration, no doubt, focuses on what might be construed as acts of shared confession and repentance. The criticism that such practices are negative or paralyzing, however, is itself suspect. We cannot simply be "inspired" into gospel fidelity. Individual and collective examination of conscience and ongoing acts of repentance are also essential. The over-reliance on techniques aimed at "inspiring" youth into fidelity over the long run, while ignoring the hard work of resistance in the short term, are for this reason profoundly misguided.

10. Brueggemann, *Prophetic Imagination*, 11.

The practice of sacred commiseration is for this reason something quite different from mere personal sharing, because it aims at uncovering and re-sisting idiosyncratic elements of enculturation. Neither is it a form of public confession. Culture tricks such as self-serving procrastination are not simply or even mainly our own creations.

My colleague-collage is a case in point. Though in part idiosyncratic, my colleague-collage is hardly unique. It is, in a sense, already out there, on the loose, and it speaks to others, as well as to me. It whispers seductively, accus-ingly, incessantly. It influences life decisions, sets the tone at conferences and faculty meetings, sways committees reading grant proposals, and nudges peer reviews and tenure decisions this way or that. Above all, the colleague-collage deflects criticism of the status quo in academia by taking the offensive, by suggesting that criticism of the way things are, the status quo, is inevitably a product of resentment, misplaced idealism, or fear of failure.

The truth is, I sometimes wonder if William James wasn't right. I wonder, that is, in the case of academic theology and Christian theological education whether in fact "verbality" may not have "stepped into the place of vision" and "professionalism into that of life."

Edward Said, speaking of academia, echoes James's sentiments and takes them a step further:

> By professionalism I mean thinking of your work as an intellectual as something you do for a living, between the hours of nine and five with one eye on the clock and another cocked at what is con-sidered proper, professional behavior—not rocking the boat, not straying outside the accepted paradigms or limits, making yourself marketable and above all presentable, hence uncontroversial and unpolitical and "objective."[11]

Of course, there is nothing wrong with professionalism as such.[12] But the apotheosis of professional advancement championed by my colleague-collage is especially odious when the subject turns to God, to justice, to the suffering of others, to issues at the very heart of theological education. In this, I be-lieve that Said, despite the harshness of his tone, may well underestimate my colleague-collage's capacity for self-serving dissimulation. For one thing, my

11. Edward W. Said, *Representations of the Intellectual* (New York: Random House, Vin-tage, 1996) 74.

12. Again, be mindful of the culture trick of substituting judgments of moral rectitude for vocational discernment. "Hey, somebody has to do it." "You're not saying there's something wrong with making a little money, are you?"

"So you think that all success is jaded, inauthentic?" No, no, and no. But because some-thing is okay, so to speak, does not mean that it is recommended, that it need be embraced, committed to as a course of action, as a life plan, that it is authentic or faithful.

colleague-collage knows better than to feign objectivity or to adopt an apo-litical posture. It knows that it is expected to say certain scripted things about justice, about sexism, racism, homophobia and the rest, and to state these things ardently when the occasion requires.

Worse yet, I fear that my colleague-collage is not above cashing in its en-lightened opinions about race and justice, poverty and nonviolence to achieve its own ends. Is it too harsh to suggest that my colleague-collage (or yours?) can sometimes cut a pose, imitating without ever embodying intense preoccupa-tion with these essential concerns? "Instead of bread, we have a stone; instead of a fish, a serpent," James says of systematic theologians a century ago.[13] But my colleague-collage has learned a thing or two in the century since the pub-lication of James's *The Varieties of Religious Experience*. Instead of bread, my colleague-collage offers a picture of bread, instead of a fish, the image of one on a bumper sticker.[14]

My colleague-collage has also learned to mimic great concern with what is now called "teaching excellence." Central to this pedagogical sleight of hand in this venue is the ability to quickly and adroitly shift the conversation from teaching excellence itself to the quantification of teaching excellence as a ve-hicle for professional advancement.

Why spend time preparing classes, my colleague-collage advises, when creating densely packed syllabi, with inordinately extensive bibliographies, printed in small font sizes with tiny margins, detailing rigid attendance poli-cies, accompanied by pretentious philosophic musings will do the trick. Then there's that matter of building an impressive collection of "unsolicited" compli-ments from former students for your files—not very easy soliciting unsolicited tributes, but well worth the effort you put into it.

Again, I wish to stress that I am not speaking either of myself or my col-leagues, but of culture tricks when I speak of the colleague-collage. We are rarely the authors of our own temptations. Nonetheless, temptations they are, and we would do well not to surrender to them. Concupiscence, the inevi-table and destructive residue of original sin, leads each of us—scholar, youth minister, pastor and priest, lay and ordained—to seek facile solutions to life's complex challenges.[15] Society, for its part, is more than happy to compliment our tendencies toward intellectual, moral, and spiritual sloth by providing

13. James, *Varieties of Religious Experience*, 446.

14. The evasive complexity of this strategy brings to mind the importance of the existen-tial insight embedded in Magritte's painting of a pipe and the sentence "*Ceci n'est pas une pipe*" ("This is not a pipe"). The image is taped to the door of my colleague Ted Brelsford's office.

15. In speaking here of the relation of individual sin to social formation and to the tradi-tional Christian notion of concupiscence, I am indebted to Juan Luis Segundo, *Evolution and Guilt* (New York: Orbis, 1974). See chapter 4 especially.

prefab answers to life's most enduring and complex problems, challenges, and dilemmas. When social scripts voiced by various and sundry colleague-collages are followed without remainder, when they are in fact not seen as scripts at all, when our colleague-collages have free and unfettered access to our hearts and minds, the result is inevitably alienation, confusion and dissimulation.

This is especially true about the turning points of life, those *kairos* moments when we start anew, when we are invited to take a different direction or to confirm one we already travel. There are no scripts for such occasions. There are, however, thank God, fellow travelers, companions to guide and support us, and the sacraments and scripture and prayer to sustain and enlighten us along the way. We need each other. We need to be able to call each other to task, even as we comfort and inspire one another. We need to talk about these things openly, prayerfully.[16]

Conclusion: Preparing for Sacred Commiseration

BEFORE CONCLUDING, I need to add by way of caveat that the practice of sacred commiseration should not be confused with informal conversation, with bull sessions, or gripe sessions, or amateur therapy sessions. The practice of sacred commiseration requires preparation on the part of youth as well as youth leaders. Above all, it requires ongoing examination of conscience on the part of all involved. Preparing for the practice of sacred commiseration entails both the willingness and the skill to uncover and study *in detail* the personal and collective constraints on our ministry with youth, even as we invite youth to study and resist their own inhibitions to embracing their own call to Christian discipleship.

Simon Tugwell, in his intriguing discussion of the wisdom of the Desert Fathers in *Ways of Imperfection*, notes that for these great Christian teachers, attentiveness to the thoughts that embodied passionate attachments that weakened faith was an essential element of spiritual practice.[17] Sacred com-

16. In the practice of sacred commiseration, the descriptions of various colleague-collages and social scripts presented by members of the group build upon and challenge each other so that the expanding image of the particularities of enculturation become more accurate, more subtle, and more complex, thus facilitating more effective resistance to them. Note the complementarity to a similar pedagogical strategy first suggested by Paulo Freire: "As each person, in his [sic] decoding essay, relates how he perceived or felt a certain occurrence or situation, his exposition challenges all the other decoders by re-presenting to them the same reality upon which they have themselves been intent." In Freirean terms each narrative in the practice of sacred commiseration can be understood as a coded situation that others build upon. Paulo Freire, *Pedagogy of the Oppressed* (New York: Continuum, 1970) 93.

17. See Simon Tugwell, *Ways of Imperfection: An Exploration of Christian Spirituality* (Springfield, IL: Templegate, 1985).

miseration assumes and builds upon something similar. The inhibitive preoccupations that stand in the way of our full embrace of Christian discipleship
will not present themselves on demand. They must be surfaced, studied, and
resisted. In my own narrative in this essay, I have attempted, especially through
my characterization of my colleague-collage, to do something like this, to share
with you in the spirit of sacred commiseration some of the thoughts and sentiments that define my own "struggles toward gospel fidelity."

I initiated a practice, "the distraction diary,"[18] that has proved helpful in
this regard—helpful, that is, in raising to consciousness what might otherwise
remain obscure and unavailable for shared conversation. I simply ask my
students to keep a notebook close to them whenever they are reading. When
they notice either that they have stopped reading—notice, that is, that they are
daydreaming or musing about things or are caught up in some worry, fantasy
or planning session—they simply write down whatever it is they were thinking when they caught themselves at it. After writing this initial collection of
thoughts, I ask them to do their best to trace their train of thought as far back
as they can. As these observations accrue over time, insights into what actually
preoccupies the students becomes a little clearer.[19]

It is also important that youth leaders give careful attention to the structure
and flow of the conversation itself. One model I have found particularly helpful
in this regard is the model of group spiritual direction,[20] which proceeds by
focusing on one person in the group during each session and follows strict
guidelines for structuring group interaction.

Not only that, but the struggle for gospel fidelity never ends. We are fellow
travelers for the length of the journey, not for some part of it. For this reason,
and as valuable as the enthusiasm and empathy of youth ministers in their
twenties and thirties can be, there is an essential place for those at mid-life and
beyond to enter into relationship with youth.

In his remarkable essay "Good and Evil,"[21] the eminent Jewish philosopher
Martin Buber considers five psalms, placing them in a sequence that presents

18. See *FOOP*, 34–36.

19. The examination of conscience, or examen, provides a good model. For a deceptively
simple text treating the examen (and one I recommend particularly for youth), see Dennis
Linn, Sheila Fabricant Linn, and Matthew Linn, *Sleeping with Bread: Holding What Gives You
Life* (Mahwah, NJ: Paulist, 1995).

20. See Rosemary Dougherty, *Group Spiritual Direction: Community for Discernment*
(Mahwah, NJ: Paulist, 1995), and David F. White, *Practicing Discernment with Youth: A
Transforming Youth Ministry Approach* (Cleveland: Pilgrim, 2005). Also see Katherine Tur-
pin's excellent new book *Branded: Adolescents Converting from Consumer Faith* (Cleveland,
OH: Pilgrim, 2006) especially chapters 8 and 9.

21. Martin Buber, *Good and Evil* (Upper Saddle River, NJ: Prentice Hall, 1997) 3–60.

the reader with a series of complex images and reflections of the progress and reversals, of the joy and near despair, that punctuate and constitute the life of one who struggles, year after year, decade after decade, toward authenticity and faithfulness. Buber's vision of authenticity, of faithfulness to God, to vocational call, is not dependent on whether at any given moment one is elated or discouraged, effective or ineffective. Indeed, each stage in the life of the Psalmist appears to include significant alternations in this regard. Of particular interest in the present context, however, is the fact that it is only when the Psalmist is apparently more than halfway through life's journey that he comes to the full recognition of his own attachment to what he has hitherto opposed—the life and values of the ones he calls "oppressors" and "liars."

In the earlier psalms—those more descriptive of youthful enthusiasm, of confident condemnations of the powerful, rich, and unjust, and of great confidence that God's kingdom is about to be realized at any moment—we find the initial blossoming of the Psalmist's passionate commitment to God's way over and against the ways of the world in thrall to power and wealth. Later in the Psalmist's life, however, the distinction between the righteous and unrighteous and the divide between oppressor and oppressed is no longer only an external reality but is now understood to divide his own heart. In fact, life has taught the Psalmist to find the oppressor within as well as without and to engage in ongoing repentance, even as he maintains opposition to the unjust social order:

> But as for me, my feet had almost stumbled;
> my steps had nearly slipped.
> For I was envious of the arrogant;
> I saw the prosperity of the wicked.
>
> For they have no pain;
> their bodies are sound and sleek.
> They are not in trouble as others are;
> they are not plagued like other people.[22]

Our youth need to be granted the freedom to confess the specificity of their own attachments to the glitzy Siren call of consumerism, even as we encourage them (and are encouraged by them) to stand in prophetic resistance to these same distorted realities. To do so, to repeat this for a final time, we will need to risk speaking humanly and in detail about our own struggles for gospel fidelity.

22. Ps 73:2–3. Note again that the Psalmist's personal confession also includes something akin to social analysis. He knows that his own moral and spiritual confusion is in part a function of the power of "the lie" perpetuated by the culture of the oppressor, the dual presence of seduction and threat. "They scoff and speak with malice; loftily they threaten oppression. They set their mouths against heaven, and their tongues range over all the earth."

Finally, let me add that engaging in the practice of sacred commiseration is less like following this or that surefire technique or some set of instructions that promise immediate results. I think perhaps it is more like the adopting of a prayerful posture, one of trust, willingness and expectation before God, and then putting this to words.

So let me close with a final suggestion in the form of a prayer written a half-century ago by Thomas Merton. I recommend this prayer to introduce a time of sacred commiseration, to set the tone for it, to help cultivate an openness to God and one's companions that is essential to it. It is a prayer, I believe, that has equal relevance for those struggling with the significance of AP scores in relation to the life of faith and to those of us who have finally, if reluctantly, come face-to-face with our own attachments to the very realities we have condemned in others and out there in the culture. Our acts of sacred commiseration, after all, come from the sometimes obscured depth of our own longings—our longing to express our gratitude to the One who has called us into being, and for whom we wish to live our lives in love and fidelity. You may already be familiar with this prayer. Nonetheless, it bears repeating:

> My Dear God, I have no idea where I am going. I do not see the road ahead of me. I cannot know for certain where it will end. Nor do I really know myself, and the fact that I think that I am following your will does not mean that I am actually doing so. But I believe that the desire to please you does in fact please you. And I hope I have that desire in all that I am doing. I hope that I will never do anything apart from that desire. And I know that if I do this you will lead me by the right road, though I may know nothing of it.[23]

---

23. Thomas Merton, *Thoughts in Solitude* (New York: Farrar, Straus and Giroux, 1987) 83.

PART FOUR
CONCLUSION

This final chapter is a transcribed and edited version of a conversation among the three authors several years ago at a Benedictine retreat center near Boston. Our hope is that this informal dialogue provides insight into the authors' shared commitment to youth ministry and youth ministers, as well as a sense of what stands behind and animates these commitments.

7

Talking It Out

Further Musings on Youth Ministry

Encouraging the Implausible

DAVID: Just to state the obvious, we all three sense that there is something going on in culture that inhibits human flourishing. And we've named it in different ways: market economy, greed, convenience, competition, manipulation, desire, and professionalism. We sense that there's something going on in culture that inhibits our love of God and neighbor.

MIKE: Yeah, I would add that this cultural shift distorts our perception. That's part of my concern—the impact of culture on how we perceive the world and our place in it.

BRIAN: We've used several terms in our essays, such as *human flourishing*, *the love of God and neighbor* as expressed in the beatitudes, and others. We've also used the language of *Christian discipleship*, and we've spoken of the *imagination of Jesus*. Essentially, I think we're illuminating tensions between our preoccupations with faithfulness to the Gospel and our preoccupations with professionalism, materialism, and consumerism. But we might also want to talk about the specific manifestations of these in ourselves, in youth, and in culture.

DAVID: Another thing runs through our work. We talked some about how
           our work is really in different contexts, but I think we need to identify
           again in a specific way that the faithfulness the Gospel calls for is not
           limited to an otherworldly kind of pursuit; it's a concern for human
           flourishing here and now, and it's a concern for the suffering of the
           world, and it's a concern for healing relationships within the world.

MIKE: So it's about the here and now, about the condition of the world so-
           cially and how it affects us.

BRIAN: I think one thing that David and I saw in your work, Mike, is your
           sense that in religious education and youth ministry, we have tended
           to think about formation as something we add to someone to help
           them become more faithful—you know, deeper, more intensely held
           beliefs and commitments and all that kind of thing. You take care to
           stress that how we are already living can be a profound inhibition to
           the possibility of being transformed by the Gospel. I think all three of
           us agree that, in different ways and in spite of our different contexts,
           we need to investigate the particularities of everyday life that stand
           in the way of our living out our Christian vocations. And we need to
           know these things in their particularity. Again, I mean about our-
           selves, our churches, and the youth we serve.

MIKE: I was thinking about this note I made yesterday, about the people
           I've met who have profoundly influenced me. They were people who
           invited me to embrace an alternative way of living. But it wasn't that
           they spoke about an alternative. It was the way they lived. I'm think-
           ing of Dennis Flynn. His religious name was Bartimeo. The guy was
           such a marvelous human being. All day, he used to visit people in
           hospitals and in nursing homes, and he was in his late seventies. And
           he had a fantastic sense of delight. He would tell a story and think it
           was funny. To me, this was very revelatory of who he is. He went to
           a nursing home once and was talking with a woman there for maybe
           ten or fifteen minutes, and she asked him if he would get into bed
           and hug her. And he said that he'd love to do it but he didn't think he
           should. And he'd tell the story with a twinkle in his eye. And this per-
           son, he had a profound influence on me, way more than my ability to
           ever name it. So, yes, he didn't add something to me. I just saw how
           he was. And when we meet a person who has a genuinely alternative
           way of living, it's a huge influence.

BRIAN: Let me ask you a follow-up question, then, Mike. What you're saying is that there are these—well, saints, or folks that have inspired us to live a different kind of life. But in a certain sense that's also adding. How do we take your observation about these particular lives and relate it directly to your own insight about what gets in the way of our living out our vocation? How do we learn from those lives? It's not exactly imitation, is it?

MIKE: I think the only point I want to make about this is that introspection reveals to us the people who've influenced us. You don't influence people's lives by saying I'm going to influence them. But if you go as deep as you can in what you're doing, basically, it will influence people. You can influence them towards superficiality, or the kind of influence I'm talking about.

This kid who was in my YCS group in the early '60s became an internist. He called me one day from the seminary in Baltimore and asked, "Is this Michael Warren, and did you ever teach at St. John's University?" I said, yeah. He told me that he'd left his practice and he went into the priesthood. And he said that his being ordained was directly related to being in the young Christian students group that I directed. Now, I wasn't doing high-powered youth ministry. We just looked at the Gospels and we tried to apply them. Now, how it happened I have no idea.

People used to ask, "Mike, why are you dealing with these kids? There are only six of them. These kids are nothing, the non-leaders in this school. You don't have time for that." So I used to always say that I wanted to "ring a dead stick"—you know, it's an old monastic thing. And, here's this kid saying that those discussions with his friends—they all became friends—were decisive.

BRIAN: So, is that the point—that when people get into discussions where they share what's going on in their everyday lives, they are better able to resist those elements that militate against Christian discipleship?

MIKE: Right. In other words, we're talking about an alternative consciousness, an alternative way of being a person. And you can't just decide you're that and then do it. But you can decide, okay, whatever I do with these young people, I'm going to try to go for some kind of gospel depth. I'd say probably the three of us could name people in the past who've exhibited elements of this stuff. They might be surprised if we told them.

DAVID: Brian, let me try to frame this in the terms that you were suggesting earlier about inhibitions. It seems to me—just reflecting on my own life and our conversation tonight—that one inhibition that I'm aware of is thinking that this radical alternative way of living is not plausible; you know it's just not possible. And you can name that as despair. But, seeing someone who is living in this way that I only dream of helps me to get in touch with that possibility, with what I really yearn for, and it sparks that possibility in a different way.

MIKE: So it becomes incarnate in a way, the alternative becomes incarnate.

DAVID: It becomes plausible. I mean, the expectations and values that are normalized and given to me as what counts, for example, as professionalism or middle class status. You know, however you want to name it, that's not the only reality, or even the best reality, even though it's the only one that we ever see around us. So meeting someone who's living that alternative gives, helps me, sparks for me, reminds me of what I really want and reminds me to live a different way.

BRIAN: I often draw insights—inasmuch as I have them—from my teaching. I was trying to say this earlier, that I've noticed a kind of flickering reality about these saintly types as invitations to live an alternative kind of a life. At times, they seem to inspire students, as you've been saying. But at other times, maybe when the plausibility structure is weak (to use David's term), my students seem to find these lives accusatory rather than inspiring. Saints become what Freud thought saints were: representatives of the cultural superego—what we're supposed to be like, not what we're inspired to be like.

MIKE: I think that's very true. I think that's very good. I presume that the things that a person exhibits that are most inspirational, the person is unconscious of—like if you're teaching, and the subtext, which you're not fully conscious of, is "Ain't I something?" And so you're always working at this curse of professionalism.

BRIAN: Or "Ain't I nothin'?"—if you're trying to live up to the virtue of humility.

MIKE: Yeah, yeah. And so, people pick that up and that's the thing that you don't even know you're exhibiting because it's unconscious, it's not in your notes. A girl met me about eight weeks ago on the stairwell at St. John's and told me that my marriage course had changed her life. And it was very important to her at that time because she was in a crisis.

I don't know what it was—maybe the permission to trade anxieties back and forth in the class—but somehow, she remembered that. In working with youth, we're not just collecting turkeys, or having car washes, or collecting money for our ski trip. There's something deep that's meant to go on. A lot of youth ministers I meet don't seem to have this thought. They're playing on the surface of things, trying to keep kids out of trouble. They're doing this lowest level exhortation about the Gospel that doesn't catch anybody. But there's something mystical, in a way, for a person who is working with the young and is attending with one eye to the radicalness of Jesus' proposals and with the other eye to the possibilities of young people.

BRIAN: I've got a question for David on that. I think what Mike is saying relates to something we were talking about the other day, which was the observation you made that after a time in youth ministry, the youth from your groups would divide into two different groups. One group would become more or less assimilated to the culture at large, with its stress on the expected social scripts—you know, what Walter Brueggeman calls "royal consciousness"[1]—and the second group would often think the only way to live a faithful life of Christian vocation was to go into the ordained ministry. And I wonder if you can expand on that? As I recall, for you that seemed like a really unacceptable disjunction—that you either got assimilated into consumerist culture or became a minister. Could you talk more about that?

DAVID: Well, in watching that happen over twenty-three years now, one of the things that occurs to me is that if you ask any of them from that first group—the ones who got assimilated into the dominant values of the culture—"Are you Christian?" most of them would probably say, yeah. They would self-identify as Christian, but what that means for them is often an odd and truncated form of faith—it gets stapled onto the edge of the middle-class life and it doesn't really integrate or reshape that middle-class life. It never is allowed to take the center of life, to become a central preoccupation, and reshape all of those relationships in more redemptive ways.

MIKE: And one of the reasons it doesn't is because there's very little discourse about the connection between discipleship and wealth. There's a disconnect in the way churches process this.

---

1. Walter Brueggemann, *The Prophetic Imagination* (Minneapolis, MN: Fortress, 1978).

DAVID: But also it seems to me that we live in a culture that increasingly doesn't allow space for alternatives. When I think back on some of the historical work that I've done, I can recall previous generations in which you can see that, yes, professionalism was still a part of the culture, and consumerism was still part of the culture, but it didn't dominate the imagination in the way that it does today. It seems increasingly like folks are forced to live out alternative values in the cracks and crevices of an increasingly monolithic social structure. And so, as youth begin to look at the world and their possibilities for living faithfully in the world, if they can't see ways for changing the structures that are out there or if they can't see the possibility for living a faithful alternative to their culture, well, the ministry is one place they can see to do that.

BRIAN: So you're saying that those who entered the ministry maybe did so because it was the only way they could imagine living out their faith deeply and authentically?

DAVID: That's right. And some of them, like myself, I'll just speak about myself, but I don't think that I was particularly gifted for ordained ministry. I did it and I think I did a good job. But looking back on my life and my vocation as an adult, I think I was just trying to find some space that would allow me to live faithfully as a disciple of Jesus. And a lot of the kids who are in my youth groups have followed similar paths. And some of them went to seminary and started working in churches but some of them have gradually kind of moved into things like pastoral counseling as a vocation—looking for different ways of trying to live faithfully.

BRIAN: Can I just follow up on that, David? In a certain way, you're suggesting that the folks who didn't go into the ministry were often in danger of succumbing to the general culture somehow. But what about the folks who did go into the ministry? Once that decision was made for discipleship, did they find themselves in institutions and with other people who would encourage that initial commitment to Christian discipleship, or did they also end up facing the very same dilemmas?

DAVID: Yeah, sure. You don't fully escape all of that by going into the ministry. But, I think all in all, I think those folks feel like they're living in a world where those ideas of the Gospel still have some power and a currency and are still kind of the narrative around which they want to create faithful lives.

MIKE: There's a metaphor I want to put in here, on this struggle towards faithfulness—the metaphor of a refuge. Brian, the retreat house where you live is a refuge so people can step back and get back in touch with these deeper calls. And if people are doing youth ministry to provide a refuge, they're doing something similar. It's a place where you can be sane again—you know, kind of like *The King of Hearts*?

BRIAN: I love that movie. It gives the sane "lunatics" power over the insane institution.

MIKE: So that's a very important point here—that sometimes people who knew us when they were young come back to touch base because we might again provide a refuge, a place to remember insights they once had and they've let go. So, anyway, seeing a youth group as a place for alternatives—for deep alternative possibilities—needs to be pushed, I think. Because basically, a lot of youth groups are the opposite. There's nothing distinctive about them. They're basically a rotary club under a very thin Christian veil.

DAVID: Let me just express another thought that I've had about young people who have gone into the ministry. They are often very poetic and artistic and they really have soul, and when they look at the world and the possibilities for work in the world, they're looking at the corporate world that dominates the imaginations of youth about their future work. But there's really no place in our culture for artists or saints to really make a living and for that to be vocation. Or at least that space is very small and risky for those youth who are artistic or just want to work with the poor and be a force for redemption in the world. And when they looked at the options that were there, there just aren't a lot of structures that are validated in our culture that allow people to have a family and to sustain themselves in this kind of creative or redemptive work that does not enhance the machinery of consumerism. And so the ordained ministry seemed like an option that provided an opening for them.

Brian: That's really an essential point for me. A place where I've always taken issue with the book *Habits of the Heart*[2]—a book that's been influential with youth ministers and teachers—is that the authors imply that the reason many youth are not able to live more ethically or authentically or maybe compassionately is that they're lacking a language to interpret and guide their ethical lives. And so the implication is that they've never really tried to live an alternative life. What I think you're saying is that often they've tried but they've found that it's very difficult to live out this kind of life in discipleship. This has led me to the conclusion—I'd like to know what you think of it—that the apparent selfishness associated with consumerism and the success ethic is not in fact about selfishness or egoism but is more the result of a kind of quiet despair about the possibility of living the life of discipleship. Have we supported youth in this, or have we blamed them?

Mike: I would like to connect with what you just said, because I like the idea of plausibility structures. I mentioned the refuge as a place where people go to get back in touch with their deepest yearnings for God and neighbor. But another metaphor is that of a chorus. Most people can't sing, can't carry a tune by themselves, but they can when they sing with a chorus. And so people meet with others who convince them that they're not nuts for having these yearnings for a deeper fidelity. Here are other people who are struggling the same way. So it becomes like a point of orientation. And the key is the possibility of speech, of speaking about these struggles and hearing other people speaking about these struggles.

Brian: So how would you translate what you just said as advice for youth ministers and other folks ministering to youth in the church?

Mike: Well, there's a very interesting program that we ran in New York. We did our youth ministry from a specific theoretical angle. It was a discernment process in which we were trying to understand the different kids who were ready to move deeper. And they would tell us, give us clues, questions that had been raised for them that they needed to pursue. So we would often go on retreat with the group and then have a chance to talk to them about themselves and so forth. For many, the next step was prayer, a systematic way of attending to the

---

2. Robert N. Bellah, Richard Madsden, William M. Sullivan, Ann Swidler, and Steven M. Tipton, *Habits of the Heart: Individualism and Commitment in American Life* (Berkeley: University of California Press, 1985).

presence of God and slowing down. So, we set up what we called NEXUS groups, New Encounter with Christ (X) Using Scripture. And we trained them, we showed them how to create space in their own rooms—their own space to sit on the floor so that it was a comfortable place to be—and we asked them to spend ten minutes every day, very loosely looking into the Gospels.

Money, Food, and Talking about Our Lives

BRIAN: Mike, once when we were talking about all this, you were worried about what you called a kind of negative spirituality in which people become constantly engaged in thinking about debt—financial debt—in the way that we might hope to be thinking about living an authentic Christian life.

MIKE: Yeah, because you're not centered on your need for wholeness, or your need for companionship, or your need for humor and comedy and joy—but you're centered on a need for money. I need more money, more money, more money, more money—you know, it gets inside you. When you're focused on your need for money, you're not focused on your gifts or the giftedness of life. Oh, it's a very tough sort of thing . . . well, you know, one of the things that I haven't said in this conversation about young people. I think among some young people it's not uncommon to have this kind of a sense of self that says, I want this, I want this, I want this, I want this, why don't I have the things that I want? It's an insistent thing. I should have the things that I want! And sometimes they can get very angry with their parents. Why aren't you giving me the things that I want, making it possible for me to have the things that I want?

DAVID: In a little book about Christian practices, *Way to Live*,[3] that I participated in, one of the chapters that I found most compelling was the chapter about how we take food in this culture. In this culture food is seen both as fuel just to gobble on the run just to keep going, and also as a way of kind of rewarding ourselves when we've done something, it serves a lot of functions. But in contrast, when we look at the way Jesus related to food, for Jesus taking food was an opportunity to reflect on the source of the food, an opportunity to reflect on the earth and the workers and an opportunity to share food with

3. Dorothy C. Bass and Don C. Richter, *Way to Live: Christian Practices for Teens* (Nashville: Upper Room 2002).

people around him and beyond even his closest circle to the multitudes. It was an opportunity for building connections, making those connections to the creator, to the earth, to laborers, to friends and strangers. And it occurs to me that living in a convenience culture, what happens is that everything is flattened out and is perceived in terms of how I can consume it. What can be most easily consumed by me? And what happens is that the otherness or the giftedness of everything, the holiness, and the mystery is flattened out into how it serves me immediately.

Mike: That's very interesting. So you're saying that Jesus sees food as a means of relationship, of drawing all things into relationship. And so the central symbol in the Eucharist is food and drink, and it's obviously relational and built right into the ritual, that when you eat this bread, you become united. It can become an empty symbol that doesn't touch anybody, you know, people don't realize that they're eating their way into one another's spirits, and sometimes the priest or pastor doesn't get it.

David: I think it is increasingly important, particularly for youth growing up in this interconnected global community, to understand the complexity of their relationships, the way in which food consumption is related to food production, which is related to exploitation of workers and to the degradation of the environment—which is all related to our spirituality. It's important for them to understand the web . . . to understand the world not just as a marketplace where I can pick and choose what I want but also as participating in a web, a network of relationships. And, I'm saying that I think that's central for faith in this century.

Brian: How would we—if we're addressing this to youth ministers, youth workers, pastors, volunteers in the church—help youth understand this web of relationships?

Mike: Well, one thing you could do, is find those who are ready to talk about the Gospel, then allow them to come together each week in small groups to do the lectionary or scripture readings and talk about what they mean in their lives, how their lives are interconnected, and how the gospel speaks in this web of relationships. Then, it would be important for the priest or pastor somehow to have some report of that discussion so that he or she is speaking not just at the community but also out of the wisdom of the community.

BRIAN: Now that's really interesting. So the priest or the pastor would learn from the wisdom of the group . . .

DAVID: . . . about the struggles and blessings of their lives, and how they are touched by the web of relationships throughout their communities and the globe . . .

MIKE: A second thing you could do is begin to assemble those who want to talk about the readings. And the priest might give a summary of the readings and say, "Now, what do you have to say about this?" And these people can speak. Speech like this does something. This might have the effect of keeping the gospel closer to their lives, responding to them and calling them beyond themselves into the world.

DAVID: I too kind of see a role of adults working with youth as collaborators in exploring their world and their experience of the world. What I've done with youth is helped them to surface the themes of their life experience and then in collaboration with adults, to problematize them and to explore the causes and the influences. And I actually had them create charts where they had the themes listed and then all of the networks and influences. Sometimes it's helpful for them to have a visualization of the network of influences and how this theme, of say poverty or homelessness, surfaces in a particular context of powers and principalities.

BRIAN: I met a Catholic priest several years ago who was working with gangs just outside of Los Angeles. I asked him how many of the youth he worked with he would still lose to gangs. He answered my question obliquely. He said, "If you gave me enough adult volunteers, we wouldn't have to lose anybody." And he said that a problem he faces is instilling confidence in adult volunteers. They think they have to know more or be holier or something before they minister to the youth. And no matter what he said, he couldn't convince them otherwise. He found this extremely frustrating and disappointing. So that suggests how important it is, not maybe to just rely on the pastors and the youth ministers, but to empower the adults within the church, doesn't it?

DAVID: Two insights—the first is a story of working with the youth group in California. We'd been working for some time in kind of the traditional youth group model. We did some rigorous training with adult workers to prepare them for working with youth. And, it was not an unsuccessful program—we had numbers of youth and everything. But at some point, we shifted the whole program and we intentionally tried to frame youth ministry as adults collaborating with youth in Christian formation and seeing themselves as partners on the journey. And we made some real structural changes to reflect this sense of partnership on a journey. I had one of the adults come to me after youth group one night and say, "You have no idea the kind of burden I feel lifted off my shoulders." You know, she said, "I have felt all of this weight of having to lead these youth and wondering myself if I had the intelligence and faith resources to do it." And she said, "Being a partner with them in this has really been liberating to me."

BRIAN: David, we've often talked about burnout with youth ministers. If they were collaborating with other adults in the way you just described, do you think they would feel less marginalized—that there would be less burnout?

DAVID: Yeah, yeah, absolutely. I'm reminded of another conversation you and I have sometimes about the nature of relationships generally. We have said in those conversations that sometimes we think in relationships that we have to solve all of our issues and problems in abstraction from that relationship before we're ready to be in that relationship. And that's a mistake, I think. Sometimes you don't even know what your problems are or your potential. You come to know yourself in relationship, and it's the relationship for me that becomes the source and context for me to reflect more deeply on who I am. And it becomes a way for me to extend, expand my own self. Working with young people can be for many adults a spiritual discipline. I've seen adults begin to address issues that could only surface in working with teenagers.

BRIAN: That could bring us back to how we invite adults into youth ministry. If what inhibits adults who are not professionals in youth ministry are thoughts like "I don't know enough, I don't know the Bible well enough, and I don't know any theology" or "I'm not living a good enough life," what can we do to help? On the one hand, we could say, you're being invited to collaborate with youth. And on the other hand, we could say, you're being invited to join with clergy leaders to explore your own faith and to learn even as you teach and to bring your own life experience and faith to this. I think with these under-standings, those adults would not be so intimidated.

DAVID: Just thinking about the charism of adults, I like Walter Brueggemann's discussion about the Biblical canon, in which he describes the Torah, the Prophets and the Wisdom Writings.[4] And the role of the adults is especially in regards to the Torah, to tell the story and help the youth to understand the images and ideas as the context for our faith, the larger story that our little lives fit into. And I think that's one charism of adults, helping us connect our individual lives with the larger story. But I also like the way that he says that the Story was told. Brueggemann says in the Torah typically it's not adults impos-ing a story onto youth. Instead the story is told as a gift, in the context of a Sabbath ritual in which youth ask questions. What makes this night so different from any other night? It's an existential question that emerges from youth and an answer comes from the tradition, from the adults who say this is our understanding of what this is about. I think youth and adult relationships could have something of that character. In the best of cases I have seen adults standing alongside youth, responding to their questions and framing their response within the larger story of God and God's work in the world. Connecting their lives to God's story in itself can be healing for youth who often feel adrift in an overheated image culture in which the story changes weekly, in which young people have a difficult time having any strong sense of their place in the world.

MIKE: And with regard to those existential questions to which the gospel gives context, I am concerned with engaging youth in telling their own stories. I am talking about the things that we dare not talk about—like our pain.

DAVID: I was teaching a class at Bethany Theological Seminary in Richmond, Indiana. I do a similar thing with the course that I teach as I do with congregations—I help them reflect on the themes, the experiences of their young people, and think critically and theologically. But in the end, I ask them to do some very focused strategizing around the aims that surface, the limit-situations that surface. You know, I'm always surprised. These become a context in which people really do struggle and create new congregational strategies for youth ministry.

4. Walter Brueggemann, *The Creative Word: Canon as a Model for Biblical Education* (Philadelphia: Fortress Press, 1982).

A few weeks ago we were struggling with the issue that they named, that had surfaced from their congregation—the alienation between youths and adults. And we had done our critical reflection, we had talked about the social issues and the social forces that had shaped that alienation. We talked theologically about the importance of a beloved community and how youths have important gifts to offer. But then we were strategizing. One youth minister said that their congregation had realized that their habits around the ways they related to youth were dysfunctional, and that they needed to dehabituate, to break their bad habits of relating to youth, and to re-habituate. Not only did they make sure that youth were well represented in every group and committee in the church, but they created structures in which youth can participate more fully. They decided that whenever an adult spoke, a youth had to follow them, in an alternating conversational pattern. It's not a hugely radical idea. But what it does is force a different pattern of relating. And it forces youth to move out of that domesticated role. And it forces adults to make space for them. One of the other things this youth minister was telling me was that it also kind of created a situation in which the church saw the importance of preparing youth for participating in its conversations. And so every youth on these committees had adult sponsors who met with them, and briefed them about the business of the church and the community beforehand, and kind of helped draw out their thoughts and opinions, and eventually helped give voice to their concerns in these committee meetings. So I thought it was an example of the way congregations can rethink their habits about how they relate to youth and begin to try to relate to them in more faithful ways.

MIKE: Over the last two years I have been using a similar concept in my courses. I am talking more and more about the idea of a self that stands for various things. I used to talk about individuals, individualism. But now I ask, "What sort of a self are you?" And that means, "How do you relate to other selves? What are your commitments to the world of selves?" Actually, in the course of a semester, the young people seem to adopt this language, and to understand it. I got this way of thinking about the self from Charles Taylor's *Sources of the Self*.[5]

---

5. Charles Taylor, *Sources of the Self: The Making of the Modern Identity* (Cambridge, MA: Harvard University Press, 1989).

Confessions about Our Own Caughtness

BRIAN: Of course, we don't stand outside of the situations we've been describing and criticizing. We're also caught up in the distortions we name and resist. The three of us are involved in academics and in our own stories of professional success and failure—you know, all that talk about knowledge as a commodity and about cultural capital and so forth. Any thoughts on that?

MIKE: Well, about being caught, when I first came to Saint John's University, one particular encounter I remember was outside a building where a senior faculty member said—I guess I had spoken up at a faculty meeting and maybe raised some issues that others didn't want me to raise—and she said to me, "Mike, keep a low profile until you get tenure." And, I said to her, "If I have to shut my mouth and can't speak in order to get tenure, then I don't want tenure, I don't need tenure." But I realize now that I was interested in getting tenure, to have a safe position, so I could do what I wanted, so that I didn't have to do what other people wanted me to do. Now, once you reach that point, then the question is what do you want to do because the pressures aren't there?

BRIAN: There's another question there, though, isn't there? If you get a PhD—I don't want to forget about youth here, but there are parallel structures in our own lives to youth. If you get a PhD, in a certain sense you're told, to—well, you know, hold your horses, conform, write this kind of dissertation, do this kind of work. So, that's maybe five or six years of formation. But the next step is that you're told—well, you know, wait until you have tenure, then you can really tell the truth. So then you're formed for another five or six years to conform to another kind of professional expectation. My question is, after more than a decade of conforming to expectations so that you can be free, how can you possibly be free? What you've probably learned best is how to conform—while making it seem like you're not conforming. It's a valuable skill.

The Culture of Youth Ministry

MIKE: I have to do a bit of autobiography here. When I was young I joined a wonderful religious order specializing in work with youth. Eventually, after several years of training, I taught in an all-boys high school.

My work there fascinated me. But gradually I came to realize that I only knew these kids in the context of a classroom. I didn't know the neighborhoods that they lived in. I didn't know their friends. I didn't know what movies they saw. I didn't know their girlfriends. I didn't know their crowd. Basically I came to see I couldn't know them. I saw that the school was a very confined space—excluding a lot of important information from me. And so I became interested in the aspects of their lives hidden from me. There was a gulf between us—let's call it the "school gulf."

As it turned out, the Brothers who led our order were asking us teachers for volunteers to work with youth outside the schools—on the streets, in their neighborhoods. This was new, and I jumped at it and volunteered. At that moment, I was the head of the religion department, in this huge school of 1400 students. Two others from other schools also volunteered. Lucky for me, the other two who volunteered were also heads of religion departments. We had much common background and university training. We worked with young people in eight Roman Catholic parishes in the Northern Virginia suburb across the Potomac River from Washington, DC. I did that work for three years. It was difficult but fascinating and rewarding. In my so-called "spare time," I was working on my PhD at Catholic University in Washington. For a dissertation I studied the youth work done by a French theologian who specialized in youth ministry and who wrote several important books on the topic.

And graduating, I looked for a teaching position at a university. I couldn't find one. I was invited to accept a position at the United States Catholic Conference in Washington, as assistant director for youth catechesis in the country. So that meant I went all around the country trying to assess what the situation was in youth work. From that position I got to meet all the leaders, all the diocesan leaders, and people who weren't named the leaders, but I thought were the real leaders. And then two years later, I accepted a faculty position at St. John's University in New York City. To New York I brought my broad connections with youth leaders across the U.S. They would ask me to come and speak about the various issues that they were concerned about, and out of that came my published material about youth ministry. However all that time, my deepest interest was not in youth ministry at all but in what I call "adult formation." And of course, to do that work, one had to be very focused on the social context in which people lived. My doctoral minor area of study was the sociology of religion. I had been interested in social contexts long before I ever took a sociology course.

BRIAN: Who was the French theologian?

MIKE: Pierre Babin.

BRIAN: Oh, yes. Did he have a lasting influence on your life and work, do you feel?

MIKE: Oh, yeah. He has wonderful published and non-published writings. They were in French and so I had to translate them. The task of translation pushes you deep into the meanings you are trying to retrieve. Babin trained young seminarians—this was in Corsica—how to go into towns and not say anything but just observe and sop up the feelings that you're getting, and see how the kids come together—just watching, trying to find out what their songs are and what stories they tell. I do think Babin is a genius for his insights into such matters. He knew the writings of Paulo Freire, the Brazilian liberationist educator. Freire's stuff on culture analysis had a big influence on me. Babin's writing—most of which has never been translated into English—influenced and helped me a lot. His writings are always in the background of my own. And so my youth ministry work has been based in practice, surely, but much more in theoretical material, like Babin's and Freire's.

DAVID: Yeah. I am projecting a lot onto your situation. But I would say—from my understanding of your work, and your life and your ministry—I think you're right, I think you are concerned about a whole ecology of issues. And one of those is how youth are formed in this culture. And I think that's a huge gift to congregations who are serious about their youth. One of the limits of youth ministry in this country has been its overly narrow focus. And I even think youth ministry has developed its own culture.

MIKE: Yeah, it has. One of the reasons I am disappointed that I haven't had the chance to work with doctoral students is that I haven't been able to reproduce my own concerns among future scholars. These are the people who are going on to careers as scholars and so forth. The students at the MA level that I've taught, they come from the university with important understanding and convictions, but they haven't had the time to work out the sort of understanding a doctoral program provides, or should provide. I'm saying I would have had a different kind of influence had I been working with doctoral students.

BRIAN: Well, but your books have touched all of us. And doctoral students read your work.

MIKE: Yes, I realize and appreciate that fact. I don't want to go into this in too much detail, but my own decision to work with youth seems to me almost weird. I have a distinct memory of when I decided my call was to work with youth. I don't think I've ever told this to anyone, because of how weird it seems. I remember walking to school one day. I was probably in the seventh or eighth grade. It occurred to me that God wanted me to work with the young. It was a sense that came to me in such a way that I can remember it. God wanted me to work with the young. And there was some "thing" that I might be able to do. As I say, it's a distinct memory, but I can't remember exactly how old I was. I was walking all by myself, and it just struck me that this is what I should do. Weird . . . It's very weird, how could you have that type of a sense at that age. I must have been a spooky kid.

I guess part of it was that I had a teacher in the sixth grade who was a Xaverian Brother. He was young, he had a sense of humor. He liked being with us; you could see it in his eyes. His name was George Randall. He went on to work several years in Africa as a teacher. I was privileged to be able to be at his deathbed and talk to him the day before he died three years ago. At any rate, my class had been taught previously by nuns, some wonderful nuns. However, the previous nun, in the fifth grade, hated kids, hated being a nun, hated being in the class, and I hated her. So when Brother Kenny came into my sixth grade classroom with the look of care and fun in his eyes, I was elated.

And so I found someone who had joy in his life, and I wanted to be like him. And it was out of that that I saw a lot of stuff going on among kids, like stealing, fighting, unhappiness, and stuff I thought was strange. And I said, maybe this is what I should do; maybe God wants me to do that. Yeah, I mean, I think vocational decisions are shrouded in mystery.

BRIAN: Sounds right.

DAVID: Amen.

LIFE IN WELLINGTON'S ARMY

LIFE IN WELLINGTON'S ARMY

Antony Brett-James

London · George Allen & Unwin Ltd
RUSKIN HOUSE   MUSEUM STREET

First published in 1972

ISBN 0 04 940042 8

Printed in Great Britain
in 11 point Plantin type
by Clarke, Doble & Brendon Ltd
Plymouth

To Jeffery and Sheila Switzer
friends of long standing and proved quality

Preface

During the long war against French Revolutionary and Napoleonic France the first loyalty of a British cavalryman or infantry soldier was to his regiment, yet most officers and men would have agreed, whatever branch of the army they belonged to, that the division was normally the highest focal point of military devotion. The same was true during the first and second World Wars. In Wellington's day this sense of loyalty to a division, which came into being in 1810 and in most cases numbered about 7,000 men, was bound up with the personality of the commander, whether the friendly, controlled, warm-hearted Rowland Hill, who was regarded with real affection and respect, or the bluff, fierce, impetuously brave and pugnacious Picton, who was held in awe, even fear, by members of his 3rd Division. Divisions as well as regiments earned nicknames while campaigning: 'the Gentlemen's Sons', 'the Observing Division', and 'the Fighting Division', to name but three.

However strong their sense of belonging to a good, experienced, battle-hardened division, those who served in the Eighth Army in North Africa or the Fourteenth in Burma will know the pride which can derive from membership of such a force. An army can grow to greatness by virtue of its record of success, often achieved as the culmination of years of depressing setbacks and retreats in a particular theatre of war; by virtue of its commander, who impresses a definite character upon the officers and men, inspires their confidence, and arouses their enthusiasm. Now and then soldiers will be proud to belong to an army which fails, appears to be hard done by, and becomes a centre of controversy. An army does not require to be huge to be famous. While it is true that Napoleon's *Grande Armée* numbered close on 600,000 when he led it into Russia, Wellington's Peninsular army never had more than 51,000 troops effectively on the field of battle, and neither in Portugal nor in Spain, nor even at Waterloo did he command more than 36,000 British soldiers. His army bore no number, for it was the only one

7

which Britain could put in the field against Napoleonic France, and he had always to take care lest he expose it to excessive risk.

From 1810 onwards he had the excellent help of the King's German Legion, and of Portuguese troops trained and led by his own officers. In 1809 and again in 1813 he had direct support from regular Spanish troops, while throughout the Peninsular War the efforts of his force were seconded most effectively by guerrilla bands, who helped to whittle down French numerical superiority by compelling Napoleon's marshals to waste thousands of troops in escort, guard post and garrison duties.

In Wellington's army, and in Sir John Moore's before Corunna, we find much with a modern ring: a sense of belonging to a home from home, a widespread determination to struggle on when sick rather than drop out and leave well-tried comrades. Anyone who has campaigned with animal transport will recognize both the confusion and clutter which can develop along inadequate tracks and the wonderful achievement of horses and mules in difficult country. Veterans will recall, besides the unaccountable halts, the stumbling and tripping and muttered curses and the snap of dead branches underfoot when marching in darkness, the peculiar feeling of naked exposure in moonlight. How familiar the heat of metal in the sun and the tackiness of warm water in bottle or canteen; the reports and returns which had to be filled in at every level! Laxity of dress strikes a recent chord, and so does the friendly scorn of troops up forward for base wallahs, be they 'Belem Rangers' in Lisbon or Cairo's 'Groppi Light Horse'.

Like their successors, Wellington's men made comparisons between the Peninsular and India, Malta, Egypt, Canada, Holland or wherever else they had seen active service. They contrasted the lamentable state of countries under enemy occupation, or ravaged by war and the passage of armies, with untramelled Britain, giving thanks that the homeland was spared such horrors as they saw around them. Britain became, inevitably, the yardstick for comparisons, be the subject roads or women or the theatre; and in their estimation the British version did not always come out on top. They learnt not to brood about death or the loss of good friends killed at their side, for life and war had to go on and work remained to be done. Cheerful laughter and joking in discomfort and adversity were appreciated and proved infectious, though grumbling was also widespread. Resourceful improvization ranked high among their military virtues. As now, so then, letters, newspapers and parcels formed a precious link with home; the supply of books never sufficed for those who loved reading. Maintenance of high morale preoccupied Wellington's best officers, many of whom had learnt the secrets while serving under Moore's far-seeing and benevolent command.

In the course of a year most of the troops spent few days actually fighting. True it is that they marched or rode long distances, sometimes advanced, sometimes retreated, and on half a dozen occasions laid siege to a fortress town, but except for the light cavalry squadrons deployed right forward to keep watch upon French movements, and the Light Division engaged on outpost duty, the soldiers spent over half the year in bivouac or billet. This does not mean they that were idle: there was always work to be done, be it repairs, foraging, administration or training; but it does mean that opportunities arose, and were eagerly taken, to indulge in a variety of pastimes.

In this book I have tried to depict the daily life of the Peninsular and Waterloo armies when not engaged in battle; to show the nature of campaigning and of 'the gipsy mode of life' they led; to indicate the relationship between officers and men, and between the military and the local population in Portugal, Spain, southern France and Flanders. Given the comparative smallness of Wellington's army, and the degree of illiteracy then prevalent, the Peninsular War is remarkably rich in private memoirs, journals and correspondence; and from these sources, written by rank and file as well as by officers, a very detailed picture emerges of how the army went about its business, the conditions under which it lived and worked, and the factors which contributed to keep men's spirits high. Certain aspects, like the army on the march, the baggage, ladies at the front, and the spiritual life, have already been dealt with in Sir Charles Oman's *Wellington's Army*, but he devotes most of his space to Wellington, his lieutenants, his tactics, and the organization of the army and the regiment; in S. G. P. Ward's *Wellington's Headquarters*, which is mainly concerned with administration, staff work and supply; in *Wellington and his Army* by Godfrey Davies; and, on a smaller scale, in my *The British Soldier in the Napoleonic Wars*.

I conclude this preface by quoting what Lord Wellington told his friend Samuel Rogers about one visitor to the Peninsular Army:

'——,when at our headquarters in Spain, wished to see an Army, and I gave directions that he should be conducted through ours. When he returned, he said, "I have seen nothing—nothing but here and there little clusters of men in confusion; some cooking, some washing, and some sleeping." "Then you have seen an Army," I said.' *

* Rogers, 204-5.

Acknowledgements

It is agreeable for an author to thank those who have helped in one way or another towards the writing and completion of his book. On this occasion I am very grateful to the following friends who have given me hospitality and kindness: Michael and Daphne Bolton, in whose home in County Wicklow I began the writing; Rien and Gon Zappey, living in northern Holland, enabled me to draft several chapters in their canal-side house, and Edmund and Edith Ronald did the same for me in Portugal; John and Diana Bailey's stimulating household in Hampshire saw the writing of other chapters at weekends; and in Diana Barry's peaceful French home I revised the text to the sound of a rushing weir and a turning mill wheel.

I am particularly indebted to Elizabeth Webb for devoting time and her experience as a writer to helping me revise the book by suggesting many sound improvements which I have been glad to accept. George Ward, himself an authority on Wellington, has kindly allowed me to quote from the journal of George Eastlake. From F. L. M. Dawson I derived some valuable information and comments based on deep and practical professional knowledge.

Lt.-Col. Alan Shepperd, MBE, and the staff of the Central Library at Sandhurst, especially Mr R. W. Meadows, have been most helpful and quick in obtaining books on my behalf from other libraries. The Leicester Library provided me with a photo-copy of Bugler William Green's rare book, *A Brief Outline of the Travels and Adventures. . . .* I owe thanks to the Director and staff of the National Army Museum, in particular Mrs Elizabeth Steele and Miss D. Paul, who showed me several exhibits concerned with the Peninsular War and gave me facilities for consulting various manuscript sources.

Dr Anne Ward's careful editing has eliminated numerous minor errors and infelicities. Once again I am glad to record my gratitude to Shane Jones for typing the book from a difficult manuscript.

September 1971   A. B-J

Contents

Preface   *page* 7
Acknowledgements   11

 1 *On the March*   23
 2 *Billets*   38
 3 *Hosts and Landladies*   53
 4 *Campaigning Kit*   66
 5 *Threadbare and Patched*   78
 6 *Bivouac Life*   87
 7 *Rations*   107
 8 *Wartime Dinner Parties*   121
 9 *Learning the Language*   135
10 *Pastimes*   145
11 *Come Dancing*   167
12 *Horses and Forage*   179
13 *Field Sports*   195
14 *Outdoor Pastimes and Routine Work*   214
15 *Chaplains and Religion*   228
16 *The Wounded and Sick*   250
17 *Army Wives*   271
18 *Fraternization*   292

References   311
Bibliography   329
Index   345

Illustrations

PLATES

1 Guns and carts approaching and crossing a bridge
  A baggage column on the march in 1811   *facing page* 64
2 The 3rd Division crossing the Tagus in May 1811
  Hat worn by Sir Thomas Picton at the battle of Vitoria   65
3 The Bishop's Palace at Pinhel
  General Graham's toilet set   96
4 Top layer and case of Lord Lynedoch's toilet set
  Sir John Moore's cutlery   97
5 Sir John Moore's key-ring and seals
  A watch belonging to Sir John Moore in 1808–9   160
6 Telescope used by Wellington at the battle of Waterloo
  Troops in bivouac in May 1811   161
7 Freineda: Wellington's headquarters for two winters
  Wellington's camp bed   192
8 Learning to smoke and drink grog
  Poor Johnny Newcome on the sick list   193

MAPS

1 Portugal, Spain and Southern France   17
2 The frontier area of Portugal-Spain where the army spent   18
  several winters
3 The area around Lisbon   19
4 The Pyrenees region   20
5 Flanders – the Waterloo campaign   21

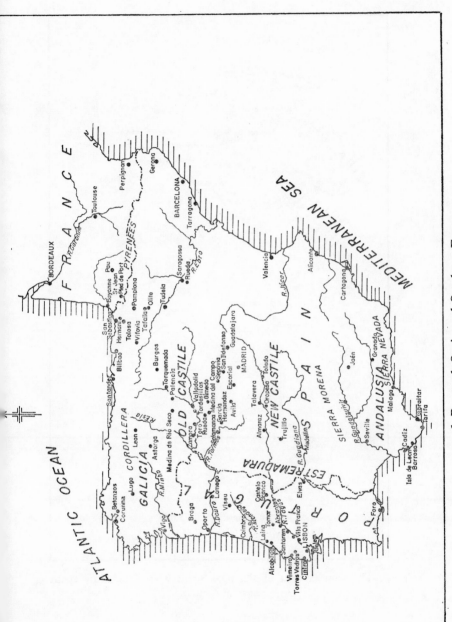

1. Portugal, Spain and Southern France

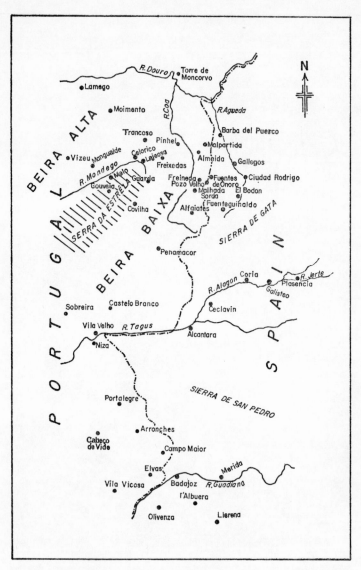

2. The frontier area of Portugal-Spain where the army spent several winters

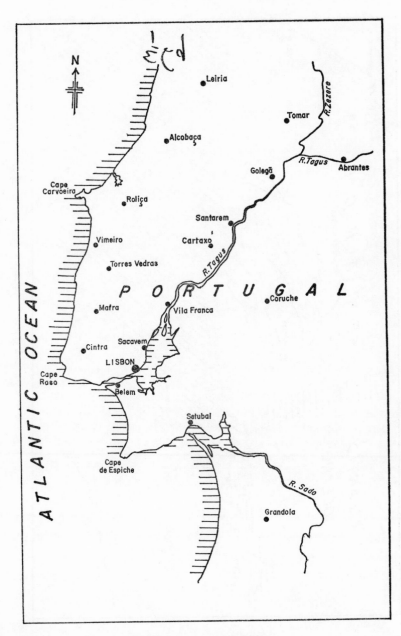

3. The area around Lisbon

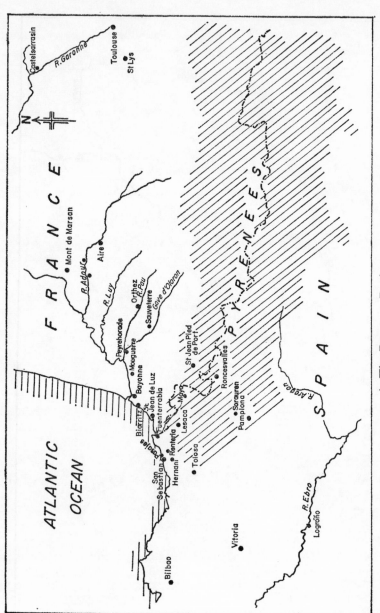

4. The Pyrenees Region

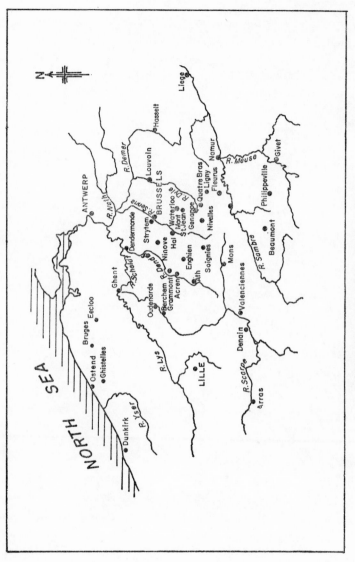

5. Flanders – the Waterloo campaign

Chapter 1

ON THE MARCH

'Salisbury Plain was a joke to what we met with in the country through which we passed, for the eye could not reach the extent of the plains over which we marched.'[1]
Lieut.-Colonel Charles Steevens, 20th Foot, June 1813

'The heat is extreme. We are all getting very brown and our lips are so painful that we can hardly touch them.'[2]
Lieutenant George Woodberry, 18th Light Dragoons, 24 May 1813

'We are generally kept warm on the line of march, trudging along in our wet shirts, which dry on our bones when a blink of the sun favours us.'[3]
Lieutenant George Bell, 34th Foot, April 1814

The Peninsular landscape across which for five years the army marched and campaigned varied as sharply as did the bivouac sites, ranging from thick brushwood and heathland at Roliça to granite rocks and stone walls along the river Coa; from vineyards near Tordesillas or Rueda to the sunburnt, parched, uncultivated wilds and brown stubble round Palencia.[4] Whereas at Busaco Wellington's troops fought on a ridge covered with gorse and heather, above a hillside seamed by ravines and strewn with boulders, earlier that summer of 1810 the light dragoons moved over a treeless plain of wheat near Gallegos, and then through rye, which 'reached nearly to our knees as we rode, and the grain flew out at every step'. Three years later regiments again marched through one continuous cornfield, trampling down twenty yards of wheat or barley on either side of the road which ran across northern Castile above Palencia and Burgos.[5] One British brigade storming the heights of Vera had to contend with large stones being rolled down upon the men, as well as with trees, brushwood and briars so prickly that hands and legs were pierced with thorns and trousers were literally torn off in shreds; but when they crossed the Bidassoa the face of the countryside altered suddenly, hedges appeared, heathland was interspersed with fields, and soldiers were reminded of England. Round St Jean Pied de Port the country was studded with country houses, meadows, vineyards, wooded hills, and large sheets of water in the valleys, while the landscape between St Jean de Luz and the Nive was remembered for its orchards and woods, its fortified châteaux and its farmhouses.[6]

In most regions the roads were bad, yet how much worse were the straggling village streets. In Portugal they appeared to visitors as invariably bad, especially in winter. The centre of the road from house to house was like a brook of mud with deep holes, some deep enough to swallow up a mule. Since the footpaths were of rough stones three or four feet high, to move from place to place was not without danger, and 'required the precaution used by the inhabitants, who carried a stick about seven feet long with an iron spike at the end'. Armed with one of these and wearing wooden shoes, Lieutenant William Hay and his friends in the 12th Light Dragoons amused themselves at the close of 1812 by visiting each other in their billets.[7]

Although the approach roads to small towns and to villages were paved for a mile or two on either side, they had usually not been repaired since first made, so were in a dreadful state by 1811 – broken up and nearly impassable. Moreover, the orchard and garden walls on both sides of the road had been pulled down or else had fallen into the road, thus blocking it in many places. 'As it is everybody's business & nobody's, there they remain,' wrote Captain George Call in his journal.[8]

During the closing weeks of 1813 the army experienced particular trouble with the roads of France: heavy in the extreme, with horses sinking to their knees in stiff mud and clay, carriages overturning, and men falling down at every step.[9] 'This is the most infernal country to campaign in I ever met with,' complained Colonel Vivian to his wife on 18th December. 'For ten days I have been covered with mud. You can have no conception of the sort of lanes – I can't call them roads – that we have here; up and down stiff hills, knee deep in mud. From head to foot we are all covered. . . .'[10]

Wellington laid great store on the ability of his troops to march and on at least three occasions during 1811 and 1812 alone he issued orders to the army requesting divisional commanders to exercise their regiments and to keep them in the habit of marching, because 'the celerity and accuracy of the officers and troops in manoeuvring are so essential in all operations'.[11]

On several occasions during the war detailed orders were issued for a column of march. When the country was open, two or more divisions of infantry or brigades of cavalry, moving from the same camp, were to march half an hour after each other; in close country they were to march at one hour intervals. The baggage was to be formed in the following order: oxen for the day's provision of meat; wheel carriages drawn by horses or mules; wheel carriages with iron axle-trees drawn by bullocks; mules with ammunition; the baggage of the staff; mules carrying camp-kettles or tents; the baggage of the regimental officers; the commissariat upon mules.[12]

Half-way through the war Wellington forbade the use of bullock carts for removing reserve and depot ammunition in the line of march, as a result of troops having endured long hold-ups in narrow roads when faced with a convoy of a hundred such carts. In the Light Division, at least, regimental baggage followed the line of march, the mules of each company being tied together and conducted by two batmen in rotation, right or left in front, while each regiment provided a subaltern, and each brigade a captain, to superintend this baggage column.[13]

A normal day's march was fifteen miles, the men sometimes setting out at sunrise and marching till ten o'clock, when they bivouacked or, more frequently, moving off when the bugles sounded at four o'clock. One particularly long and tedious march was now and then 'interrupted and impeded by other divisions from the roads often crossing each other'.[14] During that same advance towards the Pyrenees, several regiments marched for thirty-two days on end, with only two regular halts. Men suffering from sore feet were obliged, unless totally incapable of going on, to keep marching until their blisters and sores were healed; thus Captain Cooke often saw blood 'soaking through the gaiters, and over the heels of the soldiers' hard shoes, whitened with dust'.[15]

In describing General Craufurd's regulations for marches by the Light Division, John Cooke states that after each hour there

25

would be a ten-minute halt, and arrangements were made so that company commanders could close any gaps caused by obstacles and rough ground. The code of discipline was very strict, but every man knew exactly what was required of him, and humanity leavened the system. If a soldier found himself exhausted between halts, the senior company officer would order him to be given a ticket. This authority for being absent from his regiment he had to surrender on arrival in camp or to show to anyone who might question him on the road.[16]

Sir John Colborne, that splendid commander of the 52nd, confirms that Craufurd was the first man to introduce a proper system of marching. 'Sit down in it, sir! Sit down in it,' he used to call out if he saw a soldier stepping across a puddle. 'That was the way he got them to march so beautifully.'[17]

Probably the most celebrated forced march undertaken during the war was made by Craufurd's Light Brigade in July 1809 to the field of Talavera. This account is taken from the diary kept by Lieutenant Samuel Pollock of the 43rd Regiment.

'Left Coria on the 24th for Galesta [Galisteo]; on the 25th to Malpartida, a distance of four leagues, under soaking rain. Next a.m., 26th, about three leagues, crossed the river Pietar, and after marching two leagues found we had taken the wrong road; obliged therefore to cross the country about two leagues, where we halted, having marched upwards of seven leagues; next morning marched for Naval Moral, four leagues. Next a.m., 28th, the brigade marched at 1 o'clock with the intention of only going four leagues, but before we had got so far we met the Spaniards running away in all directions, with baggage, etc., and who reported an engagement; proceeded therefore about six leagues to Oropesa, where we filed off to a wood and stopped until 4 o'clock, when we again continued the march at a very quick pace until 11 o'clock. The brigade then lay down with their arms in their hands and after remaining in that situation for three hours again marched and reached the ground where the action had been fought the day previous – a harrowing march of *sixty-six miles in thirty hours*.'[18]

This achievement is justly famous, but many troops made longer if less dramatic marches, both in advance and retreat. We have a record of the distance covered by two regiments, one cavalry, the other infantry, and both for the year 1812. Between 12th May and 19th December the 13th Light Dragoons covered a total of 1,746 miles. Writing to Lord Malmesbury from Portugal on 10th December, Captain George Bowles declared that the Coldstream Guards had marched upwards of 1,700 miles. 'You may,' he added, 'form some idea of the severity of our services when I tell you that during that time I have lost *six mules*, who have all but one dropped dead from absolute fatigue (a tolerable expense for a poor man); and my case is by no means singular. . . . You will hardly believe that in the Coldstream there are only *four* officers who have stood the *whole* campaign, one of whom is your humble servant.'[19]

Other regiments of Guards have left records of their longer marches. Four companies of the 3rd/1st Guards left Cadiz on 1 September 1812 and reached Talavera on 18th October, having marched 404 miles via Seville, Medellin, Trujillo and Almaraz, at an average of sixteen miles a day and with only two days' rest. Three halt days were allowed when the 1st Guards Brigade marched from Oporto in July 1813 to join Wellington's army outside San Sebastian – a distance of 268 miles covered in twenty-two days and including three river crossings.[20]

To cross a river on the march usually presented hazards as well as discomforts, for there was seldom a bridge. Between 19th May and 17th June the 3rd Division marched from Vila Flor to Vitoria, crossed the rivers Esla and Ebro, halted for one whole day every ten, with some additional halts while waiting for a pontoon bridge to be laid or for the weather to improve. The Esla was the deepest and most dangerous. On this occasion the infantry took off their pouches and placed them on their knapsacks, then marched into the water, only to find the water was too deep and the current too swift for a man to keep his feet. Some sank to the bottom, borne down by the weight of firelock, knapsack and pouch containing sixty rounds. Others were rescued by light dragoons who dashed to their aid, grabbed the muskets, and allowed the struggling foot soldiers to cling to stirrup, horse's tail or mane, or wherever they could lay hold.[21]

Things went more smoothly in October 1813 when the army, using three fords indicated by local shrimpers, crossed the Bidassoa estuary, which was only mid-thigh deep at low tide. At

27

the Gave d'Oloron the ford was waist deep and the current fast flowing, so that once again the infantry required help from the cavalry so as not to be swept away, once again ammunition pouches were taken off and buckled on top of the knapsacks, once again stirrups and tails served as tow-ropes.[22]

During the army's pursuit of the retreating French towards St Sever, the Gave de Pau had to be crossed by ford, the wooden bridge having been destroyed on this occasion. The ground was white with frost and the water so intensely cold as to take a man's breath away. The depth being nearly five feet, extra precautions were taken by the 6th Division: ropes, attached to two field-guns deliberately placed in the stream, were thrown across for the men to hold, while dragoons rode into the river to pick up anyone who lost his balance or his grip.[23]

If river crossings were difficult, so too was marching by night when close to the French. For instance, on one occasion the 13th Light Dragoons were ordered to move sword in hand lest their rattling in scabbards be heard by enemy outposts.[24] When, in November 1813, the 2nd Division did a night approach march near Sare, the moon shone so brightly as to render conspicuous the highly polished 'Brown Bess' muskets and the brass plates on the front of the soldiers' shakos. To obviate the risk of any glint being seen by the French, even at a distance, orders were given for the men to march with arms reversed and their shakos turned back to front.[25]

The 5th King's German Legion did much the same when close to Urrugne, groping their way down a hillside, skulking along ditches, no one venturing to speak of orders about keeping silence. The men carried their muskets horizontally to prevent the gleam of bayonets from betraying their approach.[26]

Occasionally a local guide would lose his way in the dark and either lead the column an extra eight or ten miles or else have cavalry squadrons riding around the woods for half the night. When General Graham's force had to follow the Spanish army in a march from Tarifa to Barrosa, the guides undoubtedly got lost, Graham observing that his men had already been twice round a certain hill in the course of the night.[27]

One of the most difficult and memorable night marches was

made when Cole's 4th Division had to retreat down the Ronces-valles Pass from the heights of Linduz. A fog came down late on 25th July, while the action was still in progress, and it hung on the mountains for several hours after sunrise next morning. This fortunate occurrence enabled the heavily laden troops to get away unseen by the French and to ascend the very steep Mendichure Pass. Lieutenant John Bainbrigge of the 20th Foot described the scene for his children many years later: 'It became pitch dark as soon as we entered the beech wood, above the village of Espinal, and men frequently fell into deep holes or stumbled over roots and boughs of trees, and unavoidably tripped up others in their fall. These accidents, though trifling in themselves, caused in-finite confusion and many tedious and vexatious halts.'[28]

So far most of the marches referred to were conducted in fine weather, but conditions and strain became a good deal worse during periods of rain, above all in the retreat of Wellington's army from Burgos to the edge of Portugal in November 1812. That the horse artillery in this retreat travelled axle-deep in mud, passing the dead and dying on the roadside, was bad enough, but what hurt the officers most was that orders forbade them to give the walking wounded a lift. These poor fellows faced the grim alternatives of being left behind and falling into French hands or of being dragged along willy nilly by two comrades from their regiment. Captain Thomas Dyneley of 'E' Troop Royal Horse Artillery wrote frankly to his sister Dora:

Judge of my feelings on being obliged to refuse application after application to carry these unfortunate beings on our gun-carriages. Many of them, to excite compassion, would pull their clothes aside to shew their wounds, but we were obliged to turn a deaf ear to them or risk the loss of our guns by overloading the horses.[29]

When, early in 1814, the army fought on French soil under frequent and torrential rain, marching troops were splashed up to their shakos, and hundreds walked barefoot in calf-deep clay.[30] Five brigades of artillery managed to get along one road near St Lys, thanks to better horses and lighter carriages than the French, who had reckoned the road impassable to guns.

On 17 June 1815 when the 7th Hussars, covering the army's retreat from Quatre Bras to the Waterloo Ridge, came to Genappe and halted to face the pursuing French the road was one mass of liquid mud and the men were so covered with it that it was virtually impossible to distinguish a feature in their faces or the colour of the lace on their jackets.[31]

Scenes on the march varied with conditions: what was the weather? Was it an advance or a retreat? When troops were moving back near the Lines of Torres Vedras the road was crowded for miles with 'soldiers' wives and children, some on foot, some on mules and asses, pet goats, with sheep and dogs, led with cords, in loose array, with quantities of baggage'.[32] That is one scene. How different the spectacle of the 3rd and Light Divisions marching to Campo Maior after the storming of Badajoz! Many of the soldiers' torn, bloodstained uniforms were further discoloured by explosions; not a few men had one arm in a sling, while others had bandaged heads, or limped as a result of wounds inflicted by iron 'crows' feet' which the French garrison had strewn along the ditch.[33]

The scene might well be a halt on the march, as Charles Leslie of the 29th saw it in 1808 before the battle of Roliça:

'Some sitting on their knapsacks, others stretched on the grass, many with a morsel of cold meat on a ration biscuit for a plate in one hand, with a clasp-knife in the other, all doing justice to the contents of their haversacks, and not a few with their heads thrown back and canteens at their mouths, eagerly gulping down his Majesty's grog, or the wine of the country.'[34]

Right at the end of the Napoleonic Wars, on the march from Waterloo to Paris, infantry and cavalry regiments followed each other in constant succession down the road near Bavay, intermingled with, and striving to pass, the file of waggons, baggage carts and animals, led horses, convoys of stores and batteries of artillery. Servants, sutlers, stragglers and women increased the confusion. 'As far back as I could see,' noted Captain Cavalié Mercer of the R.H.A., 'the same swarm covered the road – the troops seemed to form the smallest part of the crowd.'[35]

Mercer also described his gunners on the road between Ostend and Ghistelles, this time *before* the campaign of Waterloo, moving along a straight, ill-paved, muddy causeway between stunted willow trees and ditches full of stagnant water. The men, their

30

uniforms soaked and mud-splashed, their sabres rusty, looked jaded under their bearskins which the rain had flattened – 'the mounted gunners leaning to windward, with one hand generally upraised holding on their helmets; the limber-gunners sitting sideways, turning their backs to the gale'.[36]

Much as the troops suffered from exposure to rain, no steps were taken to protect them with waterproof capes that could have been slung over the greatcoat when required. Many of the officers had purchased oil-cloth cloaks, and something of the sort should have been neither too expensive to provide for the rank and file nor too heavy for them to carry.[37]

A few officers are on record as having used umbrellas. During the retreat of 1812 Captain Lord Saltoun carried a large and strong one, which served as a walking stick and saved him from many a wetting, as he had waterproofed it with oil varnish. That same autumn Thomas Dyneley assured his sister Dora that despite the recent heavy rains he had managed to keep remarkably dry at night by means of blankets and of Mrs Lyon's umbrella fastened to the head of his bed.[38]

Four years earlier George Landmann had spent the day after Vimeiro putting together the reports and sketches of Engineer officers, writing his official despatch to the Inspector-General of Fortifications, and letters to his family – all under the shelter of an old umbrella which he had fortunately picked up on the battlefield. This someone held over his head to keep the papers from being drenched.[39]

That Wellington did not entirely approve of umbrellas on campaign was shown during action near Bayonne, when the 1st Foot Guards were holding a redoubt near the high road. He happened to ride past and, on looking round, was surprised to see a great many umbrellas, which officers were holding up to keep off the rain. He at once sent a staff officer galloping over to say: 'Lord Wellington does not approve of the use of umbrellas during the enemy's firing, and will not allow "the gentlemen's sons" to make themselves ridiculous in the eyes of the army.' Several days later he rebuked the commanding officer, Colonel Isaac Tinling, and observed: 'The Guards may in uniform, when on duty at St. James's, carry them if they please; but in the field it is not only ridiculous but unmilitary.'[40]

Nevertheless, at Orthez on 27 February 1814, when Wellington sat down on the grass, took out some paper and began writing, only to find himself inconvenienced by drizzling rain, he was very pleased when two officers, noticing his plight, procured an umbrella and fixed it so as to shelter his paper.[41]

Two commanders of the 3rd Division used umbrellas to keep off the sun. Sir Thomas Picton, to shade his eyes on the march, usually carried a huge white umbrella lined with green, and Sir Edward Pakenham was seen by a German officer in his division riding in the column protected by a large green sunshade.[42] That was three weeks before the battle of Salamanca. General Picton, who suffered with particular severity from the intense glare in summer, found a brimless cocked hat of little help, so he wore instead a wide-brimmed round or top hat.[43]

For most of the troops crossing the open plain near Malpartida in July the sunshine was hotter than they had ever experienced, and the glare caused some officers to use green eye-shades. Major George Bingham of the 53rd Foot could not help laughing when he saw a Guards officer, 'just from the shady side of Pall Mall, reposing under the shade of a green silk umbrella, and coiling up his legs that they might partake of the benefit of the shade'.[44]

As early as May every man in a cavalry regiment like the 18th Dragoons wore oak branches in his helmet against the sun. Despite such precautions on a summer's march not a few soldiers would be overcome by the heat. Soon after the battle of Fuentes de Oñoro two men of the Foot Guards and one from the 50th Regiment fell down dead. In this respect the Light Division was peculiarly vulnerable because morale was so high – the tribute comes from a cavalryman – that riflemen would struggle gamely on rather than quit the ranks while on the march. Consequently good men lost their lives through heatstroke and exhaustion, as happened to a couple when clambering up the river bank after crossing the Tagus.[45]

When the Coldstream Guards went over the same river at Vila Velha, also in June 1811, the columns marching through valleys studded with gum-cistus shrubs, which gave off a powerfully aromatic and rather sickening scent, were shrouded in dust, and the men's haversacks became soaked with sweat oozing through shirts and red jackets. Though most of the regiment stood up well to the heat during the first two days of the march, General Sir Brent Spencer wisely ordered the columns to set off an hour after midnight so as to reach their daily destination before the heat grew intense. Considerate commanders did their best to ensure that soldiers began such a march at one or two o'clock in the morning, so as to get most of the march over in darkness or the early cool, though now and then a march had to be postponed for several hours to give the artillery time to climb a long hill; and whenever the countryside allowed it, to direct regiments to march in the shade of pine woods and olive groves, as happened for two days on end during July 1810 between Leiria and Tomar.[46]

To combat thirst and a parched mouth soldiers used to suck a small pebble and thereby gain some relief, because water in the canteens was frequently so warm and unpleasant that it made them sick to drink it.[47] Drinking wine in moderation, few of the soldiers came to much harm, but when marching in hot weather far too many persisted in eating more fruit than was good for them and, when hot, drinking very cold water. Consequently they went down with fevers.[48]

Dust was always a curse of summer. Witness a road where troops and guns moving towards the front overtook large droves of cattle being driven to feed the army, and met the French ordnance captured in the fort of Salamanca going down to Lisbon, each group shrouded in deep layers of dust.[49]

Landmann of the Engineers recalled a march near Alcobaça in August 1808 when the dust was particularly thick and suffocating. The blend of dust and scorching sun produced serious inflammation of everyone's under-lip, which swelled up and then burst open. At length, someone suggested that a leaf placed between the lower teeth and the lip would effectually protect it from the rays of the sun, from the dust, and from the moisture of the mouth. This proved to be an excellent cure, and those who went through the painful experience were never again so afflicted, at least during the rest of that summer. Major-General Henry Fane suffered badly on that August march, and Landmann noticed that when he ordered the Light Brigade to halt his under-lip was so parched and so ripe with inflammation that it split in two places and blood ran down his chin.[50]

The heat of central Spain was often so intense that not only

B

33

would bacon fat dissolve rapidly even when placed in the shade, but metal objects like swords, bayonets and buttons would, if exposed to the sun for even a short time, blister the finger that ventured to handle them.[51] Near Elvas one June the heat was so fierce that only with pain could a man take hold of his sword scabbard. Brigadier-General R. B. Long found much the same at Villa Garcia, where the hilt of his sword became so hot that he could not grasp it for any length of time, and the heat of his stirrup-irons was no less trying. 'The whole atmosphere,' he noted, 'was black with heat, and a distressing sirocco wind prevailed, which passing over the burning fallow ground felt to the hand, when extended, like burning steam.'[52]

Under these conditions routine activities like shaving, washing and, in particular, drying oneself with a coarse towel became painful. Ink thickened on pens as fast as they wrote.[53] A veteran campaigner like Major John Blakiston began to imagine himself back in India, especially when he received nocturnal visits from mosquitoes, 'to which I thought I had bidden adieu when I quitted the shores of Madras'.[54]

Now and then river bathing afforded relief. In May 1811 the Connaught Rangers, for example, enjoyed themselves when they emerged from olive groves and plunged into the Guadiana when the regiment bivouacked on the banks of the Jerte, and both men and horses, almost suffocated by the July heat, bathed in the milk-warm water.[55] One summer the whole army bathed and washed clothes in the dirty warm Caia, in which cattle drank and soldiers drew their drinking water, even though the stagnant stream abounded in snakes, leeches and 'all manner of devils'.[56]

Major Smith, commanding a detachment of the 45th, seems to have been a good officer, for while quartered near Lameiros he had his soldiers strip off their full marching order after church parade and plunge into the river which flowed past the village green. The men stayed in the water until a bugle sounded, whereupon they formed into line along the bank while Smith carried out a strict inspection, thus acting, as Private William Brown expressed it, 'in the triple capacity of commander, doctor for the body, and physician for the soul'.[57]

Of course the best plan, at least during the wellnigh insufferable month of July, was to stay indoors till evening once the morning's business had been done, because, to quote Captain Gomm in 1810, 'to stir out during the heat of the day, unless by special order, is accounted an act of heroism, and bordering very near upon insanity'.[58] Such a policy was no doubt wise but seldom practical, since work had to be done, cavalry patrols had to ride out, foragers were required to go questing, and such duties could not invariably be limited to the cool parts of the day. In any case, July 1809 saw Wellington's army fighting at Talavera; two years later it was marching and fighting outside Salamanca, where one day a soldier of the 43rd put up a blanket to keep the sun's rays off Lord Wellington, and the rest of the Light Division followed suit by hoisting blankets in the same way. July 1813 saw the army campaigning in northern Spain at the approaches to the Pyrenees and France.[59]

Quick, abrupt changes in temperature sometimes imposed the greatest discomfort. Whereas on the first days of a July march several men died on the road from excessive heat, the next two nights would be marked by torrential rain and cold winds.[60] We find General Graham at Freineda on 6 May 1813 saying: 'It is so cold here that I am writing by a fire and yet my face and hands are blistered and swelled with the sun to a degree.'[61]

Probably the sharpest contrasts in climate occurred when the army was fighting in the Pyrenees, charging up and down rugged mountain-sides, exposed almost simultaneously to the intense heat of July and to the cold of winter. In the words of Lieutenant Robert Blakeney:

'Dripping with perspiration from hard fighting and scorching rain in the valleys, we had immediately to clamber up to the top of high mountains and face the extreme cold naturally to be found there and dense fogs, which soaked through us and are more penetrating and oppressive than heavy rain.'[62]

Despite the long distances marched and the normally high morale of Wellington's army except during a retreat, when the Peer faced the same problems of indiscipline as Sir John Moore had contended with on the road to Corunna, there are surprisingly few mentions of music on the march, and British troops do not appear to have sung as the King's German Legion did. But we know that in July 1811, when the 43rd marched to Portalegre,

35

martial music struck up, the word passed down the column to march at ease, the men lit their pipes and began talking.[63] Towards the end of 1808 the 50th Foot moved through the Portuguese frontier region in such intensely cold weather that, in order to keep the men alive, the band and drums were frequently brought into service, and this music had a marvellous effect. The commanding officer, Major Charles Napier, occasionally ordered some well-known quickstep to be played, and 'in a moment, as if by magic, those who were tired and jaded sprang up, imbued as it were with additional life and vigour'.[64]

St Patrick's Day was a favourite quickstep. We know that the 43rd marched to the breach at Ciudad Rodrigo preceded by their band playing the popular *Downfall of Paris*, and *The British Grenadiers* was played when the army crossed the Garonne in April 1814. It also is on record that when the 28th marched out of Brussels at 4 a.m. on 16 June 1815, bound for Quatre Bras, the regimental drum-and-fife band played *The Young May Moon is Shining, Love*.[65]

In many a camp the most picturesque scene at twilight would be the German troops seated in groups outside their tents, 'canopied in clouds of tobacco smoke, chanting together their native airs and anthems'. Their cavalry also sang on the march, three or four voices leading and the whole squadron joining in the chorus.[66] Whereas most British dragoons rode on, many of them silent, some chatting of this and that, others 'humming or whistling those tuneless airs in which the lower orders of our countrymen delight', the Germans sang beautifully.

A German officer from the Brunswick Oels corps, the 'Black Brunswickers' who served in the Light Division, described one June evening in 1810 when he and a group of British and German cavalry officers bivouacked in a large circle round a blazing fire, and drank punch out of silver mugs. A group of singers sang soldiers' songs, the favourite being Schiller's *Reiterlied*, which begins:

> *Wohlauf Kameraden, aufs Pferd, aufs Pferd!*
> *Ins Feld, in die Freiheit gezogen. . . .*

He went on to say that even the cold, proud Wellington stopped his horse and listened to this fine singing, the like of which he would never hear from his British troops, who 'either marched in sullen silence, or, as soon as they became a little tipsy, shouted their songs in a raucous roar.'[67]

Captain Cooke of the 43rd affords us an excellent vignette of the King's German Legion during the army's advance from Salamanca to Vitoria during June 1813.

'The German Hussars rode up, smoking their pipes, and singing some delighful airs, their half squadrons at intervals joining in the chorus. We had heard that the hussar brigade was to supersede these veterans, and to act with our division. The whole of us left our canvas, and lined the road to greet our old friends and companions of out-post duty. The hussars became so much affected by our cheering, that tears rolled down many of their bronzed faces. "Oh!" they said, "we are always glad to see the old *lighty* division, who will ever live in our hearts." '[68]

Chapter 2

BILLETS

'Somebody declares that the furniture of a Spanish house consists
chiefly in cobwebs, mousetraps, slips of old tapestry lying about
the floor, interspersed with fractions of pier-glass. Mine is a ready-
furnished apartment, saving the mousetrap.'[1]
Captain William Gomm, 20 July 1810

'The Billet got, they travel to explore
For Rua Sacra, Casa, Number Four.
The House was found, but wanting Door or Casement,
"Is this the place?" says John in wild amazement.
"Is it to such D——n'd sties as these they send us?
"A pretty way they treat their Brave Defenders!" '[2]
Ensign John Newcome in Lisbon

Whenever Wellington's army was on the move, the usual method
of taking billets was for quartermasters to go in advance to the town
concerned. Here a member of the Quartermaster-General's
department, having divided the place – Portalegre, for example –
into districts corresponding to brigades and battalions, would
allot certain streets for each unit, whereupon the individual
quartermaster would select and mark with chalk the best houses
for the commanding and field officers, the next best for the
captains and subalterns, and so on down the line. Every house
taken for the rank and file would have the number of men it was
to accommodate chalked upon the door.[3] When, for instance, the
Light Division entered Portalegre in 1812, streets were marked
off for the different regiments, and the houses subdivided amongst
officers and men, 'the butt ends of the soldiers' firelocks serving
as knockers, to rouse the sulky inmates, who would fain plead
ignorance of the arrival of so many guests'.[4]

General Orders emanating from Wellington's Headquarters
throw considerable light upon the routine management of

38

cantonments. At the end of May 1809 it was laid down that on halting days an officer from each company would visit his men's quarters four times a day, and on marching days twice after the men had moved in, and once before the soldiers marched away in the morning. The purpose of these visits was to ensure that the men conducted themselves regularly, and were in their quarters rather than marauding in search of plunder, and to discover any complaints made by landlords.[5]

According to another order issued when the army reached St Jean de Luz, care was to be taken that all wet straw and other dirt were removed, that fern or other bedding materials were rolled up and floors swept, and that whenever the weather was dry, blankets should be put out to air. Floorboards, staircases, doors and windows were not to be cut down or damaged, nor were farm gates to be removed. The streets occupied by each regiment – this was in Portalegre in July 1811 – had to be swept every morning, and 'the heaps of dung and filth in the unoccupied places in all the towns in Portugal' destroyed by quick lime. Furthermore, sentries were to be posted over fountains to prevent anyone from fouling the water supply.[6]

In the case of individual officers a different system applied for the allocation of quarters. On reaching a town or village, the officer showed his official route to the *juiz de foro*, equivalent to a Justice of the Peace, who was responsible for giving him a billet in the house of a local resident.[7] A General Order dated 14 March 1809 laid down that in Lisbon colonels would be entitled to four rooms, field officers three, captains two, subalterns one room each. No one under the rank of General Officer was to require more than two servants' beds. On 13 December that year Wellington had occasion to reiterate an order of his predecessor, Sir John Cradock, by which it was clearly to be understood that cover was all that any officer had a right to expect, and that he had no pretensions to ask for either a bed or furniture. 'When such articles are supplied it is a matter of civility on the part of the owner, and must be received as a favour and not as a right.'[8]

In September 1811 the Commander of the Forces felt obliged to return to this matter as a result of frequent complaints about officers' conduct towards their landlords, principally in the Commissariat and Medical Departments. He made it clear that in villages and smaller towns officers could not expect the sort of accommodation allowed in Lisbon, and that no officer had a right to demand more from his landlord than 'house-room and stabling for his horses, if the building shall afford any'. Anything beyond this must be the result of good-will from the inhabitants, and nothing like compulsion was to be used.[9] Statements by officers vary as to precisely what the householder was bound to provide, but it seems to have been a room, something to lie on, a basin, water, and a towel. In his first Lisbon billet Francis Larpent had four small rooms furnished with two tables, a dozen chairs, a bedstead and mattress, a worked flounced quilt and some fine sheets but no blankets. Later he got a silver basin and ewer, some knives and forks, and a supply of water. As will be seen, reality sometimes exceeded, sometimes fell short of, expectation.[10]

When the British Army first arrived in Portugal the villagers usually offered the best they had, and thought themselves honoured if it was accepted. Furthermore, wherever an officer was quartered, the people of the house took offence if he did not live with them. But, as Cornet Francis Hall of the 14th Light Dragoons observed wryly in October 1811, 'they have since grown poorer – and wiser!'. Regrettably the soldiers did sometimes burn a house for firewood or steal what few belongings the French Army had left to the inhabitants.[11]

Even if such depredations were not committed – and their occurrence was comparatively rare – the billets required for British troops grew too numerous and eventually wearied the Portuguese, many of whom became less civil and forthcoming.[12] A further deterrent to supplying accommodation was the lamentable conduct of certain officers who undoubtedly failed to behave like gentlemen. The whole position and change of attitude is explained by Colonel David Roberts of the 51st Foot in a scathing indictment:

'At the commencement of the Campaign on the Peninsula, the Portuguese certainly treated the British officers in the most generous manner, – voluntarily and hospitably received them into their Houses, and externally carried their liberality to great excess; giving up their most elegant Apartments, supplying them with a portion of Plate, Linen, Fuel, and Wax Candles; but it is with regret that I am obliged to state that this indulgence and hospitality was, in many instances, scandalously abused, and the most ungentlemanlike, ungrateful, indecent, and ungenerous returns were often made. What was the consequence? So many complaints were made against the Officers for abusing their Billets, that a General Order was issued, stating the number of rooms each rank was entitled to, and restricting the *quantum* of Furniture to one Table, one Chair, and one Lamp, and an allowance of Oil for each Apartment, with the use of a Kitchen.'[13]

There is no doubt that many of the inhabitants did have cause for complaint. In a village near Fuente Guinaldo, some officers of the 14th Light Dragoons were understandably refused admittance to a billet by the priest on the grounds that a British General who had lodged there the previous night had stolen his sheets. Now and then local inhabitants would refuse admittance on less reasonable grounds: under plea, for instance, of there being a person with an infectious disease in the house. This could, of course, be genuine, but more often it was false; and officers became too accustomed to hearing this excuse to be alarmed over their health.[14] Certain householders on whom officers were officially billeted were reluctant to provide facilities. When Lieutenant William Swabey presented his billet at a house in Elvas, the landlord very politely declined to allow any wood for the fire, whereupon Swabey, not to be outdone, thanked the Portuguese for his extreme civility in such terms that the man actually blushed 'for his want of gratitude and generosity'.[15]

Both sides erred from time to time, but Wellington was always ready to investigate complaints. When the Inquisitor General of Coimbra objected to giving accommodation to a major because he was married and had children, Lord Wellington replied in harsh terms, expressing surprise at receiving 'frivolous and manifestly unfounded complaints', and emphasizing that Portugal's unfortunate situation had necessitated the collection of a large army in order to defeat and frustrate the designs of the French. He added: 'It is not very agreeable to any body to have strangers quartered in his house; nor is it very agreeable to us strangers, who have good houses in our own country, to be obliged to seek for quarters here. We are not here for our pleasure; the situation of

41

your country renders it necessary; you, a man of family and fortune, who have much to lose, should not be the first to complain of the inconvenience of our presence in the country.'[16]

The prior tenure by junior officers of a billet could sometimes be overridden by the demands of a general or the officious conduct of his staff, and more than one officer was turned out of his quarter or his stable. Even Wellington's Judge-Advocate General, Larpent, had to move his animals into a back kitchen when General Stapleton Cotton arrived in Aire with about a hundred animals belonging to himself and his staff.[17]

A general and staff were blamed for taking up as much space in a town as a regiment of dragoons; and even allowing for military hyperbole, some of these important officers, once installed in their quarters at other people's expense, tended to plague their neighbours by stupid orders and tiresome complaints.[18] Nevertheless, the majority of general officers were unable to secure much in the way of superior accommodation. At Vizeu in February 1810 General Picton complained cheerfully of 'cold rooms, hard beds, bad fare, but good civility and respect from all classes, and a most inveterate hatred to the French'. When he reached Trancoso a month later, he occupied what the locals called the Casa Real, 'which was destined to receive the Prince whenever he made visits to this part of the kingdom'. Yet it provided miserable accommodation, for all its size, lacking as it did 'any of those conveniences which contribute to what we call *comfort*: a word peculiar to the English Language'. And at Albergaria just before Christmas the following year Picton, like his officers and men, wrote with mild exasperation to a legal friend of the village houses being 'all miserable sheds with earthen or brick floors, and without chimnies, carpets. . . .'[19]

When Captain Edward Codrington of the Royal Navy stayed with General Graham in the Governor's House outside Cadiz, he was a little disappointed to discover that the only dormitory his old friend could offer was 'a mere and miserable mattress and tiny pillow upon a bare bedstead, in a high barn of a room, with whitewashed walls, and unprovided with even a looking-glass by way of furniture'. Here Codrington found himself assailed by fleas, mosquitoes, and the mid-June heat.[20] Eighteen months later, after he had joined Wellington's main army in northern

Portugal, Thomas Graham fared little better in the Bishop's Palace at Pinhel for the great house had been gutted of everything and, apart from 'one comfortable cabinet with a good chimney', the walls were bare.[21] Yet he and Picton installed their headquarters in the palace more than once, because it provided good stabling for thirty horses and inferior stables for thirty more.

In October 1812 Francis Larpent, on arrival in Castelo Branco, was assigned the quarters used by any general who passed through the town. In the ruin of a fine house he had a big room with four large unglazed windows and four doors. 'Gold frames around without their looking-glasses in them, fine chairs without bottoms, etc. etc.' In this handsome but dilapidated setting Larpent had a mattress on the floor and fleas innumerable.[22] Few billets were free of vermin, and these were no respecters of rank. General Picton, quartered at Linares in August 1810, found it impossible to sleep 'for Buggs and Fleas'. One had no need to sleep in a straw loft to be devoured all night.[23] Several gunners were so tormented by fleas in a Lisbon barracks that they preferred to lie out under the gun carriages.[24] That was in the summer, but the fleas had not diminished by November, and to avoid their attentions many a man always slept on the ground or on hard chairs.[25]

Up in the villages of Beira Alta the people were seldom without fleas, and their beds were stocked with them. Some houses had rats too, and officers often slept on top of a large chest, hoping to keep out of harm's way. Of course fleas and lice were not exclusive to the frontier districts.[26] Quite the reverse. Troops coming ashore at Belem were astonished to see Portuguese people sitting in rows, picking the vermin off one another. 'There was,' wrote Sergeant Joseph Donaldson, 'none of that *modest pressing* between the finger and thumb, for fear of being seen, which we may observe in our dirty and indigent neighbours at home. It was absolute open murder!' Rich and poor alike went in for uninhibited public delousing, to the point where strangers could be pardoned for thinking it the most interesting of their forenoon pursuits.[27] Soldiers could watch a group of between six and eight females sitting each in the lap of the one behind, with the oldest woman usually at the head of the line. 'The lady in front, having nothing else to do, begins to chant some favourite air, whilst the others, with nervous paws, get all ten fingers to trace their game through the almost impenetrable forest [of hair] before them.'[28]

The pastime was neatly summed up by Colonel Roberts of the 51st in *The Adventures of Johnny Newcome*:

'It is a fact well known, the Portuguese
Cherish voluptuously both Lice and Fleas;
Some Bramin-like, are influenced by Piety,
But mostly for Amusement and Society;
For Females oft in parties will arouse
Scratching each other's Heads, t'entrap a Louse,
Whilst on their skins, the Fleas will skip, & Scramble,
And wanton Lice through all their ringlets ramble.'[29]

Billets were found in the most varied buildings. They ranged from an onion loft to a nobleman's room painted with military trophies; from the dark cell of a chapel with its cold, damp and clammy walls to a water mill turned by the river Nive and where to grow used to the clack of the wheel and the cascade of water took more than a day.[30] When a picket of the 15th Light Dragoons and 43rd Light Infantry lay down with their horses under the sheds of another water mill, the officers slept on sacks just over the wheel, and emerged next morning as white as millers![31]

One could be in a Lisbon cook-shop, or asleep at Alverca among old chairs, fishing nets and a barrel of salt in what must have been a Tagus fisherman's home before the war. Infantrymen slept one night in the public walk at Salamanca, because their regiment arrived so late that the civil authorities and most of the inhabitants had long since retired to bed.[33] Others lay out under the piazzas in Alcala during Wellington's retreat of 1812.[34]

Harry Smith of the Rifle Corps was fortunate to occupy the same quarter in Arronches on four separate occasions, and the poor family were always delighted to see him.[35] During 1809 alone Major Alexander Dickson, serving with Portuguese artillery, lived in the town hall at Ovar, an abandoned house in Pombal, another in Grijo which had been occupied by French soldiers on the previous night, and a viscount's palace at Condeixa. Dickson's experience could easily be multiplied.[36] For instance, a cobbler's shop in one Spanish town, a cobbler's cottage on a country road in the hills of Portugal; a convent near Santarem and another in Mafra; a large building which had formerly been occupied as a charity-school; a French post-house, though this was afterwards forbidden by Lord Wellington; the immense royal palace at Mafra, which accommodated seven regiments with ease.[37]

The great convent of Batalha was equally capacious. In October 1810 all the British regiments in Picton's division were quartered under its roof, and this was by no means the first time a division had passed that way.[38] Largest of all was the Escorial Palace outside Madrid, where at least four of Wellington's divisions settled in August 1812. Hill's 2nd Division lodged in the galleries, courtyards and outer halls of the Escorial without needing to use any of the private apartments. 'Our brigade,' wrote Lieutenant Patterson of the 50th, 'marched up the great staircase, with ample space to move along in sections.'[39] With so much space it is disagreeable to learn of strife and pettiness, but one German officer so hated the bickering of the British officers about who should have each room that he went outside and pitched his tent under a fig tree in the gardens.[40]

Commissary Richard Henegan found himself billeted at Pasajes in a tumble-down old house, with a wooden terrace literally overhanging the harbour. It was, he noted, 'as full of long passages, iron gratings, and trap doors, as any locality ever selected by Mrs Radcliffe for the theatre of her monstrosities'. If Henegan compared his billet with the gloomy setting for *The Mysteries of Udolpho*, Ensign Cowell Stepney likened the village room he shared with four others near the coast to 'a space about the size, colour and appearance of a respectably-proportioned coal-hole in the neighbourhood of Berkeley-Square'.[41]

Where else did soldiers sleep? Two companies of riflemen were quartered in the Convent de la Carma in Lisbon, the monks having given up some two hundred cells to accommodate them.[42] Charles Madden's troop of 4th Dragoons obtained billets in the Duke of Cadabalo's empty castle at Tenteixa, near Coimbra, and had a fire lit in the large unfurnished hall, which was sixty feet long and distinctly gloomy by the light of one candle.[43] 1814 saw Wellington's army lodged in French homes and other buildings such as a wine house near Grenade, where the 95th Rifles slept among barrels of wine, without one man ever appearing the least in-

toxicated throughout the time they spent there.[44] Near Toulouse
infantrymen sometimes slept in the numerous large farm-houses
and even in round pigeon-houses, eating pigeon pie, omelettes
and eggs in such profusion that French people exclaimed: '*Diable!
Comme les Anglais mangent des oeufs!*'[45]

The changes and chances and contrasts of a military life in
billets were aptly summed up by Major-General William Wheatley,
writing from Madrid to his wife Jane, in August 1812, just two
weeks before he died of a fever:

'I am lodged most magnificently here with 4 or 5 rooms to myself,
a handsome suite of apartments for my aide-de-camp and similar
accommodation for my Brigade Major. . . . On the day before
Campbell and myself thought ourselves highly fortunate in getting
into a ruinous old chapel and putting our beds in a gallery with
the rooks and crows; on the following day we are superbly lodged
in the house of a Spanish Grandee (the Don, however, is gone with
all his family to Majorca).'[46]

And more succinctly by Frazer, who wrote on the last day of
January 1813, with a great deal of campaigning still before him:
'Our gipsy mode of life is quite whimsical. I am become a
complete wanderer without a home, or rather equally at home in
all places.'[47] Soldiers were men who had next of kin but no fixed
abode while campaigning abroad.

Most of the Portuguese houses in which officers and men had
to take lodging were miserable, above all in winter. If the doors
and window shutters had not already been used for firewood by
French or British soldiers, then the occupant was fortunate.[48] Or
was he? Holes in the roof let in water, the camp bed got soaked,
and an officer's basin and whatever broken jars he or his servant
could procure had to catch the raindrops.[49] Whether a man was on
Beresford's staff or on Wellington's, he was still liable to be
uncomfortable. When Larpent, the Judge-Advocate General,
spent weeks in Malhada Sorda, a poor little village which housed
part of Headquarters near Freineda, his room had no ceiling –
only open, loose pantiles, with holes to let out the smoke of a fireplace without a chimney. Through a hole in the floor he could
look at his five animals and three servants sleeping on straw below
him.[50] It was typical to have the ground floor set aside for horses

and mules. This happened even in a town like Peñamacor, where in most of the houses the next two floors were for the inmates, while servants occupied the garrets or cocklofts. In one garret the cooking was often done, the fire being laid and lit on a thick stone in one corner after two tiles had been removed to allow the smoke to escape.[51]

Seldom did a house have glass in the windows. Indeed, many a village contained not a single pane, even in the Chief Magistrate's house, reckoned to be the best. No fireplaces, no proper chimneys, and roofs that let in snow and rain. Some windowless inside rooms had no other light but that which came in at the open door. Here is how Ensign Cowell Stepney of the Coldstream Guards described their billets when frost lay hard on the ground: 'The hovels of Navé D'Aver formed but a *polite excuse* for a covering. We sat, when indoors (for *in-windows* we could not call it, there being none beyond broken shutters), wrapped in our cloaks, on the family household chests, round a brazarico [*brazeiro*], or pan of hot ashes, to warm the extremities of men.'[52]

So often the kitchen was the only comfortable room, and soldiers used to adjourn there after dinner and sip wine or roast chestnuts. There might well be a pan of charcoal instead of a fire, but to use this without first opening the shutters was to court a headache from the trapped and bitter smoke. The alternative was to put up with draughts strong enough to extinguish a flambeau.[53] When a room was filled with smoke, one could barely see across from one blackened wall to the other; and if the fire was made of heather or broom, then troops unseasoned to the acrid fumes had smarting eyes. Indeed, several officers of the 32nd sat round a pierced earthen vessel full of charcoal embers for several evenings without feeling any ill effects until a visitor, who was in delicate health, suddenly fell from his chair in a kind of stupor while the officers were at dinner. Shortly afterwards, on walking across the room, Captain Harry Ross-Lewin also collapsed. Still they did not suspect the true cause of these fits – not until the colonel was seized with convulsions, several days later.[54]

No wonder many old women had shrivelled faces which reminded some of the witches in *Macbeth*. But the daughters could look attractive with their eyes as black as sloes, though they also might be forced to huddle round the fire, each holding a

47

string of beads and a cross and, if Private Wheeler's imagination did not outstrip reality, relating some horrid tale of friend slaughtered by the French.[55]

The soldiers' attitude ranged from disgust or exasperation at Portuguese filth and apathy, to compassion for their miserable lot, above all when the children ran around almost naked and half starved as well as verminous. The majority of troops deplored their extreme slovenliness, the indolent carelessness in their domestic arrangements. As Broughton wrote of Lisbon in January 1813: 'The dirt is rarely swept from the floors, and to the comforts of a scrubbing-brush and soap and water they are total strangers. In order to dissipate the effluvia pretty generally prevailing in this town they are accustomed to burn dried lavender in all their rooms.'[56]

Those who journeyed along the Douro valley and in northern Portugal certainly found the village people of the lower and middle classes extremely dirty, their rooms unswept, their furniture covered with dust. What is more, their eating and drinking habits disgusted many a British soldier, because at dinner the cutlery was not changed.[57] Charles Napier came to the conclusion that the Portuguese, in the belief that fires were dangerous in the keen air, supplied warmth 'by cherishing filth with a load of greasy cloaks on their shoulders'. Perhaps they were right but Napier, feeling perished with cold, would willingly have run the risk of a blazing fire instead of trying to stop his teeth from chattering like castanets.[58]

It is true that occasionally the décor presented a violent contrast to their primitive poverty. At Estremoz, for instance, Cornet Francis Hall slept in a room hung round with tapestry representing the Trojan War and ornamented with a dusty chandelier of antique cut-glass.[59] When Captain Swabey spent a March night in Azeuchal, near Vila Franca da Xira, his room also had tapestry on the walls, he was pleased to find curtains in the windows and matting on the floor, and the bed he slept in had a counterpane of green flowered satin with a broad silver-lace edging and fringe.[60] Larpent had the good fortune to stay in the house of the *capitan mor* at Torre de Moncorvo near the Douro, and this had painted ceilings and apricot-coloured silk hangings, with chairs and sofas upholstered to match.[61]

Comfortable but in appalling taste was the sitting-room allotted to Major-General F. P. Robinson at Torquemada in October 1812: measuring forty-two feet by thirty-four, and eighteen feet high, it was 'hung with the most paltry daubs representing the birth of Christ and, in order to make the Virgin Mary as conspicuous as possible, her wedding is represented – she is in the Spanish costume, and ought to have been married at least eight months before'.[62] The General seldom indulged in such tart observations.

Outside the principal towns, and especially in the poorer regions of Portugal where Wellington's army spent two winters cantoned in a score of small villages and hamlets which were marked only on superior maps, tapestries, curtains and upholstery were distinctly uncommon. One reason advanced for all this inattention to comfort was that for much of the year a fine climate allowed the Portuguese to spend their time out of doors, lounging in the square or some coffee-house. Having little to do indoors but sleep and eat,[63] they seemed to understand little about the use of fireplaces and fires, and whenever a shivering fit came on they simply retired to bed.[64]

'Quarters in a Portuguese village,' wrote Cornet Hall of the 14th Light Dragoons, 'are beyond comparison more dull and lifeless than the "country quarters" in England. I don't think the poor people have even time for scandal: their hours are sufficiently occupied in gaining a miserable subsistence.'[65] The poor Portuguese appeared not to know the meaning of comfort and, wrapped in large cloaks, looked very pictures of misery. 'What inestimable service a visit from a colony of Hollanders, well provided with their brooms and water-engines, would render to Portugal.' There spoke a survivor of the Walcheren campaign of 1809; but such comparisons helped little, and in most cases the army had to turn to its own ingenuity and resourcefulness.[66]

Faced with spending long winter evenings in such discomfort, many of the troops set about improving their quarters. In villages round Lajeosa, for example, bricklayers in the ranks of the Guards began to build chimneys in their cottages with expertise derived from past practice.[67] They built fireplaces, repaired doors, made window-frames and filled them with oiled paper. For lack of glass windows, most houses had large shutters with a small aperture to

49

admit the light, and over this soldiers stretched either a piece of fine cambric muslin or else the oiled paper. If no such aperture existed, then one would be cut.[68]

That the landlords did not always favour such improvements, carried out in the name of British comfort, is hardly surprising. When it was done in their absence they knew nothing about the alterations until they returned home, but more often they were in residence and had to watch the military bricklayers and carpenters, some of them unskilled in their new-found crafts. Le Mesurier met a typical reaction at Travanca in January 1812;

'The Portuguese are not very partial to our improvements, not even of our fireplaces; whilst we were building a very elegant one in the place, our Landlord came in and did not appear greatly pleased. On our enquiring the cause, he said it was not the Custom to have chimneys in their houses, and that he would have the trouble of pulling it down when we were gone, or people would would laugh at him for having two kitchens.'[69]

While this may have been a shortsighted, even stupid local view, the soldiers were often rather naive in expecting their efforts to be welcomed on sight. Several officers of the 95th living in a first floor granary at Arcangues were so plagued by a bitter December wind that they provided a fireplace and went on filling this up with such a load of bricks and mortar that the first floor nearly became the ground floor. They then had to cut down the only two fruit trees in the garden so as to prop up their edifice. 'We were rather on doubtful terms with the landlord before,' wrote John Kincaid, 'but this put us all square – no terms at all.'[70]

In sharp contrast to this abrasive encounter is William Swabey's experience at Salgueira in the autumn of 1811. Allotted a tiny room which had but one window from which most of the panes of glass had been broken by the passage of time and the French, he soon made some glazed paper to keep out the cold with the smallest possible loss of light. As a result he was requested to stop all the broken panes of glass in the spacious *quinta*. 'Amongst these simply people,' wrote Swabey, 'I believe I passed for a prodigy of human ingenuity just caught from a manufacturing, machine-loving scientific country.'[71]

The Spaniards appear to have been more enterprising and more energetic than their Portuguese neighbours in repairing damage soon after the warring armies left their district. They replaced tiles, rebuilt walls, and above all whitewashed the insides of their houses. Towards the Pyrenees they returned with doors and shutters which they had prudently carried off and concealed. They got back to work on their farms more quickly than did the Portuguese peasants, though in very few areas was the damage so widespread or repeated as in certain parts of Portugal.[72]

They seem to have accepted improvements more readily, though not always from the best motives. When, for instance, the 20th Regiment was quartered near Almendra, masons in the ranks were set to work. The landlord and his family were so delighted with the results that they had fireplaces put in several rooms so that their house was superior to any other in the village. A case of one-upmanship?[73]

Passing reference has already been made to chapels. A company of the 40th Foot was billeted in one at Portalegre in 1811, at night lying on straw, which had to be rolled up neatly in the men's blankets each morning to make the place look comfortable and tidy during the day.[74] Now and then troops found themselves put to sleep in a lofty church, as happened in May 1809 to the 7th Fusiliers when pursuing the French near Braga. Sergeant Cooper vividly portrays the scene:

'In a minute or two the band had possession of the altar, and the big drummer of the pulpit. All were cold, hungry, tired, and ill-humoured. Fires were wanted, and fires were made. Smash went the forms, down came the priest's stalls. The crashing of wood, the bawling and swearing of hundreds in the blinding, choking smoke that completely filled the edifice, were awful; and when darkness set in the place was a perfect pandemonium. During the uproar, a box of large wax candles used at the altar was found. Many of these were distributed and lighted in different parts of the church, and the scene was complete and fit for Hogarth's pencil.'[75]

At much the same time Colonel Bingham and the 53rd bivouacked in a convent church near Alconchel. He managed to preserve the handsome and profusely gilded altar intact only by placing the regimental colours on the high altar and posting two sentries to

51

prevent any soldier passing inside the rails.[76] The 15th Light Dragoons were not so well behaved at Astorga in 1808, for the horses, stabled in a convent chapel, were tied to the brazen font, which also served as manger, and one horse was tethered to a large image of the Virgin Mary.[77]

Two years later, when the army was holding the Lines of Torres Vedras, Moyle Sherer of the 34th slept with his company in Bucellas church, where the senior officer had the sacristy, the next in rank was allotted a recess behind the high altar, and the remaining officers made themselves comfortable in the spacious organ loft. Sherer used to lean out of the gallery to watch the incongruous scene below: 'How a sober citizen from St. Paul's Churchyard would have stared to see a serjeant of Grenadiers writing his reports on the communion-table, a fifer lounging at his ease in the pulpit and practising his favourite quick step, and the men dividing and calling off their rations of raw beef on tombs of polished marble.'[78]

A further case occurred on the night after the battle of Vitoria when officers of the 16th Light Dragoons took over an ancient church and installed themselves in the chancel and sacristy, with the colonel eating his meal in a very large loft and the chargers stabled '*à la Cromwell*'.[79]

Chapter 3

HOSTS AND LANDLADIES

'To have your house beset day after day by officers or soldiers, for whom personally you can care nothing, and whom you may never see again, is certainly most annoying. It must be enough to wear out the patience of a Saint, much more the hospitality of a mortal.'[1]
Major John Blakiston

Those upon whom members of Wellington's army had billets comprised as diverse a crew as that by which plum stones are counted on one's plate at lunch: wine-merchant, politician, doctor, poet, peasant, Knight of Malta, Colonel. The Bordeaux wine-merchant had two beautiful daughters who were carefully looked after by their mother, but he himself was most hospitable and friendly.[2] The Spanish politician who lived in Madrid asked John Daniell in August 1812 what had become of the famous Sir Arthur Wellesley, who had commanded the English troops at Talavera. Why had he not been at the battle of Salamanca? Daniell gave his host an agreeable surprise by declaring that Lord Wellington and Sir Arthur Wellesley were one and the same person![3]

One Portuguese doctor in Leiria wore a jacket and slippers, and resembled Don Quixote when he strutted about Captain Gomm's bedroom. Being something of a hypochondriac, he used to croak *'Ah! la Guerre! la Guerre!'* two or three times a day in Gomm's ear. The doctor found it very strange that while *he* was doing all he could to keep men alive, *they* should be hard at work putting one another to death in war. Somebody must be wrong.[4] As for the poet, he was blind, but of an evening he used to enjoy squatting on a low chair in one corner of his large kitchen chimney and there reciting verses for the edification of several junior officers in the 29th Regiment of Foot.[5]

The peasant from a mountain village in Estremadura was very

poor and lived in a humble dwelling. Dressed in sheepskins, he herded goats all day on the hills, and returned at night to the family meal, which he always prepared and which never varied. A loaf of brown bread would be sliced into a wooden bowl, some olive oil poured over it, hot water added, and the whole dish mixed up. Father, mother, children – no one spoke a word until the meal was finished. 'In their simplicity and poverty,' wrote Ensign Bell, 'there was a courteous hospitality, such as never sitting down without asking me to partake of their supper. I had a little sort of bed in a recess in the kitchen, near the fire, where we all sat of an evening by the light of some sticks, a very taciturn party.'[6]

Two Engineer officers, John Burgoyne and Charles Boothby, both lodged with the Bailli Carvalho, a Knight of Malta, when they passed through Lamego, east of Oporto, in May 1809. Besides entertaining sumptuously and with perfect manners, the Bailli and his Maltese servant took great pleasure in talking about Malta with his two 'guests', who had visited the island only two years before – much more recently than Carvalho had.[7] At another country house, this time in Mangualde, Major Alexander Dickson found the whole family playing cards. It was explained to him that three of the men present were Commanders of Malta, and a fourth member of the Order of St John was away from home – an extraordinary feature of this noble family.[8] Finally, the old Portuguese colonel in Elvas: he had served for forty-eight years, and enjoyed taking about the campaigns of Count de Lippe.[9]

When he first reached Lisbon in 1809 Captain Neil Douglas received a billet on the Viscondesia de Miroquotella, two of whose sons invited him to dinner; and he liked their family custom of going up after the meal and kissing their mother.[10] Whereas Thomas Bunbury of the 20th Portuguese Infantry Regiment lodged at nearby Belem with the Marques d'Alvito, who spent most of each day playing the French horn, his host in Torre de Moncorvo insisted not only on giving him a side of bacon every day, but also on his sleeping in his own bed, because it was an English one.[11] We find P. W. Buckham of the Staff Corps at the beginning of 1813 quartered in the house of a fidalgo named Leopold Henriques, who kept his large family of daughters totally invisible, in women's apartments which were 'as closely secured as any Turkish harem', and who asked his British guest innumerable questions during supper respecting female education in England and Catholic convents there, as he had it in mind to send his girls over to be educated.[12] Surgeon Walter Henry spent three months at Trujillo, the birthplace of Francisco Pizarro, and lodged in the mansion of an elderly descendant of the great conquistador who, in right of his ancestor, always wore with great pride a small gold key outside the flap of his right coat pocket.[13]

Whether in Portugal or Spain, British officers found themselves billeted most often with a priest or other dignitary of the Church, and these men were usually courteous, hospitable and kind. There was, for instance, the canon of Coimbra Cathedral who insisted on giving dinner every day to officers of the 29th Foot. They in turn insisted that he accept their rations; he did so, but added many capital dishes, as well as confections, dessert and good wine.[14] Equally generous was a canon of Toledo who, besides lodging Moyle Sherer most comfortably in a bed with sheets of the finest linen trimmed with muslin, had chocolate, fruit and sweet biscuits laid out ready in the early morning when the bugle sounded for his guest to leave. Sherer had earlier spent twelve days in the house of another canon, this time in Portalegre, who had placed at Sherer's disposal his library containing a good selection of French authors and some handsome editions of the classics.[15]

In February 1813, when Augustus Frazer stayed in a prior's house near Busaco, his host produced sausages, eggs, rice, pumpkins and apples, refusing to accept any payment either for this food or for the straw consumed by Frazer's mules and horses, though he did insist on reviewing the political situation throughout Europe for three hours at a stretch – and in Portuguese, no doubt encouraged by Frazer's moderate understanding of his language.[16]

Later that year Sir Edward Pakenham, Wellington's brother-in-law, lived in a priest's house at Lesaca, south of Vera. The Spaniard invariably prescribed what he called 'chicking broth' for any British invalids he heard of, without, so the General informed his mother, making 'the smallest distinction even in quantity from Fever to fracture, and he declares that he has lived Twenty Years, inspite of the village doctor's constant sentence, on the same sustenance. The Padre is not fat.'[17]

Towards the end of 1813 Major Blakiston was quartered for two days with the kind-hearted old priest of St Estevan. Imbued with

55

an inveterate hatred of the French, he inflicted upon Blakiston the penance of listening to a lengthy poem he had composed in praise of Lord Wellington and his victories, at the same time begging his guest to gain him an introduction to his Lordship, 'that he might have the honour of laying the epic at the feet of its hero'. Blakiston had managed to avoid doing anything of the sort by the time his regiment marched away to Vera, but some days later whom should he see arriving on muleback but the worthy priest of St Estevan – a ludicrous figure in clerical dress, cocked hat and spectacles. He had come to repeat his request for an interview with Lord Wellington, for which purpose he had brought the manuscript of his epic.

'He was much mortified when I stated my inability to comply with his wishes; but to make up in some sort for his disappointment, I submitted to hear his last canto on the battle of Vittoria, which he had completed since our departure, and also to listen to a repetition of some of the favourite passages of his poem.'

The harassed Blakiston listened to the sonorous language, spoken with a theatrical manner, and it *sounded* mighty fine, but knowing enough to perceive that the poem was 'a tissue of nonsensical bombast', he positively refused to recommend the priest's turgid offerings to Lord Wellington's attention and patronage.[18]

One of the most likeable priests was Padre Oliveira, on whom Assistant Commissary Richard Henegan was billeted in Vera that October. 'Next to his parishioners the simple-hearted man loved best his bees; from bees to flowers, the step is short, but with him it led to still higher researches, and as a botanist and naturalist he was held in no mean repute.' The household was managed by a much younger sister named Agnese who, to Henegan's disillusionment when he made the astonishing discovery, was visited secretly at night by Brother Antonio, a Franciscan monk whom the priest, ironically enough, held in high esteem. When Agnese bore Antonio an illegitimate child, the father killed it and buried it by night in the garden.[19]

Most flirtations and friendships with local women started because troops were quartered on a family which had several daughters, or on some attractive widow, or because adjacent houses contained girls who enjoyed conversation. Thus, when William Gomm spent July 1810 in Tomar, he had next door the prettiest girl in the town. 'When she looks out of the window and I look out of the window there are not above three long long yards between her nose and mine.' He observed that looking out of windows was a primary occupation among the ladies, who often gathered, two or three together, at the same window, and spat frequently. Gomm's girl had two sisters, and the three of them played and sang every evening, and occasionally treated the English captain to 'God Save the King'. He always acknowledged this with a low bow.[20]

Surgeon Henry had similar neighbours in Lisbon, who sat on their handsome gilded balcony in the cool of evening and amused themselves by playing tricks on the Galician water-carriers passing underneath. As soon as a carrier approached, one of the two girls would accost him. '*Tio, Tio!* [Uncle!]' The man would look up and receive a spit in the eye. He retaliated by squirting water from his little painted barrel at the ankles of the giggling girls, who came from a respectable family. Henry soon introduced himself across the narrow street and as darkness fell they all exchanged compliments, he praising their brilliant eyes, they congratulating him on his very good teeth. As far as Henry could see, these girls never went out except to church, never paid visits or drew or read books or worked, or did anything except play popular songs on a guitar. 'Their whole employment, during the time I was their neighbour, appeared to consist in lounging through the house, looking out of the window, lolling on the couches, amusing themselves with the Gallegos, and making love to me, after the fashion above described. And such was the general outline of unmarried Female life in Lisbon.'[21]

Other military men recorded as highlights of life in quarters the ignorance of Portuguese and Spanish women. Surgeon Charles Boutflower, for example, when talking to the *juiz de foro's* daughter in Cano, near Estremoz, was overwhelmed with questions about English customs. Having been taught to believe that an Englishman was not limited in the number of his wives, she was particularly curious about the marriage ceremony.[22] Then we have the lady living in Old Castile who was sadly puzzled to make out what sort of country England was. She had been assured it was

57

surrounded by water, but she could not understand how this was possible, and even if it were, how anyone could reach England. Since she had never seen a craft larger than a ferry-boat on the rivers of Spain, she had no notion of large ships, still less of the sea.[23]

More often than not soldiers and civilians lived cheek by jowl in the frontier villages, sometimes sharing one room with the owner, his wife and children, his servants, a goat, two dogs and a heap of baggage. That was the experience of Lieutenant Hough and a doctor at Souto east of Sabugal.[24] The resilient George Woodberry of the 18th Light Dragoons, having decided to keep his horses in a living-room and his mules in a sort of bedroom, had no option but to sleep in the kitchen along with his landlord and various animals. No wonder he was distracted all night by the grunting of pigs and the crying of children.[25]

Another cavalryman, Major Edwin Griffith of the 15th Light Dragoons, told his sister Charlotte in September 1813 how he was quartered with a young Spaniard, his wife and *her* sister, who was an uncommonly fine girl, 'and so fond of battledore and shuttle-cock that I get worked to death by her. . . . They usually breakfast upon the stair case, little cups of chocolate being ranged along the banisters.' It comes as no surprise to learn that Griffith's command of Spanish improved rapidly in such a billet.[26]

General Picton, though enjoying the luxury of a straw bed with a couple of blankets, was under the necessity of passing through the curate's bedchamber to reach his own. We find that Ensign Stepney and a brother subaltern were quartered in the front hall of a cottage, which served for a parlour, kitchen and all. They doubled up with half a dozen inhabitants, who cooked and ate there, slept in the smoky atmosphere, and used the exit to the village street.[27]

Such proximity did not always lead to harmonious relations, yet disputes were few. Though most British officers and men preferred Spain to Portugal as a country, they were divided in their views of the two nations who lived there with more friction than friendship. Opinions varied on the Spaniards, a majority finding them cleaner and better dressed than their neighbours. While the men looked more muscular and athletic, less diminutive in stature, the women were handsome, and had more graceful figures and better complexions. Spaniards had a staid manner and a dignified deportment which the British found very prepossessing, whereas the Portuguese had suffered more from the desolation and iron hand of war.[28] Some drew a sharp distinction between the fine Spanish peasantry on the one hand and, on the other, the indolent townspeople and members of the higher social classes. 'Their greatest luxury,' wrote Lieutenant Charles Leslie, 'is to stand idly, wrapped up in their large *capas*, smoking cigars, or gambling in the evening. Assassination is horridly common, many being stabbed at noonday.'[29]

According to Sir Robert Ker Porter, who observed the Spaniards closely as an artist, they never condescended 'to run the risk of being fatigued with any employment more active than *idleness*'.[30] Leslie ascribed the indolence, improvidence and quarrelsome nature of so many Spaniards to the immense wealth imported formerly from South America and to the facility with which fortunes had been made there. Certainly few of the master craftsmen and artisans were native born: German tailors, French watchmakers, Italian innkeepers, and Irishmen ready for work of all kinds abounded.[31]

By and large, Wellington's army found the Portuguese, as individuals, a good-natured, kind-hearted race, usually more welcoming, friendly and hospitable than their Spanish neighbours. Admittedly they appeared comparatively helpless and lacking in boldness, energy and enterprise; but when it came to billets, the Portuguese received them eagerly, and shared such food as they had – a contrast to the cool, indifferent reception accorded by so many Spanish households.[32] 'These,' wrote Lieutenant Peter Le Mesurier of the 9th, 'whenever we wished to have anything cooked, appeared displeased and grumbled; those, always received us with politeness; and if an officer happened to come in when at their meals, they appeared hurt if he did not sit down to take something with them.'[33] The Spaniards' great pride, and the superiority they felt over every other nation, especially over Portugal, aroused dislike, while what Blakiston called the rather grovelling deference shown by certain of the Portuguese was viewed by some with disfavour.[34]

Notwithstanding these opinions about national characteristics,

59

relations were normally smooth, especially where the soldiers could help the people on whom they were billeted. When Private John Green stayed in the house of an old widow at Castelo Branco, he ingratiated himself by repairing a large image of Saint Louis from which a hand had become detached.[35] At Maureville in south-west France Lieutenant Woodberry, on learning that the family in whose home he was quartered had one son a prisoner of war in England, promised to get letters through to him.[36]

Tears sometimes marked the beginning or end of a stay in billets. When Lieutenant Carss left a very kind old lady's house after two singularly agreeable months in Olivenza near Badajoz she cried bitterly to see him go; and General Long's mere arrival at a quarter south of Aranjuez caused the landlord to throw his arms round the cavalry commander and burst into a flood of tears.[37]

Contrary to expectation, Wellington's army was treated with friendliness once it crossed the Pyrenees into southern France. Individual attacks in the Spanish guerrilla style had been anticipated by many, yet the very reverse occurred. When Harry Smith and his young Spanish wife arrived at Mont de Marsan during March 1814, Juana was suffering intensely from the cold so their hostess, a widow, lit a fire and soon produced *bouillon* in a handsome slop-basin of Sèvres ware, saying that this had been given to her many years before on her wedding day and had never been used since her husband's death. 'She therefore,' wrote Smith, 'wished my wife to know how happy she was to wait on the nation who was freeing France of an usurper. The widow was a true "Royaliste".'[38] William Freer's beautiful hostess in Ustaritz liked to talk about the war and especially the Bourbons, whom she desired to see on the throne again. William Graham found that when, unwittingly, he asked the old lady who owned his billet what she thought of Napoleon she suddenly burst into tears, because her seven sons had been conscripted one by one, five of them she knew to be dead, and she had a presentiment that the other two had gone the same way. Graham was very upset by her story and dropped the subject. In Peyrehorade Larpent had a particularly civil host. He, his wife, his mother, and two daughters joined the British officer at dinner, when roast beef *à l'anglaise*, duck and chicken were served. The eldest son, who had intended to enter the legal profession, had been conscripted into the French Army and wounded at the battle of Leipzig the previous October, since when the family had heard nothing of him. Fortunately the second son, aged sixteen, was still at school. Larpent, while conceding that he and his companions were welcome guests, suggests a secondary motive – 'the expectation of having coffee and sugar cheap for grandmamma, and English linens, muslins, etc. for the two ugly misses'.[39]

Certainly this may sometimes have been the case, but far more often the goodwill was wholly genuine. Here is the spontaneous opinion of a private in the 43rd named John Timewell, who spent seven weeks near Toulouse just after the final battle there, and wrote in his diary: 'Never was men better used than the inhabitants done to the English soldiers; the friendliest people I met with in all my travels; never was soldiers used half so well in England. . . . There we had puncheons of wine in every house, as good as you pay in England five shillings a bottle. If you had but seen the soldiers in glory there, with fifty glasses on their table all full from morning to night, and even washed potatoes in it, it was so plenty.'[40]

Similarly cordial relations were noticeable when the army went to Flanders in the following year, even though some of the people in Ghent, for example, appeared to be wanting in modesty and respect. Dr William Gibney for one was a trifle put out to find that his landlady entered his room just as she pleased, without knocking – 'bedroom or sitting room, it was all the same to her'. Perhaps Gibney was annoyed at being made a captive audience for a recital of her numerous complaints, but in any case was he no veteran of the Peninsula.[41]

More typical was the experience of those old campaigners, the 16th Light Dragoons, who spent part of April 1815 in Eecloo. Once again drink became a problem, only this time it was not wine but spirits. 'The men cannot stand the good treatment they receive from the persons on whom they are billeted,' noted Captain William Tomkinson, 'and some instances of drunkenness have occurred. The old Peninsular men know their best chance of good treatment is by being civil (which at least they attempt in the first instance), and the inhabitants finding them not inclined to give trouble, generally repay them by something to drink.'[42]

When the 51st Regiment were at Grammont during May they had good quarters and the people showed great kindness. Sergeant Wheeler and another man were quartered at a tobacconist's, and took meals with their landlord and his family.

'Coffee stands ready for use all day long, when we get our rations we give it to the Mistress of the house, except our gin, this we takes care of ourselves. . . . As soon as we rise a cup or two of good coffee. Eight o'clock breakfast on bread and butter eggs and coffee. Dinner meat and vegetables, dressed different ways, with beer, afterwards a glass of Hollands grog and tobacco, evening, salad, coffee, etc., then the whole is washed down by way of a settler with Holland's grog, or beer with a pipe or two, then off to bed.'[43]

Just how friendly relations were between soldiers and civilians is shown by the fact that when the regiment left Grammont for a week and then returned, the townspeople not only welcomed them effusively but, finding they were not to be allotted the same men again, they gathered round Colonel Hugh Henry Mitchell and begged him to let the men return to their old quarters. Although some had already been given new billets and were on their way, buglers were ordered to sound the 'Assembly', and every man was re-allotted to his former billet. Such was the general rejoicing that a stranger would have thought that the 51st 'had been raised in the town and had just returned from a long campaigne'.[44]

On 9 July 1813, many weeks before the army fought its way into France, Wellington issued a General Order calling upon his troops to treat with courtesy the French inhabitants and their property:

'The officers and soldiers of the army must recollect that their nations are at war with France solely because the Ruler of the French nation will not allow them to be at peace, and is desirous of forcing them to submit to his yoke: and they must not forget that the worst of the evils suffered by the enemy, in his profligate invasion of Spain and Portugal, have been occasioned by the irregularities of the soldiers and their cruelties, authorised and encouraged by their chiefs, towards the unfortunate and peaceful inhabitants of the country.

'To revenge this conduct on the peaceful inhabitants of France would be unmanly and unworthy of the nations to whom the Commander of the Forces now addresses himself, and, at all events, would be the occasion of similar and worse evils to the army at large than those which the enemy's army have suffered in the Peninsula; and would eventually prove highly injurious to the public interests.'[45]

Wellington had particularly in mind the Portuguese and Spanish troops under his command when addressing the army. Whereas the former behaved in a largely discreet and disciplined way, certain Spanish units began serious plundering once they had crossed into France, to the point where they had to be packed off home lest they ruin the good name earned by the British regiments.

To start with caution was exercised, but fears of active hostility were soon dispelled, and commanders were saying in tones of relief that to ride around in southern France was as safe as in Leicestershire. Indeed, Wellington's implacable insistence on strict discipline throughout the war and his severity towards any who transgressed against the local populations now earned massive dividends. Had the French acted like the Spanish guerrillas, then Wellington would have had to use far too many troops keeping open his lines of communication, escorting convoys of ammunition and supplies, protecting couriers and garrisoning strong points along the main routes – all tasks of a defensive nature calculated to reduce severely his effective strength, to render much of his offensive action impossible, and, to quote Larpent once more, 'half our army, by straggling about, would have been knocked on the head'.[46]

Instead of the whole country being up in arms, so that 'a soldier durst not go a hundred paces from the battalion without being liable to be murdered by some injured connection, whose misfortunes had driven him to desperation', it was possible for a young officer like James Gairdner of the 95th to write in mid-February: 'How ridiculous now appear to us those doubts and fears we had held out to us of the peasantry rising in arms and the impolicy of entering France. We never have been better treated in Spain or Portugal, and the further we advance we find them more glad to see us.'[47]

63

This welcoming attitude clearly surprised the troops no less than their own good conduct came as a pleasant surprise to the inhabitants of town and village alike. To take one instance: when the 13th Light Dragoons entered Hasparren – the first British regiment to do so – the mayor came out to enquire what sum of money he would be required to levy from the townspeople. He took a great deal of persuading that the proposal to pay cash by weight for all forage was a serious one; indeed, he was not fully convinced until the money had actually been handed over next morning.[48]

How different the French military system had been! On all sides British soldiers heard comparisons made between their conduct and the treatment meted out by French troops to their fellow countrymen. Time and time again Wellington's men found themselves hailed as deliverers from French depredations, in contrast with which the burden of quartering the British army was almost a welcome relief.[49] Many inhabitants who returned to their villages declared that they had been forced by their own troops to quit their homes, with the threat of being hanged and having their houses burnt if they disobeyed. Besides ravaging parts of the region and using oppressive measures, the French army had forcibly taken young men to the colours or demanded crippling ransoms in lieu.[50]

Since 1813 the Cossacks had become the 'bogeymen' of Europe, and their approach was viewed with apprehension. Nevertheless, the level-headed Hussey Vivian, commanding a cavalry brigade, felt justified in telling his wife: 'Buonaparte may collect *procès verbaux*, and publish accounts of the Cossacks, but nothing can equal the "vandalism" of his own troops.'[51]

The Duke of Wellington laid down the same policy of good conduct and restraint, and the same advantages accrued, a year later at the opposite end of France, when his victorious army was advancing on Paris after the campaign of Waterloo. A General Order was issued to the effect that France was to be considered a *friendly* country. No article was to be taken without payment, and commissaries were to give vouchers and receipts for all transactions. Consequently Sir Augustus Frazer was able to write to his wife ten days after the battle that everybody spoke well of the British. One elderly French woman had told him: 'We had more

Plate 1. Guns and carts approaching and crossing a bridge. (*Photo:* National Army Museum)

A baggage column on the march in 1811. From a water-colour by Major Thomas St. Clair, 1st Foot. (*Photo:* National Army Museum)

Plate 2. The 3rd Division crossing the Tagus at Vila Velha in May 1811. From a painting by Major Thomas St. Clair. (*Photo:* National Army Museum)

The wide-brimmed round hat worn by Sir Thomas Picton at the battle of Vitoria. (National Army Museum. *Photo:* R. P. Fleming)

trouble to satisfy two Prussians who were in one house than thirty English who were in another.'[52]

Indeed, Wellington, his generals and their staffs could aptly have quoted Shakespeare when he has King Henry V say: 'We give express charge that, in our marches through the country, there are nothing compelled from the villages, nothing taken but paid for, none of the French upbraided or abused in disdainful language; for whom lenity and cruelty play for a Kingdom, the gentler gamester is the soonest winner.'[53]

Over and over again British officers, having witnessed the destruction and misery inflicted by war on civilian populations, drew sharp contrasts between, on the one hand, the wretched circumstances of the Portuguese and Spanish people and, on the other, their fortunate fellow countrymen at home. How happy the people of England ought to consider themselves, who were strangers to such horrors and lived under laws by which their lives and property were secure.[54]

'Oh, my countrymen of England,' wrote Major Harry Smith, 'if you had seen the twentieth part of the horrors of war I have, readily would you pay the war-taxes, and grumble less at the pinching saddle of the National Debt! The seat of war is hell upon earth.' Or again we have another Rifle Corps officer, this time Lieutenant George Simmons, expressing similar views in May 1811: 'O happy, happy country! You are ignorant of the miseries and wretchedness that one half of Europe is continually exposed to, and may you ever enjoy the same happiness!'[55]

That was, of course, the usual attitude, but just occasionally a note of irritation creeps in over the attitude of those at home, almost as if a touch of war at close quarters and of French depredations would jolt them out of their complacent groove and teach a salutory lesson. 'Ye gentlemen of England, who sit at home at ease, how would you like such visitors along the coast of Kent or in your snug little country towns?'[56]

Chapter 4

CAMPAIGNING KIT

'How different was Tom, marching to school with his satchel on his back, from Tom, with his musket and Kitt.'[1]
A Soldier of the 71st

Pococke of the 71st Regiment carried in his knapsack two shirts, two pairs of stockings, one pair of overalls, two shoe brushes, a shaving box, one pair of spare shoes, and a few other items. On top of the knapsack he had a greatcoat and blanket. Over one shoulder was slung a three-pint canteen of water, across the other a haversack containing enough bread and beef for three days and, on top of all, sixty rounds of ball-cartridge and, whenever it was the individual soldier's turn, a camp-kettle which, along with a bill-hook, he shared with five other men.[2]

A tradesman – what Rifleman John Harris called 'a handicraft' – might well have extra articles to load on his back. As regimental cobbler Harris had a haversack stuffed full of leather for repairing the men's shoes, besides a hammer and other tools. 'The lapstone I took the liberty of throwing to the devil.'[3]

A foot soldier usually carried a load of around sixty pounds, varying with the number of rounds of ball-cartridge and the provisions on issue. To learn the weight in pounds of individual items we can hardly do better than reproduce a list of kit (showing the weight in pounds) carried by each man of the 7th Fusiliers during the march towards Vitoria.

'1 Fusee and Bayonet, 14; 1 pouch and sixty rounds of ball, etc, 6; 1 canteen and belt, 1; 1 mess tin, 1; 1 knapsack Frames and Belts, 3; 1 White Jacket, $\frac{1}{2}$; 2 shirts and three Breasts, $2\frac{1}{2}$; 2 pairs of shoes, 3; 1 pair trousers, 2; 1 pair gaiters, $\frac{1}{4}$; 2 pairs stockings, 1; 4 brushes, button stick, comb, 3; 2 cross belts, 1; pen, ink and paper, $\frac{1}{4}$; pipe clay, chalk etc., 1; 2 tent pegs, $\frac{1}{2}$.'

66

To this was added three days' bread (3 lb.), two days' beef (2lb.), and the weight of water in the canteens (3 lb.).[4]

Another list of kit furnished by a former Sergeant-Major named Murray in the Scots Fusilier Guards tallies in most respects, but he gives the weight of *his* great-coat as 5 lbs. 10 oz. instead of 4 lbs.

A cavalry trooper had on his charge many other articles of equipment, ranging from a water sponge and corn bag to a watering bridle, nosebag and horse picker. A man serving with the Royal Scots Greys had a mane comb and sponge, a curry-comb and brush. His personal kit list included a blacking ball, three shoe brushes, a soap box, scissors, a hair comb and razor, three shirts at 9s each, a foraging cap priced at 3s 6d, three pairs of worsted stockings costing 3s 2d each, two pairs of shoes worth 8s 6d a pair, and one pair of long black gaiters.[5]

So much for the rank and file. Officers were usually left to their own devices when it came to equipping themselves for a campaign. On first landing in Portugal they would repair to the Rocio, an open space on the northern side of Lisbon, where a market for horses, ponies and mules was held every Thursday. Major George L'Estrange of the 31st Foot, who visited the fair in December 1812, paid a hundred dollars for a little black English pony, and eighty for a long-legged ugly mule. He invested in an English saddle and bridle for the pony and, for the mule, a country pack-saddle across which were slung two panniers covered with cow-hide and containing all his worldly goods, while between the panniers were loaded a six-foot stretcher, a small hair mattress and two blankets. Finally he brought a voluminous camlet cloak, and thus equipped he felt prepared 'to meet the world in arms'.[6]

Veterans were always ready to proffer advice, usually sound, to friends and relations who wished to come soldiering in Portugal and Spain. Thomas Dyneley of the Royal Horse Artillery coun-selled a friend to buy a tall stout baggage mule on arrival in Lisbon: 'They will ask about twice as much as they ought for him, but that he must not mind; a weakly one cannot go long marches, nor a low one cross deep water'.[7] Pack-saddles, of course, had to be fitted with great care, otherwise the mule would have a sore back within two days of leaving Lisbon.[8] By contrast Lieutenant George Simmons of the 95th advised his parents to equip his young brother Joseph with a dark fustian haversack, a tin pot for wine, soup and tea, a large clasp knife, and a fork and spoon. Three shirts and three pairs of socks would suffice, along with three little towels and two or three toothbrushes.[9]

Major-General William Wheatley, writing in July 1812 to his brother Harry in case he and his regiment were ordered out to Spain, not only recommended such items as a tent, a large portmanteau, a bed and bedstead, and a hair-cloth or bearskin. He also advised Harry that his baggage 'must consist of great things, no small packages; my breakfast canteens would be as good as any you can buy. They were made by Nickells in the Hay Market.'[10]

One trouble was to know whose advice to accept, when so many things were recommended. Lieutenant Peter Le Mesurier, who arrived in August 1811, met four officers of the Norfolk Regiment, to which he also belonged, who had just left the army on grounds of ill health. They suggested he take a tent and purchase a horse, but Le Mesurier reckoned that if a soldier could march with his knapsack and carry sixty rounds of ammunition, besides his arms, he himself would be able to keep up on the march. However, he proposed to go shares in a mule with another officer and to walk as far as the army. Then, if he felt too fagged, he would buy a pony as well. At all events, he would, in the face of conflicting counsel, take nothing except what he supposed to be essential.[11]

A commissary like Alexander Dallas appears to have had no trouble in procuring *three* mules to carry his personal baggage: one for his desk and papers, with a guitar-case on top; the second for his clothes and equipment; and a third to carry his tent.[12]

On first landing at Belem, the army's base by Lisbon, Ensign George Bell of the 34th bought a silver spoon and fork, tin plates and dishes, a frying pan, and tins for salt, pepper, tea and sugar. Having purchased a donkey he stuffed all his personal kit into an old leather trunk on one side of the saddle, balancing the load with a sack containing his camp-kettle, frying pan, reaping-hook, and various odds and ends, together with his servant's knapsack.[13] Individual officers, even junior ones, had all sorts of comforts with them. Lieutenant Boothby of the Engineers, for instance, had a blue patent, silver-mounted morocco writing-case full of 'letter-paper, pens, ink, letters, secrets, verses, etc.'[14]

Many an officer invested in a spy-glass in a strong leather case which was slung over the left shoulder. Engineers might well have a surveying pocket-compass. Robert Fernyhough of the Rifle Corps purchased, even before he left England, a saddle and bridle, and 'portable soup', as well as a spy-glass; and G. S. Reddell, sword cutter and accoutrement maker of 188 Jermyn Street, made for him an excellent tempered sword, as he had done for numerous generals.[15]

It is when we come to the generals that the bulk baggage – and animals to carry it all – really presents a problem, and this excess of essentials was in no sense exclusive to the Peninsular War. Major-General Robinson was serious, not sarcastic, when he wrote home in July 1813: 'You may judge of the severe hardships General officers endure by a description of my establishment, which is very low in comparison with any other – 12 men employed in various ways – Four horses, Ten mules, Five sheep, Two goats, and a large Dog – This is besides my Aide de Camp and Major of Brigade who live with me.'[16]

Certain items of campaign kit belonging to Wellington and other generals have been preserved and form part of the collection in the National Army Museum. The travelling dressing-case which Sir Rowland Hill took through the Peninsular War has seven silver-topped glass bottles and fourteen toilet instruments. Sir John Moore's campaign cutlery includes four dessert knives, two dinner knives and forks, a long steel-bladed knife with a well ground blade, and two silver knives, each with two iron prongs. Two of Wellington's shaving mirrors have survived: the first measures seven by five inches and is of silvered glass; the second has wooden protective flaps and is twelve inches across and twenty deep.

Major-General Lowry Cole, commanding the 4th Division, liked his comforts, and in order to enjoy them was obliged to travel with a dozen goats for milk, a cow, and about thirty-six sheep, complete with a shepherd. 'When you think of this,' commented F. S. Larpent, 'that wine and everything else is to be carried about, from salt and pepper and tea-cups to saucepans, boilers, dishes, chairs, and tables, on mules, you may guess the trouble and expense of a good establishment here.'[17]

Of all the establishments, the largest was General Graham's, whose baggage was said to require forty mules to transport it. Of course he had half a dozen officers to lodge and board apart from himself, and there would be several visitors, invited or otherwise, whom he had to feed. Certainly a general needed private means to run such an establishment, since to do so was reckoned to cost more than £2,000 a year, over and above the initial outlay.[18]

As early as 1808, during Sir Arthur Wellesley's first campaign in Portugal, certain officers had come to the conclusion that they overloaded themselves, in particular when means of transport were so difficult to procure. A heavy boat cloak, three days' rations in the haversack, an extra pair of boots or shoes and a supply of rum if obtainable, were all taken. To quote Robert Blakeney of the 28th: 'Each young warrior too hampered himself with a case of pistols and a liberal supply of ball-cartridge, and generally a heavy spy-glass.' To march thus laden when the August temperature was 95°F was quickly seen to be absurd, and a light cart was allowed to each regiment for the convenience of the officers, most of whom were new to campaigning.[19] In 1809, when he returned to Portugal, Sir Arthur found that by order of his predecessor, officers were required to carry their own packs, the same as the rank and file. He changed this, observing that officers would be too tired at the end of a day's march to attend to the comforts of their men.[20]

However careful junior officers might be to keep their kit to a minimum, with or without the use of a cart, their seniors were liable to indulge themselves more liberally, above all those who had transport readily to hand: the artillery, for instance. Thus we have Major Dickson in February 1810 listing the following items of baggage:

'1 large chest   1 sword
2 portmanteaux   1 cheese in bag
1 carpet bag with
  liquor canteens
2 canteen baskets   1 box with papers
1 cot and bedding   1 bag with papers and
2 camp-kettles   orderly books.'[21]
1 tent with poles

One would like to know the contents of the canteens, for instance, when what Blakeney regarded as 'a rough-and-ready canteen for officers of the line only' contained, besides a little stock of tea, sugar and brandy, a tin kettle which also acted as teapot, *two* cups and saucers, in case of company, two spoons, two forks, two plates of the same metal and 'a small soup-tureen, which on fortunate occasions acted as punch-bowl but never for soup'.[22]

Several descriptions of an officer's campaign canteen are extant. According to the surgeon of the 12th Light Dragoons at Waterloo, this pretty 'display of curious and ingenious contrivance' contained cooking utensils, breakfast and dinner equipage, candlesticks, lamps and much else, within the compass of a moderate-sized portmanteau. 'Solid and rough, seldom neat, and never gaudy, should be the furniture of such a convenience.'[23]

A clear notion of the extensive kit an officer might have with him while campaigning is given by the following list of effects belonging to Captain Dugald Ferguson of the 2/95th Rifle Corps, who died from wounds received at the battle of Salamanca. His effects, auctioned on 17 August 1812, and shared among fifteen officers, were as follows: 1 tarpaulin bed, 1 pair saddle bags, a set of handkerchiefs, 1 portmanteau, 1 pair gloves and braces, 1 morning gown, 1 writing case, 1 pair spurs and hooks, 6 old towels, 1 silver watch, 1 horse, 1 mule, 2 pairs trousers, 1 saddle and bridle, 1 set of old boots, 1 boat cloak, 2 boots, 8 silk handkerchiefs, 1 belt, 1 pair boots, 1 pair gloves, 1 canteen, 1 waistcoat, 1 spy glass, 1 sword, 6 shirts, flannel drawers and waistcoat, 1 sash, 1 looking-glass, 11 pairs socks, dressing brushes, 1 shaving case. From this total of $467\frac{1}{2}$ dollars, the equivalent of £100 at the time, were deducted funeral expenses amounting to $14\frac{1}{2}$ dollars:

'Paid nurse	3 dollars
For digging grave	3 dollars
Batman	2 dollars
Coffin and other funeral expenses	$6\frac{1}{2}$ dollars.'[24]

As in many wars, when an officer was killed, his effects, apart from personal, sentimental and valuable items, were put up for auction among his companions. After Captain Carew of the 18th Light Dragoons was killed at Vitoria, brother officers paid high prices, such as 35s for two bottles of sauce, 63s 6d for seven pounds of cheese, and 27s for two tongues. Lord Worcester bid 34s for a pair of bronze spurs.[25] After Talavera Commissary Schaumann watched several auctions held in regimental bivouacs and from the effects of Colonel Gordon, who had been killed by a howitzer, he bought very cheaply a fine pair of dark blue over-alls with two rows of buttons, which he wore for a very long time.[26]

When Richard Henegan arrived at Lesaca, just in time for the sale of belongings of a Captain Cardew, who had been killed with the 95th at Vera, only his sword and watch were reserved as mementoes for relatives; otherwise everything went piecemeal to those who had lived and worked with the deceased. 'As I entered, the half worn-out jacket, and still glittering chacot [shako] were held up to view by the military auctioneer. Such objects usually go to the regiment, and bidders were not slack in their endeavours to obtain some relic of their lamented comrade. In some short moments, the limited wardrobe was dispersed in divers hands.'[27]

During a third such auction, this time at St Jean de Luz, of Captain Henry Watson of the 3rd Foot Guards, Judge-Advocate General Larpent bought a very tolerable saddle with holsters, half worn, for eighteen dollars. He bid 10s for a curry-comb and brush, 'bad, but of English make, and in England worth about 3s or 4s – it went for a guinea!' He was also outbid for a Suffolk Punch horse, though he went as high as 200 dollars.[28] At another St Jean de Luz sale attended by Larpent, just before Christmas, items which had belonged to a Colonel Martyn went for ridicu-lously high prices. Two second-hand night-caps, which cost about 1s 6d each at home, fetched 13s. Old towels were sold at 5s apiece, and blankets at 25s. 'This,' observed the Judge-Advocate General, 'results partly from distress, partly from fun in the bidders. I always feel hurt at seeing all an officer's stock sold in this way, even to his ragged shirts and stockings, tooth-brushes, etc; everything ransacked.'[29]

Somehow there always seemed to be at least one officer's kit being disposed of in this way, especially after a bloody event like the storming of Badajoz, or a battle such as Waterloo, and it could be a melancholy business, at least for a short while, though George Bell, who was anything but callous and insensitive, probably summed up the normal attitude when he wrote:

'There was no real grief for any one beyond a week or two – all a shadow that passed away. . . . We bought their clothes and wore them, and they were sold again perhaps in a month, being once more part of the kit of deceased officers killed in action.'[30]

Quite a different type of auction took place after the successful storming of a place like Ciudad Rodrigo or Badajoz. On these occasions the soldiers would lay out for sale their different articles of plunder, and Spanish villagers clustered round as would-be purchasers. Lieutenant William Grattan watched his Connaught Rangers as they did just this in January 1812. Bolero dancers arrived to rattle their castanets; pig-skins of wine were carried into the British bivouac and sold for a trifling sum; and soon the Rangers were drinking hard, while their less fortunate companions, 'either hastily flung into an ill-formed grave, writhing under the knife of the surgeon or in the agonies of death, were unthought of, or unfelt for – *Sic transit gloria mundi!*' The soldiers were allowed three days in which to dispose of their plunder, but long before the time expired they had scarcely a rag to sell or a coin of the proceeds left in their pockets.[31]

The booty from Badajoz far exceeded that removed from Rodrigo. A great crowd of Spaniards thronged into the 3rd Division's camp, which soon resembled a vast market. Despite a lack of auctioneers, the sale proceeded briskly until all saleable goods had been carried off by eager purchasers. 'Some men realised upwards of one thousand dollars (£250), others less, but all, or almost all, gained handsomely by an enterprise in which they had displayed such unheard of acts of devotion and bravery.'[32]

British troops always enjoyed wandering round a local fair whenever the Portuguese or Spaniards established one. Wise commanding officers usually kept the booths at a reasonable distance from the regimental camp or line of guns and increased patrols to prevent disorders by their men. At Sobreira Formosa in September 1809, for instance, nearly a thousand people came to the fair. On sale was ordinary cloth from which the peasants made their cloaks, green cloth for petticoats, and salt fish and salt.[33] A month later, at Certaa, Major Dickson actually moved his guns when he discovered that they were on the stretch of ground customarily used for the fair. This was a far better show, with permanent booths fitted up as shops along the convent wall, and a street of temporary booths as well. Here could be purchased hardware and hats, cotton goods and cloth. Gold and silver ware had been brought in by traders from Oporto, who offered knives, forks, spoons, teapots, spurs, gold chains, crosses and ear-rings. Then along the river bank and under trees were people selling local cloth, common woollens, and the usual salt fish, as well as poultry, flax, vegetables, and coarse pottery. Dickson himself bought four pairs of worsted stockings, a silver purse, and enough linen to make two shirts. He was thankful to record in his journal that the day passed without any disorder or irregularity on the soldiers' part.[34]

Some towns had special fairs once or twice a year, though a place like Certaa held one every Sunday so that country people could dispose of the fruits of their labour and buy whatever they required for the week ahead. They began arriving early in the morning, and by nine o'clock the main street was crowded all the way to the market place. Business continued till dusk, and Dickson thought 'the crowd and bustle of the scene infinitely greater than the generality of country fairs in England'.[35] He took a more active part in a special fair late in 1809 at Golegã, where preparations were made over several days, what with the erection and sale of booths, the arrival of an immense quantity of goods and dozens of horses. Having done his best to help by ordering out one officer, one sergeant, one drummer, four corporals and twenty-five men to furnish patrols and prevent disturbances throughout the fair, Dickson felt so unwell he had to take to his bed, but could not sleep for the noise of the fair. Three days later he managed to visit the booths, in fine weather after some severe and hostile rainstorms, and on this occasion his main purchase was a pocket sun-dial.[36]

Sometimes, as at Espinal, the fair took a more casual and chaotic form, with the town swarming with pigs, and with women, outnumbering the men by ten to one, offering for sale straight out of hampers bread, rice, peas and beans.[37] Coimbra, though larger, had an equally simple fair. Again the women predominated, bringing everything on their heads: 'Leather, wood, salt fish, poultry, grass, and straw, and down they squat in the middle of a dirty street, and there's the market. Poultry of all kinds, tied together in whimsical confusion.'[38]

Goods on sale were normally of local make or produce, but at a fair at Alfaiates in September 1811 one officer at least was surprised to find that two-thirds of the articles were of English manufacture.[39]

Major-General Henry Mackinnon, writing from Guarda, noted that 'the greatest ornaments of the fair are the silversmiths' stalls, whose goods are in great request, as you seldom see a beggar in this country without a gold chain about his neck and gold earrings'. He also recorded that British soldiers often bought the coarse local cloth for making into trousers.[40]

While it is true that soldiers picked up at auctions and markets some of the items they needed to improve their comfort and diet, to replace worn parts of their wardrobe, to make good losses and to alleviate the rigours of campaign life, they could not buy locally so much as half of what they fancied. This applied to officers in particular, and few of them neglected to write to England for this article and that. Their list of requirements is lengthy, including as it did such things as lavender water, Seidlitz powders and packages of Smyth's Windsor soap; sets of toothbrushes, also from Smyth, perfumers of 110 New Bond Street; razors and strops, and boxes of Wayne's white tooth powder.[41] Ready-cut pens were acceptable, and so were almanacks and pocket books for the coming year. While acting as Wellington's Adjutant-General in March 1811, Edward Pakenham asked his brother for a plain box covered in Russian leather, containing a silver ink bottle with a screw top, a box of patent pens, and common note-paper. He stipulated that the box must measure ten inches by seven by three-and-a-quarter, and have a carrying strap besides a strong leather cover.[42]

When Lieutenant Dyneley was robbed of a silver pencil case given him by his brother Charles, and a pocket comb and lip-salve from his sister Dora, he was very concerned; but what worried him most was the theft of a watch, so he wrote home to his mother asking her to arrange with Dubois and Wheeler to make an exactly similar watch, 'excepting the stop-hand, which must be in front of the watch; having to open the watch behind to stop it was very inconvenient'.[43]

More unusual was Alexander Dickson's request to a friend living in James Street, Adelphi, London, to procure for him from Watkins, optician at 5 Charing Cross, 'a pair of silver mounted and double armed spring spectacles set with Concave glasses, No. 8. Desire that the bridge may have an outward bow to bring the glasses nearer to the eye.' Dickson, who dated his letter from Almeida on 11 December 1811, needed six spare pairs of glasses and a strong case. The arms of the spectacles had to be strong and with such a spring that they would stay on firmly when he was riding 'at the hardest'.[44]

Items of clothing, uniform or otherwise, were in frequent demand, and many had to be tailor-made. Whereas flannel for shirts and cloth for overalls could sometimes be found in the Portuguese capital, more complex and elegant garments, for instance a light dragoon's jacket and pelisse, had to be ordered from a London tailor.[45] Thus Pakenham begged his brother Lord Longford to have sent out to him by the first safe opportunity, from Place, the famous tailor and radical politician, enough cloth for a regimental coat, blue cloth for the facings, cuffs and collar, and three dozen staff buttons; and William Coles of the 4th Dragoons needed enough light grey pepper and salt cloth to make two pairs of overalls. Dyneley asked his brother to send him by the next packet a foraging cap from Hawkes, military cap and hat makers of 24 Piccadilly: 'Tell him to let it be much such another as Lieutenant Macdonald of Ross's troop had of him a short time since. If Hawkes does not recollect, send me one "neat but not gaudy".' Three months later he also required a sword and sabretache, the latter from Hawkes again. The sabretache was to be of his latest pattern, with ink-stand, lock and key, with two knots. General Long, too, wanted from Hawkes a couple of sword belts, embroidered or stitched with gold.[46]

We have Peter Le Mesurier writing for some flannel waistcoats to keep him warm when the 1812 campaigning season opened, and Lovell Badcock wanting six shirts and three pairs of flannel drawers in addition to the popular flannel waistcoats. Edward Freer's sisters, Anne and Martha, made his shirts and Mrs Freer sent them out, together with pocket handkerchiefs, two pairs of sheets, a pillow case, two towels and two table cloths. 'The sheets are brown,' she added, 'but in washing will soon be white – they are our spinning – you will like them better for that.' In January 1814 Hussey Vivian, commanding a cavalry brigade, asked his wife to pack up and send from home six shirts, four pairs of net pantaloon drawers, four net under-waistcoats, twelve pairs of thin worsted half stockings, six black neckties, six white waistcoats, half a dozen pairs of nankeen overalls and white trousers for summer wear.[47]

Officers also needed new boots. William Warre wrote from Lisbon to his father to order from George Hoby, boot maker with premises at 163 Piccadilly, who already had his measure, two pairs of long Regent boots: these arrived six months after Warre's initial request.[48] Hoby crops up again when Colonel Burgoyne sent money to a brother officer of Engineers stationed in England, requesting him to pay a series of bills 'with Mr Hoby, Bootmaker, St James's Street, about £30; Mr Cuff, Saddler, Curzon Street, Mayfair, about £16; Mr Prater, Linen Draper, [6] Charing Cross, about £30; Mr Buckmaster, Tailor, Old Bond Street, on account £30'. 'Send me their several receipts,' added Burgoyne, 'that they may not call upon me again.'[49]

Captain Samuel Hobkirk of the 43rd is on record as spending nearly £1,000 a year on dress. The result was seen when he was taken prisoner and at dinner with Marshal Soult was at first mistaken for a British field-marshal, so rich and elegant was the uniform he wore.[50]

Chapter 5

THREADBARE AND PATCHED

'My once gay coat in tatters hangs about,
    with many vary coloured pieces patch'd,
From ghosts of shoes, my wounded feet creep out,
    Thro' thread-bare gaiters, how my legs are scratched.'[1]
'The Subaltern's Complaint', 1811

'No one thought about the cut of a coat, or the fashion of a boot, or looked coldly on his neighbour because his ragged garment was less fashionable than his own; sufficient was it that he had a coat on his back.'[2]
Ensign Frederick Mainwaring, 51st Foot, 1811

One reason why senior officers and those with money wrote home for clothing and negotiated with London tailors was the tattered, greasy condition of all but the newest uniforms during the Peninsular War. Officers were allowed considerable latitude in what they wore, but to keep themselves looking respectable, let alone smart, proved very difficult. As for the rank and file, they did all that ingenuity and resourcefulness could achieve by way of make and mend.

Wellington was something of a dandy himself: not for nothing was he nicknamed 'the Beau' by his officers. He dressed simply, without ostentation, yet immaculately. Larpent says he had the skirts of his coats cut shorter in the Peninsula to make them look smarter, and one day in 1813 he found Wellington discussing with his servant the cut of his half-boots and suggesting alterations.[3] Wellington sometimes wore a plain grey frock coat, more often a dark blue overcoat, with a round hat or a little, flat cocked hat. Grey pantaloons, a white waistcoat, and a white instead of the regulation black neckerchief completed his costume,

78

though towards the close of the war he took to wearing in bad weather a short white cloak captured from a French dragoon. Private Green, who often saw Wellington walking to and fro in Freineda's tiny market place, thought he dressed 'as plainly as though he had been a captain or a subaltern officer'.[4]

Grattan of the Connaught Rangers declares that in matters of dress, if in little else, Wellington was an indulgent commander.

'Provided we brought our men into the field well appointed, and with sixty rounds of good ammunition each, he never looked to see whether their trousers were black, blue, or grey; and as to ourselves, we might be rigged out in all colours of the rainbow if we fancied it. The consequence was, that scarcely any two officers were dressed alike! Some with grey braided coats, others with brown; some again liked blue; while many from choice, or perhaps necessity, stuck to the "old red rag".'[5]

Overalls were in vogue among not a few infantry officers, who in consequence resembled cavalry troopers. Dandies had a field day, and to be different or even *outré* was all the rage. Witness the cut down hat adorned with a bizarre looking feather or distinguished by having no feather at all.[6]

Much the same sartorial freedom prevailed during the Waterloo campaign, officers being encouraged by Wellington's indifference to indulge their fancy. Notable in this were certain members of the Royal Horse Artillery. Mercer recalled how at one inspection in May 1815 Major Norman Ramsay wore a light-cavalry belt instead of a sash. The regimental pantaloons were pepper and salt, with straps of brown leather inside the legs and round the bottom, and a red stripe down the outside seam.[7]

With few exceptions, everyone's uniform, from headgear to shoes, quickly lost shape, smartness and colour. In May 1809 supplies of clothing were so inadequate that the officer commanding the 5/60th had to allow his men to cut away the skirts of their jackets so as to patch the upper part. After Talavera the 29th Regiment could not obtain any red cloth for patching, so grey, white, even brown had to be used instead.[8] One subaltern went so far as to have his coat mended with material from the breeches of a dead Frenchman found on the field of battle. At the end of 1812, when several regiments marched into Coria, the men's jackets, which had once been scarlet, now possessed a variety of repairs. Some of them had black sleeves fastened to a red body, others blue, and many had brown cloth sleeves to a patched body. Indeed, scarcely two were mended alike.[9]

The Rifle Corps were no better off, though the green jacket, in spite of shreds and patches, retained about it something of the original. However, several officers had brown instead of green jackets. Even when not patched all over, the uniforms had worn threadbare and very few did not have at least the elbows patched. In short, it was sometimes difficult to tell to which regiment any group of soldiers belonged, since each man's jacket resembled Joseph's coat of many colours.[10] Lord Wellington, when he rode into Ciudad Rodrigo as the 95th marched out to cantonments after the siege, was so puzzled by the rare vestiges of uniform that he had to ask the leading company commander which regiment it was. 'Some of them were dressed in Frenchmen's coats, some in white breeches and huge jack-boots, some with cocked hats and queues, most of their swords were fixed on their rifles, and stuck full of hams, tongues, and loaves of bread, and not a few were carrying umbrellas.' This was an extreme example, partly caused by the plundering that went on for several days after the troops had stormed their bloody way into the fortress town.[11]

Trousers were in very much the same state as jackets with their motley patches. Until 1811 most of the infantry wore white breeches and gaiters; then they changed to trousers of a blue-grey cloth, with a half gaiter of the same material. Since the long gaiter had been found to produce sores on the march, the new trousers would, by leaving the knee and calf unconfined, be more suitable for marching. Dress regulations for the Royal Scots added that trousers, when worn out, could be used for repairing gaiters. Men of the 20th Regiment, whose old threadbare greys had become terribly worn during fighting in the mountain passes, were highly amused to find that several of their comrades, getting ready for the battle of the Pyrenees, had obtained and chosen to wear trousers belonging to some French *tirailleurs*.[12] When the 43rd Light Infantry approached Mont de Marsan, most of the men wore trousers made from blankets, and the French people flocking out to watch *les étrangers* expressed wonder at seeing the troops of the richest nation in the world so threadbare and poorly clad.[13]

Among the soldiers of the 57th Regiment six inches of bare thigh or arm were often visible through the patches, and some had nothing but linen pantaloons to wear during the winter months. Cavalry regiments also showed the effects of weather and constant duty. For instance, the men of the 13th Light Dragoons had patched their overalls with various colours, in particular with red oilskin taken from baggage wrappers.[14]

The kilt did not always prove to be a practical garment for campaign life. While advancing toward the heights of Puebla during the battle of Vitoria, the 92nd had to cross ditches so thickly lined with thorns and briars that the blood ran trickling down many a soldier's leg.[15]

At one stage company commanders in the Gordon Highlanders were instructed to have all batmen and servants give up their kilts for the purpose of mending the kilts of the duty men, and march in pantaloons until new clothing was issued. Any man in the regiment who had a knowledge of tailoring was to assist the company tailors with repair work.

By February 1814, at the time of Orthez, the Black Watch was the only regiment in the Highland Brigade still wearing the kilt, and even these men were beginning to lose it by degrees, partly because those who fell sick and were left behind often had the kilt made into trews. When they rejoined the battalion no plaid could be supplied for new kilts, so a great want of uniformity soon prevailed.[16]

Shirts were also missing in too many cases, and had it not been for the occasional capture of some French shirts, many soldiers would have been almost naked. Soldiers of the 68th Regiment had two spare shirts when they left England in June 1811, and within three months of reaching Portugal each man was issued with a full-sized, long-sleeved flannel shirt which was thought to preserve health more effectively than did linen shirts. Despite this, they soon ran out of wearable shirts.[17]

Most serious of all was the shortage or worn-out state of the soldiers' shoes. Indeed, the situation became so bad that a single regiment could have a hundred men without shoes at a time. Far more attention should have been paid in England to the quality of footwear served out to the Army, because the shoes were generally of the very worst kind.[18] Ever since Sir John Moore's army had retreated along the mountain roads of Galicia, this had been scandalously true. All too often during that march the soles and bottoms had fallen off, leaving the upper leather laced round the ankle and the poor soldier walking barefoot. Bugler William Green of the 95th Rifles summed up the prevalent anger:

'We said the soles and heels had been glued or pegged on, as there could not have been any wax or hemp used, and the person who contracted with the government ought to have been tried by court-martial, and to have been rewarded with a good flogging with a cat-o'-nine-tails.'[19]

That poor quality persisted is demonstrated by the fact that shoes drawn from store were in tatters after only a week of marching and fighting. If shoes instead of boots had to be issued, then something better than the ordinary gaiter strap should have been devised to prevent the shoe from being torn off the foot in thick mud. In 1812 we find cases of men who, after marching their shoes off, adopted the system of Spanish muleteers. They placed their feet on the warm raw hides of bullocks which had just been killed for their food, cut out a piece to shape, and fashioned a sandal, which proved so comfortable that when a large quantity of French shoes was captured in Madrid the men were reluctant 'to quit the easy, well-fitting, and pliant sandal for the hard and cumbrous leather shoe'.[20] Next year the Guards, among other regiments lacking shoes, were provided with light hempen sandals made and worn by the local people and admirably adapted to the steep and slippery Pyrenees.

Occasionally, after a particularly severe march, Lord Wellington might sanction a free issue of shoes, but otherwise the cost of new ones, over and above the allowance of two pairs a year, was stopped from a soldier's pay. Naturally the troops had a pecuniary interest in the length and roughness of the marches they undertook.[21]

Most headgear was quick to wear out and become misshapen. When the 16th Light Dragoons received new helmets from England in September 1810 the old ones were so warped by the sun that they were scarcely wearable – another example of poor quality. The silver edging came off, the first downpours of rain put the helmets out of shape, and they looked smart for at most a few months.[22] In several regiments the troopers were reduced to wearing forage caps or even a handkerchief tied round the head. On reaching Portalegre, the Royal Dragoons were greeted by their quartermaster with a much needed consignment of hats he had just brought up from Lisbon. And not before time, since the discarded hats were in a terrible state. 'No dustman in London ever wore so filthy or so dirty an apology for a hat; not a vestige of its former shape was to be seen.'[21]

Infantry regiments fared little better. When the shako was authorized in 1811, officers of the line wore one made of felt, with a napped surface and a lacquered top, whereas the other ranks' shako was made of stout felt all over. In undress, the rank and file had a black cloth forage-cap with an oilskin cover – an excellent addition for bad weather. Officers usually made their own arrangements for waterproofing hats. When Le Mesurier was stationed in Gibraltar early in 1810 he still wore the hat he had bought on first entering the Army. After one campaign in Spain he had it covered with oilskin, and wore it for the disastrous Walcheren expedition of 1809. Next he had the oilskin taken off and turned. 'It is rather shabby now,' he noted on 24th March, 'but it must see the Summer out and then I may lay by the Veteran.'[24]

Greatcoats also wore out. In the second half of the war infantry officers and men usually wore in the autumn and winter months a grey greatcoat with a stand-up collar and a cape to protect the shoulders. To have a grey one turned scarcely improved its appearance, for the inside was of a particularly coarse material and had to be worn out also. Wellington's staff at least appear not to have bothered overmuch, if we can judge from Augustus Frazer's comment to his wife: 'Blue or grey slouch great-coats are worn by all; one may almost say the shabbier the better.'[25]

So much for outer garments. Matters were often worse still when when it came to what were called regimental 'small-clothes'. Referring to 1810, Kincaid wrote: 'They could only be replaced by very extraordinary apologies, of which I remember that I had two at this period, *one* of a common brown Portuguese cloth, and the *other*, or Sunday's pair, of black velvet.'[26]

One major cause of clothes wearing out so fast was the extreme difficulty of getting any laundry done while campaigning and marching. For one thing, soldiers often went weeks on end without taking off their clothes. For another, they were to start with very unskilled at laundering their own linen, and as will be seen, the number of women to do this work was never enough. Kincaid of the Rifle Corps summed up the situation quite frankly when he wrote: 'the ceremony of washing a shirt amounted to my servant's taking it by the collar, and giving it a couple of shakes in the water, and then hanging it up to dry. Smoothing irons were not the fashion of the times'.[27]

For one period of six days the Connaught Rangers did not see their baggage, and therefore had no change of linen. Having lain on dirty straw for the six days they agreed that a bathe in the nearby Dos Casas stream would be delightfully refreshing. So it was, but Lieutenant Grattan and half-a-dozen others hankered after clean linen as well as clean skins, so they proceeded to do the laundry. 'As this was the first appearance of any of us in the character of a *blanchisseur*, we all acquitted ourselves badly, but I worst of all.' Grattan was not being over-modest: he lost his shirt in a tiny whirlpool![28]

While at Deleytosa in 1809, the 7th Fusiliers used to go down to a river, pull off their shirts and wash them with or without soap, banging them on flat stones at the water's edge as they had seen the Spanish women do. Then they would hang the shirts on bushes or rocks, pick off any lice, and, when dry, put them on again.[29] A year later, whenever British infantrymen garrisoning in Cadiz had clothes to wash, they had to go outside the city walls to nearby cisterns. 'It was here,' Sergeant Donaldson recalled, 'I first learned to wash my own clothes. I was awkward enough when I began, but practice soon made me expert at it.'[30]

During the army's great advance across the Ebro in 1813 the soldiers used, if possible, to spend a short time after dinner washing themselves and their linen before enjoying a pipe and a cup of grog as a nightcap.[31] And when the 34th Regiment of Foot camped in the beautiful valley of Bastan to rest after two months on the move and in action, 'the men wanted washing, and shaving, and patching, and darning, scrubbing up, and a bit of polish for the next fight'.[32]

The state of uniforms was not improved by the fact that in war few concessions were made to the extremes of climate. However, there is evidence that in July 1811 the light infantry and riflemen marched across Portugal 'with their brawny necks loosened from their stocks'; and during the summer heat of 1812 it was the fashion, in the Light Division at least, to wear the jacket open.[33] For the storming of Badajoz earlier that year the 71st were allowed to discard their high leather stocks and knapsacks, and to have shirts open at the neck and trousers rolled up above the knees. Nearly every face, blackened by exposure, was covered by an unkempt growth of beard.[34]

Captain Landmann of the Engineers recalled how one day when the army was advancing across Portugal in August 1808 the dust penetrated thickly into everyone's clothes and became fixed there by the heavy dews and misty rains. Major-General Fane and he were riding side by side. Henry Fane placed his arm beside Landmann's and observed that there was scarcely any difference between the colour of his red coat and the Captain's, which was blue.[35]

That was early in the Peninsular War. By the time a regiment had campaigned for three, four, even five years, the red had turned almost to black – 'as ragged as sheep and as black as rooks' is one admirable description.[36] By the close of 1813, when the army crossed the Pyrenees into south-western France, the state of their uniforms was very poor indeed, but the opening of harbours along the north coast of Spain, such as Bilbao and Pasajes, and of St Jean de Luz, which were all much closer to England than Lisbon had been, enabled the remedy to be provided more quickly.

During the opening weeks of 1814 Wellington sent regiments in relays to be fitted with new uniforms. It was high time too. Dragoons were issued with good strong grey overalls. The 91st Argyllshires, to cite one example, purchased 705 soldier's red jackets, 56 sergeant's and drummer's jackets, and 727 black leather stocks. Some infantrymen, though issued with new clothing, had to carry it northwards on top of their knapsacks for several weeks until the garments could be altered or made up.[37]

The sartorial pay-off to all this shabbiness came in Paris after the Waterloo campaign when the British Army was reviewed by the Tsar, the Emperor of Austria and the King of Prussia. The troops paraded in the same clothes in which they had marched, slept and fought for weeks on end. Captain Mercer was present and described the uniforms:

'The colour had faded to a dusky brick-dust hue; their coats, originally not very smartly made, had acquired by constant wearing that loose easy set so characteristic of old clothes, comfortable to the wearer, but not calculated to add grace to his appearance. *Par surcroît de laideur*, their cap is perhaps the meanest ugliest thing ever invented. From all these causes it arose that our infantry appeared to the utmost disadvantage – dirty, shabby, mean, and very small.'[38]

There wrote a horse gunner, but his criticisms are confirmed by a Frenchman who, as a student, watched Wellington's Waterloo army march down the Champs-Elysées. He had already seen the fine, well turned out soldiers of Russia and Prussia, the hussars from Brandenburg and Silesia, and many another imposing martial figure. And now! 'Oh! it was really like being defeated twice over, *bis mori*, to have been beaten by an army as badly turned out as the English army was. . . . How could one be a good soldier under that little sugar-loaf of a peak, with the inelegantly cut red jacket, those grey trousers clinging to knock-knees?' That was humiliating and quite intolerable to many of the French.[39]

Chapter 6

BIVOUAC LIFE

'I make no apologies for the dirt of this note; for flead, bugged, centipeded, beetled, lizarded and earwigged, cleanliness is known to me only by name. Moreover a furze-bush makes a bad table for writing on, and a worse chair, when breeches are nearly worn out with glory, oh! oh!'[1]
Charles Napier to his mother, 21 March 1811

'Hungry, wet and cold, and without any covering, we lay down by the side of the river. I put one hand in my pocket and the other in my bosom, and lay shivering and thinking of the glorious life of a soldier until I fell fast asleep.'[2]
Lieutenant George Simmons, 1 July 1809

Ensign George Bell of the 34th Foot spent his first Peninsular campaigning days in a rainswept October. He had an old boat cloak and a blanket for his bed and bedding, he never undressed, he was never thoroughly dry, he had to live out on the sod in all weather, 'like any other wild beasts, and always up and armed ready for anything one hour before daylight, and never dismissed until we could see a white horse a mile distant'. When asked, as a 'Johnny Raw' officer, how he had slept after one very wet night, he answered: 'Slept like a fish. I believe they sleep best in water!' 'Bravo! You'll do,' came the reply, and young Bell was accepted by his fellows in the regiment.[3]

He and everyone else in the army needed such humour and resilience right through to the end of the war, because in the summer months heavy dew wetted them nearly as much as a shower of rain, and a 'Portuguese storm' in September could last for eight hours.[4] William Swabey relates how, when the 'turn-out' sounded after such a night, he was half drowned in getting his troop of horse artillery harnessed. 'The few men who had pulled off their boots and set them upright were fair subjects for laughter, except that it was too serious a matter for joking, for when they tried to pull them on in the dark, they were astonished to find them full of water.' A soldier made such a mistake only once.[5]

Time and again the officers and rank and file had no option but to lie out under the stars or clouds with no covering but a blanket, and sometimes with nothing at all.[6] On one Pyrenees mountainside soldiers of the 40th did their best with grass, sticks and stubble to build a kind of wall to keep off a little of the wind and beating rain.[7] Frequently after a long march in wet weather men had to bivouac before their camp equipage came up on mules, or else they waited sitting ankle-deep in mud so long that they sought sleep only after copious use of grog and cigars.[8] One night in France it was so cold and frosty that William Surtees of the Rifle Corps found his cloak frozen to the ground when he tried to rise next morning.[9] When, after crossing the Nivelle, the Black Watch bivouacked in a field, Sergeant James Anton and his wife Mary had to lie down for the first time with nothing but a blanket between themselves and the sky.[10]

We find soldiers bivouacked in vineyards outside Orthez and in a turnip field near Biarritz, under cork trees beside the river Jerte and chestnut trees by the Coa. One day a battalion of the Guards sheltered under the widely-spreading chestnut branches during a torrential autumn downpour, on another six officers and their servants found ample accommodation in the hollow trunk of one such tree, which made an excellent dining-room.[11] In fact, in summer time a good tree with foliage thick enough to afford shelter from sun and rain was so coveted that on halting for the night the officers chose their trees by seniority. Mules and horses could be tethered to tree trunks and baggage unloaded there also.[12]

Many descriptions exist of routine life in bivouac and of the scenes a visitor might have witnessed there. The camp would be marked out, if possible on the edge of a wood and close to a stream or river, and the troops halted. Once their arms had been piled and the necessary pickets and guards paraded and posted, the soldiers would go about their several tasks: some fetched large stones to form fireplaces, others walked off with kettles and canteens to fetch water, while the wood resounded to the chopping of branches and boughs. Horses were being watered, articles of baggage carried across the bivouac, and muleteers were singing the long nasal notes of their hymn to the Virgin Mary. In one camp bullocks were slaughtered and the meat rations distributed; in a cavalry regiment's bivouac detachments would ride in with bundles of forage, while at a divisional Headquarters aides-de-camp, staff officers and orderlies dashed to and fro.[13]

Moyle Sherer described what his brother officers in the 34th regiment might be doing at such a time: fetching bread from a nearby village, or milk from a flock of goats grazing within view, or building shelters.[14] Here is part of one officer's portrait of an encampment in a magnificent chestnut grove during June 1811:

'A few boughs hastily piled together in part screen the simple toilet of an officer, who is preparing to enjoy his rice broth, as we may gather from the preparations his servant has made, by covering the canteen with a napkin, which seems intended to be occupied as a dinner-table by two performers. . . . In the distance of this part of the scene, a Portuguese boy, with shining face, is seen blowing the fire and stirring the pot. The officer's servant is actively employed in waiting on his master, as well as attending to the horses and holding Antonio in surveillance, lest on the one hand he allow the pot to go out, or on the other, the bishop to put his foot in the pot which contains the mess of four or five hungry men.'[15]

Various methods of combating the weather, be it good or bad, were devised by those without tents. Portuguese soldiers were issued with large blankets which, for convenience, had loops at each end and at the corners, one such blanket serving for three men who would, by means of upright sticks, made a 'tent', while the other two blankets were used to sleep in. Some Portuguese gave up their bedding and with two blankets and two muskets made a very good 'tent' for two. After the battle of Vitoria there was so much plunder that a good sack or piece of carpet could usually be added to shield the rough weather side.[16] Provided that nothing was allowed to touch the overhead blanket, it would deflect a good deal of rain, but if anyone disobeyed this rule, then the water soon came seeping through. The Portuguese derived sufficient benefit from this method for Wellington to order commanding officers to have the corners and outside selvage of the blankets strengthened in order that the soldiers might pitch them without injury to the blanket,[17] not only against rain but 'in case it should be necessary to shelter them from the sun'.[18]

One night during the retreat from Burgos, the 71st piled arms near the Agueda and began to cut wood to lay under themselves in the hope that the rain would run underneath. 'We might as well have lain in the river,' remarked Thomas Pococke. 'Next morning blankets had to be wrung out and shoes emptied of water. Each man was trembling like a leaf.'[19]

Greater success attended the efforts of an eccentric subaltern of the 32nd Foot who, when the battalion took up ground for the night, 'used to stretch himself at full length on the grass, and direct his servant, a Kerry mountaineer, to proceed forthwith to thatch him; this was done by first bending twigs over him, so as to leave him just sufficient room to roll from one side to the other, and then covering the arch thickly with straw or sedge'. In this ingenious way the officer kept dry and warm while his companions lay cold, wet and comfortless.[20]

The actual 'beds' on which men lay were made in many different ways, as experience grew and hints and tips circulated. Sergeant Cooper tells how men of the 7th Fusiliers, having to fight the Talavera campaign without blankets, inverted their greatcoats, thrust their legs into the sleeves, tucked one half of the coat under them, and the other half over, knapsacks doing service as pillows, and forage caps being pulled down over the ears.[21]

Lieutenant Leslie of the 29th Foot made up his bivouac bed from a sedge mat about the size of a hearthrug, on which he slept like a top, wrapped in a large cloak and with a leather nightcap. Soon afterwards he recommended a waterproof bag palliasse to hold straw and form a bed, two blankets, one pillow, one waterproof nightcap, plus a large, well lined camlet cloak – light to carry and quickly dried after rain.[22]

Experience in Canada had taught George Landmann that the tops of pine or spruce trees could make a very comfortable bed if laid out evenly on the ground to a depth of six or eight inches above the damp earth and if the delicate tips covered the stems or stiff wood parts. Another night he lay down on a deep layer of dried Indian corn leaves.[23] Many campaigners learnt to construct little field bedsteads of branches, raised some nine inches above the sodden ground and covered with straw, grass or bracken, or with rushes cut on the banks of a nearby stream. Then, exhausted by marching or fighting, they slept 'as comfortably as we ever did on the best down bed in England'.[24]

On the battlefield of Vitoria George Bell picked up a large 'royal sack' from King Joseph's abandoned baggage, filled it with ferns, dried grass and chopped straw, and slept very well. Blakiston had a bearskin mattress stuffed with fern.[25] Some officers stitched two blankets together into a sleeping bag, crawled inside, and slept well with a good sod and a smooth stone for a pillow, and if possible a soft underlayer of fragrant wild lavender. More primitive and less comfortable was the bed of one blanket taken from under the horse's saddle and spread on the ground whenever the regiment halted for the night.[26]

A few officers like Captain Henry Goldfinch of the Engineers enjoyed the luxury in hot weather of a 'portable bed with mosquito net', and others, in the days before groundsheets, used what they called the Barrosa bed. Ross-Lewin of the 32nd Foot, who had fought in the battle of Barrosa outside Cadiz, described the bed as consisting of 'a case, made of tarred canvas, and lined with ticken, which, when filled with straw, may be laid on the wet grass without any danger that the damp will penetrate, and when empty it may be rolled up into a very small compass'.[27]

What is presumed to be Wellington's campaign bed was in two parts: a brass-framed chair having leather straps and horsehair arms covered in canvas. To the front of the seat could be hooked the bed section which had legs at the foot and half way back. The canvas was attached to the brass sides and joined by a cord threaded criss-cross through eyes down the centre. The chair could be dismantled and the bed part folded in half. On top were laid several internally sprung horsehair cushions, measuring thirty by twenty-four inches and covered in off-white hessian with a blue and white patterned loose cover. Another of Wellington's camp beds had a heavy iron frame, originally lacquered in black, the canvas being strung together by ropes.

Some regiments now and then had the benefit of tents during the first years of the war. When a number of men of the Royal Artillery working at the high fortress of Almeida in 1809 were ordered by the Governor to camp on the glacis because there were not enough huts, tents had to be loaned from the arsenal.[28] The

Light Division was also supplied with small Portuguese tents outside Badajoz in 1812; one battalion which had tents that summer used to strike camp by starlight at one o'clock in the morning, march through the cool night hours, and pitch the tents again shortly after sunrise.[29]

Quite apart from certain regiments being issued with tents, a number of individual officers managed to live intermittently under canvas throughout the first half of the Peninsular War. Their journals and letters refer to tent pickets and mallets, to poles and tarpaulin sheets, to marquees and, more often, to bell-tents. Landmann, as chief engineer, obtained one of these for his sole use after the battle of Vimeiro. In certain infantry battalions the company officers shared such a tent between three or four during the spring of 1809; and a young officer of dragoons is on record as halting one day to choose a set of poles for his tent, and then cutting them with the help of two peasants.[30]

Finally, before the campaign of 1813 began, tents were made a general issue for all British and German infantry regiments. By an order dated 1st March, officers were to draw tents on the following scale: one for each field officer, one for the company officers, one each for the adjutant, the quartermaster, the medical staff, and the paymaster. For the N.C.O.s and men three tents, with poles and iron collars, two mallets and forty pins per tent, would be issued to each company, and although it was realized that this number would be insufficient in a regiment which was up to strength, the A.Q.M.G. of each division was empowered to allot extra tents as he saw fit in order to ensure that every man was covered.[31] Even so, twenty soldiers slept to one bell-tent; and this meant, according to Sergeant Cooper, that when they had all lain down, 'none could turn without general consent, and the word "turn" given'.[32] By contrast the cavalry and the Portuguese troops had no tents for this campaign. The former, at least, were philosophical about the lack, consoling themselves with the prospect of getting into villages more frequently than the infantry ever would.

In sceptical mood George Woodberry of the 18th Light Dragoons took extra precautions, buying sixteen yards of thick material and various fittings in order to have a tent made. It cost him twenty dollars. Several officers came to admire it, and one of them offered Woodberry sixteen dollars, but he refused to sell at a loss.

Anyway, he was vain enough to believe that he had the best tent in the regiment.[33]

These bell-tents were conveyed on special mules, which hitherto had carried the heavy iron camp-kettles and now, under charge of an officer, immediately followed the regimental column on the march, preceding all other baggage. On arrival at the night's bivouac, tents were to be pitched in column on the alignment given to each battalion, brigade and division, and as much as possible out of the enemy's sight. The men took turns to carry on top of their knapsacks the lighter tin camp-kettle, and in order to relieve them of part of the weight they would otherwise carry, they were ordered late in April to leave behind their greatcoats.[34]

Despite the unquestioned benefits derived from this new policy in rain and snow, especially on exposed ridges in the Pyrenees, the tents were anything but stormproof. Most of them had come out from England at the start of the year, having been a long time in store, so that the tent-cloth had frequently rotted. All too often mountain gusts and drenching rain tore the wooden pegs out of the mud and left the soldiers to flounder in horrible, enveloping wet folds of canvas.[35]

Sometimes the tents were blown away like balloons from over the sleeping soldiers, guy-ropes snapped, or a pole was forced up through the rotten tent cap. Down about their ears came the dripping canvas. Victims of this abrupt discomfort had to leave their warm blankets, snatch a mallet, and rush naked into the storm to pitch and peg the tent again. The military discovered, not for the last time, that canvas when once sodden allowed water to pass through it like a sieve. They could easily find several inches of water inside the tent, or a stream coursing through as an overflow of the trench dug round the outside. Muskets, belts, pouches, hats and all other kit were in wretched confusion. Ammunition might be rendered useless, and everything wore a dismal, drowned appearance. One night on the heights of Maya few out of fifty tents in one position were left standing at daybreak. During the October snows one or two regiments had frequently to be dug out of their tents of a morning by the pioneers.[36]

There was really nothing to do except grin and bear it. Some laughed, others swore. The 34th officers certainly laughed, if Bell's testimony is to be relied on: battalion wags nicknamed the

Colonel's marquee 'the church', and the rest of the tents 'the town'. One day 'a hurricane floored every house in the town, church and all'.[37] 'Nothing,' observed Lieutenant Gurwood, 'but the passing joke of "Boat ahoy!" or the roars of laughter caused by some wag, who turns this acme of misery into mirth, could re-animate them to the exertion of scrambling out of these clammy winding-sheets.'[38] To take the weather too seriously was not approved of, and provoked teasing or blatant mockery, to judge by Alexander, Lord Saltoun's comment to his fiancée: 'We have famous fun with the gentlemen amateurs from England with their water-proof coats and ultra pelisses, which they find of very little use here, and they must be content, as we are, to get wet with philosophy, and dry as soon as they can'.[39]

It was often hard, nevertheless, to crack a joke or see a shred of humour. The 42nd in bivouac on the heights by Roncesvalles felt more like weeping when snow fell and hailstones as large as nuts came thudding down. They had to shield their heads with knap-sacks, while the poor mules, without such protection, ran crying to and fro, stung by the stones. 'Often, for whole days and nights, we could not get a tent to stand,' wrote Sergeant Anton; 'many of us were frostbitten, and others were found dead at their posts. . . . Frequently have I been awakened, through the night, by the sobs of those around me in the tent, more especially by the young soldiers, who had not been long from their mothers' fire-sides. They often spent the darkness of the night in tears.'[40]

Private William Brown of the 45th relates how after the battle of Orthez the men were so weary that they either could not or would not pitch their tents, and simply threw themselves on the ground. The officers, anxious for their soldiers' welfare, ordered them to put up the tents. They obeyed most reluctantly, and few actually went inside, despite a keen frost, preferring to sit or lie round bivouac fires.[41] Indeed, this was often the only way to keep cheerful and warm in bivouac. Sometimes officers and men could be seen toasting their toes round a cheerful blaze while waiting for the camp-kettle to boil or the beef to fry.[42] Those fortunate enough to have a tent might well contrive to enjoy a wet evening with mulled wine round a kettle-lid filled with hot ashes by way of a fire, on the style of the charcoal footwarmers. But the rank and file, with their forage caps pulled down over their ears, huddled

94

together under banks and walls, or else crowded round cheerless smoky fires, 'cursing their commissaries, the rain, and the French'.[43]

Sherer describes how one day the 34th, marching with the army's rearguard, did not reach their bivouac until after nightfall. They saw numerous camp fires which had mostly been made in hollow cork trees – 'the red fires in their fantastic cavities, and the bright and consuming flames issuing from their tops, lighting up the pale branches, causing a red atmosphere above, and showing to great advantage the troops, their arms, and horses'.[44] When Ensign Stepney, a newcomer to the Peninsula in 1810, saw the 1st Division, to which he belonged, in camp near Busaco, he noted specially 'the glare from the bivouac fires glancing on the arms, accoutrement, and hard visages of the men, the dark olive foliage overhanging this picture of apparent confusion'. The Division were encamped along the side of a crescent-shaped hill; and on this particularly dark night the regular lines of fires formed a most beautiful sight, like an amphitheatre.[45]

This was all very picturesque and pleasant. But up in the passes of the Sierra de Gata, south of Ciudad Rodrigo, infantry pickets would dig a large hole in the snow, light a fire of furze and dry bracken in the centre, and sit round the fire to keep warm, or to dry themselves if, while collecting fuel, they had inadvertently sunk to their armpits in a hole just when they thought the snow was firm. Sometimes, fortified by brandy and tobacco – 'articles as necessary to a winter's campaign as powder and ball' – the soldiers would lie round a large fire, their feet to the flames, while one man kept watch to feed the fire and to prevent anyone's toes from being burnt. This is how the Portuguese Caçadores managed when near the river Nive with nothing but cloaks and blankets to cover them.[46]

The Black Watch had to do much the same on the Bayonne road when, their tents not having arrived from the rear, the soldiers were obliged to bivouac in the wet clothes in which they had forded a river, 'with nothing but the sky for a great-coat'. And the same battalion, ordered to camp in a newly ploughed field which had been transformed into a mire by violent rain, still succeeded in getting a hundred or so fires blazing alongside the fences bordering the field. Some officers of the 82nd even lit a fire inside their tent, and then escaped the smoke by lying flat on the ground.[47]

One of the most disagreeable nights ever endured by Wellington's

95

army was that spent on the Mont St Jean ridge just before the battle of Waterloo. It was all very well for veterans to remind each other and raw companions that a storm on the eve of a Wellington battle boded well for the morrow – they instanced Salamanca – but the night was no less wet and horrid for such expectations; to lie down was out of the question for most troops, to stand up all night was almost equally so, and to get a fire alight proved exceedingly difficult, the chances being that another downpour would dowse the reluctant flames. In the 73rd Regiment the rank and file could devise only one plan for the night: they gathered armfuls of the standing corn and, in the words of Sergeant Morris, 'rolling it together, made a sort of mat, on which we placed the knapsacks, and sitting on that, each man holding his blanket over his head to keep off the rain, which was almost needless, as we were so thoroughly drenched'.[48]

Each regiment found a solution or, at least, a means of survival. The mud was deep on all sides, so the 15th Light Dragoons, to quote one example, collected straw and branches and with these tried to lessen the mud and make rough shelters against the torrential rain. The dragoons could find neither food nor drinking water in the nearby villages. Only those who had any provisions were comparatively fortunate, like Dr William Gibney, the regimental surgeon, who had a thimbleful of brandy and a bit of tongue, which tasted rather queer but was undoubtedly welcome. Once he had made himself a drier place to lie on, he slept 'like a top'.[49]

The gunners of Captain Mercer's 'G' Troop Royal Horse Artillery stowed themselves under the gun-carriages and spread out the painted tarpaulin covers as additional shelter. The officers, finding the only nearby farm and outbuildings crammed with troops of every arm and allied nation, set up a small tent, crept inside, rolled themselves in wet blankets and huddled together for warmth, but very few achieved more than a fitful doze.

'I know not how my bedfellows got on [wrote Mercer], as we all lay for a long while perfectly still and silent – the old Peninsular hands disdaining to complain before their Johnny Newcome comrades, and these fearing to do so lest they should provoke some such remarks as "Lord have mercy on your poor tender carcass!

Plate 3. The Bishop's Palace at Pinhel. A side view of this massive building, now a school and police post, which housed the headquarters of Generals Graham and Picton at various times. (*Photo:* the Author)

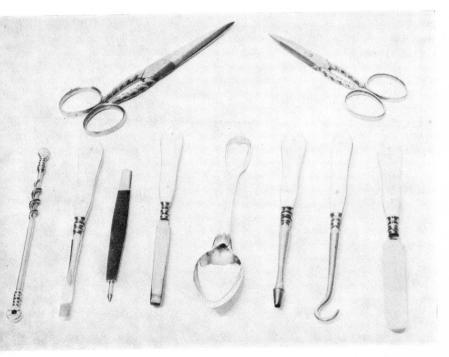

General Graham's toilet set, used after he had been elevated to the peerage in 1814 as Baron Lynedoch. (*Photo:* National Army Museum)

Plate 4. Top layer and case of Lord Lynedoch's toilet set. (*Photo:* National Army Museum)

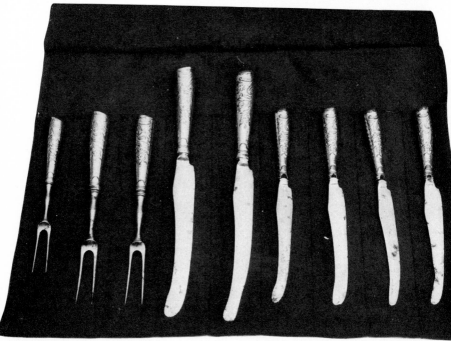

Sir John Moore's cutlery, made of Sheffield plate and used in the Peninsula. Moore left it to his old friend, Lt.-Col. Paul Anderson, who was present at his death.

what would such as you have done in the Pyrenees?" or "Oho, my boy! this is but child's play to what *we* saw in Spain." So all who did not sleep (I believe the majority) pretended to do so, and bore their suffering with admirable heroism.'[50]

On the night *after* the battle, Mercer pulled down the painted cover of a gun limber over the foot-board, in the manner of a tent roof, and crept under it. Though he found himself very cramped, he was far too excited by the events of the day to sleep.[51]

The principal reason for issuing tents had been to protect the health of the army. By the end of 1812 it had become abundantly plain that campaigning, and especially the arduous retreat from Burgos to Portugal, had caused the troops severe suffering and widespread sickness from exposure and bad weather. By the end of 1813 it was realized that many lives had been saved by the tents which, inadequate as they undoubtedly were, had preserved infantrymen in particular from cold, from unhealthy dews, and from drenching downpours.[52]

The summer of 1812, when much of the army had been marching and manoeuvring round Salamanca and Madrid, had been especially hot on the open plateau. Consequently the cavalry had been allotted the few trees available to shade their horses, while those infantry who had tents found it impossible to stay in their stifling, oven-like interior by day.[53] Major-General Wheatley, a newcomer to the Peninsula, thought himself fortunate to have procured a small round tent from his commissary. None-theless he felt provoked to write home to his brother: 'His Lord-ship certainly never spares the soldiers. A campaign under his order is no sinecure'.[54] Nor was it. Wellington, however, was not unaware of the rigours. He himself appears never to have slept out of his clothes for three years, and he always said: 'The worst house is better than the best tent'.[55]

Frances, Lady Shelley tells us how, after the war, the Duke of Wellington admitted to her that bivouacking had been bad for the troops, since it had prevented them from getting regular rest, and had got them into the habit of sleeping for an hour at a time or whenever they felt drowsy. 'Nothing,' said the Duke, 'wears out the troops so effectually.'[56] Though few constitutions could stand

D   97 indefinitely the extremes of heat and cold to which constant bivouacking subjected the troops, numerous officers recorded their astonishment at the manner in which the soldiers endured bivouac life with heavy dews at night, especially when their clothing was old and their covering restricted to a single blanket or a greatcoat. No doubt in the beginning wet clothes frightened them, but after being soaked through for weeks on end and sleeping in fields in winter, they discovered that good health could still be enjoyed, and they took pride in hardships cheerfully endured.[57] In November 1813, when most of the Light Division's tents were declared unserviceable from rents and other damage, the soldiers were still reported as healthy, to everyone's surprise, not least the doctors'. That same month Lieutenant James Hope noted that he had slept only thirteen nights under a roof out of the one hundred and eighty-one days the campaign had lasted.[58]

On many occasions an alternative to canvas was provided by huts. British troops several times had a chance to inspect hutted camps erected by their opponents, as when Wellington occupied Lisbon in 1808 after Junot's army had departed, and French huts were found to have been not only thatched but also constructed with corn in the ear, which shed grain on the ground. The French soldiers had built with branches an immense *salle de spectacle* and, reprehensibly enough, had cut down a number of the largest olive trees and, by sticking their pointed ends into the earth, had formed an avenue leading to this hall.[59] Near Talavera, after Marshal Victor had decamped in a hurry, the British found similar huts roofed with unthrashed wheat. Matting had been stripped from local churches and convents; the windows in most of the officers' huts had been glazed; and all in all it was the best camp the British had ever seen. When, two months earlier, the 29th Regiment occupied a French bivouac near Oliveira, many of the huts, arranged in regular streets, were adorned with evergreens, and in the grass had been cut such devices as *'Vive l'Empereur!'* and *'Vive la France!'* Every hut in this permanent camp had been well provided with tables, chairs and cooking utensils carried out from Portuguese houses in the town.[60]

To shelter their forward pickets in Sobral the French collected a number of immense pipes, or wine hogsheads, from nearby stores and by laying them on their sides and staving in one end, they made very comfortable quarters for half a dozen men. In addition they erected some matting huts and then tiled them.[61]

A fourth example comes from the river Nivelle district towards the end of the war, when the French had to give up defences which they had occupied for a long time. The huts, as usual, were extremely neat and comfortable. Many of them, we learn from George Bell, 'had their green blinds over their little lattice windows; their neat little fireplaces, bedsteads of green boughs, shelves for their prog, and arm-racks, so like the natty Frenchman in camp'.[62]

Wellington's army followed the French example, and whenever there were no billets and no tents but plenty of timber, the officers and men would, if time allowed, build rough and ready huts in which to sleep. To do this presupposed ordinary woods, because to cut any olive or other fruit trees was strictly forbidden, since they constituted the peasants' means of livelihood. When the 4th Dragoons bivouacked in a pine wood near Abrantes, the whole regiment was soon hutted, ten dragoons to a hut. Not far away men of an infantry battalion, the 53rd, constructed a pretty little town of fir huts.[63] Bill-hooks, hatchets, even swords came into action, hewing and hacking at every tree and bush within reach; and if at first the soldiers made awkward huts, they soon became skilled at this mode of building with branches, tree trunks and earth. Regular squads were formed for cutting branches, others for drawing them to the bivouac, and others again as architects for constructing the huts. 'This was an amusement more than a duty,' writes Gurwood, 'and it was quite wonderful to see how speedily every one was under cover. It was the pride of the company that the officers' hut should be the first and best built.' Some huts would hold a score of men, but this was exceptional, though the 40th did build spacious cook-houses.[64] These 'green retreats' could be less comfortable than they looked, for in wet weather heavy rain found easy entrance through the roof – rushes or straw resisted better than heather. During the full heat of summer huts, like tents, became little ovens soon after daybreak 'whence came forth for parade an almost *baked* battalion,' to quote Ensign Stepney of the Coldstream Guards. Not everyone agreed about the heat, and some considered huts to be cooler than tents.[65]

The precisest description of just how these huts were built comes from the pen of Charles Leslie:

'Two upright posts, about seven feet high, with forked ends, were planted in the ground about fifteen feet asunder. On these was placed a ridge-pole, or roof-tree, against which other poles were placed on each side in a slanting position, so as to form the frame of a roof. The whole was then covered with pine branches, or heath, broom, or straw. One end was closed up with poles placed nearly close together, and stuffed in the joints with grass or moss. The other end, which was left open for the entrance, had for a door a movable screen of wicker-work. Where we could find a tree, we always built the huts a little to the north-east of it, so as to have as much shade as possible.'[66]

Some of the most permanent British huts were built while the army was defending the Lines of Torres Vedras, but snags occurred. The Connaught Rangers were not alone in having to use heather for thatching because straw was unobtainable, and heather afforded a comparatively weak defence against heavy winter storms. Lieutenant William Grattan describes the scene inside his uncomfortable hut:

'At one end might be seen a couple of officers, with their cloaks thrown about them, snoring on a truss of straw, while over their heads hung their blankets, which served as a kind of inner wall, and for a time stopped the flood that deluged the parts of the hut not so defended. . . . In another corner lay some one else, who, for want of a better, substituted a sheet or an old tablecloth as a temporary defence; but this was even more disastrous than the blanket. . . . Others, more stout and convivial, sat up smoking cigars and brandy punch, while waiting for the signal to proceed to our alarm-post, a duty which the army performed every morning two hours before day.'[67]

In one Black Watch bivouac Sergeant Anton became a Robinson Crusoe and, whenever regimental duties allowed, built a hut thatched with broad ferns. Assisted by a few comrades who were rewarded with a small drop of spirits, which his wife Mary had carefully saved from the daily allowance, Anton worked hard for three days to make the hut waterproof. 'I dug an ample space within, three feet deep, and a trench around the outside, four feet deep; this was to carry off the water from the roof, and the latter

I secured more substantially than many of our Highland bothies are in the north of Scotland. . . .'

He improved the hut over the next two weeks and even built a fireplace under the roof, but as so often occurs in time of war, he and his wife had suddenly to quit their comfortable shelter when the 42nd received orders to move. Anton wrote afterwards: 'On leaving the camp that night, many of the married people set fire to their huts, but I left mine with too much regret to become its incendiary; and my poor Mary shed tears as she looked back upon it, as a bower of happiness which she was leaving behind.'[68]

The arrival of British troops several weeks after their victory at Waterloo made a strange alteration to the appearance of the Bois de Boulogne. Not content with tents, the soldiers had to have huts. In fact, the single men slept in tents, eighteen to a tent, with arms and accoutrements fastened round the centre pole. The married men built themselves a line of huts, parallel to the tents. Consequently the wood, thickly planted when the army first camped there, had so many of its trees cut down for the construction of huts that there was ample space for parade grounds. 'Such is the quantity of wood destroyed that we can see the river in our rear, altho at our first coming we could scarce enter the break.' That was written on 1st August. By mid-September the 51st Regiment for one had built a very large hut in which to receive company and had named it 'The British Hotel'.[69]

All bivouacs, whether men slept in tents, in huts or under the sky, were vulnerable to certain pests, and Wellington's army did not escape. Two of the plagues were insects and reptiles. Tortured all night by gnats and midges, a soldier would wake up to find his face swollen with bites. Mosquitoes near Plasencia stung so badly that officers' and mens' eyes swelled till they could not see out of them for hours on end. Scorpions and lizards frequented many a camp site. Turn up a flat stone and there lay a scorpion.[70] When the Hussars of the King's German Legion bivouacked in stifling heat among cork trees near the river Caia, men moved all the stones out of the way to make the place more comfortable for the horses, and in so doing they dislodged scores of angry scorpions, which troubled men and horses alike.[71] The scorpions appear to have been two inches long and an inch wide, with crab's claws, eight legs and a round tail, at the end of which was the dreaded sting.[72]

Near Oropesa in 1809 a soldier of the Buffs died from a scorpion bite in the head, but such fatalities were few. A certain officer, in putting on his shoe one morning, found that he had squeezed a scorpion to death in the toe of it.[73] The 82nd amused themselves by catching scorpions after one man had lost an eye from their sting and several other soldiers had been badly hurt. According to Captain George Wood the method was to turn up a large stone under which two scorpions usually nestled together. Then 'throwing a thread with a noose in it over them, and touching them at the same time with a straw, they would instantly dart long tails over their heads to sting; and by drawing the noose tight we caught them alive, and hung them on a tree as a punishment'.[74]

In June 1811 the 14th Light Dragoons bivouacked in an oak forest beside the Caia. The sunbaked ground was quickly pulverized by the trampling of men, horses and cattle. Soon the camp became so infested by ants that the soup could never be served up without numerous small bodies floating on the surface. Several men were bitten by snakes outside Talavera, but a fusilier named Barber marched four miles with a snake in his dress cap and came to no harm. The snake had apparently crept inside during the night. Snakes abounded in woods near Sabugal, and also at Monte Reguengo, where the 95th Rifles camped during July 1811.[75] They were particularly noticeable in a decayed tree full of holes, against which the officers of one rifle company built their straw hut. 'I have often seen fellows three feet long winding their way through the thatch,' wrote Kincaid, 'and voting themselves our companions at all times, but the only inconvenience we experienced was in a sort of feeling that we would rather have had the hut to ourselves.'[76]

Finally a more unusual plague: toads. Up in the Pyrenees at Santa Barbara in August 1813, officers of the 43rd Light Infantry discovered that if, because of heavy rain and mountain mist, they omitted for two or three days on end to remove or take out to dry their mattresses stuffed with fern, they were sure to uncover a few bloated, speckled toads as large in circumference 'as a small dessert plate'.[77]

Even if the soldiers were not bitten or stung or harassed by insects and reptiles, they were liable to be disturbed by a nocturnal concert of toads and frogs, which we are assured unkindly were

102

'by no means unlike Portuguese women in a market!'[78] Few soldiers who have ever camped out in countries round the Mediterranean and even farther afield will forget the chorus of frogs and crickets. After Waterloo, when British troops went into camp on the outskirts of Paris – close to the Seine at Neuilly, for example – they might well have expected freedom from insects, but not a bit of it. No scorpions, certainly, but black worms got between the sheets, and at night earwigs crawled up the tent poles and clustered there like a swarm of bees.[79]

However strong their dislike of insects, the officers and men were normally delighted to welcome human beings to their camps, especially female visitors, but on occasion they could be a mixed blessing if not a pest. Whenever regimental bivouacs remained near towns for more than a few days, the local inhabitants were likely to pay visits. Near Salamanca in June 1812 the Spaniards established a well-stocked market in the camp, and every afternoon people came out from the city in their thousands to enjoy themselves, singing and dancing until the military pipes, drums and bugles warned civilians and soldiers alike that it was time for bed.[80] A year later the Gordon Highlanders, serving in Sir Rowland Hill's 2nd Division, bivouacked less than a mile from Salamanca, and were visited by numbers of upper class citizens. Such was the ladies' curiosity that they would pull aside the tent doors without ceremony, in order to have a full view of *los Ingleses* – a disconcerting habit.

Near Segovia the ladies came to see over an artillery park – since to examine guns and limbers at close quarters was a new and gratifying experience for them. Several Portuguese families at Covilhã were equally thrilled to watch two guns fired and two fir trees cut down by the shot.[81]

The Portuguese were also prepared to set up a market in camp, once word had got around that the British army's discipline was strict and that the soldiers paid for everything. In this way the peasants from the district round Castelo Branco brought in a steady supply of bread, milk, eggs, poultry and excellent country wine.[82]

The army remained for more than four months in the Lines of Torres Vedras, and within a fortnight the people of Lisbon got over their alarm at having their defenders back close to the capital so thoroughly that ladies began to come by water to look at the French from vantage points like Alhandra.[83]

When part of the army was encamped near Cuellar in August 1812, after a long, 'fagging' march from Valladolid through pine woods and over sandy ground, many Spanish women came to see the camp. 'After some persuasion,' records Peter Le Mesurier, 'we made them dance on the Sand; but as we had no refreshment for them save some Adam's ale, they did not keep it up long, and went off well powdered from the Dust.'[84] Things went better ten months later near Palencia, for British troops had not traversed that part of Leon since Sir John Moore's time, so were welcomed with cheers, particularly at Medina de Rio Seco, where a large number of pretty girls came into camp, despite wet weather, and waltzed with officers of the Brunswick Oels Regiment.[85] Major-General Robinson had a different and even more memorable experience while at Montdragon in July 1813, because no British soldiers had passed that way before. Consequently the local people came in their hundreds and walked many miles out of sheer curiosity to see the regiments, whose camps aroused no less astonishment than admiration, the Spaniards being very taken with the good-humoured civility of officers and men alike. Robinson described the scene as follows:

'I dined with one of my Colonels in his tent, and we never had less than seven or eight women in it, besides ten times as many outside, admiring our dress and everything belonging to the dinner table, with more delight than ever a child did a pantomime at Christmas. . . . The Band was ordered to play for them, and in an instant their heads, hands and feet were actively employed – I never was more pleased than with the *tout ensemble*.'[86]

When the army lay outside Bordeaux for five or six weeks, the citizens made many excursions, especially on Sundays, to see the troops. Costermongers came daily to sell wine, spirits, bread, meat, fish and fruit. Sergeant William Lawrence of the 40th describes how 'every Sunday afternoon the bands of all the Regiments played, while the French amused themselves with dancing, many of them, both male and female, on stilts, which entertained us more than anything, and besides this there were all kinds of jollities in which our soldiers freely joined'.[87] Much the same occurred wherever the army went, so even when Wellington's men camped in the Bois de Boulogne during July 1815, the Parisians flocked out of the city. 'We are amused with thousands of visitors,' wrote Sergeant Wheeler. 'Some of the young lasses are truly the most engaging little devils I ever saw.' French traders set up in the camp a market which was 'overglutted with everything the heart can desire'.[88]

Of course the troops, after several months of bivouac life, longed to be back in a good billet, especially a winter cantonment, because they enjoyed the luxury, inconceivable to those who have not experienced it, of undressing after wearing their clothes for days, sometimes weeks, on end. Indeed, William Hay of the 52nd Light Infantry never had his clothes off his back or his shoes off his feet on any night during the winter of 1810–11 while the Light Division was defending the Lines of Torres Vedras. Even Wellington himself admitted to his friend Samuel Rogers: 'I undressed very seldom, never in the first four years'. The troops relished, too, a sense of absolute enjoyment after pulling off their boots, while to sleep on a bed with sheets and pillows was a pleasure which some had almost forgotten.[89]

Paradoxically, too, the officers and men got so accustomed to the hardships of bivouac life that they were initially disconcerted by the comparative comforts of a billet. Indeed, many of them considered a camp more agreeable than a Portuguese hovel. And it was possible for a level-headed, well-informed observer such as Frazer to write quite seriously to his wife soon after reaching St Jean de Luz: 'The troops have not yet been long enough in cantonments to feel the inconvenience of being comfortable. How strange this sounds! Yet the thing is very true.'[90]

It could happen that the occasional transition from primitive conditions to comfort proved to be too abrupt. Sergeant Lawrence relates how he and a private of the 40th, billeted in a gentleman's house near Bordeaux, retired to rest in a fine feather bed which, being a luxury they had not experienced for many years, was too soft for their bones, and they could not sleep. The soldier soon jumped out of bed, exclaiming: 'I'll be bothered, sergeant. I can't sleep here.' 'No,' said Lawrence, 'no more can I.' So they prepared their usual bed by wrapping themselves in a blanket, lying on the

105

floor, and placing a knapsack as pillow. Both men slept soundly, but had to do some explaining next morning when the landlord asked if there were fleas in the bed![91] At Cartaxo in December 1810 Stepney of the Coldstream Guards was able, after sleeping for three months in his clothes, to undress and go to bed in a billet. 'I shall never forget,' he records, 'the comfortless feeling experienced in confiding my person, for the first time, to a pair of cold stark naked sheets. I could not sleep a wink.'[92] As for Captain Jonathan Leach of the 95th, when he and a brother officer went on leave to Lisbon and stayed in Latour's Hotel, he found that, after exactly a year of outpost duty, sleeping in clothes in a bivouac or in some hovel of a picket house, he felt like a fish out of water. 'When I got into a regular-built bed, I could no more sleep than I could have taken wing and flown across the Tagus.'[93]

Chapter 7

RATIONS

'When a man entered a soldier's life, he should have parted with half his stomach.'[1]
Sergeant J. S. Cooper, 7th Royal Fusiliers

'Supplies, the mainspring of happiness in a soldier's life, plentiful.'[2]
Major Harry Smith, June 1813

'The Rations now arriv'd, each took his share,
And eagerly devour'd the scanty Fare;
And scanty Fare it was, consisting chief
Of flinty Biscuit, tough and stinking Beef. . . .'[3]
The Military Adventures of Johnny Newcome

The soldier's daily ration varied from time to time, depending upon the season, the distance of the army from its base, the local resources, and the amount of transport available in terms of bullock carts and mules. However, the usual daily issue was supposed to be 1 lb. of meat, $1\frac{1}{2}$ lb. of bread or 1 lb. of ship's biscuit, and either $\frac{1}{3}$ pint of rum or a pint of wine. Officers, other ranks and drivers received the same rations, and they were scarcely adequate unless supplemented by fair means or foul.[4]

The meat was fresh or salt, according to what the commissaries could procure. Because the bullocks for slaughtering were tired, feeble and reduced to skin and bone after long marches, meat on the hoof was often tough and lean like boiled leather, and, in Sergeant Anton's opinion, it would not have been allowed a stall in the poorest market in Britain. Lieutenant Robert Knowles of the Royal Fusiliers wrote to his father: 'The meat we have is so poor that it would be burnt if exposed for sale in Bolton Market.' 'It was,' says Ross-Lewin, 'rendered doubly unwholesome by overdriving, which caused the poor animal to enter the camp in a burning fever. I have often seen the Portuguese drivers hold a

107

little corn in their hands near the mouths of the wearied and famished beasts to coax them a few paces further. As soon as the skin was whipped off, the meat was served out.'[5]

However lean and stringy the beef, it usually arrived on time, but the bread ration was quite another matter, and over and over again the troops went short. Moreover, when it did come, the bread was sometimes uneatable. Three examples will suffice: in July 1809, when rations reached the 7th King's German Legion, the bread on the carts was covered in dust and looked as hard as stone;[6] after going without bread for more than a fortnight while pursuing the French from the Lines of Torres Vedras, the Gordon Highlanders were eventually overtaken by the bread they should have received on the march but as it had been newly baked when packed for dispatch, it was now unfit for use; having fought at El Bodon the 45th Foot found its bread allowance cut from 16 ozs. to 8, and that was mouldy biscuit.[7] Wellington himself had become aware of this sort of thing after Talavera, and had written: 'The soldiers seldom get enough to *eat*, and what they do get is delivered to them half mouldy, and at hours at which they ought to be at rest'.

Various alternatives to ration bread were tried. Occasionally a little flour would be issued, much of it conveyed by ship from America to Lisbon until the war of 1812. One day at Puente del Arzobispo in August 1809 the commissaries had no bread to give out, so the 7th Fusiliers were marched into a newly reaped field of wheat, and each man was allowed to carry away a sheaf; but this was of little use because they had no means of grinding it.[8] However, when a handful of Indian corn was issued to each man during the retreat from Burgos, they all began pounding it between large stones, 'which strange hand mills they passed from one to the other, keeping up such a noise throughout the whole night, that no one in camp could possibly have closed his eyes'.[9]

More than once after a battle bread was taken from the knapsacks of French soldiers who had been killed in the action.[10] Several writers describe how one day a divisional commander rode up to the colonel of the 95th who had halted beside a corn field and said: 'The men had better carry some of the wheat, as there is no prospect of any provisions'. So the riflemen stuck sheaves on their bayonets and when they camped for the night did their best to cook it. First they cut off the heads, put them into their haversacks and thrashed them with a ramrod, before winnowing with their breath. No water could be found anywhere near, nor could any salt be purchased. However they managed to boil some of the grains, but next morning not a few men had such swollen stomachs that they were unable to march.[11]

One sergeant who carried a wheatsheaf for many miles on top of his knapsack rubbed the ears between the palms of his hands whenever he had the chance, and ate the extracted grains with rapture. At night he used to spread his greatcoat on the ground, lay out a little more of the grain on top, and then thrash it. Such was the pressure of famine that officers and men tried to outbid each other for a goat's offal, sold at double the normal price for an entire goat.[12] When several herds of swine were encountered, feeding in the woods, many of the soldiers ran among them, shooting, stabbing and, like men possessed, cutting off the flesh while the pigs were still alive.[13] Much the same occurred during the November retreat of 1812.

Now and then bread could be purchased from Spaniards at a shilling a pound, and as high a price as seven shillings and sixpence had to be paid for a three-pound loaf. That was in the summer of 1811. Two years later, near the Pyrenees, Spanish peasants brought a few loaves into camp and sold them at two shillings and sixpence the pound, yet even at this price, regarded as enormous by the troops, the loaves were eagerly bought.[14]

The summer campaign of 1813 again saw the advancing army frequently short of bread, and the situation would have been worse but for the fortunate discovery by batmen from one regiment of several bags of meal while passing through a wood; a waggon load of flour captured from the French when the 53rd Foot had received only a pound and a half of bread in eight days; the presence on the soldiers' route of several water mills, which gave a chance of grinding corn to flour at a time when they had, just before fighting the battle of Vitoria, neither the time nor inclination properly to boil wheat or rye.[15]

On several days in June 1813, just before and after this battle, rations, and in particular bread, were so short that when troops marched past a field of beans they were quite capable of breaking ranks, dashing into the field, and pulling up armfuls of beans by the roots before resuming their march.[16] Bean fields were numerous in that part of Spain, but the beans were barely half grown, though the men were not deterred from boiling the leaves and tender tops and then devouring them. The 45th Foot for one had little else to eat for five days before the battle, and several officers confirm that had it not been for the impromptu picking of horse-beans, the battalion could not have withstood the protracted fatigue.[17]

Ration biscuits were particularly bad during the early months of 1811, yet even here the soldiers were inconsistent, even perverse, in their attitudes. Thus on 17th February a large quantity of biscuit was condemned and thrown into the streets, only to be picked up greedily by the troops who 'would throw away as a Ration what they seemed so anxious to possess as *condemned* food'.[18] A more usual response was voiced by Charles Napier when he wrote in April to his mother: 'We are on biscuits full of maggots, and though not a bad soldier, hang me if I can relish maggots'.[19]

Biscuits appear to have arrived in one of three states: hard, jaw-breaking and alive with maggots, as Napier indicates forcibly enough, or crushed to crumbs and mouldered to dust, or sometimes good but old. One day in November 1813 each man in the 43rd Light Infantry secured a biscuit of American make: nearly an inch thick, they were so hard as to require the stamp of an iron heel or some such hammer to break them. These American biscuits were even thick enough to save a man's life. During the march to La Petite Rhune a fortnight before Christmas 1813 the officers of that regiment ate some for breakfast at two o'clock in the morning, when Lieutenant Wyndham Madden remarked that their thickness would turn a bullet aside, at the same time stuffing one into the breast of his jacket. 'Never was prediction more completely verified,' wrote a brother subaltern, 'for early in the day the biscuit was shattered to pieces, turning the direction of the bullet from as gallant and true a heart as ever beat under a British uniform.'[20]

In all this much depended upon the commissaries. Though verdicts differ on their zeal and competence, though some were found wanting and a few proved to be dishonest, indulging in irregular if not fraudulent practices, they were mostly sound men who learnt from experience and from being chivvied by commanding officers. Only at three periods of the war did they really lose control of a situation which by the nature of things was precarious enough: in the weeks after Talavera, when Spanish promises of help were not fulfilled; during the army's pursuit of the French from the Lines of Torres Vedras in March 1811; and on the retreat from Burgos to Ciudad Rodrigo eighteen months later. Just before that retreat Captain George Bowles of the Coldstream Guards declared: 'We have never for a day failed in a regular supply since the commencement of the campaign, which considering the rapidity of some of our movements, is paying no small compliment to our commissariat.'[21] And Sergeant Wheeler, looking back in 1816 when the wars were over, set down a similar tribute: 'It is true we were sometimes badly off for biscuit, but taking everything into consideration no army could be supplied better. Indeed it is a mystery to thousands how we were supplied so regular as we were.'[22]

In a short work entitled *On Commissariat Service* Sir John Bissett, who was Wellington's Commissary-General for part of the war, explained that when Sir John Moore's army first entered Spain and so much criticism was levelled against the inefficiency of the British Commissariat,

'Arrangements had not yet been made in respect of the discipline of the Department, and the appointments to it, with a view to furnishing a set of officers trained in some measure to the duties to be required of them; such training could not be the work of a day; also, prior to this, many gentlemen got commissions in the higher ranks of the Commissariat, who had not passed through the lower gradations, or acquired any of the practice, which a regular probation would have produced. The numbers, too, were defective. . . .'[23]

Perhaps this statement accounts for Wellington writing that it was very necessary to attend to detail, 'and to trace a biscuit from Lisbon into a man's mouth on the frontier, and to provide for its removal from place to place, by land and by water, or no military operations can be carried on'.[24]

In good times and bad the soldiers lost no chance to supplement the rations with whatever came to hand on the roadside: geese,

111

turkeys and ducks near Segovia; country wine, lemons, and a leveret; cherries picked from orchards below the Pyrenees; or chestnuts taken from a wood near La Rhune and boiled to make a good substitute for potatoes.[25] Larpent records that near Tafalla at the end of June 1813 the officers of Wellington's headquarters bought cherries at about a penny a pound, as well as pears and plums, and that onions, beans, peas and lettuces were equally good and cheap. More than two years earlier, when the 48th were marching across the Zezere river prior to fighting at Busaco, the Portuguese brought out peaches, plums, grapes and wine, which they sold cheaply to the officers and generously gave away to the men for nothing.[26] During the 1812 retreat, and occasionally in the previous year, some regiments had to subsist for three or four days on acorns, but these were not like those they knew in England; they were nearly as good as the Spanish chestnuts when roasted.[27] In the following summer, after Vitoria, Bell and two other young officers of the 34th who 'chummed together' for messing often enjoyed large, ripe chestnuts, roast or boiled. 'They filled up chinks, and were a good standby, better than acorns.'[28]

Foraging for food was everyone's duty or pastime or need. In districts where the villages had been deserted by their inhabitants, not much was to be found, though troops would occasionally come on a little corn in sheaves, or a bullock or two fell into their hands on some foraging excursion.[29] During one march after dark near Santarem the 71st were thrown into confusion and quite a few soldiers knocked over by the sudden onrush of a herd of goats, but some of these were caught and they made a delicious supper that evening. Now and then fatigue parties would be sent off to search for maize and herbs for the pot. During the pursuit of Marshal Massena's army in March 1811, when Wellington's troops had outmarched their supplies, one soldier was fortunate enough to fill his haversack with Indian corn heads, which the soldiers nicknamed 'turkeys'. 'I was welcomed with joy,' he relates; 'we rubbed out some of our corn, and boiled it with a piece of beef; roasted some of our turkeys, and were happy.'[30]

Although many a soldier had no compunction about taking crops, vegetables or livestock when it was a case of 'forage or starve', not a few felt some remorse in so doing. Swabey, for instance, wrote in May 1812 that he was ashamed to show his face in Vila Franca,

112

because he and his companions found themselves obliged to press for bread, and this requisition fell heavily on the local population. But – and it was a sizeable 'but' – he could see plainly that 'if we do not adopt the plan of taking for the use of troops whatever we can get, we never can advance into Spain. War and charity are two things truly incompatible with each other.'[31]

Sometimes the troops could supplement their rations by accepting or paying for a local meal. For example, one February night in Sacavem a detachment of the 14th Light Dragoons found a shabby inn which produced an excellent dinner of boiled Tagus salmon, roast pork, salad, wine, porter and oranges.[32] Most of them found local dishes unpalatable except when very hungry, at which point garlic, 'so grateful to the Spanish appetite, but so uncongenial to the English stomach', became tolerable, even enjoyable.[33] When Augustus Frazer and several officers had an excellent dinner at a *posada* in Pamplona, the various courses, which included stewed partridges, woodcock, and roast meat, were dressed without oil or garlic, at the officers' earnest entreaty.[34]

Although a few British officers grew to tolerate a touch of garlic, Spanish cooking did not suit them. Captain James Hughes of the 18th Light Dragoons described it as 'oil, fowl, and molasses, and enough to kill one accustomed'.[35] A harsh verdict, maybe, yet Major Berkeley Paget had his breath taken away near Corunna in 1808 when 'a sausage as large as a line-of-battleship's mainyard, cram full of garlic, a dish of macaroni poisoned with saffron, and a salad mixed with lamp-oil' were placed on the dining table. As Paget was a guest, he felt obliged to eat it all out of politeness, and to lie through thick and thin by saying that he found it delightful.[36]

Often while in a village billet British soldiers watched their hosts prepare and eat the usual dish of *gaspacho*, made with garlic and pods of red pepper, pounded in a mortar. Oil, then vinegar, then water were added, and once this had been well mixed, bread was sliced in. 'This simple mixture,' observed Lieutenant Leslie near Cadiz, 'is the universal food of the peasantry, particularly during harvest.'[37]

British military cooking appears to have been basic and largely unskilled, a state of affairs caused partly by necessity and partly by sheer inexperience. One soup would have to be thickened with the crumbs and dust of ship's biscuit, in default of vegetables or rice; another soup was made of wine with eggs beaten into it, followed by fried steak and onions, and a glass of grog by the kitchen fire which had been lit in a convent vintage house.[38] Most old campaigners could brew tea, make dumplings and cook a sort of plum-pudding and thin flat flour-cakes or scones. In the 40th Regiment after Talavera the men cooked wheat by boiling it like rice, or sometimes they would crack the kernel between two flat stones and then boil it, making a kind of thick paste.[39]

If the troops had no bread, they experimented with several ways of cooking dumplings or doughboys. When Cooper of the 7th Fusiliers tried, the mixture would not stick together, so he put it into a camp-kettle in large lumps. 'When boiled, the dumplings looked like little frightened hedgehogs. To get a mouthful, I had to pick lots of prickles from the mess. The material turned out to be barley meal unsifted, and was meant for the French cavalry.'[40] Sergeant Lawrence of the 40th was more fortunate. When, after Vitoria, an Irishman brought a shirtful of flour into camp, Lawrence mixed a little salt and water with the flour and put the dumplings into a kettle swung over a fire, gipsy fashion, on two vertical sticks and a crossbar. Though lacking in fat or suet, the dumplings turned out hot and well cooked, and definitely passable in the soldiers' hungry state.[41]

Time and again the cooking of a meal was suddenly interrupted by war: the bugles would sound to arms, and barely warm food would be snatched off the fire and eaten raw later on; at Salamanca the 3rd Division was suddenly ordered to attack, so camp-kettles were overturned in an instant and packed on the mules, which started for the rear; other cooking was disturbed by the appearance of the French, or shelling, or a false alarm.[42]

Obtaining enough fuel for cooking fires always posed a problem in Spain, because large areas of campaigning country were so devoid of timber that some officers wondered how or where the Spaniards had ever got the wood used in building their convents and churches. On the field of Albuera the butts were knocked off thousands of discarded muskets and burnt on the camp fires all night. All too often houses left unoccupied on account of the war became the prey of soldiers who in desperation tore up floors, removed doors and windows, and even dismantled the roof, either to save themselves the trouble of cutting firewood after a long day's march or because there simply was no other wood in sight.[43] Occasionally, when the nights were excessively cold and hoar frost covered the ground every morning, the commissaries came to the rescue by purchasing some old, derelict houses, and serving out the beams and wood to regiments in need. Although the 51st, when manning pickets up in the Sierra de Gata above Ciudad Rodrigo during January 1812, had to burn furze and fern on their large camp fires, the 9th Foot in the Serra da Estrêla near Travanca in a previous winter found no shortage of firewood, especially pine, and three hundred soldiers at least were employed in fetching it. 'I sometimes think,' wrote Peter Le Mesurier, 'if a Portuguese Army was in England, how sour an English Farmer would look at a Party of this kind going out to cut down his trees. God grant we may never see that day.'[44]

At the close of 1812 the Sherwood Foresters, having discarded their hatchets during the retreat, had to tear off overhanging branches by brute force, but as everything was sodden wet no one knew how to get a fire alight until the men opened their knapsacks and contributed something that might serve in lieu of dry kindling wood. Thus Private Brown gave one shirt, three brushes, and a button-stick; forty such lots were consumed before their efforts at firelighting were crowned with success.[45] Normally when it came to lighting a fire, the soldiers used flint and steel and either tinder or gunpowder. In the case of some Scottish regiments a man would kneel to fan the flames with the apron of his kilt, which became known as 'the Highland man's bellows'.[46]

In summer time the troops often had to go through the tedious business of cooking their food with stubble or dry grass – near Salamanca or in districts like Pollos on the Douro where, even at the best of times, the inhabitants had only the prunings of their vines for fuel. When the army was outside Salamanca in June 1812 many of the local people spent all day long bringing wood and drinking water from city to bivouac, because no tree grew on the position and the little water there was fit only for boiling.[47]

At certain stages of the war even officers who gave convivial parties in their tents had little except rations to subsist on. When at St Jean de Luz the Black Watch usually had beef all through the meal: the first course 'soup made of beef boiled to rags – course second,

115

beef roasted – course third, beef stewed – and course fourth, beef steaks'.[48] A similar monotony appears to have prevailed in the 43rd Light Infantry, to judge by Captain Cooke's terse account of a dinner produced when a lieutenant of the Rifle Corps was entertained: 'The soup was made with bullocks' tails, the spiced minced-meat was of bullocks' heads, and the third course consisted of a bullock's heart'.[49]

Nothing was wasted, even the blood, which was caught in camp-kettles while the butchers were at work and boiled or fried; when eaten, it was found to be very good. Indeed, whenever a bullock was killed, there would be a scramble for the blood and offals, though a bullock's tail could fetch sixpence or a shilling, and its liver five shillings. Sergeant Anton remarked that very wholesome messes were made from these, but cleanness was out of the question, 'and might well have justified the saying of my Cannongate [Edinburgh] landlady, "It takes a deal of dirt to poison sogers!" '[50]

November 1813 found Wellington's army consuming some three hundred bullocks a day, with the commissariat department holding about six weeks' reserve, based on this daily rate of slaughter.[51] One year earlier, during the retreat to Portugal, the baggage went ahead of the marching troops but the bullocks travelled with them, ready for slaughter at the daily halt. A man would cook his beefsteak at the end of a ramrod, or put his poor little ration on a stick or the point of his sword, broil the meat on wood-ashes, and eat it half-smoked and half-raw, without knife or fork.[52] Even in good times the meat was more often broiled on a wooden spit than boiled in a kettle.

That circumstances were not always so rough, and indeed for officers at least were far more favourable than the above account would suggest, is indicated by this detailed description written by Leslie of the 29th.

'Our standard dishes for dinner were a certain portion of ration beef made into soup, with rice, turnips, carrots, onions, and tomatoes. These being long stewed, the soup was nutritious and the beef was always tender. Another portion of our ration beef was made into steaks, fried with onions. . . .

'When dinner was served up, the camp-kettle was placed in the middle as our soup tureen; another camp-kettle, with boiled beef,

116

was placed at the top; and a third, with beefsteaks, was placed at the bottom of our table; and the vegetables, when we could get them, were placed at each side.'[53]

Until March 1813 the army used the heavy 'Flanders' kettle weighing between 2 and $2\frac{1}{2}$ lb. One such iron camp-kettle was carried for every ten soldiers. It was then replaced by the lighter 22 oz. tin kettle, which was issued on a scale of one per six men. Instead of being transported on a mule, this kettle was carried in a bag by the men, who took turns, while the company mule could be used for moving tents instead. Each soldier had, besides, a 'little semi-circular tin saucepan, with its soup-plate in it'.[54]

Captain Cooke often observed how, when provisions ran short, the ponderous Flanders pattern kettles were turned bottomside up and 'encircled by ten or twelve weatherbeaten soldiers, who, with empty stomachs, stepped forward, one at a time, and each of them in turn rubbing his blacking-brush on the sooty part of the kettle, blacked his dusty shoes, cap-peak, canteen strap, and knapsack'.[55]

Many are the vignettes in diaries and letters of a chance, timely, and memorable meal: on the evening of Salamanca Captain von Wachholtz dozed for an hour, then woke his servant, and was soon enjoying tea and biscuits;[56] William Harding of the 5th Foot, on reaching Salamanca during the retreat from Burgos, found the square so crowded with baggage and officers that only with great difficulty was he able to procure a small cup of coffee and a sponge cake; Wellington ate a beefsteak by the roadside near Pamplona; the sixteen-year-old Ensign George Keppel on the march to Paris after Waterloo kept hunger at bay thanks to an occasional hard-boiled egg from the pistol holster of a friendly field officer.[57] When Ensign William Leeke travelled part of the way from Ostend to Ghent by canal-boat in May 1815, his only fellow passenger was Major-General Sir James Kempt. 'He was very kind to me. When, after some hours' abstinence, we began to feel hungry I volunteered to go and see what was the state of the larder, and came back with the report that there was literally nothing to eat on board, the general produced two gingerbread nuts from a paper, and gave me one of them.'[58]

The breakfast most frequently recalled in diaries and memoirs

117

was that eaten on the morning of 18 June 1815 along the ridge of Mont St Jean. In the 52nd, for instance, each officer had one biscuit and a half-mouthful of soup served in a servant's mess-tin – the only nourishment Ensign Leeke enjoyed until after the battle was over, when he obtained from a French loaf a lump of bread about as big as his fist.[59] To judge from Verner, officers in the 7th Light Dragoons fared better, for after going without food for two days, they welcomed their servants who appeared on the ridge from Brussels, bringing cold pies and other eatables, as well as a plentiful supply of brandy.[60] As for the 95th, they made a fire against the wall of a cottage occupied by Lieut.-Colonel Sir Andrew Barnard, and brewed a huge camp-kettle of tea, to which milk and sugar were added. 'As it stood on the edge of the high road, where all the big-wigs of the army had occasion to pass, I believe almost every one of them, in the early part of the morning, from the Duke downwards, claimed a cupful.'[61] Gunners of 'G' Troop, Royal Horse Artillery broached a cask of rum and filled their canteens. Then a supply of oatmeal was quickly converted into porridge, or 'stirabout' as they called it.[62]

When the army went to Flanders and were cantoned in villages round Oudenarde, to name but one district, the men were better off than their officers could ever remember. They received a pound of meat a day, a pound of bread, both of good quality, plus a pint of gin to six soldiers, and in general they gave their rations for cooking to the person on whom they were billeted. Even after the battle of Quatre Bras there was not a mess in the Black Watch without a turkey, goose, duck or chicken floating in the seething kettle; and an abundance of vegetables from neighbouring gardens added richness to the soup.[63] As for the officers, in many regiments they would dine together at an inn at two francs or so a head. Champagne was cheap, and flowed as freely as excellent wines from Rheims, from Burgundy and, to quote one who had campaigned in south-western France a year before, a Bordeaux which certainly did not come from Bordeaux. Bread was three times cheaper than in England.[64]

On active service in the Peninsula it was seldom feasible to have a regimental officers' mess as in Britain, though now and then units managed something like it while cantoned for the winter months. But when actively campaigning the officers tended to divide themselves into small groups – the officers of a particular company, or less frequently, a trio or quartet of friends.[65] This certainly applied to the 3rd and 48th Regiments of Foot in the summer of 1809, and to the 34th in 1812 after the storming of Badajoz, although at one stage this proved to be impossible, so scattered was the battalion. One little mess in the 3rd Foot was nicknamed 'the Kidney Club', because Captain Thomas Bunbury, one of the four officers, was acting for the quartermaster who had been sent on duty to Lisbon, and was alleged to gain such perquisites as kidneys by virtue of holding this temporary office. The 29th Foot followed the pattern of company officers messing together, and so did the 95th Rifles.[66]

We find mention of a Royal Artillery mess in Lisbon, in the house of a nobleman who had been proscribed as a traitor and whose goods had been confiscated. For eighteen months up till February 1810 the Royal Engineers occupied Number 33 Rua do Aleirim as mess, office and quarters, at the end of which time, as the owner had been extremely civil in providing whatever they required, and his house had suffered damage, the officers sub-scribed £50, of which £20 were for repairs and £30 were laid out in a gold snuff-box.[67] Colonel Henry Watson, commanding the 7th Portuguese Cavalry Regiment in Portalegre, presided over a very agreeable regimental mess, in which nine or ten of his officers, mostly *fidalgos* talking French or English, lived har-moniously together.[68]

High in the Pyrenees and just prior to the battle of the Nive, the 31st Regiment managed to keep the appearance of an officers' mess going; at one stage they built a sort of mess room out of branches covered with the fresh hides of animals recently slaughtered for rations. These made a tolerable roof in fine weather, but, as L'Estrange explains, when several feet of snow lay on top, 'the internal heat from the dinner-party, the dinner, and the cigars, which were constantly burning, naturally melted the snow on the top of the fresh sheep or goatskins, and a ruddy drop kept per-petually falling into our *potage* or our glasses of grog'.[69]

The 95th had done rather better the winter before in Alameda by taking possession of a barn, through the roof of which they built two large chimneys. They next made a rough but serviceable long table and benches, purchased wine-glasses and tumblers, and so had a good regimental officers' mess, thanks to a supply of good

119

Douro wine, which brought to light many singers of whose musical talents their comrades had been unaware. When the 4th Dragoons spent part of February 1810 in Montemor Velho, the officers lived in cells in a convent and used the friars' library for a mess room.[70]

What must have been the largest mess during the Peninsular War was that run by the 28th stationed in Tarifa, Europe's southernmost town. The battalion had a very spacious mess room, with an anteroom at each end. In February 1810, however, when a British force under General Graham stopped in the place for a week on its way from Cadiz to the battlefield of Barrosa, 150 officers from various regiments dined there daily, and such was the crowd that tables were put in every room in the house, many an officer being glad to get a meal in the kitchen. The demands on the 28th's cellar were so heavy that on the second day of the 'invasion', the host officers passed a resolution limiting each officer to a pint of port and half a bottle of claret a day; but despite this precaution, a pipe of port was run dry in under four days. Porter and brandy, being more easily obtainable, were not rationed. When Graham's force moved on again the 28th calculated that, including port, claret, brandy and porter, two thousand bottles had been emptied in a single week. The sergeants had also procured a room and enjoyed their mess as much as the officers had.[71]

One of the most expensive regimental messes must have been that of 'E' Troop, Royal Horse Artillery, at least in January 1814 when Lieutenant Richard Hardinge wrote with indignation: 'The messing is so expensive that we three subs are going to have a talk against it. 60 dollars for December, which amounts to my full Horse pay, which is truly absurd, as I have never had a single friend of mine to the Mess in the three months, and am paying the piper for quality friends who don't acknowledge me at other times.'[72]

Chapter 8

WARTIME DINNER PARTIES

'Tell my mother to send me out some good tea and a little pounded ginger; these canteens will hold a variety of good things if properly packed and filled. Remember the cherry brandy, etc.'[1]
Lieutenant Thomas Dyneley, 25 July 1812

'I decided to be gay today, because God alone knows if I shall see another birthday. . . . I gave them an excellent dinner; fish, poultry, beefsteaks, omelettes and rice cakes.'[2]
Lieutenant George Woodberry, 13 April 1813

Attempts were made throughout the war to obtain extra and traditional food for Christmas Day, but few precise details exist of such festive meals before 1811, in which year different messes in the Light Division dined alternately with each other to eat lean roast beef, poultry and plum-pudding, and anything else that money could buy. A German officer serving with the hussars of the King's German Legion attached to that division in 1810 had noted that the festival was celebrated cheerfully with punch, plum-pudding, roast beef, and even a Christmas tree in the form of a lemon tree decorated all over with lights and oranges. On Christmas Eve 1812 the commanding officer of the Gordon Highlanders requested his company commanders 'to give their men as good dinners as they possibly can tomorrow and something (extra) for breakfast, as it is Christmas Day, and that they will see them at it'. He did the same for New Year's Day.[3]

Lieutenant Henry Hough took the chair at a lavish Christmas dinner for artillery officers, who did full justice to 'soup, salt fish, roast beef, boiled beef, mutton, vegetables, etc., etc., and a remove of turkey, fowls, ham and tongues – afterwards pastry'. No plum-pudding, but plenty of wine, so that once the table-cloth had been removed the company drank toasts to 'All absent friends

121

and the Compliments of the Season to them', to the King, the Prince Regent of Portugal, to England, to Lord Wellington, and to the British Navy, to name only the principal toasts.[4] Wellington's Christmas guests at Freineda in 1812 shared two turkeys and some tins of mince-meat which arrived by post from Lisbon.[5] Only at Christmas the following year, when the army had reached southern France and the benefits of a much shorter sea route, was it possible for the 7th Fusiliers, and doubtless several other regiments also, to keep Christmas for the first time in the Peninsular War. At Arcangues every man contributed meat, wine or money, several sheep were bought and killed, mince pies and plum-puddings were baked, apples were passed round as dessert, and then the men warmed their toes by dancing jigs and reels to the music of several bandsmen.[6] Richard Henegan of the Field Train of Royal Artillery celebrated Christmas in St Jean de Luz that year, and after dinner a regulation was adopted to disperse the guests, 'which movement was only to take place when the empty champagne bottles met in the centre of a long dinner-table, forming an uninterrupted line of communication between the President and Vice-President'.[7]

So much for the usual conviviality and hospitality. The simplest, most touching vignette of that 1813 Christmas Day we owe to the pen of Captain John Cooke who was on duty with the 43rd Light Infantry:

'Just before dark, while passing a corporal's picquet, an officer and myself stood for a few minutes, to contemplate a poor woman, who had brought her little pudding, and her child, from her distant quarters, to partake of it with her husband, by the side of a small fire kindled under a tree.'[8]

From time to time senior officers at least were invited to attend celebration dinners, the anniversary of a victory being the most frequent occasion. For example, on 16 May 1813 Wellington honoured Marshal Beresford with a dinner to mark the battle of Albuera, won two years earlier. Guests assembled in a large tent in the village of Freineda, most of them wearing stars, medals, or the Portuguese Order of the Tower and Sword. Joe Kelly, a well-known singer who was serving in the Life Guards, entertained the company.[9]

The year 1813 appears to have been a bumper season for such dinners: 6th April found Wellington inviting all officers who had been present at the storming of Badajoz; on 5th May he did the same for survivors of the battle of Fuentes de Oñoro; the victory at Salamanca was celebrated by a great dinner in Lesaca outside San Sebastian on 22nd July, and the same village was the scene, on 27th September, of festivities to mark not only the battle of Busaco three years before but also the investiture as Knights of the Bath of Generals Lord Dalhousie, Sir William Stewart, Sir Henry Clinton, and Sir George Murray.[10] On 21st August Wellington marked the fifth anniversary of the battle of Vimeiro by inviting all officers in the 4th Division who fought there to dine with him; about fifty sat down to a splendid dinner, well laced with claret and champagne. His Lordship was very affable, and after the meal he looked round the table and said how happy he was to see so many of his old friends who had been with him in the battle. The toast of 21 August 1808 was then drunk 'with great glee'.[11]

If it wasn't a battle, then there was another reason for dining at Lord Wellington's: on 13th August, again at Lesaca, a party of thirty-six sat down to keep the Prince Regent's birthday – he was fifty-one. Eight mules laden with special food and wines came up from Bilbao, so the feast was a good one. According to Judge-Advocate General Larpent, who was present: 'Two bands were in attendance – those of the Fusiliers and the 7th. Fuento, the Spanish Commissary, gave us "God save the King" and Lord Wellington's favourite "*Ah, Marmont, onde va Marmont?*" '[12] Larpent got the words slightly wrong. This song, which the Spaniards sung to celebrate Marshal Marmont's defeat at the hands of Wellington's army at Salamanca, went as follows:

> '*Adonde vayas, Marmont,*
> *Adonde vayas, Marmont,*
> *Tan Temprano de la mañana*
> *Si te coge Velington,*
>   *Ah, Marmont, Marmont, Marmont!*'[13]

Now and then the senior officers would attend an investiture dinner, such as occurred on 7 November 1810 when Sir William Carr Beresford was installed a Knight of the Bath in the immense palace at Mafra. Lord Wellington took this opportunity to give a

123

splendid dinner for two hundred people and later in the evening a proportion of the officers were invited to a ball and supper. There must have been nearly five hundred Spanish, Portuguese and British officers present, and most of the generals, together with several members of the Regency of Portugal and Ministers of State. Wellington was in the highest spirits, according to observers.[14]

When Sir Lowry Cole was invested with the Order of the Bath at Ciudad Rodrigo on 13 March 1813, Wellington, who was Duke of that town, did not neglect to give a grand dinner, ball and supper there. Sixty-five senior British officers and Spanish military authorities as well as civilians of rank were invited. All the plate at Headquarters had to be requisitioned, and this produced just enough for one change of silver at the dinner. The supper was half cooked in advance at Freineda and taken to Ciudad Rodrigo in waggons or on mule back. Claret, champagne and port were also sent, while from Almeida, twenty-five miles away, the Governor dispatched a caravan of glass and crockery. The bare walls of the ballrooms were hung with yellow damask satin with a silver border, opening at each end in festoons like a tent; lavish crimson and gold were used in the supper rooms, Spaniards having brought all the hangings from the palace of San Ildefonso to save them from the French.

Larpent relates that everything went off very well except for the extreme cold, 'as a few balls during the siege had knocked in several yards of the roof of the ballroom, and a hard frost lay at the time. Lord Wellington stayed at Freineda until half-past three, and then rode full seventeen miles to Rodrigo in two hours to dinner, dressed in all his orders, etc., was in high glee, danced himself, stayed to supper, and at half-past three in the morning went back to Freineda by moonlight.' Toasts were drunk to 'Ferdinand the Seventh', 'The next campaign', and 'Death to all Frenchmen', to such good effect that by five o'clock in the morning certain Spaniards and Englishmen were chairing the Prince of Orange and Major-General Vandeleur, whom they let fall.[15]

The story is told of a newly joined staff officer who, on being asked to dine by Lord Wellington, explained with embarrassment that he felt very honoured by the invitation, but was already engaged to dine that day with General Hill.

'Go, by all means,' came Wellington's reply. 'You will get a much better feed than here.' Then the Commander of the Forces went on: 'As you are a stranger, I will give you some useful information. Cole gives the best dinners in the army; Hill the next best; mine are no great things; Beresford's and Picton's are very bad indeed!'[16]

Guests probably agreed that Picton's table compared unfavourably with that kept by the other divisional commanders. but he made people welcome and could be very genial company indeed. In the case of Sir William Beresford opinions differed. Certainly when Lieutenant George Woodberry dined with Beresford at Cintra on 24 February 1813, in the actual room where the notorious Convention had been signed, excellent food and wines were enjoyed by sixteen people, who included an admiral, two generals, two Portuguese gentlemen and various British field officers. After coffee Woodberry played whist with the admiral and two others, and lost five dollars.[17] In spite of Wellington's verdict, Beresford was said by some officers to keep the best table of all the general officers and to provide excellent food, served on superb plate. Small wonder, if it was in fact provided by the Regency of Portugal. But to be invited to dine with Lord Wellington carried the greatest *cachet*. Not that the prevailing atmosphere was likely to be a relaxed one, to judge from two accounts of dinner with the Commander of the Forces during 1812. The first we owe to Major Augustus Frazer, commanding the Horse Artillery, who was invited after a review of the Light Division. The party of twenty-eight had to sit until half-past eleven, because no one except the young Prince of Orange ventured to move from table until after his Lordship had risen. Frazer, who was amused at the eager looks of several companions anxious to catch a smile from the hero of the day, found Wellington to be affable and good-humoured, and a general favourite. 'All however seemed unnecessarily in fear of the great man; on his part he talked with apparent frankness.'[18]

The second description, of a dinner at Lesaca that September, comes from the pen of Mr George Eastlake, who was paying a short visit as secretary to an admiral. This time twenty officers were present and Wellington received his guests in a most gracious manner. They sat down to eat at half-past three. Eastlake thought the cooking excellent, and the company drank port, claret, madeira and a light Spanish wine.

'Lord Wellington carries himself with much dignity at table and is treated with profound respect when addressed. Indeed it seems impossible to take a liberty with him. He drank wine with no one, and I learned that this was his habit. . . . The wine – and the water – was in black bottles, there being no decanters. Silver goblets supplied the place of tumblers and some short thick wine-glasses not very liable to break were the only articles of glass at table.'[19]

The meal ended with very good coffee served in 'dragon-china basons'.

By virtue of his post as Judge-Advocate General at Headquarters, Francis Larpent often dined at Wellington's table and found him easy to converse with. Once, at Vera in November 1813, the Peer talked for two hours about the Poor Laws, the Catholic question, the state of Ireland, and other topics, just as if he had nothing else on his mind. When Larpent dined there again a week later and stayed until nearly ten, Wellington was 'all gaiety and spirits'.[20] Ensign Cowell Stepney also had the good fortune to be invited frequently to dine at Headquarters, and describes one occasion at Elvas in March 1812 which appears to have been a more informal and jolly affair altogether. The guests included the local authorities, several ladies, two commanding officers from regiments of the Guards, and some young, lively officers belonging either to Wellington's personal staff or to the units bivouacked nearby. Lord Wellington was in high spirits and most attentive to two pretty Portuguese girls, who inevitably formed the centre of attraction. They spoke French well and displayed liveliness and good manners.

'In the course of the evening the two young ladies, under the sanction of their respectable bundle of maternity, gratified Lord Wellington's taste for music by singing many pretty airs. . . . A gallant troubadour, Colonel [the Hon. Thomas] Fermor of the [3rd] Guards, was so inspired as to indulge the ladies *en revanche* with several French romances. Thus concluded an agreeable evening, which carried with it some humanizing remembrances.'[21]

Individual regiments would occasionally take it upon themselves

126

to celebrate a particular day. When 25th August, the 95th Rifle Corps' regimental anniversary, was celebrated in 1813 by seventy officers of the three battalions, two trenches for the diners' legs were dug in the turf, the earth between served as a table, and behind was the seat. The French looked down on the scene in astonishment.[22] St Patrick's Day was normally marked with enthusiasm by the Irish regiments under Wellington's command. On 17 March 1809, for instance, the 87th, or Royal Irish, held a grand gala in their Lisbon mess; the band played national airs, there was a constant round of toasts and cheers, and the officers sang – all to the great astonishment and delight of the Portuguese crowds which gathered under the windows to watch.[23] At Guarda the following March several regimental bands played through the streets, from midnight onwards, and on hearing it the Portuguese inhabitants were elated with hope, believing that the musicians must be celebrating the arrival of some great piece of news. They were disillusioned next morning.[24] On another 17th March, this time in 1813, the officers of the 88th, or Connaught Rangers, gave a grand dinner to Colonel John Keane and his brigade staff. Soon after five o'clock dinner was announced in the usual way by the tune of 'The roast beef of old England', and more than fifty officers sat down. The very large number of toasts drunk that evening included:

'St Patrick (three times three)   (*Tune :* 'St Patrick's day in the morning')

Shelah, St Patrick's wife

The King   (*Tune :* 'God Save the King')

The Prince Regent of England   (*Tune :* 'The Prince and Old England for Ever')

The Duke of York and the Army   (*Tune :* 'The Duke of York's March')

The Wooden Walls of Old England   (*Tune :* 'Rule Britannia')

The Marquis of Wellington, and success to the next campaign   (*Tune :* 'The Downfall of Paris')

General Picton and the 3rd Division   (*Tune :* 'Britons strike home')

General Pakenham and the Battle of Salamanca.   (*Tune :* 'See the conquering Hero come')

Colonel Keane and the right brigade (three times three)   (*Tune :* 'British Grenadiers')

127

St Patrick, the Shamrock and the Land
  of Potatoes
St George, the Rose and Prosperity to
  England
St Andrew, the Thistle, and the Land
  of Cakes.'[25]

On the last day of July 1811, on the eve of marching out of Lisbon to join Wellington's army, the 28th Foot held a dinner. Prospects of the campaign ahead were overcast by the recollection of having taken the same route in 1808 under Sir John Moore's command, and by thoughts of friends who had been swept away since that time at the battles of Corunna, Talavera, Barrosa and Albuera.

Robert Blakeney of the 28th described what happened after the eating was done:

'The cloth being removed, a bumper was proposed to the memory of the immortal Moore. It was drunk in perfect silence and, as it were, with religious solemnity. The martial figure and noble mien of the calumniated hero stood erect in the imagination, and was perfect in the memory of all. . . .

'Our next bumper was to the memory of our late gallant comrades, who gloriously fell since our last march from Lisbon gallantly maintaining the honour of their country and Corps. This toast was also drunk in solemn silence, while many an eye swam at the recollection of scenes and friends gone for ever. . . .

'Our third and last bumper was "To our next happy meeting; and whosoever's lot it be to fall may the regiment soon and often be placed in a situation to maintain the glory of their country, and may they never forget the bravery and discipline which won the 'back-plates' ".* This sentiment was received with wild enthusiasm and so loudly cheered by all that gloom and melancholy were frightened out of the room.'[26]

Lastly there were dinner parties given by individual officers. While in Olite towards the end of October, Hussey Vivian had his general, Lord Edward Somerset, to dine, with four other officers, and they did themselves proud. In order to assure his

---

*The 28th won the distinction of wearing its badge on the back as well as the front of the cap in recognition of repulsing the French when attacked simultaneously in front and rear, on 21 March 1801 outside Alexandria in Egypt.

wife that he had not starved his guests, Vivian listed the numerous
dishes:

First Course	Second Course
Salt fish and potatoes	Roast partridges
(i.e. 'chowder')	Apple stewed
Removes	Rice pudding
Roast saddle of mutton	Tart
Stewed beef, roast potatoes	Mushrooms
Steaks	Omelet
Boiled chicken	
Soup removed	
Ham	

They rounded off the meal with grapes for dessert.[27]

Junior officers, whether to celebrate a birthday or promotion or
merely because they were feeling 'flush', also invited their friends
to dinner. While the 18th Light Dragoons were at Olite during
July 1813, two of the officers, Smith and Christopher Blackett,
asked Captain Simon Stuart and Lieutenant Seymour of the 10th
to dinner. They flattered themselves that a good meal had been
prepared, but alas! When they sat down they found that the pigeon
pâté had been burnt to cinders, and the mutton resembled charcoal.
Smith, Blackett and Stuart took the misfortune with laughter,
but Seymour saw nothing to laugh at. Having eaten a few scraps of
pâté and vainly scraped the mutton bones, he left and went to dine
in his own quarters. Smith, in particular, was very offended by
this behaviour.[28]

Entertaining became easier once the army had crossed into
France, particularly for those who had quarters in or close to St
Jean de Luz, a once flourishing town which had fallen into some
decay. Larpent described the town as 'all a market or fair, and full
of Spaniards and Portuguese, as well as French and Bascos, all
pillaging poor John Bull by selling turkeys for 25s. and 30s., and
fowls for 12s. and 14s. . . . Every shop crowded with eatables –
wines, sauces, pickles, hams, tongues, butter, and sardines.' On
the strength of this abundance, Larpent gave a grand dinner in
the French Café. Ten sat down and were served ten dishes for the
first course, two removes for the soups, ten for the second course,
rôtis and sweets together, and ten for dessert, plus excellent

E   129 champagne, very fair Madeira and sherry, moderate port and claret, and outstandingly good *pâtisseries*. The entire bill came to forty dollars.[29]

On the occasion of his being appointed lieutenant-colonel, while in Brussels in May 1815, Sir Augustus Frazer gave a very good dinner to all the Horse Artillery officers, both British and German, in the Hôtel de la Paix on the Place Royale. Claret, sauternes and champagne flowed freely, and the utmost hilarity prevailed. Captain Mercer, who attended, wrote afterwards: 'Many of us then met for the first time, many after a separation of years, and many for the last time'.[30]

Clearly all this entertaining would have been impossible on local food resources. Luxury items, but much else besides, had to come from England or at very least from Lisbon. Major Dickson's petty cash book shows that he was able to purchase in Portugal two tongues, ten dozen anchovies, a ham, three bottles of mushroom ketchup, and two pounds of refined salt. On rare occasions foodstuff could be brought straight off a ship, as happened when a brig came into St Jean de Luz from Dartmouth. Word spread that her cargo included porter, ale, beef and cheese as well as five tons of potatoes, and there ensued an astonishing scramble of officers on board to see and buy.[31]

However, the great majority of items calculated to improve and supplement the daily rations had to be ordered from across the seas, either direct to the supplier or indirectly through the good offices of family or friends. Thus in May 1811 we have Major-General Robert Long writing to his brother asking him to procure 'some Wiltshire cheeses, tongues, portable soup, vermicelli for soup, vegetable powder for ditto, some bottles of best burgundy, vinegar and a supply of good tea'. Eighteen months later he is again commissioning his brother to get Mackay to send out two small hampers containing 'a cargo of cheeses, spices, peppers, mustard, pickles (particularly walnut), currie, vinegar (burgundy and raspberry), hams or tongues to fill up vacancies, *ad libitum*'.[32]

Another cavalry general who wrote home for delicacies was Hussey Vivian who, once the northern port of Bilbao was in use, begged his father to send him four hams, eight tongues, together with butter, cheese, and wine. Wives and mothers despatched patties of game and venison. Sir Rowland Hill was sent some coffee essence, and Sir Thomas Graham received from the postmaster in Perth a consignment of salmon and sheep with which to entertain the Cortes and Grandees in Cadiz.[33] A senior captain of the 95th received from England two immense pies, each weighing nearly a hundredweight and packed in a tin case. 'They were,' writes William Surtees, who lived in the captain's mess, 'composed of every kind of game, and the best description of fowls, such as turkeys, etc., with the bones taken out, and the meat baked till it became like brawn when cut in slices.' One ensign of the 1st Foot Guards not only brought with him from England to St Jean de Luz many hampers full of wine, liqueurs, ham, potted meat and other delicacies; he also provided generous hospitality thanks to some first-rate cooks, a cosmopolitan host of servants, and a great deal of money. On one occasion he was honoured by Lord Wellington's company at dinner. He spent so lavishly and lived so magnificently that he got seriously into debt and was eventually obliged to leave his regiment. As Gronow, a fellow Guardsman, summed up the affair: 'He and his friends had literally eaten up his little fortune'.[34]

Those – the large majority – with no relatives at home who had the means of executing such commissions on their behalf had to rely on canteen goods which might now and then become locally available. A prudent officer setting forth from the base at Lisbon would lay in a good stock of tea, sugar, coffee, hams and tongues to take with him on campaign. Occasionally someone would have an opportunity to visit Lisbon or Oporto or, in 1814, St Jean de Luz, and bring back stores for his companions. When part of Headquarters was in the remote hamlet of Malhada Sorda during the winter of 1812–13, a couple of mules would occasionally be despatched to Coimbra, returning with a load of wine, cigars and other creature comforts.[35]

While the 28th Regiment was resting below Roncesvalles late in August 1813 some of the officers requested Colonel Belson to send a detachment to the nearest port, Pasajes, in order to purchase tobacco for the men and tea and sugar for the officers. Two thousand Spanish dollars were soon collected for this purpose and entrusted to a sergeant and six grenadiers who, on arriving outside San Sebastian, then under siege, obtained permission to join the stormers of the town, played a notable part in the assault, emerged unscathed, went on to Pasajes, made their purchases and returned to battalion headquarters.[36]

Otherwise the troops had to do business with the few sutlers who followed the army and, whenever units remained stationary for a week or two, opened temporary shops and supplied – at famine prices – what one officer termed 'the requisite necessaries, and many of the luxuries, of refined life'.[37] For a list of some of these gastronomic necessities and luxuries we can hardly do better than quote the experience of Johnny Newcome when he went to buy his stock from a Lisbon supplier.

' "Pray, sir," says John, "do you sell Hams, and cheese?"
"*Si, Senhor*, I do sell all vat you please;
Biscuits, & Porter, Tongues, Hollands, & Brandy."
John crack'd his Whip, and swore 'twas all the dandy.
"Tea, Sugar, Salt, and vat of all most nice is,
Pickles and Soda, good Segars and Spices." '[38]

An Italian named Sanguinetti was the most constant sutler, and perhaps the most extortionate one too. His visits, at long and uncertain intervals, were a necessary evil for men who had to rough it willy-nilly.[39] More accommodating and good-natured was Tamet the Turk, who gave some people tick until the next issue of pay. Tamet may well have been the Moor or Mohammedan whom Charles Leslie had in mind when he described the method of a sutler who, apart from a few words of Spanish, spoke no language but his own.

'To the many who had no money he handed a slip of paper with pen and ink. Each one wrote down the articles he wanted, with a promise to pay for them when the money should arrive. No further security was required, so great was his faith in British honour. Now considering that we were all and each of us liable shortly to go into action and be killed, or to die of fever, he really ran no small risk in giving such unlimited credit, and his charges, even under these circumstances, were by no means exorbitant.'[40]

One major problem with buying delicacies from Portugal and Spain, and from Britain to a lesser extent, was the sheer lack of cash. Very seldom during the Peninsular War was Wellington's army paid up to date – a factor which influenced many other, more important aspects of living and fighting. In October 1811 it was three months in arrears of pay, bills on England were difficult to cash and, even if cashable, were taken at a most unfavourable exchange rate of six shillings for the Portuguese dollar when the current value was under five.[41] By late November a quarter of a month's pay had been issued, but this amount solved little, and whenever carriage was lacking to bring them up from Lisbon supplies remained difficult to buy locally, for the villagers had grown tired of promissary payment and often concealed their corn and other stocks.[42]

August 1812 found officers complaining that seven months' pay were due to the army. Consequently, few men could muster any dollars at all with which to purchase bread, wine and other goods; Jonathan Leach of the 95th was obliged to sell some silver spoons and a watch 'to raise the wind, considering a loaf of bread, some chocolate, and a few other things of the kind far more necessary than plate'.[43]

The position improved very little until May 1813, just before the opening of the new campaign that would carry the army to the Pyrenees and beyond. Major George Bingham of the 53rd, who had received no pay since December and had £150 owing to him on 24th April, commented without enthusiasm three weeks later: 'One piece of liberality. We are to be paid up to January 26th before we start, but we are warned that it will be a long time before we are to expect another issue'.[44]

In mid-August Captain Bowles of the Coldstream Guards was able to write home that the army had just received two months' pay – in new guineas minted in 1813 – and was paid up to March.[45] Even at the end of the year, when the army had reached St Jean de Luz, ready money was so scarce that the patient, loyal muleteers had to accept payment in Treasury bills, and so did French people who sold cattle and food to Wellington's commissariat. By this time the army was again six months, and the staff seven, in arrears.[46] The situation had scarcely improved when the troops were outside Toulouse in April 1814, but they were optimistic from a belief that England was a good paymaster, and the money would all come in a heap someday, if they lived to see it.[47] At long last, near Bordeaux

133

in May, six months' back pay was issued in gold. The problem was how to spend it. 'There was,' wrote Bell, 'no lack of wine-houses and restaurants, dominoes, pitch and toss: Heads, I win! – tails, you lose! – anything to catch the penny. So their thirty or forty dollars did not last long.'[48]

Chapter 9

LEARNING THE LANGUAGE

'*No pretty girls*, which I lament, as it assists me in learning Spanish, in which I have attained great proficiency, and I am sorry only at my having left my grammar and dictionary behind me. Pray send me one of each.'[1]
Colonel Hussey Vivian to his wife, 20 October 1813

At least a handful of officers set out from England prepared to learn a language during the sea voyage to Lisbon, and to this end they purchased a grammar and maybe a dictionary also, only to find that life on board ship in the Bay of Biscay and off Cape Finisterre was not conducive to study. Consequently some were embarrassed to discover that, on reaching a Lisbon billet, their acquirement amounted to half a dozen Portuguese words and a solitary sentence: 'bread', 'wine', 'water', 'fish', 'tea', and 'how do you do?'[2]

When one regiment disembarked after dark from a collier at Belem on Christmas Eve, 1808, great confusion and scramble ensued in the streets since neither the English troops nor the Portuguese civilians could understand each other, and the allocation of rank and file to barracks and of officers to private houses proved difficult to organize".

The experiences of Ensign George Bell, 34th Regiment of Foot, on first landing in Portugal were not unusual. Knowing barely 'three words of the Portuguese lingo', he left his billet to go for a walk, lost his way and wandered about Lisbon for some hours until rescued by an officer who had travelled on board the same ship. Next day he walked out of the city to enjoy the country air, and seeing a fine vineyard and the gate open he went inside and found the owner. This Portuguese gentleman invited Bell to sit

135

down and then talked at length to the seventeen-year-old ensign, who could understand only a few words such as 'Wellington, and the *guerra*, and Marshal Soult', and felt so small at his inability to comprehend, let alone reply, that he resolved at once to learn the language. Some days later, after a bout of illness, Bell was invited to dine by the landlord of his billet, and with the aid of a dictionary he managed to converse with the family. When he set off with some convalescent soldiers to join the army at Portalegre, he found the marches sometimes long and dreary, and rendered more tiresome still by problems of language.

'No one knew the distance; meeting a solitary peasant now and then we would ask "Quantas leaguas, señor, a Sacavem?" Answer, "Dos leaguas e pokito, señor"; march on another league and meet pizaro the second, and ask the same question, "O señor, Sacavem, *tres* leaguas e no mas (just three leagues)!" No milestones, no hotels, inns, or refreshment houses.'[3]

Neither Tomkinson nor any other officer in the 16th Light Dragoons could speak Portuguese on arrival in Lisbon, and when Tomkinson himself missed his way while *en route* for a billet in Torres Novas, he spent hours wandering round without knowing more of the language than the name of his destination. The sergeant and dragoon with him were equally at a loss.[4] The same sort of thing happened six years later when another British army under Wellington's command assembled in Flanders. Although in a village like Ghistelles many of the inhabitants spoke or understood a little English, this was not the case in isolated farms. Consequently British horse gunners could not understand their billets, nor could they ask the way, so it became necessary for officers to accompany their men and ensure that they were safely housed. Even the officers had great difficulty, because most of the local people spoke nothing but Flemish, and as one cornet explained: 'The only answer I can ever obtain is "yaw", in English "yes".'[5]

With notable exceptions, the rank and file did not manage well as linguists. As an officer of the 11th Light Dragoons explained:

'I doubt if many of them ever thought, before their arrival at Lisbon, that there was any other language than English; and I can easily believe the joke, however stale, of the astonishment of some of them on finding that even the smallest and youngest children spoke Portuguese! Though they make but little progress beyond the names of the few necessaries of life, they are highly enraged at the peasantry if they do not understand a whole sentence of English, in which a single word of Spanish or Portuguese is introduced; and in such cases damn them roundly for "not knowing their own language!" I leave you to judge of the correctness of the pronunciation when they use "hogwar" for *"aqua"*, . . . "akefent" for *"aqua-ardiente"* "pebble" for *"pueblo"*, "fogo" for *"fuego"*, and so on.'[6]

In fairness one must add that many officers achieved scarcely better results, and some who asked in English for whatever they wanted, at a hotel in Corunna for instance, seemed astonished at not being understood by the puzzled waiters, whom they damned as stupid scoundrels. Since, however, this particular establishment bore the name Hotel de Inglaterra, perhaps the officers, who soon nicknamed it 'The British', had some reason for expecting to be understood.[7]

During the winter months spent in cantonments quite a few officers devoted several hours a day to studying Portuguese or Spanish with the aid of books, and so did some of those convalescing from wounds or a fever. William Guthrie's *Geographical, Historical and Commercial Grammar*, published in 1770, proved a helpful guide to Portuguese, and Mordente's Spanish Grammar was in regular demand.[8] In August 1812 *The Royal Military Chronicle* published, to quote the words of its advertisement:

'A Spanish Grammar for the use of officers, price two shillings and sixpence, arranged upon the plan of the Eton Latin Grammar, i.e. so as, by the omission of what is superfluous, and the fullest exposition of what is necessary, to write the greatest brevity with the fullest explanation, and thereby to assist the memory, and enable every one to instruct themselves. The Publisher is enabled to say, that this is not only the cheapest, but likewise the best Spanish Grammar extant; inasmuch as it is not the work of an ignorant foreigner, but of an elegant scholar, for his own use.'[9]

According to the publisher, an officer would be able to instruct himself in a mere two months. However, when Captain George

137

Call of the 9th Light Dragoons set about the task in December 1811, using other books, he tried to make even quicker progress, and wrote in his journal on the 7th:

'This day commenced studying the Portuguese, resolving to learn it in 6 weeks – having leisure hours on my hands – propose passing the day in the following way –

Study from	11 to one
Practise the Flute	1–2
Writing on various subjects	2–4
Bodily exercise	till dinner

From eight till breakfast transact business, write Invitations. After breakfast attend Stables and arrange Domestic concerns.

'In the Evening from 9 till 11 – read or write English letters.'[10]

To teach yourself Portuguese or Spanish was one method. Another was to hire a local teacher. P. W. Buckham of the Staff Corps was one who elected to do this. Having decided, while in Oporto, to devote a portion of each day to the study of Portuguese, he obtained from a friend the name and address of a teacher. The Portuguese, wearing black silk breeches, silver-buckled shoes, and profusely powdered hair, called next day, and began to read aloud in order to afford Buckham some idea of the harmony of the language. Buckham was not impressed.

'Such words as not, then, are, etc. being in constant recurrence, and these, written naô, saô, entaô, being all pronounced nông, sông, entông, you may form some tolerable notion how extremely melodious such a language must be! My mouth has been nearly twisted awry in submitting to half-a-dozen lessons; and then there is a sort of high and low tone to be acquired, which leaves me in despair of ever attaining to proficiency.'[11]

On hearing Portuguese spoken while he still could not understand what was said, Buckham simply burst out laughing. Quite the reverse occurred when he had an opportunity to compare it with Spanish, which 'is grand and sonorous, and seems to confer an elevation of character upon the speaker'. Whereas the Portuguese spoke in a dilatory, even drawling manner, the Spaniard, at least to Buckham's ear, was prompt, energetic and precise.[12]

We find General Graham, who already spoke French, German

and Italian as well as Spanish, describing Portuguese as 'infamous – such a nasal-clipp'd pronunciation with much affinity in words, that makes one quite afraid of chang'g the little Spanish we know for this abominable sister'.[13] Lieutenant Allen of the Royals noted that the Spaniards appeared to aspirate every word: 'Don Julian they pronounce Don Hoolian; General, Heneral; and so on'. He found Portuguese much more readily understood, but Spanish a finer and more sonorous language. 'They do not, in this respect, differ so much as the inhabitants of Cheshire and Flintshire, divided by the river Dee only, and who are altogether unintelligible to one another.'[14]

One problem was the ease with which the two languages of the Peninsula could be muddled in the mind. 'We had no sooner become familiar with the squeak of a Portuguese,' observed William Gomm, 'than we were led away to listen to the gargling tones of a Spaniard.' Soldiers who learnt Spanish first sometimes had great difficulty in speaking Portuguese, except in a mingled and inelegant form, while those who eagerly practised Spanish tried to throw their Portuguese into the background as rapidly as possible.[15]

Various other methods were used for gaining and improving a knowledge of the language. Some soldiers were encouraged to read Spanish newspapers because they enjoyed the abuse of King Joseph and other members of the Bonaparte family. Most officers took every opportunity of chatting with their landlords as a means of acquiring fluency and a richer vocabulary. A few, like Alexander Dallas of the Commissariat in Cadiz, learnt to play the guitar and to sing Spanish songs to his own accompaniment, as well as paying great attention to his grammar. To procure and read a few Portuguese and Spanish books was a more scholarly approach, but less popular than mixing in local society. In fact, some ability to speak was an essential passport to most evening parties, so the inducement to learn was strong.[16]

Easily the most popular and certain method of making rapid progress was to learn from pretty girls, whether on walks, while flirting, at meals in billets or when dancing. To receive Spanish or Portuguese lessons in exchange for English lessons was great fun and reasonably effective, though not in the circumstances described by Swabey at Salgueira in the winter of 1811, when the bright-

139

eyed niece of their landlord was enthusiastic to teach the Portuguese langauge to those who would go to school to her.

'In return we undertook to teach her English which I cannot say we did with that commendable fidelity which would have better become us. I fear we rendered Portuguese, of which we were asked the English, into all sort of ridiculous expressions causing the most ludicrous dilemmas that can be imagined. I do not think this was justifiable, but I have bound myself to speak the truth, and this was one of our follies, yet on the whole our conduct was most gallant and decorous.'[17]

Just how many became really fluent in one or both languages of the Peninsula, or in French, is impossible to say. Certainly those who had most frequent business with the local inhabitants – commissaries, engineers, the provost, members of the Quartermaster-General's department, and the few officers who rode into danger as Wellington's eyes and ears – were obliged to gain at least a reasonable command of the spoken word. Major Harry Smith reckoned that by the end of 1811 he could speak Portuguese as well as English and when he married his young Spanish bride from Badajoz, he rapidly became admirably fluent in her language also.[18]

Conversation with priests could sometimes be carried on with the aid of mongrel Latin blended with stumbling Spanish or Portuguese, but Captain William Bragge of the 3rd Dragoons, while agreeing with a correspondent that priests ought to understand Latin, said that in his experience not one in five hundred knew a little of it.[19] A few well-educated *fidalgos*, unacquainted with French and having no English except some oaths picked up indiscriminately from British troops, could manage a little Latin. Certainly Surgeon Walter Henry found such a man in Lisbon who understood the doctor's overtures because he had been taught to pronounce Latin in the broad Continental and not the English manner. Henry describes their halting exchanges on the events of the day thus: 'the *"bellum internecinum adversus Gallos"* – the great *Dux* Wellington, the *"exercitus Britannicus"* – the *Rex Georgius* – the *"spes Lusitaniae"* and so on for half an hour'.[20]

Several instances are on record of individuals overrating their abilities to serve as interpreter. One commissary, perplexed to know how to convey his meaning to a party of muleteers, eventually turned to some British officers standing nearby and asked if anyone could help. One officer immediately stepped forward. 'I think, sir, that I can explain to them anything you need.' The commissary was delighted. 'Then, sir, be so kind as to tell them that they must be here early in the morning with their mules.'

The interpreter addressed the puzzled muleteers as follows: 'Portuguesios, the commissario – wants the mulos – tomorrowo – presto – la, la,' and pointed to the village of Vimeiro. 'Oh, sir!' cried the commissary, who was very disappointed by this ludicrous performance, 'I feel much obliged to you, but I can go as far as that myself.' For months after this episode the self-styled linguist bore the nickname of 'Jack the Interpreter'.[21]

That was Portugal. As for Spain, when officers went to new billets, their servants would often take charge of proceedings as soon as the landlord appeared. A conversation like the following would then take place. 'Shove off, señor, ondigesta el salo? ondigesta el cama? cama bono for official inglesy, es bon Christiano; quero pong [bread], vino, montecy [butter], akydenta [brandy] for soldados, quero leche [milk], oily for de lampy, you intende? Me parly bon Spanole.'[22]

After Waterloo, when the army was advancing on Paris, several regiments wasted hours wandering about the countryside, thanks to the inflated self-esteem of a brigade major, who prided himself on his colloquial command of the French language. In fact he was lamentably deficient, yet too proud to ask for the services of an interpreter. Consequently the cavalry brigade went much out of its way while trying to reach Le Cateau. Instead of saying *'où est le chemin au Cateau?'* he persisted in asking: *'Où est le chimeney à Catty?'* so that the person thus interrogated, being too polite to admit he did not understand, pointed out the way to any town or village whose name bore the slightest resemblance to Catty.[23]

A few senior or well-endowed officers played safe and hired someone to interpret for them, at least in the early weeks of Peninsular service. Thus we find John, Lord Burghersh, a lieutenant-colonel on the staff, attended constantly by a Portuguese priest who acted as guide and interpreter; and Major-General Houston had with him for the same purpose a Mr

141

Pedroso.[24] British officers who were seconded for service in Beresford's Portuguese army had, of course, to speak the language; and a General Order dated 6 May 1809 wisely laid down that any officers commanding a brigade to which Portuguese troops were attached would employ an interpreter, who would receive the pay and allowances of an ensign and be entitled to draw forage for one horse.[25]

One way to secure the services of an interpreter was to take into service a servant boy who looked after animals and went foraging. Officers picked up these boys in varying circumstances. Some were taken on in Lisbon, especially if they could speak broken English; others were hired in less ordinary circumstances. For example, one was captured from the French during a cavalry skirmish early in 1811 and remained for years with the regiment, as servant to Lieutenant Lockhart, eventually accompanying the 16th to England.[26] When William Hay exchanged from the 52nd Foot into the 12th Light Dragoons, a fellow officer wished to buy part of Hay's uniform, but having no money offered his Portuguese servant boy in lieu. Because Hay considered Francisco 'an active, neat, intelligent lad and the very thing I most wanted', the bargain was struck, and he rode away on one pony, the boy on the other, carrying two wicker panniers packed with clothing and ham.[27] Simmons accidently met a half-starved Portuguese boy in a street of Castelo Branco and engaged him on the spot.[28] Surgeon Henry did much the same, when he saw a Portuguese lad dozing in the shade of some chestnut trees near a convent gate in Coimbra. 'He said he could cook, and brush my clothes, and polish my boots, and groom a horse. He had no certificates, for he had never been in service – but he had an honest as well as a comely face. . . . I hired him at once – appointed him my Major Domo and Factotum, and directed him to look after my rations.' Antonio proved his worth, groomed the horse very well, and served faithfully until June 1814.[29]

While the army was quartered near Ciudad Rodrigo in January 1812 not a few villagers brought their teenage sons and begged the officers to take them as servants. Some offered their services at twelve years old in exchange for their keep and an almost nominal gratuity.[30] After a little training most of them became 'famous foragers and efficient interpreters'. Indeed, foraging was one of their principal tasks. Kincaid relates how, during the army's pursuit of the French across Portugal in March 1811, the officers of each rifle company had a Portuguese boy in charge of a donkey.

'He carried our boat-cloaks and blankets, was provided with a small pig-skin for wine, a canteen for spirits, a small quantity of tea and sugar, a goat tied to the donkey, and two or three dollars in his pocket, for the purchase of bread, butter, or any other luxury which good fortune might throw in his way in the course of the day's march.'[31]

Not only officers had such servants. A majority of the women, British and Portuguese alike, had a boy assistant; many of the dragoons paid boys to help them; and the hussars of the King's German Legion, divided into groups of ten or twenty, each kept a flock of sheep or goats in the charge of a Portuguese lad. Since his other main duty was to go out and steal, he was nicknamed a 'romp boy', from the word *rompere*, 'to destroy' or 'to steal'. The officers in the 1st King's German Legion Hussars also had them – smart fellows who seldom returned empty-handed when sent out with canteen and sack.[32] Foraging they were certainly good at, but was this enough? Taking care of animals and baggage was also required of them, at least by the officers of the Royal Engineers. When they signed a memorial to the Inspector-General of Fortifications, dated 20 August 1813, they asked that their extra pay be doubled on the grounds that, not being allowed the attendance of any servant, and the expense of an English servant who was not a soldier being entirely beyond their means, they were 'reduced to take into their employment Portuguese or Spanish lads, Deserters or other dangerous characters, without any previous knowledge of them or written proof of honesty'.[33]

Though I have found no record that any boy was killed or wounded in battle, things did not always go smoothly for them. For one thing, there was generally a feud between Spanish and Portuguese servant boys. For another, they sometimes could not stand up to the fatigue and fevers, especially during the retreat of 1812, and several perished on the roadside. Swabey lost a boy named Manuel in bivouac, after months of faithful, efficient service, when one of his horses suddenly took it into its head to roll while saddled. The boy, in trying to prevent damage to the

143

saddle, imprudently hit the horse, which lashed out with both hindlegs, caught Manuel on the forehead, and killed him.[34]

A lighter note was struck the following summer when, after Wellington's resounding defeat of the French army at Vitoria, all the Portuguese boys copied the soldiers by dressing up in over-large French uniforms, even those which had belonged to generals, and parading about the battlefield.[35]

The most detailed account of these Portuguese boys we owe to Harry Smith, who records that most officers in the Light Division had goats, and each company officers' mess had a boy who took charge of them on the march and in bivouac, and also milked them. Smith's boy had a flock of fifteen to look after.

'We observed extraordinary regularity with these goats, and upon enquiry we found out the little fellows organizing themselves into regular guards. They had a captain, quite a little fellow of dear old Billy Mein's 52nd Regiment; their time of duty was as regular as our soldiers; they had sentries with long white sticks in their hands, and Mein's little boy held a sort of court-martial, and would lick a boy awfully who neglected his charge. My little boy's name was Antonio, and when he was for guard, I have seen him turn out unusually smart, with his hands and face washed.'[36]

Late in May 1814, when all Portuguese troops left Wellington's command and returned home, British officers were ordered to send away their Portuguese and Spanish servants, so that they would travel under control and protection. That this order caused disappointment is shown by the case of Lieutenant Woodberry's faithful 'Sparem Joe', as he was nicknamed, who had a year before been recommended by a beautiful young lady, and had set his heart on accompanying Woodberry to England and now could not do so.[37] Some British officers gave their goats to their servant boys as a leaving present, in the hope that the herd would be the basis for future prosperity as goat-proprietors.

Chapter 10

PASTIMES

'No set of persons could more industriously strive to unite mirth with hardships, and relaxation with severe duty. . . . In our quarters we lived gaily and well. A spirit of good-fellowship and hospitality everywhere prevailed; and in the midst of war, – balls, private theatricals, and agreeable parties were things of continual occurrence.'[1]
Lieut.-Gen. the Marquess of Londonderry

No opportunity was neglected of finding relaxation and enjoyment. As normally happens, the officers fared better than the rank and file, but many pastimes were open to all. Whenever the army settled for several months on end, facilities for entertainment were at their best, yet even a brief stay could produce an amusing activity, for certain ways of passing the hours required no special conditions, and could be indulged whatever the season and weather.

Conversation was one such way, and occupied a good deal of time. Apart from talking 'shop', and praising or picking holes in senior officers, comparing notes about last night's party, and complaining about the arrears of pay, the postal delays, the toughness of the ration beef, or the awkwardness of some local magistrate, there was a lack of well-worn subjects. 'You would laugh if you could hear our conversation here,' wrote Augustus Frazer to his wife from Pasajes in July 1813; 'one moment spherical case and round shot, the next tea or shoes or Russian ducks.'[2] Of course the army discussed sensational items of news like the assassination of Spencer Perceval, the Prime Minister, in the lobby of the House of Commons and Napoleon's invasion of Russia; they speculated about Lord Wellington's intentions, and tried to forecast when the army would take the field; they conjectured the probable area and aim of the next campaign. Lost friends were remembered, and so were past battles and marches.

Beyond the topics of the day a few of the officers would argue about some pamphlet, or a review already a year old.[3] They might wax passionate about transfers, promotions, and the filling of vacancies. Captain Charlie Beckwith expressed it well in a letter dated 1 May 1813 to William Napier, who was back in London:

'The monotony of the scene is only varied by the reports of Monday which are well found to be lies on Tuesday morning. Sometimes 40,000 Frenchmen march out of the country, sometimes they march in; sometimes the Spaniards have 150,000 men, sometimes 50; sometimes we have plenty to eat and drink, and sometimes we have not.'[4]

One special pleasure which could seldom be enjoyed was to meet friends from one's home county or district. Thus we find Private Green of the 68th on board a boat gliding up the Tagus from Lisbon and accidentally meeting a man named Parker who also came from Louth in Lincolnshire. 'No man can imagine,' wrote Green, 'how pleased I was with the man: because he was a fellow-countryman.'[5] On a September day of 1812 Lieutenant Hough, Royal Horse Artillery, met the assistant surgeon of the 16th Light Dragoons, Mr John Evans, waiting with sick and wounded soldiers. They spent the day together and chatted about Gloucester and Monmouthshire, Evans showing a letter in which his mother had mentioned a visit from Hough's sister and brother. Three days later, while in Torquemada, Hough met a Lieutenant William Pearce of the 44th Regiment who came from Gloucestershire, was most friendly, had been at school with Hough, and talked about Hough's brothers.[6] To meet a schoolfellow at war often meant more than a similar encounter would have done at home. Certainly Cornet Francis Hall was delighted to run into a fellow Wykehamist who commanded a troop in the Royal Dragoons; and three days before the Waterloo campaign began, Ensign George Keppel of the 14th Foot spent his sixteenth birthday very pleasantly with some 'Old Westminsters'.[7]

Partly because of the hardship of campaigning life and partly by association with the Spaniards, the habit of smoking cigars, usually spelt 'segars' at the time, became widespread, until for some it served almost as food or sleep.[8] Beckwith of the 95th Rifles assures his friend William Napier: 'Our mode of life is exactly the same as when you left us. I ride about all the morning in pursuit of nothing. Barnard smokes segars until the very atmosphere between the Coa and the Agueda is impregnated with the "herbiforous herb" as Doctor Morgan says.' And on September evenings later that year, 1813, officers crowded into a well-known Bilbao coffee-house to drink punch, lemonade, and coffee, and to smoke cigars for an hour or two. Peter Le Mesurier smoked two or three cigars a day and thought them excellent things for health.[9]

In bad weather pipe smoking becomes for many a soldier the greatest luxury he can enjoy. He smokes a pipe to keep warm or to pass the time or to keep the ague at bay; he smokes leaves and herbs when tobacco runs out.[10] This happens on the eve of Vitoria to the 71st Regiment until their colonel rides off and somehow procures half a pound per man. Such a deficiency seldom occurred, because its portable nature, low price and constant sale usually enabled the sutlers to have a supply;[11] but in 1813 the war with America produced a severe shortage of tobacco in Portugal, except for the Brazil product, which was rated villainous stuff to smoke and by no means 'the great comfort of a Soldier's life'.[12]

Two memorable Peninsular vignettes concern smoking. The first came during the army's retreat from Burgos in November 1812. On a raw cold morning, when the troops were standing in close column waiting for orders to move on, a regimental doctor 'often noticed among comrades the short pipe handed about from one to another, that each might enjoy a couple of whiffs – its warmth and stimulus solacing and comforting the inward man'.[13] The second was penned by an officer in the Black Watch when his regiment and others, including the King's German Legion, spent a month near St Jean de Luz: 'The most picturesque scene our camp exhibited was the space occupied by the German light troops, who, during the twilight, sat in groups before the doors of their tents, canopied in clouds of tobacco smoke, chanting together their native airs and anthems'.[14]

Instead of smoking, certain officers took snuff, though supplies were often erratic, especially in crucial times of rapid movement by the army and consequent confusion and inability to cope by the sutlers who tried to follow the troops or at least to pay regular visits. Perhaps the best example of a timely arrival of good things from England was the box of biscuits and supply of snuff sent by

147

Mrs Swabey to her son William, who was a great snuff-taker and used, apparently, to place a box at each end of his pillow when he went to bed, so as never to be at a loss for a pinch. A brother officer brought the parcels from Lisbon, arriving outside Burgos just in time to return to Portugal the hard way with the retreating troops. In his letter of thanks, written after the retreat was over, Swabey declared: 'As for the snuff, oh, ye gods! I literally had taken the last pinch I had not ten minutes before I opened the box containing that article'.[15]

The praises of smoking whether in bivouac, during a night march, under rain or snow or on campaign were rarely sung more persuasively than by the admirable Jonathan Leach, who under-valued his recollections by calling them 'Rough Sketches':

'If a man in England, after having eaten an alderman's dinner, and lounged on a sofa, with a Turkey carpet under his feet, a blazing fire before him, and a cigar in his mouth, fancies that he really knows the comfort of tobacco in that shape, he is very much mistaken; as is in like manner the equestrian or pedestrian dandy, with unshorn lip, who whiffs his cigar all over London, and through the Park, on a fine, bright, butterfly morning. He must rise, wet to the skin and numbed with cold, from the lee side of a tree or hedge, where he has been shivering all night under a flood of rain, – then let him light his cigar, and the warmth and comfort which it imparts is incredible. Or let him march, night after night, until he is so over-powered with sleepiness as to tumble off his horse during his momentary doze, (sleeping as he rides along, and falling in amongst the column of soldiers, who are in a similar plight); or if he is marching on foot, rolling about in the ranks in a state between sleeping and waking, – let him then apply his cigar, and he is awake again.'[16]

Some soldiers smoked and talked, some smoked and pondered, while a minority smoked to accompany their perusal of a news-paper, whenever a batch of them arrived in the mail. Many would have agreed that a newspaper was the most acceptable present which any friend could send during the Peninsular contest. Moreover, to have one sent out from home enabled the recipient to oblige his companions; and any officer who had no access to a regular paper was likely to feel peeved with his neglectful friends for whom war was a very distant affair. They should, he felt, take a trip to some foreign land in order to learn to sympathize in the want of 'those consoling little papers', even if much that they printed about the war struck the troops as a pack of lies.[17] The *Globe*, the *Morning Post*, the *Day*, the *London Chronicle* and many other newspapers reached the army, until nearly every officer at least could read one if he so desired. They were avidly perused for old news of the soldiers' own doings, and for the endless editorial speculations about the outcome of the war. 'With one we were all glorious and successful,' wrote Cowell Stepney, 'with another Lord Wellington was an ignoramus and we were all going to a place not to be named in print.'[18] Wellington himself read *The Times*, but also took the *Courier*, as he told Larpent at the end of 1812, to know what the British Government intended to do and 'as a decent paper to show General Castaños', the Spanish commander.

Of all those who read newspapers the most avid were probably the amateur politicians, so much so that one officer remarked how soon the interest people took in politics was lost when they had no means of being daily informed of the turns they took.[19] When a mail arrived up from Lisbon or Pasajes or St Jean de Luz, the eager politicians would assemble round a tree or tent appointed as the regimental news-room and explore the pages of the weekly packet of London and Edinburgh papers.

On going to Spain with his battalion, Colonel Edward Sebright of the 1st Foot Guards, a well-known eccentric, left directions for newspapers to be forwarded to him regularly. Whenever they arrived at regimental headquarters he had his servant damp them with water. Then, holding them to the fire, he would exclaim: 'Why, my papers smell as if they were only printed last night'.[20] It should be explained that at this period paper was damped before proofing, so that it could be dropped without too much pressure on to the uneven handset type.

A newspaper was what Lieutenant Rice Jones termed 'the greatest curiosity we can get'. One method, perhaps the most reliable, of dispatching a newspaper from Britain was via the Foreign Branch of the General Post Office. Newspapers giving news from Wales or Scotland were very welcome, and local papers such as Motley's of Portsmouth, which Colonel Fletcher, the chief engineer, received irregularly and late, had their devotees. Second-hand pamphlets and political caricatures, after relations and friends had finished reading or looking at them, were welcome. If a weekly or monthly printed the *London Gazette* promotions, that was an attraction. From early 1811 onwards certain officers received a new publication, *The Royal Military Chronicle or British Officer's Monthly Register and Mentor*. This contained biographies, topographical accounts of garrisons, copies of the gazettes, military promotions, obituaries and letters to the editor, plus a course of tactics and practical engineering and various military essays.[21]

Readers in the Peninsula derived considerable amusement, also exasperation, from learning what impression recent events in their war had produced upon the population at home, by the time William Cobbett, the *Morning Post* and *London Chronicle* had played their parts.[22] When Hill's headquarters were at Coria during the winter of 1812–13, regimental and staff officers alike were fascinated to read detailed accounts of the Russian campaign and of Napoleon's disaster there. In March 1813 they were depressed to read of the proceedings to be instituted against the Princess of Wales. 'May God grant her victory over her enemies. That is my wish and the whole army's,' declared George Woodberry.[23] No less disagreeable to peruse was 'the ridiculous nonsense put in the English newspapers by the friends of young men who are as ignorant as themselves'. Thus wrote Lieutenant Simmons, who in May 1811 begged his parents never to publish his letters to anyone, as the consequences could only be unpleasant. Many of the private letters which did appear in the press contained erroneous statements and, though treated with ridicule by those actually fighting the war, were probably accepted as accurate by people at home.[24]

In August 1810 Wellington, well aware of the mischievous effects of such letters, issued a General Order against officers who communicated 'the number and dispositions of the different divisions of the army, the formations of its magazines, preparations for breaking bridges, etc'. It was plain that more than once the French plans had been founded on such information, extracted from the English press. If officers chose to communicate facts of this kind, then they simply must 'urge their correspondents not to publish their letters in the newspapers, until it shall be certain that the publication of the intelligence will not be injurious to the army or to the public service'.[25]

Wellington, who set his face against the habit his staff and other officers had of 'writing news and keeping coffee houses', also deplored the irresponsible manner in which editors forecast events or gave accurate accounts of, for instance, the batteries and siege works at Cadiz and the calibre and number of guns each was to contain. Yet there was no censorship, and he did not advocate such a measure. 'I have done everything in my power by way of remonstrance,' he told Lord Liverpool in March 1811, 'and have been very handsomely abused for it; but I cannot think of preventing officers from writing to their friends.'[26] Besides disliking the irresponsible lack of security, Wellington condemned the widespread 'croaking' among officers, which occurred in his army, especially in 1810. Many failed to see how the war could possibly be brought to a successful conclusion. Even a man of pugnacious character and determination like General Picton was sometimes a prophet of gloom; and a few officers went so far as to advocate a policy of 'give up and get out'.

Lieut.-Colonel Frederick Ponsonby wrote to his mother as late as February 1812 to complain of the croakers and false prophets and those gentlemen who saw the black side of everything. 'They exaggerate the numbers of the French army and diminish our own, they would believe that the Emperor of China had landed 500 thousand men to assist the French, but they give no credit to a report of reinforcements landing for us. It makes one a little sick to be in a room with them.'[27] Fortunately they were few in number by that time. The course of the war had taken a more favourable turn by 1812, but eighteen months earlier the pessimism was more understandable though no less mischievous to the cause, and 'highly injurious to the public service', as Wellington chose to express the matter to the British Minister in Lisbon on 11 September 1810. 'I must devise some means of putting and end to it, or it will put an end to us. Officers have a right to form their own opinions upon events and transactions, but officers of high rank or situation ought to keep their opinions to themselves: if they do not approve of the system of operations of their commanders, they ought to withdraw from the army.'[28]

Perhaps the 'croakers' should have spent more time reading books, except that even those officers who enjoyed reading rarely had enough books, at least during the winter months when time was liable to hang heavily. To make the evenings bearable, to relieve themselves of *ennui*, they read anything that came to hand. It was easier for those who knew Portuguese, Spanish and French, because sometimes they could borrow books from the families on whom they were billeted. Some of the priests had a fair collection, though most of their books were lives of the saints or religious works,[29] and occasionally they picked up volumes abandoned by or captured from the French. Thus we find one officer at Tomar deep in a history of Don Juan de Castro, a Portuguese who flourished during the reign of Charles V; another in April 1809 read Fénelon's *Télémaque* left behind by a Frenchman who had occupied the same quarters before the battle of Vimeiro.[30] Charles Boothby, living in the house of an asthmatic priest in Elvas who understood French, could take from the library works by Racine, Molière and Voltaire and could even have perused a Portuguese translation of Milton's *Paradise Lost*.[31] Numerous French books were found among the baggage on the battlefield at Vitoria, and in the town itself one excellent bookseller had for sale some of the classics and the best French authors, in pocket-size Paris editions and unusually cheap. He assured Moyle Sherer that he had sold more books to the British in the course of one fortnight than he had disposed of in two years to the French troops constantly passing through the city; and expressed great surprise 'that among our officers so many reading men should be found'.[32]

Linguists certainly had no great problem in laying in a stock of books for the winter if they could read the works of Florian and Madame de Sévigné in the original text.[33] Naturally books of this kind became easier still to procure once the army entered France, but officers who had to rely on English books continued to be deprived. Not a few wrote home to request family or friends to send out a list of works, ranging from a small edition of Shakespeare, *Tristram Shandy*, and any of the novels of Smollett or Fielding to Henry Swinburne's *Travels Through Spain*, published in 1779.[34] That books about Spain were in demand and thought worthwhile is indicated by the fact that Swabey read Jean

Benjamin la Borde's *Itinéraire descriptive de l'Espagne* and
Carleton's *Memoirs*, which had been recommended to him as a
book 'very well adapted for perusal by all officers in Spain, being
partly an account of Lord Peterborough's campaign in Valencia,
Murcia, etc. in which Captain Carleton served'. Since the book is
believed to be spurious, and since Wellington's army did not
campaign in Valencia or Murcia, one is hardly surprised to learn
that Swabey found the book little calculated to give instruction.
William Napier, meanwhile, was studying *Mémoires de la Guerre
des Basses Pyrénées*.[35] However, for knowledge of Spain and the
Spaniards, British officers relied on Cervantes' *Don Quixote* and
on the adventures of *Gil Blas* by Lesage, though the latter never
visited Spain and painted Parisian life adapted by what he had
heard tell of the Peninsula. They would have echoed Swabey's
declaration that the book 'certainly contains the most faithful
picture of Spanish character, and that even without any high
colouring. Such adventures as its hero met with I believe daily to
take place in Spain, where jealousy and intrigue are the common
pursuits of all ranks in society.'[36]

Since most references to reading books are to be found in the
letters and diaries of Wellington's officers, it is good to hear of a
sergeant in the Foot Guards who, near Seville, asked Captain
John Harley, 47th Regiment, whether he had read *Gil Blas*, and
then quoted several passages, in particular the lines;

> 'He that has not Seville seen
> Never has a traveller been.'

When they entered Jafra, the sergeant was delighted, this being a
place much written of by his favourite author.[37]

Other works mentioned by name include *Hudibras*, Samuel
Johnson's *Rasselas*, and *A Young Man's Book of Knowledge* which
led William Bragge boldly to attack 'a position defended by
Multiplication and Division'.[38] When Edmund Wheatley was
recovering from wounds at Urugne in November 1813, his friend
Lieutenant Alexander Carmichael drank tea with him and read
aloud Robbie Burns' poems until eleven o'clock at night. In the
same month Major Frazer gleaned much useful information from
reading Vauban's standard work, *The Defence of Fortified Places*.[39]

Many officers appear to have been sufficiently familiar with the

153

novels of Mrs Ann Radcliffe for the sight of a monk and a muleteer in a dark and narrow glen to suggest an appropriate frontispiece to one of her works. A particular favourite was her romance entitled *The Italian,* a story of spies, dungeons and monks, especially a crafty monk named Schedoni who, for all his talents and energy, was a detestable, unfeeling hypocrite and profligate.[40]

As the heat of summer was conducive to reading, officers are now and then mentioned as 'lounging' over a favourite author till the heat of the day had passed. As early as May Vila Franca was so hot between the hours of eleven and five that a thoroughly energetic character like Swabey stayed indoors reading a serious professional work, Charles Pasley's *Military Policy of Great Britain.*[41]

It would probably be true to say that all officers liked to see the latest issue of the Army List as soon as it came out, but surely of no one else except Colonel John Frederick Brown, commanding the 28th Foot, could it have been truthfully said: 'He never had but one book, and that was the Army List'[42] – or to give it the full title, *A List of all the Officers of the Army and Royal Marines on Full and Half-Pay,* published annually by the War Office of the day.

While convalescing from fever at Coimbra Rice Jones was able to buy Lalande's Tables of Logarithms because it would no doubt be useful for his work as a Royal Engineer, and he borrowed from a wounded officer a copy of *On Solitude* by Zimmermann, a Swiss doctor who had been summoned to attend Frederick the Great in his last illness, and whose book, first appearing in 1755, had been translated into the principal languages of Europe.[43]

William Gomm, of the Quartermaster-General's Department, laid aside a translated biography of Marlborough's ally, Prince Eugene, to write to his wife: 'You know his life was one of my school books and half the events he relates are still fresh in my recollection, but his biographer could never give them the interest that he does himself'. It is Gomm who affords us a most agreeable vignette when he describes how, at Alpedrinha near Fundão, he lay under a tree throughout one day, reading the Italian poet Ariosto, and soon became aware that the surrounding scenery of hills thickly treed with oaks and chestnuts 'was almost in reality what Ariosto fancied'.[44]

It was all very well collecting several dozen books, either sent

154

from England or picked up while campaigning or in billets; but most officers had no means of carting them to and fro across Portugal and Spain. Just picture the young subaltern in the 48th Regiment of Foot who found himself with fifty volumes which a friend had purchased for him in London! In any case, whatever the resources of reading matter, good or bad, a portable library was less essential than, and had to take very much second place to, what Leach described as:

'a portmanteau containing a few changes of linen, boots, etc. etc., to say nothing of tea, sugar, chocolate, rice, bread, meat, a pig's skin of wine, a keg of spirits, cigars, spare horse-shoes and nails, etc. etc. . . . Our half-starved animals had more than enough to do in scrambling along with such matters on their backs, without the additional weight of libraries, even had it been possible to have procured books. A good telescope and correct maps of the country were indispensable.'[45]

Officers would write home to fathers or friends to order a good map of Portugal and Spain or of Portugal on its own. That published by William Faden, 'geographer to his Majesty at 5 Charing Cross', was about the best, but it had to be pasted on canvas and sent in a strong case. One description says it consisted of four sheets 'and, when joined together, will fill the whole side of a moderate sized room'. The other excellent map of Spain was that by Lopez, 'in sheets of provinces', for which William Napier, when ordering it from London, was prepared to pay up to twenty guineas.[46]

So much for the quieter, more solitary pastimes. Many more officers and men relieved boredom and enjoyed convivial evenings in social pursuits of one sort or another. Card parties became very popular, particularly among those who spoke the language and had the *entrée* to local society. Play was usually for small stakes,[47] but officers on leave in Lisbon sometimes spun out a night at the faro tables and, according to a lieutenant in the Brunswick Oels Regiment, play was often for very high stakes indeed. During the winter of 1810–11, having seen thousands of guineas laid on a single card, he commented: 'When once the rich Englishman became addicted to the game, they indulged it relentlessly, in a manner I have observed in no other nationality'.[48]

Of course the great majority could not afford to gamble in this way, nor had they the inclination. What most of them preferred was a quiet game of whist among their friends or a party of faro in a friendly Portuguese household. Take the case of that distinguished gunner, Major Dickson. When quartered at Golegã in November 1809 and serving with Portuguese troops, he was often invited by the *juiz de foro* or by an elderly colonel who had an English wife. After tea, cards were introduced, and the company played faro, casino and whist.[49] A few officers at Alcobaça had the good fortune to be billeted on a man who invited his neighbours to meet the British – and, after tea and coffee, to listen to music, play cards and enjoy a hot supper.[50] While at Covilha some of Wellington's artillery officers played 'a rub of cribbage' after a dinner at which they had drunk 'Arthur's good health'.[51] Several members of the 18th Light Dragoons appear to have had so little to do when the army reached southern France at the end of 1813 that they played cards from daybreak until dinner in Hasparren. The ever observant, critical Woodberry noted of his companions in boredom: 'P. & H. seem to be among the losers, and poor P. swears every day he won't play again, but next day it is he who starts'. P. was Lucas Pulsford, the regiment's assistant-surgeon.[52]

General Picton was a keen card player and his aide-de-camp, Captain T. Edwardes Tucker, thought it worth noting in his journal for 29 January 1814 the following item: 'Remarkable Event. At whist this evening, in one of the deals, Sir Thomas Picton and his partner, Colonel Stovin, were without a single trump in either of their hands, and it is therefore to be premised that their adversaries must have had thirteen between them.'

The rank and file were often as keen on cards and gambling as the officers were, though in different settings. For instance, when the army was unsuccessfully besieging Badajoz in April 1811 the 7th Fusiliers were on duty in the trenches, and one day when it was Sergeant Cooper's turn to warn of any approaching shot or shell, the rest of his company, having to wait while the Engineer officer staked out some more work, sat down and played cards in the trench.[53] No less than their British companions, the Portuguese *caçadores* had an itch for gambling, and even when a few minutes' halt was called on the march, they could be seen grouped in impromptu card parties.[54]

For officers, one of the best ways of spending a social evening was to get on the invitation list of a *tertulia*, which may be translated 'assembly' or 'reception'. When Buckham of the Staff Corps was quartered near Tolosa in 1813 he had a choice of two *tertulias*: one a ladies' party, the other a sort of club, where the men discussed the gazettes and pamphlets of the day over cigars and hot chocolate.[55] The latter style was comparatively unusual, and most of Wellington's officers describe 'at homes' given by ladies of some wealth and distinction.

To judge by contemporary letters, memoirs and journals, Badajoz provided the most memorable brand of *tertulia*. During 1809 a certain Donna Payna opened her house every evening to the best local society and also to British officers, whom she received with the utmost courtesy. Its blend of conversation, cards, song and dance reminded some officers of a London rout. On the night of 14th October, celebrated as King Ferdinand VII's birthday, Lord Wellington and members of his staff attended, and besides an exhibition of a bolero and fandango danced by the hostess and a second lady, a handsome widow named Donna Manuela sang a Spanish ballad accompanied on the guitar.[56] Another leading Badajoz hostess, the Marchioness of Monte Salud, who was no beauty but a highly intelligent woman, liked to entertain her guests at the piano, while several of the party accompanied her on the flute and guitar. Captain Gomm, who was invited to her home one August evening in 1810, recalled that generally from ten to twelve people gathered in the room, all men with dusty boots who walked in and out just as they pleased.[57] This casual entry and exit is confirmed by others. The usual procedure was for a lady to announce that a *tertulia* would take place at her house on certain nights and then, without further invitation, anyone of her own social class who chose to call after nine or ten o'clock merely sat down, with so little ceremony that there was no need even to acknowledge one's hostess.[58]

After George Scovell had attended a Badajoz *tertulia* on 19 September 1809 he described it in the following terms:

'I was much amused at the manner of arranging the chairs, it showing how determined they were to have conversation, exactly opposite to each other, and touching. It seemed to be very lively,

157

and I could easily perceive that the *double entendre* was the grand substitute for real wit. Singing was a part of the evening's amusements. It finished with dancing Cotillions, Country dances, etc. There was one Card table but no high play. Water was the only refreshment given, nor is any other necessary as they all sup before they assemble.'[59]

Alexander Gordon, who had spent an occasional evening the previous year in Corunna, found such parties exceedingly dull. For one thing, most of those present were priests and friars. For another, the room was often ill-lit. Then sugared biscuits and lemonade were sometimes offered though usually dispensed with. Worst of all, both sexes had the abominable habit of spitting on the floor. The men smoked cigars and passed them from mouth to mouth.[60] Burgoyne noticed the same habit in Badajoz. The Spaniards rolled their own cigars and, when half smoked, often gave them to their neighbours to finish. He was more surprised by the indelicate stories and conversation which passed before the most respectable women who, far from appearing in the least shocked, constantly joined in the hearty laughter. 'Their actions and manners are on the same free and easy system: a young man making love will light his cigar, and will accompany a pretty speech with a volume of smoke plump in the face of his *innamorata*.'[61]

At Cadiz, another centre of gay social activity because after 1809 it became the refuge of the Spanish Government which had been obliged to leave first Madrid and then Seville, officers also found behaviour to amaze or shock them. Here, for instance, is what Captain Neil Douglas of the 79th (Cameron Highlanders) found at a large party one Sunday evening:

'As it was Carnival time all form, and even what in England might be termed common decency, seem'd to be laid aside. Some of the Ladys appeared in Men's Clothes, and the men again in those of the Women. One great piece of wit amongst the Men was the dropping of handfuls of a very small sweet meat down the backs and Bosoms of the Ladys who though of course much annoyed took it all in good humour.'[62]

The pattern here was much the same as at Badajoz. Five or six houses were open every night, and British officers had free access to Spanish society. An officer had only to be presented by a friend to the lady, and she would give him a cordial invitation, offering a free *entrée* to her house for as long as he remained in the city.[63] Visitors would sit down and talk until tired, then walk out again to some other *tertulia*, but here they did at least greet the lady of the house. The Anglo-Spanish families provided tea instead of or as well as the water and the bottle of wine which normally stood in one corner of the drawing-room. Some houses contained a separate music room, others kept a long gambling table crowded with fashionable men and women, all eagerly engaged in playing faro.[64]

Once Wellington's army had withdrawn to the Lines of Torres Vedras in October 1810, Lisbon became more lively and gay, owing in part to the arrival of numerous sutlers, loose women and other people who eagerly sought to tempt soldiers and officers to part with their pay. Amusement and relaxation after the hardships of campaign life were to be found in the capital, where young officers spent money in reckless fashion. Certainly German officers serving under Wellington's command in the King's Legion and the Black Brunswickers were surprised at some of the attitudes and goings-on. One such officer tells us that although a bottle of champagne always cost a guinea in the best restaurants, he nevertheless watched one young officer in the Royal Dragoons entertain to breakfast six of seven brother officers and four or five very attractive girls, and pay for forty bottles of champagne out of his own pocket. What is more, drunken officers threw half of these out of the window between the laughing, gaping Portuguese street boys.

As for the wanton girls, the prettiest of whom had come to Lisbon from Andalusia, the sums they took off the officers in the way of money is almost unbelievable, and the disorder reached such a pitch, especially between the common prostitutes and the drunken English soldiery, that Lord Wellington saw himself obliged to take active steps to prevent it. Accordingly he had several shiploads of the most brazen girls sent away.[65]

A favourite pastime for the inactive winter months was amateur dramatics, or 'private theatricals' as they were often called. The enterprise developed in the Lines of Torres Vedras, with the Light Division always to the fore, producing plays in a style which most officers found astonishingly good, given the difficulties of procuring suitable costumes. It seems, however, that the first effort was a flop and derived from the bragging talk of a French aide-de-camp who, when the two front lines were close together in January 1811, mentioned the theatre which Massena's *Armée de Portugal* had established in Santarem. Determined not to be outdone, one Rifle Corps company converted into a theatre an old house in which olive oil had formerly been made. Jonathan Leach records that the result was not a success: 'The blankets and great-coats of the soldiers made capital side-scenes; and had not too much wine and grog found their way behind them, no doubt the piece would have gone off with great *éclat*. But, as the truth must be told, they all forgot their parts; and it was a toss-up whether our attempt at horse-racing or play-acting was the most perfectly ludicrous.'[66]

By the time the next winter came round, the Light Division had changed its method, and it was left mostly to officers to produce and act. A ruined chapel on the outskirts of Fuente Guinaldo became the theatre for an ambitious performance of Shakespeare's *Henry IV* with scenery painted by Captain John Bell, the Deputy Adjutant-General, who many years later became Governor of Guernsey. A dress rehearsal was held on 16th November, and the play was publicly performed two days later,[67] the village being filled 'like a beehive' with officers who, wrapped in camlet cloaks, had ridden a considerable distance on donkey, mule and horse from other divisions to see the show. The best account of what occurred comes from the fluent pen of Captain Cooke of the 43rd.

'Tickets being issued for pit and boxes, we moved in Bacchanalian groups towards *el Teatro* (or chapel). It was crammed to excess, as we had not forgotten to reserve some seats for *los soldados*. The curtain no sooner drew up, than the wonder of the *muchachas* knew no bounds, and they became so loquacious in admiration of the scenery and dresses, and in disputing among themselves which was *el Principe*, and which of the various characters the officers were to personify, that it was a considerable time before they could be so far tranquillized as to permit the performance to proceed, which, however, went off with great éclat.'[68]

160

Plate 5. Sir John Moore's key-ring and seals. (*Photo:* National Army Museum)

A watch belonging to Sir John Moore in 1808–09. It was made by Collier of London. (*Photo:* National Army Museum)

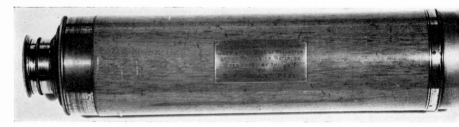

Plate 6. This telescope was used by Wellington at the battle of Waterloo. Made by Matthew Berge, optician, of 199 Piccadilly, it was given to the Duke by Sir Robert Peel. (*Photo:* National Army Museum)

Troops in bivouac in May 1811. Note the various tents, the goat boys, the officers at table, and the barber. (*Photo:* National Army Museum)

The audience thoroughly enjoyed the evening, and Captain John Kent of the 95th displayed such genuine talent in the role of Hotspur that he was the star performer and, as will be seen, became a draw whenever he was billed to appear.

Elsewhere a large barn was transformed into a theatre, and several popular comedies were staged. Regimental bands provided music, and a very high standard of acting was attained. Indeed, Schaumann, the Hanovarian assistant-commissary, picked out one infantry subaltern who 'as regards costume, mimicry, dancing, and singing, impersonated a *prima donna* with such inimitable skill and comicality that he might without fear have appeared on any stage'.[69]

The most talked-about performance of all was probably *The Revenge*, a tragedy by Edward Young which had been first produced at Drury Lane in 1721. Young, who was at one time chaplain to King George II and then Rector of Welwyn, had taken as hero of his play a Moor named Zanga, who having been captured by the Spaniards and condemned to slavery by a certain Don Alonzo, took his revenge by exciting the Spaniard to jealousy. The tragedy was re-enacted on 30 October 1811 by officers of the Light Division, with Kent in the role of Zanga. At a subsequent appearance Lord Wellington and his staff were in the audience. Next day the Peer took the field with his foxhounds and in the heat of the chase Captain Kent was thrown from his horse into a stream. Lord Wellington witnessed the mishap and enquired who had fallen. 'It's only Zanga washing his face, my Lord!' replied a colonel who was riding by.[70]

At Nave de Haver some officers of the Coldstream Guards converted an old room into a theatre and there rehearsed a comedy entitled *The Heir at Law*, by George Colman the Younger, which had been performed in London in 1797. Unfortunately the Coldstream version was interrupted by what Stepney referred to as 'The Tragedy of the Siege and Capture of Ciudad Rodrigo'.[71]

While in Madrid during September and October of 1812 officers of the Light Division, anxious to show off their talent as actors to their beloved *señoritas*, once more began the process of ordering dresses and learning their parts. The play they chose to produce was again Young's tragedy, *The Revenge*, with Kent of the Rifle Corps playing the part of Zanga the Moor, but this time

F

161

in El Teatro del Principe instead of a ruined chapel. Cooke of the 43rd has again left the most detailed description of the performance:

'The piece went off in silence, until he began to move backwards and forwards, like the pendulum of a clock, his sinewy arm and clenched fist, cased in a black silk stocking, or glove, encircled by a shining bracelet – which caused the muleteers in the gallery to roar with laughter. The *señoras* tittered, and held their fans to their faces. During the remainder of the evening poor *Zanga* was treated more like a comic than a tragic character, and whenever he raised his arm, which he had frequent occasion to do, the same round of salutations greeted him on all sides, such as "Arré Múlo", etc. etc.'[72]

All in all, the evening was *not* a success, and the play was the first and the last attempted by the British garrison in Spain's capital city. Grattan of the Connaught Rangers explains that, despite Kent's fine acting, the play would never have been allowed to proceed by the audience had not the actors been British officers and the play put on to raise money for poor relief. 'Whether it was that the other characters were ill cast, or that the tragedy was too dull for the Spaniards to relish, it is a positive fact that, long before the second act was finished, the audience were heartily tired of the play . . . from the moment "Zanga" (or *El Preto* as they styled him) appeared, there was one universal buzz of disapprobation.' Perhaps the Spaniards' dislike of the Moors was the reason. Fortunately, Samuel Foote's popular farce entitled *The Mayor of Garratt*, first produced in London in 1764, followed as an agreeable contrast and restored the audience to a good humour.[73]

In the winter of 1812–13, this time at Gallegos, the Light Division established a theatre which, according to Leach, 'might have vied with half the provincial ones in England, if we could have procured female performers'. The theatre was fitted up in an empty chapel, and the Bishop of Ciudad Rodrigo appears to have cursed the Light Division for its sacrilege.[74] On Saturday evening, 6th March, two pieces were given. The first, *Fortune's Frolic*, had six male parts, played by subalterns in the 43rd and 95th, while the three female roles were taken by Lieutenant the Hon. Charles Gore, a son of the Earl of Arran, Lieutenant Lord Charles Spencer, and Lieutenant Thomas Grubbe. The second play was a farce entitled *Raising the Wind*, acted by five subalterns from the Light Division and a Captain William Cator of the Royal Artillery. As for the two women's parts they went to Lieutenant Edward Freer and Captain Samuel Hobkirk, both of the 43rd.

The handbills, printed on the Headquarters press at Freineda, ended with the words:

NO ADMITTANCE BEHIND THE SCENES
VIVAT WELLINGTON[75]

The next major performance, at the 'Light Division Theatre, Gallegos', took place on Thursday, 13 April 1813, when Sheridan's comedy, *The Rivals* was given. This time Hobkirk played Mrs Malaprop, a Lieutenant Pattenson took the part of Sir Anthony Absolute, and William Cox was Sir Lucius O'Trigger. Also on the bill was a farce called *The Apprentice*.[76] Leach, who attended that evening, recalled long afterwards how ludicrous it was to see Lydia Languish and Julia 'performed by two young and good-looking men [Gore and Spencer], dressed uncommonly well, and looking somewhat feminine on the stage, drinking punch and smoking cigars behind the scenes, at a furious rate, between the acts'.

When Wellington attended an earlier performance of *The Rivals*, one of the actors forgot his lines at a critical moment and things looked awkward until the Marquess rose to his feet and began clapping and shouting 'Bravo!' This demonstration restored the actor's confidence and he remembered his part. After the show Wellington and his staff rode back a dozen miles in darkness over terrible roads to headquarters at Freineda.[77]

Apparently the Spaniards were reluctant to patronize these theatrical performances. For one thing, they could seldom understand what was being said. For another, the ladies were revolted by the idea that men should play the female parts and 'turned up their pretty noses at the want of grace and elegance on the stage. The masculine strides in petticoats upon the boards must have been an utter abomination in the eyes of those mincing beauties, whose largest step would not be more than three or four inches.'

At the same period Sir Rowland Hill was encouraging an

163

amateur theatre down at Coria. His 2nd Division also had some capital actors and scene-painters. Slim-delicate-looking, pale-faced ensigns distinguished themselves in petticoats, and the overall standard deserved a larger audience. Bell, who took part, writes: 'We had some very handsome Spanish señoras, who looked on and laughed through their bright eyes, but understood nothing'. After the play all the actors and 'actresses' were invited to General Hill's supper table. The same happened a year later at Vieux Mouguerre, above the Adour, where Hill once again patronized an amateur theatre and entertained the whole *dramatis personae* after the play.[78]

Besides these amateur performances, opportunities occurred now and then, especially for officers, to attend the professional theatre or opera. Those quartered, convalescent or waiting in Lisbon were well placed to spend an evening in the dull, heavy, badly lit opera house. The British may well have enjoyed themselves there, but many were highly critical. First they disliked the way in which actors repeated word for word what the prompter told them, he being sometimes more audible than the cast.[79] Secondly, some of them deplored the indelicate style of dancing there. Lieutenant Simmons of the 95th waxed eloquent to his parents on the subject of the Lisbon audience in July 1809:

'The Portuguese ladies seemed to enjoy the performance with great rapture, which must make a Briton turn from them with disgust, and awake in the soul those refined sentiments for delicacy and virtue which characterise our British dames; and at all public entertainments a man possessing any degree of feeling for the honour of the sex, must be disgusted with such immodest performances.'[80]

Dickson enjoyed the music of an opera called *Ouro nao compra amor* ['Love is not bought for Gold'], and Larpent had misgivings about the buffo-style comic masks which appeared to be the favourite fashion among Portuguese opera-goers. *Macbeth* was turned into a pantomime: 'the death and dagger scene very fine, but the whole effect marred by the mummery of fantastic dancing and skipping witches'.[81]

On 25 October 1809, to mark the fiftieth anniversary of King George III's accession to the throne, many officers went to the

Opera to watch the performance of an appropriate ballet.[82] Moyle
Sherer, while convalescing in Lisbon early in 1810, used to steal
in a cabriolet to the Opera Buffa or the San Carlos Theatre, and
enjoyed the admirable acting and pleasing voices of Vaccani and
Scarameli, while in September that same year Captain Neil
Douglas of the 79th attended a special benefit performance, at
which the battle of Oporto was represented on the stage with
the aid of infantry, cavalry and artillery manoeuvring in great
style.[83]

Oporto had its opera, which a few Engineer officers attended,
and an ill-lighted theatre. In January 1813 Frazer found the performances so dull that he and his friends left in the middle of a
popular play about King Frederick of Prussia yielding to the
entreaties of a lady on behalf of her husband, who had been
sentenced to death for some military offence, the nature of which
they could not discover.[84] Salamanca also boasted a theatre, where
the performances were often poor, the prompter took his place in
front of the stage and where, above the upper tier of boxes, ran a
sort of gallery 'for the admittance of *women only* – such women as
go alone go there'.[85] Opinions varied sharply about the theatre in
Madrid. On Sunday, 16 August 1812, when Lord Wellington and
his staff occupied the royal box and the house was crowded,
scenery, dresses, and acting were excellent, and between the acts
the audience was entertained by music and high-quality dancing
of the bolero and fandango. In contrast, a month later the company
of comedians struck British officers, at least, as weak; apparently
the most applauded actor obtained his laughs in the closing scene
by using a chamberpot and pulling off his breeches prior to going
to bed.[86]

Early in 1814 we find members of the army enjoying themselves
in St Jean de Luz's theatre, but more dramatic were the performances in Toulouse. Here an actor announced Napoleon's
abdication at Fontainebleau,[87] and the theatre was opened free
to British officers, some of whom misbehaved themselves to the
point where Sir Rowland Hill, Wellington being absent, issued a
General Order desiring officers to control their conduct by the
rules of propriety belonging to England, and forbidding them
to appear on the stage, 'which is by no means their proper
theatre'.[88]

165

Finally, in Brussels during the month before Waterloo, officers went now and then to the Salle des Nobles, either to hear the celebrated Madame Angelica Catalani sing an Italian opera in good voice and exquisite manner, or to a concert attended by Wellington and all the 'grandees'.[89]

Chapter 11

COME DANCING

'We had waltzes, boleros and fandangos, dark eyes, favourable glances, agreeable smiles, white teeth, charming figures, and graceful movement. We actually began to feel a little humanized.'[1]
Ensign John Cowell Stepney, Coldstream Guards

'At these balls there was no supper, only slight refreshments, such as iced lemonade, iced cream, chocolate, coffee, and sweet cake, with plenty of wine. . . . Occasionally we might have 300 present.' [2]
William Graham, with the 4th Dragoons at Lerin, August 1813

The best known giver of balls during the Peninsular War was, of course, Lord Wellington himself, whether he issued a general invitation to all officers who cared to attend or, as in Madrid, confined his invitation cards to field and staff officers.[3] In Brussels on 8 June 1815 he gave a grand rout attended by the Prince of Orange, the Duke of Brunswick and the British and foreign nobility then living in the city, on which occasion four invitation cards were received by each regiment. Wellington, standing apart, received his guests after they had walked through an illuminated garden and before they began dancing.[4]

Most celebrated of wartime balls was the Duchess of Richmond's given a week later in a large room which had been used for a coachbuilder's warehouse and, more recently, by her daughters as a schoolroom and for games of battledore and shuttlecock on wet days. Of the 220 people who went to the Richmonds' house that night, six were to be killed in the battle of Waterloo, one lost an arm, another a leg, and four more received wounds.[5]

According to Sir Hussey Vivian, so little did the Duke of Wellington expect the French to advance that he was to have given a ball on 21st June, the second anniversary of the battle of Vitoria.[6] Indeed, one can say that, as in the case of dinners, balls

167

were given now and then to celebrate a special event like the King's birthday on 4th June, or the installation of a general as a Knight of the Bath, or the anniversary of some battle.[7] On 28 July 1812, for instance, Lord Wellington gave a dance for the principal inhabitants of Olmedo to commemorate Talavera, while in January 1813 the Spaniards marked the storming of Ciudad Rodrigo in similar style. Six months later Wellington's victory at Salamanca was recalled by a ball organized by the heavy dragoons at Tafalla.[8]

Occasionally a regiment would arrange a dance merely as a social event in an otherwise bleak calendar. Thus we find the 1st Hussars entertaining the ladies of Covilha in December 1811, the officers of the 3rd Dragoons each subscribing one dollar for a dance at Fuente del Maestre, close to Niza, and, during the early months of 1813, the 95th Rifles giving a ball nearly every week to the ladies of Alameda and the surrounding villages, who did them the honour of attending.[9]

When the 9th Foot were quartered in Leomil during May and June 1812, Lieutenant Peter le Mesurier noted how the ladies of the town appeared not to be fond of dancing. 'They are,' he wrote, 'the laziest set of Mortals on the face of the Earth, so that we are obliged to have Officers for partners.' Yet when the regiment marched away, the same ladies wept, declaring that they had never spent such an agreeable month. What is more, the balls were well attended latterly, and with eagerness.[10] Other, less personal factors could hold sway when it came to finding partners. Two officers gave a splendid ball and supper in Cadiz on Saturday, 7 April 1810, and the affair went off very well, lasting until after two o'clock in the morning, although a number of the ladies sent their apologies because it was Easter.[11] On several occasions Lent imposed an initial restraint, though the Spaniards and Portuguese were often prepared to defy this in order to enjoy a supper and dance.[12] In the political, patriotic sphere the pressures could also be strong, as when the local *junta* of Salamanca gave a ball for Wellington's army in June 1812 – a month before the victory there – and many people declined to come lest the French troops return and penalize their fraternization on the dance floor. Or again, soon after the British set foot on French soil, the young ladies of St Jean de Luz were at first doubtful as to the propriety of joining enemy officers in gaieties, but they consulted together and apparently arranged matters with their conscience.[13]

St Jean de Luz must have been especially difficult in respect of female partners. With their defeated army evicted from Spain and retreating across south-western France, the people had every reason to resent and suspect the incoming British army, and to start with many ladies were, as already indicated, too patriotic to dance. Consequently, when the local mayor, thinking to please Milord Wellington, gave a ball at the Hôtel de Ville, the only lady present was Countess Waldegrave, then living at headquarters with her husband John, a major in the 15th Dragoons. What was one partner among two hundred men? Inevitably the ball was an utter flop, despite the personal efforts of the Mayor who entertained the officers by dancing an English hornpipe which he had learnt while a prisoner of war at Plymouth.[14]

Things went better on 11 February 1814 when about thirty local ladies arrived to dance at the *Salle de la Mairie* – none of them very handsome or of high social standing. Nevertheless, everyone enjoyed the cotillions, waltzes and country dances, and Wellington, Beresford 'and all the smarts' were present.[15] A month later the 43rd suffered a social setback near Mont de Marsan. The senior officer gave a dance in the *château* in which he had quarters, and only one girl appeared on the scene so, making a virtue of necessity, the officers took turns to waltz with her until she was exhausted, at which point everyone had supper.[16]

There was usually a senior or junior officer ready to arrange and finance a local dance whenever opportunity occurred. Sir Stapleton Cotton, the cavalry commander, was a generous patron, and offered a ball at Covilhã in February 1812 and another at Zafra two months later. Lower down the hierarchy we learn that while in Madrid Captain Samuel Hobkirk of the 43rd gave a ball and supper which cost him three hundred dollars;[17] and at Sanguessa Charlie Gore, detached from the Rifle Corps as an aide-de-camp, laid on a ball at which, to quote Harry Smith, 'there was as much happiness as if we were at Almack's, and some as handsome women'.[18] The town of Olite appears to have generated special gaiety, because during July 1813 at least three dances are on record, given by Lieutenant James Conolly of the 18th Light Dragoons, by Henry, Marquess of Worcester, and by that observant if caustic diarist, George Woodberry, also of the 18th, at whose *soirée* forty-two of the local ladies attended.[19]

Cadiz, far to the south, was a particularly gay social centre. The streets were as busy as those of London: crowded with two armies, with members of the Spanish Court and Government, with a great influx of refugee families, and with scores of Galician porters who, because the streets were mostly too narrow to admit coaches or even carts, carried the city's loads on their shoulders. On the open gardens of the *Alameda*, where towards evening people of rank and fashion promenaded or sat resting on marble seats in the shade, the embroidered uniforms of Spanish officers mingled with the black dresses, coloured gloves and fluttering fans of the local beauties. Whenever a man wished a light for his cigar, one of the attendant fire-boys would strike a match of combustible rope on the ground; and *boca* boys, carrying baskets filled with the claws of small crabs caught in the nearby marshes, wormed their way through the crowd and gave shrill cries of '*boca fresca de la Isla!*' At sundown a bell rang from every church tower, and silence fell upon the people, who stood up for evening prayer. Later still, they attended the theatre, or danced in the ballroom of a well-known local dancing-master. Sometimes, when Andalusian women were dancing with castanets to the accompaniment of a guitar, the dance would be interrupted by the whine of an enemy shell, by screams of '*Caramba*'*!* and by prayers to the Holy Virgin.[20]

Perhaps the best known of the balls there in 1810 was that given by Alexander, Lord Saltoun, a captain in the 1st Foot Guards. One brother officer who attended was Frederick Trench, then holding a staff post. He described the scene as follows:

'There was an immense crowd & but very few that looked tolerably well in evening dresses – indeed it is an observation that everyone must make that the women when out of the streets are peculiarly ill-dressed – their finery hangs on in a loose slovenly manner & the hair not well managed & above all or *below* all I shd. say their bosoms are absolutely frightful. Nature has not been particularly partial to them in this point – they wear no stays, the climate hot, their modes of life relaxing, which added to a bad skin and bad taste makes the thing very bad indeed. They danced country

dances to a very slow waltz time & with a fantastical sort of figure
but which kept you perpetually in contact with your partner –
instead of change sides or a Gentn. setting between two Ladies
here after several difficult evolutions of the arm the lady throws
herself into the joined arms of two men on her back & as if
fainting etc. When the waltzing began there was a pretty lively
girl whose name I forget who exhibited all she well could before
so mixed an assembly of the best attitudes. She played with her
partner, encouraged him – was then coy, then modest, then
shocked, turned away her head & hid her face with her hands
(her *burning* not flushing Face). Next she laid her head on one
hand as if asleep (while *he* hung over her), the other hand hanging
dead; by degrees she recovered a little but suddenly fainted away,
throwing herself quite back in his arms, her head hanging down &
her arms lifeless! He holds her clasped round the waist & while
they glide round now quicker pressed close to him in the most
sensative [*sic*] points of contact. In short nothing can be more
expressive & till now I never saw a *Waltz* – the Spanish men
seem to enjoy the dance & all dancing as much as any Frenchman
or Italian. Many of [the] women wore their wide white mantilla &
neck covered & they looked not as if they came to dance but as if
they had been picked up walking in the streets & brought in!'[21]

As might be expected, local dances evoked the most comment
by British soldiers. Although some thought the *fandango* gay,
pleasing and admirable, others considered it scarcely decent, even
immodest or obscene.[22] 'This dance,' wrote one Scot, 'had a great
effect upon us, but the Spaniards saw it without being moved, and
laughed at the quick breathing and amorous looks of our men.'[23]
The other principal Spanish dance, the *bolero*, invented in about
1770 by a Murcian named Bolero, aroused equal disapproval
among British observers of the scene. After watching an exhibition
of it during a ball given at Ceclavin near Plasencia in November
1808, Sir Robert Ker Porter remarked on the female dancer's
great dexterity in keeping time not only with her castanets but
also with 'the silent movements of her bottom, which in elasticity
far exceeded the quickness of her feet. . . . Disgusting as it was to
our eyes, the honest Ceclaviners liked it well, and a frequent
repetition of the amusement took place during the evening.'[24]

171

Officers and men were fascinated by the intricate movements of these country dances, but found them exceedingly difficult if not impossible to learn, despite numerous demonstrations at balls attended by the British.[25] In return, the Portuguese and Spanish ladies were taught the steps of several English country dances, including the Sir Roger de Coverly, and after a few lessons from officers turned ballet-masters they could usually perform these admirably. By contrast, they found the greatest difficulty in learning reels.[26] 'Fancy a parcel of people,' wrote Lord Saltoun to his future wife after attending a ball in Lisbon, 'whom God never meant to be active, striving to dance Scotch reels, while the fiddlers were doing their best to play them as like waltzes as the *music* will admit of.'

One ball at Isla de Leon outside Cadiz was marred when a Highland steward ignored remonstrances and insisted on introducing a blind piper from the 79th Regiment. He was led up the room, 'playing a Pibroch as loud and discordant as any of his breechless brethren could wish. The affrighted Spanish ladies putting their fingers in their ears ran round the room in amazement wanting to know from me what was the matter. At length, finding that this uproarious noise was likely to continue, as these Cameronian fellows were preparing for a Highland fling among themselves, the damsels fairly fled into the garden.'[27]

For music the officers could normally rely upon the services of a regimental band such as that of the King's German Legion, the 18th Light Dragoons or the 1st Portuguese Caçadores, but if these were not available, then the dancers had to be content with a fife and drum, or with local fiddlers and guitarists. Once in 1808 the 15th Light Dragoons danced to a spinet and a square tambourine, covered with parchment on both sides and without bells.[28] When Alexander Dickson gave a dance in his house for the artillery officers and their partners, he provided two guitars to accompany them. However, the Royal Horse Artillery and others quartered in Medina del Campo on 1 August 1812 were fortunate in that two bands, those of the 2nd and 61st Regiments, who happened to be marching to join the army, were prevailed upon to play English and Spanish country dances, and not a few waltzes at a hurriedly improvized dance, which lasted till midnight and produced 'a very fine assemblage of beauty'.[29]

Supper at these dances ranged from roast chestnuts to sweet-meats brought from a town held by French troops. In the villages of Portugal all the girls wished for and expected – and all the younger officers could afford – was cakes, fruit, lemonade, and sometimes a local wine, iced in summer time.[30] Woodberry of the 18th Light Dragoons offered his guests sandwiches, *négus*, lemonade and pastries, to such good effect that on leaving, most of the men were drunk and the women very gay. While the girls loved to eat grapes and chocolate, the men enjoyed their cigars.[31] Particular care was taken to refresh the chaperoning duennas, 'those Cerberuses of young hearts', with ample wine, punch and cake and as good a cold supper as local resources allowed.[32]

Now and then a ball acquired a measure of notoriety thanks to a social *gaffe* or explosive quarrel. For instance, at a masked ball held at Fuente Guinaldo early in 1813, many of the light infantry officers wore disguise and masquerade, a few dressed as women and one as a Spanish farmer, and one or two of their partners dressed as British officers. The harmony was broken by a dispute between the two leading beauties.[33] Jealousies of another kind erupted when some British commissaries organized a ball at Tolosa and omitted to invite the Spanish officers from the local garrison, whereupon the latter held a second dance and deliberately left off their invitation list any lady who had attended the commissaries' ball.[34] If Woodberry is to be credited, the Marquess of Worcester's ball was nearly ruined by a ludicrous if not scandalous episode. When musicians hired for the evening failed to turn up at the appointed time, a British N.C.O. was sent in search, and found them intoxicated and dancing in the nude except for a pelisse thrown over their shoulders. They had some women there, but Woodberry never discovered whether they too were dancing naked.[35] Sometimes a scandal would be caused when, escorted by the officers who had chosen to invite them, ladies of doubtful reputation appeared at a dance. This would be the signal for respectable ladies to leave the ballroom in disgust and embarrassment, though their action provoked mocking laughter as often as shame from the men concerned. Woodberry was displeased to note that Major Hughes of his own regiment, the 18th Light Dragoons, brought to his ball in Olite one of the most notorious local women, who had formerly belonged to the Pamplona theatre company. However, when it came to dancing, she was in a class by herself and aroused general admiration by the graceful manner in which she waltzed.[36]

Kincaid of the Rifle Corps probably expressed the view of many when he wrote:

'A woman was a woman in those days; every officer made it a point of honour to marshal as many as he could to the general assembly, no matter whether they were countesses or *sextonesses* [at Rueda he fell desperately in love with a sexton's daughter and took her to the ball]; and although we, in consequence, frequently incurred the most indelible disgrace among the better orders of our indiscriminate collection, some of whom would retire in disgust, yet, as a sufficient number generally remained for our evening's amusement, and we were only birds of passage, it was a matter of the most perfect indifference to us what they thought; we followed the same course wherever we went.'[37]

Here are two further examples of the type of incident or contretemps which could make an evening embarrassingly memorable. In August 1812 a grand ball in King Joseph's country house near Madrid was marked by the excellence of its food, but also by a trying experience for Colonel Frederick Ponsonby, who wrote home: 'In waltzing *after* supper I got in a tumble by sticking my spurs into a lady's gown, and brought half Madrid down with me. The room was large, a whole crowd waltzing, so, as the circle approached the spot where I and half a dozen more lay down, they came in rotation.'[38] No less awkward an event, though in a quite different way, occurred at a ball in Cadiz on 28 May 1810, when the guard had the utmost difficulty in keeping out a large number of Spanish officers who tried to get in without tickets. Captain Neil Douglas relates that, despite every exertion by the guard, many of these officers forced an entry and, 'what is scarcely credible, they pocketed every thing that came in their way'.[39]

Most of the dances continued till one or two o'clock in the morning, but from one of General Cotton's dances, attended by about a hundred people, the cavalry officers left at daybreak, mounted their horses, and marched.[40] Towards the close of a ball given by Lord Wellington at Olmedo, orders to advance arrived an hour before daylight. In his memoirs Cooke of the

43rd Light Infantry recalled the droll sight of officers sleeping as they rode along, 'still dressed in their ball attire, such as crimson, light blue, or white trowsers, richly embroidered with gold or silver, velvet and silk waistcoats of all colours, decorated in a similar manner: dandies ready alike for the dance and the fight'.[41] On the field of Quatre Bras the bodies of several officers were found, lying dead in the silk stockings and buckled shoes which they had worn at the Duchess of Richmond's ball the previous night. Their servants had hurried with the baggage to join the columns when the call to arms sounded, so making it impossible for their masters to change out of their full-dress uniforms.[42]

During the Peninsular War Wellington's troops were quick to observe and note down minor differences in female dress. While most women from the higher social strata wore black, either because it was the fashion or because it was a symbol of wartime, the village women usually went in for bright colours: red stockings in Toro, brown ones in nearby Zamora, and yellow in the Ebro valley and between Llerena and Seville. While the buxom girls of Malpartida encased their legs in blue stockings with scarlet clocks, those in Alcántara wore black worsted.[43]

On first entering Spain Sir John Moore's soldiers were struck by the yellow skirts worn by the peasant women. Sometimes the petticoats were very short, like tiny aprons, and made of red wool or brown cloth, occasionally figured with 'ridiculous patches of red cloth', as in Almeda and the villages along Spain's mountainous frontier with Portugal.[44] Riding from Freineda down the Portuguese side of that frontier in November 1811, Captain Call of the 9th Light Dragoons noted that the ladies of quality dressed in a manner close to the English style. As for the middle classes, they wore 'mantles or cloaks with sleeves and hoods, and only thrown over the shoulders – the lower orders and market women a short woollen petticoat of home manufacture, no stockings & seldom shoes – a handkerchief tied round the head or a large woollen mantle covering the head, shoulders, & part of the body'.[45]

Hair styles also varied: often worn very long, plaited behind, and neatly tied with a bow of ribbons or else descending in long plaits gay with ribbon, as at Fuente Guinaldo on Palm Sunday.

Whereas in some villages the women covered their heads with a sort of black cowl which hung down the back in long folds, in Lisbon the lower classes wore a white handkerchief over the hair, while the middle classes arrayed themselves in black lace veils.[46] In Badajoz all the women dressed in black when they walked on the public promenade from six o'clock onwards on a Sunday evening. They wore black at *tertulias*, with lace veils thrown back. Indeed, it seemed that the face was never covered by the mantilla. Apparently the town prided itself on the beauty of its women, though opinions differed on this score: while Gomm, having seen enough to convince him to the contrary, thought this conceit sheer affectation, Stothert noticed several beautiful women who attracted attention 'by their engaging yet not immodest looks, and the graceful ease of their carriage. . . . The *tout ensemble* of their simple and elegant dress is admirably suited to display a fine form to the best advantage.'[47]

Colonel Bingham gave his opinion that Spanish ladies looked more to advantage in the mornings, and in their native dress, because of an evening they dressed in the French fashion, and in white, which did not suit their sallow complexion. Those who wore native dress were the village girls. Round Palencia, for instance, the favourite colours at a dance were neither black nor white but red, yellow and green, with a white handkerchief covering the shoulders. Massive gold ear-rings and necklaces terminating in huge crosses gleamed in the lamplight.[48] Large bows of ribbon decorated their pigtails, which hung flauntingly down their backs, whereas further north, at Olite, the plaits were gathered on the left shoulder at a dance, which gave a charming effect. As for the women of Estremoz, they favoured a sort of black silk cloak fastened to the waist and brought over the head and shoulders like a hood.[49]

Some diarists were more discriminating and less enthusiastic than others, tempering praise of the women with an awareness of their faults. It was fun to be welcomed with guitars, castanets and pretty dancers; soldiers enjoyed it whenever Spanish girls came into a regimental camp and danced for them. They had watched young villagers put flowers in their hair and dance fandangos and boleros on the green outside the church. Dancing, and flirtation, had been the strongest incentives to learning the language. But oh! the suffocating smell of garlic![50] William Freer of the 43rd, when describing a Portuguese wedding dance, observed: 'Some of them now and then opened the wind-passages and left in the room (which was small and full, we having that day a large party to Dinner) perfumes agreeable to none but themselves'.[51]

The habit of spitting, which is prevalent to this day in Lisbon, shocked Wellington's troops who saw Portuguese women doing it without regard to time or place. And how soon the climate made them old and ugly, with a tawny, walnut complexion – not so much the society ladies, but the peasantry and those loquacious orange-women selling in the Lisbon markets.[52]

Woodberry, writing in Olite during August 1813, noted another custom of the Spanish women which struck an Englishman as indecent. If you had your back to a woman and she wanted to attract your attention, she would not tap you on the shoulder; instead she was likely to give you several hefty smacks on the bottom. Woodberry himself was greeted in this fashion one morning in the market place and everybody roared with laughter at his embarrassment.[53]

Whatever their shortcomings, Spanish women rated higher in the army's estimation than did their Portuguese neighbours in person, appearance and dress.[54] Certainly the Portuguese girls in villages near Celorico, for instance, were pretty enough, but would have been much more so had they washed their faces and combed their locks. Kind and civil they were, but why did they put on such airs and affectations?[55] Ker Porter, observing with a painter's eye, was most unflattering to the peasant girls of Abrantes and district when he saw them towards the close of 1808. In his view they attracted notice solely by their neglect of all cleanliness and total want of all beauty. 'Not even a tawdry attempt at taste ever appears to vary the sad surface; all is one sombre mass of dirt; a very sympathizing covering with such rugged efforts of nature.'[56] He was exceptionally harsh, for by and large the British were struck by the women's elegance, their dainty, inimitable, dignified carriage, their graceful figures, their dark, expressive eyes, and a certain bewitching air. Even the peasant girls had a poise and confidence which many officers had met nowhere else in the same social class.[57]

177

Surgeon Walter Henry, who first entered Spain in March 1812, summed up widespread approval by a, for him, unusually emotional panegyric.

'They are such semi-divinities – they skim over the ground so aerially, and wear the basquina and dear little mantilla so gracefully, and their Cinderella shoes so daintily; and manoeuvre their fans so coquettishly, and have such magnificent eyes and lovely shapes; and talk so endearingly, and lisp so prettily, and smile so affectionately, and waltz so charmingly – that I wonder I brought away the bigness of a hazel-nut of heart untouched out of the country.'[58]

So much for the Portuguese and Spaniards. As for the French the army found them a gay and lively people, intent on pleasure and friendly and welcoming, especially after the fighting had ended.[59] In the expectation – soon to be frustrated for those ordered across the Atlantic to fight in America – of returning home shortly comparisons were made with the British women. One would like to know how many shared the opinion expressed by Lieutenant James Gairdner when he wrote of the females in and around Castelsarrasin: 'They have the compleat French manner in which I have seen nothing loose or improper, nothing that I should be sorry to see in my own wife or sister; and they have a great deal of vivacity and badinage which the British females want and which renders them more insipid.'[60]

Chapter 12

HORSES AND FORAGE

'It was new to us to go on picket, and to sit on horses as videttes, for two hours on a stretch. It was equally new to our horses to have their saddles and housings fastened on for twenty-four hours together, and to receive their food with the bits hanging at their chests, and everything prepared for action at a moment's notice.'[1]
Private George Farmer, 11th Light Dragoons

'The worst part of our misery is the seeing our horses and mules actually dying of starvation, no forage can be procured, and till the rainy season sets in they must eat flint stones.'[2]
Captain George Bowles, 20 January, 1812

To be well mounted did mean that a commander was comparatively safe when, having had to ride forward to examine the enemy's dispositions and movements, he could gallop away from any French pursuers. Sir Thomas Graham always needed a stud that was thoroughly equal to the service because it was, he said, an inexpressible comfort not to have to consider whether one's horses could bear the fatigue or not. Just before his return to the Peninsula early in 1813 he sent ten horses, 'three for servants or draught of light baggage, cart or buggy, three capital short legged hackneys (British mares) and four of a superior class for chargers, from four to six years old and from 15–1 to 15–2, with good barrels, excellent action, and unexceptionable legs and feet for the most stony country'. He also had left over from the previous year's campaign one hack mare, a strong Spanish pony which was admirable for night work, and an old hunter which had been wounded in battle and had a slight tendency to spavin. All this outfit cost the General a great deal of money, six of the horses coming to £600. Indeed, two of them cost £140 apiece, 'which is almost too much to expose to fire, but there is such comfort, safety, and satisfaction in being thoroughly well mounted on service that I could not resist the temptation'.[3]

179

Wellington, who rode at about twelve stone, worked his horses very hard and early in 1812 found himself very badly off, having lost several mounts and worn out others. 'The Peninsula is the grave of horses,' he declared, 'and I have lost fourteen upon a stud generally of ten in three years.' In requesting his brother-in-law to send him some, preferably mares, which stood the climate better, he stipulated good feet and shoulders.[4]

In the event, officers bought a wide variety of mounts ranging from an English pony to an Andalusian stallion. One purchased from a Moorish merchant in Lisbon a horse which was small and no longer young, but strong, enduring and well suited to field service; another took a fancy while at Ostend to a baggage horse because of his 'very superior powers in leaping over the very broad gutters across the street, which were filled with water by the pouring rain'.[5]

An idea of the number of horses involved is provided by returns for June 1812, just before the battle of Salamanca, when Wellington's army of 47,000, excluding Hill's corps, had 4500 cavalry mounts. Among ten regiments of dragoon guards, light dragoons and hussars the strength in horses varied between 340 and 520 per regiment, and the cavalry, British and Portuguese, at Wellington's disposal ranged from 1864 in three brigades at Fuentes de Oñoro to 8317, divided into ten brigades, for the battle of Vitoria.[6] If we examine more closely the experience of one regiment, the 14th Light Dragoons, we find that in the course of five-and-a-half years on foreign service the number of troop horses cast and sold or otherwise lost was 1564. The 14th embarked late in 1808 with 720 horses, received 664 remounts, 381 horses from other units, captured 63 from the French, and procured 13 Spanish steeds. Only 278 returned with the regiment to England in 1814.[7] Another veteran regiment of light dragoons, the 13th, was abroad for four years five months, during which it marched about 6000 miles, engaged in a dozen battles and over thirty affairs, and besides six officers and 274 men, lost 1009 horses.[8]

A sea voyage always produced serious problems for the cavalry. As late as December 1812 nine out of forty horses died aboard a single transport between England and Lisbon. When the 7th Light Dragoons, for example, landed at Corunna in November 1808 they had already lost seven horses during the passage, and another was drowned while being disembarked. This operation went deplorably on the first day, because rain fell in torrents, and the transports were unable to moor along the quayside, so horses had to be lowered on slings into the sea and then left to swim ashore.[9] Badly as the 7th fared, the 15th Light Dragoons did even worse, because Corunna could not afford stabling for the cavalry force which landed there. Consequently, part of the regiment had to wait on board ship until the troops who had landed first – the 7th and 10th Light Dragoons – had set off towards the mountain roads of Galicia. Several days' delay proved detrimental to the 15th, and many of their horses rapidly lost condition and even the use of their legs for a while; indeed some were rendered quite unserviceable by being cooped up aboard the transports.[10] Meantime the 7th, making do with poor-quality forage, had lost too many horses from lameness owing to their confinement on board for thirty-seven days and to their having moved off too soon after disembarkation. The regiment left Corunna with seventeen horses lame, had another eighteen lame at Betanzos, and on reaching Lugo had thirty-one more with lameness.[11]

As in every other branch of campaigning, lessons were learnt about horses. When the army first landed in Portugal in 1808, Colonel William Robe pointed out strongly the error of sending guns overseas without horses, and drew attention to the fact that even old, blind animals, and casts from the cavalry, were proving superior to any horses obtainable in the country, because the latter, though good of their kind, were too small and light for pulling gun-carriages. These required six horses each, while eight were needed to draw the long six-pounder gun and ten for the twelve-pounder.[12]

Spanish horses, considered by some to be too long in the neck, back and leg, and to lack the strength of British cavalry mounts, were distinctively branded with a hot iron on flank and neck,[13] such marks often helping in cases of theft. For instance, a horse purchased by an officer in the morning would be stolen at night by some peasant in the seller's employment. A few days later the very same horse was sure to be brought back by someone else and offered for sale to the rightful owner. The new vendor would be in league with the first who, to quote Henegan, 'would swear by

181

all the saints in the calendar that the animal had arrived that very morning from a distant part of Spain'.[14]

Engineer officers were especially vulnerable to having their horses worn out while accompanying generals on reconnaissance. Though Lieutenant Rice Jones derived some consolation from the excellence of Craufurd's table, he had to ride extremely hard every day to keep pace with the Light Division's leader, and his horses suffered in the process. Even the Chief Engineer, Colonel Richard Fletcher, had his stud almost exhausted when he and Wellington rode out daily all over the country for thirty miles round Lisbon, while examining sites for defensive works in what became, a year later, the Lines of Torres Vedras. Captain Thomas Pitts, who was afterwards killed, rode out with General Graham, Colonel de Lancey and a light dragoon to find a place where a bridge could be thrown across the Douro. Swabey of the Royal Horse Artillery went too, and described the great speed at which Graham led the reconnaissance party over rough, rocky ground along one stretch of river bank which was difficult of access. 'As he had fresh horses, three at different points, I only one, Colonel de Lancey two, and Pitts being only moderately mounted, we were soon left in the lurch.'[15]

The longest non-stop ride Captain Brotherton of the 14th Light Dragoons ever performed during the Peninsular War was when he carried despatches from Wellington at St Jean de Luz to the British Ambassador in Madrid, Sir Henry Wellesley – a distance of some 380 miles. Relays of horses waited ready for him all the way. William Warre once rode fifty miles straight off in August 1809 to Wellington's headquarters and then thirty-six miles back again.[16] Wellington himself was quite prepared to ride fifty miles between breakfast and dinner. He did this in March 1813 when he returned to Freineda from a visit to Lisbon in five days, using relays of horses.[17]

Another 'forced ride' was made by Charles Napier who, while recovering from a serious wound in Lisbon, heard that the French were retreating northwards from the Lines of Torres Vedras. Although his wound was still open, he rode all one night and having covered ninety-two miles with only one halt, he overtook the British army between Redinha and Condeixa. 'My poor horse had 2 lbs of Indian corn, on which he performed this severe journey in 22 hours, including the three hours halt!'[18]

Brotherton relates how, when Wellington's headquarters were at Gouveia, west of Guarda, in September 1810, the 14th Light Dragoons and 1st German Hussars were watching the French. Upon the enemy making a sudden advance one night, it became imperative to inform Lord Wellington urgently of this move, so Brotherton was instructed to ride the twenty-five miles with the news.

'I naturally chose my *best* horse, a thoroughbred one of great value, which my father had just sent me out from England, having bought him, a colt, at a sale of the King's stud, and broke him in himself, which rendered him of additional value to me. I was obliged to urge him, to perform my important mission, to such a pitch that he dropped under me, when I had reached only half-way to my destination, and I had to get a troop-horse from a cavalry regiment on the road, to conclude my journey, which nearly killed him also. I reached Lord Wellington's headquarters early in the morning, still dark.'

The only compensation Thomas Brotherton received for his valuable horse was £35, the regulation sum. This was particularly unsatisfactory in that Sir Charles Stewart, the Adjutant-General, had recently offered to buy it for three hundred guineas.[19]

Compensation for infantry subalterns who lost horses was chancy, so when they became involved in a skirmish on the line of march they quickly dismounted and sent their precious steeds to the rear, because if these were killed in action they had to bear the loss. Thus we find numerous instances of young officers writing home to father for a loan with which to buy another horse, or in some cases to send one out from England.[20]

Cavalry officers in particular had much more to contend with in respect of horses, enough anyway for Captain Verner of the 7th Light Dragoons to write quite sincerely in 1808: 'Some people fancy a Dragoon is much better off because he has a horse to ride; all I can say is, without having to look after my horse as a private has, I would many times have preferred being without one, and have from choice marched many miles on foot'.[21]

Notably in central Spain the horses suffered greatly from the heat; the glossy black coats of the Royal Dragoons' mounts, to mention one regiment, degenerated to a dingy brown or bay, and furrows appeared down the hind quarters. 'Had Don Quixote lived at this time,' wrote Leach of the 95th, 'he might have gone blindfold through our camp, quite certain to have found a Rosinante in any horse on which he first laid his hands. Chopped straw and stagnant water, with constant exposure to a broiling sun, and being picketed under a shadeless tree, reduced them to a pitiable state.'[22]

Besides prolonged, arduous spells of duty and exposure to heat and to diseases like farcy, glanders, mange, staggers, thrush, contracted feet and coughs and colds, horses on military service could die from a variety of causes: one had to be destroyed because of a kick which broke its thigh; another was stung by a viper and died. As for battle casualties, Thomas Brotherton had nine horses shot under him during the Peninsular War, yet he did not consider this a great number in view of the constant exposure to fire.[23] During the one-day battle of Waterloo it was not uncommon for an officer to have one or two horses shot under him, even three, but the experience of Captain Edward Cheney was undoubtedly rare, in that while commanding the Scots Greys for the final three hours, he had five horses killed in the space of twenty minutes. One only was his own; the rest were troopers'. He kept mounting the fresh horses 'with the same coolness that he would had they been at his own stable door'.[24]

Then we have the problems of accommodation for horses in Portugal and Spain, coupled with that of the most suitable, enduring mounts for campaigning life. As in so many aspects of military affairs, advice flew to and fro. Thomas Dyneley, writing home in March 1812, suggested that his brother William should buy small, stout nags, about six or seven years old, because these required less to eat. He added another cogent and often overlooked reason for his advice: one was much more likely to find a stable for a small horse, the ceilings and doors of Peninsular stables being mostly very low, having been constructed to shelter mules and donkeys.[25]

In that miserable village, Malhada Sorda, where the Artillery established their headquarters near to Wellington's at Freineda, the filth and poverty were extreme, yet because the place afforded reasonably good stabling, this advantage compensated for wretched accommodation. On being allotted a capacious stable as a billet,

Richard Henegan turned his animals into it and installed himself in the loft above;[26] but matters often worked out less conveniently, as Commissary Daniell discovered when he and his companions, unable to find a billet in Santarem, were obliged to stay in the stable into which their horses had been settled. Here a party of muleteers had already kindled a fire and assumed occupation, so the British officers were distinctly cramped and, with the non-arrival of their baggage, spent some comfortless hours. The following night they put up in a different stable, this time at Golega, and lit a fire to dry their clothes, which had been soaked by the streams they had forded on the way.[27] Captain Bull's troop of horse artillery had a more dramatic experience while lodged in the castle of Vila Viçosa. They were looking out of the third floor windows, when suddenly some of the horses fell through the ceiling, 'to the great astonishment of their fellow brutes in the storey below them'.[28] At the close of 1808, during Moore's campaign, cavalry horses were sometimes crowded into convent cloisters or into a chapel, as occurred in Astorga, where Gordon of the 15th Light Dragoons found one troop horse tied to a massive image of the Holy Virgin and several others tethered to a brazen font, which also served on this occasion as a manger.[29]

So much for stabling. A greater source of wear on horses was the lack of proper roads in the Peninsula, apart from a few highways linking the principal cities. Indeed, the majority of roads and tracks were found to be so rough that it sometimes proved impossible to keep the forge carts near enough to the cavalry regiments to enable the forges to be used during an advance. Fortunately by 1812 ingenuity had devised a substitute: in each squadron a small anvil and bellows were carried by one mule, and charcoal and iron by a second. These mules marched with the baggage and were normally up to the front.[30] At the end of each day's march the farriers – some writers called them 'the sons of Vulcan' – would make several sets of shoes. 'Puff went the bellows; clink, clank hammer and anvil.' But they were often short of fuel, and on several occasions troopers had to turn hewers of wood and burners of charcoal.[31]

If the poor roads delayed forge carts, they also wore down horseshoes, especially on the long march of 1813. In the 13th Light Dragoons, to name only one regiment, the stock of iron

185

became exhausted, but by sheer good fortune a timely supply of bar-iron was discovered in a foundry near Roncesvalles, thanks to which all the horses were new shod and each dragoon was given enough raw material for a second set of shoes.[32] When Colonel Vivian reached St Estevan with half his regiment, having scrambled for six hours over mountainous country, he wrote to his wife Eliza: 'You may guess what the roads were when I tell you that in one troop alone upwards of twenty horses lost their shoes; and so full of rocks and loose stones are they that without a shoe it is impossible to move an inch; so the farriers are hard at work in the rear'.[33]

As early as Vimeiro horseshoes were so scarce that parties of men were sent across the battlefield to knock them off dead horses for use by the farriers.[34] Many a horse was lost for want of shoeing. One morning during the retreat to Corunna in 1808 the 7th Light Dragoons had to leave sixty behind from this cause. All the more exasperating was it to come later upon kegs full of spare shoes and nails which, had they been up with Moore's army, would have saved a great many horses – at least for a week or two. William Verner always carried spare nails in the top of his cap, and when his own horse cast a shoe this was luckily picked up and, in the absence of farriers, fastened by an infantryman. As a result of this campaign every man in the regiment was provided with one set of spare shoes and a supply of nails, which he carried on the saddle. What is more, certain dragoons in each troop were trained in shoeing, and Verner himself attended instruction in the farrier's shop.[35]

An N.C.O. relates that in April 1813 every man in the 3rd (King's own) Dragoons carried a spare set of horseshoes, with a stock of nails. The shoes were not to be touched, though a few of the nails were eventually used.

'Woe to him that disturbed the repose of the former in the valise, except from the most urgent necessity. So sacred was this reserve store considered, that I think I can, without fear of uttering an untruth, affirm that scarcely a set was called into requisition from their first deposit at Lisbon to the landing of the regiment at Dover from Boulogne [1814].'[36]

It was all very well to make such rules, but a shortage of shoeing smiths often contributed to the difficulties of keeping horses on the road. The resources of Spain did not afford any who knew how to shoe in the British manner. A further snag experienced by gunners at least was that the four shoeing smiths on the strength of each artillery brigade were not mounted, as they should have been, and therefore had difficulty in keeping up with the guns and limbers.[37] By 1811 the authorities had at last realized that one farrier per cavalry troop was wholly inadequate, so a second was allowed, besides a squadron farrier with the rank of corporal whose job it was to supervise the work, especially when a regiment was scattered about the countryside in detachments.

Farriers continued to do blood-letting, to cut numbers in the horses' hair, and to dock tails. These short tails were the universal sign by which all armies in the Peninsula could recognize British cavalry at a distance. The civilian population also used the same means of identification, to the point where a miller's son at Obidos asked Captain Burgoyne whether English horses were born with short tails![38] One suspects that in many cases the tails were docked because it saved the trouble of daily combing and brushing, and of pulling the top of the tail regularly to obtain a fly-whisk appearance. Cavalry officers, many of them from the big landed families, were too often impatient, dashing and fond of fun, but not so ready to supervise stable duties. Indeed, some felt too grand to look after the veterinary side because at home they usually had a good stud groom on the estate, where the farrier had a light forge and not so many horses to shoe at any one time. Few officers knew much about their horses' feet; and the troopers were harder to discipline in painstaking, fiddling jobs than were their French opponents, who came from a much wider cross-section of the community and whose officers had risen by merit rather than purchase.

It is surprising that the troopers were not trained in cold shoeing, but maybe their officers did not know how to do it and the farriers lacked the capacity to instruct in the practice. To have supplied all cavalry regiments with sets of ready-made shoes would have paid off handsomely so long as they were expendable and not intended merely as an untouchable item on the equipment returns. Those who came off worst in all this were the infantry officers, because once the mounted regiments had been served, most of the

187

remaining good farriers were taken by the generals or staff, and often the inferior ones only were left for anyone else. Consequently numerous valuable horses were lost and officers rendered temporarily incapable of performing their duties in the best manner.[39]

Those who looked after their horses best were the Hussars of the King's German Legion, and even British cavalry officers, Colonel Hugh Owen for one, frankly admitted that they were *our first masters* in outpost duties'.[40] The cosmopolitan Legion, which recruited just over 30,000 officers and men between November 1803 and the battle of Waterloo, had in its ranks Poles, Swedes, Hungarians, Russians, Dutch and French, as well as Saxons and Prussians.[41] Kincaid of the 95th, who served alongside the 1st German Hussars for many months on end, confirms their excellence in this vital work and states that their movements were always regulated by the importance of their mission. 'If we saw a British dragoon at any time approaching at full speed, it excited no curiosity among us, but whenever we saw one of the first hussars coming on at a gallop it was high time to gird on our swords and bundle up.'[42]

Time and again the British had to concede that the Legion's horses were in far better order than those of their own cavalry regiments. Gleig accounted for this by the fact that, in his words, 'an Englishman, greatly as he piques himself on his skill as a groom, never acquires that attachment for his horse which a German trooper experiences'.[43] Attachment and attentiveness were the key words in this superiority. The men, who almost lived with their horses, could often be seen lying on the ground fast asleep, while their horses stood between their legs, and though the animals were tormented by flies and constantly stamping, their masters never feared an injury.[44] Early in 1814, when hay and corn were totally deficient, the condition of the German cavalry provoked astonishment among the British generals. The secret was that the German troopers shared their own bread ration with their animals, which had nothing else but turnips and crushed pickle-broom.[45] Another theory was that the soldiers of the King's German Legion were not so fond of drink as their British comrades. More certain is that they did not cheat their horses by selling their forage. Burgoyne gathered that they fed their horses when they pleased, but that if a horse known to be of a good constitution lost condition, then the rider was punished. 'These people are great plunderers, but with respect to their horses, they steal for them, and not from them, and take great pains to provide them with some sort of litter to lie down in.'[46]

The correct ration of forage for all the mules and horses with the army was fourteen pounds of hay or straw, twelve pounds of oats, or ten pounds of barley or Indian corn. When the commissary issued English hay, the ration was to be ten pounds, but when he issued straw or any other local forage, it was fourteen pounds. In January 1810 this had to be reduced to ten pounds but the ration of Indian corn or barley was increased to twelve pounds as a partial compensation. Whenever green forage was issued, the ration was to consist of twenty-eight pounds.[47] On Boxing Day 1812 artillery officers drew from the commissaries twelve pounds of corn and the same weight of straw to last two days; two months later light dragoon officers were issued with six pounds of hay and eight pounds of corn.[48]

On service a light dragoon's horse carried three days' rations, the corn being stuffed into a sack balanced behind the saddle, and the hay or straw packed into nets and slung across the saddle bow.[49]

The winter of 1811–12 had a serious effect on the horses, many of which, from starvation, threw out mange. The 16th Light Dragoons had scarcely a Portuguese dollar in cash for buying medicines, and if a druggist in the village of Aviz had not given the regiment some on promise of payment, they would have been very hard pressed to cope. Furthermore, this regiment frequently went eight or nine days without corn, and in consequence lost many horses. Since no straw was to be had either, the famished animals ate withered grass – so eagerly that they swallowed many stones at the roots, and died.[50]

With March came green forage, the barley being just fit to cut, and the horses' condition improved quickly. Every spring it was the same: soldiers out cutting green wheat. But before this abundance forage was extremely scarce, and regiments, or individual officers, had to buy small cakes of Indian corn-flour, such as were eaten by Portuguese peasants; and after a day's march the men would be sent off to cut withered grass in the woods.[51]

Bad as this winter undoubtedly was, the most serious period for horses going short of forage was the army's retreat from Burgos and Madrid to the frontier villages of Portugal in November 1812. Some units managed better than others, but every horse suffered, and so did the men; although the situation was nowhere near as terrible as that of Napoleon's *Grande Armée*, which was in the process of losing 160,000 horses in Russia, it was grim enough. We have the assurance of two Royal Horse Artillery officers that during four days of the army's retreat the horses had no forage whatever, so they ate the harness off each other's backs as well as limber-box lids. One horse was fed with a double handful of sandstone which, so Captain Dyneley told his sister Dora, 'he ate as eagerly as I ever saw an animal eat beans'. Notwithstanding such adversity, the Royal Horse Artillery lost in this period only four horses and two mules.[52]

The heavy rain caused horses to sink at every step to the fetlock, and tree bark and sprigs of wild briar afforded an indifferent substitute for provender. Some regiments fed their starving horses on spoiled biscuits. One officer who paid £4 for a bushel of barley was reckoned to have a prize.[53]

The start of Wellington's 1813 campaign was held up for lack of forage, because straw, bad hay and a little Indian corn did not suit horses for very active service, and they would not be ready till they had had a month's green food. On 22nd February Judge-Advocate General Larpent reported from Headquarters that the last reserve of hay – two great stacks which had been saved on Wellington's express order – was being consumed. 'After that we must buy reaping-hooks, and try to cut grass before the green corn forage comes in.'[54] Some officers had already sent home months earlier for scythe and whetstone which would, they hoped, cut double the quantity of grass in half the time. But regiments had to send further and further afield – up to thirty miles along execrable roads – to collect any substitute for grass. Indeed, with every field eaten close and all straw and corn consumed, the cavalry had not only to collect grass along the hedge bottoms but also to take risks by foraging closer and closer to the French outposts. This proved hard work for the mules which carried back the forage during what should have been their time of rest before the big advance; it also proved to be dangerous, since mules as well as covering parties came under fire now and then, and this method of foraging was stopped after a few mules had been lost and a captain wounded in the process.[55] However, by the end of March most horses were feeding on green forage, mainly barley; some were fortunate and received up to twenty-eight pounds each per day. Whenever no green forage was to be had, as occurred at Almeida as late as May, officers bought small bundles of dry grass at about one shilling each in the market.[56]

Southern France proved to be no less hard on horses. Round St Jean de Luz in mid-December the cavalry regiments existed for five days on one pound of corn per horse and the little grazing which could be managed after the business of the day was done. Five days before Christmas Augustus Frazer announced that, after many days without hay or straw, or any substitute, the staff horses had been given a little hay. 'There is no grazing,' he wrote, 'though the exercise of moving does the creatures good.'[57]

The same shortage prevailed at Arcangues, whence the Rifle Corps had to send their baggage animals once a week on a three-day march 'through oceans of mud' to fetch corn. 'The whole cavalcade always moved under the charge of an officer,' Kincaid tells us, 'and many were the anxious looks that we took with our spy-glasses, from a hill overlooking the road, on the day of their expected return.'[58] Lieutenant James Gairdner of the same regiment set out on 1 February to procure corn at Rentoria, but on finding none he went on to the port of Pasajes and there, after a great deal of trouble, he managed to get corn off a ship and hire boats at his own expense in order to bring it up to Rentoria.[59]

When the army was around Vera, Hasparren and St Jean de Luz the forage situation became so bad that horsemen tried mixing bruised furze with Indian corn or, in the absence of hay and straw, they fed furze on its own. Most horses seemed very fond of it and kept their condition surprisingly well, but horses in low condition and infected with farcy were liable to show signs of the disease under this diet; and an outbreak in May 1814 at Mont de Marsan caused many to be destroyed. Cavalry who were a good deal on duty and had no corn issued for several consecutive days found their horses losing flesh and even becoming mangy. Dragoons were sent off to cut furze, gorse and also bracken, which they pounded with a mallet before cutting up fine into a sort of paste. The young shoots made a very palatable, wholesome food for horses doing moderate work. Senior staff officers who had no time to go in search of furze found themselves obliged to pay five shillings for one sack of chopped furze in the local markets.[60]

Thistles which flourished on the heaths round Hasparren were also chopped and then mixed with corn and hay, but because of prickles the thistles had first to be crushed; otherwise the horses would not touch them. To do this, men would lift a barn door off its hinges, lay it on the ground, place the thistles on top, and then beat them flat with clubs.[61]

On rare occasions a squadron would have a stroke of luck, such as the discovery in stables at Grijo of a plentiful supply of green forage which had been cut for French horses and then abandoned. In contrast, a regiment could suffer a particular misfortune, as when two squadrons of the 16th Light Dragoons, having found abundant green forage in one village, were ordered to move away to another, principally because the Colonel thought his quarters bad. 'This with him,' observed the normally temperate Tomkinson, 'is the first consideration and his regiment the last.'[62]

An awkward, petty or self-indulgent cavalry commander could by various means add to the already exhausting trials of a commissary's life. During the oppressive heat of July 1809, for instance, Schaumann and his men began to cut whole cornfields for forage, and were in the throes of doing so when Major-General Payne 'raved and annoyed us as usual, for he deplored the fact that we commissaries could not perform the impossible feat of carrying home 100 sheaves on our backs and stuffing the beloved dragoon horses with it'.[63]

A constant and more serious problem was the detrimental effect foraging could have upon relations with the civilian population outside the towns. When the 14th and 16th Light Dragoons stayed at Tomar in June 1809, certain fields were allotted to Schaumann by the local magistrate, and he and his staff had to cut the poor people's corn. He had also to compensate the Portuguese peasants for their loss by giving them a requisition receipt on Headquarters, though most of them preferred their own corn to cash, because fresh supplies were not easily purchased. The people would howl and cry, tear their hair, and go on their knees, begging him to spare their property, but he could not do

Plate 7. Freineda: Wellington's headquarters during two successive winters in Portugal.

The steps on the left lead to the house he occupied. In the back part of the white-fronted building is a large room, with ornamented ceiling, which was probably the scene of the Duke's dinner parties. This photograph shows the market place where Wellington paced to and fro with members of his staff, and one end of the church, the bell of which used to toll for hours on end. (*Photo:* the Author)

Wellington's camp bed, according to family tradition. (*Photo:* National Army Museum)

Plate 8. Learning to smoke and drink grog. One of Thomas Rowlandson's illustrations to *The Military Adventures of Johnny Newcome*. (*Photo:* John Freeman)

Poor Johnny Newcome on the sick list. Etching by Thomas Rowlandson. (*Photo:* John Freeman)

so, since he was answerable for the cavalry horses being in fit condition to do their work. 'It is my most solemn duty,' wrote Schaumann, 'to enter the town every day at the head of the regiment, laden with corn and the curses of the inhabitants.'[64]

Officers and men soon realized that, in their zeal, nay desperation, to obtain forage for precious horses, they were bound to impose hardship on the local peasantry. A requisition for Indian corn would be enforced on the *juiz de foro* of a group of villages, a search made, and the corn seized. 'All I can say in extenuation,' wrote William Swabey, 'is that it is better to supply their defenders, even with the necessaries of life they need themselves, than to have their houses pulled down and their lives endangered by the cruelty of their neighbours.'[65] One August day in 1810 the 4th Dragoons, on being ordered to procure forage in fields near Guarda, were obliged to bring in wheat just ready to be cut, though it constituted the sole dependence of many poor families. In the following summer General Craufurd angered members of his own Light Division, as well as the inhabitants of Peñamacor, by seizing all forage, preventing the townspeople from entering after eight o'clock at night, and, perhaps worst of all, refusing to allow the owners of forage to retain any for their own cattle. 'This order so far in the rear was very unnecessary and tyrannical,' commented Downman of the Royal Horse Artillery.[66]

However well-disposed the Spaniards and Portuguese felt towards British troops billeted in their villages, the moment the officers had to set about the disagreeable duty of seeking forage, they could not escape abuse and grumbling. Call it what one chose – 'a calamity of war', 'very hard on the inhabitants' – foraging had to go on, because the animals had to be fed, and whenever the commissariat could not procure enough by regular methods, the soldiers had to do it themselves. Hence the hostility of women and children, who begged the dragoons and hussars to hand back something to keep starvation at bay.[67]

Inevitably the villagers became progressively more skilled at concealing their stocks of forage – initially from French soldiers, but in the end from Wellington's men also. Inevitably, too, the soldiers, at their wits' end for supplies, grew more canny – and ruthless – at searching. With the onset of winter the peasants hid their straw with the greatest care, this being their only chance of

G

keeping alive till the spring their few remaining oxen, which they badly needed for working the land. 'They hid their straw behind stores of wood laid by for fuel, which two or three dragoons would remove with several hours' work, and possibly not find above 3 or 4 days' supply for 3 or 4 horses. . . . The scarcity towards the last was so great, we took it out of the beds they lay upon.'[68]

Cavalry and horse gunners alike searched chimneys, ovens, cupboards and beds, rummaging right through towns in this way. Swabey relates how, in January 1813, he and his men outwitted a fat rich priest in Melo. 'A large cellar with nothing apparently but wine in the barrels contained pipes of straw; and cupboards with doors pasted up with paper, and false roofs gave us a plentiful harvest; last year we did not know how to play these tricks.'[69]

Looking back on the Peninsular War, another Horse Gunner, Captain Edward Whinyates, confessed that he had risked so much in foraging for his troop that if the Spaniards and Portuguese had not been his personal friends but had reported him, he would have been tried by court-martial and most likely broken.[70] How utterly different was the position when the army found itself in Flanders! The men obtained forage in every stable they entered, and while quartered near Ostend and Bruges, to mention but two examples, all ranks were delighted with the abundance of the country and could not avoid contrasting the Low Countries with Spain and Portugal. They did not regret the change.[71]

Mercer relates that the forage allowance, though sufficient to keep horses in reasonably good condition when idle, was inadequate when they were hard worked. 'Nor was it sufficient at any time,' he adds, 'to put on them that load of flesh, and give them that rotundity of form which Peninsular practice had established as the *beau ideal* of a horse entering on a campaign, the maxim being – "The more flesh a horse carries, the more he has to lose, and the longer he will be able to bear privation".' Accordingly, cavalry and horse artillery had to borrow from local farmers and were able so to do thanks to the opportune and superb crop of clover that year.[72]

Chapter 13

FIELD SPORTS

'We care nothing about "the season", there are no game laws, and, as for the "campaign" being opened, we can just find time to fight and course too.'[1]
Captain Thomas Dyneley, Royal Artillery 3 March 1812

'Sir Rowland Hill came riding by with his pack of hounds at his heels. With his invariably kind and almost bashful manner, he said: "I am going to put my hounds into this little wood; they may perhaps flush a woodcock, and you get a shot." '[2]
Captain George L'Estrange, Vieux Mouguerre, near Bayonne, 1814

Lovers and riders of horseflesh were always prominent whenever opportunities for field sports occurred in between, and even amid, campaigns. Race-meetings were organized whenever possible. In Cadiz the course was laid out below an entrenched camp, with spectators getting a fine view from one of the redoubts. General Graham always gave a meal afterwards in order to maintain harmony between the British troops and the local population.[3]

Portalegre, with its large garrison, contained many sporting characters among the officers, who set up a committee, or miniature Jockey Club, laid out a reasonably good one-mile course on the plain, appointed stewards, and conducted everything under the patronage of General Hill, who was himself 'a great amateur in horse-flesh and had always a capital stud'.[4] When September 1811 came round the Portalegre races took place on the 18th, partly for the benefit of the local girls; and if the horses were not very brilliant, donkey and mule races made up the deficiences. Ensign Bell affords us this vivid description of the Portalegre event:

'The Derby never created more fear or excitement than our race-ground on the olive plain. All the Tats in the Garrison went to the post very smart, and ready to win the bag of dollars hanging on the big olive-tree; first away often last in the race – the real

195

winner sometimes losing his race by dismounting before coming to the scale to be weighed – one or two disappearing as bolters amongst the trees. A jockey with perhaps a red night-cap going right off to his stable in the town, and knocking down two priests in the gateway. Then the donkey race; every Jock sitting with his face to the tail, a smart fellow running in front with a bunch of carrots.'[5]

Donkey races were always popular, and in July 1810 the people of Tomar, and the troops cantoned there, enjoyed two excellent ones, each of three heats and run on the Portuguese drill-ground. Racing began at midday, and there was plenty of punch to drink.[6]

Of two sweepstakes which have been recorded, one for ponies at Covilhã in March 1813 was a great success, being won by Lieutenant Henry Hough of the Royal Horse Artillery and watched by a number of ladies who also enjoyed the refreshment tent with its wine and cakes.[7] As for the other, held near Valle when the army was defending the Lines of Torres Vedras, the horses entered were badly out of condition after a diet of chopped straw and winter grass. Consequently, before they had covered a hundred yards one horse fell down from sheer debility, and those immediately behind ran foul of him. As Leach observed afterwards, 'a greater burlesque on horse-racing never was witnessed'.[8] Grattan of the Connaught Rangers watched some admirably contested horse-races in the Lines, and noted: 'Jockeys, adorned with all colours, were to be seen on the course, and the harlequinade appearance of these equestrians was far from unpleasing'.[9]

We owe to an anonymous writer a description of the 7th Division's race-meetings in the spring of 1813. The stewards, judge, clerk of the course and most of the riders were officers of the 51st, and the first meeting of the Moimento Races was attended by large crowds, who included the divisional commander, Lord Dalhousie, and many Portuguese and British officers.

'Major Roberts' bay mare, *Countess*, beat Captain Kelly's chestnut horse, *Slyboots*; one mile heat, *Countess* the favourite. Surgeon Reid's Portuguese horse, *Lancet*, beat Captain Byrne's grey horse, *Dashaway*; one mile heat, *Dashaway* the favourite but having bolted, was distanced. Major Roberts' *Brown Bob* beat the

Assistant Commissary's grey horse, *Wagtail* – odds five to four on *Brown Bob*.

Sweepstakes of Country Horses – all ages.

Captain Smellie's *Bonny Robin*	1
Lieutenant Jones' *Corsair*	2
Lieutenant Simpson's *Doctor*	3
Captain Douglas' *Rockaway*	4

'Hard running between *Bonny Robin* and *Corsair*.

'A Silver Cup for Mules.

Paymaster Gibbs' *Money-Bag*	1
Lieutenant Minchin's *Pat*	2
Lieutenant Frederick's *Beau*	3
Captain Keyt's *Nimble Dick*	4

'A hard race and showed much sport.'

Afterwards the officers all sat down to a handsome dinner and then attended a grand ball, for which the local ladies had, strange to relate, been specially provided with shoes and stockings.[10]

While the army was assembling in Flanders during April and May 1815, several race-meetings took place. On the afternoon of Friday 28th April, for instance, on the road between Berchem and Oudenarde, the officers of the 10th Light Dragoons lost to those of the 18th. A return contest was planned for the following Monday, and the first race was about to start when a staff officer arrived from Brussels with urgent orders for the cavalry brigade to move to the Dender because of reports that Napoleon was in Valenciennes [11] – a false alarm. On 23 May eleven races were run near Grammont, and afterwards the 10th gave a strawberry feast, with plenty of champagne and hock.[12]

The last day of May saw more important races at Op Hasselt, to which the Prince of Orange came, and so did Lords Uxbridge, Hill, Fitzroy Somerset, Generals Vivian and Vandeleur, and many other commanders of high rank. Wellington and Blücher had planned to attend, but were prevented by atrocious weather from so doing. Twenty mounted dragoons kept the course clear, and at one time close on two thousand horsemen were on the scene, most of them officers. The meeting began with a race for thorough-breds, with nine runners, and then a race for half-breeds; but the second part of the programme had to be abandoned because of the rain.[13]

A week later officers' chargers, owners up, were to compete at Grammont for a sixty-guinea gold cup offered by Lord Uxbridge. The race would run over a course of 280 yards – two posts had been erected seventy yards apart, and the horses were to go twice round each. Every officer was to ride with sabre drawn, and anyone touching the reins with his right hand would be disqualified. Large crowds had gathered on the course by midday when the meeting began. First eleven three-parts-bred horses raced, then thirteen thoroughbreds. There followed several entertaining races for ponies and mules, but at this juncture the weather intervened once again. A violent storm broke out and did not clear until late in the evening, so seventy officers of the light dragoon brigade sat down to a dinner which had been arranged at their request by the Mayor of Ninove. Within two hours the assembled company had eaten a very good meal and had got themselves so drunk on champagne that one young officer of the 10th Light Dragoons stood on a table and began to smash all the crockery, bottles and glasses with a heavy stick. Then the rest of the officers mounted their horses and set off for the race-course. Half of them fell off on the way, and riderless horses galloped back to their stables. The wildest members of the party rode off into the night on a steeplechase, and alarmed the local inhabitants by shouting '*Vive Napoleon!*', overturning two carts, and charging at peasants like Cossacks. Not surprisingly, the brigade commander received numerous complaints, and the damage had to paid be for. The actual meal, with drinks, cost each officer fifty francs.[14]

Wellington's Waterloo army, whatever he said of its military virtues and experience, loved horseflesh and the associated sports. Unfortunately for the enthusiasts, hunting had already been proved a great failure by British regiments quartered round Brussels in 1814. The farmers could not see the propriety of officers riding across their land, and the Prince of Orange, as commander-in-chief, had felt obliged to pay a considerable sum to indemnify them for alleged damage to their crops. Furthermore, as Basil Jackson of the Royal Staff Corps sardonically remarked: 'The Belgian foxes had no idea that they were to run before the hounds, not being trained, I presume, to do so from their birth like our own'.

Officers tried hunting in the Forest of Soignies, but once again the stupid foxes would not run.[15]

Things had been very different in the Peninsula, though the countryside had been too often unsuited to fox-hunting. In the winter of 1809 General Hill went coursing three times a week from Montijo, with now and then a fox-hunt around Badajoz, where the Spanish huntsman blew, to quote the General himself, 'not a vulgar tin horn such as our huntsmen use, but a sort of pipe-lute, or whistle, with which the bearer occasionally plays a tune, to collect the dogs and animate the sportsmen'.[16] But this hunting was done with very scratch collections of local dogs. Only in 1811, with the arrival from England of two good packs of hounds at a time when the army was in winter quarters among the frontier villages of Portugal, did fox-hunting become properly established and popular.

Both packs came out in late September: that belonging to George, 8th Marquess of Tweeddale, a captain in the 15th Regiment of Light Dragoons, was loaned to Wellington's headquarters at Fuente Guinaldo;[17] while south of the Tagus a pack sent from Shropshire would, as Hill declared in a letter of thanks to his elder brother who had made the arrangements, 'afford great amusement to the officers of this part of the army, who, I am persuaded, are entitled to every recreation circumstances will permit of'.[18] Sir Rowland Hill was always prominent in the Peninsular hunting field, so much so that Blakeney, one of his infantry officers, wrote that the General 'was as keen at unkennelling a Spanish fox as at starting a French general out of his sleep, and in either amusement was the foremost to cry "Tally ho!" or "There they go!" '[19] Round Portalegre and Cabeço de Vide his pack enjoyed many a good run of an hour or so, but seldom caught a fox, because the country was unfamiliar, rocky and stony, and very bad for the feet of horses and dogs alike. Moreover, the foxes were too plentiful for sport, the hounds continually dividing in every direction, until confusion reigned. Once or twice when Reynard sought refuge in a rabbit burrow he was dragged out and dispatched by the hounds.[20]

On one much talked of day it was the fox which became a victim of confusion. A strong field found early outside Coria and galloped off in ardent pursuit with only one brief check. After running for two hours the hard-pressed fox made for his earth in a steep bank of the river Alagon, but being flustered by the long chase went sheer down a hundred and fifty feet instead of making an oblique descent. Five couples and a half of the best hounds followed over the edge and were all killed, their bodies lying on top of the dead fox. The remainder of the pack would have shared the same fate had not the most forward riders, Hill among them, arrived in time to flog them off. The horsemen were themselves fortunate to escape, for the treacherous bank gave no indication of danger until almost too late.[21]

This accident more or less put a stop to hunting on the southern front for that season, but away to the north Lord Tweeddale's pack was providing reasonable sport for officers within reach of Headquarters. The Coldstream Guards supplied a huntsman dressed in a long bright scarlet coat: this was Tom Crane, who later spent many years with the Fife Hunt. Few of the officers knew much about hunting, but General Graham, who had arrived from Cadiz to command the 1st Division, was an outstanding horseman who had first ridden to hounds in 1758 and had subsequently hunted for many seasons in Leicestershire with his friend Hugo Meynell, founder of the Quorn. There he had earned a reputation for riding at any fence and disdaining to dismount for anything; and though the Peninsular countryside was almost free of hedge and fence, the General hunted with the same skilled impetuosity.

Graham's laconic journal for November and December 1811 refers frequently to hunting round Lajeosa, San Pedro and Pinhel: 'Bad sport, cold and wet, and bad scent'; 'Found a fox in the first cover we drew, and ran almost without a check for 35 minutes very hard, and killed in the open field'; or again, 'went over to headquarters and accompanied Lord Wellington to hunt. Drew the cover near the Quinta D'Aguila, and found a fox, which, after a pretty run of about three quarters of an hour over a fine country, we killed in the open field'.[22] Finally we may quote his entry for Christmas Eve: 'We had excellent sport yesterday, probably the best fox chase ever run in Spain – 95 minutes *without a check* over an open country. . . . The fox died just in time for I cd. not have held my place three minutes longer.' Graham was another who liked to be up in front, and he was sixty-three at the time.[23]

Wellington's letters on military affairs at this period to his second-in-command, Thomas Graham, often have a postscript such as: 'The weather does not promise much, but if it should be fair, the hounds will go tomorrow to Pozo Velho at $11\frac{1}{2}$'; or 'The rivers are so full that I am afraid it will be impossible to hunt tomorrow.'[24] One officer wrote that Lord Wellington did not mind what the hounds ran so long as he got a good gallop. This was just as well, for to begin with Lord Tweeddale's hounds were familiar with neither their huntsman nor the Portuguese countryside. The earths were so numerous, and the difficulties of stopping them so great, that sport was poor more often than not. If the foxes, being too fat, were not killed almost at once, then they ran to ground among rocks where the horses' feet soon suffered to excess.[25] Indeed, sarcastic observers were quick to comment that more horses were killed than foxes, and fatal accidents were gloomily predicted for hard riders, not least for Wellington himself. 'He got a tumble two days ago and hurt himself a little,' wrote a Guards officer, who added: 'He will certainly break his neck some day.'[26]

The Peer did nothing of the sort, but one of his aides-de-camp, the young Prince of Orange, took a severe toss, and George Murray, the Quartermaster-General, broke his collar-bone, the doctors observing that he had only to hold himself up 'like a boarding-school miss' to be very soon well again.

Wellington might not mind what the hounds ran, but one winter day in 1811 the pack ran something which was more than even he had counted on, and the ludicrous incident aroused particular hilarity in non-hunting circles. The hunt had galloped several miles down a road, the hounds in full cry, when they drew up round a local cart and made the mortifying discovery that they had been chasing a load of salt fish! This had, of course, made an excellent drag.[27]

The next winter, 1812–13, Major James Stewart, a Rifle Corps officer who held the post of Assistant Quartermaster-General, had an excellent pack of harriers to which Harry Smith acted as whipper-in; and Commissary Haines had a pack of beagles. That January, once more round the village of Freineda, foxes were plentiful, but they escaped all too easily into holes among the rocks by the Coa. Faced with this problem, Captain Charles Wood of the

201

52nd, a Deputy Assistant Adjutant-General, who was in charge of the sixteen couple of foxhounds which straggled about and ran badly for want of a huntsman, used to ride out and stop the holes overnight, give a loud 'halloo!' and then gallop sharply away. Despite his efforts, in the course of one month, hunting usually three times a week, the hounds killed one fox only, and that was 'mobbed'.[28]

One day the hounds started a large wolf which was chased for several miles until it escaped into a hole. Another time a wild cat fell victim to the pack. Nonetheless, Wellington, who according to his Judge-Advocate General knew 'nothing of the sport, though very fond of it in his own way', was always eager for the chase, so much so that on hunting days Mr. Francis Larpent found that he could get almost anything done, because the Peer would stand, whip in hand, impatient to be off, and therefore quick to dispatch the business of the day.[29] Near Freineda in May, just before the 1813 campaign opened, we glimpse Wellington with his long whip and a terrier dog, trying in vain to dislodge a fox which had gone to ground under a rock just when it seemed certain he must be caught. Three couple of hounds, followed by the Commander of the Forces on 'Copenhagen' and by a young subaltern of the Rifle Corps, had outdistanced the others across a soggy ploughed field and a series of stone walls, only to be thwarted of the expected reward for bold riding and bolder jumping. Wellington never swerved to right or left, but took every wall in his way.[30]

When the Pyrenees were reached, that assiduous gossip, Ensign Gronow of the 1st Guards, recalled seeing at a meet 'about two hundred officers assembled, some well mounted, but the majority on "screws", ponies or even mules – a strange contrast to the Quorn and Pytchley gatherings'. The best riders, largely because they owned the best horses, were officers of the 14th and 16th Light Dragoons.[31]

There was the rub: one had to be well mounted to participate. It was all very well for Lord Wellington, with a good stud of eight hunters and sometimes up to fifteen chargers, to gallop about the country round St Jean de Luz, as on the occasion when only the Spanish General Freire, as a former cavalry commander, managed to keep up, and all the staff were left far behind. Wellington did not have good horses merely to keep them idle, so he worked them hard.[32] Hunting became a totally different, and far more risky, business for an officer who had a single horse for all purposes. Fitness for active service had to take priority over a sporting pastime which might so easily injure the officer's one and only mount. Thus we find Captain Henry Goldfinch of the Royal Engineers writing to a friend at home:

'I ventured yesterday to show my only horse . . . with Lord Wellington's foxhounds, and, tho' resolved only to see the burst and not follow, had one of the hardest rides I ever remember. The Duque and all the field . . . were thrown out. We did not kill, but tally-ho'd the rogue, dead tired, just as the hounds ran off on a fresh scent. Various are the deaths and casualties among the sportsmen's cattle.'[33]

Another example is Ensign John Mills of the Coldstream Guards who, with one horse, found that, especially when forage comprised a little rye-straw and even less corn, he could not take the liberty of pursuing the foxes. He remarked, perhaps with a trace of satisfaction, 'Lord Wellington has worn out all his horses'. Back in December 1811 General Long had, on the same grounds of inadequate forage, foreseen that this amusement would cost too dearly to be indulged in frequently.[34]

Wellington, who at this stage of the campaign wore a black cape and sky-blue frock-coat, the colours of the Hatfield Hunt and a gift from his friend Lady Salisbury, took the field regularly twice a week whenever military operations permitted, 'as if he had been a denizen of Leicestershire, or any other sporting county in England. . . . When the hounds were out, he was no longer the Commander of the Forces, the General-in-Chief of three nations, and the representative of three sovereigns, but the gay merry country gentleman, who rode at every thing, and laughed as loud when he fell himself as when he witnessed the fall of a brother sportsman.'[35]

In order that hunting should be enjoyed in safety from French interference, lookouts were often posted at intervals over a dozen miles of countryside, but even this precaution could not always have averted trouble had not the French been forbearing in their attitude to wartime hunting. In 1810 at Cadiz General Graham and his officers chased stray dogs instead of foxes and hares among the salt marshes and redoubts, and in their zeal often rode to the very outposts of the blockading French, who wondered not a little at the 'view halloo!' from their enemies, yet fired not a shot of defiance.[36] One autumn day when the hounds near Freineda chased a fox into enemy territory, Tom Crane and the hounds were captured, only to be sent back next morning to Wellington's outposts under a flag of truce. Towards the end of 1813 a Spanish dog fox, being hard pressed by the hunt, took it into his head to swim the Bidassoa into France. Regardless of danger, the hounds and huntsmen followed. Shaking themselves on the far bank, they set off in full cry and soon afterwards killed. What, meanwhile, of the enemy troops? A French drum-major was instructing a score of boys in a quiet spot on the river bank and, far from showing fight, they were so alarmed by the noise of the dogs that they scampered away. The rest of the hunt had remained on the west side of the Bidassoa, watching the sport from what they complacently assumed to be a safe vantage point. Of this illusion they were soon robbed when suddenly the French brought up a field battery and opened fire. Now it was the hunt's turn to scamper away as if 'Old Nick' had been at its heels.

Tom Marsden, a hard-drinking 'gentleman horse-dealer', had recently collected this and another pack, thanks to the efforts of, among others, the Marquess of Worcester who, on leaving the Peninsula, had sent out some of his father's (the Duke of Beaufort's) hounds. Marsden was not going to let the French have them without a struggle, so he rode to the water's edge and, waving his white handkerchief as a flag of truce, asked permission of the battery commander to cross the river and explain matters. His request was granted. On learning the cause of all this unusual flurry, the French officer graciously allowed the huntsman and hounds to return to Lord Wellington.[37]

The same courtesy was extended to coursing, and when the 95th, for example, were in the Lines of Torres Vedras, the French never interfered with their sport, though British officers frequently coursed hares and shot quail within half range of their carbines.[38] Three years later, at daybreak just before the battle of Toulouse, the 28th saw a fine hare playing in a cornfield between the French and British outposts. A brace of greyhounds was unslipped and after a hard course the hare was killed – within the French lines.

The owner of the dogs bowed to the French officer and called them off, but his opponent politely sent back the hare and his compliments, with a note to say that the British required the hare more than he and his companions did.[39]

In the autumn of 1809 General Craufurd ordered that the battalions of his Light Brigade should frequently be marched down to the river Caia to bathe. Every battalion except one marched as fully armed and accoutred as if they were about to 'mount guard in some stiff-starched garrison'. The exception was the Rifle Corps, whose commander, Sydney Beckwith, told his men to wear light fatigue-dress and to carry nothing except a stick, while the officers were to take their greyhounds and fowling-pieces on this bathing parade. Once clear of Campo Maior, where they had quarters, the riflemen extended in one long line, and in this skirmishing order set off straight across the plain towards the river bank. Hares, rabbits and partridges were soon startled, whereupon, in the words of Jonathan Leach, 'such shooting, coursing and knocking down with sticks and stones, and such *mobbing* of quadrupeds and birds commenced, that a game-preserving John Bull would undoubtedly have stigmatised us as a most nefarious corps of poachers'. Once the men had bathed, dried themselves and dressed, the same happy scene took place on the return march, and everyone arrived back in high spirits. Colonel Beckwith certainly knew about morale.[40]

The sport was not always so prearranged, though the heartening effects could be similar. For example, in October 1811, when marching across an extensive plain near Malpartida, Almeida and the Spanish frontier, the 92nd Highlanders were entertained when several officers on horseback accidentally started a hare, whereupon every greyhound belonging to the regiment was sent in pursuit. At length the hare 'fell under the snouts of its numerous pursuers'. Realizing how delighted the soldiers had been at this impromptu sport, the officers set about coursing in earnest, and continued to do so until they reached the end of the plain. 'Time was so wonderfully beguiled,' wrote James Hope, 'that on the arrival of the column at Alcuesca, many of the men conceived that they had not marched above half the distance they had really done.'[41]

Six months later a much larger body of troops – three infantry divisions and two brigades of cavalry – were advancing across a wide, treeless plain of coarse grass and wild garlic in order to cover the siege of Badajoz. No living thing was to be seen except the countless hares which sprang up among the marching columns. 'The men's shouts drove them like shuttlecocks from one to the other, till, bewildered by noise, and surrounded by foes, followed by every yelping cur, galloped after by every officer they approached, they fell a sacrifice in endeavouring to force their way through our ranks. Most were killed while trying to escape, and close on fifty hares were cooked over bivouac fires that evening.'[42] Much the same occurred when Hill's 2nd Division, not in the presence of the enemy, was heading for Salamanca across the plains and Sir Rowland indulged officers who owned greyhounds by allowing them to course hares alongside the column. Many a hare made for the marching columns, only to be killed and added to the pound of ration beef.[43]

Good coursing was to be had round Covilhã in January 1813, even though the dogs often failed to kill, so 'strong' was the country. One Sunday the officers collected every cur they could find in the town and spent a diverting day, though they killed only one hare, which they were obliged to shoot, for in Portugal it was 'all for the pot'.[44]

As the war went on, several officers made collections of dogs of one sort or another. William Hay, serving with the 12th Light Dragoons, never lost the chance of picking up a good-looking greyhound, and by July 1813 he had at least half a dozen 'large, rough, handsome dogs'. General Hill also had some fine dogs, and so did Robert Long, commanding a cavalry brigade: 'mine I think are as good both in nose and foot,' he told his brother, 'and yelp as harmoniously'.[45] Harry Smith, an enthusiast for coursing as for everything else, whether on the plains near Santarem or snatching time after duty in the trenches outside Badajoz to chase hares along one bank of the Guadiana, had thirteen greyhounds and dogs by the end of 1812, including a famous Spanish greyhound named 'Moro', which had been bred at Zamora.[46]

The army's sporting characters frequently discussed the comparative merits of English and Spanish greyhounds, until one October day in 1811 the matter was put to the test near Fuente

Guinaldo. A capital hare was put up over a particularly fine stretch of coursing country and chase was given by two English greyhounds, which had recently been sent out from home to the 43rd Regiment, and by a highly esteemed Spanish hound. The hare was killed by the English dogs, but these were so exhausted by the heat and the severity of the course that one of them died immediately and the other was saved only with great difficulty by bleeding. As for the Spanish hound, he was accustomed to the climate, but in any case he had taken particular care not 'to distress himself by an over-display of zeal', and so arrived several minutes after the hare and the English hound had died. Undoubtedly the heat enervated the limbs of English dogs, while the native hounds were inured to it. William Graham had two greyhounds, one English, the other Portuguese, and although the former was considered excellent at home he was left far behind by the Portuguese dog and eventually died on the march just before the battle of Vitoria.[47]

Sir Thomas Graham's journal at the close of 1811 contains many a terse entry such as 'Rode out with the greyhounds. . . . Killed one hare' and 'Rode out coursing; greyhounds killed a fox'. But the country round Lajeosa near Guarda, where he spent that winter, proved on the whole too rocky for coursing.[48] That Lord Wellington himself was quick to seize a chance of chasing a hare is indicated by an incident which occurred on the heights of San Cristobal outside Salamanca during June 1812. The Anglo-Portuguese army was faced by Marshal Marmont's. It appears that while the Peer was riding along the British line under artillery fire and accompanied by a large group of staff officers, a brace of greyhounds passed near him in pursuit of a hare. At that moment Wellington was deep in conversation with the Spanish General Castaños, but he instantly gave the 'view halloo!' and galloped after the hounds, leaving Castaños and other foreigners to exchange looks and remarks of utter amazement. Wellington did not stop till he had seen the hare killed, whereupon he rode back and resumed his post as commander-in-chief, just as though nothing had happened.[49]

We have seen how coursing could sometimes be a sport in which a whole battalion at a time could become involved. Fishing, by contrast, was normally the sport of the solitary or of two officers

207

together. Most units had several expert fishermen, and these would supply not only their own table with fish but would also help their friends to eke out and give variety to the rations issued.[50] Much depended on the standard of tackle available whenever an opportunity occurred. Alexander Dickson writes in his diary on 10 October 1811: 'prepared fishing tackle'. Surgeon Henry always carried with him a cane-rod, but was often badly served, because Spanish-made hooks were very clumsy, and those the British had to use for fly-hooks had a hole or eye at the top, and almost invariably broke. By the summer of 1813, when fishing enthusiasts had reached the Bidassoa, the ports of northern Spain were open to English ships, so William Surtees for one procured some good-quality tackle which a captain in his battalion, the 95th, had just brought from home.[51]

Best of all rivers for trout was the Bidassoa where excellent sport, relaxation and a few fish were to be had by the persevering and fortunate. But each river across the Peninsula became noted for its speciality: the Guadiana was well stocked with fine mullet, the Mondego with dace, and the Tagus with salmon; barbel were to be found in tributaries of the Tagus and in the Agueda, which abounded with trout and also with a type of roach named 'rock-fish' by some of the military fishermen. In southern France the fine, clear tidal waters of the Nive yielded both sea and fresh-water fish.[52]

No expertise was required to catch carp from the fish-ponds of a stately mansion just in front of the British outposts south of Toulouse. It belonged to a Monsieur Villeneuve, but as all the furniture had been destroyed, he and his family were not in residence. Several officers of the 95th caught a number of the carp with hooks but, far from being a treat for their mess-mates, the fish turned out to be extremely muddy and not worth eating.[53] Even less skill went into fishing out of a palace window at Vila Viçosa in 1808. Major Steevens of the 20th Foot had no tackle except a piece of stick for a rod and a string with a bent pin tied to it, yet he and a brother officer managed together to catch some-thing now and then. 'I am ashamed to say what they were,' he confessed later; 'nothing more nor less than *gold and silver fish.*'[54]

As with fish, so with game: it made a welcome addition to the lean ration beef in the pot. Officers, however, went shooting for different motives. George Gleig wandered about the western Pyrenees with a gun over his shoulder, not only in quest of birds but also to view the country to the best advantage and to observe the positions of the opposing armies. Some officers regarded shooting primarily as good exercise, and at a time when hundreds of men in the Light Division near Campo Maior were suffering from agues and fevers, Leach of the 95th attributed his good health to living in the open air with gun or greyhound and to constant exercise. Sometimes only the keenest sportsmen could endure the intense heat – 97° 'by Fahrenheit's thermometer' in September 1811.[55]

Many opportunities for shooting occurred while on the march across country full of game. When a regiment of light dragoons advanced near Plasencia, two officers, merely by staying on the flank, with one old gun between them, killed a fine bag of Spanish partridges and wild pigeons. Eagles and vultures hovered above the army's rearguard near Castelo Branco in 1809, and several times these sinister birds came within fair shot.[56] One of the most memorable vignettes of shooting comes from the pen of Captain Michael Childers, 11th Light Dragoons, who was in El Bodon during part of September 1811. Quails, partridges and hares abounded there. Whenever Childers went shooting from Pays, which had a wood reckoned to be forty miles square, he used to amuse himself 'in setting fire to the country to burn out the rabbits. You can have no idea of the rapidity and fierceness of one of these fires, it makes a noise like the sea in a dreadful gale of wind. I believe it is the only way they manure the ground in this country, the atmosphere is always hazy from the number of fires.'[57]

One gathers that the Spaniards preferred the sport of shooting rabbits to any other, and thought anyone who said he preferred eating a hare to a rabbit must be joking. British officers went after any game they could put up: wood-pigeons, doves and quails near Niza and Rendo; wild duck, teal and grouse, even stone curlews around Medina del Campo; red-legged partridges and snipe. Woodcock were plentiful near Pinhel and Lajeosa in November 1811, and along the Tagus banks by Abrantes.[58] Bustards were seen occasionally – they were numerous in districts such as Plasencia; and at Abrantes an officer of the 30th managed to kill two of them with a single shot by patiently staying buried in sand until he could seize his chance. Another officer shot a bustard which weighed twenty-two pounds and measured six feet between the wing tips. He and a companion found the bird excellent to eat, like turkey. As for Captain Bowles of the Coldstream Guards, he was so proud of having killed a bustard that he had a pen made of its feather, and mentioned this fact to several correspondents.[59]

More often than not, an officer would go off alone or with one friend and perhaps a single Spanish pointer, and spend the day in quest of partridge, hare and quail.[60] Large bags were seldom brought home, because ammunition was often not of the best, even being made by officers themselves. 'We could never discover,' observed L'Estrange, 'the means of depriving the shot of long tails that appertain to the home manufacture of this necessary article, and consequently our aim was not as deadly as if it had come from our friend Mr Walker's round tower at Chester.'[61]

Then most of those who went shooting had no dog to point or rouse the birds, and even those with dogs were sometimes foiled by the demands of war, as happened when Captain Neil Douglas went out near Busaco with Dr Miller, surgeon to the 79th. No sooner had their dogs got upon game after infinite labour and hard walking in the sun than suddenly the 'Assembly' was sounded by a distant bugle, and the two men had to call off the dogs and hurry back to their billet.[62] Perhaps the officers of the Coldstream Guards were favoured, for when Headquarters were at Cartaxo early in 1811, Wellington kindly allowed officers of his acquaintance to take his own dogs, and they frequently did so, to their pleasure and profit.[63]

On occasion some of Wellington's staff, assisted by half a dozen riflemen, went after boar in the Sierra de Gata south of Ciudad Rodrigo. Rifleman Costello was one of the 95th who had the good fortune to be selected in July 1811, and he found the hunt very exciting, particularly from the ferocious nature of the quarry. 'I well remember,' he recalled, 'the first wild boar I saw in one of these hunts: he was a huge fellow, with tusks of a most alarming size, but although we fired several shots, and the hounds pursued him, he escaped.'[64] Captain Warre, serving with Portuguese troops, spent one May day hunting boar and achieved nothing except to get soaking wet. The procedure was for those who were armed to post themselves behind trees or rocks or in the brushwood, forming a chain round a small area in the same mountain range, while the remainder went in with dogs and by their shouting and noise drove the animals. Unfortunately not a boar or a wolf made its appearance, and the party returned home eight miles in despair and drenched.[65]

Now and then a General such as Rowland Hill or Lowry Cole would organize a wolf-hunt, but there is no evidence that the effort was adequately rewarded. Wolves posed an occasional threat to the army, especially to soldiers on outlying picket duty in the mountains. Near Cartaxo in November 1810 dragoons on sentry were often attacked at night and could only keep the wolves at a respectful distance by carbine fire. To be posted in some lonely wooded gorge or on a hillside, with the French in front and the wolves howling all round, was a gruesome experience, especially after several troopers of the 15th Light Dragoons had been attacked up on Monte Salguessa as they lay sleeping in extreme cold.[66] Sometimes soldiers could frighten off the wolves by making a flash of powder in the pan of their muskets, or could keep them at bay on the plains surrounding their bivouacs near Albuera by large fires which set them howling pitiably.[67]

Wolves would come down from the Serra da Estrêla near Certaa and besides making serious depredations on sheep, goats and pigs belonging to the local peasants, they attacked the army's commissariat herds more than once. Horses and cattle had to be shut up at night, for wolves had been known to eat part of an animal alive. One priest lost seven pigs in 1809 despite having a large dog which gave chase whenever the alarm was sounded and which bore scars from fighting with wolves.[68] Round Coimbra the story was much the same. It was not unusual for wolves to attack oxen and horses in the middle of the day, and it was much worse after dark. At Pinhel wolves took a fancy to the Coldstream Guards' oxen, destroyed half a dozen of them, and dispersed the remainder.[69] Just after Easter, 1813, a wolf went for three Guardsmen and severely lacerated the arm of one before his companions succeeded in stunning and then killing the wolf.[70] Commissary Dallas was riding up a slope of the Sierra Morena when there walked out of the forest the largest wolf he had ever seen: 'it looked like an English ass in size'. It stood in the road and stared at

211

Dallas, opening its mouth to show tremendous fangs. The commissary's horse gave a screech of fear and would have turned and fled if Dallas had allowed him to do so. He made the horse stand still and then, hoping he might in some way alarm the wolf, gave a sudden and violent shout. 'He did not move, and I gave another, and after a pause he walked as quietly into the wood on one side as he came out of it on the other.'[71]

Wolves, however, were not always so responsive, as William Hay found when the 52nd were marching through wild, uncultivated country covered with thickets and gum cistus shrubs, and packs of wolves boldly followed the army. Hay was in the lead one day when he suddenly came on four fierce animals who paid no heed to his appearance and went on eating. To Hay's relief, his men caught up, whereupon he borrowed a sergeant's musket and fired one shot. This only had the effect of making the wolves retreat for a few moments until the soldiers had passed.[72]

While the 82nd Foot were quartered in Santa Marhina it became very difficult to obtain forage for their cattle, so detachments had to be sent across the Serra da Estrêla in search of supplies. So steep were the tracks, so slippery was the ice, that villages were reached only with great difficulty. What is more, the inhabitants, who were extremely civil and kind, declared that the French had never ventured to pay them a visit. On one such excursion Captain George Wood lost a mule: it slipped down a precipice and was killed. 'On returning,' wrote Wood, 'we found the animal nearly devoured by wolves, which prowl about in packs on these heights. One of them stood and looked at us with great ferocity; but on coming closer it made off, just as one of the men was about loading his piece to shoot it, which I ordered him to do, being myself a very bad shot.'

Wood also relates that when pressed by hunger, these wolves came down by night to the 82nd's villages and, scratching open the graves of recently buried soldiers, preyed upon their flesh.[73] When the 95th visited the battlefield of Sabugal in June 1811 they found that nearly all the dead had been torn from their graves and devoured by wolves, which were numerous in the wild rocky district. Maybe Thomas Dyneley had such horrors in mind when, a year later at Garcia Hernandez, he had to shoot his horse 'Old Maida' after a gun-carriage had smashed one of her hind legs. He buried the mare in a grave six feet deep and then filled the top with broken bottles to deter the wolves from scratching her up.[74]

Those who simply *had* to keep the wolves at bay were the local shepherds, many of whom were watched by Wellington's men and figure in their journals and memoirs. High in the Sierra de Gata shepherds would set fire to the heather in order to frighten the wolves from the neighbourhood of their flocks, and in a favourable wind could quickly kindle the whole mountainside.[75] Most often they wore a black or white dress of sheepskin, woolly side outwards, to protect the thighs as well as breast and back. They carried a carbine or a long Spanish gun, and were accompanied by very large wolf dogs, whose necks were encircled by strong iron collars bristling with protective spikes.[76] Colonel Vivian remarked that their costume gave one 'more the idea of Lapland than of Spain'.

Chapter 14

OUTDOOR PASTIMES AND ROUTINE WORK

'[On picket duty] we amused ourselves generally at night watching the shells exchanged between the besieged and the assailants, the sight was very beautiful, sometimes as many as seven or eight-and-twenty crossing each other, like so many comets.'[1]
Sergeant Edward Costello, 95th Rifles, outside Ciudad Rodrigo, June 1810

'The Commander of the Forces wishes the Commanding and other Officers of regiments, particularly the Field Officers, to recollect that there is a great deal to do to keep their regiments in order upon service, besides attending to the parades and drills of the men.'[2]
General Order dated 24 September 1809

We find recorded the most varied, even unlikely outdoor pastimes: watching fish swimming under a bridge, throwing stones at pigs, standing at Punhete on the bridge of boats to see the local fishermen hauling their nets to catch Tagus savey – a fish of the salmon type, though with whiter flesh. When Tomkinson was recovering from wounds in Oporto, the cats made such a dreadful noise at night that he could not sleep, so he and his friends sat by an open window, and shot with a pistol at the cats moving along the roof of a house across the street. At Valle towards the close of 1810 some of the 95th, for want of a better pastime, managed to construct a still with which they made spirits from dried grapes found in an old wine house there, but the pastime was shortlived, because the still was discovered and promptly destroyed by Captain O'Hare.[3] High in the Pyrenees near Roncesvalles the principal amusement of subalterns in the 28th and 34th Regiments was to loosen huge rocks and let them roll down the French side of the mountain. Amid tremendous noise, limbs and branches were torn off forest trees by the crashing boulders. Young officers would spend hours

214

doing this: to quote George Bell, 'it sometimes occupied three or four of us for an hour engineering at a great rock to get him up on the right end for a start'.[4]

Long rambles occupied some days; energetic members of the 43rd chased herds of shaggy wild ponies barely larger than wolf-hounds, or they fired with ball ammunition at eagles and vultures circling high overhead, or wandered up among the giant cliffs, perched themselves in some cranny, and sat for hours gazing at the Atlantic and passing ships, with emotions which they felt, but could not describe.[5]

A few of the officers at least were rather ashamed at indulging in such activities, but they had nothing else to do at certain periods of the war. And no one had cause to feel embarrassed over the majority of pastimes, whether walking along the sea wall at St Jean de Luz, scarcely able to stand in the wind and drenched by spray, or riding and walking outside Lisbon to get exercise in fresh air away from the city's filth and unwholesome atmosphere.[6] There would be an occasional excursion on horseback to some Portuguese *quinta*, crossing the Tagus by ferry and dining with a local magistrate, which was how fourteen officers and four ladies spent one November day; or now and then a picnic in the forest, everyone contributing something towards the *al fresco* feast.[7] While at Covilhã, some of the King's German Legion used to make excursions into the surrounding country to visit farms and taste the very good apples or else, having almost no duties to perform in winter quarters, they went riding after breakfast; and if that occupation palled, then they sat on a low wall in the market-place and cracked jokes to kill time until the trumpeters blew a four o'clock fanfare to summon them to dinner in the mess.[8]

A few landowners, notably General Graham, took opportunities to send home trees, livestock, dogs and other things which impressed them favourably in Portugal and Spain, and which they hoped would flourish in Britain. Thus we find Graham in 1811 dispatching to Perthshire some Spanish broom seed and several bags of the ilex and cork tree acorns, because he anticipated that the dwarf sort, growing bushy, would make an admirable cover for game. While at Lajeosa in October that year he ordered Spanish chestnuts from Oporto for plantation at home, besides

215

some berries of a Portuguese laurel he had found 'which is quite a *tree*'.[9]

Sightseeing was another pastime which had numerous devotees. Portugal and Spain were rich in churches, cathedrals, monasteries, aqueducts and other antiquities to explore whenever opportunity occurred. One day it would be a mosaic, some valuable marbles or a solid silver altar, on another an ancient foundling hospital in Salamanca or Roman remains in Merida. Lieutenant Hough and his friends paraded most of the streets in Madrid, spent a Sunday visiting the public walks and botanical gardens, wandered round the museum, and sauntered one evening in the Prado, which reminded them of Hyde Park in London. This was in August 1812, and Henry Hough was so enthusiastic that he declared roundly: 'Madrid, to speak plain, is in my opinion far superior to London'.[10]

After the fall of Pamplona Augustus Frazer and two brother officers spent a whole day walking attentively over the citadel and defence works, visiting the cathedral and other churches, 'and poking into several shops in search of we knew not what'.[11] Battlefields were favourite haunts, especially those on which the visitors had not themselves fought. They would, as Frazer did at Busaco more than two years after the action, stand with outspread map on the very spot where Wellington had stood to conduct operations – a projecting rocky knoll – while a captain who had taken part in the battle explained it in detail.[12]

At every stage of the Peninsular War the officers rode or walked to see the local sights; the Fort de Lippe at Elvas; the museum in Coimbra with its collection of shells, fossils, stuffed birds, beasts and fishes; or Pizarro's mansion in the market square of Trujillo. And Sergeant Donaldson, with many other rank and file, peered at exhibits in one of Madrid's museums, enjoying some enormous boa-constrictors and a heavy lump of gold brought from South America.[13] When Frazer paid a visit to Dax, he said on entering the inn: 'what is there to be seen in your town?' The good-humoured French landlady replied: 'There are, sir, many things. There is the boiling fountain, the cathedral, an excellent hospital, and the mud baths'. So Frazer, an indefatigable and eager sightseer, trudged away to see what Dax had to offer.[14]

Probably the best country in which to indulge this pastime was Flanders when Wellington's army assembled there in 1815 for the

Waterloo campaign. Captain Mercer, who had not served in Spain or Portugal, voiced the sentiments of many when he wrote: 'After being shut out from the Continent so many years, the novelty of everything one saw enhanced this interest amazingly'. At Bruges he wandered round the town hall, the ramparts and Church of Notre Dame, and he visited the cathedrals of Ghent as well as Brussels, but he also enjoyed the vegetable and flower market.[15] Frazer, still busy seeing new places and describing them to his wife, appears to have concentrated on art, picking out two Rubens paintings in the cathedral of Antwerp, in which city he visited several private collections, the house where Rubens had lived, and the painter's tomb. What struck him most in a Brussels museum was a coat worn by the Pretender Charles Stuart.[16]

By and large Wellington's was an army of doers rather than watchers, but from time to time regiments were exposed to watching a bullfight laid on by local authorities to celebrate the departure of French troops and to welcome the British. In this way the inhabitants of Trujillo laid on a grand bullfight as a mark of respect and gratitude for the services rendered at Almaraz by General Hill and his 2nd Division. Here the market square was turned into a bullring. Apart from similar opportunities in Seville, Cadiz and Bilbao, there were smaller, more impromptu affairs at Villa Real and Coria, and a particularly impressive bullfight in Madrid, where, on the evening of 31 August 1812, the Junta organized a *fiesta* in honour of Lord Wellington's entry. Five hundred tickets were given for the British and Portuguese officers, and a thousand for the rank and file.[17]

Few British soldiers enjoyed their first bullfight, the majority considering it a wretched attempt at sport, a cruel and disgusting one, which 'to a mind tinctured with the smallest degree of humanity cannot be witnessed without horror'. For one thing, the bulls that were brought into the arena to be goaded and killed were often in little better condition than the bullocks driven into camp to supply the troops' daily meat ration. For another, they found it hard to understand how the Spanish populace could flock to this, their favourite spectacle, when the shouts of applause were in exact ratio with the degrees of cruelty practised;[18] and when, if the unfortunate bulls were killed without half a dozen horses and at least one of the fighters being victim, the disappoint-

217

ment was extreme. This was the view of Surgeon Boutflower, who felt bullfighting to be a stain upon the national character of Spain, and declared that the spectacle so accorded with the ideas of Spaniards of both sexes than many a poor family who had no money to buy bread to eat would sell the clothes they wore or their bed in order to procure the wherewithal to pay for admission to a bullfight.[19] This statement is confirmed by Elizabeth, Lady Holland, who attended bullfights in Madrid and Seville during 1803 and noted that the rage for bull festivals was so great that women sold 'their shifts, and finally *persons*, to procure sufficient to obtain a seat'.[20] Some soldiers who persevered and went more than once to a bullfight found that habit overcame and deadened their more refined sympathies. Thomas Bunbury, for one, admitted that, having felt sick the first time he watched the barbarous scene, he became less chicken-hearted. And how could things have been otherwise, when the Spanish girls he knew laughed at him and persuaded him to pay a second visit to the ring?[21]

When it came to doing, the army played almost every conceivable outdoor game with gusto, however primitive the conditions, however makeshift the equipment. The 30th Regiment, who spent the winter of 1811–12 near Abrantes, played fives, and so did certain officers of the 11th Dragoons at Chamusca. A year later saw the 3rd Dragoons playing the game in Larrega Churchyard. Rackets, or an apology for that game, was also popular, played with wooden bats against the side wall or tower of a village church, be it El Bodon, Gallegos or Martiago near Ciudad Rodrigo.[22] William Napier showed his ingenuity by making balls out of worsted stockings. During November 1813 the 4th Dragoons, quartered in villages outside Pamplona, found a rackets court in some nobleman's house and on hearing of this, Sir Stapleton Cotton, who commanded Wellington's cavalry, rode down from Headquarters to join the subalterns of the regiment in a game. Battledore and shuttlecock was in vogue for indoor exercise with the 18th Light Dragoons near Pamplona and Hasparren during periods of incessantly bad weather.[23]

Opportunities for games and sports varied considerably from one unit to another, depending on the officers' attitudes to such activities. The artillery were usually keen on football, and in a match at Covilhã between sixteen men of Captain Parker's brigade and sixteen of Colonel May's, the latter won after a hard struggle. The 71st Highlanders spent their time playing football when off duty one winter, and after the battle of Fuentes de Oñoro the French brought down several bands to a level piece of ground between the two sides and played music until sunset, while the Highlanders danced and amused themselves at football.[24]

Prior to the Waterloo campaign, when regiments were quartered in the villages and small towns of Flanders – Dendermonde, Acren, Strytem, Enghien and the rest – time would often have hung heavily had it not been for numerous pastimes of all sorts. A swim across the Dender, a stroll into Grammont to meet friends of other regiments or an excursion to Antwerp or Brussels were three ways of preventing boredom. While some officers spent their mornings 'knocking about the balls at a miserable billiard table upon the rickety floor of an upstairs room in a neighbouring cabaret',[25] soldiers of the 14th Foot off duty were to be seen helping the peasants in their various labours. The Earl of Albemarle, who was Ensign George Keppel in May 1815, states that before they left the cantonment the men had weeded the flax and the corn, and that year's potato crop was entirely of their planting.[26] Whereas several officers of the Royal Horse Artillery liked to take a short ride after dinner before seeing their horses done up for the night, Captain Mercer preferred 'the calm beauties of evening with my cigar under the splendid avenue of beech in rear of the chateau, and when night closed in, retired to my antique saloon, which a blazing fire of fagots and a couple of candles made tolerably comfortable. Here I buried myself in Madame de Genlis's *Life of Henri IV*, sometimes until midnight, tranquil and happy'.[27]

In a meadow outside Enghien on 6th April the grenadiers of a Guards battalion played football, and the following month a great cricket match took place there, watched by a very large crowd which included the Duke and Duchess of Richmond and their daughters. There are one or two references to games of cricket in Portugal and Spain, notably at Guarda in August 1810, when Surgeon Boutflower wrote: 'From the ground where we play we can distinctly see the Fire from the Garrison of Almeida. From the Spirit with which the officers in general enter into this game one would hardly suppose there was an enemy within an hundred

Leagues of us'.[28] And at Sabugal in the following June Captain Gomm and his companions played cricket till their legs were tired, and chess till their heads were, so that they almost forgot 'the sound of drums'.[29] After Waterloo, when the army was quartered on the outskirts of Paris, the 52nd sometimes played cricket in the Champs-Elysées, and crowds of French people, to whom the game was quite unknown, turned up to watch. Ensign Leeke of the regiment overheard one illuminating French comment to the effect that 'no wonder the English were not afraid of cannon-balls, when they could so fearlessly meet and stop those dreadful cricket-balls coming towards them with such terrific force'.[30]

Five officers in the 12th Light Dragoons were so much at a loose end while in quarters near Oudenarde during May 1815 that whenever the weather permitted, they would knock a hand-ball against the blind wall of a large farm-house, and deceive themselves 'into a belief that we were in a racket-court'. In bad weather they were reduced to getting the local boys to buy them some marbles – 'the only weapons of dissipation the little chandler's shop afforded. These amused us on a barn floor for a day or two.'[31] On 15th June some of the officers and men of the 73rd Highlanders were playing at ball against the gable-end of a house when an orderly dragoon brought orders from the brigade commander to fall in immediately and move to nearby Soignies. Drum rolls and bugle calls quickly assembled the scattered soldiers, and soon the battalion was marching to battle.[32]

One result of games in which the officers played with the men they led was to enhance morale and, in the words of Mrs Fitz Maurice, to 'soften "the rugged features of war" '. In the Rifle Corps those who promoted cricket, football, rackets, leaping, running and casting the stone were as well remembered for this leadership as for their gallantry in the field.[33] While at Leomil in February 1812 the 88th Regiment got up a sort of ball court and there officers and men alike amused themselves to such good effect under the brigade commander's approving eye that one writer felt justified in declaring: 'it is attributable to those trifles that the soldiers of the "Connaught Rangers" were so devoted to their officers and their colours'.[34] Colonel Sydney Beckwith, commanding the 95th Rifles, stood out by his encouragement of foot-races, football, rackets and chasing a greasy pig, believing as he did that 'to divert and to amuse his men, and to allow them every possible indulgence compatible with the discipline of the battalion, was the surest way to make the soldiers follow him cheerfully through fire and water, when the day of trial came'.[34]

Just as it is wrong to think of troops solely in terms of the battlefield or the long march, so it gives a false picture if one thinks of pastimes and forgets the hundreds of hours of routine work which is seldom mentioned in journals, letters and memoirs just because it was everyday routine and taken for granted. Yet each arm of the service had its own tasks to perform and problems, both human and material, to solve.

For the infantry during the Peninsular War may be quoted what Cooper of the 7th Fusiliers wrote under the heading 'WORK':

'To be tolerably fit for parade required three hours' work. His pouch, magazine and bayonet scabbard were covered with heel-ball like his cap. The barrel of his musket; the outside and inside of the lock; the bayonet, and the ramrod, must be polished like a razor. In addition, to the above, he had to clean white leather gloves, cap and breastplate; his great coat must be neatly rolled up and be exactly eighteen inches long. When blankets were issued, they had to be folded to suit the square of the knapsack. Many other things required polishing besides those already mentioned, as the gun brasses, picker, and brush and bayonet tip, etc. etc.,[36]

Throughout the year the cavalry had numerous tasks which ranged from protection of foragers to finding fords and then sounding them. Regiments like the 16th Light Dragoons spent many weeks on outpost duty with the Light Division, when they never unsaddled except in the evening, in order to clean the horses. At night the men slept holding their bridle reins and ready to turn out at a moment's notice. In June 1810, along the Agueda for instance, the dragoons turned out at two o'clock in the morning and remained on the alert until the pickets had been relieved.[37] These pickets on duty along a chain of posts often comprised one officer, one sergeant, two corporals and eighteen men, usually supported by infantry at night, and also by two guns. They waited on bridges, at fords or by water-mills. Sometimes cavalry patrols would ride among the hills to watch for any changes to French camps, or to stop enemy soldiers from plundering the villages. To give but one example: in January 1811 a lieutenant and six dragoons fell in with twenty *chasseurs* who were loading horses with Indian corn. The officer led a charge, and eight Frenchmen and a dozen horses were captured. When these horses were sold each dragoon's share amounted to over £20.[38]

In the winter and spring months artillery batteries had a great deal of work to do to prepare for summer campaigning. Gun-carriages and harness had to be repaired and cleaned. Wooden axle-trees were regularly greased. Several hundred canvas painted covers, 7 ft 6 in. by 6 ft 6 in. and marked ORDNANCE, had to be made. One day wains were loaded with musket ball ammunition; next day the same carts had to be unloaded so as to enable the Medical Department to use them for transporting the sick. Gun-carriages were repainted. Stores had to be packed and distributed – and what a miscellany of stores! Sponges, wad-hooks, ladles and handspikes. Kegs of grease, spare linch pins, washers and axle-trees. Lanthorns, water buckets, tool chests, large and small tarpaulins. Twine, hoops for powder barrels, hand hatchets, felling axes and broad axes, claw hammers, 'lintstocks with cocks dressed to match', spades and shovels, tubes, wet clay, fuses, and many other items.[39]

Captain Robert Lawson's diary of summer 1812 affords interesting sidelights on life and work in a Royal Artillery brigade of heavy six-pounders. His men oiled the harness and trained the horses. After green fir wood had been tried in vain for repairing the back axle of a forge cart, Lawson himself went into Ciudad Rodrigo and obtained some dry elm for the job. One day the brigade was employed on gun drills and exercised the tangent scales. On another the officers and men repaired and collected sacks, fitted up new stable collars, and made canvas nosebags. While outside Madrid in August the wheelwrights were kept extremely busy mending wheels, which were all giving way owing to the heat and to the roughness of the roads. 'The tyre nails all dropping out,' noted Lawson, 'the wood having receded from them. 6 fellies, 3 spokes, & two naves requiring repairs.'[40]

From officers of the Royal Engineers a multitude of duties were required. Whereas during an advance they went ahead to

reconnoitre roads and repair bridges, when the army had to retreat some of them accompanied the rearguard, destroying bridges
and preparing obstacles with which to impede the French pursuit.[41]
They had to observe the state and width of roads and tracks and
report whether they were practicable for artillery. Any districts
which were sufficiently open and level to enable cavalry to act with
advantage were to be noted; so, too, was the breadth and the depth
of rivers. Bridges were always important, so engineers reported
whether they were built of stone or wood, whether they could
bear the weight of guns and, of course, their length and breadth.
Whenever they came to a village or town they were accustomed to
estimating the number of billets that could be provided, as well
as the likely resources in water, fuel and provisions. Any fortifications and military works had to be accurately sketched, and
calculations made as to water supply, how far bomb-proof, how
many troops needed for defence, and the nature of the soil. Details
of any good camping sites were of value, especially when the
officer noted down whether water, fuel for cooking fires, and
timber for building huts were close at hand. These *Instructions for
Officers of the Corps of Royal Engineers when attached to columns,
or moving through the country* summed up by declaring: 'whatever
can facilitate or retard the march of an army must be carefully
attended to, and the whole digested into a written report, accompanied by such sketches as circumstances may admit of. Whenever
the army or a column takes a position, the Engineer will make a
sketch of the ground upon a scale of 3 in. to a mile'.

Preparing for a siege – and there were half a dozen during the
Peninsular War – involved the Engineers in heavy, often dangerous
work. Few in number, they had assistance from officers of the line,
but these had first to be trained; from N.C.O.s and men of the
Royal Military Artificers or, later, from the first companies of
Royal Sappers and Miners; and from carpenters, masons and
miners drawn from the infantry. They had to train soldiers to
make fascines – those bundles of brushwood which were thrown
into ditches to form a sort of bridge; gabions – baskets which when
full of soil made a sound protective parapet; and pickets of prescribed dimensions.[42] At Ciudad Rodrigo they made at least 2500
gabions, 2,500 fascines, and 10,000 pickets; and we know that
during the siege of San Sebastian 2,726 gabions, 1,476 18-ft.

fascines, and 20,000 sandbags were used. All these bulky items, prepared out of sight of the garrison, had then to be moved up in every cart that could be collected for the purpose.

Royal Engineers officers took turns in command of working parties digging saps and parallels close to the ramparts of a town under siege, sometimes in snowstorms, sometimes with rainwater lying deep in the trenches, and almost always under enemy fire. This was never popular work for infantrymen, so much so that Wellington had to issue an order which stated that to work during a siege was as much a part of a soldier's duty as to engage the enemy in the field. Scaling ladders were made, thirty feet long, two feet wide at the top, and one and a half at the bottom. Other ladders, twelve feet long, were used for getting into an outwork or descending into some defensive ditch, while ladders double that length were required for scaling walls. Certain men had also to be practised with axes in cutting down gates and palisades.[43]

About a mile from the place under siege the engineers' park would be concealed by a hill or ridge, and here all the officers of engineers, those acting temporarily in this role, and the soldiers brigaded as sappers, miners and artificers would bivouac. Here, too, the tools, fascines, gabions, platforms, scaling ladders, sandbags, and other stores would be regularly piled or laid out in rows of fixed numbers, so that they could be readily counted in a moment, or that a demanded number of one or other item could be issued without confusion in the dark. In the words of that distinguished engineer, Sir John Jones: 'The saw-pits and places of work for the carpenters, the forges for the repair of tools, and the spaces for re-tying and re-making damaged fascines and gabions, and generally for every species of labour which could be performed out of the trenches, were also established within the park boundary line, for the convenience of overlooking the workmen, and the security of the materials'.[44]

Sometimes, as at San Sebastian, mine shafts had to be sunk in order to blow down a wall. When the French threw up light balls to discover the working parties, bold engineers had to run and extinguish these flares as they fell by smothering them with filled sandbags or shovelling earth on top of them. Occasionally the French garrison, as at Ciudad Rodrigo and Badajoz, would make a sortie to frustrate the workers and if possible destroy what they had done, so it might fall upon an officer of Royal Engineers to form up the pickets and working party and repulse this attack. Even more dangerous was their task of guiding the stormers to the breach on the night selected for the assault.

Always Wellington's army suffered from a shortage of trained engineers, and their casualities were heavy: 7 out of 19 were killed and wounded at Ciudad Rodrigo, 13 out of 24 at Badajoz, 3 out of 5 at Burgos, and 11 out of 18 at San Sebastian, including their chief, Lieut.-Colonel Richard Fletcher. The allowances of spades, shovels, pickaxes, crowbars and other tools was inadequate and, more serious still, their quality was inferior – either they were local country ones, too small for the men, even when inclined to do much work with them, very easily broken and still more easily buried and lost; or if of the common English pattern, they were far too large and heavy. In particular the pickaxes, from the length of their helves and iron heads, caused not a few accidents at night among workmen when thickly crowded.[45] Not without good reason did Wellington complain and protest to Lord Liverpool about the Storekeeper General: 'Every thing in the way of intrenching tools and cutting tools supplied by his department is so bad as to be almost useless. . . . It would be cheaper for the public to pay larger prices, if that is necessary, in order to get better goods. . . . The cutting tools which we have found in Ciudad Rodrigo belonging to the French army are infinitely better than ours. Is it not shameful that they should have better cutlery than we have?' The French ones were lighter, much more portable, and less awkward to use.[46]

No regular army can exist without administration and this means office work, which in turn entails the filling up of returns, reports, and a sheaf of routine or special documentation. Wellington's army was no exception. A much-quoted letter which has been attributed to the Duke runs as follows:

'If I attempt to answer the mass of futile correspondence that surrounds me, I should be debarred from all serious business of campaigning. I must remind your Lordship – for the last time – that so long as I retain an independent position, I shall see that no officer under my command is debarred by the futile drivelling of

H   225 mere quill-driving in your Lordship's Office from attending to his first duty, which is, and always has been, so to train the private men under his command that they may, without question, beat any force opposed to them in the field.'[47]

One cannot be certain that Wellington ever wrote this letter to the Secretary of War, though it is in character. Nevertheless, whatever he wrote to London, he did insist on efficient, punctual administration within his army. Charles James's *Universal Military Dictionary* of the period defines 'returns' as being of various sorts, 'all tending to explain the state of the army, regiment, troop, or company; namely, how many are capable of doing duty, on duty, sick in quarters, barracks, infirmary, or hospital; prisoners, absent with or without leave; total effective; wanting to complete to the establishment, etc.'.[48]

In the early years of the Peninsular War most staff and regimental officers lacked experience, and administration appears to have been very inadequate, if one judges from this General Order issued from Badajoz on 24 September 1809. 'The mistakes in the returns and states sent from many of the regiments of the army are so frequent and so glaring, that the Commander of the Forces apprehends that the proper mode of keeping an account of their men is neglected or is not known in these regiments.'[49]

A half-yearly return of casualties was required to show the number of recruits joined, men dead, killed in action, discharged or deserted, plus a record of transfers given and received. Officers commanding regiments were sometimes irritated to learn that they had to certify on the back of the monthly returns they submitted the dates of all General Orders received during the preceding month and to certify that such orders had been duly entered in the regimental orderly books.[50] Every regiment was required to render to the Adjutant-General's department a daily state and a ration return. The cavalry version of the former had columns in which to indicate the number of officers, sergeants, trumpeters, rank and file – and horses – who were present, absent, on command, prisoners of war, and missing. Another column asked for 'alterations since yesterday', such as joined, dead, discharged, deserted, promoted, and reduced. As for alterations to horses, they might have joined, died, been sold or cast or transferred. No doubt they too deserted now and then. On the ration return an officer or clerk would fill in the number of persons, horses, mules and oxen, followed by a receipt for so many pounds of bread, biscuit, meat, barley, Indian corn, straw, green forage, and wood, and so many pints of wine and spirits.

Then there were promotion recommendations, court-martial proceedings, pay certificates and affidavits. All General Orders had to be entered in divisional and brigade orderly books and these would be called for every two months, checked and signed as correct by an officer of the Adjutant-General's branch. In the words of one instruction dated 1810, 'the General Orders are to be kept at one end of the book, and the Division Orders at the other; when they meet, a new book is to be procured, which is to be charged to the contingent account'.[51]

Every regiment had also to fill in and submit a return of field equipment. This comprised three main categories; camp equipage; entrenching tools; pack-saddles and mules; and each item had to be marked as 'received', 'serviceable' or 'unserviceable', or 'wanting'. As usual, the cavalry had to cope with a longer and more complex list. Such things as water decks, corn sacks (one per horse), hair nosebags (also one per horse), breast lines, reaping hooks (ten per troop), bridles and collars, picket posts and 'great mallets' were added to the usual bill-hooks, spades and shovels, felling axes and baggage straps. Besides one picket rope for every nine horses, there were supposed to be half a set of forage-cords (i.e. two cords) per horse.[52]

During the dangerous crossing of the River Esla in May 1813 the cavalry lost a good deal of equipment, and if the 1st (King's) Regiment of Dragoon Guards were typical, the river was blamed for every subsequent loss sustained by the troopers. At the commanding officer's inspection, before each day's march, one man would be asked what had become of his canteen, another where his forage-cords or nets were. The invariable reply was: 'Lost in crossing the Esla'. 'Bless me!' the commanding officer would exclaim. 'That Esla must be choked up with camp equipage.' In the end it became necessary to have an inventory made of every article of equipment in each man's possession in order to stop 'further calumnies against Father Esla'.[53]

Chapter 15

CHAPLAINS AND RELIGION

'The church bells of St. Sebastian remind me that to-day is Sunday.
I hope you are quietly preparing to go to church. How much better
suited to the day are your employments than mine!'[1]
Major Augustus Frazer to his wife, 1 August 1813

Whether among the officers or the rank and file, it was rare for a
soldier to read the Bible. George Bell, when he came to write
down his recollections of the war, could not remember seeing one
do so in the course of three years, but he quickly added that some
good and pious men were to be found campaigning in Portugal and
Spain who were not ashamed to

> 'Kneel, remote, upon the simple sod
> And sue, *in forma pauperis,* to God.'[2]

An officer who returned from the army in Spain stated the
melancholy fact that in the 23rd Regiment it would have been
difficult at times to procure even *one* English Bible, and he gained
the impression that the same scarcity existed throughout the army.[3]
Now and then we find an officer or N.C.O. taking steps to remedy
this lack of Bibles in his particular regiment. While in Brussels
during April 1815 Lieutenant John Sperling of the Royal Engineers
received a chest of Bibles and Testaments, but as the British troops
were stationed near the French frontier and did not wish to be
encumbered with any extra weight, he decided to send the books
to a chaplain in Antwerp, where they could be distributed among
sick and wounded soldiers. Apparently many to whom Bibles were
issued enquired what they should do with them. 'With those who
know their value,' wrote Sperling, 'this will not be the case, but
with others who see not in them the word of Life, and the precious
companionship they afford, they care not to inconvenience themselves with the burden. I cannot say much for the moral state of

228

our soldiers. From the facilities which present themselves, drunkenness and vice are sadly prevalent.'[4]

There is evidence that, during the Peninsular War, a few officers read prayers on a Sunday to the men they commanded: Captain John Eligé of the Royal Artillery was one, Major Smith of the 45th Regiment another;[5] and when Frazer took over Captain Robert Bull's troop of Royal Horse Artillery in March 1813 he found that Bull had been in the habit of reading prayers to his troop whenever field duties allowed. Frazer was glad to follow this good example and continue the practice.[6]

Such individual efforts could not fail to be inadequate within Wellington's army as a whole, for besides a lack of piety and a lack of Bibles, there was a shortage of clergymen of the right sort who could be persuaded to become chaplains and minister to soldiers in the field. In February 1811 Wellington wrote to the Adjutant-General to say that he was not getting enough respectable chaplains for the army, largely because the terms of service were still not good enough, despite recent efforts to improve them. Adequate as the pay abroad might be, that of retired chaplains was not. In his opinion the period of service ought to be reduced from ten to six years, the pension should be augmented, and the six years of service should be without leave of absence except on grounds of ill health. As things were, most of the chaplains who had arrived in Portugal had promptly applied for home leave, so that besides one chaplain in Lisbon he had only Rev. Samuel Briscall at headquarters. He was an excellent young man of refined manners and a good presence, but he alone could not take all the services required nor give the troops the advantage of religious instructions – 'the greatest support and aid to military discipline and order'.

That was one reason for Wellington's letter. There was a second and more pressing one: the rapid spread of Methodism in the army. At Cartaxo he had heard of two if not three Methodist meetings, at which soldiers gathered of an evening to sing psalms and now and then to hear a sergeant preach. In the 9th Regiment of Foot two officers attended such meetings, and their colonel had not been able to prevail upon them to desist. Such activities were, in the abstract, perfectly innocent, 'and it is a better way of spending their time than many others to which they are addicted; but it may become otherwise'. Nevertheless, in Wellington's view, a respectable clergyman could, 'by personal influence and advice, and by that of true religion, moderate the zeal and enthusiasm of these gentlemen, and prevent their meetings from being mischievous, if he did not prevail upon them to discontinue them entirely. This is the only mode in which we can touch these meetings.' A decade later, Wellington was to write of Mr Briscall: 'By his admirable conduct and good sense I was enabled more than once to get the better of Methodism, which had appeared among the soldiers, and once among the officers'.[7]

What worried Wellington most was the possible effect upon discipline if officers and N.C.O.s met together to hear the exhortations of their juniors in rank. Undoubtedly the Methodists had a beneficial influence among the rank and file in certain regiments, the Guards for example. Sergeant Stevenson pasted up in the Sergeants' Mess of the 3rd Foot Guards a verse which ran as follows:

'It chills the blood to hear the Blast Supreme
Rashly appealed to on each trifling theme,
Maintain your rank: vulgarity despise;
To swear is neither *brave*, *polite* nor *wise*.'[8]

That Wellington's insistent letters bore fruit is indicated by the fact that in November 1811 the Duke of York, as Commander-in-Chief, set the chaplains' branch on a new footing, and assigned to each chaplain the pay and allowances of a major. A number of men had been selected with the utmost care by 'the first prelates of this country', and certain instructions drawn up for their conduct were explained to Wellington in a letter from the Adjutant-General which said that, by command of the Duke of York,

'the Chaplains shall visit the sick and hospitals of their respective divisions or garrisons at least twice in each week, and diligently perform the requisite duties therein; that divine service shall be performed each Sunday: and His Royal Highness particularly enjoins that more men shall not be assembled, for that purpose, at a time, than the voice can reach – a precaution very necessary to insure the attention of the soldier; but that the Chaplain shall perform the service successively to the different corps of his division: and His Royal Highness desires that the service may close with a short practical sermon suited to the habits and understandings of soldiers. To this last part of the service the Commander-in-Chief attaches much importance, as being in conformity to the custom of the established church; and more than ever required at this time, which is peculiarly marked by the exertions and interference of sectaries of various descriptions.'[9]

Chaplains were appointed to each division of infantry and cavalry, to the troops in Lisbon, and to the hospitals at Coimbra.

Some of the new chaplains not only had little experience of life, they were also naive and slow to adapt themselves to campaigning conditions. At one church parade in June 1812, attended by Sir Rowland Hill and members of his staff, three infantry battalions, the 50th, 71st and 92nd, formed a square and their drums were placed in the centre. The clergyman appeared on what was, in fact, his first parade, walked up to these drums and then, looking about him, placed both hands on the rim of the bass drum and nimbly jumped on to the drumhead, mistaking it for a platform or a pulpit. The whole brigade tittered with laughter, everyone expecting to see him vanish inside the drum. Hill sent an aide-de-camp hurriedly across to suggest to the chaplain that he would be more at ease on the ground. Accordingly the latter jumped down and began the service. All appears to have proceeded smoothly, but the incident was laughed about for a long time afterwards.[10]

A similar parade service near Pamplona in 1813 had a more dramatic ending. On this occasion a drum had been placed within the square for the clergyman's books, and a knapsack for him to kneel on. He had read part of the service when all of a sudden he jumped up with his traps and bolted out of the square as fast as his legs would carry him, amid the applause and laughter of the assembled troops. They had no idea why he had fled, until a large body of French soldiers appeared on the scene, whereupon the congregation also ran about pretty smartly and prepared for action. The ensuing engagement lasted hotly until nightfall.[11]

When the Light Division bivouacked on the river Caia near Elvas, they were joined by a chaplain who, though no doubt a good man, was unprepossessing in appearance and manners.

231

Kincaid relates how, on the first Sunday after his arrival, the troops were paraded for divine service, and were kept waiting in square until at length

'he rode into the centre of it, with his tall, lank, ungainly figure, mounted on a starved, untrimmed, unfurnished horse, and followed by a Portuguese boy, with his canonicals and prayer books on the back of a mule, with a hay-bridle, and having, by way of clothing, about half a pair of straw breeches. This spiritual comforter was the least calculated of any one that I ever saw to excite devotion in the minds of men, who had seen nothing in the shape of a divine for a year or two.'[12]

Private Wheeler, lying wounded in the hospital at Fuenterrabia, deplored the way in which British soldiers, especially the dying, were neglected in respect of spiritual aid. Surely the Reverend Gentlemen should be stationed at the sick depots and made to visit the hospitals instead of following the army with a brace of dogs and a gun. 'It is true,' he declared, 'that there are chaplains with the army who sometimes perform divine service, but of what use are they, the service they perform has no effect, for their mode of life do not agree with the doctrine they preach. I have often heard the remark that a Chaplain is no more use to the army than a town pump without a handle.'[13]

When a very severe contagious fever broke out in 1812, the chaplain of the 5th Division at the time, the Reverend Mr Browne, carried out his duties of visiting the sick with such devotion that he caught the disease and died, to the sincere regret of all ranks.[14] In somewhat humorous contrast comes the story of Mr Heyward, the chaplain at Cadiz in 1810, who was most anxious to be at the bedside of soldiers dying from a virulent fever which ravaged the garrison, yet was equally keen not to fall a victim to the disease. The extraordinary measures he took to avoid contagion became a source of jokes among the troops. Henegan explains why.

' "Which way does the wind blow?" were his first words on entering a sick ward, having been admonished by the surgeon to keep on the windward side of the patient. In following this advice there was, however, some difficulty; for as the beds of the sick lay in different directions, the same breeze that placed poor Heyward in safety on one side wafted the contagious air over to him from the other; and so there he used to twist and turn like a weather-cock in a hurricane, facing the four cardinal points in turn, without the power of commanding his own stability. No doubt his disinclination to quit this world arose from the great enjoyment he felt in it.'

At least Mr Heyward ventured into the wards, but Samuel Briscall so shrank from encounters with pain and sickness that he refrained from visiting the hospitals at all.[15]

Given the diversity of the chaplains sent to the Peninsula, it was inevitable that the quality and appeal of church parades should vary sharply. For troops to have to parade in full marching order, with a field-day to follow divine service, was not conducive to a quiet mind or pious thoughts. There would be restless hitching of knapsacks, and many wry faces during the ceremony. 'I dare say,' observed Sergeant Donaldson, 'the anticipation of the drill that was to follow prevented them from feeling much benefit from their devotions.'[16]

In contrast to such inept handling by the brigade commander or his staff, we find Private Green of the 68th on guard duty near Pamplona when divine service was performed nearby. 'I stole from the guard, got into the rear of one of the regiments, and heard the prayers read; after which a short sermon was preached. This was the only sermon I had ever heard since May 1811, it being two years and three months.' When the sermon was over, Green returned to his guard and was relieved to find that his absence had not been noticed.[17] On Sunday, 14 February 1814 the 18th Light Dragoons and other troops paraded for divine service in drenching rain, and no chaplain came, whereas three weeks later, in the same town, the same troops stood under a beating sun for a service well-conducted by the brigade chaplain. On the whole the sermons appear to have been of good quality.[18] To take one example: at Vera F. S. Larpent went to a military church for the first time in fourteen months. The service, held in a large building which had just been made water and windproof for a hospital, was 'short, plainly read, but tolerably well; the sermon homely and familiar, but good for the troops, I think, and very fair and useful to any one. Lord Wellington was there'.[19]

The arrival of Headquarters in St Jean de Luz made regular services possible again, and more attention was paid to religious devotions than had been customary. Divine service was performed either on the beach or on nearby sand-hills for the Foot Guards. The Commander of the Forces and his numerous staff placed themselves inside the regimental square, composed of some 2,500 men, and Lord Wellington always appeared to listen attentively while Briscall read the service and usually preached a good and appropriate sermon. He apparently did just this on Christmas Day, yet the congregation found many distractions when attending service in the open air. It was to Briscall that Wellington had remarked, three years earlier at Cartaxo when he regularly went to the Coldstream Guards' church parade: 'Say as much as you like in five-and-twenty minutes. I shall not stay longer.'[21] By standing near the preacher Wellington was able to hear, but usually the parade was too large for a service in the open air, and many could not hear what Briscall said.

Rather the reverse had happened to a chaplain with the British troops in Cadiz. One Sunday he had gone through the morning service before Major-General Graham arrived, having been unavoidably detained. Graham's aide-de-camp took a message asking that the sermon, which was nearly finished, should be recommenced for the General's benefit. The chaplain obeyed. Afterwards he was teased by several young officers about the extra labours he had undergone.

'Now acknowledge, Doctor,' said one of them, 'that you thought it a terrible bore.'

'Indeed, sir, you quite mistake my thoughts. Few divines have enjoyed, like myself, the gratification of having their sermon encored.'[22]

Undoubtedly the most written-about and admired chaplain was Edward Cockayne Frith who went by the name of 'the fighting parson' in the 2nd Division to which he was attached. Besides being an excellent 'expounder of the sacred text', he was a gallant soldier, who considered it part of his duty to accompany the troops into action, when he often wore a red hussar jacket and exposed himself to the hottest fire.[23] Displaying great courage and physical strength, he rescued wounded soldiers in several engagements, and at the battle on the heights of Maya, for instance, carried on his back, one by one, three or four badly wounded officers to the village a mile and a half below.[24]

Several anecdotes are told about Mr Frith. On 31 July 1813, being up with the leading columns and noticing that the artillery officer was at a loss to find a road through a wood that was hindering progress, he immediately placed himself at the head of the guns and led them through to the spot where they were to open fire on the retreating French. On seeing the chaplain in this new role some of the Gordon Highlanders felt inclined to treat themselves to a laugh at his expense, and Lieutenant James Hope records the exchange of dialogue that ensued:

'One of them vociferated, "gude guide us, look at the clergyman leading the artillery;" to which a second having added, "Am sure *he* has nae business to place himself in danger," a third, by way of rejoinder, said, "Haud your tongue, ye gowk, he's the very man that should be here – *he's prepared.*" '[25]

Another day a party of staff officers were trying to find a ford for the passage by the army of a deep and rapid stream. Most of their horses refused the water, but up rode Frith. 'I dare say my nag will take it,' he remarked. Within a few minutes he had reached the far bank and then returned to show that it could be done.[26]

He preached an excellent sermon in one of the squares of Brussels a week before the battle of Waterloo; and an even more impressive one afterwards when, Wellington's victorious army having marched into Paris, the 5th Division camped near Clichy, then two miles from the city. Charles Cadell was present on the next Sunday when the Division paraded for divine service in a *château* park, and in a history of the 28th Regiment described the occasion:

'The beautiful manner in which he dwelt on the battle, and the sad and sudden loss of friends and comrades, drew tears from many; and when he wound up with the sad pangs it would cause at home, to the widows and orphans, the parents and friends of those that had fallen, concluding with the text, "Go to your tents and rejoice, and return thanks to the Lord for the mercies he has granted you," there was hardly a dry eye in the whole division, and it had an excellent effect on the men.'[27]

235

Burial of the dead was a haphazard business in wartime, above all for the rank and file. After a battle such as Talavera when the summer's heat was intense, the smell of corpses became so horrible that an order was given for them to be collected in large heaps, covered with branches cut from nearby trees and then burnt.[28] After roadside engagements one sometimes came upon a new-made grave, with a musket-barrel or a laurel-bough planted at its head – 'a sure sign that its inmate had been a favourite with his comrades'. Two Gordon Highlanders who died of fever in December 1808 were buried in the ruins of an old house, while for a dead seaman off H.M.S. *Audacious* two pioneers dug a grave in a vineyard and under an olive tree. When one officer, one sergeant and ten riflemen lost their lives in a skirmish at Barba del Puerco they were buried in a communal grave. This often happened.[29]

George Gleig, who after the war took Holy Orders and became chaplain to the Royal Hospital at Chelsea, declared that in his experience as a subaltern with the 85th Regiment, reading the burial service over the dead was a thing unheard of. 'Into huge pits dug to receive them the slain in battle were cast, as manure is cast into a trench, and the victims of fever and privations were in a somewhat similar fashion disposed of. Even the officers, though interred apart, had no prayers read beside their graves, for this, among other reasons, that the chaplains of the army were very few in number, and of these few, not one, so far as I know, cared to make more than a convenience of the service.' A harsh condemnation, and one to which not a few exceptions are to be found.[30]

An extra effort was certainly made to have individual officers interred in a properly prepared grave. After Vitoria Major Frazer buried George Thelusson close to a chapel and placed a crucifix over his head 'to protect his remains from insult'. He took charge of his watch, ring and locket until he could find an opportunity of sending them to England by some naval officer.[31] In the pursuit of Massena's army across Portugal during March 1811 Lieutenant James Stewart of the 95th was killed in action, so at dawn next day his body, wrapped in his cloak and deposited in a chest for a coffin, was buried in the village of Alverca, in front of Colonel Beckwith's quarters and in the presence of the entire advance-guard – riflemen, hussars and artillery. Yet when three subalterns of the same regiment died while defeating a French attempt to force their way across a bridge, the trio had to be buried in a single grave, with their clothes on and without a coffin.[32]

Two generals perished in the storming of Ciudad Rodrigo: Henry Mackinnon and Robert Craufurd. The former was extricated from under other bodies in the ditch and carried by a sergeant's party to Espeja, where he was buried with full military honours, his remains being followed by his brother officers of the Guards to a grave dug in the village market-place. Ensign Stepney had previously cut off a lock of hair to send to Mackinnon's widow.[33]

It was decided that General Craufurd should be buried in the breach where he fell, so his Light Division assembled outside the house in which he had died near the San Francisco Convent, and with arms reversed marched between a double row of soldiers of the 5th Division who, with muskets also pointing to the ground, lined the road on either side as far as the breach. The coffin, carried by six sergeant-majors and with six field officers walking as pall-bearers, was followed first by General Stewart and Craufurd's aide-de-camp as chief mourners, and then by Lord Wellington, General Castaños, Marshal Beresford, and a long procession of staff and general officers. In front moved several military bands playing slow and mournful airs. The regiments took post round the grave as best they could among the rubble, while the coffin, now headed by a chaplain, came to the spot. The music ceased, and no sound was heard save the voice of the clergyman, who faltered over the solemn declaration, 'I am the resurrection and the life'. After the service came a salute of musketry and gunfire.[34]

The set-piece funeral at which Wellington was most conspicuous was that of Major Charles Somers Cocks. Of this brilliant officer, killed at the siege of Burgos in October 1812, Wellington said in one vehement outburst: 'Had he outlived the campaigns, which from the way in which he exposed himself was morally impossible, he would have become one of the first Generals of England.' Then he relapsed into glum silence. He and Generals Cotton, Pack and Anson, with the whole of the staffs and the officers of the 16th Light Dragoons and 79th (Cameron Highlanders), in both of which regiments Cocks had served with exceptional distinction, attended his body to the grave in the 79th's camp ground. At the funeral Wellington looked so gloomy, so forbidding and so much affected that no one ventured to speak to him.[35]

Sometimes, for lack of a chaplain, one of the officers would have to read the burial service over a soldier like Driver William Weeks of the Royal Horse Artillery who died after a long bout of dysentery. Certainly Lieutenant Robert Knowles of the Royal Fusiliers not only supervised the funeral of a man who had died of disease in his company, but also took the place of the clergyman and read the service. Having attended a similar funeral at Alfaiates, Ensign Allen of the Royals observed that an officer turning parson was a novelty, 'but an evident impression of awe and devotion accompanied it, which gave solemnity to the ceremony'. Even more impressive was the occasion when, there being no Prayer Book from which to read the burial service over an officer in the Fusilier Brigade, Lieutenant George Brown of the 23rd stepped forward and repeated the service from memory and with remarkable accuracy.[36]

One virtually insuperable problem regarding burial was the refusal of Peninsular priests to allow Protestant heretics to be interred in local graveyards. The military dead were not allowed to rest in consecrated ground unless they were Catholics, and with few exceptions, none but the Irish regiments qualified on these terms. The Reverend James Wilmot Ormsby, who served as a chaplain during 1808, had much to say on this matter. 'It is not the opinion of partial bigotry, but the universal conviction, that the English are not Christians, and when any officer announces himself an Irishman, there is an immediate exclamation of pride and joy, 'Es Catolico, es Irlandes'; and he is thenceforward treated with the warmest cordiality of friendship by every member of the family.'

Whenever Bell visited a certain monastery in Lisbon, the monks supposed him to be a good Catholic because he admitted to being an Irishman, his family home being on the shores of Lough Erin. That was one question the monks never forgot to ask, since they considered all Irishmen to be Roman Catholics. 'Regarding myself,' declared Bell, 'they were quite out of their reckoning, for there never was a more staunch, loyal Protestant subject.'[37]

Since no good office could wipe out the stain of heresy, sometimes the only solution was to pass for an Irishman and, thereby, for a good Christian.[38] This is why, when a particularly well-loved company commander in the 95th Rifles, Captain John Uniacke by name, was killed at the assault on Ciudad Rodrigo, his pay-sergeant resolved that he should by some means or other be buried in consecrated ground. The Spanish priests naturally refused, because Uniacke was a heretic, but Sergeant Fairfoot insisted that he was an Irishman. On these grounds permission was granted, so Fairfoot selected the finest tree in Gallegos churchyard, 'and there I laid his head'.[39] Not long before the retreat from Madrid in 1812, Swabey had several men of his artillery troop die of a fever. The French being not far away, the local Spaniards ventured to refuse burial in their graveyard because the dead soldiers were heretics. Swabey would not accept their refusal, and took it upon himself to bury his men by force. 'But I have often since thought I was wrong,' he wrote later, 'for who can say after we were gone whether these superstitious people dug up my poor comrades and gave their bodies to the wild birds of the wilderness.'[40]

Such attitudes undoubtedly rankled in the minds and memories of many British soldiers under Wellington's command. As Protestants tinged with Puritan traditions, they were surprised too, and shocked, by what they considered to be the ignorance, superstition and bigotry prevalent among all classes in Portugal and Spain. In British eyes the two nations were ridden by priests whom Lieutenant Simmons, for one, portrayed as 'fat-sided and sleek-faced rascals who, under the pretended semblance of soul-savers, congregate in large bodies, gourmandising the richest viands and drinking the best wine'.[41] He was writing of Salamanca in 1812 – a city which abounded in churches, convents and monasteries; but much the same could have applied to numerous towns on both sides of the frontier, though his acid view overlooks many priests of high worth and real humanity.

Officers commented adversely on the fact that the clergy in Lisbon displayed great skill at cards and that the city's most fashionable gambling house was kept by a dignitary of the Church who 'with his black-cross hanging from his neck did not scruple to sit as bank between his assistants'.[42] Many British military men found it paradoxical that so much general licentiousness should prevail notwithstanding works of devotion in the streets, the constant ringing of church bells, long prayers said in every family, and strict observance of the ceremonies of religion.

Was it, asked Surgeon Boutflower, because the people had the form of religion but not the spirit? 'A Religious Mind,' he wrote in Badajoz towards the end of 1809, 'cannot but feel shocked at the profane manner in which the Sabbath is observed here. It is not sufficient that Amusements are partaken of in the same manner as on other days. Sunday is always selected as a Day on which they are pursued with unusual avidity. Neither is working, buying or selling generally abstained from.'[43]

Sergeant Joseph Donaldson of the 94th Foot, who spent part of one winter in Fonte Arcada, summed up widespread opinion within the army when he wrote:

'Religion with them appeared to be from mere habit, religion with them played on the surface, but did not reach the heart. When the bell rang at stated periods for prayer, each rosary was put in requisition; but this did not interrupt the conversation, they managed to pray and converse at the same time. As bigotry is always the attendant of ignorance, they were no way liberal in their opinions concerning us; and so contaminated did they consider us by heresy, that they would not drink out of the same vessel. But to tell the truth, I believe they did not understand the principles of the religion they professed, and the 'Padre Cura' of the village (a gross and most unspiritual looking piece of furniture) did not seem much qualified to inform them.'[44]

Another thing which, for very different reasons, the soldiers held against many families in Portugal and Spain was that daughters were shut away in convents, 'doomed by their parents from superstitious bigotry to be secluded from the world and live entombed in a vile prison, like common felons and miscreants, not fit to be at large'. George Simmons was exaggerating, but many shared his views. Sometimes a British officer tried to reason with one of the parents, venturing to talk of cruelty, and seldom was any attempt made to justify the practice by argument. Swabey, for one, was drily informed by an old gentleman, who had taken him to glimpse the nuns in a convent near Melo, that his only daughter was to go there in a year's time, solely because he was determined to have a male heir and, as he had no son, she stood in the way of a nephew to whom he wished to leave all his property.[45]

The nuns' most dramatic experience of war and invasion probably occurred in October 1810, when Wellington's army, having defeated Marshal Massena on the high ridge of Busaco, withdrew south across Portugal to the Lines of Torres Vedras. One day the 40th Foot halted for twenty minutes by a nunnery outside Leiria, and nuns crowded the balconies to watch the British soldiers. As the French were following close, the 40th's commanding officer ordered the convent doors to be broken open by a section of grenadiers, of whom William Lawrence was one. He relates that the poor women seemed very glad to get their liberty, 'for they came out as thick as a flock of sheep and set off for Lisbon'.[46] It may have been the same nuns who, when Captain Brotherton was passing with a squadron of the 14th Light Dragoons, implored him to save them from the French. Brotherton could not stop to protect the distracted creatures, nor could he bear to leave them to their fate, 'though they were neither young nor handsome, but old and sallow, from penance and vigils, no doubt,' so he had the twenty-two of them placed *en croupe* behind as many of his dragoons, whom they clasped tightly round the waist, and brought them to safety within the Lines, being complimented on his chivalry by a much-amused Wellington.[47]

During this retreat each division was accompanied, and sometimes impeded, by a pathetic band of refugees as large as itself, either walking or else mounted on horse or donkey. Trudging along among women who led children by the hand or carried them on their backs were several nuns who had managed to leave their convents and, 'quite strange to the world, either wandered about helplessly, beside themselves with fear, or else, grown bold, linked arms with the soldiers and carried the latter's knapsacks'.[48] A similar scene occurred three years later when the forward British divisions suffered a temporary reverse in the Pyrenees at Maya and retreated down the valley of Bastan. Many civilians went too, including some escaped nuns who mingled with the troops along the dusty road – 'their pale faces hectic with unwonted exertion, alarm and exposure'. This time, instead of having their knapsacks carried by nuns, the soldiers displayed commendable respect and tenderness as they carried the little bundles of portable property

241

and helped the elderly nuns. 'Assuredly,' comments Surgeon Henry, 'it was a high compliment to the character and discipline of the British Army.'[49]

War in the Peninsula certainly hit the convents hard and brought to their inmates experiences which were at once terrifying and horizon-widening. When one nunnery had to remove itself to Cadiz, the Lady Abbess took up residence in a relative's house, and in so doing crossed an outside threshold for the first time in forty-eight years.[50] Gomm never forgot meeting the Abbess of Santa Clara at Montijo, while riding from Merida to Badajoz in 1810. She came from an excellent Spanish family, and between the age of eleven and the coming of the French – a period of sixty-five years – she had never moved out of her convent. Then the French troops had plundered the place, so the nuns had gone home, while she, disorientated and careworn, had lived on the charity of some poor people nearby. Attempts were being made to restore the ruined convent, and she hoped one day to reunite her flock and resume the way of life to which she had been accustomed, but she was already seventy-six.[51] This pattern became familiar to the army. At Coria, for example, only seven nuns had returned by 1812 out of thirty who had left their convent two years before when the French drew close. Before 1808 the Convent of Santa Clara in Certaa had been occupied by at least eighty sisters, yet by September 1809 only seven remained, with a dozen 'seculars, that is to say, girls for education'. Special dispensation was granted for nuns to leave their convents at the approach of Napoleon's troops, and as happened at Guarda, all but two or three left their 'sacred prison'.[52]

At Badajoz in 1812 certain of the nuns became involved in war in a different way – not as refugees but as nurses. After the storming and capture of the town many of Wellington's wounded were looked after with kindness and skill by sisters who had taken temporary shelter in a deserted house and devoted themselves to the care of the sick and the dying. Now, for a few days, they nursed the wounded soldiers until bullock-carts were ready to take away those who could stand the jolting journey.[53]

Early in 1810, men of the Rifle Corps passing through a Portuguese village near Celorico were greeted by nuns with reiterated cries of 'Viva'! and white handkerchiefs waved from the convent windows. Very much the same occurred two and a half years later, when the Gordon Highlanders marched into Llerena and were greeted by nuns who cheered through the gratings of their cell windows. 'As long as any of us were in sight,' wrote Lieutenant Hope, 'they waved their lily white handkerchiefs, and hailed us as the deliverers of their country.'[54] The same fluttering of handkerchiefs could be seen during the retreat of 1812, but this time the nuns crowded apprehensively at the grilled windows of a Salamanca convent and waved a frightened farewell to the 24th Regiment of Foot on its march towards Portugal.[55]

Many convents were not difficult to visit, though restrictions varied. Whereas at Castro near Braganza the authorities had no scruples about opening the upper half of the vestibule door and allowing British officers to converse with the nuns – under surveillance by one or two elderly members of the order – officers quartered in Portalegre had only, if Kincaid is to be credited, to ring the bell and request the pleasure of half an hour's conversation with one of the prettier nuns to have their wish indulged. Of course they took pains to ascertain beforehand the names of those few girls who might be termed 'pretty'.[56] Indeed, the soldiers' main interest and hope, and their principal source of disappointment resided in the looks of the nuns, given the fact that a life of vigils, fasting, restraints of many kinds, and the lack of fresh air and proper exercise were in themselves enough to cause beauty to fade. 'All the nuns I have ever seen,' wrote Colonel Wilkie, 'bore evident marks of premature old age.'[57] Others were more fortunate in their encounters and gave less harsh verdicts, having been rewarded with sight of one very pretty nun at Penafiel, a number of young and handsome ones at Vila Viçosa, and several in Coimbra who would have been considered handsome in England. Pairs of sparkling black eyes were usually in evidence, even if in the older nuns there were no other remains of good looks.[58]

Almost always the nuns were half obscured by close iron gratings, and conversation had to be carried on through double rows of bars which were so contrived that you could merely shake hands. Not that such hampering grills deterred officers in convent parlours from talking to the inmates for hours on end. Some admitted to paying a daily visit, for it was a means of banishing boredom and sometimes an adventure of the heart.[59]

243

Most of the nuns were inclined to be chatty, and 'there was a good deal of King Ferdinand's Spanish murdered in endeavouring to make ourselves understood'; and Portuguese too, of course. At Vila Viçosa in 1808 officers of the 20th Foot found that the Lady Abbess and some of her nuns spoke French as well as Italian, so they managed between them to get along well, especially as the women were most agreeable in conversation. Those at Portalegre enjoyed a good joke and nonsense as well as anyone else, while nuns at Vizeu displayed intense curiosity about events in the outside world.[60] Sometimes they were gay and vivacious, sometimes, as at Merida, they lamented their unhappy fate and pined for liberty. 'We are here,' they would say, 'like birds with clipped wings, powerless.' Then 'a little noise' – George Bell does not elaborate – and they would fly off like chamois, calling '*Adios, adios, caballero. Otro tiempo.*'[61]

On being told that the nuns of Olite were not allowed – on God's account – to speak between eight o'clock at night and seven next morning, Lieutenant Woodberry replied that he thought God would be better pleased with the nuns if they were to dance fandangos with the 18th Light Dragoons instead of remaining dumb for so many hours, during which their thoughts might not be entirely good and innocent. He was not consistent, however, for on asking to see the nuns after Sunday service and being told by the Abbess that they were going to confession, he said to himself: 'In heaven's name, what sins can they accuse themselves of?'[62]

Commissary Dallas, who took Holy Orders after the war, describes how surprised the British were at the large amount of liberty allowed to the nuns – very different indeed from the notions prevalent in England; and he instances an experience while quartered on the upper storey of a large house in Trujillo.

'Immediately opposite to my window was the principal convent of the town, and on a level with it were several small windows with iron bars across them. The street was very narrow, we could almost have shaken hands across. During many parts of the day those windows in the convent were occupied by the nuns, many coming in succession to chat with me and any officer who happened to be with me, in very lively conversation.'[63]

By contrast, certain nunneries proved very hard of access. At

244

Coimbra, for instance, due to there being many heretics in the area, the nuns were preserved with more than ordinary care from all possibility of the most harmless meetings, and even the customary grill and 'turning box', also called 'the whirligig concern', were blocked up.[64] Subterfuge was occasionally used to gain admittance. When Frazer wanted to visit a convent in Tolosa, he and his companions were taken there by the *alcalde*, who looked, or pretended to look, for horses, while in fact they scrutinized the nineteen nuns: they were all ugly and old, yet delighted to receive a visit. Boutflower managed to enter a Portuguese convent in Guarda with a staff officer who obtained permission to do so on the pretext that he had to measure the altitudes of surrounding mountains from a high tower belonging to the convent. The abbess was completely taken in by this story, and as two confessors were available to accompany the officers, they were admitted, and met the abbess, attended by twenty nuns. Boutflower takes up the story:

'As soon as we thought we had been a reasonable time in measuring distances, we proposed to descend, when one of the Nuns whispered us to ask permission to see the whole of the Convent, which the Abbess at once granted. So pleased were the Sisterhood with this visit (the first they had ever known), that there was not a Nook, Cranny, or Corner, they did not in a whisper suggest to us to ask the Abbess to be permitted to see. . . . Being a Medical Man I was allowed to visit their Infirmary.'[65]

One place where soldiers had an opportunity of seeing the nuns and hearing them sing was in convent chapel. 'Twenty-five ladies came out and played bo-peep with us,' wrote Wellington's Judge-Advocate-General.[66] Officers of the 3rd Foot Guards who entered Coimbra on Christmas Day 1809 were able to attend High Mass in the nunnery of Santa Clara on the opposite bank of the Mondego, where they watched the Mother Superior, her train borne by two of the oldest nuns, walk solemnly to a seat at the upper end of the chapel. A beautiful girl, Donna Antonia Maria by name, wearing the habit of a novice, played the organ with a masterly touch, and when the sisterhood sang in full chorus, officers could distinguish by its sweetness and variety of tone the fine voice of Maria Benedita who, at the age of seventeen, had taken refuge

245

within the nunnery walls at the first invasion of Portugal by the French and, after a short novitiate, had voluntarily taken the veil.[67] When William Stothert attended another High Mass on St Benedict's day at the end of February, Sister Joanna Perpetua sang a solo, and so did Maria Benedita, 'who acquitted herself with much taste and execution in a difficult hymn'. Then a Franciscan friar came in and delivered a sermon extempore from the pulpit, but appears to have made little impression upon the congregation by his preaching.[68]

In June 1810 Lord Wellington himself took the opportunity afforded by inspection of a Portuguese brigade in Trancoso to visit the local nuns. Accompanied by commanders and staff, and granted admittance by the porteress, he rambled all over the convent – a place marked by poverty and dirt, apart from some of the cells, which were reasonably neat. Most of the nuns were at prayer, and were astonished to see a large party of men appear at the chapel door from the *inside* of the convent. Those officers who noticed several pretty faces hoped to have a chance of talking to the girls afterwards, but prayers went on so long that they could not stop. 'This visit of the great people,' observed William Warre to his father, 'will furnish conversation, I dare say, for years.'[69]

Often visitors would be treated to large dishes of very sweet sweetmeats and sugared cakes ornamented with flowers cut from coloured paper, or to cups of chocolate, or to nosegays and preserved fruits, in return for little notes or love letters, written in villainously bad Portuguese.[70]

When, at the special request of the fifty nuns at a large convent in the Serra da Estrêla outside Coimbra, who wished to see the troops and hear their band, the 53rd Foot marched through the courtyard, they were showered with oranges from the window gratings. At Portalegre a military band often played in the outer court of two nunneries, and the same happened in Salamanca, where the nuns loved to have a regimental band brought up for their entertainment.[71] One day an elderly nun begged that the band would play the tune used when the regiment went into battle, so next day the drums were ordered to accompany the band and treat the sisterhood to the 'Reveille'. The noise, which was normally enough to start the heaviest sleeper when the drummers performed in the streets of a town, can be imagined when concentrated in a convent parlour. It appears that the first crash of the drums sent the frightened nuns squeaking and scuttling into the convent 'like a parcel of rabbits'. By and by they took courage and returned cautiously one by one, and were in the end so delighted with the noise that they requested its frequent repetition.[72]

Soon after his first arrival in Lisbon in September 1811 Captain George Isaac Call of the 9th Light Dragoons was taken by a Portuguese friend to visit the nunnery of the Order of San Domingo. On arrival they heard the last part of the Mass in the handsome church and saw the nuns indistinctly through a grating.

'We then proceeded to the Hall, knocked at the Door, & were rec.d by the Porteress, who is a fine middle aged women & has been in her youth very pretty. . . . We ordered some sweetmeats, & then went up stairs to visit the Nuns. On our arrival at the Room I beheld the Iron Grates – doubly protected from us Mortals – Having waited a short time a lady appeared, dressed in the order – a white woollen dress with large sleeves fastened by a loop at the Shoulder – a slip of the same suspended from the Bosom to the Feet which hangs loose & which hides the key of their Room & the Cross. The Dress is tied round the waist with Black Ribbon, the Neck & Arms covered with white Muslin. A white cowl with the hair neatly braided behind, none in front – over this a white hand-kerchief or veil and a black broad Band pinned at top of the head, & hanging down behind – a neat clean dress & very becoming. We were joined by her Sister who came to reside there for pleasure. She is 50 and has been a very handsome Lady in her younger days. We conversed with her for a long time – a young Lady now made her appearance with Flowers etc., niece to the above ladies – an interesting circumstance – 23 years of age, had taken the veil at 17 – was quite happy – she played on the spinnet & sang and talked on different subjects . . . .

'The doors into the Gallery were left open and the Seculars were peeping in, & also the nuns who had not permission from the Abbess – the old Lady was too ill to come, & lived at the furthest end of the Convent. At first the girls were shy, but after conversing a short time became very agreeable – they sang duetts & trios – and the Aunt who had taken the veil took the Bass – the Elder has

247

a fine treble voice & the Aunt a beautiful strong bass. They sang with great taste, first without music & afterwards with the spinnet. The Elder & Aunt by turns sang solos. I was highly delighted. The Seculars were looking on – some very pretty – their eyes were not idle, nor were their fingers. I made myself understood without speaking. The three sisters had their eyes on me and the eldest passed some compliments. I told the Friar to say that I was so captivated with her singing that I could not help admiring her voice as well as her person, & that I regretted the Grating was between us. She answered she knew I understood music, but that my eyes were fixed upon prettier objects than her, but hoped I would favour them with a song, which I was obliged to decline.'

George Call had spent three most agreeable hours in the convent, and on getting up to go he asked if they would let him have the music and words of songs he had heard. He and his friends were asked to write down their names, and his name was repeated over and over, particularly by the young nun who seemed to Call to have lost her heart. 'On my making my congée she repeated "George", "George" with great emphasis. . . . Had I a heart to give, I might have given mine.'[73]

The nuns at Olite told George Woodberry that one of their number had eloped with a French officer in 1811, but he had been compelled to return her to the convent, where she had spent two weeks in solitary confinement. Even after hearing this story, Woodberry felt sure that the nuns would willingly leave their community to follow the fortunes of the 18th Light Dragoons, despite the vows they had taken.[74] Kincaid went further by claiming that he never asked a nun if she would elope with him but she immediately consented – and unconditionally. 'To show that in accepting it they meant no joke, they invariably pointed out the means, by telling me that they were strictly watched at that time, but if I returned privately, a week or two after the army had passed, they could very easily arrange the manner of their escape.'[75]

Let us give John Kincaid the final word about nuns in the Peninsula, as he bids farewell to Portalegre in 1812 for the fourth and last time:

'Dear nuns of Santa Clara! I thank thee for the enjoyment of many an hour of nothingness; and thine, Santa Barbara, for many of a more intellectual cast! May the voice of thy chapel organ continue unrivalled but by the voices of thy lovely choristers! and may the piano in thy refectory be replaced by better, in which the harmony of strings may supersede the clattering of ivories! May the sweets which thou hast lavished on us be showered upon thee ten thousand fold! And may those accursed iron bars divide thee as effectually from death as they did from us!!!!'[76]

Chapter 16

THE WOUNDED AND SICK

'I am obliged once again to cry shame against the regulations for the transport of the sick. The unfortunate beings, more fit for their death beds than for being moved from one place to another, are daily passing through here [San Payo] on cars without springs, every jolt of which is sufficient to fracture a limb; others dying are left neglected and unpitied by the road side, two hundred probably having only one hospital mate to dress their wounds or minister to their diseases.'[1]
Captain William Swabey, 7 December 1812

'Using my firelock as a crutch. . . . I kept hopping along until I came to a large white house where many wounded men were waiting to be dressed. Here I found the surgeon, Dr. Beattie, who came at once to me and dressed my leg and put a bandage on it. He then gave me a drink of water and told me I had got it at last. I, smiling, replied, "Long run the fox, but he is sure to be caught at last." This made many smile whose bones were sore enough.'[2]
Sergeant Daniel Nicol, 92nd (Gordon Highlanders) 28 July, 1809, after Talavera

To discover and collect the wounded on a battlefield, especially after dark, was a tremendous problem. At Salamanca a large part of the field was grown over with shrubs, and the ravines were full of nearly ripe corn, where many a wounded soldier died in concealment before he could be found. On the slope of one hillock about two hundred men had crept or been collected, and were waiting to be removed when Commissary J. E. Daniell saw them, 'each man wrapped in his blanket, by which they might be distinguished from the dead lying about'.[3] Such were the difficulties of collection after a major battle that wounded men sometimes remained for two, even three days on the field. Some crawled by degrees to the nearest village, and peasants, round Vitoria for instance, would bring them into a military dressing station or

250

hospital, but hundreds lay without food or having their wounds attended. When Judge-Advocate General Larpent rode past the field two days later, he was taken by some men to be a doctor from his black plume. They appealed to him in so affecting a manner that he immediately removed the feather in order not to be thought unfeeling enough to pass by without noticing their plight.[4]

Once the fighting was over, troops from individual regiments were sent all over the contested ground in search of wounded comrades, and hospital waggons also plied to and fro, but during the action it was the task of buglers and bandsmen to carry those who had been hit to the regimental surgeon, using either a wooden stretcher or blankets. Sometimes a blanket would be tied between two sergeants' pikes; but more often a hole had been worked at each corner of the bandsmen's blankets, and through these two poles could be run, thus forming a litter carried by four men.[5]

On flat ground this could be reasonably comfortable, but not so in the Pyrenees. When Robert Blakeney had his leg shattered in the battle of the Nivelle he was left among the dead and dying until Assistant-Surgeon Simpson came on the scene. Having no leg splints Simpson had to make do with arm splints. When some of the band arrived he had Blakeney placed in a blanket and carried down the hill, but as the slope was extremely steep the blanket contracted in the middle under his weight, his damaged foot drooped beyond the blanket's edge for want of proper long splints, and the poor officer suffered excruciating pain until he was laid in a cottage.[6] In default of blankets, the wounded might be carried on branches, on great-coats, even on bed sheets taken from nearby houses. One officer of the Sherwood Foresters, having been shot through the leg, was carried to a house from the field of Busaco by four Portuguese in one of the bearers they used for burying their dead.[7]

The experience of Bugler William Green when he volunteered to join the 'forlorn hope' at the storming of Badajoz was typical. He had already taken part in two dozen engagements and never been wounded, but on this occasion, 6 April 1812, he was not so fortunate, being hit in the thigh and left wrist. A kindly sergeant gave him a little rum to drink, and when the firing slackened, Green managed to hobble a short distance to the rear, holding his

251

injured hand with the good one, until he felt so faint through loss of blood that he was glad to lie down again. Soon afterwards four bandsmen from another regiment came up and carried him on a stretcher made of sacking nailed to two poles. Before setting off, Bugler Green asked the stretcher-bearers if they could give him a drink of water. They told him they had none. However, one bandsmen added: 'There is some a little way off, but there are both dead men and horses in it. You cannot drink it.'

Green takes up the story:

'I replied "my good fellow, run and fill your canteen." It held about three pints; I drank if off. He ran and filled it again; I then got into the stretcher, they carried me shoulder high, and at the distance of about a mile we reached the tents, where there were about 50 staff and regimental doctors. I was so thirsty that I had emptied the three other pints before they set me down; I hobbled into the tent, there was a doctor standing by the tent-pole, with his coat off, a pair of blue sleeves on, and a blue apron; a large wax taper was burning, and there was a box of instruments laying by his side. The tent was full of wounded, all laying with their feet towards the pole.'[8]

The doctor tore off most of Green's trouser leg to expose the thigh wound, then made his finger and thumb meet in the hole, and said 'The ball is out, my lad!'. He put on lint and strapping. After examining the wrist he inserted an instrument and pulled out a half-inch piece of the thumb bone which had been broken off and driven to the back of the wrist. The ball itself could not be extracted, so the doctor dressed the wound and told Green to lie down outside the tent. When a corporal from the same company of 95th, who had a shoulder wound, proposed that Green should try to walk to the regimental tents, about a mile off, the bugler said he was willing. 'I made the attempt, but before we had walked 20 paces, my thigh being bare of covering, the bleeding had parted the lint and the strapping from the wound. The night was very cold, so that every step I took was like a penknife in the wound, and I was two hours going the mile.'[9]

In a skirmish on 23 July 1810 Rifleman Edward Costello of the 95th received a shot under his right kneecap. With a tremendous effort he dragged himself back over the Coa bridge and then, faint with loss of blood, he persuaded a comrade to help him up the hill to a chapel which had been converted into a temporary hospital. Here the surgeons soon dressed his wound. Having no mules or waggons, they advised anyone who could move to make his way to Pinhel as quickly as possible. Accordingly about seventy disabled soldiers set off, helping one another to hobble along. Costello had a couple of rifles as crutches and in this way reached the nearest village, at which point the magistrate had the worst of the wounded placed in bullock carts. Costello was fortunate, and thought it a blessing, 'although crammed with six others into a wretched little vehicle, scarcely capable of accommodating more than two'. Painfully they dragged on all night. Next morning Wellington and his staff rode by, noticed the overcrowding, and gave orders for additional carts to be procured. Eventually, on the last day of July, they reached Pinhel, but no further medical attention was given until at Freixedas, nine miles on, the Coldstream and Scots Guards looked after the wounded. Costello's wound was dressed, and he got rid of a comrade who had bled to death on top of him in the cart and lain there for many hours because the Portuguese driver positively refused to remove the body.[10]

It was torture for wounded soldiers to travel to hospital either sitting or lying in these rudely-constructed Portuguese carts, with small solid wooden wheels revolving on unoiled axle-trees, and drawn by a pair of bullocks, yoked at the head. Such carts travelled at about two miles an hour. A peasant, armed with a long stick having a sharp nail at one end, walked in front of the bullocks and occasionally prodded his goad into their shoulders to hasten them along, though all it succeeded in producing was an awkward zig-zag trot for a few yards and increased torment for the wounded. On narrow stony tracks the jolting often tore off plasters and opened up wounds.[11] It was believed that the Portuguese never greased the wheels because the dreadful squeaking frightened away the Devil.[12] The most precise description of such carts we owe to Sergeant Donaldson:

'They were about five feet long, and two and a half broad; but, instead of being boarded at the sides, there were stakes placed in holes about eighteen inches apart; the wheels were about two feet in diameter, rather octagonal than round; and, as they were not girt with iron, it was quite a common thing to have a piece broken out of the circumference, and, of course, every time the wheel turned, the whole cart would be violently shook.'[13]

One day in December 1812 Captain Swabey, riding near San Payo, caught one of the bullock drivers, 'the lowest coward perhaps in creation, beating with a stick an unfortunate wounded soldier . . . because he was too helpless to dismount from the cart to walk up the hill. The revenge I took on the miscreant was simple and severe. I actually beat him till I could not stand over him.'[14]

The sick were transported in similar carts which, even along good roads, invariably moved at a pace slow enough to exhaust the patience of any healthy man. When Cooper of the 7th Fusiliers travelled in this way to Vila Viçosa, he could not endure the jolting and noise on top of the fever and dysentry. What is more, his nose began to bleed violently and continued to bleed until he had tied some thin cord very tightly round his two little fingers.[15]

English spring waggons, though less uncomfortable than local carts, also come in for criticism in the diaries, letters and memoirs of this period. Even an officer with a shoulder wound who had a waggon all to himself found the jolting between Busaco and Pombal so painful that time and time again he was tempted to get out and lie by the roadside; yet somehow he stuck it out to journey's end.[16] Better by far were artillery carriages on the few occasions when these could be used for such a purpose. After the battle of Barrosa, near Cadiz, Major Duncan had all the spare ammunition removed from his carriages in order to make room for as many wounded officers and men as he could manage, and in this way a good number were evacuated from the battlefield without delay.[17] Other means of conveyance for the wounded were mules or asses harnessed with pack-saddles, but many a soldier, unwilling to tolerate the uneasy, precarious business of sitting astride, preferred either to hobble on so long as his legs would carry him, or to make two muskets serve as crutches.[18]

More comfortable than cart or spring-waggon was the local sedan-chair, but few had the comparatively good fortune to travel in one. Harry Smith did after the battle of the Coa, where he was wounded in the ankle-joint. A local Portuguese gentleman produced such a chair, slung between two mules, and Smith was the only wounded soldier who could manage to ride in it, by laying his injured leg on one seat and sitting on the other.[19] Colonel Alexander Dickson, recovering from a fever, journeyed from Oporto to Lamego in such a litter to escape from the September sun. His particular chair had no front seat, so he was able to stretch out his legs.[20] Captain Tomkinson was another beneficiary of the sedan-chair. After being wounded in the neck and both arms during a cavalry engagement, he was carried on a door into Grijo and there spent a delirious week in the priest's house before he was fit enough to resume his journey northwards to Oporto. In the chair it took about two and a half hours to cover the eight remaining miles. Tomkinson felt extremely tired, and kept on begging the carriers to stop and let him rest a little. 'I was dreadfully irritable and wished the dragoon to *shoot* the Portuguese who held up the curtains of the sedan windows to look at me, which they repeatedly did on my entering the town.'[21]

A severe fever left Colonel Neil Campbell, who commanded a regiment of Portuguese infantry, so weak that he could barely talk or turn over, and he also travelled in a large sedan-chair, though not before some peasants had carried him in his bed to Pinhel. Instead of men to lift it, Campbell's litter had a mule in front and another behind, with poles fixed on their sides, the points of these shafts passing into strong eyes in the saddle.[22] Besides jolting up and down, the chair swayed backwards and forwards over the white glaring roads. When he could no longer stand the litter, Campbell had himself lifted on to his horse, and then back again, twenty times a day until shelter for the night could be found in a village. Such were the pain and exhaustion that Campbell could not tolerate more than one day of this torment, so his attendants hired a cart drawn by two oxen, but the jolting was still violent enough for Campbell to discharge the cart after two days of it and to make the rest of the hundred-mile journey on horseback – at a walk. 'So feeble was I,' he wrote, 'that I could not move two paces without a supporter, I generally managed to travel five miles in the morning, and again from two to seven in the afternoon and evening, frequently resting for twenty or thirty minutes under the shade of a tree, to slumber on my cloak.'[23] Campbell made the last part of the journey to Lisbon by boat picked up in Coimbra, and by the time he reached the capital his health had greatly improved.

By far the most comfortable and least dangerous means of conveyance was undoubtedly a boat. A trip down the Mondego was good enough, though this route did involve being transferred to a sea-going ship at the river mouth. Better still was to be taken along the roads to Abrantes, and thence down the Tagus all the way to Lisbon in a boat with tall, picturesque white lateen sails. Mrs Fitz Maurice, whose husband was an officer in the Rifle Corps, accompanied a party of soldiers who had been wounded at the storming of Badajoz. 'I have often heard described the luxury of sitting on the gunwale, with a broken leg in the water, eating delicious oranges; – luxury dearly purchased at the expense of much previous suffering. During three days the boats glided down the beautiful stream.'[24] Costello of the same regiment also made the last stages of a long, painful journey by water, first in a river boat down the Mondego to Figueiro da Foz, and thence to Lisbon. On the way to the coast the intense heat affected the wounds, and the very few doctors had no time to give proper attention. Consequently this neglect

'caused maggots to be engendered in the sores and the bandages, when withdrawn, brought away on them lumps of putrid flesh and maggots. Many died on board, and numbers were reduced in consequence to the necessity of amputation. By care and syringing sweet oil into my wounds, I however had managed to get rid of them.'[25]

One corporal with a musket-ball in the right shoulder was in such pain after three days' neglect that he said to the doctor: 'Sir, for God's sake dress my wound. I cannot live in such agony.' The doctor took from his pocket a small vial of spirits and poured some into the wound, thereby bringing out hundreds of maggots. 'There,' he said. 'You will now have some ease and sleep.'

On arrival in Lisbon, Costello and his companions were carried to hospital on stretchers by men of the Portuguese Militia. He recovered to endure many more campaigns, and survived this wound by fifty-nine years.

One of the most exhausting and painful journeys by mixed

means from field of battle to base hospital was that experienced in 1810 by Lieutenant George Simmons of the 95th. When, at the battle of the Coa, he was wounded in the thigh, a neckerchief was tied round the limb and twisted tight with a ramrod to stop the bleeding. Then he was propped on a horse and taken first to the church of Alverca to join many badly wounded soldiers who were laid in all directions on the stony floor. After several hours he was placed in a clumsy bullock cart which took him to the bishop's palace in Pinhel. Next, after a visit from the surgeon, Simmons was lifted into a spring waggon drawn by mules. He shared it with three brother officers, and reached Celorico after suffering torture throughout the day. 'The springs of this machine were very strong, and the rough ground we passed over made them dance us up and down in an awful manner. Bad as the movement of the bullock car was, this was ten times worse, if possible.'

The Portuguese muleteers vanished with their mules, so the wounded officers had to be transferred from the spring waggon to bullock carts once more, a change which pleased them in anticipation yet proved to be a nightmare, because several soldiers died, several more neglected to keep their wounds covered and soon found them a mass of maggots until an application of oil was found to kill them, while flies and mosquitoes tormented the convoy, which moved so slowly that the sun's rays beat down with no respite. Salt meat was a diet to turn the strongest stomach in such conditions, and the biscuit was usually full of worms or mouldy. At one point Simmons was thrown out of his cart when the bullocks, managed by a soldier servant in default of the Portuguese driver, careered along out of control. Miraculously he landed on top of his palliasse on the only bit of soft ground in sight. At long last, after covering at least a hundred miles in a week, they came to the Mondego and were taken on board a river boat for the journey to Coimbra and thence to the coast at Figueira da Foz.[26]

A shorter journey, but scarcely less arduous for it was unrelieved by water transport, was that described by Private Green of the 68th who, after being wounded below the heart in the Pyrenees, had to wait three days until a surgeon arrived with thirty mules to carry away the wounded. As they descended the mountain paths, these mules kept slithering several yards at a time, so much so that one sergeant fell off his mule and narrowly missed plunging down a precipice. When at last the party reached Wellington's head-quarters at Lesaca they were put in the town hall and had to lie on the bare stone floor. Off again next day to renewed suffering down the steep tracks. Green never expected to reach the bottom alive. 'It was like cutting my body to pieces. I cried, screamed, prayed, and wished to die: my companions were in the same way.'

At last they reached flat ground and were lodged overnight at General Graham's headquarters in the village of Hernani, where once again they had to lie on a bare floor. On the following day they came to the little port of Pasajes and entered the general hospital there.[27]

Conditions in the hospitals were all too often appalling. One of the main centres was Celorico, near Guarda in north-eastern Portugal. In 1810 Sergeant Cooper, 7th Fusiliers, was there in two small unventilated rooms, with eleven other men, most of whom were either unconscious or bawling out incomprehensible jibber. 'There was not a single chamber utensil.' he wrote. 'A blanket was spread on the floor instead. Some made use of the window for every purpose. I saw neither basin, soap, nor towel.'[28] There was no good reason, at least on paper, for such shortages of equipment, since a hospital for 500 patients had in its authorized stores 200 chamberpots, 6 bedpans and 6 stool-pans. Other items included 500 spoons, 200 trenchers, 200 pint-pots, 100 quart-pots, 100 bowls, 10 basins, and 200 linen shirts and nightcaps in addition to one palliasse, one blanket, one pair of sheets, one coverlid and one bolster-case per bed.[29]

In practice the hospitals were overcrowded to the point where, in Celorico during the autumn of 1811, two patients occupied each bed. When one died, another was brought in to fill his place and, in the words of Cornet Francis Hall, to 'share in mind as well as body the infection of his disease'. Celorico was not alone in having dreadful conditions. At Vila Viçosa, where a convent had been converted into a hospital, the windows were small, ventilation was lacking and about 150 patients lay in the corridors, alongside multi-purpose barrels or tubs. Since the inevitable stench was horrible, fir logs were burnt at the four corners of the convent to drive away the infection and mitigate the smell. These fires no doubt afforded some relief, but sick and wounded men found the smoke made their eyes smart painfully.

Cooper also had to sample the military hospital in Elvas, this time housed in a bomb-proof barracks. As usual, there was next to no ventilation, and one door only to the ward. Of his own condition he wrote: 'Shirt unchanged and sticking to my sore back; ears running stinking matter; a man lying close on my right hand with both his legs mortified nearly to the knees, and dying. A little sympathy would have soothed, but sympathy there was none. The orderlies were brutes.'[30]

All too often this was true. Whereas most of the doctors were devoted to their work and humane in character, many of the orderlies were neither. Augustus Frazer, an authoritative witness who wrote day by day to his wife Emma at home, was depressed by the need for more medical aid, for improvement in arrangements for the sick, and, not least, for humanity, even tenderness, towards sick men. 'I fear, in many cases, both have been wanting.' That was written in January 1813, by which time matters had improved not a little.[31]

Once the sea routes had been shortened by use of northern harbours like Bilbao and Pasajes, near San Sebastian, hospital conditions did improve. On 8 September 1813, stores arrived from England, and in Pasajes hospital each man was provided with 'a harden bed-tick filled with straw, two blankets, one pair of sheets, and one rug: this happy change caused us partly to forget our late misfortunes'. The surgeons came round the wards twice daily to dress wounds, and everything that attention could achieve was done for the men's recovery. Later that month Green of the 68th and some of his companions were sent by ship to a convent where all their regimental uniform was taken away and replaced by a suit of hospital clothing. This comprised a long coat, a flannel waistcoat, a pair of trousers, and a shirt, all in white. A flannel cap was also issued for good measure.[32] On leaving this hospital, some of the soldiers were housed in prefabricated huts made and put together in England. Each section was numbered, so to assemble and erect them was easy, though the finished product was by no means perfect, given that high winds sometimes tore off part of the roof and left the convalescents exposed to the rain.[33]

One of the most depressing aspects of any hospital was the way in which the dead were disposed of. After Talavera a main hospital was established in Elvas, and several thousand British

259

soldiers died there. George, one of the famous trio of Napier brothers, records how the dead cart used to go round three times a day laden with naked corpses, which were tumbled into a hole outside the town.[34] Bugler William Green was in Elvas at the same time and relates that the men who died, mostly of fever, were buried between eleven o'clock and midnight, without any religious service or military honours. A friend of his named John Moore fell seriously ill of the fever and was, in error, taken to the dead-house and laid on a plank with his feet tied together, ready for burial that same night. However, the sentry on duty there, hearing a noise, called the corporal of the guard. They opened the door and found that Moore had fallen off the plank and was trying to untie his feet. Moore recovered and rejoined his company and friends.[35]

Two years later, at Celorico, between fifty and a hundred men were buried daily, and even in the winter months from ten to twenty corpses were carried through the streets 'with scarcely the fragment of a tattered cloak, or a few boughs, to shroud their ghastly remains, and in this state were flung into a hole, which constituted a common receptacle without the town. Death was too common a fault to be treated ceremoniously.'[36]

It was normal for each regiment, whether cavalry or infantry, to have one surgeon and two assistant surgeons. Several of these doctors left behind recollections of campaign life, but they make little mention of the medical work. One exception is Walter Henry, who does afford an occasional glimpse of his professional duties, especially during the 1813 advance. On the day of Vitoria he and three colleagues spent many hours in a large wheat field, collecting wounded soldiers, dressing their wounds, performing amputations and sending survivors to the rear.[37] Henry tells us that when he went to attend a new batch of wounded, he would carry his instruments and surgical apparatus, while an orderly brought the tray of plasters and bandages. Among the surgical instruments provided for use in the field were an amputating saw and knife, a metacarpal saw, two scalpels, a screw tourniquet, a pair of bullet forceps, twelve curved needles and thread for ligatures, a tenaculum for picking up arteries and veins, two catheters, one of silver, the other of elastic, two trephines or circular saws for removing part of the bone of the skull, and instruments for withdrawing fluid.

After one severe action near Pamplona at the end of July, Henry was sent by the staff surgeon to a village church at which the wounded were being collected. There he spent five days and nights, with scarcely an hour's respite; indeed, for the first two days he appears to have had no medical assistance whatever. Help eventually came from two surgeons who were attached to regiments of cavalry.[38]

Opinions vary sharply on the competence and humanity of the army surgeons. Many were ornaments to their profession, but some arrived with grossly inadequate experience and, as Sergeant Donaldson puts it, 'were thrust into the army as a huge dissecting room, where they might mangle with impunity, until they were drilled into an ordinary knowledge of their business'. A number of the hospital orderlies were callous brutes, not above beating patients with a broomstick.[39]

Whatever the quality and character of the medical staff, it cannot be denied that the soldiers of that period endured pain with remarkable toughness and fortitude. Some of the wounds were indeed dreadful, and in the conditions of the time recovery was astonishing. Take the case of Corporal James Buchanan of the 13th Light Dragoons, who was attacked by three French dragoons at Aire on the Adour in March 1814 and either killed, captured or wounded his opponents, in the process receiving fifteen wounds. One bone of his forearm was severed and his nose was cut off, yet he recovered, thanks to the skilled attention of Surgeon Henry. An infantryman who took part in the storming of Badajoz had thirteen bayonet wounds in various parts of his body as a result of the French defenders throwing down the scaling ladders. While in hospital he stripped every morning for the doctor to dress his wounds and by good treatment he got well again.[40] In the fighting at Waterloo the French lancers inflicted numerous wounds, and many of the Scots Greys, to mention only one regiment, recovered from ten to a dozen lance thrusts. And one private named William Lock, wounded in seventeen places, lived to tell the tale.[41]

No more gallant officer campaigned under Wellington's command than Colonel John Colborne, afterwards a field-marshal. At the storming of Ciudad Rodrigo while in command of the 52nd a bullet struck his right shoulder and passed some way down the arm, carrying part of the gold wire of his epaulette into the wound.

He could not lie on his left side, as it hurt the other to be raised, and the pain of lying on his back became so dreadful that his bed had to be lifted off the ground on one side to give him ease. The day after the battle a surgeon cut the wound across and across, probing for the ball, but he could not find it, and fifteen months were to elapse before it was extracted. Harry Smith, who knew him well, wrote long afterwards: 'The pain Colborne suffered in the extraction of the ball was more even than his iron heart could bear. He used to lay his watch on the table and allow the surgeons five minutes' exertions at a time, and they were three or four days before they wrenched the bone from its ossiffed bed . . . of course the shoulder-joint was anchylosed, but he had free use of the arm below the elbow.'[42] At one stage of the journey to Coimbra, whither he was carried on twenty mens' shoulders, Colborne felt so weak and his nerves were so upset that he used to be obliged to say 'Give me a glass of wine, I am going to cry'. 'I could not help crying continually. Once I felt it coming on as I was being carried across a stream in my journey and a good many soldiers were looking on, but I was so ashamed of their seeing me and thinking I was crying because I was hurt, that that, I think, prevented me.'[43]

It sometimes happened that a musket ball could not be extracted. This was the experience of William Napier, who received a severe wound in the back, and of Lord March, afterwards Duke of Richmond, who still had a ball in his chest in 1828, fourteen years after being gravely wounded at the battle of Orthez.[44] As for the ball which lodged in Costello's thigh in 1810, it was not cut out until after his death almost sixty years later.

When Charles Napier was wounded at Busaco, a musket ball entered one side of his nose, passed through, and lodged in the jawbone on the opposite side. It was extracted with great difficulty, a large part of the jaw coming away with the ball, as well as several teeth. During this long and painful operation Napier never uttered a word or winced while under the surgeon's hands, Indeed, this surgeon told George Napier that he had never seen anyone bear pain so patiently and so manfully.[45]

Lest gangrene set in, the surgeons frequently decided to amputate a soldier's arm or leg, and this was done without anaesthetic, except sometimes a gulp of rum, and with the patient only on rare occasions requiring to be held to the operating table. Landmann visited a field hospital near Obidos in 1808, and was shocked to see two surgeons just completing the amputation of a soldier's leg below the knee. Landmann started back and said rather quickly: 'I beg pardon'. Meanwhile the patient was seated on a table, holding up the stump of his leg with both hands, and singing 'God save the King' in a lusty voice. 'But on my begging pardon and turning away, he suspended his song, and exclaimed with a strong Irish accent, "Walk in, sir. No offence at all, sir . . ." Outside the cottage door two little drummer boys were engaged in warming long strips of adhesive plaster in the sunshine.'[46]

Captain Charles Boothby, Royal Engineers, had one leg badly mangled by a musket ball at the battle of Talavera, and the staff surgeons decided to amputate. Boothby is candid in his account of the operation he underwent after the instruments had been laid out and a mattress placed on the table.

'One of the surgeons came to me and exhorted me to summon my fortitude. I told him that he need not be afraid; and Fitzpatrick stopped him, saying that he could answer for me. They then took me to the table and laid me on the mattress. Mr. Miller wished to place a handkerchief over my eyes; but I assured him that it was unnecessary – I would look another way. The tornequet [sic] being adjusted, I saw that the knife was in Fitzpatrick's hand; which being as I wished, I averted my head. . . .

' "Is it off?" said I, as I felt it separate.

' "Yes," said Fitzpatrick. "Your sufferings are over."

' "Ah, no! You have yet to take up the arteries!"

' "It will give you no pain," he said, kindly; and that was true – at least, after what I had undergone, the pain seemed nothing.

'I was carried back to my bed, free from pain, but much exhausted. The surgeons complimented me upon my firmness, and I felt gratified that I had gone through what lay before me without flinching, or admitting a thought of cowardly despair.'[47]

Whenever such operations were being performed, terrible sights met the eye, horrible sounds struck the ears. From the windows of one convent amputated arms and legs were flung down into a square among wounded soldiers who lay waiting their turn to go before the surgeons, if they lived long enough.[48] Vimeiro churchyard after the battle contained unpleasant evidence of surgery: a heap of legs that had just been amputated, and a large wooden dish filled with severed hands.[49] After Ciudad Rodrigo, when George Napier had his arm cut off, Surgeon Guthrie took a long time to do the job – at least twenty minutes – so blunted were his instruments from the number of amputations he had already performed. 'I thanked him for his kindness,' wrote Napier, 'having sworn at him like a trooper while he was at it, to his great amusement.'[50]

Of all the descriptions of amputation horrors, perhaps the most graphic and gruesome comes from the pen of Lieutenant William Grattan of the Connaught Rangers, whose attention was arrested by an extraordinary bustle and a kind of half-stifled moaning in the yard of a *quinta*, or nobleman's country house, a mile or two from the battlefield of Fuentes de Oñoro.

'I looked through the grating, and saw about two hundred wounded soldiers waiting to have their limbs amputated, while others were arriving every moment. It would be difficult to convey an idea of the frightful appearance of these men; they had been wounded on the 5th [May 1811], and this was the 7th; their limbs were swollen to an enormous size. Some were sitting upright against a wall, under the shade of a number of chestnut-trees, and many of these were wounded in the head as well as limbs; the ghastly countenances of these poor fellows presented a dismal sight. The streams of gore, which had trickled down their cheeks, were quite hardened with the sun, and gave their faces a glazed and copper-coloured hue, – their eyes were sunk and fixed, and what between the effects of the sun, of exhaustion, and despair, they resembled more a group of bronze figures than any thing human, – there they sat, silent and statue-like, waiting for their turn to be carried to the amputating-tables. At the other side of the yard lay several whose state was too helpless for them to sit up; a feeble cry from them occasionally, to those who were passing, for a drink of water, was all they uttered.

A little farther on, in an inner court, were the surgeons. They were stripped to their shirts and bloody; – curiosity led me forward; a number of doors, placed on barrels, served as temporary tables, and on these lay the different subjects upon whom the surgeons were operating; to the right and left were arms and legs, flung here and there, without distinction, and the ground was dyed with blood. Doctor Bell was going to take off the thigh of a soldier of the 50th, and he requested I would hold down the man for him; he was one of the best-hearted men I ever met with, but, such is the force of habit, he seemed insensible to the scene that was passing around him, and with much composure was eating almonds out of his waistcoat-pockets, which he offered to share with me, but, if I got the universe for it, I could not have swallowed a morsel of any thing. The operation upon the man of the 50th was the most shocking sight I ever witnessed; it lasted nearly half an hour, but his life was saved.'[51]

The medical machinery usually worked more smoothly when-ever a battle was fought near a large town or city, because the surgeons could find much better accommodation in which to operate and to house the wounded. Also, the energy and resources of the local population became instantly available. On 22 July 1812, for instance, many inhabitants of Salamanca came out, carrying with them tea, coffee and other refreshments, while carts laden with fresh fruit, provisions and containers of water squeaked their way to the scene. Women back in the city had already pre-pared a large quantity of lint and rags for binding up wounds, and many Spanish girls were to be seen that evening supporting from the battlefield those among the wounded soldiers who were able to walk. They also carried their knapsacks and muskets. The local doctors, too, came out by torchlight with jackasses laden with bandages and other stores in order to dress the wounded – or some of them at least – on the spot.[52]

The other notable instance of local help from a city is Brussels, though the city lies five times as far from the battlefield of Waterloo as does Salamanca from Los Arapiles. On the eve of the battle the Mayor of Brussels invited his fellow citizens to send him every mattress or palliasse, bolster, sheet and blanket they could possibly spare. Anyone who had old linen or lint was requested to give it without delay to his parish priest.[53] Many families, including several British ones who had rented houses in Brussels that year, took wounded men into their homes, sent for surgeons, and did their best as amateur nurses. In the streets and squares thousands of wounded were laid on straw; and since not nearly enough doctors were available to cope, the ladies worked as hard and humanely as they could to make up for this lack. While some of them scraped lint, others prepared cherry water for the wounded.[54] One of those cared for in this way was Sergeant Edward Costello, who wrote of these untrained nurses: 'numbers were busily employed – some strapping and bandaging wounds, others serving out tea, coffee, soups, and other soothing nourishments; while many occupied themselves stripping the sufferers of their saturated garments, and dressing them in clean shirts, and other habiliments'.[55]

Even two weeks after the battle of Waterloo, Brussels was full of wounded. Upon many a door were written the words in white chalk: *'militaires blessés'*, and sometimes, in the case of officers, the actual number of wounded in the house. When Miss Charlotte Waldie walked through the streets on her return from Antwerp, she saw at every open window the wounded troops, 'languid and pale, the ghosts of what they were'. More encouraging was the sight, in Brussels' Park, of a few officers, lame, disabled, or supported on crutches, with their arms in slings or their heads bandaged, 'slowly loitering in its deserted walks or languidly reclining on its benches'.[56]

Emphasis has been laid upon the medical care of Wellington's wounded, yet in the Peninsular War, as in more recent wars, a far larger number of soldiers went sick and even died from fevers than from wounds received in battle. Between 1 January and 25 July 1812, the 1st and 3rd Battalions of First Guards had 801 rank and file die of fever, while in the first five months of 1813 they buried 800 out of 2,000.[57] The officers suffered just as badly. One evening after dinner in August 1811 Lord Wellington talked in confidence of the many sick officers: 700 absent as against 1,400 present. Their constitutions must all be broken, he observed. And a month later when, in the high districts round Guarda and Celorico, nearly half the newly arrived troops lay in hospital, veterans of the Walcheren campaign shook with fever, and one division had as many soldiers sick as were fit for duty, Wellington declared: 'We are an army of convalescents'.[58]

Conditions had not improved greatly since General Hill had written from near Merida on 10 November 1809 that the army was much reduced by disease.

'It is generally supposed that we have upwards of 30,000, but I assure you we could not bring more than 13,000 into the field. The sickness which prevails is dreadful, and the mortality melancholy. There are not less than 10,000 in the hospitals, besides some hundreds in a convalescent state. The deaths during the last three weeks have, upon average, been little short of fifty men a day.'[59]

Sometimes the call and excitement of battle can act as a cure, if only a temporary one. In the Peninsular War the majority of sufferers had to rely on it. Here are three examples. On 7 July 1813 Bell of the 34th had a particularly severe fit of the ague, and felt so ill and had so bad a headache that he lay down under an apple tree. The intense heat merely increased his sufferings. Suddenly the drums beat to arms, the bugles sounded the 'Assembly', and everyone hurried to his alarm-post, orders having come to march up the mountain as fast as possible. Bell struggled to his feet, joined his company, and dragged himself along, feeling faint and weary. 'It was a point of honour,' he says, 'not to be detained by any trifling illness, and so I stuck to my trade as usual.' In the excitement of battle he forgot his fever, and afterwards lay out all night in a cold damp fog. 'The ague took flight and never returned during the war! Some fellows said that it was frightened out of me! Maybe so. I wish it had been frightened out of me sooner.'[60] When the 52nd were withdrawing to Busaco in 1810 George Napier suffered from fever every night, yet such was the effect of mind over body that the moment he engaged with the enemy he felt strong and fit and able to do his duty as well as any other officer of the regiment. But when they halted at night he felt weak and wretched again.[61] Then there was Colonel Frederick Ponsonby commanding the 12th Dragoons who, on the morning of Vitoria while awaiting orders to move, asked William Hay to accompany him to the front. After riding five miles or so, and reconnoitring the French positions, Ponsonby said in an undertone: 'Hay, I am very ill. This is my ague day, and I feel it coming on.' He led his horse into some undergrowth beside the road and said he simply had to lie down till the fit was over. Hay and the Colonel's orderly were to keep a sharp lookout and, if the enemy moved in such a way that the regiment would have anything to do, he was to send word immediately. Meantime Hay was to tell nobody that the Colonel was unwell. At about ten o'clock the regiment rode up from the overnight bivouac, and Ponsonby resumed his work.[62]

Doctors were by no means immune from sickness. Larpent records that five medical men died in Ciudad Rodrigo alone during the winter of 1812–13. So it comes as no surprise to read of Surgeon Henry's exasperation at finding himself attacked by his old enemy, the tertian ague, while quartered near Plasencia early in 1813. For two weeks he dosed himself with normal remedies like quinine, but to no avail: at noon every second day his teeth began to chatter. Determined to defeat his enemy, Henry prepared a tumbler of hot spiced wine for half past eleven, ordered his horse to the door, swung into the saddle, drank the mulled wine, and then cantered across the open plain. At noon, when he felt 'the ague-fiend's cold fingers' grasping his loins, he set spurs to his horse and pushed him into a full gallop, riding until he had outdistanced the pursuing fever. Next time he tried this plan with equal success, and on the return of the third period, when the fit came on, he was delighted to find himself comfortable. 'My spine,' he tells us, 'did not turn into a great icicle, nor my grinders commence their former hornpipes.' Henry never had the ague again.[63]

Cures for ague were varied, even bizarre sometimes. Simmons, who had a daily attack in November 1811, was so weak that he stayed in bed and took large doses of opium and quinine bark. Whenever he felt a cold fit coming on, he placed two hot stones on his chest and two at the soles of his feet. By treating himself in this way he got rid of the fever and slowly recovered.[64] Assistant Commissary August Schaumann tried similar orthodox remedies, but nothing relieved his shivering, not even the strongest doses of quassia, quinine, or a blend of quinine and black pepper. In the end he lost patience, disregarded the doctors' restrictions on diet, ate and drank whatever he pleased, and just got on with his work. Eventually he, too, felt well again.[65]

Several tried a form of water cure. When Swabey had a violent headache followed by a fit of the ague, he was attended by Surgeon George Peach of the 9th Dragoons who made him get into water during every hot fit and repeat the operation several times. 'This getting into water in a fever makes one shudder almost as much as if told to get into a furnace.'[66] Hay of the 12th Light Dragoons was another who, during the retreat from Burgos in 1812, had an attack every other day. Wet to the skin and trembling from head to foot, he had difficulty staying in the saddle. One evening, however, with a tree root for a pillow and his feet near the fire, which his batmen got burning with green branches, Hay lay down, covered by his sodden cloak. 'This,' he wrote, 'acted like the fashionable "water-cure", as, most extraordinary to relate, I never had a return of the ague from that day.'[67]

A far more drastic water-cure was practised in the hospital at Elvas during the autumn of 1809. Bugler William Green of the Rifle Corps was quartered in the town, and when off duty he and his companions took turns to sit with the sick until about midnight, when they took fever patients out of bed and led them to a flight of steps. As the sick wore no shirts in bed they were naked, so two buckets of cold water were poured over each. 'They were so deranged they knew nothing about it. I have put my finger into their hand, when they would jump out of bed, follow me, and sit quietly while we poured the contents of the buckets over them, and would be led by the finger back again to bed, and never utter one word.'[68] The regimental officers and doctors believed this mode of treatment had a beneficial effect, and no doubt it did for some of the afflicted. Costello, also of the Rifle Corps, was one of them. He recovered after six weeks, thanks to a strong constitution and, so he believed, to the doctors' cure of frequent drenching in cold water.[69]

One of the strangest 'cures' for ague was the spider's web. While Sergeant Donaldson was in hospital with fever, General Sir John Hope paid a visit and in going round the wards asked the staff surgeon which was the prevailing disease. 'Fever and ague,' replied the surgeon. Hope said he had heard of an allegedly infallible cure among the old women of Scotland. The surgeon begged to hear what it was. 'It is simply a large pill formed of a spider's web, to be swallowed when the fit is coming on.' Hope had never tried it himself, so could not guarantee its efficiency.

'The staff surgeon,' wrote Donaldson, 'gave a shrug, as much as to say it was all nonsense, looked very wise, as all doctors endeavour to do, and the conversation dropped.'

Donaldson overheard this exchange and was impressed, so when

269

the general and surgeon had left, he hopped out of bed, soon collected a spider's web or two, and next time a fit of ague came on, he confidently swallowed the dose. He recovered rapidly, was soon strong enough to rejoin his regiment (the 94th) and never had another fit of fever.[70]

Chapter 17

ARMY WIVES

'In quarters they were assailed by every temptation which could be thrown in their way, and every scheme laid by those who had rank and money, to rob them of that virtue which was all they had left to congratulate themselves upon. Was it to be wondered at, then, if many of them were led astray, particularly when it is considered that their starving condition was often taken advantage of by those who had it in their power to supply them, but who were villains enough to make their chastity the price?'[1]
Sergeant Joseph Donaldson

By regulations and custom, only six wives were allowed to travel on service with each company. The women drew lots as to which should go, and this casting of lots was usually left until the last evening before a regiment embarked for the war.[2] Tickets inscribed 'To go' and 'Not to go' were put in a hat, and when the moment of suspense and destiny arrived, most affecting, pathetic scenes occurred, because wives left behind often faced starvation or charity, though individual regiments did give allowances to carry the women and children home. This was done when the 18th Light Dragoons sailed for Lisbon in 1808 and ninety-one wives had to be refused permission to follow their husbands. The 23rd Foot, on assembling at Falmouth to sail for Corunna, took forty-eight women and twenty children in addition to forty sergeants, nineteen drummers and 575 privates.[3]

A return of the British women with the 4th Division in November 1813 shows that the 7th Fusiliers had seventeen, the 20th Regiment had twenty-two, the 23rd Fusiliers twenty-five, the 27th Regiment thirty-four and the 40th Regiment twenty-four. The 48th Regiment had nineteen and the single company of the 60th only two, while the 2nd Provisional Battalion numbered six wives. This makes a total of 149. As for the three Portuguese infantry battalions serving in the Division, they were accompanied by ninety women.[4] For the Waterloo campaign the 13th Light Dragoons took to Ostend twenty-eight women and nine children.[5]

Regiments had to submit regular returns showing the names of each woman on strength, the husband's name, rank, troop or company, the woman's age, her height in feet and inches and the colour of her eyes, hair and complexion. Other columns required details of the children, whether boys or girls, and their respective ages.[6]

Few of the wives are on record as having been killed by enemy action, but two at least died in this way. During the army's retreat in October 1812 the 51st Light Infantry had to fight when the French tried to force the bridge at Valladolid. A cannon-ball struck Sergeant Maibey's wife while she was eating breakfast at her husband's side, carried away her right arm and breast, and killed her. One fusilier whose leg was almost severed at the battle of Toulouse had lost his wife twenty months before at Salamanca, where she had been killed while bravely giving a drink to a wounded soldier.[7] In addition, a number of women had narrow escapes from death. Here is an example. One evening at dusk, when pursuing the French towards Aire and the river Adour, the 66th halted in column on the road, whereupon a shot from one of the enemy's guns knocked over a soldier's wife who had always managed to keep up with the regiment on the march. Surgeon Henry hurried across and found she had no more than a graze and some bruising on the shoulder. On learning that no real harm had been done, the woman was so relieved and delighted that she 'pulled a fowl out of one enormous pocket, and half a yard of black pudding out of the other, of which she begged my acceptance. I cannot say I pocketted the fee, but we regaled on it at our bivouack that evening.'[8]

Now and then a few of the women became prisoners of war, though seldom for long. During the retreat to Corunna several women belonging to the 95th fell into the hands of the French who, after using them as they pleased, gave them some food and sent them back to the regiment. At the battle of El Bodon in 1810 some women belonging to one of General Picton's brigades were captured by the French, along with stores and baggage. Private William Brown recalled that their 'co-mates' appeared to be so little affected by this occurrence that when one Irishman, seated round a camp fire that evening, was commiserated with on losing his wife he replied: 'Faith, boys! I would not have cared a straw about it at all, but Jenny had got my pipe away with her!' Let us hope she still had the pipe when, a few days later, she and her companions were escorted to the British outposts by French cavalry and restored to their husbands.[9]

Occasionally a woman would turn up on a field of battle. An instance of this occurred during Wellington's first action in Portugal – at Roliça. While riding between two regiments Captain George Landmann, the senior Royal Engineer that summer of 1808, overtook a woman dressed in a nankeen riding-habit and a straw bonnet, who carried a parasol and a large rush basket. Shot was making dust fly on the road. Several men lay dead, others were gravely wounded, so the woman was obliged to step over bodies in order to get forward. Landmann, thinking she must be either unaware of the danger she was in or else so bewildered by the battle that she did not realize that she was heading towards the enemy, could not resist saying to her, *en passant*, that she had much better go back for a short time, as this was a very unfit place for a lady to be in. 'Upon this she drew herself up,' writes Landmann, 'and with a very haughty air and, seemingly, a perfect contempt of the danger of the situation, evidently proceeding from extreme agitation, she replied, "Mind your own affairs, sir. I have a husband before me." I obeyed.' Landmann never discovered who she was.[10]

One of the most remarkable ladies who went to the Peninsular War was Susanna Isabella Dalbiac, whose husband Charles commanded the 4th Dragoons, in which regiment her father had served and her eldest brother was then a captain. Married in 1805, the Dalbiacs had one daughter, Susanna Stephanie. Mrs Dalbiac, having hurried out from home to nurse her husband through a fever contracted in the summer of 1810, had enjoyed campaigning enough to stay on after the Colonel had recovered.[11] She was to be seen riding at the head of the 4th, carrying a little haversack and bottle on the pommel of her saddle.[12] She slept at his side, whether under a roof, in a tent, or beneath the stars and clouds. For two nights down by the malarial Guadiana river she lay out in pouring rain, with nothing to cover her but a single blanket.[13] When her husband's brigade commander wanted to lighten the burden that her affection imposed upon her, he was unable to do

273

so: 'She is inexorable, and rejects prayer, petition or remonstrance'.[14] One must add that, back in England, Susanna Dalbiac had been considered delicate, so her friends were astonished at the way in which, without injuring her health, she stood up to fatigues under which many a soldier had collapsed.

Her most testing ordeal came at Salamanca in 1812. On the night of 21 July, the 4th Dragoons were bivouacked on a height near the river Tormes. The men lay asleep beside their picketed horses, and a short way down the slope stood several guns. The evening had been ominously sultry, and a sudden flash of lightning and a violent thunderclap woke the dragoons and startled their horses. Indeed, the latter were so alarmed that a number of them broke away from their pickets and galloped down the hill. Fortunately the Dalbiacs were not asleep at the time, but seated on the ground near the artillery. The Colonel just had time to snatch up his wife and place her on one of the guns – a prompt action which saved them both from being trampled to death or seriously hurt by the frightened horses dashing past on either side. Eighteen men in the cavalry brigade received injury, and next morning thirty-one horses were missing.[15]

Next day Wellington's army fought and won the battle of Salamanca. Susanna Dalbiac's conduct on this occasion was praised by several contemporaries: Sir William Napier singled her out for an exceptional eulogy in his famous *History of the War in the Peninsula*: 'Forgetful of everything but the strong affection which had so long supported her, she rode deep amidst the enemy fire, trembling, yet impelled forwards by feelings more imperious than terror, and stronger than the fear of death.'[16] Ensign, afterwards Major-General, George Bell declared vehemently: 'There was no man present that did not fight with more than double enthusiasm seeing that fair lady in such danger on the battlefield'.[17]

Dalbiac and the 4th Dragoons took part in the great charge of the Heavy Cavalry Brigade in which General Le Marchant was killed. For many hours afterwards Colonel Dalbiac's wife believed her husband had suffered a similar fate, so at dusk, when battle was done, she set off with one dragoon to search for him. Unfortunately she lost her escort in the darkness, and for some time wandered alone among the dead and wounded – a gruesome experience. Eventually she learnt, to her joy and relief, that the Colonel was safe and unhurt. Still she did not rest, for next morning she was back in the city of Salamanca, tending the wounded and summoning doctors to dress their wounds.[18] One of those lucky enough to be nursed by Mrs Dalbiac was Lieutenant Norcliffe of the 4th Dragoons, who had been wounded in the head, captured by the French and then released when the latter were obliged to retreat. He had run back to the nearest British infantry, whence he was carried to the rear in a corporal's blanket, suffering agonizing pain all the way. The Northumberland Fusiliers' surgeon bandaged his head, and next morning Norcliffe was taken on a mule to his regiment, where Mrs Dalbiac, 'whose kindness I shall never forget, got me carried into Salamanca and washed my head and put me to bed; she then got Dr Gunning to come, who dressed my wound properly and bled me'. Not only did Norcliffe recover, but he later became a major-general, surviving Salamanca by fifty years.[19]

Once she had assured herself that Norcliffe was in expert hands and out of danger, Mrs Dalbiac set off to rejoin her husband and the regiment, who were already on their way to Madrid; she had to ride all through the night before she overtook them. She seems to have been much in demand as a nurse, and as competent as she was ready to oblige. The 4th was something of a family regiment, for its officers included a brother-in-law, George Dalbiac, and two nephews, one of whom, Cornet John Luard, went down with fever in the malarial Guadiana valley. She took charge and he soon recovered, thanks to 'a dose of salts, an emetic, and the kindness of Colonel Dalbiac and Aunt Susan'. When Luard took ill again fifteen months later, this time with dysentery during the army's retreat from Burgos in November 1812, he jolted feverishly along in a local cart, soaked to the skin and feeling so unwell that he could not keep down even liquid nourishment. 'I was left in a wayside inn outside Ciudad Rodrigo,' he wrote, 'and would probably have died had not Aunt Susan sought me out and rescued me. She was already nursing Colonel Charles Dalbiac and looked after me as well.' When news that the French were approaching caused the sick and wounded to be evacuated as far as the high fortress of Almeida, just inside Portugal, the river Agueda flooded as they were crossing and the carts had to be

275

abandoned in midstream. 'Susan came to the rescue once more and got us safe across.' But for her devotion and determination, it is unlikely that John Luard would have recovered. He later described her as 'one of the wittiest, if not necessarily the most beautiful, women that I have ever met'.[20] Many years later Charles Dalbiac himself, writing to a friend, paid his wife a most graceful tribute:

'Whenever the Regiment took the field Mrs Dalbiac accompanied me on horseback and such was the case on the date of the battle of Salamanca, up to the moment when the action commenced. She then remained near the extreme right of our position, whence the heavy brigade of Cavalry had moved for the attack, and she could distinctly discern most of the operations in that quarter. . . . Here she had the fortitude to remain during the whole of the action, tho so completely within Cannon range that shots from the enemy's guns frequently raked up the dust near her horse's feet.

'Of this incomparable wife I will only add that with a mind of the most refined cast, and with a frame of body alas too delicate, she was, when in the field, a stranger to personal fear.'[21]

In northern Spain and the Pyrenees another officer to be accompanied by his wife was John, Earl Waldegrave, a major in the 15th Dragoons. Lady Waldegrave was a beautiful woman, an admirable horsewoman, gracious and sweet of manner, and she was also courageous. 'I have seen her for 4 days together amongst the skirmishers,' noted Cornet Shakespear of the 2nd Dragoons.[22] 'Her conduct,' Captain Gronow assures us, 'was the theme of the army and she won universal praise and admiration. She was a perfect heroine.' After the war she would tell stories of the many risks she had been exposed to in the several cavalry charges led by Lord Waldegrave. On one occasion she was nearly taken prisoner, but she boldly presented her pocket pistol at the breast of a French cavalryman who threatened her, whereupon he dropped his sword and allowed her to escape.[23]

Probably the finest act of personal bravery performed under fire by a British army wife during the Peninsular War occurred at Cadiz in 1810. The woman's husband, Sergeant Reston of the 94th Regiment, was one of a detachment ordered to hold the fort of Matagordo when it was under bombardment from French guns across the bay. Matagordo Fort, being only a hundred yards square, was a place of danger, and as the bomb-proofs were too small to contain the whole garrison, some of the men lived in huts, as did Mrs Reston. One day when the French batteries opened fire, she was woken by a twenty-four pound shot striking a fascine just beside her head. Undaunted, she took her four-year-old boy down into a bomb-proof, and there assisted the surgeon, Dr Bennett, to dress the wounded soldiers as they were brought in. To do so she tore up her own linen and also her husband's.

A drummer-boy, on being ordered to fetch water from a well in the centre of the fort, seemed very reluctant to go, and lingered by the bomb-proof door, bucket in hand.

'Why don't you go for the water?' asked the surgeon.

'The poor thing's frightened, and no wonder at it,' said Mrs Reston. 'Give it to me, and I'll go.'

She walked to the well, and under fire filled the bucket. Scarcely had she done this when a shot severed the rope, so she asked a sailor to help her, recovered the bucket, and brought it full of water to the bomb-proof. When not attending to the wounded, she carried sandbags for repairing the battery, handed ammunition along, and took wine and water to the gunners. Next morning Mrs Reston was still at her post, though two other women, who had been in hysterics inside a bomb-proof, had left the battery. Ammunition was exhausted, and the French, seeing the delapidated state of Matagordo, prepared to assault the place. Although their first attack was beaten off by fire, and more ammunition arrived, the fort was found to be untenable. Accordingly the survivors of the small garrison were evacuated by naval boats.

Donaldson, who was present throughout the action, wrote as follows: 'Mrs Reston still exhibited the same undaunted spirit. She made three different journeys across the battery for her husband's necessaries and her own. The last was for her child, who was lying in the bomb proof. I think I see her yet, while the shot and shell were flying thick around her, bending her body over it to shield it from danger by the exposure of her own person.' Mrs Reston excaped unhurt and survived the war, but never received the smallest token of approval for her courageous conduct and the service she had rendered.[24]

We have a record of several more excellent wives who came out to join their husbands. Captain Charles Tonyn of the 48th Regiment, for example, learnt of his wife's arrival in Lisbon at the end of August 1811. Mrs Hogan, wife of the 7th Fusiliers' quarter-master, made the journey in November 1812, although he did not wish her to run the dangerous chances of war; it must have been a disagreeable voyage, for she lay below with sea-sickness until the ship came in sight of Belem Castle. Mrs Edward Currie used to make tea for General Hill and his staff and held little receptions whenever the 2nd Division settled down for a few days at a time. Captain Currie was Hill's aide-de-camp, and his amiable wife always dined at the General's table, with the result that, in Blakeney's words, officers present 'neither forgot the deference due to beauty nor the polished manners of the drawing-room'. And Mrs Berry, wife of the paymaster of the Buffs, Marlborough Parsons Berry, was seen at table in front of a chapel near Portalegre, dining *al fresco* with a party of officers.[25]

That a wife was sometimes close enough to nurse her husband is shown by the story of Major-General Robert Ross, who was severly wounded on 27 February 1814 at the battle of Orthez. His wife hurried the ninety miles from Bilbao to St Jean de Luz over bad roads to be with him, yet took five days on the journey. Ross wrote home to a relative: 'She is now at my elbow, having on the receipt of mine mounted her mule and in the midst of rain, hail, mud and all other accompaniments of bad weather, set off. . . . Our little boy is left at Bilbao with his nurse.'[26] Although this episode ended well, Mrs Ross's happiness did not last, for within six months the General, having won the battle of Bladensburg and captured Washington, had died of wounds received while fighting at Baltimore.

It was, of course, inevitable that certain wives who accompanied the army should have to mourn their husbands. Lieutenant-Colonel George Grey died of his wounds at Badajoz on 7 April 1812 while his wife was living in Lisbon. The news of this successful but costly siege reached the capital while she was seated upstairs on a verandah. She heard shouting in the streets – important news from the army. Then her husband's name was mentioned. Immediately imagining the worst she was taken in premature labour and on 14th April gave birth to a boy, whom she named after his father. He became Sir George Grey, Governor successively of South Australia, New Zealand, and Cape Colony, and then Premier of New Zealand.[27]

At the close of the 1811 campaigning season Major-General Andrew Hay sailed for home in order to bring back to Lisbon his wife and daughters, accompanied by a raw-boned Scottish servant. Several officers sent for their wives at this period, and Richard Henegan, who travelled with the Hays from England, was prompted to express disapproval of the system. In his view – and he was not alone in holding it – a heavy burden of sorrow and anxiety was imposed on the wives. 'How many could be named, who, at Lisbon, suffered torments from the effects of idle rumours and false reports, fabricated for local purposes only, and thus anticipated, over and over again, the bereavement that they were perhaps destined to be spared.'[28] As soon as Wellington's army reached southern France, Mrs Hay and her three daughters decided to join him, but three days after they had completed the overland journey from Lisbon to Biarritz, the General was killed at Bayonne – on 14 April 1814. On his round of the pickets he said to the soldiers with a note of glee in his voice: 'No more fighting, my lads! Now for your homes, wives and sweethearts.' Three hours later he died, just as he gave the order to hold on to the church at St Etienne at all costs, the French garrison having made a sortie.[29]

At Toulouse, the last battle of the Peninsular War, many distressing scenes occurred because the baggage camp was near the field of action, and women could not be prevented from coming up to enquire after their husbands. Most of those who made the journey found that their men had been either killed or wounded. When one gunner died of his wounds in a nearby château, his widow became so frantic with grief that she ran out and deliberately exposed herself to the enemy's fire and had to be dragged to safety by a sergeant.[30] In sharp contrast we have the wife of Sergeant Dunn of the 68th. He was killed early in the battle of Salamanca, and she became nearly frantic with shock, yet within a week she took up with a Sergeant Gilbert Hubbs of the same company, and lived with him thereafter. 'This poor woman was unlucky,' observed Private Green, 'for she had lost five husbands.'[31]

Her experience was by no means uncommon. In fact, many of

279

the women became widows two or three times over, and were seldom without offers of marriage from other soldiers in the regiment. The alternative to taking on a new man was usually to go home by ship, probably to an uncertain welcome and precarious future. Although most of the wives remained faithful until death did them part, several found themselves another man with remarkable speed and nonchalance. This was the more unusual when the woman concerned was an officer's widow. Major Harry Ross-Lewin of the 32nd came across one notable case when, after the battle of Salamanca in which he was severely wounded in the left arm, he was carried to the city and left in a miller's house. Soon afterwards two English ladies were brought in: one was married to a subaltern who had been reported as badly wounded but of whom no further news had been received; the other, a very beautiful girl, had lost her husband, a captain, in the fighting. For some time the captain's widow sat motionless, with a vacant stare. Then, as if remembering where she was, she made signs to her companion, who said to Ross-Lewin: 'It is her husband's watch that she wants'. The watch was found fastened under her habit, and she kissed it repeatedly before laying it against her bosom. The old miller and his family were moved to tears by this scene, even the Spanish mule driver burst into tears, and his mules stopped turning the mill wheel as if in sympathy. As for the widow, she had violent hysterics and floods of tears. When Ross-Lewin rose next morning he learnt that the two ladies had taken a carriage and moved to another billet. A few days later, while walking in Salamanca's magnificent square, he was astounded to see the captain's widow, whose grief had caused such a stir, leaning on the arm of a young commissary who wore two gold epaulettes. She was evidently in good heart, and on the following day set off with her new beau for Ciudad Rodrigo.[32]

Quite apart from suspiciously short and cheerful widowhoods, by no means every marriage mentioned in the Peninsula was harmonious, for a variety of reasons. This appears to have been true of one notorious couple in the 18th Light Dragoons. In his journal George Woodberry frequently mentions Lieutenant Morris, a brute of a husband who broke a bottle over his wife's head, for which act he had his rum ration stopped. In making enquiries, however, the officers discovered that the wife was, in fact, the guilty party, so her rum was also stopped! She followed the regiment on foot into southern France, and even though she was, in his view, an absolute bitch, Woodberry felt sorry for her. Yet when he offered to take her child on horseback with him one day she refused with an unladylike oath, cursing everyone in general and the regiment in particular. Morris himself nauseated his brother officers by talking freely and at length about the harsh treatment he meted out to his wife, however much they might feel she deserved it.

When the 18th Light Dragoons reached Mont de Marsan early in March 1814 Mrs Morris managed to persuade her husband to buy her a grey pony. Woodberry summed up the *ménage* by writing: 'Surely no regiment has ever been so compromised by an officer's wife as the 18th has been by Mrs Morris' behaviour'.

Early in 1813 a major in the 4th Dragoons kept a lady named Margaret who was 'a very termagent for temper'. One day he said something that displeased her, so she grabbed the tablecloth and sent everything on to the floor, spilling the soup and smashing crockery and glasses. 'This, to her, was genteel and in style,' observed William Graham, who was present. 'That night she got drunk with brandy, saying it was the finest comfort in nature.'[33]

Certain of the rank and file wives showed themselves to be very undisciplined. Even while carrying children in arms, they would break into Portuguese cellars with the men and take wine from staved-in casks. Wellington himself wrote in 1850 to Lady Salisbury: 'It is well known that in all armies the Women are at least as bad, if not worse, than the men as Plunderers! and the exemption of the Ladies from punishment would have encouraged Plunder!'[34] Indeed, the assistant provost-marshals would now and then catch them at it, or else the matter would be reported to some general officer. To take one instance, on arrival at a small Spanish town in July 1809 several women belonging to the 29th Regiment, having got ahead of the column, helped themselves to vegetables and other food. On hearing complaints of their activities from the wronged inhabitants, General Hill consigned the culprits to the provost who, in the words of Lieutenant Leslie, 'exercised schoolboy discipline on a few as an example to the rest'.[35] Peter Le Mesurier of the Norfolk Regiment believed that the women sometimes behaved worse than the men and relates how one

281

summer's day in 1812 the provost of the 5th Division desired one of them to leave a field where she was busy digging potatoes; otherwise he would punish her. With a tremendous oath she replied: 'You may flog me every day, for a meal of praties', and then walked off well loaded. A year later, when on baggage guard near Palencia, Le Mesurier was astonished to see four or five troops of Portuguese women marching in the rear with the baggage. Hitherto they had scattered across the country, plundering relentlessly in all directions until it became necessary to find a remedy for their depredations. As Le Mesurier explained, 'none was found to answer so well as keeping them in Flocks, and placing a Guard over them; for the Cat could not deter them from plundering on the March; it has been tried, and found not to answer so well'. No wonder, if they were all as brazen and *insouciant* as the potato woman.[36]

Sergeant Nicol of the 92nd, who was taken prisoner at Talavera, tells us how, one Sunday while a column of British prisoners was being escorted across northern Spain, some of the women went begging to the chapel doors. They obtained so much money that they were soon the worse for drink and began to riot and even to fight with their husbands. 'It is a great pity,' he comments, 'such vagabonds should be allowed to go abroad with the army.' The six women were later sent back to England by the French.[37]

Bell writes of two soldiers' wives who, during the retreat from Burgos to Portugal, 'stuck to the army like bricks', and sometimes impeded progress in their indisciplined way. Mrs Biddy Flynn and Mrs Betty Wheel were supposed to follow their respective regiments, but often blocked the narrow paths until an exasperated Wellington had to order the donkeys to be shot unless the women obeyed. They paid little attention to the order. Led by Mrs Skiddy, a squat little Irishwoman, very broad in the beam, who rode a donkey named 'the Queen of Spain', they tried to get ahead of the column. Alas! the provost-marshal had laid an ambush and several donkeys were shot as a deterrent. Undaunted, though bitter in lamentation and curses, the women marched on, the devoted Mrs Skiddy still eager to forage and cook for her husband Dan. As she remarked: 'We must risk something to be in before the men, to have the fire an' a dhrop of tay ready for the poor crathers after their load an' their labour'.[38]

Mrs Skiddy and her friends may well have been a trial to the provost-marshal, but their motives were understandable, and they certainly put their husbands' interests first.

Indiscipline apart, by no means everyone considered that army wives, be they officers' or other ranks', were an asset on campaign. On hearing that two young officers of the Corps of Royal Artillery Drivers had arrived at Sabagul in May 1813, accompanied by their wives, Augustus Frazer, whose own wife was in England, wrote: 'What will these ladies do? I cannot conceive a situation more uncomfortable than that of women following an army. I fear they will find neither the reality nor even the appearance of civility from any one: all are occupied with their own business and their own comforts'.[39]

These clearheaded but rather pessimistic views were expressed just as Wellington's army was setting off for the great summer offensive which was to lead to Vitoria, the Pyrenees and San Sebastian. They would no doubt have deterred Emma Frazer had she been contemplating the sea voyage to join her husband. They also reflected the belief that the two wives in question would have no time in which to settle down and become used to army life before having to travel with the troops day by day. Yet these conditions were favourable compared with those endured on a retreat in winter. No wonder another artillery officer, Captain Adam Wall, took a jaundiced view of the women who set off with General Sir David Baird's force from Corunna in December 1808, and whom he termed 'this everlasting clog to a British Army'. Sir David, realizing that he would be unable to help these women, arranged for them to return to England in empty transports, but they were averse to such a plan, and persevered in marching either in front of or behind the several brigades, with the result that the children died of exposure, and the women were reduced to raggedness and starvation. In his diary for 20 December 1808, Wall made the following harsh condemnation:

'It is a most mistaken idea to suppose that women can possibly be of the smallest use to an Army upon active service. The supposition of their washing for the soldiers is a delusion, for washing is a comfort the soldiers never sought, and the women never able to inclined to supply. I believe both officers and men were glad to get

283

an opportunity of washing a shirt, when halted for a few hours; but the women, from excessive fatigue, were incapable of helping themselves, much less of washing for the men.'[40]

This was an early and, on the whole, unfair judgement, for many veterans paid tribute to the darning and laundering and cooking which the women performed. The conditions in which Moore's army retreated over snowbound mountain roads were the harshest of all. In the words of Charles Steevens, an officer in the 20th Regiment of Foot, 'there ought not to have been any women with our army, after we commenced our retreat. Our women received a liberal allowance to pay their was back to Lisbon; but, after being absent a few days, they again made their appearance, and many of them, poor things, perished.' One woman he remembered especially, because she had been with the 20th for ten years and more, had a delicate constitution, and was an example of good conduct. Along the road to Corunna she went missing one dark night, and her daughter, quite a young girl, had to trudge to Corunna by herself. The mother was never heard of again.[41]

Other women were remembered on that arduous march: Mrs Munday, wife of the 28th Regiment's orderly-room sergeant, carried a lapdog in a basket over her arm and brought the pet safely to England; another sergeant's wife, Sally Northey, attended a Cornish officer, Honey by name, who was very ill in a roadside hovel, but she had to leave him when the French cavalry came in sight;[42] Sally Macan, wife of a soldier in Captain Diggle's company of the 52nd, noticed Charles Diggle falling behind on account of illness and fatigue, so she whipped off her garters and secured the soles of his boots which were separating from the upper leathers – an action which set him on his feet again and enabled him to reach Corunna.[43] He had an opportunity to repay her kindness a year or so later by offering her a lift on his horse the morning after she had given birth to a child in the regimental bivouac.

During the army's other two retreats – from Busaco to the Lines of Torres Vedras in October 1810 and, in particular from Burgos back to Portugal two years later – it was the women who suffered most. Those in poor health sat in bullock carts and added their sobs to the squeaking of ungreased wheels. 'If you asked them

284

where they were going,' wrote Surgeon Burroughs, 'they said they did not know. They were going with the English.'[44]

At all times on the march the women were exposed to great hardship and sometimes to danger, above all whenever the army had to cross a river. In May 1813 the left wing under General Graham's command made the difficult crossing of the Esla in flood – the cavalry by fords, the infantry by means of a pontoon bridge, about twenty feet wide and protected by railings on either side, Fortunately the French offered no resistance, which was just as well, because not a few horses and men were lost in the ravine, some of the foot soldiers were dragged across while hanging to a stirrup or horse's tail, and Graham had good cause to write afterwards: 'a more unpleasant operation I never desire to be concerned with'.[45] William Maginn, who watched the scene while awaiting his turn to cross, states that the river was as broad as the Thames at Richmond or Windsor. From ten o'clock in the morning until five in the afternoon columns of troops, horses, muleteers, mules, baggage, artillery, stores and much else went across the bridge, while Maginn and his companions sat under trees, eating cold beef and biscuit. 'Many elegant English ladies – wives of the officers – were to be seen upon the rock which overhung the river, with their gay parasols and waving feathers.'[46] For the women of the army, this proved to be a comparatively safe passage. At another crossing, however, one wife accidentally slipped into deep water and would have drowned had her two greyhounds not swum hard for the shore, dragging her to safety by their lead.[47]

Orders for an opposed crossing of the Nive were received by the 34th Foot on the night of 8–9 December 1813. Ensign Bell relates how the regimental wives reacted to this news.

'The women were all astir in a moment, lighting their fires "to have a dhrop of tay" for their respective warriors, "just to warm their hearts before plunging into the river, bad luck to the French". . . . This intended advance bothered them. How were they to cross the river and follow the troops, against a positive general order? The ladies assembled round a big fire on a dark winter's night to discuss this point. Mother Skiddy, Brigadier-General of the Amazons, so called, addressed the meeting. "I have the weeest donkey of you all, an' I'll take the wather if I'm to swim for it, but let me see

285

who's to stop me, Bridget Skiddy, who travelled from Lisbon here into France. If Dan falls, who's to bury him. God save us! Divil a vulture will ever dig a claw into him while there's life in Biddy, his laful wife. Now, girls, you may go or stay." and so she began to saddle her ass.'

The 34th fought its way across the swollen river under cover of guns, and once a footing had been secured on the far bank, Mrs Skiddy and the wives joined their menfolk.[48]

When the Black Watch and other regiments crossed the Adour, the stones in the bottom were so slippery that men had to support each other to stop falling. One sergeant's wife tried to make the passage on a donkey, carrying a child in her arms, but suddenly the animal stumbled, the child gave a start and fell into the swollen river, whereupon the mother, with a distracted shriek, jumped in to rescue her child. Both were swept away by the current. The husband, walking nearby, plunged into the ice-cold water in a vain bid to save his family, and he himself was rescued only with the greatest difficulty. This accident induced the other women to wait until a bridge had been repaired before they ventured to cross.[49]

These were all dangers while marching in the company of troops. Even more trying could be the long lone march across Portugal or Spain to rejoin a husband or to return to the comparative comfort of a base such as Lisbon. There is the case of an officer's wife who rode alone by mule from Lisbon to join her husband at the front. Near Celorico the armed Portuguese peasantry, noticing her somewhat masculine appearance, which the habit and black hat she wore did nothing to minimize, arrested her on suspicion of spying, marched her all the way back to Lisbon and there handed her to the proper authorities. Fortunately for the poor lady, the assistant surgeon of her husband's regiment happened to be in the capital, and his testimony on her behalf extricated her from prison and embarrassment.[50]

Captain John Harley of the 47th Foot relates how, whereas several hundred wives enjoyed comparative ease in Lisbon while their husbands were exposed to the discomforts and chances of war, one captain's wife was so attached to her husband that she determined to join him in the field, even though the army was then besieging distant Burgos. On arrival there she found herself in a deplorable situation because the captain was kept so busy that he could speak to her for only a few minutes each day. Moreover, he was unable to give her any money, since the pay was in arrears. What he did do was to collect about sixty pounds from his brother officers, obtain for her a horse, a mule, and a Portuguese servant lad, and then he prevailed upon her to go back to Lisbon. Though most reluctant to do so, she eventually consented and set off on the long journey. Several weeks later Wellington's army retreated from Burgos, and the regiment in question overtook the lady. What was her husband's horror to find her walking barefoot. No horse, no mule, no Portuguese boy, and no money. Apparently at one stage of the journey she had ridden through a wood and reached a *posada*, where she soon discovered that her purse was missing. She had been in the habit of fastening it on the crutch of the saddle each morning, and supposed that it must somehow have got caught in the undergrowth; so she returned to the wood and searched the path minutely, but in vain. Tired and miserable, she rode back to the inn, where on learning of her misfortune the Spanish owners were kind enough to lodge her free of charge. Next morning she set off again, but her troubles were by no means over, for during the night the Portuguese boy absconded with her horse and mule, and all the clothing she had brought for the journey. There she was, alone and stranded without money or transport in a strange country; yet she did not despair, and persevered on foot, trudging towards Portugal until her shoes were worn off her feet.[51]

In March 1813, while at Coimbra, Major Augustus Frazer met a blind Connaught Ranger, who was accompanied by a decent-looking wife. She carried an infant of five weeks, while a two-year-old girl ran beside her, because although they had started the march with a donkey, this had been stolen. The soldier, on his way to Lisbon to be invalided home, was cheerful though anxious about his little daughter whom he was now and then obliged to carry. She, poor mite, was frightened and hurt each time he stumbled or fell because of his blindness. Frazer was so impressed by their cheerfulness and resignation that he went to the commandant and secured for the soldier's family a passage to Lisbon in a Tagus sailing boat. Six months later Frazer met another army wife who was making her painful but uncomplaining way to the harbour of

Pasajes, next to San Sebastian, trying to lead a stubborn donkey and at the same time to look after two ragged children, one of them still at her breast. Her husband had been wounded and was coming by boat so as to get aboard a transport bound for Bilbao.[52]

Occasionally the means of carrying babies was more sophisticated. On 8 June 1813, near Palencia, Frazer passed an ass laden with the best pair of hampers he had ever seen – flat-sided, comfortably roofed and snug. He was surprised to notice that in one of the hampers, lined with scarlet cloth, a pretty child lay sleeping. On enquiring from the donkey boy, Frazer discovered that the child belonged to the mess sergeant's wife of the 23rd Foot. When the mother came riding by she told the major that she had already carried her little one in this way, and safely, for more than a year.[53] No less elegant and practical was the bassinet described by Baron Louis-François Lejeune, who found himself a prisoner of war in Olivenza on the first day of May, 1811, and watched a picturesque small British cavalcade pass by.

'First came the captain in his scarlet uniform, mounted on a beautiful horse, and carrying a large open parasol; behind came his wife, elegantly dressed and wearing a very small straw hat. Seated on a donkey she held up an umbrella and caressed a little black and tan King Charles spaniel on her knee, while she led gracefully by a blue ribbon a tame goat, which was meant to supply her with cream for her cups of tea night and morning.

'At Madame's side walked an Irish nurse, carrying slung across her shoulders a bassinet made of green silk, in which lay an infant, the hope of the family. Behind Madame's mule marched a huge grenadier, the captain's faithful servant, with his musket over his shoulder, urging on with a stick the lady's long-eared steed. Behind him again came a donkey laden with the voluminous baggage of the family, surmounted by a tea-kettle and a cage of canaries. A groom or jockey in livery brought up the rear, mounted on a sturdy English horse, with its hide gleaming like polished steel. The groom held a huge posting whip in one hand, the cracking of which made the donkey mind its pace, and at the same time kept order among the four or five hunting dogs – hounds, spaniels and greyhounds – which served as scouts to the captain during the march of his little cavalcade.'[54]

288

Several soldiers' wives gave birth during the retreat of Sir John Moore's army over the mountain roads of Galicia to Corunna. At one place, under an overturned cart which had been drawn into the shelter of a rock, a woman lay with twins not two days old. She was dead, but the children still whimpered and several officers who came trudging past promised a good sum of money to another woman riding in a bullock cart if she would care for the infants. She did so.

A wife in the 92nd Regiment adopted on the spot a fine little boy whose mother had not survived a terrible child-bed. The sturdy Irish wife of a rifleman named M'Guire was taken in labour while on the march and had to lie down in the snow. Most of the regiment thought she was doomed, but not a bit of it. Next morning, to everyone's surprise and relief, she and her husband, who had not left her side, overtook the column, carrying the babe in arms. They got their son safely to Corunna and thence to England, where he survived.[55]

These women must have been tough indeed if the example of the 7th Fusiliers' march from Oropesa to Plasencia before the battle of Talavera is anything to go by. When the regiment halted for the night one wife was delivered of a child. Next morning she and the baby were placed on a horse and moved with the column.[56] Two years later, in July 1811, an hour before the Gordon Highlanders were due to march out of Bienvenida, the wife of a private soldier named Watt presented her husband with twin boys. When the two babies were given to him, he exclaimed in despair: 'Gude preserve me, Betty Watt. What can I do wi' them?'[57] When the 95th stormed the heights of Vera in October 1813, one rifleman had a son born to him by his Portuguese wife, who gave birth soon after the battle, having been taken in labour while clambering up the mountainside. She appears to have been quite unperturbed by the whole affair for, as Kincaid relates, she, her child and her donkey 'came all three screeching into camp, immediately after, telling the news, as if it had been something very extraordinary, and none of them a bit the worse'.[58]

Then we have Mrs Cowell, who cooked for the officers of the 47th. An excellent woman, she followed the regiment from Cadiz to Madrid, despite every remonstrance because she was near to her confinement, so near, indeed, that on the night of her arrival she was delivered of twins. As the 47th had no tents, she had to lie out under a tree, and the soldiers took off their coats to cover her. Two days later the army had to retreat. Poor Mrs Cowell took the twins in her arms or on her back as she walked through rain and hailstones, frequently having to wade knee-deep through streams. More than once she and the infants came under fire, yet they escaped unharmed and eventually reached Ciudad Rodrigo. On getting to Lisbon she embarked with the children for England. Her husband, Sergeant Cowell, was killed eight months later at the storming of San Sebastian.[59] Near Orthez in southern France, Sergeant Donaldson saw one poor soldier whose wife had died, leaving him an infant of a few months old. Although he might have persuaded one of the women of the regiment to look after the baby, he preferred to take personal charge, and for many a long day's march it sat on top of his knapsack. Eventually he fell sick and went to hospital, carrying the child with him. Donaldson could never discover what happened to them both.[60]

The Waterloo campaign provides at least one case of pregnancy and childbirth in arduous circumstances. When Ensign Thomas Deacon of the 73rd Highland Regiment was shot through the arm at Quatre Bras he was taken with the baggage train to Brussels for treatment. His wife and three children had been left in rear with the baggage guard, and she spent the night of 16th–17th June anxiously searching for her husband among the wounded, because someone had told her he had been hit. Not for many hours did she learn that he had gone to the city. Of course she resolved to join him there, but could obtain no means of conveyance, even though she was in the last stages of pregnancy. And so, leading the children by the hand, she stumbled through a violent thunderstorm which lasted for ten hours. Soaked. exhausted, and feeling faint, clothed only in a black silk dress and a shawl, she eventually reached Brussels on the morning of 18th June, and there found Thomas Deacon in comfortable quarters. On the very next day she gave birth to a fine baby girl, who was christened, aptly if rather unkindly, 'Waterloo' Deacon.[61]

Several other wives were present at Waterloo. Mrs Alexander Ross, wife of the 14th Foot's quartermaster, stayed with the Regiment for some time after the firing began. This was by no means her baptism of fire, for in 1807 she had been severely wounded during General Whitelocke's shameful campaign at Buenos Aires, when her husband had been a sergeant in the 95th. Now, at Waterloo, she was eventually prevailed upon to withdraw, and climbed to the church belfry and watched and listened from there.[62]

There died at Rolvendon, Kent, in October 1903 a Mrs Barbara Moon, whose father was mortally wounded during the battle. Like Ross a sergeant in the 95th Rifles, he had served through much of the Peninsular War, notably at Badajoz and Salamanca, accompanied by his wife. Their baby daughter, born with Wellington's army in 1811, was four years old at the time of Waterloo, and rode in a waggon across the battlefield an hour or two after the fighting ended. Another little girl who saw something of the battle was Elizabeth Gale, whose father Daniel fought on 18th June while his wife and five-year-old daughter worked in the nearby women's camp. Elizabeth, who was born at Beaminster in Dorset on 31 January, 1810, remembered cutting up lint and seeing many dead. She later married a man named Watkins and was still living in Norwich in 1903 – reputedly the last British eyewitness of Waterloo.[63]

Chapter 18

FRATERNIZATION

'I was highly amused, just before dusk, by observing many of our soldiers run into a field between the hostile pickets, and dig with their bayonets. Soon after I saw many of the enemy do the same thing: they did not molest each other, but appeared even familiar, laughing and joking promiscuously. How strange, thought I, that these men, who tomorrow would be slaying each other, should now be so good-humouredly employed together! They were digging potatoes.'[1]
Lieutenant George Wood, 82nd Foot near Pamplona, 1813

'I should hate to fight out of personal malice or revenge, but have no objection to fight for *"Fun and glory"*.'[2]
Colonel George Napier, 1828

For much of the Peninsular War Wellington's men referred to their enemies the French by such expressions as 'Johnny Crapaud' and 'the rascally frog-eaters'. It was rare for personal animosity to show its head. Indeed, a measure of chivalry and courtesy prevailed between British and French contenders, however barbaric, cruel and uncivilized the encounters between the French army and the bands of desperate, revengeful guerrillas. There were, in any case, certain approved exchanges, usually after a battle and concerned with collecting the wounded with the least possible delay, and sometimes Wellington himself would correspond with an opposing French marshal about the exchange of prisoners.

On perhaps a dozen occasions one or other side used a flag of truce in order to search for the wounded and carry them off the field of battle. Such a halt in the fighting occurred at Busaco, when the 52nd and their opponents spoke to each other without the least animosity or angry feeling. Captain George Napier recalled one sad little incident during this peaceful encounter. 'One poor

German officer in the French army came to make enquiries respecting his brother, who was in our service in the 60th Regiment, which was at the time composed principally of foreigners, and upon looking about he found him dead, the poor fellow having been killed.' Very soon Wellington and Massena had the retreat sounded, and the soldiers of each army scampered off to their own positions 'like a parcel of schoolboys called in from play by their master'.[3]

Part way through the battle of Fuentes de Oñoro a suspension of hostilities was agreed upon for the purpose of carrying away the wounded and the dead. Joseph Anderson, in charge of one fatigue party engaged in this work, relates how after one hour 'the bugles of both armies sounded "To arms!", on which the French troops near us immediately fell in, shouldered their arms, and taking off their caps, gave us three cheers'. The British soldiers shook hands with some of their opponents, ran back to their own lines as fast as they could, took off their caps and returned the cheers. Only then did the battle start again and continue furiously until nightfall.[4] At the end of the battle of Sorauren Marshal Soult sent over a flag of truce for permission to bury his dead and attend to the wounded. This was granted, and British troops lent a helping hand. When the job was finished, Highlanders and French soldiers could be seen digging potatoes together in perfect amity, just as they did on several other occasions. Next day the French again had flags of truce, this time for passing baggage belonging to their officers who had been taken prisoner in the battle. Everyone was very friendly, meeting half way and shaking hands.[5] During the 1812 retreat, when French cavalry cut off the 7th Division's baggage, among those captured were several children who were travelling in panniers carried by donkeys. The French had no wish to be encumbered with these children, so a few days later they sent them back under a flag of truce.[6]

Merely to watch the French activities provided an inexhaustible source of interest. With a glass one might see clearly the soldiers in the windows of Santarem or standing round fires outside the town. Gillmor and a general's aide-de-camp watched seven blue-clad French soldiers eating soup at a table. At each spoonful each man looked round, so that the two British officers likened them to seven blue pigeons feeding. On the Cartaxo road out of Santarem

293

British officers and men could, from Almeirim, watch the enemy posting his pickets, and his fatigue parties felling trees, digging trenches or constructing breastworks; while on the road leading north could be seen French orderlies, detachments and forage parties moving to and fro.[7]

Lieutenant Moyle Sherer frequently spent whole mornings observing the scene with the aid of his field-glass.

'Here I would see a troop of their dragoons exercising on the plain below the town; there a general officer riding out with his staff; here some field-officer visiting his guards and picquets, and there several of their men washing and cleaning their arms and appointments on the very brink of the stream. You constantly heard the sound of their voices; and, on a still day, might readily distinguish what they said.'[8]

One July day near Vera in 1813 the Rifle Corps saw a gay assembly of French officers and well-dressed women dancing quadrilles to the music of a band in front of their tents across the valley – so close that the British could distinctly make out the tunes to which they 'capered away', and, with telescopes, could see their faces.[9] And from a camp above Urrugne at the end of October that year Captain Gubbins of the 85th Foot was able to watch with the naked eye French troops at drill. Infantry on picket duty outside Bayonne in February 1814 were also amused to watch the French drilling their conscripts and to listen to their military bands playing nearby. Sometimes a conscript, tired of the harrying life he led, came across to the British lines.[10]

Flags of truce produced beneficial results, and gazing through telescope and field glass was a harmless pastime, but whenever the French and British armies faced each other at close quarters for more than a day or two, the soldiers were liable to fraternize. Two periods in particular are studded with examples of this friendly, spontaneous relationship: between October 1810 and March 1811 along the Lines of Torres Vedras, and towards the close of the war when such rivers as the Bidassoa, Nive and Nivelle formed the dividing line between friend and foe. We have seen how in the realm of field sports cordial courtesies were exchanged when a foxhound, even a huntsman, ran into the opposite camp by mistake, or when British greyhounds killed a hare within the French positions. Matters were often taken a good deal further, and there could be implicit dangers in the practice.

During at least one period of the Peninsular War troops from both armies bathed amicably in the same river – the Douro at Pollos early in July 1812. The arrangements began with British soldiers being allowed to cross unmolested to the French side in order to cut wood for building huts; and it soon became the practice for the men to bathe together with the greatest confidence and cordiality and sometimes to exchange rations such as biscuits and rum for brandy and wine. It was noticed that the French troops studiously avoided approaching the Portuguese, whom they recognized by the dark colour of their skin.[11] Surgeon Boutflower says it was not uncommon to see up to five hundred of the enemy and as many of our own troops bathing in the Douro together like this, while the cavalry of both sides came down on respective banks of the river to water their horses, it being perfectly understood that neither party should ever approach when bearing arms, and that any infringement of this understanding would draw immediate fire.[12] During the battle of Talavera both armies went to a brook for water as if there had been a truce, 'looking at each other, drinking, and wiping the sweat from their brows, laughing and nodding heads to each other, all thoughts of fighting for the time being forgotten'.[13] At the time of Salamanca a stream with numerous fords ran between the opposing armies, and although British troops lived all night in a state of alarm, expecting to be attacked, the French allowed them to water their horses and bathe. Hundreds of soldiers took a chance and bathed every day.[14]

Whenever the advanced pickets of both armies were close to each other, French and British troops were liable to converse about a wide range of subjects. Up near Guarda in 1810 the French were saying it was nothing less than madness for the British to remain in Portugal, and that unless they hurriedly flew to their ships they would all be eaten up.[15] At Abrantes the first question a French officer was likely to ask a British one was: 'When are you going to have another field-day?', because the 13th Light Dragoons had them frequently on a large plain near the Tagus, and these proved a great source of interest to the French, it being said that on one occasion Marshal Massena and his staff were keen spectators.[16]

Across one stream French officers expressed admiration for British horses, spoke of good King George, and sang the praises of Lord Wellington. In mid-September 1812 two French cavalry officers talked of nothing but joining Napoleon's Grand Army in the north and even said the Emperor had reached St Petersburg. He had just entered Moscow, but they could not possibly have known this yet.[17]

During the retreat from Madrid in 1812, when French and British pickets faced each other across a bridge, several officers from each army crept on to it and sat 'upon the opposite ruins of an exploded arch with their legs hanging over the water'. The conversation, good-humoured, courteous and friendly, concerned, on the French side, the vigorous march they had made, and on the British, attempts to show that although the French might think they were advancing, their movement was in fact a retreat.[18] Similar fraternization occurred a year later across the Nive, when French officers and those of the 28th Regiment used to meet on a narrow stretch and talk over past campaigns. The French would never believe, or pretended not to anyhow, the reverses suffered by Napoleon's army in Germany, in particular at Leipzig. Nor would they credit the news of the *'Orange Boven'* uprising in Holland against the French occupation troops, so one British officer took a copy of the *Star* newspaper, wrapped it round a stone, and tried to throw it over the river. Unfortunately the stone went through the paper, which fell in the water. Very quietly the French officer said: 'Your good news is very soon damped!'[19] In an effort to convince two French officers who were on picket duty nearby, Lieutenant Gairdner of the 95th gave them two books containing all the bulletins – from various Allied generals and from the British Ambassador in Russia – dealing with the recent, and for the French disastrous, campaign across Germany.[20]

Earlier, when Wellington's army was holding the Lines of Torres Vedras, an intriguing incident with newspapers puzzled even the Commander of the Forces. Word reached him that General Maximilien Foy had established communication with the British outposts and was constantly sending flags of truce in order to borrow English newspapers. Wellington instructed Baron Trip, who was conducting this affair, not to send the papers next time, but to ask instead why General Foy wanted to see them. Foy replied that he had been speculating in English funds, and was very anxious to know the price of the three per cents![21]

One day Captain George Landmann of the Royal Engineers overheard a close-quarters exchange between two sentries on opposite banks of a stream.

'I say, mounseer, how do you do? Parle vou france? I say, how is master Nap?'

The Frenchman did not understand, and replied: *'Que dis-tu, mon sacré goddam? Combien te donne-t-on par jour?'*

This enquiry about his daily rate of pay was lost on the English soldier, who came back with: 'What's that you say, you hungry frog?'

Perhaps the Frenchman guessed from the tone of voice that this remark was none too complimentary, for he half turned his back after shouting: 'Ah, you f—— *bête!'*

The redcoat was not to be put off. In friendlier tone he asked: 'Where's your rod and hook? What's the use of bait without?'

'Allons, John Bull, *veux-tu une miche?'* said the other, throwing across the stream a piece of bread after rummaging in his haversack. John Bull, not to be outdone in generosity, held up his canteen and called out: 'I say, come here. You're a good fellow. Come down here and take a drop of rum to old Georgey's health.'

Though the Frenchman missed the reference to the King, he could not misunderstand the offer of a drink, so down he went, touched his cap, drew apart his bushy moustaches, wiped his mouth on his coat sleeve, and took a good swig of the rum. Then, to mark his gratitude, he threw his arms round his enemy's neck and kissed him. This characteristically Gallic gesture was too much for stolid John Bull, who angrily tore himself from the embrace and said: 'Do you take me for a girl, or what sort of pranks would you be after?' Then he slapped the French cheek, whereupon a French sabre was drawn from its scabbard.

Landmann, who had so far remained unnoticed, now intervened hurriedly to prevent a violent quarrel, and thanks to his good command of French was able, though not without difficulty, to resolve the tension to the satisfaction of both parties. Even so, the insulted Frenchman kept on muttering: *'un soufflet ne se pardonne pas'.*[22]

One day in February 1811 Sherer of the 34th Foot was walking

297

along a river with several friends when he saw an unusual crowd on the opposite bank. Some French officers saluted with the greeting *'Bonjour, messieurs'*; and they fell into conversation, asking after Lord Wellington, saying he had done wonders with the Portuguese troops, and praising him warmly for his conduct of the campaigns. They next enquired whether King George was dead, and on being told that he was not, one of the Frenchmen said something, but inaudibly. Another, in a louder voice, repeated: *'Le général dit que tout le monde aime votre Roi Georges, qu'il a été bon père de famille et bon père de son peuple.'* The French officer thus divulged the high rank of his companion. Sherer continues: 'They asked us how we liked bacalhao [codfish] and arete, instead of English roast beef; and we, what they did at Santarem without the restaurateurs, cafés and *salles de spectacle* of their dear Paris.'[23]

George Woodberry of the 18th Light Dragoons tells us how, as soon as he arrived on picket duty at Bonloc near Hasparren on 23 January 1814, a Sunday, he was invited to go to the bridge to talk to a general's aide-de-camp. This Frenchman wanted English newspapers, and as a means of introducing the subject gave Woodberry the latest gazettes he had received from Paris. Woodberry, promising to let him have some papers next day, asked several questions about the Emperor. These were side-stepped, and eventually the aide-de-camp said: 'You imagine, just because we let you stay in this country, that things are going badly for us, but you will soon realize your mistake and will be only too glad to recross the Pyrenees'. Woodberry did not pursue the subject, as he saw that they would never agree. The French officer then enquired how the British spent their time, and was told that they organized balls at Hasparren. There was to be one that very evening at General Cotton's house. The aide-de-camp expressed a keen desire to attend, on account of a beautiful lady in Hasparren, his girl friend, who was to be there.[24]

Such fraternization was to be found among all ranks, and many owed life or freedom to what was referred to as 'civilized warfare'. This was particularly true once the French army was defending the motherland. To give three examples: soon after the battle of the Nive, Colonel Alexander of the 1st Foot Guards was riding back from the front on a very dark and stormy night when he missed his way, the horse fell over a bank and came clattering

298

down with its rider head over heels into a lane – close to a sentry, who instantly challenged. The Colonel, hearing the shout of *'Qui vive?'* and the click of the enemy's musket, thought he was going to fire. *'C'est l'officier du poste anglais. Ne tirez pas!'* he shouted, with admirable presence of mind. *'Non, mon colonel,'* came the reply. *'J'espère que vous n'êtes pas blessé.'*[25]

On 15 December 1813, when Lieutenant James Gairdner of the 95th was at dinner, a rifleman came up to report that the officer of the French picket wished to speak to him. Gairdner went forward and was met by two officers who shook his hand very warmly. 'When I asked them if they wanted anything they produced a keg of brandy and said they only came to drink my health and chat a little, which after doing so we parted. They were very civil.'[26]

Lastly we have the episode at Arcangues when three French officers took a table and chairs out of a house in front of the 95th, carried them into the middle of the field which separated the two armies, sat down within a hundred yards of the British picket, and drank wine. Each time they did so they held up their glasses as much as to say: 'Your health'. 'Of course we did not molest them,' comments William Surtees, 'but allowed them to have their frolic out.'[27]

The outposts often made arrangements not to molest each other and to give warning of any change of policy. At one point the French had double sentries, and whenever a British soldier approached they would strike the butts of their firelocks as if to say: 'We are here, and there is no room for both of us'. Up in the Maya Pass in 1813 the advanced sentries were in many places scarcely ten yards apart, particularly at night, yet they never interferred with each other and seldom spoke, even the usual words 'All's well'. Lieutenant Blakeney relates how

'this monotonous roar was superseded by "stone chatters" – white polished stones, about two pounds weight each, were placed on the spot where each sentry was usually posted at night, and he struck them against each other twice in slow time. This was repeated along the chain of sentries. Should any sentry neglect this for more than five minutes, the next sentry instantly struck the stones three times and quickly; this rapidly passed along the line and a visit from the picquet immediately followed. . . . It was rather remarkable that whatever signals our sentries made were immediately repeated by those of the enemy.'[28]

At Hasparren early in 1814 the outposts were for the umpteenth time on opposite sides of an easily fordable stream, so Colonel Vivian, commanding a cavalry brigade, came to an agreement with the French not to fire except in case of serious attack; and he told his wife Eliza: 'So we now ride along side by side, within five yards of each other, without any more danger of being shot than you are when hunting on the town burrows. This is doing as gentlemen should. They really are devilish civil, honourable fellows, and know how to make war.'[29]

When the 34th Foot held one bank of the narrow, fast-flowing Nive, French troops planted pickets on the other, with an understanding that there would be no hostilities without due notice. Officers conversed across the stream in tones of good-humoured badinage, the French telling stories of many escapes in action, pointing as they did so to bullet-holes in their hats, and the British declaring how happy they would be to meet their opponents in Paris soon.[30]

The rank and file also developed friendly relations across the water, making themselves very agreeable to the French soldiers because they knew there was brandy in France. The problem was to get hold of it. They used to call out things like *'Bono-frances'*, *Fromage*, *Cognac*, and *Tabac*, and despite faulty pronunciation, they made themselves understood. A series of stepping-stones which were visible whenever the river was low helped to a solution. George Bell takes up the story.

'They subscribed their coppers, put them into a mess tin, gave it a rattle to draw the attention of the sentry, and without any arms in hand, one of the picket stepped down to the water, gave his tin another rattle, placed it on the centre big stone, called out "Cognac!" and retired. By and by it was taken away, and returned in the evening full of brandy (not likely of the best quality). The relieving picket was let into the secret, and the trade went on for a while. . . .'[31]

Once over the Pyrenees into France, any lull in hostilities enabled the soldiers, using their smattering of Spanish as a *lingua franca*, to establish a traffic in tobacco and brandy with their opponents. That much ingenuity was displayed in this barter is indicated by the fact that when the 28th were manning pickets at a barrier between St Pierre and Bayonne, they placed a large stone in the rivulet along which their line of sentries was posted, and on the stone an empty canteen and a quarter dollar. For this price it was soon filled with brandy by a French sentry on the opposite bank.[32]

French officers were extremely polite and offered to send to Bayonne for anything their British counterparts wanted. Money had to be paid in advance, and soon French watches, rings, trinkets, silk dresses and lengths of cloth, used by one officer to make up 'a new Sunday Pair of inexpressibles' [trousers] were brought to the outposts. The chief commission was brandy, which was plentiful and cheap, and in exchange tea was offered. Many of the Frenchmen had learnt to like it, some of them while prisoners of war in England; and these ex-captives occasionally sent letters to sweethearts beyond the Channel, British officers being quite ready to receive and forward such *billets doux*. One received as a souvenir from a lieutenant in the 10th Chasseurs a sheet of the latest fashionable ladies' bonnets from Paris![33]

Another incident occurred when Captain Parker Ellis of the 1st Guards was on outpost duty with a German officer in front of St Jean de Luz. As good relations had been established with the French, Ellis wondered whether he might not be able to get a case of claret from the other side. When he and the German went forward they were joined by a French officer who said he would like to oblige them but could not afford to purchase the wine out of his own pocket, with the chance that he might lose his money in the event of a move by either army. However, if Ellis was prepared to take that risk and entrust him with the money, he could buy it and deliver three days later, when his regiment would next be on outpost duty. He was true to his word, and on the third day a case of most excellent claret was waiting, which had been brought on a mule from St Jean de Luz.[34]

One December day in 1813 a French lady came out from Bayonne to see *les habit rouges* of the English troops, who happened to be the 43rd Regiment. Her poodle approached the British lines and was so frightened by French whistles to recall it that the little creature dashed over and crouched at the feet of Captain Cooke

301

and some of his companions. 'Without a moment's delay we sent it back by a soldier to its anxious mistress, who was highly delighted, and with her own delicate hand presented a goblet of wine to the man.' The Englishman drank it down, touched his cap, and rejoined his regiment, with a pipe in his mouth and a store of tobacco which had been presented to him by the French soldiers.[35]

Many were the activities to which fraternization extended. Foraging parties did not poach or come to blows. Commissary Schaumann explains how if a French party discovered his men already loading up near Torres Vedras, they would halt and wait patiently until he had finished and gone away; the British would reciprocate. 'If, however, we had met unexpectedly, or on a reconnoitring patrol, we would have fought to the death.'[36] Three years later, up by the river Bidassoa, a certain valley became a neutral ground where French and British foragers often met and good humouredly helped themselves so long as any forage remained. Much the same occurred near St Jean de Luz, only this time it was a village, not a valley: a tacit understanding was reached whereby neither side interfered with the other when collecting forage. The French usually went in first, and when they had finished they rang the church bell as a sign that the British were free to come.[37]

Near Arcangues that December a dozen soldiers of the 43rd Light Infantry were reported absent one evening at roll-call, so an officer and patrol went in search of them. The officer was astounded to find his men in a nearby apple store, fraternizing happily with an equal number of enemy soldiers who had also arrived, unarmed, to raid the apples. Their friendliness had been given additional warmth by the discovery that both parties belonged to the 43rd Regiment. When the British officer and patrol came on the scene, the Frenchmen fully expected to be taken prisoner. Instead, to their grateful surprise, they were told to hurry back to their own lines, while the errant light infantrymen, well laden with apples, returned to their comrades.[38] An even more remarkable coincidence occurred in July 1811 after the battle of Fuentes de Oñoro, when the British outposts were separated by a stream from the French, who had been driven from the village. It was agreed between the officers commanding the opposing pickets that their men should take water unmolested. A French officer, when posting his pickets, said to his British counterpart: 'When you want water, and our sentries challenge, call out *"aqua"* and you shall have it. Have the goodness to give your lads similar orders.' On the first night a French sergeant was captured by the 52nd Oxfordshire Regiment. He had not been fetching water, so was taken in front of Captain James Frederick Love. Under questioning the sergeant admitted that he had crossed the stream in order to take leave of a Spanish girl in Fuentes de Oñoro. 'Love, sir,' he explained, 'has made me your prisoner.'

'Well, then.' came the reply, 'we will not be too hard on you for once. Go back to your Captain and tell him that if Love got you into this scrape, Love gets you out again. My name is Love, and you will not forget it!'[39]

The 1st Guards, helping to invest Bayonne, occupied a large building in St Etienne which had formerly been a convent and stood very close indeed to the French outworks. One day Captain Parker Ellis and a brother officer were playing a game of 'pitch and hustle' in the garden by the picket house when a British sentry at the bottom of the garden walk called them down. He pointed out a French sentry who had just been posted immediately beyond the hedge and within our lines. Colonel Alexander happened to come forward, went over to the Frenchman and told him he must withdraw, but the sentry replied that he dared not leave his post. However, when the relief came he would tell *Monsieur le Caporal* what the Colonel had said. Alexander requested him to beckon up someone from his picket, which he did, and a French N.C.O. came forward and agreed to send for the officer. When the Frenchman arrived Alexander said that he had no wish to harm the sentry, but if he was not withdrawn within a quarter of an hour he would be shot. 'The French officer,' writes Parker Ellis, 'was a very reasonable and gentlemanly young man, and after many bows and the exchange of a pinch of snuff he went back to his party, taking the sentry with him.'[40]

Fraternization led to some extraordinary incidents. In November 1813 up in the Pyrenees the French troops, with their fruitful country just behind them, were better off for supplies than were the British, particularly in respect of brandy, and the French seized every opportunity at night to offer their opponents a dram.

That they never abused this confidence is shown by what happened to a British soldier who, not content with a single glass of brandy, unwisely accepted an invitation to drink more, not with an individual sentry but with the main body of the picket. There he got so drunk that, when an officer came on his rounds, the French had to conceal the Englishman under greatcoats. He remained undetected, and once the coast was clear he was carried back to his own post. His watch, which he had lost or which the Frenchmen had removed, was returned to him on the following night.[41]

Ellis recalled an episode which occurred in a small chestnut grove outside St Jean de Luz. One night a British sentry who stood right forward called the attention of his officer to the French sentry who could be seen clearly in the moonlight leaning fast asleep against a tree, with his musket by his side. The British officer crept up, took possession of his musket, and then woke him. The Frenchman was very frightened at finding himself thus disarmed and a prisoner, but the Guards officer handed back his firelock, merely observing that it was lucky that he, and not one of his own officers, had found him asleep at his post. The poor Frenchman was immensely grateful and tried to explain that, having marched for many hours along bad country roads and immediately been sent on outpost duty, he had been overcome by fatigue.[42] Something similar had occurred three years before near Torres Vedras, where the Buffs used to drink with the nearby French sentries until one night a private of the Buffs left his musket behind. Luckily for him one of the Frenchmen brought the weapon after him and saved his name.[43]

Occasionally matters could have had a less agreeable outcome. Kincaid was on picket at the end of a bridge one December night when a musket ball from a French sentry struck a burning log in the fire round which the riflemen were sitting. Next morning the French sent in a flag of truce to apologize for the incident, explaining the shot had been fired by a stupid sentry who had imagined that enemy troops were advancing upon him. Kincaid says that the 95th Rifles accepted the apology, even though they knew perfectly well that it had been done by a malicious rather than a stupid fellow.[44]

The river Nive afforded numerous occasions for fraternization. Here, too, the central section of the Ustaritz bridge had been blown, though the abutments remained on each bank. One December day Buckham watched a French sentry with his long musket, white cap, and loose grey great-coat, slovenly thrown over his shoulders; twenty yards away stood a Black Watch private. No molestation was offered by either side. French and British troops alike came down to water their horses, while their women washed the regimental linen nearby. Often French soldiers would try to entice their opponents to desert. Their methods were to stick a piece of beef on the point of a bayonet or to hold out a canteen and shout: 'I say, come here! Here is ver good ros-bif. Here is ver good brandy.'[45] Similar exchanges went on at the bridge across the Nive at Cambo. British troops being very badly off for salt, the French would occasionally let them have a supply; and one colonel sent a bundle of newspapers now and then to General Hill.[46] Handbills which often found their way into British camps also offered such inducements to desert as a comfortable house, or permission and encouragement to pursue any trade for which the would-be deserters had been trained. A few soldiers availed themselves of this offer, so officers on duty at the outposts received orders to prevent any communication between the armies; but however vigilant, they could not wholly stop it.[47]

When the 16th Light Dragoons were holding pickets near Rio Maior and Calares, several French officers, having first taken off their swords, came down from the heights opposite to speak to Captain Tomkinson and his companions. Their object, they said, was only foraging, and the English should not put themselves to any inconvenience, because they would soon withdraw again. 'They complained much of the way they were going on, and hoped to put an end to the business one way or other. They did not appear to think things went on well for them. They invited us to a play in Santarem they had got up, and we them to horse-races, football, and dog-hunts. The communication was put an end to by general order.'[48]

By the time Lord Wellington ordered his officers to stop accepting French invitations to theatricals, many had already enjoyed an evening in Santarem, received most hospitable treatment, and exchanged very amicable teasing. For instance, the French let it be known that they were performing nightly a play entitled *L'Entrée des Français dans Lisbon*, whereupon the

British retorted amid general laughter that they would shortly act a piece called *The Flight of the French*.[49]

Only a month before General Rowland Hill had felt obliged to put a stop to the intimacy which had developed between the opposing armies along the Lines of Torres Vedras: soldiers from each army picking grapes from the same vineyard, water from the same well, and inviting each other to drink wine. He had even learnt of a few cases of British officers sending to nearby Lisbon for boots and shirts for some of 'their *friends* at outposts'. In telling this to his sister, Hill felt it would appear rather extraordinary to her that British and French troops were perfectly good neighbours who would never think of molesting each other.[50] More than this, the soldiers exchanged compliments by shaking hands, until it was properly stopped on the grounds, according to Boutflower, 'that the Simplicity of our Fellows was no match for the Cunning of a Frenchman'. Hill considered the balance much more equal, and was grateful for the intelligence he had procured thereby.[51]

One day, when a picket of the 52nd Regiment was on guard at a ford near Gallegos, and a French picket was on the opposite bank, several of the French soldiers asked Captain George Napier's permission to come across and get tobacco, as they had none. Napier allowed two of them to come. They immediately stripped off their clothes and swam over – he would not let them try the ford. The Frenchmen obtained the tobacco they required, related the news from France, and returned quite happy. When describing this incident for the benefit of his children in 1828, Napier added the following comments:

'Now this was all wrong, because, when a man is placed in charge of a post, he should never permit his enemy to come within reach of being able to observe what he is about, the strength of his party, or the nature of his defences. The safest plan is to keep him at a distance, and to allow of no familiarity or intercourse between your men and the enemy's.'[52]

Most of Wellington's army would no doubt have agreed with these observations, yet circumstances sometimes made it difficult for a man to act harshly. Take the case of the 71st, whose outposts in the Lines of Torres Vedras were divided from the French by a deep ravine. The Scots realized well that their own privations were mild when compared with those endured by their opponents, who were extremely short of food, even to the point of living on mules and donkeys for meat. One day the officer of the French picket opposite was fortunate to secure a bullock, but just as he was about to slaughter the beast, it made its escape and took refuge among the 71st, who eagerly seized it. The Frenchmen were in such want that they took the risk of following their bullock across the ravine and begging a part of it. Lieutenant John Graham who was in local command, generously gave them what they asked for, and then allowed them to depart. For this he was severely reprimanded.[53]

Accounts of fraternization from the French side are rare. Lieutenant Charles Parquin, however, was in Spain throughout 1811 and writes that in May near Ciudad Rodrigo a British unit was encountered while a French detachment was out on reconnaissance. Major de Vérigny was eager to meet some enemy officers, so handing over a bottle of good French brandy, he instructed Parquin to gallop close to the British line, wave a white handkerchief, and say he had come to offer them a drink. 'If they accept, then I and the other officers with me will gallop over to join you.'

Parquin stuffed the bottle into his sabretache and followed his instructions, whereupon an officer of the 10th Light Dragoons rode forward and asked what he wanted. The Frenchman explained; his offer was accepted; and they were joined by about ten officers from each side. The bottle was passed round and soon emptied. They all agreed the brandy was excellent, and the British officers, having expressed their thanks and appreciation, asked how long Parquin and his companions had been in Spain.

'Only a short while. This time two years ago we were fighting the Austrians, and we have just come from France to make your acquaintance, gentlemen.'

'You are most welcome,' they all replied together.

One of the Englishmen enquired whether anyone came from Moulins and would be kind enough to take a letter and forward it to a fellow countryman who was a prisoner in that town. It so happened that an officer of the 13th Chasseurs named Dulimbert lived at Moulins – indeed, his father was prefect there – so he gladly offered to do so. Accordingly, the letter was sent next day to Dulimbert under a white flag. Parquin goes on to say that this meeting with the English officers had apparently lasted longer than their general wished, and several shells fell near the group, thus closing the conversation, though not before the Frenchmen had drunk the rum which their opponents had offered as a return of hospitality.[54]

Later that year, if Parquin is to be trusted, the French cavalry officers in his brigade still drank glasses of rum and brandy with their British counterparts, but the rank and file *chasseurs* had a less polite way of procuring rum. It was not unusual to hear one of them call out: 'We've no brandy left. Who's going to catch a *goddam*?' This French nickname for the English derived from the oath. The *chasseurs* took it in turns to capture an Englishman and the flask of rum he always had with him. A *chasseur* would also make a profit of three napoleons, which was the fixed price paid for each horse captured.

Parquin adds that the English officers were very brave and excellent company, but prone to make caustic remarks. They loved to joke and banter.[55]

In his memoirs the French General Lamarque laid stress on the goodwill which existed between opponents who had fought each other, and there is evidence from French sources of the courteous relations maintained on both sides. A certain Captain Guillet received from the arms of some Highlanders a four-year-old son he had lost three months earlier during the *débâcle* at Vitoria. Several correspondents, moreover, refer to British truce parties who came with money or even servants for onward dispatch to fellow countrymen who had been taken prisoner.[56]

During a long war marked by severe hardships, great discomfort, very intermittent and inadequate welfare, and primitive facilities even for the period, it is pleasant to record that, against a background of bitter, revengeful, hate-ridden atrocities committed by French troops on the one hand and Spanish guerrilla bands on the other, a friendly feeling so often prevailed between British and French soldiers at war. The phenomenon is rare, even surprising, although other instances occurred in Napoleon's time and a few more recent examples could be cited. In trying to account for the Peninsular War friendliness, Sergeant Joseph Donaldson put it down to mutual respect for the others' bravery and a generosity of sentiment.

'How different were our feelings in this respect from many of our countrymen at home, whose ideas of the French character were drawn from servile newspapers and pamphlets, or even from so low a source as the caricatures in print shops; but I myself must confess, in common with many others, that I was astonished when I came in contact with French soldiers, to find them, instead of pigmy spider-shanked wretches, who fed on nothing but frogs and beef tea, stout handsome looking fellows, who understood the principles of good-living as well as any Englishmen amongst us; and, whatever may be said to the contrary, remarkably brave soldiers.'[57]

References

CHAPTER 1: ON THE MARCH

1 Steevens, 93–4
2 Woodberry, 68
3 Bell, 129
4 Tomkinson, 175, 178, 203
5 *Ibid.*, 29–30, 239
6 Frazer, 300, 372; Cooke, ii, 25–6, 46, 50–1
7 Hay, 92–3
8 Call MS.
9 Cooke, ii, 46, 50–1; Frazer, 323, 371
10 Vivian, 176–7
11 Gurwood, 108
12 *Ibid.*, 73
13 Dickson, 448–9; Cooke, i, 160
14 Daniell, 199
15 Cooke, i, 285
16 *ibid.*, i, 87
17 Colborne, 172
18 Levinge, 125 [Pollock]
19 Barrett, i, 199; Malmesbury, ii, 332
20 Hamilton, ii, 433–4, 454
21 Wheeler, 112–3
22 Smythies, 157
23 Ross-Lewin, 232
24 Barrett, i, 157
25 Bell, 32; L'Estrange, *The Buffs*, 1, 383–4
26 E. Wheatley, 14
27 Malet, 18; Brett-James, *General Graham*, 203
28 Smyth, 394
29 Dyneley, 50
30 Larpent, ii, 228
31 Verner, 41
32 Gillmor, 155
33 Cooke, i, 157–8
34 Leslie, 38–9
35 Mercer, 202–3
36 *Ibid.*, 18
37 Donaldson, 88
38 Saltoun, i, 248; Dyneley, 48
39 Landmann, ii, 251
40 Gronow, ii, 11
41 Ross-Lewin, 230
42 E. Fraser, 288
43 Wachholtz, 290
44 Gomm, 275; Bingham MS.
45 Woodberry, 72; Tomkinson, 106
46 Stepney, 124–5; Garrett, 7; Stothert, 103; Gomm, 152
47 Pococke, 92
48 J. Green, 63
49 Hough, 853
50 Landmann, ii, 115–6
51 *Journal of an Officer*, 141–2
52 Long, 202
53 Schaumann, 204
54 Blakiston, ii, 142
55 Grattan, 90
56 Schaumann, 165, 312
57 Wylly, *Sherwood Foresters*, i, 168
58 Gomm, 167, 161
59 Cooke, i, 166
60 Moore Smith, 138
61 Graham of Fintry, 166

62 Blakeney, 301
63 Cooke, i, 79
64 Patterson, 63–4
65 Cooper, 114

66 Malcolm, 263; Kincaid, *Random Shots*, 162
67 *Wider Napoleon*, ii, 37
68 Cooke, i, 245

CHAPTER 2: BILLETS

1 Gomm, 163
2 Roberts, 40–1
3 Leslie, 187–8; J. Green, 84
4 Cooke, i, 79
5 Gurwood, 43
6 *Ibid.*, 45–6
7 Larpent, i, 13; Frazer, 23
8 Gurwood, 253
9 *Ibid.*, 255
10 Larpent, i, 14, 9; Hough, 844
11 Hall, 1736
12 Larpent, i, 14
13 Roberts, 21
14 Daniell, 59
15 Swabey, 84
16 Brett-James, *Wellington at War*, 197
17 Larpent, ii, 208
18 Woodberry, 82
19 Picton, xii, 142, 143–4; xiii, 8–9
20 Codrington, i, 172
21 Graham of Fintry, 159
22 Larpent, i, 154–5, 16
23 Madden, 337
24 Swabey, 14
25 Gillmor, 156
26 Ross-Lewin, 162
27 Donaldson, 111–2
28 Hope, 69–70
29 Roberts, 54
30 Stepney, 11; Larpent, i, 9; Wylly, *Sherwood Foresters*, i, 233; Steevens, 118–9

31 Cooke, ii, 103–4
32 Pococke, 75
33 Daniell, 130
34 Gairdner MS.
35 H. Smith, 49–50
36 Dickson, 46
37 Rice Jones, 181, 322, 96; Gavin, xvii, xix; Mackinnon, 41; Gurwood, 241
38 Burgoyne, i, 116
39 Patterson, 257
40 Wachholtz, 302
41 Stepney, 69
42 Fernyhough, 211
43 Madden, 343–4
44 Surtees, 297
45 Cooke, ii, 124
46 W. Wheatley, 450
47 Frazer, 59
48 Madden, 343–4
49 Warre, 131
50 Larpent, i, 36
51 Wheeler, 71–2
52 Stepney, 191
53 Long, 154
54 Ross-Lewin, 214–5; Wheeler, 71–2
55 Wheeler, 71–2
56 Broughton, 22
57 Burgoyne, i, 46
58 W. Napier, *Life of C. J. Napier*, i, 152
59 Hall, 1320
60 Swabey, 70

61 Larpent, i, 159
62 Robinson, 158
63 Hall, 1330
64 Long, 154
65 Hall, 1735
66 Ross-Lewin, 162
67 Graham of Fintry, 157–8; Boutflower, 116
68 Daniell, 188; Stepney, 34; J. Green, 133; Le Mesurier MS; Saltoun, iii, 7

69 Le Mesurier MS.
70 Kincaid, *Adventures*, 281–2
71 Swabey, 38
72 Larpent, ii, 4; i, 54
73 Steevens, 91
74 Lawrence, 81–2
75 Cooper, 8–9
76 Bingham MS.
77 Gordon, 59–60
78 Sherer, 123–4
79 Dallas, 102

CHAPTER 3: HOSTS AND LANDLADIES

1 Blakiston, ii, 147–8
2 Gronow, i, 24
3 Daniell, 158
4 Gomm, 149
5 Leslie, 190
6 Bell, 61
7 Burgoyne, i, 47
8 Dickson, 50
9 Gomm, 177–8
10 Douglas, 101–2
11 Bunbury, i, 19
12 Buckham, 122–3
13 Henry, 55
14 Leslie, 104
15 Sherer, 206
16 Frazer, 71
17 Pakenham, 219
18 Blakiston, ii, 241
19 Henegan, ii, 98–117
20 Gomm, 165–6
21 Henry, 32
22 Boutflower, 28
23 Leslie, 132
24 Hough, 876
25 Woodberry, 74–5
26 Griffith, 145
27 Stepney, 75

28 *Ibid.*, 119
29 Leslie, 228
30 Ker Porter, 102–3
31 Leslie, 27
32 *Ibid.*, 77; Anderson, 38
33 Le Mesurier MS.
34 Blakiston, iii, 27
35 J. Green, 84
36 Woodberry, 203
37 Carss, 8; Long, 224
38 H. Smith, 167
39 Scarfe, 35; W. Graham, 77; Larpent, ii, 183
40 Mockler-Ferryman, *Regimental War Tales*, 146
41 Gibney, 165
42 Tomkinson, 275
43 Wheeler, 162
44 *Ibid.*, 163
45 Gurwood, 125–6
46 Larpent, ii, 193
47 Simmons, 329; Gairdner MS.
48 Barrett, i, 222
49 Frazer, 430
50 Lonsdale MS.
51 Vivian, 233
52 Frazer, 565, 581

53 Shakespeare, *King Henry V*, Act iii, Scene 6
54 Thoumine, 150
55 H. Smith, 102–3; Simmons, 179, 122
56 Bell, 47

CHAPTER 4: CAMPAIGNING KIT

1   Pococke, 77
2   *Ibid.*, 76–7
3   Fitchett, 18 [Harris]
4   Cooper, 80–1
5   Almack, 140–1
6   L'Estrange, 27–8
7   Dyneley, 32
8   Tomkinson, 3
9   Simmons, 209
10 W. Wheatley, 445
11 Le Mesurier MS.
12 Dallas, 52
13 Bell, 41, 35
14 Boothby, *Under England's Flag*, 262
15 Landmann, ii, 94, 143; Fernyhough, 203, 205
16 Robinson, 163
17 Larpent, i, 299
18 Ward, *Wellington's Headquarters*, 38
19 Blakeney, 19
20 Bunbury, i, 21–2
21 Dickson, 156
22 Blakeney, 209–10
23 J. G. Smith, ii, 198–9
24 *Rifle Brigade Chronicle*, 1930, 248–50
25 Woodberry, 25
26 Schaumann, 194
27 Henegan, ii, 91–2
28 Larpent, ii, 72–3
29 *Ibid.*, ii, 76
30 Bell, 90
31 Grattan, 170–1
32 *Ibid.*, 213, 215–6
33 Dickson, 73; Allen, 125
34 Dickson, 99
35 *Ibid.*, 81
36 *Ibid.*, 114–5
37 Frazer, 35–6
38 *Ibid.*, 73–4
39 Allen, 125
40 Mackinnon, 56
41 Griffith, 145; Long, 103
42 Long, 228; Pakenham, 83
43 Dyneley, 47
44 Dickson, 516
45 Badcock, 72, 74
46 Pakenham, 74; Scott Daniel, 87; Dyneley, 17, 47; Long, 213
47 Le Mesurier MS.; Badcock, 77; Scarfe, 8–9; Vivian, 190
48 Warre, 40, 65
49 Rice Jones, 'Letters addressed to', 112
50 Levinge, 205–6

CHAPTER 5: THREADBARE AND PATCHED

1   'Subaltern's Complaint', 343
2   Mainwaring, 517
3   Larpent, ii, 162
4   J. Green, 132

5 Grattan, 50
6 *Ibid.*, 50
7 Mercer, 86
8 Butler, ii, 76; Sherer, 61
9 Wood, 112; Hope, 122
10 Wheeler, 74
11 Kincaid, *Adventures*, 117–8
12 Fitchett, 272 [Anton]; Leask and McCance, 643; Smyth, 398
13 Cooke, ii, 96
14 Barrett, i, 260–1
15 Hope, 260
16 Gardyne, 323–4; Fitchett, 272–3 [Anton]
17 Hope, 122; Simmons, 184; J. Green, 70
18 Foss, 58; Donaldson, 96–7
19 W. Green, 11
20 Stepney, 181
21 Sherer, 253; Ward, *Wellington's Headquarters*, 79

22 Tomkinson, 40
23 Atkinson, 267
24 Cowper, i, 499–500; Le Mesurier MS.
25 Frazer, 128
26 Kincaid, *Adventures*, 34–5
27 *Ibid.*, 35
28 Grattan, 79
29 Cooper, 29
30 Donaldson, 55
31 *Military Sketch-Book*, ii, 124–5
32 Bell, 79
33 Cooke, i, 75, 196
34 Oatts, ii, 173
35 Landmann, ii, 105
36 Lawrence, 193
37 Dunn-Pattison, 54; Cooke, ii, 96
38 Mercer, 299
39 Brett-James, *The Hundred Days*, 214

CHAPTER 6: BIVOUAC LIFE

1 W. Napier, *Life of C. J. Napier*, i, 164
2 Simmons, 11
3 Bell, 10, 11, 54
4 Landmann, ii, 160
5 Swabey, 25–6
6 Tomkinson, 106; Cooper, 29
7 Lawrence, 169
8 Malcolm, 288
9 Surtees, 281
10 Fitchett, 250 [Anton]
11 Patterson, 170; Fitz Maurice, 179–80
12 Malmesbury, ii, 116, 118; Ross-Lewin, 149
13 Schaumann, 243

14 Sherer, 42
15 W. H. Maxwell, i, 205–6
16 Larpent, i, 297
17 Bunbury, i, 168
18 Gurwood, 35
19 Pococke, 106
20 Ross-Lewin, 208
21 Cooper, 29
22 Leslie, 83, 85
23 Landmann, ii, 279, 255
24 Hope, 350; Patterson, 149
25 Bell, 79; Blakiston, ii, 178
26 Simmons, 237; Fernyhough, 216
27 Rice Jones, 'Letters addressed to', 99; Ross-Lewin, 162

28 Dickson, 55
29 Cooke, i, 135; Daniell, 108–9; W. Verner, *History*, 170
30 Landmann, ii, 192, 270; Madden, 511; Sherer, 93; Leslie, 122
31 Ward, *Wellington's Headquarters*, 200; Bragge, 92; Kincaid, *Random Shots*, 306
32 Cooper, 146
33 Frazer, 140; Tomkinson, 235; Woodberry, 51–3
34 Surtees, 189; Gurwood, xxxvi
35 L'Estrange, 129; Cooke, i, 292
36 Surtees, 244, 249; Kincaid, *Adventures*, 261; Gleig, *The Subaltern*, 111; Hope, 302; Cooper, 103; Madden, 524
37 Bell, 95
38 Gurwood, xl
39 Saltoun, iii, 18
40 Anton, 120–1
41 Wylly, *Sherwood Foresters*, i, 266–7 [Brown]
42 Simmons, 175–6; Kincaid, *Random Shots*, 90
43 Sherer, 96–7
44 *Ibid.*, 149
45 Stepney, 16; Madden, 354
46 Blakiston, ii, 315
47 Malcolm, 269; Fitchett, 254 [Anton]; Gleig, *The Subaltern*, 152
48 Morris, 74
49 Gibney, 183–4
50 Mercer, 157
51 *Ibid.*, 182
52 Daniell, 193; Burgoyne, i, 255–6; Swabey, 182–3; Malmesbury, ii, 351
53 Daniell, 151–2

54 W. Wheatley, 443
55 W. Fraser, 52
56 Shelley, i, 155–6
57 Malmesbury, ii, 235; Burgoyne, i, 244; Simmons, 269
58 Larpent, ii, 15; Hope, 366
59 Stocqueler, i, 37
60 Malmesbury, ii, 121; Leslie, 108
61 Stewart MS.
62 Bell, 99–100
63 Leslie, 82; Madden, 358; Bingham MS.
64 Kincaid, *Random Shots*, 89; Malmesbury, ii, 118; Hall, 1543, 1545; Cooper, 15; Lawrence, 145; Gurwood, xxxvi-vii
65 Stepney, 133; Leslie, 83; Bingham MS.
66 Leslie, 83
67 Grattan, 48–9
68 Fitchett, 248–9 [Anton]
69 Morris, 92; Wheeler, 180, 183
70 *Journal of a Regimental Officer*, 83; Cooper, 64; Wood, 85
71 Schaumann, 310–11
72 Schäffer, 227–8
73 Cooper, 17; Kincaid, *Random Shots*, 229
74 Wood, 85
75 Carss, 5; Cooper, 17
76 Kincaid, *Random Shots*, 228–9
77 Cooke, ii, 3
78 *Journal of a Regimental Officer*, 83
79 Ross-Lewin, 299
80 Wheeler, 81
81 Gardyne, 271; Hough, 859, 878

82 Sherer, 101
83 Sidney, 149
84 Le Mesurier MS.
85 *Ibid.*
86 Robinson, 163
87 Lawrence, 191–2
88 Wheeler, 178–9

89 Rogers, 204; Gleig, *The Subaltern*, 152; Daniell, 46
90 Frazer, 353
91 Lawrence, 189
92 Stepney, 35
93 Leach, 192–3

CHAPTER 7: RATIONS

1   Foss, 69 [Cooper]
2   H. Smith, 94
3   Roberts, 79
4   Frazer, 17; Swabey, 33
5   Schaumann, 165; Pococke, 85; Anton, 81; Knowles, 26; Ross-Lewin, 151
6   Schaumann, 166
7   Wylly, *Sherwood Foresters*, i, 191 [Brown]
8   Frazer, 21; Cooper, 27
9   Sherer, 221
10 Carss, 6
11 Lawrence, 56
12 *Memoirs of a Sergeant*, 74–5
13 *Ibid.*, 74–5
14 J. Green, 87; Wylly, *Sherwood Foresters*, i, 233; J. Green, 184–5; H. Smith, 20
15 Cooper, 83; Bingham MS.; Wheeler, 115
16 Steevens, 96–7
17 Wylly, *Sherwood Foresters*, i, 241 [Brown]; Mill, 140
18 Stewart MS.
19 W. Napier, *Life of C. J. Napier*, i, 166
20 Mill, 138–9; Anton, 81; Patterson, 262; Cooke, ii, 41; Levinge, 194–5
21 Malmesbury, ii, 317

22 Wheeler, 22
23 Ellison, 23 [Bissett]
24 Gilby, 213
25 Boutflower, 152; Larpent, i, 157; Cadell, 161; Cooper, 104
26 Larpent, i, 213
27 Sherer, 105; Knowles, 37
28 Bell, 79
29 Schaumann, 201
30 Pococke, 84–6
31 Swabey, 90
32 Hall, 1399
33 L'Estrange, 95
34 Frazer, 397
35 Malet, 21
36 Vivian, 72
37 Leslie, 253
38 Anton, 96; Schaumann, 262
39 Cooke, i, 230; Lawrence, 56
40 Cooper, 83
41 Lawrence, 141–2
42 Pococke, 78; Wylly, *Sherwood Foresters*, i, 224; Pococke, 118
43 J. Green, 94; Wachholtz, 275; Burgoyne, i, 185
44 Ingilby, 260; Wheeler, 73; Le Mesurier MS.
45 Wylly, *Sherwood Foresters*, i, 231 [Brown]
46 Gardyne, 314

47 Kincaid, *Adventures*, 75; Donaldson, 151; Tomkinson, 167; Wylly, *Sherwood Foresters*, i, 224
48 Malcolm, 263–4
49 Cooke, ii, 22
50 Lawrence, 164; Cooper, 56; Anton, 96
51 Frazer, 333
52 Leeke, i, 75; Sherer, 219
53 Leslie, 84
54 Burgoyne, i, 255
55 Cooke, i, 243–4
56 Wachholtz, 298; Harding MS.
57 Albermarle, 158
58 Leeke, i, 5
59 *Ibid.*, i, 19–20
60 Verner, 43

61 Kincaid, *Adventures*, 329
62 Mercer, 159
63 Tomkinson, 276; Fitchett, 298 [Anton]
64 Woodberry, 259, 262, 266
65 Carss, 7
66 Gleig, *The Subaltern*, 31; Sherer, 31; Bell, 30, 22; Bunbury, i, 39; Leslie, 178; Leach, 76
67 Burgoyne, i, 68; Swabey, 14–5
68 Dickson, 361
69 L'Estrange, 130–1
70 Leach, 297–8; Madden, 344
71 Blakeney, 170–2
72 Hardinge, 165, 241

CHAPTER 8: WARTIME DINNER PARTIES

1 Dyneley, 694
2 Woodberry, 43
3 Cooke, i, 109; *Wider Napoleon*, ii, 62; Gardyne, 321
4 Hough, 877
5 Larpent, i, 44
6 Cooper, 107
7 Henegan, ii, 197–8
8 Cooke, ii, 73–4
9 Larpent, i, 144, 146
10 Graham of Fintry, 169
11 Steevens, 108
12 Larpent, i, 287
13 *Memoirs of the Late War*, 241
14 Boutflower, 69
15 Larpent, i, 90–1
16 E. Fraser, 120–1
17 Woodberry, 21–2
18 Frazer, 148, 107–8
19 Ward, *Wellington*, 90

20 Larpent, ii, 20, 27
21 Stepney, 271
22 Kincaid, *Adventures*, 246; Surtees, 233
23 Leslie, 97
24 Boutflower, 42–3
25 Daniell, 190–1
26 Blakeney, 210–1
27 Vivian, 152
28 Woodberry, 113
29 Larpent, ii, 99–100, 44–5
30 Mercer, 115
31 Dickson, *passim*; Larpent, ii, 37
32 Long, 103, 228
33 Vivian, 139; Henegan, ii, 140; Sidney, 259; Brett-James, *General Graham*, 221
34 Surtees, 258; Woodberry, 24; Gronow, i, 90

35 Henegan, i, 302
36 Cadell, 176
37 Sherer, 98; Kincaid, *Adventures*, 281; Leslie, 193
38 Roberts, 35–6
39 Stepney, 170–1
40 Leslie, 193–4
41 Stepney, 170

42 Burgoyne, i, 150; Boutflower, 118
43 Leach, 278
44 Bingham MS.
45 Malmesbury, ii, 371
46 Larpent, ii, 130
47 Bell, 130
48 *Ibid.*, 144

CHAPTER 9: LEARNING THE LANGUAGE

1 Vivian, 147
2 Henry, 22
3 Bell, 5–8
4 Tomkinson, 2
5 Mercer, 19; Almack, 8
6 E. Fraser, 295–6
7 Gordon, 15
8 Stewart MS.; Sherer, 81; Swabey, 85; Bragge, 17; Le Mesurier MS.
9 *Royal Military Chronicle* 1812, iv, 91–2, 174
10 Call MS. 38
11 Buckham, 17–8
12 *Ibid.*, 57–8
13 Brett-James, *General Graham*, 238
14 *Royal Military Chronicle*, lv, 40–1
15 Gomm, 142, 181; Dallas, 78; Woodberry, 84
16 Gordon, 36; Leslie, 80; Dallas, 26
17 Woodberry, 53, 134; Swabey, 36

18 H. Smith, 54
19 Larpent, i, 24; Malet, 19; Bragge, 125
20 Henry, 23
21 Ross-Lewin, 113
22 Patterson, *Camp & Quarters*, 135
23 Gibney, 226
24 Landmann, ii, 286; Dickson, 17
25 Gurwood, 201
26 *Wider Napoleon*, ii, 24; Bell, 76
27 Hay, 43, 46
28 Simmons, 191
29 Henry, 25–6
30 Swabey, 61; *Journal of an Officer*, 249
31 Kincaid, *Adventures*, 59–60
32 Bell, 77; Schaumann, 276
33 W. Porter, i, 350
34 Swabey, 61
35 *Ibid.*, 61; Tomkinson, 254
36 H. Smith, 129–30
37 Woodberry, 219, 67

CHAPTER 10: PASTIMES

1 Londonderry, ii, 181–2
2 Frazer, 192

3 Boutflower, 136, 105; L'Estrange, 128; Larpent, i, 40

4   *Rifle Brigade Chronicle*, 1913, 45
5   J. Green, 62
6   Hough, 862
7   Hall, 1545
8   Henegan, i, 246–7
9   *Rifle Brigade Chronicle*, 1913, 45; Vivian, 136; Le Mesurier MS.
10 Simmons, 124, 175
11 Pococke, 112
12 Le Mesurier MS.
13 'Reminiscences of a Regimental Medical Officer', 115
14 Malcolm, 263
15 Swabey, 51
16 Leach, 239–40
17 Hope, 347; Swabey, 49
18 Warre, 190; Vivian, 172
19 Larpent, i, 40; Swabey, 50
20 Gronow, ii, 289
21 Rice Jones, 'An Engineer Officer', 403; Barnard TS.
22 Gomm, 217
23 Woodberry, 37
24 Simmons, 181; Rice Jones, 'An Engineer Officer', 403
25 Brett-James, *Wellington at War*, 195–6
26 *Ibid.*, 191, 196n.
27 Bessborough [Ponsonby], 227
28 Brett-James, *Wellington at War*, 200–1
29 Swabey, 115
30 Gomm, 167; Mackinnon, 360
31 Boothby, *Under England's Flag*, 158
32 Sherer, 246
33 Le Mesurier MS.; Gomm, 328
34 Rice Jones, 'An Engineer Officer', 119

35 Long, 103; Swabey, 87
36 Swabey, 166
37 Harley, ii, 25–6
38 Bragge, 120; Sherer, 186–7; Bragge, 122
39 E. Wheatley, 19; Frazer, 350
40 Sherer, 186–7
41 Sherer, 186–7; Swabey, 88
42 Bell, 110
43 Rice Jones, 'An Engineer Officer', 105
44 Gomm, 239, 266
45 Leach, 238–9
46 Warre, 116; *Royal Military Chronicle*, 1810, i, 111; W. Napier, *Life of Sir W. Napier*, i, 109
47 Swabey, 43; Leslie, 178; 'Retreat upon Portugal', 31; W. Smith MS.
48 *Wider Napoleon*, ii, 55
49 Dickson, 112–3
50 *Journal of a Regimental Officer*, 33
51 Hough, 877
52 Woodberry, 149–50
53 Cooper, 57
54 Kincaid, *Adventures*, 197
55 Buckham, 328
56 Stothert, 122–3
57 Gomm, 177
58 Burgoyne, i, 58
59 Scovell MS.
60 Gordon, 31
61 Burgoyne, i, 59
62 Douglas MS.
63 Leslie, 234
64 Dallas, 26
65 *Wider Napoleon*, ii, 53–4
66 Leach, 190–1
67 Scarfe, 23; Cooke, i, 110–1; Swabey, 44–5

68 Cooke, i, 112–3
69 Schaumann, 327
70 Buckham, 162–3
71 Stepney, 201
72 Cooke, i, 222–3
73 Grattan, 286–7
74 Leach, 298; Kincaid, *Adventures*, 193
75 Scarfe, 30
76 E. Fraser, 292; Daniell, 191
77 Leach, 298–9; Willoughby Verner, 436
78 Cadell, 147; Bell, 63, 114
79 Woodberry, 10
80 Simmons, 14–5
81 Dickson, 149–50; Larpent, i, 10–1
82 Rice Jones, 'An Engineer Officer', 265
83 Sherer, 81; Douglas MS.
84 Frazer, 60
85 Gairdner MS.
86 Hough, 860; Bragge, 72
87 Gleig, *The Subaltern*, 157; Cooke, ii, 7
88 Gurwood, 312
89 Frazer, 500–2; Woodberry, 274

CHAPTER 11: COME DANCING

1 Stepney, 120
2 W. Graham, 65–6
3 Hough, 861; Cooke, i, 195
4 Ross-Lewin, 252
5 Brett-James, *The Hundred Days*, 41; W. Fraser, 260–6
6 Vivian, 265
7 Hall, 154; Stepney, 119–20; W. Stewart MS.; Stothert, 119
8 J. Green, 134; Woodberry, 114
9 W. Smith MS.; Bragge, 46; Simmons, 279
10 Le Mesurier MS.
11 Douglas MS.
12 Swabey, 64
13 Tomkinson, 172; Kincaid, *Adventures*, 285
14 Gronow, i, 8
15 Frazer, 403
16 Cooke, ii, 97
17 Scarfe, 29
18 H. Smith, 111
19 Woodberry, 103, 105
20 Brett-James, *General Graham*, 193–4; Henegan, i, 161
21 Trench MS.
22 J. Green, 134
23 Pococke, 110
24 Ker Porter, 110
25 Schaumann, 326
26 Larpent, i, 70; Bingham MS.; Stothert, 119–20
27 Bunbury, 65–6
28 Gordon, 89
29 Hough, 858
30 Kincaid, *Adventures*, 94; Bell, 9–10
31 Woodberry, 124
32 Stepney, 121
33 Larpent, i, 70
34 Frazer, 388–9
35 Woodberry, 107
36 *Ibid.*, 124
37 Kincaid, *Adventures*, 152–3
38 Bessborough, 227
39 Douglas MS.

L

40 Tomkinson, 153
41 Cooke, i, 195–6
42 W. Fraser, 271, 280
43 Schaumann, 370; Surtees, 196–7; Bunbury, 136; Patterson, 172
44 Frazer, 114; Simmons, 279
45 Call MS., 32
46 Frazer, 114; Hall, 1536; Ker Porter, 43–4
47 Gomm, 176; Scovell MS.; Stothert, 121
48 Bingham MS.; Ker Porter, 111–2
49 Woodberry, 106; Gairdner MS.
50 Simmons, 279; Cooke, i, 109
51 Scarfe, 17
52 Broughton, 61; Gomm, 142
53 Woodberry, 126
54 Boutflower, 14
55 Warre, 124
56 Ker Porter, 85
57 Boutflower, 156–7; Kincaid, *Adventures*, 94
58 Henry (1st ed.), 56–7
59 Surtees, 313–4
60 Gairdner MS.

CHAPTER 12: HORSES AND FORAGE

1 Gleig, *Light Dragoon*, 35–6
2 Malmesbury, ii, 252
3 Brett-James, *General Graham*, 262
4 Longford, 268
5 Gavin, xxix; *Wider Napoleon*, ii, 23; Leeke, i, 5
6 Daniell, 106–7
7 H. B. Hamilton, 158
8 Barrett, i, 262
9 Vivian, 67
10 Gordon, 17–8
11 Vivian, 74
12 Duncan, ii, 213, 198
13 E. Wheatley, 19
14 Henegan, i, 334–5
15 Swabey, 174
16 Warre, 70
17 Larpent, i, 89
18 Napier, *Life of C. J. Napier*, i, 159
19 H. B. Hamilton, 161–2 [Brotherton]
20 Bell, 62
21 Verner, 17
22 Leach, 224
23 H. B. Hamilton, 172 [Brotherton]
24 Dalton, 60; Almack, 71
25 Dyneley, 13
26 Henegan, i, 299–300
27 Daniell, 39
28 Swabey, 67
29 Gordon, 59–60
30 Tomkinson, 155–6
31 Tale, 137–8
32 Barrett, i, 217
33 Vivian, 158
34 Landmann, ii, 233
35 Verner, 15–6
36 Tale, 137
37 Dickson, 865, 894
38 Schaumann, 179; Burgoyne, i, 38
39 Surtees, 225
40 Tomkinson, 42
41 Ompteda, 170, 295; E. Wheatley, 8–9

42 Kincaid, *Random Shots*, 162
43 Gleig, *The Subaltern*, 199
44 Ross-Lewin, 304–5
45 Ompteda, 280
46 Burgoyne, i, 72
47 Gurwood, 113–5
48 Frazer, 24; Woodberry, 18
49 J. G. Smith, ii, 197
50 Tomkinson, 120–1
51 *Ibid.*, 130; Swabey, 69
52 Swabey, 146; Dyneley, 50
53 Burroughs, 61; Stanhope MS.
54 Larpent, i, 75
55 Larpent, ii, 39; Woodberry, 153; W. H. Maxwell, ii, 116; Barrett, i, 228; Frazer, 308
56 Larpent, i, 96, 44, 155
57 Frazer, 375, 377

58 Kincaid, *Adventures*, 282
59 Gairdner MS.
60 Frazer, 388, 390; W. H. Maxwell, ii, 117; Barrett, i, 228; Woodberry, 153
61 Schaumann, 400
62 Tomkinson, 263
63 Schaumann, 167–8
64 *Ibid.*, 160–1
65 Swabey, 35
66 Madden, 347; Downman, 186
67 Le Mesurier MS.; Woodberry, 67
68 Tomkinson, 128
69 Swabey, 159
70 *Ibid.*, 165n.
71 Tomkinson, 274
72 Mercer, 91

CHAPTER 13: FIELD SPORTS

1 Dyneley, 13
2 L'Estrange, 152
3 Stanhope MS.
4 Leslie, 191
5 Bell, 10
6 Gomm, 160, 165
7 Hough, 878
8 Leach, 189–90
9 Grattan, 52
10 Wylly, *History of K.O.Y.L.I.*, i, 254
11 Woodberry, 267, 269
12 Malet, 120
13 Woodberry, 295; Malet, 122
14 Vivian, 260
15 Woodberry, 299–300
16 Jackson, 6

17 Sidney, 120
18 Graham of Fintry, 157; Long, 133; Sidney, 164
19 Blakeney, 214
20 Long, 150, 153
21 Henry, 61
22 Brett-James, *General Graham*, 239–40; Delavoye, 614–5
23 Graham of Fintry, 63
24 Brett-James, *General Graham*, 245
25 Long, 135
26 Malmesbury, ii, 240
27 Long, 155
28 H. Smith, 92; Kincaid, *Adventures*, 193
29 J. Green, 132; Larpent, i, 60–1, 122

REFERENCES

30 Fitz Maurice, 193
31 Gronow, ii, 200
32 Larpent, ii, 105
33 Rice Jones, 'Letters addressed to', 103
34 Fortescue, 73 [Mills]; Long, 153
35 Gleig, *The Subaltern*, 116
36 Henegan, i, 161–2
37 Gronow, ii, 200–1
38 Leach, 188–9
39 Cadell, 223–4
40 Leach, 109–10
41 Hope, 96–7
42 Stepney, 275
43 Cadell, 149–50
44 Hough, 877
45 Hay, 117; Long, 168
46 H. Smith, 62, 82
47 Leach, 237; W. Graham, 67–8
48 Delavoye, 608, 615; Graham of Fintry, 157
49 Kincaid, *Adventures*, 75
50 Grattan, 90
51 Dickson, 480; Henry, 26; Surtees, 188
52 Grattan, 90; Henry, 26, 60, 62; W. Stewart MS.; Gairdner MS.
53 Surtees, 295–6
54 Steevens, 55
55 Leach, 155; Gleig, *The Subaltern*, 61; Leach, 107
56 *Journal of a Regimental Officer*, 82, 86
57 Williams, 125
58 Malmesbury, ii, 290–1, 304; 233, 240
59 W. Stewart MS.; Swabey, 86; Malmesbury, ii, 300
60 Leach, 101; W. Stewart MS.; Vivian, 146
61 L'Estrange, 43–4
62 Malmesbury, ii, 233; Douglas, 104
63 Stepney, 46–7
64 Costello, 71–2
65 Warre, 252–3
66 Schaumann, 274; Carnock, 11
67 Kilvert, 83; Long, 99
68 Graham of Fintry, 160; Steevens, 58; Dickson, 109
69 Malmesbury, ii, 240
70 Woodberry, 60
71 Dallas, 69
72 Hay, 32
73 Wood, 171–2
74 Kincaid, *Adventures*, 84; Dyneley, 27
75 Gomm, 235
76 Cooke, i, 86; Sherer, 71; Vivian, 94

CHAPTER 14: OUTDOOR PASTIMES AND ROUTINE WORK

1 Costello, 29
2 Gurwood, 260
3 Swabey, 168; Leslie, 183; Tomkinson, 15; Costello, 43
4 Cadell, 179; Bell, 90–1
5 Cooke, ii, 37; Donaldson, 193
6 Swabey, 168; Larpent, ii, 72, 156; Stewart MS.
7 Dickson, 116; Surtees, 157

8   Schaumann, 335–6
9   Graham of Fintry, 156–7
10 Hough, 860–1
11 Frazer, 397
12 *Ibid.*, 56–7
13 Frazer, 68–9; Donaldson, ii, 108; Sherer, 197
14 Frazer, 433
15 Mercer, 21, 24, 109
16 Frazer, 501
17 Burgoyne, i, 210
18 Blakiston, ii, 266; Boutflower, 159
19 Boutflower, 159–61
20 Holland, 66
21 Bunbury, i, 19
22 Stewart MS.; Bragge, 109; Leach, 120; Kincaid, *Random Shots*, 233
23 Cooke, i, 130; W. Napier, *Life of Sir W. Napier*, i, 124; Malet, 73, 81
24 Hough, 879; Pococke, 85, 89
25 Mercer, 55
26 Albemarle, 135
27 Mercer, 77
28 Broughton, i, 237; Vivian, 256; Saltoun, iii, 47; Boutflower, 53
29 Gomm, 225–6
30 Leeke, i, 157
31 J. G. Smith, i, 70–1
32 Morris, 66
33 Fitz Maurice, 177
34 'Retreat upon Portugal', 30
35 Leach, 120–1
36 Cooper, 149
37 Woodberry, 346; Tomkinson, 25
38 Tomkinson, 57, 70–1
39 Dickson, 488, 837, 592–3; Hough, 845, 875
40 Dickson, 700–8 [Lawson]
41 W. Porter, i, 246
42 *ibid*, i, 289–90, 278
43 *Royal Military Chronicle*, July 1814, 205; June 1814, 127–8; Frazer, 98
44 J. T. Jones, ii, 182
45 *ibid.*, ii, 192
46 Brett-James, *Wellington at War*, 232–3
47 Connell, *Auchinleck*, 501
48 James, 745
49 Gurwood, 259–60
50 *General Regulations*, 21–2
51 Gurwood, 583, 580, 170
52 *Ibid.*, 585; Ward, *Wellington's Headquarters*, 200
53 Tale, 145

CHAPTER 15: CHAPLAINS AND RELIGION

1   Frazer, 214
2   Bell, 9
3   Gilby, 225
4   Sperling, 123–4
5   Hough, 845; Wylly, *Sherwood Foresters*, i, 168
6   Frazer, 75
7   Gleig, *Personal Recollections*, 129; Brett-James, *Wellington at War*, 212–4
8   Oman, 330 [Stevenson]
9   Gurwood, 62–3
10 Barrallier, 520
11 Lawrence, 145–6

12 Kincaid, *Adventures*, 86–7
13 Wheeler, 153
14 Cowper, i, 407
15 Henegan, i, 222–3; Gleig, *Personal Recollections*, 129
16 Donaldson, 197–8
17 J. Green, 185–6
18 Woodberry, 15, 27; J. Green, 201; Le Mesurier MS.
19 Larpent, ii, 23
20 Gronow, i, 8; Larpent, ii, 136; Frazer, 379
21 Stepney, 36; Gleig, *Personal Recollections*, 129
22 Henegan, i, 223–4
23 E. Fraser, 287; Gronow, ii, 38
24 Cadell, 166–7
25 Hope, 337–8
26 Gronow, ii, 38
27 Frazer, 532; Cadell, 238
28 Simmons, 22; W. Green, 16
29 Malcolm, 279; *With Napoleon at Waterloo*, 73; Gillmor, 159; W. Green, 20
30 Gleig, *Personal Recollections*, 130
31 Frazer, 158
32 Willoughby Verner, 250; W. Green, 21
33 Stepney, 246–7
34 Craufurd, 210–2
35 Tomkinson, 210, 217
36 Swabey, 32; Knowles, 36; Allen, 125; Tomkinson, 118
37 Swabey, 32; Ormsby, ii, 46; Bell, 7–8
38 Wheeler, 72–4
39 Fitz Maurice, 183–4
40 Swabey, 134
41 Simmons, 236
42 Robinson, 154; Ross-Lewin, 216

43 Boutflower, 17–8
44 Donaldson, ii, 132–3
45 Steevens, 55; Simmons, 49; Swabey, 166
46 Lawrence, 68
47 H. B. Hamilton, 73–4
48 Schaumann, 261
49 Henry, 78–9
50 Douglas MS.
51 Gomm, 196
52 Dickson, 87; Boutflower, 52
53 Fitz Maurice, 188
54 Hope, 93
55 Burroughs, 51
56 Buckham, 130; Kincaid, *Random Shots*, 224
57 Wilkie, 101
58 Frazer, 181; Woodberry, 102; Hough, 857; Steevens, 55; Stothert, 27
59 Woodberry, 102; Frazer, 181; Sherer, 135
60 Wilkie, 102; Steevens, 55; Stothert, 147
61 Bell, 18
62 Woodberry, 137, 103
63 Dallas, 78
64 Henry, 26–7
65 Boutflower, 47–8
66 Larpent, i, 192
67 Stothert, 143–5
68 *Ibid.*, 155–6
69 Warre, 136–7
70 Steevens, 55; Woodberry, 112; Leach, 73
71 Bingham MS.; Wilkie, 102
72 W. Maxwell, ii, 257–8 [Wilkie]
73 Call MS.
74 Woodberry, 112
75 Kincaid, *Random Shots*, 224–5
76 Kincaid, *Adventures*, 143–4

CHAPTER 16: THE WOUNDED AND SICK

1 Swabey, 151
2 *With Napoleon at Waterloo*, 102 [Nicol]
3 Daniell, 141–2
4 Larpent, i, 200
5 Gavin, xxiii
6 Blakeney, 324
7 Bell, 89; Douglas, 106
8 W. Green, 28
9 *Ibid.*, 28
10 Costello, 33–5
11 Cooke, i, 84
12 Donaldson, 183
13 *Ibid.*, 181–3
14 Swabey, 151
15 Cooper, 32
16 Douglas, 105
17 Surtees, 122
18 Grattan, 220, 222
19 H. Smith, 32
20 Dickson, 461
21 Tomkinson, 12
22 Dickson, 461
23 Campbell, 24–5
24 Fitz Maurice, 188–9
25 Costello, 37; W. Green, 31
26 Simmons, 78–9, 80–8
27 J. Green, 192–4
28 Cooper, 37, 78, 150
29 Ward, *Wellington's Headquarters*, 199
30 Cooper, 150
31 Frazer, 53
32 J. Green, 198
33 Wheeler, 200–1
34 G. Napier, 112–3
35 W. Green, 17
36 Hall, 1737
37 Henry, 70
38 James, 398; Henry, 83, 81–2
39 Donaldson, ii, 92–3; Costello, 22
40 Barrett, i, 240–1; Henry, 95; W. Green, 29
41 Dwelley, *A Muster Roll.*
42 Moore Smith, 174–5; H. Smith, i, 59
43 Moore Smith, 177
44 G. Napier, 185, 245; Willoughby Verner, 128
45 G. Napier, 155–6
46 Landmann, ii, 165–6
47 Boothby, *A Prisoner of France*, 19–20
48 Schaumann, 193
49 Ross-Lewin, 109
50 G. Napier, 219
51 Grattan, 95–7
52 Daniell, 140; Burgoyne, i, 205; Maxwell, i, 356–7
53 Brett-James, *The Hundred Days*, 196
54 *Ibid.*, 201
55 Costello, 195–6
56 Thackwell, 81; Waldie, 239–40
57 F. W. Hamilton, ii, 450; Saltoun, i, 242
58 Brett-James, *General Graham*, 234–5, 237
59 Sidney, 116
60 Bell, 80–1
61 G. Napier, 138
62 Hay, 109–10
63 Henry, 62
64 Simmons, 205
65 Schaumann, 317
66 Swabey, 107

67 Hay, 79–80

68 W. Green, 17

69 Costello, 22

70 Donaldson, 95–6

CHAPTER 17: ARMY WIVES

1 Donaldson, 219
2 Gleig, *The Subaltern*, 13
3 De Watteville, 125–30; Patterson, 11; Malet, 15; Cary, i, 219
4 *Journal of the Society of Army Historical Research*, 1952, 91
5 Barrett, i, 270
6 Gurwood, 590
7 Rice, 218, 221; Cooper, 117
8 Henry, 94
9 W. Green, 9; Wylly, *Sherwood Foresters*, i, 190
10 Landmann, ii, 145–6
11 Lunt, 45
12 Longford, 283
13 Tomkinson, 188
14 Long, 93
15 Tomkinson, 185; Shelley, i, 52
16 W. Napier, *History*, iii, 66–7
17 Bell, 46–7
18 Tomkinson, 188
19 Norcliffe, 458–60
20 Lunt, 56, 66, 63–4
21 Scott Daniel, 123
22 Longford, 283
23 Gronow, ii, 213–4
24 Donaldson, 357–9
25 Swabey, 18; W. Graham, 5; Long, 137; Blakeney, 214
26 Smyth, 344
27 Bannatyne, 275
28 Henegan, i, 257
29 Bannatyne, 275; Gomm 336; Leask, 330–1
30 Daniell, 322–3

31 J. Green, 102
32 Ross-Lewin, 188–9
33 Woodberry, 160–1, 171; W. Graham 35
34 Salisbury, 110
35 Leslie, 123
36 Le Mesurier MS.
37 *With Napoleon at Waterloo*, 212
38 Bell, 60
39 Frazer, 106
40 Wall, 336–7
41 Steevens, 71
42 Wylly, *K.O.Y.L.I.*, i, 201
43 Leeke, ii, 311
44 Burroughs,
45 Brett-James, *General Graham*, 267
46 *Military Sketch-Book*, ii, 115
47 Cooper, 108
48 Bell, 107
49 Fitchett, 253 [Anton]
50 Blakeney, 163
51 Harley, 66–8
52 Frazer, 86, 212
53 *Ibid.*, 138–9
54 Lejeune, ii, 136–7
55 Fitchett, 192–3 [Harris]
56 Cooper, 17
57 Hope, 174
58 Kincaid, *Adventures*, 257–8
59 Harley, i, 65–6
60 Donaldson, 225–6
61 Morris, 70
62 Albermarle, 145
63 Dalton, 277

CHAPTER 18: FRATERNIZATION

1 Wood, 206
2 G. Napier, 177
3 *Ibid.*, 145–6
4 Anderson, 66–7; Gavin, xviii
5 Oatts, ii, 214; Carss, 16
6 Costello, 114–5
7 Madden, 506; Gillmor, 158
8 Sherer, 134–5
9 Leach, 330
10 Barrett, *The 85th*, 86; Younge, 515
11 Grattan, 230; Wylly, *Sherwood Foresters*, i, 220 [Brown]; Donaldson, 96
12 Boutflower, 145
13 *With Napoleon at Waterloo*, 100 [Nicol]
14 Bragge, 62
15 Boutflower, 49
16 Barrett, i, 124–5
17 Schaumann, 277; Tomkinson, 204
18 Swabey, 137
19 Cadell, 191
20 Gairdner MS.
21 Ellesmere, 128; Stanhope, *Conversations*, 54
22 Landmann, ii, 293–5
23 Sherer, 136–7
24 Woodberry, 150–1
25 Parker Ellis, 8
26 Gairdner MS.
27 Surtees, 263
28 Blakeney, 303–4
29 Vivian, 186
30 Bell, 105

31 *Ibid.*, 106
32 Blakiston, ii, 319–20; Cadell, 205
33 Surtees, 258; Bell, 114; E. Fraser, 300
34 Parker Ellis, 7
35 Cooke, ii, 73
36 Schaumann, 269
37 Kincaid, *Adventures*, 238; Hay, 127
38 Mockler-Ferryman, *Regimental War Tales*, 139–40
39 Leeke, ii, 334
40 Parker Ellis, 'Reminiscences of Bayonne', 68–9
41 Ford MS.
42 Parker Ellis, 7
43 H. Maxwell, i, 209–10
44 Kincaid, *Adventures*, 36–7
45 Buckham, 322–3
46 Gavin, xxv
47 Blakiston, ii, 319
48 Tomkinson, 64
49 Stepney, 43; Anderson, 52; Schaumann, 277–8; Sherer, 138
50 Sidney, 151
51 Lawrence, 70–1; Boutflower, 67
52 G. Napier, 115
53 Gavin, xviii
54 Parquin, 205–6
55 *Ibid.*, 225
56 Vidal de la Blache, i, 171–2
57 Donaldson, ii, 151

M

Bibliography

A. MANUSCRIPT SOURCES

BARNARD: Lieut.-Colonel Sir Andrew: 'Letters of a Peninsular War Commanding Officer'. Edited by Captain M. C. Spurrier, 1966. (Typescript in Ministry of Defence Library (Central and Army), London)

CALL: MS Diary of Captain George Isaac Call, 27th (later 24th) Light Dragoons, from September 1811 to February 1812.
National Army Museum 6807/150
   See also *Journal of the Society of Army Historical Research*, vol. xxix.

COLES: Letters of W. C. Coles from Ireland, the Peninsula and France, 1806–17. He served in the 4th Foot until 1809, in the 4th Dragoons 1809–12, and thereafter in the 12th Light Dragoons.
National Army Museum 6807/419

DOUGLAS: MS Diary of Captain (afterwards Lieut.-General Sir) Neil Douglas, 79th Foot, from July 1809 to October 1810, formerly in the author's possession.
See also under 'Published Sources – Douglas'

FORD: MS Journal and Notebook (No. 71) of Lieut. John Ford, 79th (Cameron) Highlanders, 1809–14.
National Army Museum 6807/71

GAIRDNER: MS Diaries of Lieut. James P. Gairdner, 95th Rifles.
National Army Museum 6902/5 Nos. 1 and 2

HARDING: MS Diary 'Peninsular Campaign MS, 1813–14', kept by Lieut. William Harding, 5th Foot, in the possession of Dr John Harding

LE MESURIER: MS Diary of Lieut. Peter Le Mesurier, 9th Foot, (1789–1813), kept from 12 September 1808 to 20 November 1813. A copy of letters to his family in the Channel Islands, loaned to me by Edward Hall Esq.

SCOVELL: Papers of General Sir George Scovell.
Public Record Office, War Office 37/6

STANHOPE: Colonel the Hon. James Hamilton:
i. 'Private Memoranda and Journal from the beginning of 1810 to the 26th of July 1812 when I returned to England.'

ii. 'Journal from the end of 1812 to end of 1813, and 1815.' Loaned to me by the late Earl Stanhope, K.G., D.S.O., M.C.

STEWART: MS Diary of Major William Stewart, 30th Foot, from 24 September 1810 to 11 May 1811.
National Army Museum 6112/33

TRENCH: Journal of Major (afterwards General Sir) Frederick William Trench (1775–1859), 1st Foot Guards. He served in the Peninsula as an Assistant Q.M.G. from 1811 to 1813.
National Army Museum 6807/261

B. PUBLISHED SOURCES
Place of publication was London unless shown otherwise.

ALBEMARLE, GEORGE THOMAS, EARL OF: *Fifty Years of My Life* (3rd ed., revised, 1877)

ALLEN, ENSIGN JOHN: 'Journal of an Officer of the Royals in Spain' (*The Royal Military Chronicle*, vols. 2 and 3, 1811)

ALMACK, EDWARD: *The History of the Second Dragoons. 'Royal Scots Greys'* (1908)

ANDERSON, LT.-COLONEL JOSEPH: *Recollections of a Peninsular Veteran* (1913)

ANTON, QUARTERMASTER-SERGEANT JAMES: *Retrospect of a Military Life, during the most eventful Period of the Last War* [*42nd Highlanders*] (Edinburgh, 1841)

'ARTILLERO': 'Newcome's Journey to Head-Quarters near Burgos' (*The United Service Journal*, 1831, Part I)

ATKINSON, C. T.: *History of the Royal Dragoons 1661–1934* (Glasgow, 1934)

BADCOCK: 'A Light Dragoon in the Peninsula'. Extracts from the Letters of Captain Lovell Badcock, 14th Light Dragoons, 1809–1814. Edited by C. T. Atkinson (*Journal of the Society for Army Historical Research*, vol. 34, 1956)

BANNATYNE, LT.-COLONEL NEIL: *History of the Thirtieth Regiment 1689–1881* (Liverpool, 1923)

BARRETT, C. R. B.: *History of the XIII Hussars* (2 vols., Edinburgh, 1911)

BARRETT, C. R. B.: *The 85th King's Light Infantry* (1913)

BARRALLIER: 'Adventure at the Battle of Salamanca; Recollections of Services in Spain and Portugal by Captain Barrallier, late 71st Regiment' (Colburn's *United Service Magazine*, October 1851 and April 1852)

BELL, MAJOR-GENERAL SIR GEORGE: *Soldier's Glory, being Rough Notes of an Old Soldier*, arranged and edited by Brian Stuart (1956)

BESSBOROUGH: *Lady Bessborough and her Family Circle*. Edited by the Earl of Bessborough and A. Aspinall (1940)

BLAKENEY: *A Boy in the Peninsular War. The Services, Adventures, and Experiences of Robert Blakeney, Subaltern in the 28th Regiment. An Autobiography*. Edited by Julian Sturgis (1899)

BLAKISTON, MAJOR J.: *Twelve Years' Military Adventure in Three quarters of the Globe : or, Memoirs of an Officer who served in the Armies of His Majesty and of the East India Company, between the Years 1802 and 1814 in which are contained the campaigns of the Duke of Wellington in India, and his last in Spain and the South of France* (2 vols., 1829)

BOOTHBY: *A Prisoner of France. The Memoirs, Diary, and Correspondence of Charles Boothby, Captain Royal Engineers, during his last Campaign* (1898)

BOOTHBY: *Under England's Flag from 1804 to 1809. The Memoirs, Diary, and Correspondence of Charles Boothby, Captain of Royal Engineers.* (1900)

BOUTFLOWER, CHARLES: *The Journal of an Army Surgeon during the Peninsular War, August 1809–May 1813* (1912)

BRAGGE: *Peninsular Portrait, 1811–1814. The Letters of Captain William Bragge, Third (King's Own) Dragoons*. Edited by S. A. C. Cassells (1963)

BRETT-JAMES, ANTONY: *General Graham, Lord Lynedoch* (1959)

BRETT-JAMES, ANTONY: *The Hundred Days. Napoleon's Last Campaign from eye-witness accounts* (1964)

BRETT-JAMES, ANTONY: *Wellington at War, 1794–1815. A Selection of his wartime Letters* (1961)

BROUGHTON, LORD (John Cam Hobhouse): *Recollections of a Long Life*. Edited by his Daughter-in-law, Lady Dorchester (2 vols., 1911)

BROUGHTON, S. D.: *Letters from Portugal, Spain, & France, written during the Campaigns of 1812, 1813, & 1814, addressed to a friend in England* (1815)

BIBLIOGRAPHY

BUCKHAM, P. W.: *Personal Narrative of Adventures in the Peninsula during the War in 1812–1813*. By an Officer late in the Staff Corps Regiment of Cavalry (1827). Published anonymously

BUNBURY, LT.-COLONEL THOMAS: *Reminiscences of a Veteran. Being personal and military adventures in Portugal, Spain, France, Malta, New South Wales, Norfolk Island, New Zealand, Andaman Islands, and India* (3 vols., 1861)

BURGOYNE: *Life and Correspondence of Field-Marshal Sir John Burgoyne, Bart*, by his son-in-law, Lt.-Col. the Hon. George Wrottesley (2 vols., 1873)

BURROUGHS, GEORGE FREDERICK: *A Narrative of the Retreat of the British Army from Burgos; in a series of Letters* [Late Assistant Surgeon of the Royal Dragoons] (Bristol, 1814)

CADELL, LT.-COLONEL CHARLES: *Narrative of the Campaigns of The Twenty-Eighth Regiment, since their return from Egypt in 1802* (1835)

CAMPBELL, MAJOR-GENERAL SIR NEIL: *Napoleon at Fontainbleau and Elba, being a Journal of Occurrences in 1814–1815 with a Memoir of the Life and Services of that Officer* by his nephew Archibald Neil Campbell Maclachlan (1869)

CARSS: 'The 2nd/53rd in the Peninsular War. Contemporary Letters from an Officer of the Regiment.' [Capt. John Carss] Edited by S. H. F. Johnston. (*Journal of the Society for Army Historical Research*, vol. 26, 1948)

CARY, A. D. C. AND MCCANCE, STOUPE: *Regimental Records of the Royal Welsh Fusiliers (late the 23rd Foot)* (3 vols., vol., 1, 1689–1815) (1921)

CODRINGTON: *Memoir of the Life of Admiral Sir Edward Codrington with Selections from his public and private correspondence*. Edited by his daughter Lady Bourchier (2 vols., 1873)

COOKE, JOHN: *Memoirs of the Late War: Comprising the Personal Narrative of Captain Cooke of the 43rd Regiment of Light Infantry* (2 vols., 1831)

COOPER: *Rough Notes of Seven Campaigns in Portugal, Spain, France, and America, during the Years 1809–1815*, by John Spencer Cooper, late Serjeant in the 7th Royal Fusiliers (London & Carlisle, 1896)

COWPER, COLONEL L. I. (editor): *The King's Own. The Story of a Royal Regiment*. vol. 1, 1680–1814 (Oxford, 1939)

CRAUFURD, REV. ALEXANDER H.: *General Craufurd and his Light Division* (1891)

CROKER: *The Croker Papers. The Correspondence and Diaries of the late Right Honourable John Wilson Croker, Secretary to the Admiralty from 1809 to 1830.* Edited by Louis J. Jennings (3 vols. 1884)

DALLAS: *Incidents in the Life and Ministry of the Rev. Alex. R. C. Dallas, Rector of Wonston,* by his Widow (3rd ed., 1873)

DALTON, CHARLES: *The Waterloo Roll Call, with Biographical Notes and Anecdotes* (2nd revised enlarged ed., 1904)

DANIELL, JOHN EDGECOMBE: *Journal of an Officer in the Commissariat Department of the Army* (1820)

DELAVOYE, ALEX. M.: *Life of Thomas Graham, Lord Lynedoch* (1880)

DICKSON: *The Dickson Manuscripts, being Diaries, Letters, Maps, Account Books, with various other papers of the late Major-General Sir Alexander Dickson, Royal Artillery.* Series 'C' – from 1809 to 1818. Edited by Major John H. Leslie (Woolwich, 1907 etc.)

DONALDSON, JOSEPH: *Recollections of the Eventful Life of a Soldier* [A sergeant in the 94th Scots Brigade] (new ed., Edinburgh, 1845)

DOUGLAS: 'The Diary of Captain Neil Douglas, 79th Foot, 1809 to 1810'. Edited by Antony Brett-James (*Journal of the Society for Army Historical Research,* vol. 41, 1963)

DOWNMAN: 'Diary of Major Thomas Downman, Royal Horse Artillery, in the Peninsula, from 30 April 1811 to 17 August 1812' (*Journal of the Society for Army Historical Research,* vol. 6, 1927)

DUNN-PATTISON, R. P.: *The History of the 91st Argyllshire Highlanders* (Edinburgh, 1910)

DWELLEY, E.: *A Muster Roll of the British Non-Commissioned Officers and Men present at the Battle of Waterloo* (privately printed, Fleet, Hampshire, 1934)

DYNELEY: 'Letters written by Lieut.-General Thomas Dyneley, C.B., R.A., while on active service between the years 1806 and 1815,' arranged by Colonel F. A. Whinyates, late R.H.A. (*Proceedings of the Royal Artillery Institution,* vol. 23, 1896)

EGGLESTONE, WILLIAM MORLEY: *Letters of a Weardale Soldier, Lieutenant John Brumwell* [43rd Regt.] (Published by the Author, Stanhope, County of Durham, 1912)

ELLESMERE, FRANCIS, EARL OF: *Personal Reminiscences of the Duke of Wellington*. Edited with a Memoir by his Daughter Alice, Countess of Stafford (1904)

ELLISON, MAJOR-GENERAL SIR GERALD: 'Army Administration' (*The Army Quarterly*, October 1921)

FERNYHOUGH: *Military Memoirs of Four Brothers (Natives of Staffordshire), engaged in the service of their country, as well in the New World and Africa, as on the Continent of Europe*. By the Survivor (1829)

FITCHETT, W. H. (editor): *Wellington's Men. Some Soldier Autobiographies* (new ed., 1912)

FITZ MAURICE, MRS: *Recollections of a Rifleman's Wife, at Home and Abroad* (1851)

FORTESCUE, THE HON SIR JOHN W.: *Following the Drum*. Contains 'An Ensign on Wellington: John Mills, Coldstream Guards, in letters to his Mother at Bisterne in the New Forest' (Edinburgh & London, 1931)

FOSS, MICHAEL: *Famous Regiments: The Royal Fusiliers (The 7th Regt. of Foot)* (1967)

FRANKLAND: *A Memoir of the early Military Life of Sir Frederick William Frankland, VIII Baronet of Thirkleby*. Written at the request of his Children and printed by them for private circulation (1874)

FRASER, EDWARD: *The Soldiers whom Wellington led. Deeds of Daring, Chivalry, and Renown* (1913)

FRASER, SIR WILLIAM: *Words on Wellington. The Duke – Waterloo – The Ball* (1902)

FRAZER: *Letters of Colonel Augustus Frazer, K.C.B., commanding the Royal Horse Artillery in the Army under the Duke of Wellington, written during the Peninsular and Waterloo campaigns*. Edited by Major-General Edward Sabine (1859)

GARDYNE, LIEUT.-COLONEL C. GREENHILL: *The Life of a Regiment. The History of the Gordon Highlanders from its Formation in 1794 to 1816* (Edinburgh, 1901)

GARRETT: 'A Subaltern in the Peninsular War. Letters of Lieutenant Robert Garrett, 1811–1813.' Edited by A. S. White (*Journal of the Society for Army Historical Research*, vol. 13, 1934)

GAVIN: 'The Diary of William Gavin, Ensign and Quartermaster, 71st Highland Regiment, 1806–1815. Being his daily notes of his Campaigns in South Africa, South America, Portugal, Spain, Southern France, and Flanders.' With a preface by Col. H. R. H. Southern and a Prefatory Note and Commentaries by Sir Charles Oman (*The Highland Light Infantry Chronicle*, 1920–21)

GEISSLER, C.: *Denkwürdigkeiten aus den Feldzug in Spanien in den Jahren 1810 u. 1811 mit dem herzogl. sachs. Kontingent* (Leipzig, n.d.)

General Orders. Spain and Portugal. vol. ii, 1810; vol. iii, 1811; vol. iv, 1812 (1811–13)

General Regulations and Orders (Horse Guards, 1 Nov., 1804)

GIBNEY, DR THOMAS: *Eighty Years Ago, or the Recollections of an old Army Doctor. His adventures of the Field of Quatre Bras and Waterloo and during the Occupation of Paris in 1815.* Edited by his Son, Major R. D. Gibney (1896)

GILBY, THOMAS: *Britain at Arms. A Scrapbook, from Queen Anne to the present day* (1953)

GILLMOR: 'The Diary of Lieutenant C. [Clotworthy] Gillmor, R.N. Portugal, 1810.' Edited by Lieutenant H. N. Edwards (*Journal of the Society for Army Historical Research*, vol. 3, 1934)

GLEIG, G. R.: *The Light Dragoon* [George Farmer, 11th Light Dragoons] (1850)

GLEIG, G. R.: Personal Recollections of the First Duke of Wellington, with sketches of some of his Guests and Contemporaries. Edited by his Daughter Mary E. Gleig (Edinburgh & London, 1904)

GLEIG, G. R.: *The Subaltern* (1st ed., 1825. Everyman ed., n.d.)

GOMM: *Letters and Journals of Field-Marshal Sir William Gomm, G.C.B., from 1799 to Waterloo, 1815.* Edited by Francis C. Carr-Gomm (1881)

GORDON, ALEXANDER: *A Cavalry Officer in the Corunna Campaign, 1808–1809. The Journal of Captain Gordon of the 15th Hussars.* Edited by Colonel H. C. Wylly (1913)

GRAHAM OF FINTRY: *Supplementary Report on the Manuscripts of Robert Graham, Esq., of Fintry.* Edited by C. T. Atkinson (Historical Manuscripts Commission, Series 81, 1940)

GRAHAM, WILLIAM: *Travels through Portugal and Spain during the Peninsular War* (1820)

GRATTAN: *Adventures with the Connaught Rangers, 1809–1814,* by

337

William Grattan, late Lieutenant Connaught Rangers. Edited by Charles Oman (new ed., 1902)

GREEN, JOHN: *The Vicissitudes of a Soldier's Life, or a Series of Occurrences from 1806 to 1815* [68th Durham Light Infantry] (Louth, 1827)

GREEN, WILLIAM: *A Brief Outline of the Travels and Adventures of William Green (late Rifle Brigade) during a period of 10 years in Denmark, Germany, and the Peninsular War,* (Leicester, 1858)

GRIFFITH: 'Peninsular War Letters written by Major Edwin Griffith, 15th Light Dragoons, and Cornet Frederick Charles Philips.' Edited by Norman Tucker (*The National Library of Wales Journal,* vol. XII, No. 2, Winter 1961, Aberystwyth, 1961)

GRONOW: *The Reminiscences and Recollections of Captain Gronow, being Anecdotes of the Camp, Court, Clubs, and Society, 1810–1860* (1st ed., 1862–66. 2 vols., 1900)

GURWOOD, LIEUT.-COLONEL JOHN: *The General Orders of Field Marshal the Duke of Wellington in Portugal, Spain and France, from 1809 to 1814; in the Low Countries and France, in 1815; and in France, Army of Occupation, from 1816 to 1818* (1837)

HALL, CORNET FRANCIS: 'Recollections in Portugal and Spain during 1811 and 1812' [14th Light Dragoons] (*Journal of the Royal United Service Institution,* vol. LVI, July-Dec. 1912)

HAMILTON, LIEUT.-GENERAL SIR F. W.: *The Origin and History of the First or Grenadier Guards* (3 vols., 1874)

HAMILTON, COLONEL HENRY BLACKBURNE: *Historical Records of the 14th (King's) Hussars from 1715 to 1900* (1901)

HARDINGE, LIEUTENANT RICHARD: 'Letters from the Peninsula, 1812–1814' with notes by Lt.-Colonel M. E. S. Laws (*The Journal of the Royal Artillery,* vols. LXXXV, 1958, and LXXXVI, 1959)

HASTINGS: *Report on the Manuscripts of the late Reginald Rawdon Hastings, Esq. of the Manor House, Ashby de la Zouch.* Edited by Francis Bickley (vol. 3. Historical Manuscripts Commission, 1934)

HAY, CAPTAIN WILLIAM: *Reminiscences 1808–1815 under Wellington.* Edited by his daughter, Mrs. S. C. I. Wood (1901)

HENEGAN, SIR RICHARD D.: *Seven Years' Campaigning in the Peninsula* (2 vols., 1848)

HENRY, WALTER: *Surgeon Henry's Trifles. Events of a Military Life.* Edited by Pat Hayward (1970. 1st ed., Quebec, 1839; 2nd ed., 1843)

HOLLAND: *The Spanish Journal of Elizabeth, Lady Holland.* Edited by the Earl of Ilchester (1910)

HOLZING, KARL FRANZ VON: *Unter Napoleon in Spanien. Denkwürdigkeiten eines badischen Rheinbundoffiziers, 1787–1839* (Berlin, 1937)

HOPE, LIEUTENANT JAMES: *The Military Memoirs of an Infantry Officer, 1809–1816* [92nd Highlanders] (Edinburgh, 1833). Published anonymously

HOUGH, HENRY: 'Journal kept by Lieut. Hough from 22 March 1812, to 13 May, 1813' (*Journal of the Royal United Service Institution,* vol. LXI, 1916)

INGILBY: 'Diary of Lieutenant [William Bates] Ingilby, R. A., in the Peninsular War (*Royal Artillery Institution Proceedings,* vol. XX, 1900)

JACKSON, LIEUT.-COLONEL BASIL: *Notes and Reminiscences of a Staff Officer, chiefly relating to the Waterloo campaign and to St Helena matters during the captivity of Napoleon.* Edited by R. C. Seaton (1903)

JAMES, MAJOR CHARLES: *An Universal Military Dictionary in English and French; in which are explained the terms of the principal sciences that are necessary for the information of an officer* (4th ed., 1816)

JONES, MAJOR-GENERAL SIR JOHN T.: *Journals of Sieges carried on by the Army under the Duke of Wellington in Spain during the years 1811 to 1814* (3 vols. 3rd ed., 1846)

JONES, LIEUT. RICE: 'An Engineer Officer under Wellington in the Peninsula. The Diary and Correspondence of Lieut. Rice Jones, R.E., during 1808–12.' Edited by Capt. the Hon. H. V. Shore, late R.N. (*The Royal Engineers Journal,* July 1912–March 1913)

JONES, LIEUT. RICE: 'Letters from the Peninsula during 1812–13–14 addressed to Lieut. Rice Jones, R.E. by Engineer Officers.' Edited by Commander the Hon. Henry N. Shore, R.N. (*Journal of the Royal United Service Institution,* vol. LXI, 1916)

Journal of an Officer in the King's German Legion: comprising an account of his campaigns and adventures in England, Ireland, Denmark, Portugal, Spain, Malta, Sicily, and Italy (1827)

Journal of a Regimental Officer during the Recent Campaign in Portugal and Spain under Lord Viscount Wellington, with a correct Plan of the Battle of Talavera (1810)

KILVERT, REV. FRANCIS: *Kilvert's Diary 1870–1879*. Selections, chosen, edited and introduced by William Plomer (1944)

KINCAID, CAPTAIN J.: *Adventures in the Rifle Brigade, in the Peninsula, France, and the Netherlands, from 1809 to 1815* (1830)

KINCAID, J.: *Random Shots from a Rifleman* (1835)

KNOWLES: *The War in the Peninsula. Some Letters of Lieut. Robert Knowles, a Bolton Officer.* Arranged by his great-great-nephew, Sir Lees Knowles (Bolton, 1909)

LANDMANN: *Recollections of my Military Life,* by Colonel Landmann, late of the Corps of Engineers (2 vols., 1854)

LARPENT: *The Private Journal of F. Seymour Larpent, Judge-Advocate General, attached to the Head-Quarters of Lord Wellington during the Peninsular War, from 1812 to its close.* Edited by Sir George Larpent (2 vols., 2nd ed. revised, 1853)

LAWRENCE: *The Autobiography of Sergeant William Lawrence, a Hero of the Peninsular and Waterloo Campaigns.* Edited by George Nugent Banks [40th Regt] (1886)

LEACH, LIEUT.-COLONEL J.: *Rough Sketches of the Life of an Old Soldier* [95th Rifles] (1831)

LEASK, J. C. AND MCCANCE, H. M.: *The Regimental Records of the Royal Scots* (Dublin, 1915)

LEEKE, REV. WILLIAM: *The History of Lord Seaton's Regiment (The 52nd Light Infantry) at the Battle of Waterloo* (2 vols., 1866)

LEJEUNE: *Mémoires du Général Lejeune. En Prison et en Guerre. A Travers l'Europe (1809–1814)* (Paris, 1896)

LESLIE: *Military Journal of Colonel Leslie, K.H., of Balquhain, whilst serving with the 29th Regt. in the Peninsula, and the 60th Rifles in Canada, etc. 1807–1832* (Aberdeen, 1887)

L'ESTRANGE: *Recollections of Sir George B. L'Estrange, late of the 31st Regiment, and afterwards in the Scots Fusilier Guards. The Peninsular War* (n.d., c. 1873)

LEVINGE, SIR RICHARD GEORGE AUGUSTUS: *Historical Records of the Forty-Third Regiment, Monmouthshire Light Infantry* (1868)

LONDONDERRY, LIEUT.-GENERAL CHARLES WILLIAM VANE, MARQUESS OF: *Narrative of the Peninsular War, from 1808 to 1813* (2 vols., 3rd ed., 1829)

LONG: *Peninsular Cavalry General (1811–13). The Correspondence of Lieutenant-General Robert Ballard Long.* Edited with a Memoir by T. H. McGuffie (1951)

LONGFORD, ELIZABETH: *Wellington. The Years of the Sword* (1969)

LUNT, JAMES: *Scarlet Lancer* [based on the diary of John Luard, 4th Dragoons and later 16th Light Dragoons] (1964)

MACKINNON, MAJOR-GENERAL HENRY: *A Journal of the Campaign in Portugal and Spain, containing Remarks on the Inhabitants, Customs, Trade, and Cultivation, of those Countries, from the year 1809 to 1812* (Bath & London, 1812)

MADDEN: 'The Diary of Charles Dudley Madden, Lieutenant 4th Dragoons, Peninsular War, 1809–11' (*Journal of the Royal United Service Institution,* vol. LVIII, 1914)

MAINWARING, FREDERICK: 'Four Years of a Soldier's Life, by a Field Officer' (*Colburn's United Service Magazine and Naval and Military Journal,* August 1844)

MALCOLM, JOHN: *Reminiscences of a Campaign in the Pyrenees and South of France* [42nd Regt] (Constable's Miscellany, vol. XXVII, Edinburgh, 1828)

MALET, COLONEL HAROLD: *The Historical Memoirs of the XVIIIth Hussars* (London & Winchester, 1907)

MALMESBURY: *A Series of Letters of the First Earl of Malmesbury, his Family and Friends from 1745 to 1820.* Edited by his Grandson (2 vols., 1870) [vol. 2 contains the letters of Captain George Bowles, Coldstream Guards]

MAXWELL, SIR HERBERT: *The Life of Wellington. The Restoration of the Martial Power of Great Britain* (2 vols., 1899)

MAXWELL, W. H. (editor): *Peninsular Sketches; by Actors on the Scene* (2 vols., 1845)

MCGRIGOR: *The Autobiography and Services of Sir James McGrigor, Bart., late Director-General of the Army Medical Department* (1861)

Memoirs of a Sergeant late in the Forty-Third Light Infantry, previously to and during the Peninsular War (2nd ed., 1839)

Memoirs of the Late War (1831)

The Military Sketch-Book. Reminiscences of Seventeen Years in the Service abroad and at Home, by an Officer of the Line. (2 vols., 1827)

341

MILL, MAJOR JAMES: 'Service in Ireland, the Peninsular, New Orleans and at Waterloo 1810–15' [40th Regt.] (Colburn's *United Service Magazine*, 1870)

MOCKLER-FERRYMAN, LIEUT.-COLONEL A. F.: *The Life of a Regimental Officer during the Great War 1793–1815*, compiled from the Correspondence of Colonel Samuel Rice, C.B., K.H., 51st Light Infantry (Edinburgh, 1913)

MOCKLER-FERRYMAN, LIEUT.-COLONEL A. F., *Regimental War Tales 1741–1919*. Told for the Soldiers of the Oxfordshire and Buckinghamshire Light Infantry (the old 43rd and 52nd) (Oxford, 2nd ed., 1942)

MOORE SMITH, G. C.: *The Life of John Colborne, Field-Marshal Lord Seaton* (1903)

MORRIS, SERGEANT THOMAS: *Military Memoirs. The Napoleonic Wars.* Edited by John Selby (1967)

NAPIER, GENERAL SIR GEORGE: *Passages in the Early Military Life of General Sir George T. Napier, K.C.B., written by Himself.* Edited by his Son, General W. C. Napier (1894)

NAPIER, COLONEL W. F. P.: *History of the War in the Peninsula and in the South of France, from the Year 1807 to the Year 1814* (3 vols., new ed.)

NAPIER, LIEUT.-GENERAL SIR W. NAPIER: *The Life and Opinions of General Sir Charles James Napier* (4 vols., 1857)

NAPIER, W.: *Life of General Sir William Napier.* Edited by H. A. Bruce, M.P. (2 vols., 1864)

NEALE, ADAM: *Letters from Portugal and Spain* (1809)

NORTHCLIFFE: 'A Dragoon's Experiences at Salamanca' [Lieut. Norcliffe Norcliffe, 4th Dragoons] Edited by Charles Dalton (*The Cavalry Journal*, Oct. 1912)

OATTS, LIEUT.-COLONEL L. B.: *Proud Heritage. The Story of the Highland Light Infantry.* Vol. 2. *The 74th Highlanders, 1787–1882* (1959)

OMAN, C. W. C.: *Wellington's Army 1809–1814* (1913)

OMPTEDA: *A Hanoverian-English Officer a Hundred Years Ago. Memoirs of Baron* [Christian] *Ompteda, Colonel in the King's German Legion, 1765–1815.* Translated by John Hill (1892)

ORMSBY, REV. JAMES WILMOT: *An Account of the Operations of the British Army and of the State and Sentiments of the People of Portugal and Spain, during the Campaigns of the Years 1808 and 1809, in a series of Letters* (2 vols., 1809)

PAKENHAM: *Pakenham Letters, 1800 to 1815* (1914)

PARKER ELLIS, LIEUT.-COLONEL C.: 'Anecdotes of Outposts' (*The Brigade of Guards Magazine.*)

PARQUIN, LIEUTENANT-COLONEL CHARLES: *Souvenirs de Gloire et d'Amour* (Paris, n.d.)

PATTERSON: *The Adventures of Captain John Patterson, with Notices of the Officers, &c of the 50th, or Queen's Own Regiment, from 1807 to 1821* (1837)

PATTERSON, MAJOR JOHN: *Camp and Quarters. Scenes and Impressions of Military Life* (2 vols., 1840)

POCOCKE, CAPTAIN THOMAS: *Journal of a Soldier of the Seventy-first Regiment (Highland Light Infantry) from 1806 to 1815* (Constable's Miscellany, vol. XXVII, Edinburgh, 1828). Published anonymously

PORTER, SIR ROBERT KER: *Letters from Portugal and Spain, written during the march of the British Troops under Sir John Moore, by an Officer* (1809). Published anonymously

PORTER, MAJOR-GENERAL WHITWORTH: *History of the Corps of Royal Engineers* (3 vols., 1889)

'Reminiscences of a Regimental Medical Officer on the Retreat of the Army from Madrid in 1812' (Colburn's *United Service Magazine*, part III, 1851)

'Retreat upon Portugal in 1812. From the Reminiscences of a Subaltern' (*United Service Journal*, September 1837)

Rifle Brigade Chronicle, The. Compiled and edited by Colonel Willoughby Verner (1913 & 1930). Compiled by Major H. G. Parkyn (1931).

ROBERTS, LIEUT.-COLONEL DAVID: *The Military Adventures of Johnny Newcome, with an Account of his Campaign on the Peninsula and in Pall Mall and Notes by an Officer* (new ed., 1904). Published anonymously

ROBINSON: 'A Peninsular Brigadier. Letters of Major-General Sir F. P. Robinson, K.C.B., dealing with the Campaign of 1813'. Edited, with an Introduction, by C. T. Atkinson (*Journal of the Society for Army Historical Research*, vol. 34, 1956)

ROSS-LEWIN, HARRY: *With 'The Thirty-Second' in the Peninsular and other Campaigns.* Edited by John Wardrell (Dublin, 1904. 1st ed. in 3 vols., 1834)

Royal Military Chronicle, The, or British Officer's Monthly Register and Mentor (6 vols., 1811-13. New Series, 6 vols., 1814-16)

SALISBURY: *A Great Man's Friendship. Letters of the Duke of Wellington to Mary, Marchioness of Salisbury, 1850-1852.* Edited by Lady Burghclere (1927)

SALTOUN, ALEXANDER FRASER, 17TH LORD: *The Frasers of Philorth* (3 vols., Edinburgh, 1879)

SCARFE, NORMAN: *Letters from the Peninsula. The Freer Family Correspondence, 1807-1814.* Reprinted from 'Transactions of the Leicestershire Archaeological Society', vol. xxix, 1953 (Leicester, 1953)

SCHÄFFER, CONRAD VON: *Unter Napoleons Fahnen in Spanien (1808-1809). Aus den Erinnerungen eines deutschen Generals.* Herausgegeben von Karl Brunner (Berlin, n.d.)

SCHAUMANN, AUGUST LUDOLF FRIEDRICH: *On the Road with Wellington. The Diary of a War Commissary in the Peninsular Campaigns.* Edited and translated by Anthony M. Ludovici (1924)

SHELLEY: *The Diary of Frances, Lady Shelley, 1787-1817.* Edited by her Grandson, Richard Edgcumbe (2 vols., 1912-13)

SHERER, MOYLE: *Recollections of the Peninsula,* by the Author of *Sketches of India* (3rd ed., 1824). Published anonymously

SIDNEY, REV. EDWIN: *The Life of Lord Hill, G.C.B.* (1845)

SCOTT DANIEL, DAVID: *4th Hussar. The Story of the Queen's Own Hussars, 1685-1958* (Aldershot, 1959)

SIMMONS: *A British Rifleman. The Journals and Correspondence of Major George Simmons, Rifle Brigade, during the Peninsular War and the Campaign of Waterloo.* Edited by Lieut.-Colonel Willoughby Verner (1899)

SMITH, MAJOR-GENERAL SIR FREDERICK: *The History of the Royal Army Veterinary Corps, 1796-1919* (1919)

SMITH, SIR HARRY: *The Autobiography of Sir Harry Smith 1787-1819* (1910; 1st ed., 2 vols., 1901)

SMITH, JOHN GORDON: *The English Army in France; being the Personal Narrative of an Officer* (New ed., 1831). [Asst. Surgeon of the 12th Light Dragoons]. Published anonymously

SMITH, WILLIAM: 'Journal of Captain William Smith of the 11th Light

Dragoons during the Peninsular War' [May 1811–Nov. 1812] (*Journal of the Royal United Service Institution*, vol. LX, 1915)

SMYTH, LIEUT. B.: *History of the XX Regiment 1688–1888* (1889)

SMYTHIES, CAPTAIN P. H. RAYMOND: *Historical Record of the 40th (2nd Somersetshire) Regiment from its Formation, in 1717, to 1893* (Devonport, 1894)

SPERLING, JOHN: *Letters of an Officer of the Corps of Royal Engineers from the British Army in Holland, Belgium, and France, to his Father, from the latter end of 1813 to 1816* (1872)

STANHOPE, PHILIP HENRY, 5TH EARL: *Notes of Conversations with the Duke of Wellington 1831–1851* ('The World's Classics', 1938; 1st ed., 1888)

STEEVENS, LIEUT.-COLONEL CHARLES: *Reminiscences of my Military Life from 1795 to 1818*. [The XX Regt] Edited by his Son, Lieut.-Colonel Nathaniel Steevens (Winchester, 1878)

STEPNEY, LIEUT.-COLONEL SIR JOHN COWELL: *Leaves from the Diary of an Officer of the Guards* [Coldstream] (1854). Published anonymously

STOCQUELER, J. J.: *The Life of Field Marshal the Duke of Wellington* (2 vols., 1852)

STOTHERT, CAPTAIN WILLIAM: *A Narrative of the Principal Events of the Campaigns of 1809, 1810 and 1811, in Spain and Portugal; interspersed with Remarks on Local Scenery and Manners. In a Series of Letters* (1812) [Adjutant, Third Foot Guards]

'Subalterns Complaint, The. On Picquet at Pena Perda, a very lofty mountain, one of the passes of the Sierra de Gata in Spain' (*The Royal Military Chronicle*, vol. 3, 1811)

SURTEES, WILLIAM: *Twenty-Five Years in the Rifle Brigade* (Edinburgh & London, 1833)

SWABEY, LIEUT. WILLIAM: *Diary of Campaigns in the Peninsula for the Years 1811, 12, and 13*. Edited by Colonel F. A. Whinyates (Woolwich, 1895)

TALE, REGTL. SGT.-MAJOR WILLIAM: *Jottings from my Sabretasch by a Chelsea Pensioner* [King's Hussars] (1847). Published anonymously

THACKWELL: *The Military Memoirs of Lieut.-General Sir Joseph Thackwell*, arranged from Diaries and Correspondence by Colonel H. C. Wylly (1908)

THOUMINE, R. H.: *Scientific Soldier. A Life of General Le Marchant, 1766-1812* (1968)

TOMKINSON, LIEUT.-COLONEL WILLIAM: *The Diary of a Cavalry Officer in the Peninsular and Waterloo Campaigns 1809-1815.* Edited by his Son James Tomkinson (1894)

VERNER, COLONEL WILLOUGHBY: *History & Campaigns of the Rifle Brigade*, Part II, 1809-1813 (1919)

VERNER, WILLIAM: *Reminiscences of William Verner (1782-1871), 7th Hussars.* Edited with an Introduction by Ruth W. Verner (Society for Army Historical Research Special Publication no. 8, 1965)

VIDAL DE LA BLACHE, LE CAPITAINE: *L'Evacuation de l'Espagne* (Paris & Nancy., 2 vols., 1914)

VIVIAN, THE HON. CLAUD: *Richard Hussey Vivian, first Baron Vivian. A Memoir* (1897)

WACHHOLTZ: 'Auf der Peninsula 1810 bis 1813. Kriegstagebuch des Generals Friedrich Ludwig v. Wachholtz' (*Beihefte zum Militär-Wochenblatt*, Berlin, 1906)

WALDIE, CHARLOTTE: *Narrative of a Residence in Belgium during the Campaign of 1815; and of a Visit to the field of Waterloo.* By an Englishwoman (1817). Published anonymously

WALL, CAPTAIN ADAM: 'Diary of the Operations in Spain, under Sir John Moore' (*Proceedings of the Royal Artillery Institution*, vol. 14, Woolwich, 1886)

WARD, S. G. P.: *Wellington* (1963)

WARD, S. G. P.: *Wellington's Headquarters. A Study of the Administrative Problems in the Peninsula, 1809-1814* (1957)

WARRE, LIEUT.-GENERAL SIR WILLIAM: *Letters from the Peninsula 1808-1812.* Edited by his Nephew, the Rev. Edmund Warre (1909)

WATTEVILLE, COLONEL H. DE: *The British Soldier. His Daily Life from Tudor to Modern Times* (1954)

WHEATLEY, EDMUND: *The Wheatley Diary. A Journal and Sketch-book kept during the Peninsular War and Waterloo Campaign.* Edited by Christopher Hibbert. [Ensign, 5th King's German Legion Line Bn.] (1964)

WHEATLEY, MAJOR-GENERAL WILLIAM: 'Letters from the Front, 1812', by G. E. Hubbard. (*The United Service Magazine*, vol. LVIII, new series, 1919)

WHEELER, WILLIAM: *The Letters of Private Wheeler, 1809–1828*. Edited by Captain B. H. Liddell Hart (1951)

Wider Napoleon! Ein Deutsches Reiterleben, 1806–1815 Herausgegeben. von Friedrich M. Kirscheisen (2 vols., Stuttgart, 1911)

WILKIE, LIEUT.-COLONEL FLETCHER: 'Recollections of the Peninsula' (Colburn's *United Service Magazine*, January 1844)

WILLIAMS, CAPTAIN GODFREY TREVELYAN: *The Historical Records of the Eleventh Hussars, Prince Albert's Own* (1908)

With Napoleon at Waterloo, and other unpublished documents of the Waterloo and Peninsular Campaigns. Edited by Mackenzie MacBride (1911). It contains the journals of Sergeant D. Robertson and Sergeant Daniel Nicol, both in the 92nd Foot (Gordon Highlanders)

WOOD, CAPTAIN GEORGE: *The Subaltern Officer. A Narrative.* [82nd Regt] (1825)

WOODBERRY, GEORGE: *Journal du Lieutenant Woodberry. Campagnes de Portugal et d'Espagne, de France, de Belgique et de France (1813–1815)*. Traduit de l'Anglais par Georges Hélie (Paris, 1896)

WYLLY, COLONEL H. C.: *History of the King's Own Yorkshire Light Infantry* (2 vols., n.d., 1924)

WYLLY, COLONEL H. C.: *History of the 1st & 2nd Battalions, The Sherwood Foresters, Nottinghamshire and Derbyshire Regiment, 1740–1914. 45th Foot, 95th Foot* (2 vols., 1929)

YOUNGE, K. E.: 'Some Peninsular Letters' [Lieutenant, 38th Regt.] (*The United Service Magazine*, vol. LXII, new series, 1916)

ADDENDA

DUNCAN, CAPTAIN FRANCIS: *History of the Royal Regiment of Artillery* (2 vols., 1873)

ROGERS: *Recollections of Samuel Rogers* (1859)

Index

1. PEOPLE AND REGIMENTS

Alexander, Col., 298–9, 303
Allen, Ensign John, 139, 238
Alvito, Marques de, 54
Anderson, Lieut. Joseph, 293
Anson, Major-Gen. George, 237
Anton, Sgt James, 88, 94, 100–1, 107, 116
Anton, Mrs Mary, 88, 100–1
Ariosto, Ludovico, 154

Badcock, Capt. Lovell Benjamin, 76
Bainbrigge, Lieut. John, 29
Baird, Major-Gen. Sir David, 283
Barber, Fusilier, 102
Barnard, Lt.-Col. Sir Andrew, 118, 147
Beattie, Dr George, 250
Beaufort, Henry Charles, Duke of, 204
Beckwith, Capt. Charles, 146–7
Beckwith, Lt.-Col. Sydney, 205, 220–1, 236
Bell, Dr A., 265
Bell, Ensign George, 23, 54, 68, 72, 91, 93, 99, 112, 134–6, 164, 195, 215, 228, 267, 274, 285, 300
Bell, Capt. John, 160
Belson, Lt.-Col. Charles, 131
Benedita, Sister Maria, 245–6
Bennett, Dr James, 277
Beresford, Lt.-Gen. (Marshal) Sir William Carr, 46, 122–3, 125, 142, 169, 237
Berry, Paymaster Marlborough Parsons, 278
Berry, Mrs, 278
Bingham, Lt.-Col. George Ridout, 32, 51, 133, 176
Bissett, Sir John, 111
Blackett, Lieut. Christopher, 129
Blakeney, Lieut. Robert, 35, 70, 128, 199, 251, 299
Blakiston, Major John, 34, 53, 55–6, 59, 91
Blücher, Feldmarschall Gebhard Leberecht, Fürst von, 197

Boothby, Capt. Charles, 54, 68, 152, 263
Boutflower, Dr Charles, 57, 218–9, 240, 245, 295, 306
Bowles, Capt. George, 27, 111, 133, 179, 210
Bragge, Capt. William, 140, 153
Briscall, Rev. Samuel, 229–30, 232, 234
Brotherton, Capt. Thomas, 182–4, 241
Broughton, Dr Samuel Daniel, 48
Brown, Lieut. George, 238
Brown, Lt.-Col. John Frederick, 154
Brown, Pte William, 34, 94, 115, 272
Browne, Rev. Frederick Harvey, 232
Brunswick, Friedrich Wilhelm, Duke of, 167
Buchanan, Cpl James, 261
Buckham, P. W., 54, 138, 157, 305
Bull, Capt. Robert, 185, 229
Bunbury, Capt. Thomas, 54, 119, 218
Burghersh, Lt.-Col. John Fane, Baron, 141
Burgoyne, Lt.-Col. John Fox, 54, 77, 158, 187–8
Burns, Robert, 153
Burroughs, Dr George Frederick, 285
Byrne, Capt., 196

Cadell, Lt.-Col. Charles, 235
Call, Capt. George, 24, 138, 175, 247–8
Campbell, Col. Neil, 255–6
Cardew, Capt., 72
Carew, Capt. Robert, 71
Carmichael, Lieut. Alexander, 153
Carss, Capt. John, 60
Carvalho, Bailli, 54
Castaños, Gen. Don Francisco Xavier de, 149, 207, 237
Catalani, Mme Angelica, 166
Cator, Capt. William, 163
Cervantes, Miguel de, 153

Cheney, Capt., later Col., Edward, 184
Childers, Capt. Michael, 209
Clinton, Lt.-Gen. Sir Henry, 123
Cobbett, William, 150
Cocks, Major Charles Somers, 237–8
Codrington, Capt. (R.N.) Edward, 42
Colborne, Lt.-Col. Sir John, 26, 261–2
Cole, Lt.-Gen. Sir Galbraith Lowry, 29, 69, 124–5, 211
Coles, Lieut. William Cowper, 76
Colman, George, the Younger, 161
Conolly, Lieut. James, 169
Cooke, Capt. John, 25, 37, 116–7, 122, 160, 162, 174, 301
Cooper, Sgt John Spencer, 51, 90, 92, 107, 114, 221, 254, 258–9
Costello, Sgt Edward, 210, 214, 252–3, 256, 262, 266, 269
Cotton, Lt.-Gen. Sir Stapleton, 42, 169, 174, 218, 237, 298
Cowell, Mrs, 289–90
Cox, Lieut., 163
Cradock, Lt.-Gen. Sir John Francis, 39
Crane, Tom, 200, 204,
Craufurd, Major-Gen. Robert, 25–6, 182, 193, 205, 237
Cuff, Thomas, saddler, 77
Currie, Capt. Edward, 278
Currie, Mrs Ann Maria, 278

Dalbiac, Lt.-Col. James Charles, 273–6
Dalbiac, Mrs Susanna Isabella, 273–6
Dalhousie, Lt.-Gen. George Ramsay, Earl of, 123, 196
Dallas, Alexander R. C., 68, 139, 211–2, 244
Daniell, John Edgecombe, 53, 185, 250
Deacon, Ensign Thomas, 290
Deacon, Mrs, 290
Deacon, Miss 'Waterloo', 290
de Lancey, Col. Sir William Howe, 182
Dickson, Lt.-Col. Sir Alexander, 44, 54, 70, 73–4, 76, 130, 156, 164, 172, 208, 255
Diggle, Capt. Charles, 284
Donaldson, Sgt Joseph, 43, 84, 216, 233, 240, 253, 261, 269–71, 277, 290, 308–9
Douglas, Capt. Charles Atoyne, 197
Douglas, Capt. Neil, 54, 158, 165, 174, 197, 210
Downman, Major Thomas, 193
Dulimbert, 307–8
Duncan, Major Alexander, 254
Dunn, Sgt, 279
Dunn, Mrs, 279
Dyneley, Charles, 75–6
Dyneley, Miss Dora, 29, 31, 75, 190
Dyneley, Capt. Thomas, 29, 31, 67, 75–6, 121, 184, 190, 212

Eastlake, George, 125–6
Eligé, Capt. John, 229
Eugene, Prince of Savoy, 154
Evans, Dr John, 146

Faden, William, geographer, 155
Fairfoot, Sgt Robert, 239
Fane, Major-Gen. Henry, 33, 85
Farmer, Pte George, 179
Fénélon, François de Salignac de la Mothe, 152
Ferdinand VII, King of Spain, 124, 157, 244
Ferguson, Capt. Dugald, 71
Fermor, Lt.-Col. Thomas, 126
Fernyhough, Lieut. Robert, 69
Fielding, Henry, 152
Fitz Maurice, Mrs, 220, 256
Fitzpatrick, Dr Percy, 263
Fletcher, Lt.-Col. Sir Richard, 149, 182, 225
Florian, Jean Pierre Claris de, 152
Flynn, Mrs Biddy, 282
Foote, Samuel, 162
Foy, Gen. Maximilien Sébastien, 296–7
Francisco, servant boy, 142
Frazer, Lt.-Col. Sir Alexander, 46, 55, 64, 83, 105, 113, 125, 130, 145, 153, 165, 191, 216–7, 228–9, 236, 245, 259, 282, 287–8
Frazer, Mrs Emma, 259, 282
Frederick II, King of Prussia, 165
Frederick, Lieut. Edward, 197
Freer, Miss Anne, 76
Freer, Lieut. Edward, 76, 163
Freer, Miss Martha, 76

Freer, Lieut. William, 60, 177
Freire, Gen. Manuel, 202
Frith, Rev. Edward Cockayne, 234–5
Fuento, 123

Gairdner, Lieut. James Penman, 63, 178, 191, 296. 299
Gale, Daniel, 291
Gale, Elizabeth (later Mrs Watkins), 291
Genlis, Mme Stéphanie Félicité de, 219
George II, King, 162
George III, King, 122, 127, 140, 164, 296–8
Gibbs, Paymaster John, 197
Gibney, Dr William, 61
Gillmor, Lieut. (R.N) Clotworthy, 293
Gleig, Lieut. George Robert, 188, 209, 236
Goldfinch, Capt. Henry, 91, 203
Gomm, Capt. William, 35, 38, 53, 57, 139, 154, 157, 220, 242
Gordon, Capt. Alexander, 158, 185
Gore, Lieut. Charles, 162–3, 169
Graham, Lieut. John, 307
Graham, Lt.-Gen. Sir Thomas, 28, 35, 42–3, 69–70, 120, 131, 138–9, 179, 182, 195, 200–1, 203, 207, 215, 234, 258, 285
Graham, William, 60, 167, 207, 281
Grattan, Lieut. William, 73, 79, 84, 100, 162, 196, 264
Green, Pte John, 60, 79, 146, 233, 257–9, 279
Green, Bugler William, 82, 251–2, 260, 269–70
Grey, Lt.-Col. George, 278
Grey, Mrs, 278
Grey, Sir George, 278–9
Griffith, Miss Charlotte, 58
Griffith, Major Edwin, 58
Gronow, Ensign Rees Howell, 131, 202, 276
Grubbe, Lieut. Thomas, 163
Gubbins, Capt. Richard, 294
Guillet, Capt., 308
Gunning, Dr John, 275
Gurwood, Lieut. John, 94, 99
Guthrie, Dr George, 264
Guthrie, William, 137

Haines, Gregory, 201
Hall, Cornet Francis, 40, 48–9, 146, 258
Harding, Ensign William, 117
Hardinge, Lieut. Richard, 120
Harley, Capt. John, 153, 286
Harris, Rfn John, 66
Hawkes, T., Mosley & Co., military cap makers, 76
Hay, Major-Gen. Andrew, 279
Hay, Mrs Elizabeth, 279
Hay, Lieut. William, 24, 105, 142, 206, 212, 267–9
Henegan, Richard, 45, 56, 72, 122, 181, 185, 279
Henriques, Leopold, 54
Henry, Dr Walter, 55, 57, 140, 142, 178, 208, 242, 260–1, 268, 272
Heyward, Rev. John, 232–3
Hill, Lt.-Gen Sir Rowland, 7, 45, 69, 103, 124–5, 131, 150, 163–5, 180, 195, 197, 199, 206, 211, 217, 231, 266–7, 278, 281, 305–6
Hobkirk, Capt. Samuel, 77, 163, 169
Hoby, George, bootmaker, 77
Hogan, Q. M. John, 278
Hogan, Mrs, 278
Hogarth, William, 51
Holland, Elizabeth, Lady, 218
Hope, Lieut. James, 98, 205, 235, 243
Hope, Lt.-Gen. Sir John, 269–70
Hough, Lieut. Henry, 58, 121, 146, 196, 216
Houston, Major-Gen. William, 141
Hubbs, Sgt Gilbert, 279
Hughes, Capt. James, 113
Hughes, Major James, 173

Jackson, Lt.-Col. Basil, 198
James, Major Charles, 226
Johnson, Dr Samuel, 153
Jones, Lt.-Col. Sir John T., 224
Jones, Lieut. Rice, 149, 154
Jones, Lieut. William, 197
Joseph Bonaparte, King of Spain, 91, 139, 174
Junot, Gen. Andoche, Duc d'Abrantes, 98

Keane, Col. John, 127
Kelly, Capt. Edward, 196
Kelly, Joe, 122

Kempt, Major-Gen. Sir James, 117
Kent, Capt. John, 161–2
Keppel, Ensign George Thomas (later Earl of Albemarle), 117, 146, 219
Keyt, Capt. John Thomas, 197
Kincaid, Capt. John, 50, 83–4, 102, 143, 174, 188, 191, 232, 243, 248, 304
Knowles, Lieut. Robert, 107, 238

La Borde, Jean Benjamin, 153
Lamarque, Gen. Maximilien, 308
Landmann, Capt. George, 31, 33, 85, 90, 92, 262–3, 273, 297
Larpent, Francis Seymour, 40, 42–3, 46, 48, 60–1, 63, 69, 72, 78, 112, 123, 126, 129, 149, 190, 202, 233, 245, 251, 268
Lawrence, Sgt William, 104, 114, 241
Lawson, Capt. Robert, 222
Leach, Capt. Jonathan, 106, 133, 148, 155, 160, 162, 184, 196, 205, 209
Leeke, Ensign William, 117–8
Lejeune, Col. Louis-François, Baron, 288
Le Marchant, Major-Gen. Gaspard, 274
Le Mesurier, Capt. Peter, 50, 59, 68, 76, 83, 104, 115, 147, 168, 281–2
Lesage, Alain René, 153
Leslie, Lieut. Charles, 30, 59, 90, 113, 116, 132, 281
L'Estrange, Major George, 67, 119, 210
Lippe Bückeburg, Count of, 54
Liverpool, Robert Bankes, Earl of, 151, 225
Lock, Pte William, 261
Lockhart, Lieut. William, 142
Londonderry, Lt.-Gen. Charles William Vane, Marquess of, 145, 183
Long, Major-Gen. Robert Ballard, 34, 60, 76, 130, 203, 206
Longford, Edward Michael, Baron, 75–6
Love, Capt. James Frederick, 303
Luard, Cornet John, 275–6

Macan, Mrs Sally, 284
Macdonald, Lieut., 76

Mackinnon, Major-Gen. Henry, 75, 237
Madden, Lieut. Charles Dudley, 45
Madden, Lieut. Wyndham, 110
Maginn, William, 285
Maibey, Mrs, 272
Mainwaring, Ensign Frederick, 78
Malmesbury, James Harris, Earl of, 27
Manuel, servant boy, 142–3
March, Capt. Charles Gordon Lennox, Earl of, 262
Marlborough, John Churchill, Duke of, 154
Marsden, Tom, 204
Marmont, Auguste-Frédéric-Louis de, Duc de Raguse, Maréchal de France, 123, 207
Massena, André, Prince d'Essling, Maréchal de France, 112, 160, 236, 241, 293, 295
May, Lt.-Col. John, 219
Mein, Capt. William, 144
Mercer, Capt. Cavalié, 30, 79, 86, 96–7, 130, 194, 217, 219
Meynell, Hugo, 200
M'Guire, Rfn, 289
M'Guire, Mrs, 289
Miller, Dr John, 210
Miller, Dr William Bowen, 263
Mills, Ensign John, 203
Milton, John, 152
Minchin, Lieut. Francis, 197
Mitchell, Lt.-Col. Hugh Henry, 62
Molière, Jean Baptiste Poquelin, dit, 152
Moon, Mrs Barbara, 291
Moore, Lt.-Gen. Sir John, 8, 35, 69, 104, 111, 128, 175, 185, 289
Moore, Rfn John, 260
Morgan, Dr John, 147
Morris, Lieut. James, 280–1
Morris, Mrs, 280–1
Morris, Sgt Thomas, 96
Munday, Sgt, 284
Munday, Mrs, 284
Murray, Lt.-Gen. Sir George, 123, 201
Murray, Sgt-Major, 67

Napier, Major Charles, 36, 48, 87, 110, 182, 262

Napier, Major George Thomas, 260, 262, 264, 267, 292, 306

Napier, Capt. William Francis Patrick, 146, 153, 155, 218, 262, 274

Napoleon Bonaparte, Emperor of the French, 150, 165, 190, 197, 242, 296–8, 308

Nickells, John, trunk maker, 68

Nicol, Sgt Daniel, 250, 282

Norcliffe, Lieut. Norcliffe, 275

Northey, Sgt, 284

Northey, Mrs Sally, 284

O'Hare, Capt. Peter, 214

Orange, Gen. Willem Frederick, Hereditary Prince of, 124–5, 167, 197–8, 201

Ormsby, Rev. James Wilmot, 238

Owen, Lt.-Col. Hugh, 188

Pack, Major-Gen. Sir Denis, 237

Paget, Major Berkeley, 113

Pakenham, Major-Gen. Sir Edward Michael, 32, 55, 75, 127

Parker, Capt. John, 218

Parker Ellis, Capt. Charles, 301, 303–4

Parquin, Lieut. Charles, 307–8

Pasley, Capt. Charles William, 154

Pattenson, Lieut. Cooke Tylden, 163

Patterson, Lieut. John, 45

Payne, Major-Gen. William, 192

Peach, Dr George, 268

Pearce, Lieut. William, 146

Pedroso, Mr, interpreter, 142

Percival, Spencer, 145

Perpetua, Sister Joanna, 246

Peterborough, Charles Mordaunt, Earl of, 153

Picton, Lt.-Gen. Sir Thomas, 7, 32, 42–3, 45, 58, 125, 127, 151, 156, 272

Pitts, Capt. Thomas, 182

Pizarro, Francisco, 55, 216

Place, Francis, 76

Pococke, Capt. Thomas, 66, 90

Ponsonby, Lt.-Col. Frederick, 151, 174, 267–8

Pollock, Lieut. Samuel, 26

Porter, Sir Robert Ker, 59, 171, 177

Prater, William & Charles, linen drapers, 77

Prince Regent, later King George IV, 123, 127

Pulsford, Dr Lucas, 156

Racine, Jean, 152

Radcliffe, Mrs Ann, 45, 154

Ramsay, Major Norman, 79

Reddell, G S., sword cutter, 69

REGIMENTS, etc.
Designation as in the 1812 Army List. This is not the order of battle of Wellington's Army.

Cavalry
1st (or the King's) Dragoon Guards, 227

1st (or Royal) Dragoons, 83, 146, 183

2nd (or Royal North British) Dragoons (Royal Scots Greys), 67, 184, 261, 276

3rd (or the King's own) Dragoons, 140, 168, 186, 218

4th (or the Queen's own) Dragoons, 45, 99, 120, 167, 193, 218, 273–6, 281

7th (or the Queen's own) Light Dragoons (Hussars), 29, 118, 180–1, 183, 186

9th Light Dragoons, 138, 175, 247, 268

10th Light Dragoons (Hussars), 181, 197–8, 307

11th Light Dragoons, 136, 179, 209, 218

12th Light Dragoons, 24, 71, 142, 206, 220, 267, 269

13th Light Dragoons, 27–8, 64, 81, 180, 185, 261, 272, 295

14th Light Dragoons, 40–1, 49, 102, 113, 180, 182–3, 192, 202, 241

15th Light Dragoons (Hussars), 44, 52, 58, 96, 169, 181, 185, 199, 211, 276

16th Light Dragoons, 52, 61, 82, 146, 189, 192, 202, 221, 237, 305

18th Light Dragoons (Hussars), 23, 32, 58, 71, 92, 113, 129, 156, 169–70, 172–3, 197, 233, 244, 248, 271, 280–1, 298

Foot Guards
1st, 27, 31, 131, 149, 170, 202, 266, 298, 301, 303

Coldstream 27, 32, 47, 99, 106, 111, 133, 161, 167, 200, 203, 210–1, 234, 253

3rd, 72, 126, 230, 245, 253

Infantry of the Line

1st (or the Royal Scots), 80

3rd (or East Kent) (the Buffs), 102, 119, 278, 304

5th (or the Northumberland), 117, 275

7th (or Royal Fusiliers), 51, 66, 84, 90, 107–8, 114, 122–3, 156, 221, 238, 254, 258, 271, 278, 289

9th (or the East Norfolk), 59, 68, 115, 168, 281

14th (or the Buckinghamshire), 146, 219, 290

20th (or the East Devonshire), 23, 29, 51, 80, 208, 244, 284

23rd (or Royal Welsh Fusiliers), 228, 238, 271, 288

27th (or Inniskilling), 271

28th (or the North Gloucestershire), 36, 70, 120, 128–9, 154, 204, 214, 235, 284, 296, 301

29th (or the Worcestershire), 30, 53, 55, 79, 90, 98, 116, 119, 281

30th (or the Cambridgeshire), 209, 218

31st (or the Huntingdonshire), 67, 119

32nd (or the Cornwall), 91, 280

34th (or the Cumberland), 23, 52, 68, 84, 87, 89, 93, 95, 112, 214, 267, 285–6, 297, 300

40th (or 2nd Somersetshire), 51, 104–5, 114, 241, 271

42nd (or the Royal Highland) (Black Watch), 81, 88, 94, 100–1, 115, 118, 147, 286

43rd (or the Monmouthshire), 26, 35–7, 44, 61, 77, 80, 102, 110, 116, 123, 160, 162–3, 169, 175, 177, 215, 301–2

44th (or the East Essex), 146

45th (or the Nottinghamshire) (Sherwood Foresters), 34, 94, 108, 110, 229, 251

47th (or the Lancashire), 153, 286, 289–90

48th (or the Northamptonshire), 119, 155, 278

50th (or the West Kent), 32, 36, 45, 231, 265

51st (or the 2nd Yorkshire West Riding), 40, 44, 62, 78, 101, 115, 196, 271

52nd (or the Oxfordshire), 26, 105, 118, 142, 152, 202, 212, 220, 261, 267, 284, 292, 303, 306

53rd (or the Shropshire), 32, 51, 99, 100, 133, 246

57th (or the West Middlesex), 81

60th (or Royal American), 79, 271, 293

66th (or the Berkshire), 272

68th (or the Durham), 81, 146, 233, 257, 259, 279

71st (Highland), 66, 85, 90, 112, 147, 219, 231, 306–7

73rd (Highland), 96, 220, 290

79th (or Cameron Highlanders), 158, 165, 172, 210, 237

82nd, 95, 102, 212, 292

85th, 236, 294

87th (or Prince of Wales' own Irish), 127

88th (or Connaught Rangers), 34, 73, 79, 84, 100, 127, 162, 196, 220, 264, 287

91st, 85

92nd (Gordon Highlanders), 81, 103, 108, 121, 205, 231, 235–6, 242, 250, 282, 289

94th, 240, 270, 276

95th (Rifle Corps), 44–5, 50, 63, 65, 67–8, 71–2, 80, 82, 84, 88, 102, 106, 108, 116, 119, 127, 131, 133, 146, 160–2, 164, 168–9, 174, 184, 188, 191, 201–2, 204–5, 208–12, 214, 220, 236, 239, 242, 252, 256–7, 269, 272, 289, 291, 294, 296, 299, 304

Royal Artillery, 91, 122, 156, 163, 181, 184, 195, 218–9, 222, 283

Royal Horse Artillery, 30, 67, 79, 125, 130, 136, 146, 172, 182, 185, 190, 193–4, 196, 219, 229, 238

— — — 'E' Troop, 29, 120

— — — 'G' Troop, 96, 118

Royal Engineers, 31, 33, 54, 68, 85, 91, 119, 143, 182, 203, 222–5, 228, 263, 273, 297

Royal Staff Corps, 54, 138, 157, 198

Commissariat Department, 39, 111, 139

Medical Department, 39, 222, 224

Foreign Corps
King's German Legion, 8, 28, 35, 37, 101, 108, 143, 147, 159, 172, 188, 215
Brunswick Oels Regiment (Black Brunswickers), 36, 104, 155, 159
Portuguese Army, 54, 95, 119, 172

Divisions
1st, 95, 200
2nd, 28, 45, 103, 164, 206, 217, 134, 278
3rd, 7, 27, 30, 32, 45, 73, 114, 127
4th, 29, 69, 123, 271
5th, 232, 235, 237, 282
6th 28
7th, 196, 293
Light (Brigade till 22. 2. 1810), 25–6, 30, 32–3, 35–6, 38, 85, 92, 98, 105, 121, 125, 144, 159–63, 182, 193, 205, 221, 231, 237

Reid, Dr James, 196
Reston, Sgt, 276
Reston, Mrs, 276–7
Richmond, Charlotte, Duchess of, 167, 175, 219
Robe, Lt.-Col. William, 181
Roberts, Lt.-Col. David, 40, 44, 196
Robinson, Major-Gen. F. P., 49, 69, 104
Rogers, Samuel, 105
Ross, Q. M. Alexander, 290–1
Ross, Mrs Elizabeth, 290–1
Ross, Major Hew Dalrymple, 76
Ross, Major-Gen. Robert, 76, 278
Ross, Mrs, 278
Ross-Lewin, Capt. Harry, 47, 91, 107, 280
Rubens, Peter Paul, 217

Salisbury, Mary, Marchioness of, 203, 281
Saltoun, Alexander Fraser, Capt. Lord, 31, 94, 170, 172,
Sanguinetti, 132
Schaumann, August Ludolf Friedrich, 161, 192–3, 268, 302
Schiller, Johann Christoph Friedrich, 36

Scovell, Major George, 157–8
Sebright, Lt.-Col. Edward, 149
Sévigné, Marie de Rabutin-Chantal, Marquise de, 152
Seymour, Lieut., 129
Shakespear, Cornet Arthur, 276
Shakespeare, William, 65, 152, 160
Shelley, Frances, Lady, 97
Sherer, Lieut. Moyle, 52, 55, 89, 95, 152, 165, 294, 297–8
Simmons, Lieut, George, 65, 67, 87, 142, 150, 164, 239–40, 257, 268
Simmons, Ensign Joseph, 67
Simpson, Dr Edward, 251
Simpson, Lieut. William Davidson, 197
Skiddy, Pte Dan, 282, 286
Skiddy, Mrs Bridget, 282–3, 285–6
Smellie, Capt. Peter, 197
Smith, Major, 34, 229
Smith, Lieut. E., 129
Smith, Major Harry G. W., 44, 60, 65, 107, 140, 144, 169, 201, 206, 254–5, 262
Smith, Mrs Juana Maria, 60, 140
Smollett, Tobias, 152
Smyth & Nephew, perfumers, 75
Somerset, Major-Gen. Lord Edward, 128
Somerset, Lt.-Col. Lord Fitzroy James, 197
Soult, Nicolas, Duc de Dalmatie, Maréchal de France, 77, 136, 293
Spencer, Lt.-Gen. Sir Brent, 33
Spencer, Lieut. Lord Charles, 162–3
Sperling, Lieut. John, 228
Steevens, Lt.-Col. Charles, 23, 208, 284
Stepney, Ensign John Cowell, 45, 47, 58, 95, 99, 106, 126, 149, 167, 237
Stevenson, Sgt, 230
Stewart, Lt.-Gen. Sir Charles. *See* Londonderry.
Stewart, Lieut. James, 236
Stewart, Major James, 201
Stewart, Lt.-Gen. Sir William, 123, 236
Stothert, Capt. William, 246
Stovin, Lt.-Col. Richard, 156
Stuart, Capt. Simon, 129
Surtees, Q. M. William, 88, 131, 208, 299

Swabey, Lieut. William, 41, 48, 50, 87, 112–3, 139–40, 143, 152–4, 182, 193–4, 239–40, 250, 254, 268
Swinburne, Henry, 152

Tamet the Turk, 132
Thelusson, Cornet George Woodford, 236
Timewell, Pte John, 61
Tinling, Col. Isaac, 31
Tomkinson, Capt. William, 61, 136, 192, 214, 255, 305
Tonyn, Capt. Charles, 278
Trench, Major Frederick William, 170
Trip van Zoutlandt, Lt.-Col. Baron Otto Ernst Gelder, 296
Tucker, Capt. T. Edwardes, 156
Tweeddale, Capt. George Hay, Marquess of, 199–201

Uniacke, Capt. John, 239
Uxbridge, Lt.-Gen. Henry, Earl of, later Marquess of Anglesey, 197–8

Vandeleur, Major-Gen. Sir John Ormsby, 124, 197,
Vauban, Sébastien le Prestre de, 153
Vérigny, Major de la Chasse de, 307
Verner, Capt. William, 118, 183, 186
Victor, Claude Victor, Duc de Belluno, Maréchal de France, 98
Vivian, Major-Gen. Sir Hussey, 24, 64, 77, 128–30, 135, 167, 186, 197, 213, 300
Voltaire, François Marie Arouet, dit, 152

Wachholtz, Capt. Friedrich Ludwig von, 117
Waldegrave, Ann, Countess, 169, 276
Waldegrave, Major John, Earl, 169, 276
Waldie, Miss Charlotte, 266
Wales, Charlotte, Princess of, 150
Wall, Capt. Adam 283
Warre, Capt. William, 77, 182, 210, 246
Watkins, J., optician, 76
Watson, Capt. Henry, 72
Watt, Pte, 289
Watt, Mrs, 289

Weeks, Driver William, 238
Wellesley, Sir Henry, 182
Wellesley, Lt.-Gen. Sir Arthur, later Field-Marshal the Duke of Wellington, 25, 31–2, 36, 39, 41, 45, 53, 56, 62–3, 69, 78–70, 82, 85, 89, 91, 97–8, 105, 108, 111, 117–8, 122–7, 131, 136, 144–5, 150–1, 157, 159, 161, 163, 165–7, 174, 180, 182–3, 190, 197, 199–204, 207, 210, 216, 225–6, 229–30, 233–4, 237–8, 241, 246, 266–7, 273, 281–2, 292,-3 305
Wheatley, Ensign Edmund, 153
Wheatley, Lt.-Col. Harry, 68
Wheatley, Mrs Jane, 46
Wheatley, Major-Gen. William, 46, 68, 97
Wheel, Mrs Betty, 282
Wheeler, Sgt William, 48, 62, 105, 232
Whinyates, Capt. Edward, 194
Whitelocke, Lt.-Gen. John, 291
Wilkie, Lt.-Col. Fletcher, 243
Wood, Capt. Charles, 201–2
Wood, Capt. George, 102, 212, 292
Woodberry, Lieut. George, 23, 58, 60, 92–3, 121, 125, 144, 150, 156, 170, 172, 177, 244, 248, 280–1, 298
Worcester, Capt. Henry, Marquess of, 72, 169, 172, 204

York and Albany, Field-Marshal Frederick Augustus, Duke of, 127, 230–1
Young, Edward, 161

Zimmermann, Johann Georg von, 154

2. SUBJECTS

Ague, cures for, 267–71
ambulance carts, 253–4
ammunition, 25, 79
amputations, 262–5
anniversaries, 127–8
artillery work, 222
auctions, 71–3

Baggage, 25, 30, 67–8. 70
balls, 145, 167–71
bands, 36, 51, 103, 122–3, 161
bathing, 34, 205, 295
beds, 42, 46, 48, 54, 58, 68, 90–1, 105–6

beef, 25, 30, 107–8, 115–6, 118
bigotry, 238–40
billets, 38–51, 62, 105–6, 136, 223
biscuit, 30, 107, 110–1, 118
bivouacs, 87–106
blankets, 35, 39, 88–91, 95, 221
boar hunts, 210–1
bolero, 73, 157, 165, 167, 176
books, 55, 137, 152–4
bread, 108–9
bullfights, 217–8
bullocks, 25, 89, 116, 217
burials, 236–8

Camp equipage, 67–71
camp-kettles, 25, 66, 93, 116–7
canteens, 70–1, 121
card games, 155–6
cavalry duties, 28, 221–2
chaplains, 228–38
childbirth, 289–90
children, 30, 122, 271, 281, 286–8
Christmas, 121-2
churches, 51–2
church parades, 34, 233–5
cigars, 88, 100, 119, 146–7, 158, 170
commissariat, 110–1, 116
complaints, 39, 41–2
convents, 45, 51–2
conversation, 145–6
cooking, 94, 113–6
Cossacks, 64
coursing, 204–7
cricket, 219–20
'croakers', 151–2

Dancing, 103, 122, 158, 167–75
dinner parties, 121–30
dramatics, amateur, 159–64
dust, 25, 32–3, 85

Engineers' duties, 222–5
eye-shades, 32

Fairs, 73–5, 129
fandango, 157, 165, 167, 171, 176
farriers, 185–8
firewood, 114–5
fishing, 207–8
flags of truce, 204, 292–3
fleas, 43–4
flirtations, 56–7, 139, 176

football, 219
footwear, 25, 81–2
forage, 188–94, 203
fox-hunting, 198–204
fraternization, 168, 203–5, 292–309
French, attitude to, 178

Gambling, 155–6, 159
games, 218–20
General Orders, 38–9, 41
generals' tables compared, 125
girls, 56–8, 104–5, 135, 139–40, 159, 195
goats, 30, 54, 89, 144
guns, 28, 103

Headgear, 31, 82–3, 86
health, 97–8
heat, 23, 32–5, 42, 70, 97, 99, 183–4
horses, 67, 179–88, 198, 200, 202–3, 212, 226
horse fair, 67
horseshoes, 186
hospitals, conditions in, 232, 258–9
hounds, 195, 198–207
hunting, 198–205
huts, 98–101

Improvements to quarters, 49–51
insects, 87, 101–3
interpreters, 140–2

Jackets, 30, 78, 80

Kit, 66–71

Landscape, 23–4
languages, learning, 58, 135–40
laundry, 34, 83–4

Maps, 155
marches, 25–7, 30
march regulations, 25–6
Methodism, 229–30
mules, 25, 27, 69, 94
muleteers, 82, 88–9, 141, 257
music, 35–6, 161

Newspapers, 139, 148–50, 305
night marches, 28–9

nuns, 240–9
nursing, 242, 265–6, 275

Office work, 225–7
officers' messes, 112, 118–20
outpost duty, 37, 179, 221–2

Pay, in arrears, 133–4, 145
Portuguese, troops' opinion of, 58–9, 175–6
priests, 41, 55–6, 239
prisoners of war, 272

Race-meetings, 195–8
rain, 29, 31, 35, 87–8, 93–6
returns, 226–7
river crossings, 27–8, 227, 235
roads, 24, 30, 163, 185–6, 223

Sedan-chairs, 255
servant boys, 142–4
servants, 30, 89
shepherds, 213
shooting, 209–10
shopping from Britain, 75–7
sieges, 131–2, 214, 223–5
sightseeing, 216–7

singing, 36–7, 88–9, 120, 123, 245–6, 249
smoking, 36–7, 146–8, 158
snuff, 147–8
Spaniards, troops' opinion of, 58–9, 176–8
stabling, 43, 181, 184–5
surgery, 251–2, 260–5
sutlers, 30, 132, 147, 159
sweepstakes, 196–7

Tents, 25, 68, 91–9, 101
tertulias, 157–9
theatres, 164–5
theatricals, private, 145, 159-64
toasts, 124, 127–8, 297

Umbrellas, 31–2, 80

Waltzes, 104, 167, 169, 171, 174
waterproof clothing, 31, 83, 94
wine, 33, 120, 129–30
wives, 30, 88, 122, 143, 271–81
wolves, 211–3
women in battle, 273–7
wounded, 29–30, 242, 250–8

G3